EVERYMAN,
I WILL GO WITH THEE,
AND BE THY GUIDE,
IN THY MOST NEED
TO GO BY THY SIDE

WILLIAM SHAKESPEARE

Histories

with an Introduction by Tony Tanner
General Editor – Sylvan Barnet

VOLUME 2

EVERYMAN'S LIBRARY

193

This book is one of 250 volumes in Everyman's Library
which have been distributed to 4500 state schools
throughout the United Kingdom.
The project has been supported by a grant of £4 million
from the Millennium Commission.

First included in Everyman's Library, 1906

These plays are published by arrangement with New American
Library, a division of Penguin Books USA, Inc.

ISBN 1-85715-193-3

A CIP catalogue record for this book is available from the
British Library

Published by David Campbell Publishers Ltd.,
Gloucester Mansions, 140A Shaftesbury Avenue,
London WC2H 8HD

Distributed by Random House (UK) Ltd.,
20 Vauxhall Bridge Road, London SW1V 2SA

HISTORIES

CONTENTS

———

INTRODUCTION

RICHARD II

What must the King do now? Must he submit?
The King shall do it. Must he be deposed?
The King shall be contented. Must he lose
The name of king? a God's name, let it go.

(III, iii, 142–5)

On her death-bed, Queen Elizabeth is said to have remarked that 'must' was not a word which may be used to princes. It is a word which comes to be used to Richard II, but only after he has consistently used the word to, and of, himself. In the scene after the one quoted above, there is the following exchange:

Richard. What you will have, I'll give, and willing too,
For do we must what force will have us do.
Set on towards London, cousin, is it so?
Bolingbroke. Yea, my good Lord.
Richard.   Then I must not say no.

(III, iii, 204–7)

Richard seems almost too ready, even eager, to put himself under compulsion – to exchange being absolute ruler for being absolutely ruled. It is not too much to say that Richard starts to abdicate ('From Richard's night to Bolingbroke's fair day', III, ii, 218) some time before Bolingbroke announces his intention to usurp ('In God's name, I'll ascend the regal throne', IV, i, 113) – though Bolingbroke's intentions are something of a mystery, perhaps even to himself. The definitive concession – self-inflicted abnegation, perhaps – occurs one scene later.

Bolingbroke. Are you contented to resign the crown?
Richard. Ay, no; no, ay: for I must nothing be.

(IV, i, 199–200)

From one point of view, this is simply a sombre recognition of the inevitable – all men must die; but, in the circumstances, it has the tremendous pathos of the anointed king, God's minister

xi

on earth, visibly, audibly confronting what has come to seem the unavoidability of, effectively, self-nihilation.

The pathos and paradox of the king who 'must' was also dramatized by Marlowe in his *Edward II* (1592), in which there is the following exchange:

> *Edward.* And, Leicester, say what shall become of us?
> *Leicester.* Your majesty must go to Killingworth.
> *Edward.* Must! 'tis somewhat hard, when kings must go.

Marlowe's play almost certainly influenced Shakespeare's *Richard II*. Both plays depict weak kings, who are irresponsible, arbitrary, and self-indulgent while they are secure on the throne (both, incidentally, from the same dynasty). They both ignore and alienate their wise counsellors and turn to favourites (perhaps not coincidentally, there are three of these in each play). I quote Geoffrey Bullough: 'In both plays the king is deposed, ill-treated, and then murdered in an interesting manner, leaving the kingdom in the hands of a better ruler. In each the king becomes more likeable in defeat than he was in power, and the play becomes an experiment in counterpointing the tragedy of a weak and erring central figure against the conflict of opposing groups ("upstarts" and true nobility). This idea was perhaps Shakespeare's biggest debt to Marlowe in *Richard II*.' With this play, Shakespeare goes back to the beginning of the sequence of events which led to the Wars of the Roses, the tyranny of Richard III, and the advent of Henry VII and the Tudors. But this second tetralogy is to be different from the first. It is more complex and subtle and, arguably, reveals a new attitude to politics. Bullough gives a conventional description of the difference. 'Whereas the first tetralogy was mainly concerned with negatives, the evils of dissension, the fratricidal strife of barons, disorder triumphant, the second group is concerned with positive values, the nature of good government, the qualities needed by a strong and wise ruler: prudence, leadership, consideration for popular feeling, ability to choose rightly between good and bad counsel, to put the public weal before private pleasures.' This is not wrong, but perhaps it makes the second tetralogy sound a shade too bland, tending towards the untested complacencies of the instruction manual. As we shall see, it is, and does, a good deal more than this.

In his portrayal of Richard, Shakespeare had two traditional versions to draw on, to be found in Tudor chronicles. One stressed the weak and irresponsible king who deserved to lose his throne: the other saw him as a betrayed martyr. In this play he is both, as if Shakespeare could see how the latter could be latent and dormant in the former, how a king could be a 'degenerate' fool *and* a Christ-like saint. And a 'nothing' too. In the first three scenes, Richard, in his handling of the quarrel between Mowbray and Bolingbroke, can be seen as behaving like a responsible king. It is not, as is sometimes suggested, a foolish and capricious act to stop the combat between the two men by throwing down his 'warder' or truncheon, and he has good reasons for banishing the dangerous and war-like adversaries, since the

> grating shock of wrathful iron arms,
> Might from our quiet confines fright fair Peace,
> And make us wade even in our kindred's blood
>
> (I, iii, 136–9)

We might pause on 'kindred's blood'. The ceremony, pageantry, formality of these opening scenes are often commented on as bespeaking an older medieval world which the more Machiavellian power-politics of Bolingbroke will, in due course, supplant. But if we listen to the language employed by Mowbray and Bolingbroke – 'rites of knighthood', 'chivalrous design of knightly trial', and talk of kinsmen, honour, blood, vengeance – we soon realize that we are hearing the older voice of feudalism. When Richard fails to dissuade the combatants from insisting on entering the lists, we are witnessing the failure of monarchy to assert its authority over the power of feudalism. I take the point from Graham Holderness, and his account of what is going on seems to me right. 'The conflict which ultimately leads to the king's deposition is not a conflict between old and new, between absolute medieval monarchy and new Machiavellian power-politics. It is a conflict between the king's sovereignty and the ancient code of chivalry, which is here firmly located in the older and more primitive tribal and family code of blood-vengeance. Richard initially acquiesces in this code ... but subsequently attempts to affirm a policy of royal absolutism, which insists on the king's prerogative overriding the procedures of chivalric law. Richard's political response to this constant clamouring for power on the part of the feudal lords, is to impose a policy of *absolutism* ... [Shakespeare] sees the deposition of Richard II, not as the overturning of a traditional order by new, ruthless political forces, but as the consequence of an attempt by a later medieval monarch to impose on feudal power an absolutist solution. The victorious forces are not new but old: feudal reaction rather than political revolution. The society we see dissolving had been an effective unity and balance of royal prerogative and feudal rights – both parties in the conflict have pushed their interests to the point of inevitable rupture.' 'We were not born to sue, but to command,' asserts Richard, perhaps a little desperately, at the end of the first scene. To the extent that the play is a 'Tragedy' (as it was entitled when first printed), it is in the painful spectacle of the King Who Would Command transformed into the King Who Must.

Richard, then, appears sufficiently, if precariously, kingly in the first three scenes, trying, though only imperfectly succeeding, to control the unruly and quarrelsome barons. But the next, more private, less formal scene, among his favourites, reveals a cynical and callous side to his character as we hear him expressing the hope that John of Gaunt will die ('God ... help him to his grave immediately!') so that they can raid his 'coffers'. And the next scene (II, i) shows him in much the same vein as John of Gaunt indicts him with his dying breath. Gaunt, at this point, takes on prophetic status:

> Methinks I am a prophet new inspired,
> And thus expiring do foretell of him:
> His rash fierce blaze of riot cannot last,
> For violent fires soon burn out themselves.

(II, i, 31–4)

and utters his famous lament over England ('This precious stone set in the silver sea'), because, under Richard, 'this dear dear land' –

> Is now leased out − I die pronouncing it −
> Like to a tenement or pelting farm.
> England ...
>   is now bound in with shame,
> With inky blots, and rotten parchment bonds.
>
> (II, i, 59−60, 63−4)

Blots on parchment, on paper, on books, on 'pride', or just 'blots' − the image occurs more often in this play than in any other by Shakespeare. It refers here, literally, to the deeds and leases by which Richard has 'farmed' out the royal demesnes − substituting economic contracts for earlier bonds of fealty; but also metaphorically to the growing evil which seems to be staining the land (not just from Richard's dissolute mismanagement; Bolingbroke is called a 'pernicious blot' by Aumerle − IV, i, 324). Gaunt repeats his reproach to Richard's face:

> Why, cousin, wert thou regent of the world,
> It were a shame to let this land by lease;
> But for thy world enjoying but this land
> Is it not more than shame to shame it so?
> Landlord of England art thou now, not king.
>
> (II, i, 109−13)

He also says something else to Richard which is more prophetic, perhaps, than he realizes:

> O, had thy grandsire with a prophet's eye
> Seen how his son's son should destroy his sons,
> From forth thy reach he would have laid thy shame,
> Deposing thee before thou wert possessed,
> Which art possessed *now to depose thyself*.
>
> (II, i, 104−8, my italics)

The second line refers, in particular, to Richard's murder of his uncle, the Duke of Gloucester (Woodstock) which was, indeed, an infamous 'blot' on Richard's reign. This murder is rather glossed over in the play − indeed, Shakespeare makes it uncertain whether Mowbray, Aumerle, or Richard was the murderer. Only the dying Gaunt speaks out unequivocally about it:

> My brother Gloucester, plain well-meaning soul
> ...

May be a precedent and witness good
That thou respect'st not spilling Edward's blood.

(II, i, 128–31)

The line I have partially italicized continues that compulsive
play on words which marks Gaunt's last speeches. He is saying
that though Richard is 'possessed' of the crown, he is now also
'possessed' in the sense of being in the grip of diabolical
influences – to the extent that he will lose the throne. But
Gaunt could not have foreseen how accurately his words
describe what we are about to see – which is, exactly and
literally, a king deposing himself.

At the news of Gaunt's death Richard continues to show his
callous side – ('His time is spent ... so much for that') – and
announces, ruthlessly, his intention to 'seize' all that Gaunt
possessed – 'for our Irish wars'. In doing this, he is robbing
Gaunt's son, the banished Bolingbroke (Hereford), of his
legitimate inheritance, his 'rights and royalties'. This provokes
another of Richard's wise-counselling uncles, the stalwart and
long-suffering York, to protest:

> Take Hereford's rights away, and take from time
> His charters and his customary rights,
> Let not tomorrow then ensue today;
> Be not thyself. For how art thou a king
> But by fair sequence and succession?

(II, i, 195–9)

Matters of 'sequence and succession' were of vital concern to
the Elizabethans, not only as they surveyed their turbulent
history, but also as they wondered whether the 'succession' to
their own Queen would be 'fair' or, in one way or another,
foul. Richard was the last king ruling by direct hereditary
right in 'succession' from William the Conqueror, and to see
him thus ignoring, or rather profaning and violating, 'customary rights', those same sacrosanct rules of inheritance which
had made him king, is, indeed, shocking. He is wilfully
disrupting those sacred continuities on which all peaceful
transactions and transmissions depend – the 'sequence of days'
no less than the succession of kings. And he will prove to be the

most spectacular victim of his culpable abrogations. But, for
now, he is mindlessly indifferent to York's warnings:

> Think what you will, we seize into our hands
> His plate, his goods, his money, and his lands.
>
> (II, i, 209–10)

and it's off to Ireland, to settle those 'rug-headed kernes' (at
which, incidentally, he was very successful – though Shakespeare leaves that out as well).

We will not see Richard again until Act III, scene ii, when
he will soon seem a changed man as the long ordeal and
anguish of his self-deposition begins. In the interim we witness
Bolingbroke's return to England, and the nobles', if not the
country's, rush to support him. And here we should note one
of those interesting departures by Shakespeare from his
sources. The Holinshed Chronicles make it absolutely clear
that Bolingbroke (Hereford, and now, after the death of
Gaunt, Lancaster) was invited back to England by the
discontented nobles ('requiring him with all convenient speed
to convey himself into England, promising him all their aid,
power, and assistance, if he, expelling King Richard, as a man
not meet for the office he bare, would take upon him the
scepter, rule, and diadem of his native land and region').
Whatever else, this at least exonerates Bolingbroke from
having initiated the idea of usurpation. Not a word of this in
Shakespeare. Instead, when the nobles collude in exasperation
after Richard has left for Ireland, Bolingbroke is already,
mysteriously, back in England, and had been waiting in
Brittany, with allies and troops, simply for Richard's departure for Ireland. This puts a very different colour on Bolingbroke's possible motives and intentions. Until he suddenly
announces that he will 'ascend the regal throne', he continually insists that he has only returned to claim his rightful
inheritance – 'I come for Lancaster', 'I am come to seek that
name in England', 'I lay my claim/To my inheritance of free
descent'. But, in the time scheme of the play, he is already in
England sixty lines after Richard announces he is going to
Ireland, which in turn occurs only some seventy-five lines after
the death of Gaunt (all in the same scene). This means that,

dramatically, Bolingbroke could hardly have known of his father's death and of Richard's infamous expropriation of the whole Lancaster estate. Or at least, to a spectator it would seem that way. It is another example of the way Shakespeare likes to problematize time, inducing, in this case, a calculated and crucial uncertainty. *Did* Bolingbroke somehow know about his father's death and the regal robbery, and did he *genuinely* come just for his 'rights and royalties' – with subsequent unforeseen circumstances somehow propelling him on to the throne? Or was he already bent on invasion and usurpation? One thing is certain – there was no prior invitation and request from the English nobles. This man came of his own volition.

The matter is of vital importance, since it was this usurpation that set in motion what would become the long train of disasters culminating in Richard III and the subsequent accession – usurpation – of the Tudors. And Shakespeare makes sure that we have no certain access to the originating moment, the originating motive, of that history-changing usurpation. Is Bolingbroke a Machiavellian who had the whole take-over plotted from day one? Or is he simply borne along on a tide of events, one thing leading to another as things do? He does not seem to exercise any cunning or special skills, and power and support just seem to melt and slide away from the absent Richard 'with the speed of an avalanche' (the felicitous image is Peter Ure's). So perhaps he is simply an angry baron who, effectively, stumbles on the crown. Yet he sometimes gives the impression of only seeming not to have any ulterior motives, while moving shrewdly if warily so that his usurpation will appear, in R. F. Hill's words, 'inevitable but undesigned'. We cannot resolve these uncertainties for the simple reason that Shakespeare gives us no insight into, indeed no glimpses of, Bolingbroke's motives, aims, and intentions. We are never let into his mind. We have seen the growing importance of the soliloquy in the history plays, and it is surely remarkable that, alone among the villains and schemers of the histories (if he is one), Bolingbroke never soliloquizes. He remains shut up, shut off, and we can never know what truly moves him. And the ambiguity is not resolved by him in

2 Henry IV. At one point he says, actually quoting words spoken by Richard II in the earlier play:

> 'Northumberland, thou ladder by the which
> My cousin Bolingbroke ascends my throne'–
> (Though then, God knows, I had no such intent,
> But that necessity so bowed the state
> That I and greatness were *compelled* to kiss)
>
> (III, i, 70–74, my italics)

then, on his death-bed:

> God knows, my son,
> By what bypaths and indirect crooked ways
> I *met* this crown, and I myself know well
> How troublesome it sat upon my head.
> ... It seemed in me
> But as an honor *snatched* with boisterous hand
>
> (IV, v, 183–6, 190–91, my italics)

'Compelled' is passive; 'met' is neutral; 'snatched' is active. The English language itself recognizes and respects the unfathomable uncertainties and ambiguities of the decision-making process – we can 'come to' a decision (that could be like meeting); we can 'take' a decision (more like snatching); or we can 'make' a decision (perhaps an altogether more responsible, artefactual matter). It is entirely possible that Bolingbroke's impulses remain mysterious to himself. He certainly shows signs of a guilty conscience (though he never reveals, or perhaps confronts, the cause), and he may indeed be – in *Richard II* – a rather unscrupulous, power-hungry, scheming politician who prefers to disavow his own deepest intentions, pretending, instead, to be 'compelled' by circumstances. Or he may genuinely not know exactly *why* he does *what* he does, not be able to disentangle and distinguish seeking from meeting, snatching from being compelled – in a word, his motives from his opportunities. All this makes him at once mysterious and human, and I think this root uncertainty or ambiguity is a masterstroke on Shakespeare's part. Such are the figures who, at once, make and are made by history.

Two short premonitory scenes, which follow one after the other immediately prior to Richard's reappearance, seem almost to prefigure what is to happen. We have seen the support of the nobles fall away from Richard in his absence (even that of loyal York), and then we watch as the Captain of the Welsh army (on which Richard is relying to fight Bolingbroke) announces that his army is dispersing because "Tis thought the King is dead: we will not stay' (II, iv, 7); and Salisbury reads the gathering omens clearly enough:

> Ah, Richard! With the eyes of heavy mind
> I see thy glory like a shooting star
> Fall to the base earth from the firmament;
> Thy sun sets weeping in the lowly west,
> Witnessing storms to come, woe and unrest
>
> (II, iv, 18–22)

It is just this 'falling' and 'setting' we are about to see. But if the King is proleptically 'dead', his rival and antagonist is very much alive, as we see in the next scene in which Bolingbroke's behaviour is almost regally autocratic as he orders the summary execution of Richard's favourites, Bushy and Green. 'See them delivered over/To execution and the hand of death.' This is the man now in charge. The king is 'dead': long live the 'king'. But we should take note of another gesture on Bolingbroke's part. Before despatching Bushy and Green, he announces: 'yet, to wash your blood/From off my hands ... I will unfold some causes of your deaths' (III, i, 5–7). This is the (would-be self-exculpating) Pilate gesture, and it is arguable that Bolingbroke, in time, plays Pilate to Richard's 'Christ'. This is certainly how Richard will come to see it:

> Though some of you, with Pilate, wash your hands,
> Showing an outward pity: yet you Pilates
> Have here delivered me to my sour cross,
> And water cannot wash away your sin.
>
> (IV, i, 238–41)

And after Richard has been murdered, in almost the last lines of the play, Bolingbroke vows:

> I'll make a voyage to the Holy Land,
> To wash this blood off from my guilty hand.
>
> (V, vi, 49–50)

He never makes that voyage to the Holy Land – though he is recorded as dying in the Jerusalem Chamber of Westminster, a circumstance which it pleases him to regard as auspicious, but which Shakespeare may have regarded more ironically. Certainly, it is not clear that he can (indeed, that *anyone* can) 'wash off' blood from guilty hands, just as it is unclear whether Richard, approaching the depths of his abjection, can 'wash away my balm' (i.e. the anointing ointment used at the coronation, IV, i, 206) – balm may stick to a consecrated head as long as blood to a guilty hand. *May*. There can be no certainty in such matters.

Richard is very conscious of being the 'Lord's Anointed', and it is very easy for him to see himself as a Christ figure, now surrounded by Judases and Pilates. (The King as God's substitute on earth, and thus a God-like figure with 'divine right', became crucial to Tudor political theory.) In three scenes – on the Welsh coast, at Flint Castle, and in Westminster – we see Richard, effectively, enduring his stations of the cross, as he suffers more and more humiliation and descends to the depths of abjectness (A. P. Rossiter suggested the possible influence of the 'staged spectacle of a sacrificial king of sorrows', familiar from the Mystery Cycles). Before considering these scenes, I want to quote a remarkable passage from Walter Pater's *Appreciations* concerning these scenes:

In the Roman Pontifical, of which the order of Coronation is really a part, there is no form for the inverse process, no rite of 'degradation', such as that by which an offending priest or bishop may be deprived, if not of the essential quality of 'orders', yet, one by one, of its outward dignities. It is as if Shakespeare had had in mind some such inverted rite, like those old ecclesiastical or military ones, by which human hardness, or human justice, adds the last touch of unkindness to the execution of its sentences ...

Richard's grief, Pater asserts, 'becomes nothing less than a central expression of all that in the revolution of Fortune's wheel goes *down* in the world'.

When Richard first lands on the coast of Wales, he touches, and conjures, and puts his confidence in 'my earth' (a much-repeated word in this play, fittingly enough as the down-sinking Richard moves inexorably 'to earthward', if I may borrow an apt phrase from Robert Frost). He starts by enunciating a conventional regal confidence:

> So when this thief, this traitor, Bolingbroke,
> Who all this while hath reveled in the night
> Whilst we were wand'ring with the Antipodes,
> Shall see us rising in our throne, the east,
> His treasons will sit blushing in his face,
> Not able to endure the sight of day,
> But self-affrighted tremble at his sin.

(III, ii, 47–53)

Wrong, of course. Richard's sun is already setting, while Bolingbroke is 'rising' – without a tremble.

> Not all the water in the rough rude sea
> Can wash the balm off from an anointed king;
> The breath of worldly men cannot depose
> The deputy elected by the Lord.

(III, ii, 54–7)

Richard had 'breathed' Norfolk into permanent exile (I, iii, 153), and commuted Bolingbroke's banishment by four years with 'a word' – prompting Bolingbroke to comment – 'such is the breath of kings'. For one last moment, Richard see himself as untouchable (out of reach of any sacrilegious 'water' and 'breath'), invincible, asserting that God and his angels will fight on his side – 'for heaven still guards the right'. But he is destined, and that shortly, to do the impossible unanointing washing and the inconceivable deposing breathing – himself.

The first piece of bad news (the dispersal of the Welsh army – admittedly a blow) seems to precipitate instant collapse – 'All souls that will be safe fly from my side.' He briefly rallies (in this scene he experiences those sudden alterations between extreme moods which often testify to some sort of severe psychic instability):

> I had forgot myself: am I not King?
> Awake, thou coward majesty! Thou sleepest.
> Is not the King's name twenty thousand names?
> Arm, arm, my name! a puny subject strikes
> At thy great glory. Look not to the ground,

> Ye favorites of a king, are we not high?
> High be our thoughts.
>
> (III, ii, 83–9)

The name 'Richard'; or the name 'King'? Can one sleep while the other wakes? (Shortly, he will lose all his names: 'I have no name, no title ... And know not now what name to call myself', IV, i, 254–8). There is more than a touch of incipient amnesiac-somnambulism here – he is losing his grip on his unitary self. And within fifty lines, in total reversal, the cry is – look *to* the ground, and *low* be our thoughts.

> Let's talk of graves, of worms, and epitaphs,
> Make dust our paper, and with rainy eyes
> Write sorrow on the bosom of the earth.
>
> (III, ii, 145–7)

He indulges what must be this pleasurable morbidity for some thirty lines, until he reaches that easeful stage of nihilism when you simply give up *everything*.

> throw away respect,
> Tradition, form, and ceremonious duty;
> For you have mistook me all this while:
> I live with bread like you, feel want,
> Taste grief, need friends – subjected thus,
> How can you say to me, I am a king?
>
> (III, ii, 172–7)

This is what he, very accurately, calls 'that sweet way I was in to despair'. He is briefly interrupted when he is encouraged to make one more, now totally implausible, gesture of regal confidence – 'An easy task it is to win our own' (III, ii, 191) – but more bad news quickly returns him to 'that sweet way'. 'I'll pine away;/A king, woe's slave, shall kingly woe obey' (III, ii, 209–10). His last words of the scene presage all that is to follow:

> Discharge my followers, let them hence away,
> From Richard's night to Bolingbroke's fair day.
>
> (III, ii, 217-18)

The next scene takes place in front of Flint Castle where the 'sacred king' (III, iii, 9) has found temporary refuge.

Bolingbroke arrives, seemingly behaving as an impeccably loyal subject.

> Henry Bolingbroke
> On both his knees doth kiss King Richard's hand,
> And sends allegiance and true faith of heart
> To his most royal person ...
>
> (III, iii, 34–7)

Yet in instructing Northumberland to convey this message to the King, he tells him to send it 'Into his ruined ears' (III, iii, 33), thus, it seems, betraying the fact that, while showing the correct courtly decorum for the moment, he can already see the actual ruined man through the fast dissolving sacred king. I use the metaphor deliberately. As Richard Altick noted in an important article: 'In no other history play is the idea of tears and weeping so insistently presented. It is this element which enforces our impression of Richard as a weakling, a monarch essentially feminine in nature, who has no conception of stoic endurance or resignation but a strong predilection for grief. This is why the play seems so strangely devoid of the heroic ...' In this play, there is, strangely, no fighting – but a lot of crying. It is, indeed, a play about a 'King of Sorrows'.

When Richard first appears, high on the walls, he is still regal – 'Yet looks he like a king,' says York – and Bolingbroke, perhaps diplomatically deferring to convention, likens him to the sun *rising*:

> See, see, King Richard doth himself appear,
> As doth the blushing discontented sun
> From out the fiery portal of the East.
>
> (III, iii, 61–3)

Yet very soon, almost immediately in fact, he is seen 'setting', literally coming 'down'. Northumberland asks him to 'come down' so that he can talk to Bolingbroke in 'the base court' (simply, the *basse cour*, the lower courtyard). Richard takes the literal request and turns it into a metaphor, working it for all it is worth:

> Down, down I come, like glist'ring Phaethon,
> Wanting the manage of unruly jades.

INTRODUCTION

In the base court! Base court where kings grow base,
To come at traitors' calls, and do them grace:
In the base court, come down: down court, down king,
For night owls shriek where mounting larks should sing.

(III, iii, 177–82)

This is the scene in which he starts to use, compulsively, the language of 'must' ('Must he be deposed?', etc.). And all this, be it noted, before Bolingbroke has issued any threats or, indeed, shown his hand at all. Perhaps this simply indicates that the prescient king has a very clear view of Bolingbroke's as yet unstated intentions. Nevertheless, it is an incredibly quick capitulation. He appears eager to give (in this case his crown), *before* he has been asked (never mind ordered or coerced). Perhaps this means that he can already see the writing on the wall; but to a certain, quite distinct, extent, he himself is doing the writing. He seems to luxuriate in long, morbid and self-pitying speeches – 'And my large kingdom for a little grave,/A little, little grave, an obscure grave', etc. (III, iii, 152–3) – and at times he talks himself into incoherence, sounding less like a king than a 'fool'. 'I talk but idly, and you laugh at me' (III, iii, 170); 'Sorrow and grief of heart/ Makes him speak fondly like a frantic man' (III, iii, 183–4). Certainly, to use his own words, he 'plays the wantons with [his] woes' (III, iii, 163). No restraint, no restraint – as Conrad might have said. Indisputably, by the end of this scene, his 'Highness' has become his 'Lowness' and not, certainly not, without his own collusion.

There is one more stage in this 'rite of degradation' to be gone through (or acted out), for the King must experience the passage from 'lowness' to nothingness. This, the third station if you like, takes place in Westminster Hall.

> *Bolingbroke.* Are you contented to resign the crown?
> *Richard.* Ay, no; no, ay: for I *must* nothing be.
> Therefore no, no, for I resign to thee.
> Now, mark me how I will *un*do myself.
> I give this heavy weight from off my head,
> And this unwieldy scepter from my hand,
> The pride of kingly sway from out my heart;
> With mine own tears I wash away my balm,

> With mine own hands I give away my crown,
> With mine own tongue deny my sacred state,
> With mine own breath release all duteous oaths;
> All pomp and majesty I do forswear;
> My manors, rents, revenues, I forgo;
> My acts, decrees, and statutes I deny:
> . . .
> God save King Henry, *un*kinged Richard says.
>
> (IV, i, 200–12, 219, my italics)

This is, perhaps, the most crucial speech in the play – and note, first, the verbs: resign, give away, wash away, deny, release, forswear, forgo, deny. This is the lexicon of compulsive, even desperate, repudiation, relinquishment, self-negation, self-erasure. This is an inverted rite, by a king, of self-stripping, denudation, which we will see again, albeit in different circumstances, in *King Lear*. The 'unkinging' king. Scholars have noted the unusual number of negative words with privative prefixes in the play – producing such unusual coinages as 'undeaf', 'unhappied', 'uncurse', 'unkiss' and – above all – 'unkinged' (twice). 'Undo' is common enough, but it is certainly not common to watch (and Richard *wants* to be watched – 'Now, mark me . . .') a king 'undo' himself, still less to witness a king 'unking' himself – the language itself resists the formulation as if it is trying to refer to something which is, or ought to be, an impossibility.

In the second scene of the play, the widow of the murdered Duke of Gloucester laments, helplessly, to her brother-in-law, Gaunt:

> grief boundeth where it falls,
> Not with empty hollowness, but weight.

She then thinks of asking York to visit her, but, on consideration, changes her mind:

> and what shall good old York there see
> But empty lodgings and *un*furnished walls,
> *Un*peopled offices, *un*trodden stones . . .
>
> (I, ii, 58–9, 67–9)

Un– un– un–. Such is the world of deprivation, loss, grief. A world of 'un' – and it is this world which Richard, perhaps the most dazzlingly and richly accoutred of all English kings (see the glorious Wilton Diptych to start with), is going to have to enter. Is this world of grief, of loss, 'empty', 'hollow' – or does it have its own 'weight'? The Duchess of Gloucester does not put in another appearance, but, in fact, this is to become *the* question of the play (so Shakespeare works – five minutes with a dispensable Duchess before, seemingly, the play has got going, and the deepest issue of the play is already adumbrated). Back in Westminster Hall, Richard, now completely deprived of any sense of who, or what, he is, asks for a mirror:

> Let it command a mirror hither straight,
> That it may show me what a face I have,
> Since it is bankrout of his majesty.
>
> (IV, i, 264–6)

Of course, it doesn't tell him anything helpful or, in more sombre terms, anything ontologically stabilizing. Simply the perennial message of the incomprehensible difference between 'then' and 'now'.

> Was this face the face
> That every day under his household roof
> Did keep ten thousand men?
> . . .
> Was this the face that faced so many follies,
> And was at last outfaced by Bolingbroke?
>
> (IV, i, 280–82, 284–5)

Hard to face that. Richard smashes the mirror.

> Mark, silent king, the moral of this sport:
> How soon my sorrow hath destroyed my face.
>
> (IV, i, 289–90)

But the 'destruction' of the living self is not so easy, as the more realistic, less metaphorical Bolingbroke points out:

> The shadow of your sorrow hath destroyed
> The shadow of your face.
>
> (IV, i, 291–2)

Bolingbroke lives in the world of power, of steel, of 'iron'; he is

not given to 'reflection' – mirrors and images are nothing to
him. But Richard is going all the other way – he takes the hint
and, crucially, turns it.

> Say that again.
> 'The shadow of my sorrow'? Ha, let's see.
> 'Tis very true, my grief lies all within,
> And these external manners of laments
> Are merely shadows to the unseen grief
> That swells with silence in the tortured soul.
> There lies the substance . . .
>
> (IV, i, 292–8)

Where lies the substance? Richard makes this *the* question. Was
it in the court that has vanished, the favourites that have gone,
the armies that have dispersed, the kingly glory that has
melted away? Was that ever-deliquescent world truly 'substantial' – did it have real 'weight'? Or was the 'emptiness', the
'hollowness' exactly there? Richard has already begun to see it
that way:

> within the hollow crown
> That rounds the mortal temples of a king
> Keeps Death his court, and there the antic sits,
> Scoffing his state and grinning at his pomp,
> Allowing him a breath, a little scene,
> To monarchize, be feared, and kill with looks,
> Infusing him with self and vain conceit,
> As if this flesh which walls about our life
> Were brass impregnable; and, humored thus,
> Comes at the last, and with a little pin
> Bores through his castle wall, and farewell king!
>
> (III, ii, 160–70)

The material world of externalities, seemingly so solid and
physical, is not, truly, the 'substance', but, paradoxically,
'hollow', a realm of shadows. Obliterated in an instant with a
pin. The *real* 'lies all within', with 'unseen grief' and the silence
of the 'tortured soul'. This is how Richard is intent, determined, on seeing things, embarking on his irreversible and
uncompromising journey into interiority. This scene – Bolingbroke quietly 'doing' himself, Richard loquaciously 'undoing'

himself – brings, and 'jars', two worlds together. Rossiter: 'One is the half-fantasy world of the Court, where Richard's half-dream kingship reigns, with angels at his beck and serpents for his foes; the other is that other dream, of action, will, and curt-worded decision, in which he is nothing, or a passive sufferer, a king of woes (or merely a king of words). In the mirror-episode the two dreams doubly confront each other.' The breaking of the mirror is the final shattering of Richard's kingly identity.

A very interesting way of considering what happens to Richard is provided by Ernst Kantorowicz's important book, *The King's Two Bodies* (1957). The title refers to a legal fiction, promulgated by Tudor jurists to support the notion of the divine right of secular powers. To simplify (though not by much), this 'fiction' asserted that the king has 'two Bodies': one is the 'Body natural' – the creatural, physical body that dies; and the other the 'Body politic', also known as the 'mystical Body', which 'contains his royal Estate and Dignity' – 'and in this Name the King never dies'. (Thus, at the time of the Civil War the Puritans could say – 'we fight the king to defend the King'.) Kantorowicz: 'The legal concept of the King's Two Bodies cannot ... be separated from Shakespeare ... It is he who has eternalized that metaphor. He has made it not only the symbol, but indeed the very substance and essence of one of his greatest plays: *The Tragedy of King Richard II* is the tragedy of the King's Two Bodies.' Kantorowicz traces out how, in Richard, these two bodies (which should, of course, be as one) fall apart, as it were, and engage in self-destructive struggle until, finally, one betrays the other. 'The Universal called "Kingship" begins to disintegrate; its transcendental "Reality", its objective truth and god-like existence, so brilliant shortly before, pales into nothing, a *nomen* ... Not only does the king's manhood prevail over the godhead of the Crown, and mortality over immortality; but, worse than that, kingship itself seems to have changed its essence. Instead of being unaffected "by Nonage or Old Age and other natural Defects and Imbecilities", kingship itself comes to mean Death, and nothing but Death ... The king that "never dies" here has been replaced by the king that always dies and suffers death more cruelly than other mortals. Gone is the oneness of the body natural with the immortal body politic, "this double Body, to which no Body is equal". Gone also is the fiction of royal prerogatives of any kind, and all that remains is the feeble human nature of a king.' In Westminster Hall, Richard's tear-filled eyes mistily make out traitors all round him, but then:

> Nay, if I turn mine eyes upon myself,
> I find myself a traitor with the rest;
> For I have given here my soul's consent
> T'undeck the pompous body of a king;
> Made glory base and sovereignty a slave,
> Proud majesty a subject, state a peasant.
>
> (IV, i, 246–51)

Richard perceives, says Kantorowicz, that 'he is a traitor to his own immortal body politic and to kingship such as it had been to his day … the king body natural becomes a traitor to the king body politic … It is as though Richard's self-indictment of treason anticipated the charge of 1649, the charge of high treason committed by the *k*ing against the *K*ing.' After this, there is only the inner world left to him. He is despatched to the Tower (later changed to Pomfret Castle).

On his way there, the people throw 'dust and rubbish' on his 'sacred head',

> Which with such gentle sorrow he shook off,
> His face still combating with tears and smiles,
> The badges of his grief and patience …
>
> (V, ii, 31–3)

Having played out his scenes before his Judas and Pilate figures, he is now approaching his Calvary or Golgotha (referred to by Carlisle in his tremendous warning to Boling-broke, IV, i, 114–49, see line 144), and, once again, he briefly takes on the lineaments and demeanour of a Christ figure. In addition to becoming a genuine figure of pathos, he now takes on a strange beauty, quite missing in his earlier appearances. His Queen, Isabel, shortly before their final parting, describes him as a 'beauteous inn' compared to Bolingbroke, who is a mere 'alehouse' (V, i, 13, 15) – odd but rather powerful metaphors. Isabel plays a very small part in the play. She is a witness in the overtly emblematic Garden Scene (III, iv); and she has an oddly premonitory early scene with Richard's favourites in which she complains of a nameless apprehension and unhappiness – 'my inward soul /With nothing trembles ... makes me with heavy nothing faint and shrink ... nothing hath begot my something grief' (II, ii), which seems to provide an anticipatory fore-echo of the 'nothing' which Richard is to become, and his dungeon soliloquy:

> But whate'er I be,
> Nor I, nor any man that but man is,
> With nothing shall be pleased, till he be eased
> With being nothing.
>
> (V, v, 38–41)

Her parting from Richard has little true pathos, he seeming to be more intent on narcissistic self-pity:

> Tell thou the lamentable tale of me,
> And send the hearers weeping to their beds.
>
> (V, i, 44–5)

Etc. ... And that is about all we see of the Queen. Isabel was in fact a very young girl at the time, and perhaps Shakespeare had that in mind. Whatever, unlike many regal women in Shakespeare, she is, effectively, kept in the margins of the play.

Richard's long dungeon soliloquy (V, v, 1–66) – the only soliloquy in the play – is not at all serene; being king of the inner world brings no royal satisfactions. He tries to fabricate an alternative world, and fails. Alone, he is everybody and nobody:

> Thus play I in one person many people,
> And none contented ...
> ...
> Then am I kinged again and, by and by,
> Think that I am unkinged by Bolingbroke,
> And straight am nothing.
>
> (V, v, 31–2, 36–8)

The question is often raised as to whether Shakespeare here achieves, or conveys, a sense of deeply felt inwardness, that authentic, anguished self-probing and analysis which we associate with the great tragedies. Or whether there is too much self-pleasing artifice in the language, too much formal antiphony, too many elegant conceits, too much smooth patterning of statement, to convince us we are hearing the urgent flow of true feeling. This is perhaps related to the question of whether or not Richard is a 'poet'. Many have thought him one. According to Walter Raleigh, 'it is difficult to condemn Richard without taking sides against poetry'. Walter Pater found him 'an exquisite poet if he is nothing else, from first to last', exclaiming enthusiastically, 'What a garden of words!' (Some have found him simply a *bad* poet.) Others have denied him the status, suggesting instead that he likes to spin out elaborate speeches because he is too weak to act (it might just be noted that he is active enough when his murderers set on him – he kills two of them, four in Holinshed!) One thing is certain – the idea and activity of 'speech' is given extraordinary emphasis. The word 'tongue' occurs more often than in any other play, and 'breath', 'mouth', 'speech', 'word' are frequent. Richard Altick thinks that this 'draws constant attention to the propensity for verbalizing ... which is Richard's fatal weakness', and, more generally, underlines 'the unsubstantiality of human language'. As I have mentioned, there is, remarkably, no fighting in the play (the knightly combat which is about to occur at the start is arrested and prevented by ceremony – this sets the tone), and Richard does at times give the impression of wishing to arrest the world with words. By contrast, Boling-broke is almost dumb about his doings and movings. It is perhaps worth remembering that Richard II's court (in the play only slightingly referred to for its interest in foreign fashions and luxury) was known for its splendour, elegance, refinement – including an interest in the arts. Chaucer and Gower wrote during his reign, as Tillyard reminds us. I don't think the question of whether Richard was a good or bad poet (or no poet at all), or the matter of the relative sincerity or 'conceit-edness' of his speech, are particularly central (or decidable). The play is contemporary with *A Midsummer Night's Dream* and *Romeo and Juliet*, and clearly Shakespeare was interested in pushing the lyric potentialities of language in new directions. Richard is plausibly presented as a medieval king of sensibility, who prefers refinement to valour, ceremony to combat, fine words to ferocious wars (perhaps that is why Shakespeare kept silent about his success in fighting the Irish). When his (too luxurious, too irresponsible) world collapses around him, he falls back on what he knows, and does, best. Into what new areas of suffering and deprivation – and 'degradation' – all this would take him, he could hardly have foretold. That is what Shakespeare shows us. The spectacle is of – the king unkinged. And it is awesome.

*

HENRY IV, PART ONE

Gadshill. Give me thy hand. Thou shalt have a share in our purchase, as I am a true man.
Chamberlain. Nay, rather let me have it, as you are a false thief.
Gadshill. Go to; 'homo' is a common name to all men.

(II, i, 94–8)

Richard II contains no comedy – and no prose. As befits, it might justly be thought, its almost continuously ceremonial, even sacramental (no matter how inverted) character. *Henry IV* very notably, indeed explosively, has both comedy and prose – and this difference allows us to glance at a major problem, or at least a determining factor, for Shakespeare when he wrote his history plays. To put it very simply, as a creative dramatist he is hemmed in by history. When it comes to events – let us unblushingly call them the facts – he is limited by, and pretty strictly adheres to, the chronicles. Of course, within these givens he can be, as we have seen, marvellously adroit and inventive, with his conflations, rearrangings, telescopings, omissions, and – though these are comparatively rare – additions. And it goes without saying that, when it comes to revelation of motive and exhibition of character, Shakespeare has and takes all the liberties he wants. Just occasionally, it seems as if he is on the brink of push-ing history off in a non-historical direction (in *King John* for example), but he always comes back to the facts as then known. His Richard III may multiply his murders unconscionably, but will have to turn up to meet his fate at Bosworth. Prince Hal can spend as many, entirely legendary, hours in taverns as Shakespeare decides, but he has a date he must keep at Shrewsbury (albeit Shakespeare takes great liberties with the ages of the leading players). And when Hal speaks as a prince, in princely mode, he speaks poetry. History, it seems, demands the muse.

But bringing in a figure like Falstaff (though, to be sure, there isn't another figure in literature 'like' Falstaff), opened up entirely new areas of possibility for Shakespeare. Falstaff is related to an historical predecessor in only the most tenuous of ways, and the origins of the Falstaff we see are, ultimately, unknowable, untraceable. From one point of view, he is not an historical character at all. Yet there he is, in history (he is at Shrewsbury, too), even while he seems to be making very free with history, indeed threatening 'history', at least in its official, chronicle form. You don't make annals out of Falstaff's anarchic antics. Yet with Falstaff, Shakespeare was able to perfect a genre of 'comic history' which added a whole new dimension to historical drama – arguably to drama *tout court*.

To get some sense of the new kind of historical drama Shakespeare was able to effect with the presence of Falstaff, I want to consider the first three scenes in some detail. We start where we might expect to start – in the King's palace in London. The King's opening speech is grave, and as so often in Shakespeare, the first lines set the tone of the play.

> So shaken as we are, so wan with care,
> Find we a time for frighted peace to pant
> And breathe short-winded accents of new broils
> To be commenced in stronds afar remote.

The immediate impression is of a strained and insecure monarch, and an apprehensive nation, seriously out of breath. We are reminded how recently it was that the 'thirsty' soil was 'daub(ing) her lips with her own children's blood', and 'trenching war' 'channel(ing)' the fields and 'bruise(ing)' the flowers. How 'opposed eyes . . . Did lately meet in the intestine shock/And furious close of civil butchery'. The King's hope is that

> The edge of war, like an ill-sheathèd knife,
> No more shall cut his master.

But there is a lot of that cutting edge and civil butchery to come. Once more the King has to defer his promised Crusade (to expiate the murder of Richard II) because of more local 'broils' in Wales, Scotland, and the north of England (uprisings and rebellions or incursions from these realms were to trouble most of Henry IV's reign, dubbed, accurately enough, by Hall 'The Unquiete Time of King Henry the Fourthe'). Westmoreland tells of the success of 'wild Glendower' and how a thousand Englishmen have been 'butchered':

> Upon whose dead corpse there was such misuse,
> Such beastly shameless transformation
> By those Welshwomen done, as may not be
> Without much shame retold or spoken of.
>
> (I, i, 43–6)

This probably refers to castration – but in due course we are to see for ourselves some 'misuse' of a 'dead corpse', different but perhaps no less shocking; and there are 'transformations' to come, how 'beastly' or 'shameless' may be individually decided.

There has also been a 'sad and bloody hour' in Northumberland against Douglas and the Scots, but here Hotspur has had success and taken some important prisoners, described by the King as 'honorable spoil', 'a gallant prize' (I, i, 74–5) – a vocabulary of robbery we are to hear much of. More to the point, the King makes it clear that he wants, and intends to have, those prisoners for himself – despoiling the spoiler of his spoils we may say, glancing ahead at what is to come. The King also reveals his discontent with his son, particularly in comparison with Hotspur – 'sweet fortune's minion and her pride' (I, i, 82). Hotspur is 'the theme of honor's tongue', while

> See riot and dishonor stain the brow
> Of my young Harry.
>
> (I, i, 84–5)

The contrast, comparison, and competition between the two

'young' Harrys will be central to the play (Hotspur was, in fact, twenty-three years older than Hal – indeed, he was two years older than the King), as will be the theme of 'honor'. In one short scene, a lot of the play has been prospectively opened up.

The language throughout is grave, compacted, dignified blank verse, and the atmosphere is of serious state business. Posts and messengers arrive; news – 'uneven and unwelcome' or 'smooth and welcome' – keeps coming in; questions are of 'power', and matters are mainly military. Speed is of the essence – 'this haste was hot in question', 'come yourself with speed to us again' – as we watch a pale and troubled king trying to manage volatile and discontented factions erupting all over the land. I note that the last word of the King's first speech is 'expedience', and with this king, in this court, the politics of expediency are paramount.

The first line of the second scene – actually set in the Prince's 'lodging', presumably in a 'tavern' part of London – introduces us to Falstaff, asking the time. 'Now, Hal, what time of day is it, lad?' This provokes, by way of a response from the Prince of Wales, a most unprincely blast of demotic prose:

What a devil hast thou to do with the time of day? Unless hours were cups of sack, and minutes capons, and clocks the tongues of bawds, and dials the signs of leaping houses, and the blessed sun himself a fair hot wench in flame-colored taffeta, I see no reason why thou shouldst be so superfluous to demand the time of the day.

(I, ii, 6–12)

Time is for soldiers and statesmen; for utilitarians and fixers; for schedulers and planners. Time is for kings, particularly if, like this king, they have a lot of 'business' (key word). 'Come yourself with speed to us again' – because we'll need all the time we can get. Hal is right. Falstaff has nothing whatever to do with such closely observed clock time. He is exclusively physical and corporeal, and is mainly concerned – still Hal's response – with eating and drinking and 'unbuttoning' after supper. The literal act is apt for metaphorical extrapolations, since Falstaff inhabits, and to some extent presides over, a world of multiple 'unbuttonings' – of trousers, morals, religion, codes, language – ultimately perhaps, the unbuttoning of value itself. We will see. Falstaff's immediate response to the Prince is characteristic – 'Indeed you come near me now, Hal.' Not only can he always deflect any criticism; he can invariably turn it to his advantage, even when it seems completely unanswerable. On this occasion he asks Hal – 'when thou art king' – to dignify Falstaff and his gang. 'Let us be Diana's foresters, gentlemen of the shade, minions of the moon; and let men say we be men of good government, being governed, as the sea is, by our noble and chaste mistress the moon, under whose countenance we steal' (I, ii, 25–30). And let them say that black is white. But how plausible-sounding, and, anyway, pleasurable, is this brazen casuistry; and he has enough bits of the lexicon of mythology and polity to make his case sound sonorous and dignified – he sounds as if he is talking a compound of heraldry and law. The pun on that last word, 'steal', is perfection – at once, telling a truth and showing a lie. Inasmuch as 'steal' can mean 'creep quietly for protection', this is just what he is doing at this moment, hiding his nefarious activities behind a mystifying mythological panoply of Diana and the moon. Inasmuch as 'steal' means steal, this is exactly what they do – they rob by night. This is pure Falstaff, of course. But by the end of the play, when we have seen and heard the nobles, the princes, the King himself, in action, we might well want to avail ourselves of Falstaff's words and ask – under whose countenance do *they* steal?

'When thou art king' – the words are often in Falstaff's mouth: 'shall there be gallows standing in England when thou art king? And resolution thus fubbed as it is with the rusty curb of old father Antic the law? Do not thou, when thou art king, hang a thief (I, ii, 61–4). Falstaff is, of course, imagining and anticipating a, to him, Utopian upside-down world of permanent carnival and anarchy – 'when thou art king'. He is, of course, to be hopelessly, cruelly?, disappointed, and in the event 'old father Antic the law' will prove to be a good deal less 'Antic' than Falstaff can ever have feared. But as long as the Prince is content to play, or be, a 'madcap', Falstaff feels free to expand, 'unbutton', and luxuriate – which is, of course, our, very considerable, fun.

But the 'fun' is full of potentially serious points and allusions (as perhaps all really good fun is). When he says to the Prince 'I would to God thou and I knew where a commodity of good names were to be bought' (I, ii, 85–6), we can recognize the shameless cynicism, but may pause to ponder where some of the established men of repute – the King, for example – procured their 'good names'. And when, after a farrago of Puritan cant (which he does very well), Falstaff announces 'I must give over this life, and I will give it over! By the Lord, and I do not, I am a villain!', we are alerted to a theme of repentance and 'conversion' (transformation) which will become crucial. The Prince deflects Falstaff 'from praying to purse-taking' (I, ii, 99–101, 107), and they are soon planning the robbery at Gad's Hill. At which point, Poins engages the Prince in his planned 'jest' to allow Falstaff and his gang to rob the travellers they have in mind, and then to 'rob' them of their booty – just what the King was planning to do to Hotspur in the previous scene. When the Prince asks how they can avoid recognition, Poins has disguises of buckram ready – 'to immask our noted outward garments' (I, ii, 184). We are still in that lawless night-time world in which robbery and jesting are scarcely distinguishable. But even at this point, as they prepare for 'fun', they are adumbrating the use of disguise and 'counterfeit' by the King at the Battle of Shrewsbury.

At the end of the scene the Prince is left alone, and he has a soliloquy (it is notable that he has just one soliloquy in each of the three *Henry* plays). Men tend to be honest in soliloquies; they are, as we have seen, often rogues who play a deceptive role to the other characters, a role which they drop when they are alone (alone with us). The Prince's speech has been seen as problematical, but we can be sure that he is speaking in his own, princely, voice; that this is the man. Significantly, he reverts to the courtly mode of poetry – buttoning himself up again we might say.

> I know you all, and will awhile uphold
> The unyoked humor of your idleness.
> Yet herein I will imitate the sun,

> Who doth permit the base contagious clouds
> To smother up his beauty from the world,
> That, when he please again to be himself,
> Being wanted, he may be more wond'red at
> By breaking through the foul and ugly mists
> Of vapors that did seem to strangle him.
>
> (I, ii, 199–207)

He's just playing with them. This is the realization that has shocked some, while others seem to think that he is revealing his true princely quality as one who can handle pitch without being defiled. It is – I think – unarguably unpleasant, and if it is so for us it is simply calumny to think it wasn't for Shakespeare. Nobody likes someone who so coldly uses other people. We don't now, and the presumption must be that they didn't then. And more:

> So when this loose behavior I throw off
> And pay the debt I never promisèd,
> By how much better than my word I am,
> By so much shall I falsify men's hopes;
> And, like the bright metal on a sullen ground,
> My reformation, glitt'ring o'er my fault,
> Shall show more goodly and attract more eyes
> Than that which hath no foil to set it off.
> I'll so offend to make offense a skill,
> Redeeming time when men think least I will.
>
> (I, ii, 212–21)

First, his patrician disgust at the company he has decided to keep – base contagious clouds, foul and ugly mists. Then, behaviour he can apparently 'throw off'; as, perhaps, he can 'throw on' royalty – this is conduct as costume. Conduct as 'commodity' we might say. Certainly, his talk of 'debt' suggests the market world of 'business', and he treats his 'reformation' as, indeed, a commodity which must be shown to its best advantage 'to attract more eyes'. There is nothing very inward going on here – in a later age, such a 'reformation' might well be termed 'other-directed'. As Ornstein points out, the Prince is talking like a clever shopkeeper who 'knows how to display the merchandise of his behaviour'. From any point of view, it is a speech of extreme and unappealing calculation. He might, he will, turn out to be a good king. But what sort of a man will he be? Rossiter once suggested that Sonnet 94 might provide a way of reading the Prince:

> They that have pow'r to hurt and will do none,
> That do not do the thing they most do show,
> Who, moving others, are themselves as stone,
> Unmovèd, cold, and to temptation slow;
> They rightly do inherit heaven's graces
> And husband nature's riches from expense;
> They are the lords and owners of their faces,
> Others but stewards of their excellence.

It may not fit in every respect, but it will do to be going on with.

The next scene opens with a speech from the King which could almost be a continuation of his son's, which it immediately follows.

> My blood hath been too cold and temperate,
> Unapt to stir at these indignities
> . . .
> I will from henceforth rather be myself,
> Mighty and to be feared, than my condition.
>
> (I, iii, 1–2, 5–6)

Myself – as king? My condition – my natural disposition? It is a wise man who knows the one from the other, if, indeed, they are finally separable. Whether Prince Hal eventually manages to bring 'self' and 'condition' harmoniously together will remain a debatable point. For a prince in line for the throne, where lies the 'self' and when and where is he most 'being' it? But the importance of this scene lies in the introduction of Hotspur – and his barely controllable fury at the King's peremptory demand that he hand over his prisoners. Hotspur is the leading representative of the third important realm of the play, termed by Maynard Mack 'the feudal countryside'. This is a world away from the court and the tavern; based in the north of England, it is more in touch with Wales and Scotland than London, though of course the lines of communication are open, and, indeed, this scene takes place in the council chamber at Windsor. But this is not Hotspur's natural habitat, and, as Holinshed rather nicely puts it, he is 'not a little fumed' at the King's arrogant and even supercilious deportment towards him. Hotspur, with his almost fanatical chivalric code, and his headlong, uncalculating (note!), impetuosities, is an almost anachronistic figure, at times made to sound foolish, even childish (petulant beyond constraining, more interested in his horse than his wife, more concerned with romantic honour than prudent strategy); yet he speaks some of the most powerful, trenchant lines in the play, and we would do well to attend to his opinion of King Henry – or, as he would more forcefully have it, 'this unthankful king, / . . . this ingrate and cank'red Bolingbroke' (I, iii, 134–5). Anger sometimes arrives at ferociously penetrating perceptions.

Harking back to a chivalric age in which he would have been more at home, Hotspur bitterly regrets that his family and friends did help 'To put down Richard, that sweet lovely rose' (I, iii, 173 – they are always good, being gone). Henry IV, he sees, is a 'vile politician . . . this king of smiles, this Bolingbroke' (I, iii, 239, 244), and he recalls 'what a candy deal of courtesy/This fawning greyhound then did proffer me (I, iii, 248–9). Readers of Shakespeare will not need reminding of the nausea associated with candy-courtesy in his plays. Hotspur and his associates plan 'revenge' (the old code). By the end of Act I, Henry is not looking so good or so secure – 'wan' indeed. He has grief from his own son whom he takes to be a derelict delinquent (in time, a would-be parricide); and he is threatened by a potentially more serious act of insubordination on the part of his wished-for surrogate 'son' (see I, i, 85–9). All my sons – and they are all against me. Hotspur is certainly after both father and son:

> All studies here I solemnly defy
> Save how to gall and pinch this Bolingbroke;
> And that same sword-and-buckler Prince of Wales
>
> (I, iii, 226–8)

And, to keep vividly alive our sense of the contrast between Prince Hal – so sunk in 'dishonor' as far as his father is concerned – and Hotspur, we have Hotspur's vainglorious address to honour:

By heaven, methinks it were an easy leap
To pluck bright honor from the pale-faced moon,
Or dive into the bottom of the deep,
Where fathom line could never touch the ground,
And pluck up drownèd honor by the locks

(I, iii, 199–203)

A lot of 'honor' is 'drowned' in this play, and how much is
finally 'plucked up' is perhaps a moot point.

The scene ends, as have the previous two, with plotting.
Hotspur, being Hotspur, can hardly wait.

O let the hours be short
Till fields and blows and groans applaud our sport!

(I, iii, 298–9)

Every realm has its sports – Hotspur's are fields and blows and
groans; Falstaff's sack and thieving and unbuttoning; the
King's are, well, the somewhat subtler sports of expediency,
counterfeit-regality, and crown-retention.

In this first Act Shakespeare has laid out the topography –
geographical and psychological – of his play, and the main
figures from each realm have, variously, 'disported' themselves. Bolingbroke, Falstaff, Hotspur – plus the, apparently,
so far disengaged and floating Prince; the main thrust of the
play will be to trace out how the Prince manages his relationship with these three men, and these three worlds. It matters;
it greatly matters – because he is unavoidably due to become
the most famous of all English kings. The King and Falstaff
look like opposites – true paternal authority and legitimate
rule versus a disreputable corrupter of youth and the spirit of
misrule. But the King's 'legitimacy' won't bear much scrutiny,
and the disorder abroad and spreading in the land is, arguably, of his own bringing and making; and Falstaff, as an
undeniable sort of father-figure, can show to the Prince a spirit
of inclusive, tolerant humanity, which his real, 'expedient',
father shows no sign of possessing. (William Empson once
wrote: 'If you compare Hal to his brother and father, whom
the plays describe so unflinchingly, it is surely obvious that to
love Falstaff was a liberal education.') Again, Hotspur and

xlii

Falstaff seem to offer the Prince quintessential examples of opposed codes – chivalry and cynicism. Yet both are rebels against the constituted authority in place; both – it is part of their undoubted appeal – are in some ways childish, retarded (from the sombre standpoint of joyless, unenthusing maturity), and both are marked, or marred, by a disabling excess; for if Falstaff drinks too much sherris-sack to be good for anything much, Hotspur so intoxicates himself with fuzzy notions of 'honor' that he finally unfits himself for efficient soldiery. There is no more apt cameo in the play than the spectacle of Falstaff carrying the dead Hotspur from the battlefield on his back in front of the incredulous Prince Hal. 'I am not a double man', he calls out reassuringly to the Prince (V, iv, 137), but Falstaff–Hotspur do, incongruously enough, make up a composite figure (a 'double' act) that Hal will have to go beyond – 'transcend' if you like (some critics do), certainly leave behind. Yet Hal is like Hotspur in being young and brave (which is why Shakespeare suggests, unhistorically, they are of an age). Hal is also like Falstaff, at least for a time, joining him in anarchic mockeries on the uncourtly side of town. Hal is also like the King – his first, calculating soliloquy reveals him to be very much his politic father's son, even if repentance and reconciliation are deferred. That is perhaps the main point. Hal is 'like' everybody, and can beat them all at their own games. He out-policies his bemused father; he outwits Falstaff in his tavern knaveries; and he defeats Hotspur at his own chosen sport – on the killing-field of chivalric combat. He knows them all. Certainly, he is the lord and owner of his face.

We have had ruthless kings and rebellious lords before. The crucial addition in the two *Henry IV* plays is, of course, Falstaff and his milieu. The court and the tavern, or the tavern revellers and the noble rebels, might initially seem worlds apart, but they are brought into all sorts of provocative relationships by what A. R. Humphreys nicely calls 'the fabric of linkage'. The behaviour, and thus the authority and proclaimed values, of the court and the nobles, are too often parodied, or travestied, or comically paralleled by what goes on around Falstaff, for us to regard them as anything but seriously challenged and called into question, if not actively undermined. Nothing and no one remains uncontaminated by the prevailing, often quite corrosive, irony – except, perhaps, our ice-cool Prince. But that might prove to be the biggest irony of them all. The point about the various alternating plots – they come together at Shrewsbury – is that 'the more they are scrutinized, the more connected they appear, the connection being sometimes of parallelism and reinforcement, sometimes of antithesis and contrast, sometimes a reversal by which serious or comic is judged by the other's values' (A. R. Humphreys). And the main point about the differing worlds is that, mutually exclusive though they may seem, they all co-exist in one world. For this is all England; and, the point enforces itself, this is all – *all* – history. Well, as far as Shakespeare is concerned.

Before considering the rest of this play, I think it might be advisable to say something about Falstaff as a character, a figure, an emanation, a whatever-he-is. There was a real Sir John Oldcastle (Falstaff's original name) who lived from 1378 to 1417. He was, apparently, a serious gentleman (though he might have been a wild youth), who became High Sheriff of Herefordshire and later Lord Cobham. A friend of King Henry, he was, subsequently, 'banished'. He was a Lollard convicted of the Wycliffite heresy, for which he was condemned, captured, and, finally, hanged and burnt. He next appears, or rather his name does, in a play called 'The Famous Victories of Henry the Fifth', probably written around 1594. This anonymous play is crude and chaotic ('like going through the *Henry IV–Henry V* sequences in a bad dream' as A. R. Humphreys says), and, apart perhaps from its depiction of the young Prince as an out-and-out delinquent, its main interest lies in the fact that one of the Prince's madcap companions is called Sir John Oldcastle. But he is neither funny nor fat, and it's not even clear that he likes a drink. He only speaks some 250 flat words, the likest of which to any spoken by Shakespeare's Falstaff are: 'We shall never have a merry world till the old King be dead' (iv, 39). From Oldcastle to Falstaff is truly a miraculous metamorphosis. (Maynard Mack pointed out another example of what

Shakespeare could do with a hint from this play. Mistress Quickly springs from an offhand reference by the Prince to 'the old tavern in Eastcheap' where 'there is a pretty wench that can talk well'.)

Of course, there are other detectable influences. John Dover Wilson set out some of these clearly enough in his *The Fortunes of Falstaff* (1943). Of first importance is the figure of the Devil, or his Vice, from Miracle and morality plays and interludes. He gives as an example 'Youth' (1520) in which Youth insolently banishes Charity to be joined by Riot who introduces him to Pride and Lechery. Youth repents, and is saved by Humility. (Falstaff is specifically referred to as riot and Vice and the Devil – 'old white-bearded Satan' – in Shakespeare.) Gluttony was a common tempter of youth in these morality plays and interludes, as was Sensual Appetite, Sloth, Idleness, and World, Devil, and Flesh (see, for example, 'The Castell of Perseverance', 'The Interlude of the Four Elements', 'The Trial of Treasure'). You can find traces, and more than traces, of all of them in Falstaff. And of many other figures too – the Clown, the Jester, the Fool, the Lord of Misrule, and the *miles gloriosus* (boasting of bravery but avoiding battle – the braggart, cowardly soldier). Throw in, too, the parasite, the sponger, the trickster – the list seems almost infinitely extendable – many of them, says Dover Wilson, 'antic figures the origins of which are lost in the dark backward and abysm of folk custom'. With all this, we must never forget that Falstaff is never remotely stupid. He is phenomenally adroit and inventive with words, endlessly resourceful, unflaggingly creative. It is interesting that, according to J. P. Collier, Coleridge said: 'It was in characters of complete moral depravity but of first-rate wit and talents, that Shakespeare delighted', and 'instanced Richard the Third, Falstaff, and Iago'. Richard III and Iago! Falstaff is certainly no Father Christmas but, while Coleridge is justified in according him a comparable mental fertility and agility, I don't believe that Falstaff deserves quite to be grouped with such unmitigated evil (would you like a meal with Richard, a drink with Iago?) Dr Johnson hits perhaps a happier note: 'But Falstaff, unimitated, unimitable Falstaff, how shall I describe thee? Thou compound of sense and vice; of sense which may be admired but not esteemed, of vice which may be despised but hardly detested. Falstaff is a character loaded with faults, and with those faults which naturally produce contempt.' Johnson lists the faults – forcefully enough, as you may imagine – and concludes: 'Yet the man thus corrupt, thus despicable, makes himself necessary to the Prince that despises him, by the most pleasing of all qualitites, perpetual gaiety, by an unfailing power of exciting laughter . . . ' The thought of Dr Johnson enjoying Falstaff is one which, I think, we can all savour. But, here again, 'perpetual gaiety' doesn't seem quite right by the end of the two plays, by which time also the Prince signals his decision that Falstaff is distinctly *un*necessary to him now that he is King. So – not *toujours Iago*, but not *toujours gai* either.

'And who, in fact, is "he"? "He", really, is the comic personality given a chance by the dramatist to revel in a comic role.' Thus A. R. Humphreys in his admirable Arden edition. And when Humphreys concludes his comments on Falstaff, he is closer to Dr Johnson than to Coleridge. 'In other words, Falstaff, though immensely "living", is not like any single real man. But he is symbolically like life itself; the large comedy of humanity is embodied in him. He expresses the indispensable spirit of fun.' This is certainly one way of looking at Falstaff, though I think it takes us a step closer to Father Christmas than is appropriate. We should, perhaps, set against this a mordant and extremely negative view of Falstaff and the whole world of the play, articulated by John Danby in *Shakespeare's Doctrine of Nature*. We have presented, says Danby, a nation 'disintegrated into mutually exclusive spheres', which is pervaded by 'pitiless fraud'. Falstaff's code of 'Commodity' is the code by which everyone, high and low, lives.

Analysis leaves us, then, with symbols of Power and Appetite as the keys to the play's meaning: Power and Appetite, the two sides of Commodity . . . The England depicted in *Henry IV* . . . is neither ideally ordered nor happy. It is an England, on the one side, of bawdy house and thieves' kitchen, of waylaid merchants, badgered and bewildered Justices, and a peasantry wretched, betrayed, and recruited for the wars: an England, on the other side, of the chivalrous wolf-pack ... Those who see the world of *Henry IV* as some vital, joyous, Renaissance England must go behind the facts that Shakespeare presents. It is a world where to be normal is to be anti-social, and to be social is to be anti-human. Humanity is split in two. One half is banished to an underworld where dignity and decency must inevitably submerge in brutality and riot. The other half is restricted to an over-world where the same dignity and decency succumb to heartlessness and frigidity.

This is eloquent, and certainly reminds us of aspects of the play(s) which we must not forget. But ultimately, this isn't quite right either.

Falstaff is not quite such a nihilistic figure as Danby would seem to imply. It is probably better to see him as, in part, embodying the spirit of carnival, as defined by Mikhail Bakhtin in his seminal work, *Rabelais and His World*. This has been done at some length by Graham Holderness (in *Shake-speare Recycled*), to which more interested readers are referred. For Bakhtin, in the Middle Ages 'a boundless world of humorous forms and manifestations opposed the official and serious tone of medieval ecclesiastical and feudal culture ... the culture of folk carnival humour'. In carnival, social hierarchy was inverted, authority mocked, conventional values profaned, official ceremonies and rituals grotesquely parodied, the normal power structures dissolved – in a word, Misrule, Riot, the world-upside-down. For Bakhtin – he has a political programme – carnival amounted to 'the second life of the people, who for a time entered into the utopian realm of community, freedom, equality and abundance'. In particular, carnival emphasized, often grotesquely, the flesh and all bodily appetites and functions – 'all that is bodily becomes grandiose, exaggerated, immeasurable'. Most of this fits 'fat-guts' Falstaff very well (his gross fleshy size and general immersion in physicality is often emphasized; on the other hand, he shows no very great interest in 'equality' – he has his own knightly contempt for the poor wretches beneath him, though he will rob and drink with them). To this extent, Holderness is justified in his general claim that Falstaff is a figure of carnival (though it should be stressed that Falstaff 'embodies' traces and vestiges and lineaments of many other figures and types – long before Walt Whitman, Falstaff 'contains multitudes').

Falstaff clearly performs the function, in *Henry IV Parts One and Two*, of carnival. He constitutes a constant focus of opposition to the official and serious tone of authority and power: his discourse confronts and challenges those of king and state. His attitude to authority is always parodic and satirical: he mocks authority, flouts power, responds to the pressures of social duty and civic obligation by retreating into Bacchanalian revelry.

Of course, carnival was a strictly controlled and temporary period of liberation and inversion – a permitted period of licence which arguably served to consolidate the social hierarchies and institutions which obtained for the non-carnivalesque rest of the year. Inasmuch as Falstaff wants carnival to be the permanent and everyday state of affairs, he represents – Holderness would argue, I think rightly – a potentially dangerous, subversive, uncontainable force or spirit. And, inasmuch as Falstaff is *not* pinned down and penned down in the chronicles – he inhabits the unconfined spaces of unwritten history – he allows Shakespeare to introduce something dangerous, subversive, and perhaps ultimately uncontainable into his history *plays*.

Act II is effectively dominated by Falstaff, though I note that it opens with carriers and ostlers talking about horses. Horses are often referred to in the play, understandably enough since it is almost seething with people on the move – messengers, traders, merchants, highwaymen, pilgrims, whole armies either advancing or scattering in retreat. (We tend to forget how crucial horses were in those days: when Vernon is trying to dissuade Hotspur from a premature attack, his reason is that the *horses* are tired – 'not a horse is half the half of himself', IV, iii, 24). Horses are also, of course, essential to chivalric deportment. Falstaff roars 'Give me my horse' after Poins and the Prince have 'removed it' (he may or may not be echoing Richard III's famous line) since it is undignified for a knight to go on foot; later, the Prince extends the, rather cruel, joke by arranging for Falstaff to lead a 'charge of foot' ('I would it had been of horse', says Falstaff, rather plaintively).

Quite apart from suffering loss of status, anyone less suited to the ambulant mode of travel than Falstaff would be hard to imagine. When Vernon describes Harry 'vaulting' so perfectly on to his horse, it is as though Hal has transformed himself into a true prince. Vernon's description inflames Hotspur with lust for combat. 'I am on fire', he says, and then:

> Come, let me taste my horse,
> Who is to bear me like a thunderbolt
> Against the bosom of the Prince of Wales.
> Harry to Harry shall, hot horse to horse,
> Meet . . .
>
> (IV, i, 118–22)

Hotspur clearly has more 'taste' for his horse than his wife (see II, iii, 75–105), and one can sense his almost erotic excitement at the prospect of meeting 'hot horse to horse'. This is very much a man's world.

The double robbery at Gad's Hill provides an occasion for plenty of ironies. The well-named Gadshill sets the tone when he boasts that he does not rob with vagabond trash, but with those 'who do the profession some grace'. There is a fair amount of punning fun with that last word: 'I am joined with . . . nobility and tranquillity' – he means Sir John, and that last word is a nice collective noun for the idle and the privileged who live life very easily and unpainstakingly – 'they pray continually to their saint, the commonwealth, or rather, not pray to her, but prey on her, for they ride up and down on her and make her their boots' (II, i, 82–5). We have already seen Falstaff shift 'from praying to purse-taking' in a trice; and there is much in the play to suggest that, more generally, there is barely a letter's worth of difference between 'praying' and 'preying' among most of the main players, the tranquil and the untranquil alike, so that, in effect, it doesn't take much rhetorical adroitness to mask or cover the latter with the former. They all ride up and down on the commonwealth – when they can find their horses.

When Falstaff finds his horse has been stolen, he memorably complains 'A plague upon it when thieves cannot be true one to another' (II, ii, 27–8) – thus, not coincidentally one feels, anticipating an outburst by Hotspur not a hundred lines ahead (there were no scene divisions, remember) when he complains (in a rather Falstaffian tirade) about fellow conspirators who have let him down. A plague upon it! After the first robbery (i.e. by Falstaff and his men), the Prince says to his fellow-plotter Poins: 'The thieves have bound the true men. Now could thou and I rob the thieves and go merrily to London.' Which is just what they do, the Prince commenting, 'Got with much ease. Now merrily to horse' (II, ii, 93–4, 105). Merrily, merrily indeed (it is a Falstaffian word – 'What, shall we be merry?', II, iv, 280). The Prince finds particularly funny the thought that the horseless Falstaff 'sweats to death and lards the lean earth as he walks along' (II, ii, 109) – there is rather an edge to his 'merriment'. Perhaps more pertinently, we may remember that Hal's father 'got' the crown from the 'true' king Richard 'with much ease' (in the next play, we will see Hal literally removing his father's crown, also 'with much ease', though it is a more complex incident). With thieves robbing thieves at every level, can we be sure that there are any 'true men' left? For Gadshill, as we have heard, when it comes to differentiating 'a true man' from 'a false thief' it is pretty much six of one and half a dozen of the other. 'Go to; "homo" is a common name to all men.'

Act II, scene iv, is Falstaff's 'biggest', longest (550 lines) scene, and is in many ways the pivotal scene of the play. Thereafter, the tavern world recedes (apart from one important scene), and we are in the politico-military worlds of the King and the rebels. All roads lead to war. But before that – Eastcheap. It opens with Hal laughing, still in a 'merry' mood, because he has been 'with three or four loggerheads amongst three or fourscore hogsheads. I have sounded the very bass-string of humility' (II, iv, 4–6). He has been drinking and ingratiating himself with a bunch of poor, illiterate sots (loggerheads and hogsheads), calling them by their Christian names, with the result – he boasts – 'I am so good a proficient in one quarter of an hour that I can drink with any tinker in his own language during my life' (II, iv, 17–19): 'when I am King of England I shall command all the good lads in Eastcheap'. They call him, he says, 'the king of courtesy'. Is

1

this a democratic feeling for the people – or is he 'slumming'?
King Henry will shortly advise him to follow his own example:

> And then I stole all courtesy from heaven,
> And dressed myself in such humility
> That I did pluck allegiance from men's hearts.
>
> (III, ii, 50–52)

Like father, like son. Hal has anticipated his father's advice –
already 'stealing' courtesy, and 'dressing' in humility (we will
later hear of 'the garment of rebellion' – all attitudes and
modes of behaviour seem available ready-to-wear, so to
speak). And 'allegiance', like 'honor' is apparently there for
the plucking. The 'proficient' Prince (son of an 'expedient'
father) says to Poins: 'I tell thee, Ned, thou hast lost much
honor that thou wert not with me in this action.' What kind of
'honor' the Prince can 'pluck' from the tavern, and just how
ironic he is being in the use of the word, is indeterminable.
Shortly after this speech, he, notoriously, plays his mocking
game with 'my puny drawer' Francis, who is gratuitously
bewildered and made to look and sound a fool. It wouldn't do
to get too soft or solemn about a bit of tavern knock-about, but
not much 'honor' accrues to the Prince from this episode. Is he
demonstrating how easy it is to fool the people, if necessary
with 'humility' and 'courtesy'? He says of Francis 'His
industry is upstairs and downstairs, his eloquence the parcel of
a reckoning' (II, iv, 100–102). Curiously – or perhaps not so
curiously in this play of endless echoing ironies – the words,
taken at a slant, are self-applicable. The Prince's 'industry' is
both 'upstairs' (the court) and 'downstairs' (the tavern).
'Parcel of a reckoning' means adding up bills, and if we gloss
that as 'calculation' – what's the profit, what's the loss? – we
can say the same of the Prince's 'eloquence'.

Immediately following this description of Francis, the
Prince rather unexpectedly invokes Hotspur – to mock *his*
'industry' (killing dozens of Scots at breakfast) and 'eloquence' (horsey, and full of martial bravado). Is this cold-eyed
young Prince measuring himself up against *both* Francis *and*
Hotspur? Perhaps. Certainly he goes on to say: 'I prithee call
in Falstaff. I'll play Percy, and that damned brawn shall play

Dame Mortimer his wife' (II, iv, 109–11). They do shortly 'have a play extempore' – where better than in a tavern where much Elizabethan drama was originally played? – but in the event they don't play the Percys – they play the Bolingbrokes. (Of course, Hal *will* 'play' Hotspur in due course – indeed *out*-play him, at his own game. But not yet.)

This 'play' comes after Falstaff's truly fabulous account of the Gad's Hill episode, followed by his quite dazzling act of self-extrication when the Prince confronts him with the truth of what happened and his own masked participation ('By the Lord, I knew ye as well as he that made ye' (II, iv, 268 et seq.). Comment here is quite superfluous. But the 'play extempore' is another matter. It comes after, and is prompted by, an interruption in the tavern by the court – upstairs reaching downstairs – in the form of a messenger described simply but significantly as 'an old man' and 'gravity'. He is a 'nobleman ... from your father' (this to the Prince) – a grave, parental surrogate sent to call the errant 'madcap' children (various) to order. 'Villainous news,' says Falstaff to the Prince, 'you must to the court in the morning.' Official history is imperiously beckoning, and will not be denied. All very disagreeable and frightening, and, as Falstaff says to the Prince, his father, the King, will give him a very hard time. 'If thou love me, practice an answer.' And the ensuing play shows us, indeed, a prince at 'practice'.

'Do thou stand for my father' (II, iv, 376). Using to-hand appurtenances which are a travesty of the adjuncts of royalty: 'this dagger my scepter ... this cushion my crown' – even here one feels a barb, for, at one level, what is kingship if not comfort (cushions) defended by force (daggers)? – Falstaff acts the King and starts arraigning the Prince. He takes the opportunity to insult the Prince's appearance and deplore the company he keeps (defiling pitch) with, of course, the exception of one 'virtuous man' often in his company – 'there is virtue in that Falstaff. Him keep with, the rest banish' (II, iv, 429–30). That's enough for the Prince, who now wants to change roles. 'Do thou stand for me, and I'll play my father.' Falstaff playing the King is one sort of a joke – we have already gathered that he is, in *some* unspecifiable sense, a surrogate father, or father-figure, for Hal. But the Prince playing the King – the son playing the father – is a different matter. 'Depose me?' complains King Falstaff, staying with the game; yet it will become at least possible that Hal would like to depose his father in good earnest, just as his father had deposed Richard. And when he *is* the king, as he surely will be, will he still be *playing* the king; how will we ever know if this player-king leaves off 'playing'? We are skirting serious matters. Hal takes his opportunity to subject Falstaff to an unrestrained hail of abuse of such virulence that it begins to sound heart-felt. Not just a 'stuffed cloakbag of guts' (par for the course), but 'reverend vice', 'gray iniquity', 'abominable misleader of youth', 'father ruffian', 'white-bearded Satan', and even, simply, 'devil'. James Winny, fastening on '*father* ruffian', has suggested that Hal is 'tacitly denouncing his father's viciousness', and that Falstaff is 'unwittingly standing in for the man whose moral character he shares'. This is possible – it might explain the sudden flow of venom if Hal has indeed found a scapegoat for his putative father-hatred; but it is undemonstrable. You just can't tell with Hal. Prince Falstaff of course puts in a spirited defence of the 'merry' old man who keeps the Prince company, ending, famously:

No, my good lord: banish Peto, banish Bardolph, banish Poins; but for sweet Jack Falstaff, kind Jack Falstaff, true Jack Falstaff, valiant Jack Falstaff, and therefore more valiant being, as he is, old Jack Falstaff, banish not him thy Harry's company, banish not him thy Harry's company, banish plump Jack, and banish all the world!

(II, iv, 474–80)

To which, the King-Prince, as famously, replies: 'I do, I will.'

At this point a chill comes over the play – over both plays – which is never quite warmed away. Partly because one of the effects of the Prince's response is that feeling you get when someone says something outrageous, or deeply disturbing, to you, at the same time maintaining an absolutely impassive face which tacitly says – I defy you to tell whether I am joking or not. Is the Prince still 'playing' the King; or is this the Prince taking the chance to rehearse ('practice') what he will do and say when he *is* king? Is he still playing at all, or has he stepped out of the game? Perhaps he stopped acting some time before this: indeed, did he ever start? Where did all the 'merriment' go? If this can worry and unsettle us, it must trouble Falstaff a good deal more. He, understandably, would like the play to go on indefinitely – 'Play out the play' – but, as if on cue, after the Prince's words, a knocking at the door puts an end to the 'sport', and this time it is the Law, in the shape of the Sheriff and the watch, breaking in on the revels. They are after Falstaff, who characteristically sleeps behind the arras while the Prince, with gracious equivocations, sees off the Law. But that knock on the door was a loud one, for history really is breaking in on the play-world of the tavern. As the Prince declares, with all due finality – 'We must all to the wars' (II, iv, 546).

The third Act shows us the three worlds for the last time. In Wales, the rebels are dividing up the map in anticipation, and Hotspur loses his temper with what he calls the 'skimble-skamble stuff' of Glendower, who is out-bragging him. Worcester reproaches Hotspur with 'Defect of manners, want of government', and tells him 'You must needs learn, lord, to amend this fault' (III, i, 183, 179). The next scene in the Palace in London, has another intemperate (or thought to be) youth being reproached by a graver elder, this time the King to his son. Rather in the spirit of the parent who says to the child, 'you have been sent to try me', the King tells Hal that, the way he is behaving, he must be serving as 'the rod of heaven/To punish my mistreadings' (III, ii, 10–11). He does not, nor does he ever, confess or spell out what those 'mistreadings' were, but he is clearly a man carrying some guilt. He alludes to 'heaven', and there are scattered references to 'sin' and the like, but – and this is also something of a departure – there is little religious sense in this play, not much 'celestial superintendence' as Maynard Mack put it, no sense of a divine or providential plan. These people, anachronistically or not, inhabit what the commentators call a Tudor Erastian world. Erastus was a sixteenth-century Swiss theologian, promoted in England by Hooker, who maintained – against the extreme Calvinists – that the civil authorities should exercise jurisdiction both in civil and ecclesiastical matters. Generally speaking, 'Erastianism' indicates the ascendancy of the State over the Church in ecclesiastical matters. The most 'religious' language is in the mouth of Falstaff, drowned in flesh and parody. The King believes in 'necessity' and regards ruling as 'business' – 'Our hands are full of business' (III, ii, 179) – a word favoured in Shakespeare, by unprincipled plotters. This is a very secular world. The King compares his 'degenerate' son unfavourably with Hotspur, but Hal promises that he will 'redeem all this on Percy's head' (III, ii, 132). His language is, again, revealing. He says he will force Hotspur to '*exchange*/His glorious deeds for my indignities'; Hal will 'call him to so strict *account*/That he shall *render* every glory up ... Or I will tear *the reckoning* from his heart' (III, ii, 145–52). This is the language of a merchant: Hal will go shopping for honour.

At the end of the scene, the King says: 'Let's away:/Advantage feeds him fat while men delay' (III, ii, 180) – to be immediately followed by Falstaff, complaining, implausibly, that he is getting thinner. 'Bardolph, am I not fall'n away vilely since this last action? Do I not bate? Do I not dwindle?' (III, iii, 1–2). This is a simple joke, but what follows has deeper resonances. 'Well, I'll repent, and that suddenly, while I am in some liking.' We have just heard the Prince promise sudden (opportunistic?) repentance, and when Falstaff goes on to admit 'And I have not forgotten what the inside of a church is made of, I am a peppercorn, a brewer's horse', we may wonder if the Prince is any more familiar with the interior of religious buildings – or beliefs. Most of the rest of the scene has Falstaff bamboozling the honest Hostess, and refusing to pay her what he owes her. Rather shrewdly she says to him: 'You owe me money, Sir John, and now you pick a quarrel to beguile me of it' (III, iii, 68–9). Falstaff is certainly not alone in using this strategy to avoid an incurred debt; indeed, it pretty exactly describes how the King has treated the rebel nobles who once helped him to the throne ('well we know the King/Knows at what time to promise, when to pay', says Hotspur, drily enough – IV, iii, 52–3). There is a lot of stealing in this play, but not much honest repayment of debt. In the previous Act, when the Sheriff arrived and the Prince tells Falstaff to hide behind the arras, he then says, 'Now, my masters, for a true face and good conscience'; Falstaff's parting line is 'Both which I have had; but their date is out, and therefore I'll hide me' (II, iv, 502–5). Their date is out. So it would seem – and the arras is not the only place to hide.

The rest of the play consists of the convergence of all the parties on war, and the concluding battle at Shrewsbury. The most important event, or phenomenon, is the almost miraculous transformation of Prince Henry. Legends of Henry's wild and dissolute youth, and the sudden change and reformation that came over him when he became king, started in his own life-time (in his youth, says a chronicler of 1516, he 'applied him unto all vyce and insolency, and drewe unto him all ryottours and wylde disposed persones'), though it appears there is no historical basis for these stories. Dover Wilson suggested that fifteenth-century allegorical (morality play) taste needed a Prodigal Prince who would then be miraculously converted into the hero of Agincourt. Perhaps. Shakespeare's cool, detached Prince (himself, not so wild after all) is a world away from the unreconstructed, vandalizing thug of *The Famous Victories*; though, interestingly, as Bullough pointed out, he diminishes the Prince's administrative work and experience (he was, in fact, governor of North Wales and the Marches from 1400). Bullough also suggests that if he did have some wild years, they would most likely have been between 1405 and 1410 (when the King was ill, and Hal was aged eighteen to twenty-three) – i.e. *after* Shrewsbury. As usual, Shakespeare wants to tell it his way.

The transformation is, certainly, 'miraculous'. It is celebrated by, occurs in, Vernon's famous 'I saw young Harry with his beaver on' speech (IV, i, 96–109), which is in answer to Hotspur's inquiry as to where the 'madcap Prince of Wales' is, and which starts:

> All furnished, all in arms;
> All plumed like estridges that with the wind
> Bated like eagles having lately bathed;
> Glittering in golden coats like images;
> As full of spirit as the month of May
> And gorgeous as the sun at midsummer

and so on. It concludes by comparing Henry to Mercury and

likening him to an 'angel' dropped from the clouds on to a
'Pegasus' who is about to 'witch the world with noble horsemanship'. The poetry of this description has been rightly
praised, but I find that there is something strange about it. It
is not just the extreme fulsomeness of the admiration, which,
understandably enough, irritates Hotspur. It is as if the words
were spoken by someone hypnotized, in a trance, as if Vernon
has seen a vision. Something similar happens when Vernon describes the exquisitely princely way in which Henry offered
his challenge to single combat (V, ii, 51–69). It sounds like an
anthology of the principles of 'courtesy', drawing from Hotspur, again understandably, the comment – 'Cousin, I think
thou art enamored.' Vernon is dazzled; and so are we. I
honestly can't quite work out what I think Shakespeare is
doing here. Miraculous transformations are, of course, peren-
nially popular, and not just in folk tale, legend, and myth.
And here the audience is given, if not quite frog-into-prince, at
least tavern layabout into chivalric hero. Perhaps it is as
simple as that. Yet Shakespeare has provided such a subtle,
penetrating portrait of this complex prince that I find it hard
to think that he intended us to forget all we have seen of the
unmoved calculator. Vernon's descriptions are marked by
excess; they are 'idealized', too much so for Hotspur and
perhaps they should be a bit too much for us. Shakespeare
likes having soldiers provoked into wonder and praise – as
with Enobarbus on Cleopatra in her barge. But I cannot help
thinking that Shakespeare would have us think that, in some
way, Vernon has been 'taken in', as we say – 'enamored' is no
bad word for his almost ecstatic evocations. Hal has 'thrown
off' his tavern role, and 'put on' the panoply of chivalry. The
indications are that this capable, controlled manipulator has
an extensive 'wardrobe'. I use the word advisedly, for it is used
later in the play, in very telling circumstances. In this connection it is worth noting that Hal is compared to Mercury, where
we might expect – because of Pegasus – Perseus. Mercury –
god of furtiveness and trickery – is always devious, and
traditionally comes disguised or invisible. Perhaps Shakespeare is giving a sign – this prince is always Mercurial. I owe
this observation to Jonathan Bate in *Shakespeare and Ovid*.

The aforementioned use of the word 'wardrobe' occurs during the Battle of Shrewsbury. Fierce Douglas thinks he has killed the King, only to be told by Hotspur that, in fact, he has killed Blunt, who is 'semblably furnished like the King himself' (i.e. disguised as the King – V, iii, 21). Hotspur explains – 'The King hath many marching in his coats' (V, iii, 25), to which Douglas – angry at the rather cowardly cheating (a true soldier would hardly stoop to this) – answers:

> Now, by my sword, I will kill all his coats:
> I'll murder all his wardrobe, piece by piece,
> Until I meet the King.
>
> (V, iii, 26–8)

When he does meet up with King Henry, he suspects another disguised substitute – another coat to kill:

> Another king? they grow like Hydra's heads.
> ...   What art thou
> That counterfeit'st the person of a king?

When the King asserts 'The King himself ... the very King', Douglas is understandably sceptical:

> I fear thou art another counterfeit;
> And yet, in faith, thou bearest thee like a king
>
> (IV, iv, 24, 26–8, 34–5)

The word 'counterfeit' was first heard in Act II, scene iv, when they are told that the Sheriff has arrived at the tavern, and Falstaff, very cryptically, says to Hal: 'Never call a true piece of gold a counterfeit. Thou art essentially made without seeming so' (II, iv, 492–3). This is a much discussed passage, of uncertain meaning and undecidable application. Who is the 'true piece of gold'? Falstaff? The Prince? And in what sense is Hal 'essentially made' (some editors rather desperately suggest it should be 'mad')? We have already seen both Falstaff *and* the Prince to be notable counterfeiters in their different ways, and it becomes evident that 'counterfeiting', in one form or another, is widespread at every level in the land. The battle scenes quite clearly and centrally present us with a 'counterfeit' king, leaving it quite uncertain how far back the counterfeiting goes; where – on all levels – it started, where it stops. Whether, that is, 'appearance' ever gives way to 'essence'; where, and if, true gold is to be found. By extension, I don't think we can ever be quite confident that we meet the 'true', the 'very', Prince – as opposed, that is, to another part of his – undoubtedly well-stocked and carefully maintained – wardrobe. And yet, in faith, he bears himself like a prince at Shrewsbury? Certainly he does. Whatever else, he is his father's son.

The danger and threat of counterfeiting (a hanging offence until comparatively recently) is that it destroys trust and devalues the currency. Something like this happens to the crucial notion of 'honor'. Hotspur, we might say, is the 'essence' of chivalric honour, albeit of a distinctly feudal kind, at times verging on hyperbolic self-parody. Prince Hal overtly parodies him, but at Shrewsbury it seems as if he is determined to replace him – on the self-equivalizing grounds that there is no room for 'two stars':

> Nor can one England brook a double reign
> Of Harry Percy and the Prince of Wales.
>
> (V, iv, 65–6)

Specifically, he is determined to take Hotspur's honour:

> And all the budding honors on thy crest
> I'll crop to make a garland for my head.
>
> (V, iv, 71–2)

A cynic might suggest that he wants the garland for his wardrobe; the line at least implies that honour is a movable, removable commodity – not, that is, of the essence. You can crop it off and put it on.

While Hotspur is being truly killed by Henry (for which, incidentally, there is no proper chronicle evidence. Shakespeare clearly wants them to seem rather like 'doubles', with one finally vanquishing the other; the Renaissance displacing feudalism, perhaps – but I won't push that), Falstaff is pretending to be killed by Douglas. Seeing him lying on the ground, the Prince bids him a fairly fond farewell and passes on. As he 'rises up' once the coast is clear (some have detected a resurrection joke), Falstaff self-justifyingly soliloquizes:

'Sblood, 'twas time to counterfeit, or that hot termagant Scot had
paid me scot and lot too. Counterfeit? I lie; I am no counterfeit. To
die is to be a counterfeit, for he is but the counterfeit of a man who
hath not the life of a man; but to counterfeit dying when a man
thereby liveth, is to be no counterfeit, but the true and perfect image
of life indeed ... Zounds, I am afraid of this gunpowder Percy,
though he be dead. How if he should counterfeit too, and rise? By my
faith, I am afraid he would prove the better counterfeit.

(V, iv, 112–23)

So he stabs Hotspur's corpse – a kind of ultimate physical
profanation and desecration of chivalry. And by the time he
has repeated the word 'counterfeit' for the ninth time, he has
done even more damage, for he has sent the word mockingly
echoing into every corner of the play. This occurs barely
eighty lines after the exchange between Douglas and the King
just discussed, and it opens up the possibility, or suggests the
thought, that perhaps the only pertinent consideration, at
every level, is – who proves the better counterfeit?

Falstaff, stabbing dead Hotspur, is 'killing' chivalry, and he
has already had a comparable deflating effect on the concept
and notion of 'honor'. We have already heard his 'catechism'
on honour on the eve of the battle – 'What is honor? A word.
What is in that word honor? What is that honor? Air – a trim
reckoning! Who hath it? He that died a Wednesday. Doth he
feel it? No.' (And so, famously, on – see V, i, 129–41.) He strikes
the same note when he comes across the body of Blunt. 'I like
not such grinning honor as Sir Walter hath. Give me life;
which if I can save, so; if not, honor comes unlooked for, and
there's an end' (V, iii, 58–61). At such moments, Falstaff is the
honest coward, laying no claim to any of the martial, heroic
virtues. (We have just seen that he carries a bottle of sack in his
pistol case.) Such words and sentiments have an irresistible
appeal to the life-at-all-costs coward who exists in, at least,
most of us. We invariably feel a spasm of pleasure and
liberation when someone 'blows the gaffe on human nature',
as Falstaff so often, consciously and unconsciously, does. By a
recognizable convention, a soliloquizing figure is telling the
truth to us, and himself, about what he is, what he believes,
what he desires, what he intends. At such moments, at least,

Falstaff is *not* counterfeit. He may not be gold, but he is, we feel, being true. The effect he has on the play can hardly be calculated. By what he says, by what he *is*, Falstaff calls into question, makes a mockery of, undermines (many verbs are applicable to his effect) the ideals, values, virtues which men cherish and invoke (if not embrace) as giving meaning, dignity, purpose to their lives. He does, indeed, seem to have the effect, intended or not, of devaluing – perhaps *dis*valuing is better – all values: not just, as we have seen, kingship and honour; but honesty, courage, responsibility ('I have misused the King's press damnably', IV, ii, 12), compassion ('food for powder, food for powder, they'll fit a pit as well as better. Tush, man, mortal men, mortal men', IV, ii, 67–8), continence, and so on indefinitely. There is no being serious about any serious things around Falstaff – he can reduce them to absurdity with a word. A great unbuttoner, indeed! Falstaff's effectual destruction of values and, let us call them, the official virtues, wherever he goes, has led some to detect more than a touch of the true Devil (Uncreator, Disvaluer Supreme) about him, and one can see why. Certainly, we can hardly take the King, Hotspur, and, I think, Prince Hal, at face value, or at their own self-estimations, with the proximity of Falstaff. We can never quite get away from the possibility that, simply, they prove the better counterfeits. Just before the Battle of Shrewsbury, the King says – 'nothing can seem foul to those that win' (V, i, 8), while after the successful conclusion, in the last words of the play, he says:

> And since this business so fair is done,
> Let us not leave till all our own be won.
>
> (V, v, 43–4)

Simple. If you win, the 'business' is 'fair'. 'Foul-ness' is losing. It is impossible not to call this Machiavellian. If Falstaff makes 'fair' things 'foul' – or simply dissolves the difference between them – he is certainly not alone in so doing.

But because there is widespread 'counterfeiting' it does not mean there is nothing 'true', nor does the shameless displaying of cowardice discount the reality of courage – even if you will find most honesty in a tavern hostess (Mistress Quickly) and true bravery in a poor country conscript, Feeble (Part Two). It may be, as Falstaff laments, 'a bad world', but it is *not* the case, as he all too self-applicably asserts, that 'there is nothing but roguery to be found in villainous man' (II, iv, 132, 125). There are no (or few) absolute conditions. Things come mixed, and in the matter of values and virtues too, it is nearly always a matter of more and less. A usurper king still has to reign, and he may be better at it than his legitimate predecessor. Shakespeare was not a nihilist, though his all-encompassing realism necessarily made him sceptical – and nowhere more far-reachingly so than in the *Henry IV* plays which comprise his finest achievement in the history genre (and in which the poetry is everywhere marked by a particular metaphorical force and pungency, abstractions constantly becoming physical – 'Supposition all our lives shall be stuck full of eyes,' says one of the rebels – V, ii, 8; I choose almost at random. There is, in the *Henry IV* plays, poetry of the sort of compact power and metaphorical velocity we associate with *Macbeth*.) What Shakespeare does, in these plays pre-eminently, is expose the realities of the amoral concern for power behind the pious orthodoxies and beneath the self-protective carapaces of men in high – and not so high – places. These words by A. P. Rossiter get it right, I think:

Because the Tudor myth system of Order, Degree, etc. was too rigid, too black-and-white, too doctrinaire and narrowly moral for Shakespeare's mind: it falsified his fuller experience of man. Consequently, while employing it as FRAME, he had to undermine it, to qualify it with equivocations: to view its applications with sly or subtle ambiguities: to cast doubts on its ultimate human validity, even in situations where its principles seemed most completely applicable. His intuition told him it was *morally* inadequate.

There is a lot of unfinished business left by the end of the play, and it seems clear that Shakespeare already had the second part in mind.

*

INTRODUCTION

HENRY IV, PART TWO

From a God to a bull? A heavy descension! It was Jove's case. From a
prince to a prentice? A low transformation!

(II, ii, 173–5)

Perhaps rather surprisingly, Shakespeare only used the word
'metamorphosed' in one play, *The Two Gentlemen of Verona*
(where he uses it twice); but the words 'transform', 'transformed',
'transformation', recur in his plays from early to late: it was a
phenomenon, a process, which continually interested him. And
this part of *Henry IV* is primarily a play of 'low transformations'
and 'heavy descensions'. The main movement is that of downward degeneration. Royalty is tired; characters are visibly ageing
or sick; things are 'dull', 'heavy', 'lead'; one image has men's
spirits frozen up 'as fish are in a pond'; a man's tongue tolls bad
news like 'a sullen bell'; the recruited militia is Feeble, Moldy,
Shadow. The scenes in Gloucestershire bring rustic provincial
England into the play, and allow some amiable intimations of
rural realities; but the supervising Justices are Shallow – a
comic analogue to the Lord Chief Justice in Westminster, who,
by a 'low transformation', has 'turned into a justice-like servingman', and whose 'justice' indeed proves to be 'shallow' – and
Silence. It is a comic enough world, but it is a world grown
senile and sleepy, ripe for falling. Falstaff has become a much
coarser, at times rather sinister, figure; the tavern has become a
brothel; Pistol's bragging, bar-room violence is a sad travesty of
Hotspur's rash, feudal valour; and the ending of the second
rebellion, in the Forest of Gaultree, is a much nastier, meaner
business than the open fighting on the battlefield at Shrewsbury.
There is *no* honour, no chivalry, not even any honest combat in
this play. 'What trust is in these times?' asks the Archbishop
despairingly (I, iii, 100), and the answer is – virtually none:
words are not kept, debts are not paid. The feeling could be
called entropic: death and termination are in the air.

When Henry IV finally appears – which is not until Act III
– he is in his 'nightgown'; it is hardly a regal entry. If he
started 'shaken' and 'wan', he is in visibly worse shape now. In
a remarkably powerful, heart-felt soliloquy, he laments his
terrible insomnia:

> O sleep, O gentle sleep,
> Nature's soft nurse, how have I frighted thee,
> That thou no more wilt weigh my eyelids down
> And steep my senses in forgetfulness?
>
> (III, i, 5–8)

Not quite 'Macbeth hath murdered sleep', perhaps; but not far from it. Certainly, when he concludes –

> Uneasy lies the head that wears a crown
>
> (III, i, 31)

– we are convinced that this head is very uneasy indeed (as usual, he never quite says why, though it becomes unmistakably clear that the cause is the 'unkinging' and murder of Richard). He is 'weary' and 'sick' throughout, complaining that 'health ... is flown/From this bare, withered trunk' (IV, v, 229). (Falstaff, the other 'father-king', is addressed as 'thou dead elm', II, iv, 339: this part of the 'forest' is failing.) Shakespeare's intention is fairly clear here. Holinshed gave Henry a healthy and active ten years between Shrewsbury and his death. Samuel Daniel, in his long poem on the Civil Wars between the Two Houses of Lancaster and York, depicts a sleepless king, beset by 'intricate turmoils, and sorrows deep' some time before his death. Shakespeare makes him continuously sick from the time of Shrewsbury. This, no doubt, because he wished to show, or suggest, a sick nation. The King sees it in these terms:

> you perceive the body of our kingdom
> How foul it is, what rank diseases grow,
> And with what danger, near the heart of it.
>
> (III, i, 38–40)

and so do the rebels:

> we are all diseased,
> And with our surfeiting and wanton hours
> Have brought ourselves into a burning fever,
> And we must bleed for it. Of which disease
> Our late king, Richard, being infected, died.
>
> (IV, i, 54–8)

In a word, each party sees the other as the source of the

'disease', but all agree there is a prevailing sickness. (The King foresees more 'rotten times' to come, when his riotous son succeeds him, though here, of course, Shakespeare, and history, have a surprise in store.) There is much talk of individual sickness – pox, gout, gluttony, apoplexy, and so on – and the need for doctoring, physic, medicines, diet, purging, and other remedies (there are a number of references to 'vomit') is often remarked on. At the very start, Northumberland is 'crafty-sick'. Then Falstaff, notably, makes his entrance asking what the doctor says 'to my water', to be told that the diagnosis is that 'the party that owed it ... might have moe diseases than he knew for' (I, ii, 5). It is typical of the rather acridly cynical turn his speech has taken, that Falstaff should say: 'A good wit will make use of anything. I will turn diseases to commodity' (I, ii, 258–9). 'That smooth-faced gentleman, tickling commodity ... this bawd, this broker, this all-changing element', as the Bastard in *King John* put it, shows here with more ravaged features. The prostitute Doll (there were no manifest prostitutes in Part One – the tavern has become more sordid) asks Falstaff when he is going to 'begin to patch up thine old body for heaven?' (II, iv, 237). And it is that 'old body' which is now very much to the fore.

Reminders of age and ageing are everywhere. The Lord Chief Justice has 'some smack of an age in you, some relish of the saltness of time in you' (I, ii, 101–2). Falstaff is not alone in being 'as a candle, the better part burnt out' (I, ii, 161). The one-time merry-making acquaintance of Falstaff and Shallow, Jane Nightwork, is old – 'Nay, she must be old. She cannot choose but be old. Certain she's old' (III, ii, 212–13). When Falstaff, preposterously, tries to pass himself as young, he gets this from the Lord Chief Justice:

Do you set down your name in the scroll of youth, that are written down old with all the characters of age? Have you not a moist eye, a dry hand, a yellow cheek, a white beard, a decreasing leg, an increasing belly? Is not your voice broken, your wind short, your chin double, your wit single, and every part about you blasted with antiquity, and will you yet call yourself young? Fie, fie, fie, Sir John!

(I, ii, 185–93)

Falstaff has a deflecting, parrying answer – he always does, and his resourcefulness is still intact; but he may have felt, as Hamlet put it, also talking about the condition of old men, 'we hold it not honesty to have it thus set down!' But Falstaff knows his condition; knows he is an 'old pike' still snapping up 'young dace' (III, ii, 341). He confesses in a soliloquy, 'Lord, Lord, how subject we old men are to this vice of lying!' (III, ii, 313). And, lying in the arms of Doll Tearsheet at the tavern, he says, with an uncharacteristic simplicity which has its own pathos – 'I am old, I am old' (II, iv, 278). He adds – ''A grows late; we'll to bed. Thou'lt forget me when I am gone,' and we feel that it is growing late in every sense, that this world is grown old and is entering a terminal twilight, moving towards its final sleep and oblivion as a last dusk settles over it. It is a curiously moving moment, in what has become a rather squalid setting. It even sets the tempestuous and rather foul-mouthed Doll 'a-weeping'.

When Doll mentions 'heaven', Falstaff gives a shiver – 'Do not speak like a death's-head. Do not bid me remember mine end' (II, iv, 240). But 'ends' – conclusions and concludings, outcomes and terminations – are constantly referred to. 'Let the end try the man,' warns the Prince while still in his tavern days (II, ii, 46): 'Well, hearken o' th' end,' says Doll, fatalistically (II, iv, 287): 'Let time shape, and there an end,' says Falstaff, with perspicuous resignation (III, ii, 343). The sense of time past, time passing, is strong in this play. 'We see which way the stream of time doth run,' says the Archbishop (IV, i, 70), referring to 'the rough torrent of occasion' which has forced them into rebellion: the rebels stand in time present, aiming to change time future. But, the 'rough torrent of occasion' is wearing them all down, sweeping them all away; and, from the court to the tavern, 'the stream of time' often runs backwards. The King remembers Richard with a guilty sadness; Hostess Quickly recalls the twenty-nine years she has known Falstaff with a forgiving fondness; Shallow casts his mind back fifty-five years to what he likes to think of as his wild youth at the Inns of Court. 'We have heard the chimes at midnight, Master Shallow' (III, ii, 220), Falstaff nods concurringly. A slightly melancholy, 'long-ago' feeling is pervasive. The 'endless end' is, of course, death, and it tolls throughout the play, from Morton bringing the news of the 'hateful death' of Hotspur – ending with 'Brother, son, and all are dead' (I, i, 81), to Shallow's intimations of mortality, 'shallow' though they may be: 'and to see how many of my old acquaintance are dead! ... Death, as the Psalmist saith, is certain to all, all shall die' (III, ii, 35–40). From Northumberland's castle, to the Court and taverns of London, to the houses of Gloucestershire – all shall die. It becomes a question whether this sick, weary, ageing, dying world can produce anything regenerative for the future; whether, that is, there is any new world waiting to be born – or, perhaps, waiting to reign.

From the beginning, when Northumberland, with 'strained passion', hysterically cries out: 'Now let not Nature's hand/ Keep the wild flood confined! Let order die!' (I, i, 153–4 – with a contradictoriness typical of the play, he talks the lion and acts the coward, persuaded by his womenfolk to flee to Scotland); to the King on his death-bed, foreseeing that, under his son, his kingdom 'wilt be a wilderness again' (IV, v, 136), crying despairingly:

> Pluck down my officers, break my decrees,
> For now a time is come to mock at form.
>
> (IV, v, 117–18)

there is a growing sense of a world about to collapse in ruin and chaos, all form and order mocked or gone. When the King dies, the Lord Chief Justice succinctly sums up the general dread – 'I fear all will be overturned' (V, ii, 19). In such a state of affairs, Falstaff would be in his element; indeed, as a kind of Lord of Misrule, he is committed to the overturning (as well as the unbuttoning) of order and form. He thinks the death of the King marks the beginning of *his* reign – 'be what thou wilt, I am fortune's steward! ... the laws of England are at my commandment. Blessed are they that have been my friends, and woe to my Lord Chief Justice' (V, iii, 132, 139–40). Given what we have seen of his 'friends', not to mention his disdain for all laws, this would promise anarchy indeed. But, there is another King and, as he and we are soon to discover, he has other ideas.

In his gross, deteriorating physicality, Falstaff almost literally 'embodies' all the diseases, corruptions, and degenerate appetites of the dying world, which must be somehow rejected, dismissed, purged, or just left behind. Perhaps, as has been suggested, he does figure the old 'god' who must be slain or banished in a sacrificial rite in order to restore health to the blighted, blasted land. He seems, curiously, at once more threatening and less powerful in this play. He still manifests, for the most part, that 'absolute self-possession and masterly presence of mind' which Hazlitt admired. He still has his adroit way of 'wrenching the true cause the false way' (II, i, 113). But when the Chief Justice says to him, almost contemptuously – 'You speak as having power to do wrong' (II, i, 133), we realize he has none in any significant sense (he can still abuse a tavern hostess or a country simpleton). His world is beginning to disintegrate around him – we last see his women being arrested and taken away, charged with complicity in some unspecified murder, and despite his boast he cannot save them. He is not the man he was, and in his ill-founded conviction of personal invulnerability and influence in high places, he is in increasing danger of emerging more clearly as the 'great fool' the Chief Justice thinks him. Crucial here is his changed relationship with the Prince, which is central to the play.

We hear at the start that 'the King hath severed you [Falstaff] and Prince Harry' (I, ii, 211), but there is much to suggest that the Prince has already started to separate himself from Falstaff. When we first see the Prince, he is back with Poins and other taverners asking for 'small beer', and of course we think he has simply regressed to his old low-life habits. (We have already heard of his – legendary – striking of the Lord Chief Justice, dramatized in the *Famous Victories*, but, perhaps discreetly, left off-stage by Shakespeare.) But the tone is different. His opening words – 'I am exceeding weary' – suggest he partakes of the general tiredness; then when he goes on to say that he is 'out of love with my greatness' (II, ii, 1, 13), we may begin to wonder how far his feelings of disaffection and alienation extend. Certainly, Poins tells him that everyone thinks he is still 'so lewd and so much engraffed to

Falstaff' (II, ii, 62), and even near the end the King is convinced (and informed) that his son is still accompanied by his 'continual followers', indulging his 'headstrong riot' (IV, iv, 62). But, even in that first scene with Poins, it is clear that the Prince no longer knows whether Falstaff frequents his old drinking haunts, and he has never heard of Doll Tearsheet. In the event, he shares only one scene with Falstaff, prior to the climactic rejection scene, and the scene merits some particular comment.

After receiving a rather pompous and patronizing letter from Falstaff, which however touches a nerve when it airily says, 'Repent at idle times as thou mayst' (II, ii, 129) – since he will have to 'repent' a second time – the Prince resolves to go to the tavern with Poins, disguised as drawers, to 'see Falstaff bestow himself tonight in his true colors' (II, ii, 170). The resulting scene is clearly intended as a dark echo of the comparable long tavern scene in Part One, and is situated at exactly the same point in the play – the end of Act II. Almost Falstaff's first words are 'Empty the jordan!' (i.e. chamber pot) which, like his opening reference to his urine, link him more firmly than ever with the lower bodily functions. He immediately engages in rather abrasive banter about venereal disease with Doll Tearsheet. The Hostess has already addressed Falstaff as 'honeysuckle villain ... honeyseed rogue' (II, i, 51) – but she means, of course, 'homicidal', and in truth much of the 'sweetness' – the more delectable part – has drained away from this coarser, 'sourer', Falstaff. 'These are very bitter words,' says the Hostess, accurately enough, about the general level of conversation in the tavern which is, by turns, salacious, insulting, and violent. Falstaff engages in some extravagant abuse of the Prince, unaware, of course, that he is listening. When the Prince reveals himself and accuses Falstaff – 'You whoreson candle-mine you, how vilely did you speak of me' (II, iv, 308) – Falstaff can only rather lamely insist, 'No abuse Hal. None, Ned, none.' It is a marked falling off from the inspired way he self-exculpatingly extricated himself from his blatant lies about the Gad's Hill fiasco. The Prince has no pleasant or fond, or even friendly, words for Falstaff. The scene is interrupted, as was its counterpart in Part One, by a knocking on the door and a summons from Westminster, and 'Falstaff, good night' are the only polite words the Prince says to his old companion of the revels as he takes up his sword and cloak and leaves. Falstaff follows soon after – they are all off to the wars – and we should note that the sorely-tried Hostess says to him 'an honester and truer-hearted man – well, fare thee well' (II, iv, 394), while Doll 'comes blubbered' (i.e. marked with weeping). The tears of a sentimental whore, perhaps: but perhaps also, the man has still 'honey' enough in him to love.

Watching Falstaff and Doll at dalliance, the Prince comments to Poins – 'Saturn and Venus this year in conjunction!' (II, iv, 270). He has already compared himself to Jove, as he disguised himself as a tavern 'drawer' – 'From a God to a bull? A heavy descension! It was Jove's case' (II, ii, 173–4). At his coronation procession (when he is finally crowned King), Falstaff, still confident of his favour, calls out to him – 'My king! My Jove! I speak to thee, my heart!' (V, v, 47) – only to receive what is, I suppose, the most famous rebuff in literature: 'I know thee not, old man.' Jove-Jupiter-Zeus (= father of the bright heaven) was the god of the new order who deposed his 'father', Saturn-Cronos (associated, it might be remembered, with agriculture and fertility, and whose celebrations – saturnalia – were periods of festivity and licence); and this is the moment when Jove-Henry V displaces, and terminates the 'reign' of, the old 'god', Saturn-Falstaff. (I think Philip Williams is justified in suggesting that the real sick, old, father-king who has to be displaced by the regenerating son is Henry IV, and that the rejection of Falstaff is, among other things, a sacrificial rite, the 'slaying' of the surrogate 'father', the scapegoat.

Much has been written justifying Hal's spurning of Falstaff at this point. History, legend, and the chronicles all required the abrupt rejection by the Prince-now-King of his former reveller-friends. And, clearly, Falstaff is a most inappropriate leader and guide (a false staff to lean on, indeed) for a king who will reign over one of the glorious periods of English history. We have seen the miraculous transformation of the madcap rioter into chivalric warrior at Shrewsbury; and, so the argument goes, we here witness the transformation of the clearly somewhat disenchanted reveller into committed upholder of justice at his coronation at Westminster – when Hal adopts the impeccable Lord Chief Justice as his appropriate new father figure: 'You shall be as a father to my youth' (V, ii, 118). Moreover, we have been well prepared for the rejection. Both Hal's first soliloquy ('I know you all' etc.), and the 'play' ('Banish plump Jack, and banish all the world' – 'I do, I will'), give clear notice of what is to come. Only recently, Warwick has sought to reassure the King:

> The Prince but studies his companions
> Like a strange tongue ...
> The Prince will in the perfectness of time
> Cast off his followers ...
>
> (IV, iv, 68–9, 74–5)

though quite how Warwick knows this when the King and the rest of the court still think the Prince to be an unreconstructed reprobate, is not clear. Some critics regard the rejection of Falstaff as a, perhaps regrettable, necessity, but certainly an inevitable one. It is pointed out that he is not *so* harshly treated, and will, in any case, be provided for. It gave Dr Johnson no problems, insisting that 'since Falstaff has nothing in him that can be esteemed, no great pain will be suffered from the reflection that he is compelled to live honestly'. All this is true enough, and, from the point of view of the theatrical effect, the rejection has to be both anticipated and, when it comes, a sudden shock. Inevitable, yes; but by any standards it is a cruel public humiliation.

> I know thee not, old man. Fall to thy prayers.
> How ill white hairs becomes a fool and jester!
> I have long dreamt of such a kind of man,
> So surfeit-swelled, so old, and so profane,
> But, being awaked, I do despise my dream.
> Make less thy body hence, and more thy grace.
> ...
> Presume not that I am the thing I was,
> For God doth know, so shall the world perceive,
> That I have turned away my former self.
>
> (V, v, 48–53, 57–9)

He has 'put on' the mantle of majesty ('I will deeply put the fashion on' – this, of mourning for his father – V, ii, 52), as his father used to 'dress' himself in humility; and, perhaps, as he put on a leather jerkin and apron to spy on Falstaff in the tavern, which he has now, presumably, finally 'thrown off'. He is, as always, the lord and owner of his face – and as unmoved as stone. Shakespeare has prepared us for this, too.

'I know you not' – these were Christ's words to the foolish virgins; He uses them again in the parable of the few who shall be saved, and the many who shall be excluded – presumably to be damned. The 'master of the house' says to those knocking on the door – 'I know you not whence ye are':

26. Then shall ye begin to say, We have eaten and drunk in thy presence, and thou hast taught in our streets.
27. But he shall say, I tell you, I know you not whence ye are; depart from me, all ye workers of iniquity.

(Luke 13)

The echo of these familiar words from the gospels would not, I surmise, have been lost on much of Shakespeare's audience. Falstaff has certainly eaten and drunk in the princely presence, and qualifies with little trouble as a 'worker of iniquity'. However, I hardly think this makes of the Prince a Christ-figure. In a play (both parts) of such multiple, trenchant, often subversive ironies, I think it is more likely to be sombrely parodic (indeed, I might even suggest that the always straight-faced Prince is permitting himself a slightly blasphemous quotation). For it is quite inconceivable to me that Shakespeare did not feel, and thus intend to portray, the inhumanity, not of the 'severance' itself (it has clearly been coming), but of the mode and manner – this actual moment – of the rejection. Falstaff may deserve what he gets, and be lucky to get off with a pension; and so, very sensibly, we could continue our justifications and extenuations. But the tavern Hostess, arguably the most honest character in the plays (though I suppose I should add the Lord Chief Justice – which makes a happy pairing!), seems to me to have the truth of the matter when she says of her old friend quite simply – 'The King has killed his heart' (*Henry V*, II, i, 91). In banishing plump Jack, Hal has not banished the *whole* world, but he *has* banished *a* world which, no matter how disreputable, coarse, and unruly, contains genuine values and important qualities not to be found at court; and, arguably, he has banished a part of his own humanity as well. (Even more seriously, for us, he has banished Falstaff from his next play. But more of that in due course.)

*

The play, unusually for Shakespeare, starts with a Prologue (or Induction) spoken by 'Rumor, painted full of tongues'.

> Upon my tongues continual slanders ride,
> The which in every language I pronounce,
> Stuffing the ears of men with false reports.
>
> (6–8)
>
> ...   The posts come tiring on,
> And not a man of them brings other news
> Than they have learned of me. From Rumor's tongues
> They bring smooth comforts false, worse than true wrongs.
>
> (37–40)

The play is full of 'tongues' (Falstaff claims to have 'a whole school of tongues in this belly of mine', and he is certainly a fit emissary of Rumor), 'false reports', 'smooth comforts false', unreliable 'news', 'rotten opinion'. The very first scene has Lord Bardolph bringing the 'certain news' to Northumberland that his son, Hotspur, has killed Prince Harry, which quickly proves to be *un*certain news indeed. ('News' also has uncertain, even contradictory effects. 'In poison there is physic,' says Northumberland, finally convinced of the truth of the news of his son's death: 'these news ... being sick, have in some measure made me well', I, i, 139. It seems there is also poison in physic: 'wherefore should these good news make me sick?' says the King, taken ill even as he is told of the successful defeat of his enemies, IV, iv, 102. Inexplicably, the people are said to be 'sick of happiness', IV, i, 64.) But nearly everyone falls victim, one way or another, to 'false report' and 'smooth comforts false'. The King believes his son has gone to the dogs,

lxxiii

while Falstaff is confident of his benevolent patronage – both are proved wrong. Falstaff, a character of 'pure fear and entire cowardice' (II, iv, 333), has gained a reputation for bravery (presumably by having claimed to have killed Hotspur) in which even the Lord Chief Justice seems to believe, and to which the genuine warrior Coleville surrenders, to be promptly executed – a rough reward for his credulity. Shallow believes Falstaff will return the thousand pounds he has borrowed; while, probably an even wilder expectation, Mistress Quickly thinks Falstaff will keep his promise to marry her. Even names can be misleading – Bullcalf is a coward, Feeble is brave, and Fang is pretty toothless. 'Words' are everywhere, but it is uncertain how many of them are to be trusted. What certainty is in these times? After the rebels have worked through a series of architectural images for their planned rebellion ('When we mean to build,/We first survey the plot, then draw the model' and so on – see I, iii, 41–62), the Archbishop says:

> An habitation giddy and unsure
> Hath he that buildeth on the vulgar heart.
>
> (I, iii, 89–90)

They want to make sure they have 'a sure foundation' on which to 'build' their rebellion, but, like so many of the structures of expectation erected by hope, desire, fear, or trust, it turns out to be 'an habitation giddy and unsure' – and not just because of the 'vulgar heart'. The lack of 'sure foundation' – grounds for total trust – is pervasive, ubiquitous. The Prince-now-King, about to effect his sudden transformation into regality, promises 'To mock the expectation of the world' (V, ii, 126). Everywhere, expectation is mocked, and people disillusioned into ruin and death.

Nowhere more graphically and shockingly than at Gaultree, when John of Lancaster (Hal's younger brother) promises the rebels that, if they 'discharge' their armies ('as we will ours'), their 'griefs shall be with speed redressed'. 'I ... swear here, by the honor of my blood,' he says. The Archbishop accepts the pledge: 'I take your princely word for these redresses.' John says, 'Let's drink together friendly and embrace' to celebrate 'our restored love and amity' (IV, ii, 54–66). They duly drink, and the rebels discharge their men who are soon dispersed. At which point, John, whose army has remained in place, arrests the rebel leaders on charges of 'capital treason' and orders their immediate execution – adding, with supreme pious hypocrisy:

> God, and not we, hath safely fought today.
>
> (IV, ii, 121)

Much the Bolingbrokes have ever cared about 'God'.

Now all this is clearly appalling. Mowbray's complaint, 'Is this proceeding just and honorable?' (IV, ii, 110), seems mild indeed. Some critics commend John for being a good Machiavel; others say he is just playing by the stern laws of 'necessity' which are constantly invoked. ('Construe the times to their necessities' – IV, i, 102 – says Westmoreland, in justification of all the King's crimes. Henry himself says, 'Are these things then necessities?/Then let us meet them like necessities' – III, i, 92–3. 'Necessity' rules all; explains all; excuses all. Henry's 'necessitarianism' might argue him a pragmatist; but it can serve as an amoral, self-exculpating creed.) I have even read one who maintains that Shakespeare would probably have approved of John's trick – on the grounds, roughly, that with rebels, anything goes. I find the suggestion utterly extraordinary. I have no doubts that Shakespeare shared the general Elizabethan horror of rebellion and civil war, and that, quite apart from his need to defer to historical fact, he would have thought that Henry, no matter how illegitimately he came by the crown, had to contain the threat of civic disorder. But the manner of the 'defeat' – the deceit, the betrayal, the smooth, unperturbed ruthlessness – is shocking; and if we find it shocking, then we may be sure that Shakespeare found it so too, and wrote it to be so. A Prince foresworn; the 'princely word' broken; the rites of reconciliation and amity profaned; God blasphemed – it is a sorry day's work. What trust is in these times indeed? (One interesting change Shakespeare made to the account of this event in his source – Holinshed has Westmoreland entirely responsible for the whole treacherous trick, whereas Shakespeare makes John of Lancaster the only begetter of the shameless strategy. Why? Perhaps he wants to show another Bolingbroke as a cool, unprincipled operator. Henry's handling of Richard; Hal's treatment of Falstaff; the way 'sober-blooded' John deals with the rebels – by this time, we may begin to think it runs in the family!)

We must conclude by considering the Prince-now-King, since clearly the end of the play celebrates a 'high' transformation – not exactly from a bull to a God; but at least from an apparent (and in Shakespeare, *only* apparent) madcap rioter capable of boffing the Lord Chief Justice, to a perfect King, implacable upholder of the Law. (To make the metamorphosis seem more sudden and miraculous, Shakespeare omits any reference to the fact that Prince Henry was active in national politics from 1410–1413, and, on his accession, was already an experienced administrator. He was also clearly ambitious and something of a schemer, trying to force his father's abdication in 1411 – Shakespeare leaves that out, too.) In short, errant Hal must now emerge, as from a chrysalis, as the glorious Henry V. The prince in waiting need kick his heels no longer. For good or bad, good *and* bad perhaps, there can, and will, be no more tavern-house regressions.

Henry IV, weary and seemingly conscience-plagued, has become a brooding pessimist:

> O God, that one might read the book of fate,
> And see the revolution of the times
> Make mountains level, and the continent,
> Weary of solid firmness, melt itself
> Into the sea! And other times to see
> The beachy girdle of the ocean
> Too wide for Neptune's hips. How chances, mocks,
> And changes fill the cup of alteration
> With divers liquors! O, if this were seen,
> The happiest youth, viewing his progress through,
> What perils past, what crosses to ensue,
> Would shut the book, and sit him down and die.

> (III, i, 45–56)

There is more than a hint of tragic feelings in these lines – more King Lear than King Henry. At the very least, we can say that Henry IV is losing his taste for history, and the making of history. But the last thing his son can do is 'sit him down and die'. His father is a dying king reigning over a dying world: England needs a new king, a new start, a new 'mood'. And this is promised. On his death-bed, Henry says to Hal:

> And now my death
> Changes the mood, and what in me was purchased
> Falls upon thee in a more fairer sort,
> So thou the garland wear'st successively.
>
> (IV, v, 198–201)

For Henry, the crown has always sat 'troublesome' on his 'uneasy' head. Because it was 'purchased' – i.e. *not* acquired by inheritance, as crowns should be. His hope is that 'succession' is hereby restored, and his son will enjoy 'better quiet,/Better opinion, better confirmation' (IV, v, 187–8). Of course, legitimate succession has not *really* been restored – and the Wars of the Roses are less than fifty years away. But for now, the death of Henry IV 'changes the mood'. And Hal has converted, apparently, to true kingliness.

As a prince, he shows no very evident desire for the crown, no usurping or parricidal hunger to take his father's place (here again, one suspects that Shakespeare is deliberately keeping his record rather cleaner than a fuller 'history' would allow; grooming him, perhaps, for repentance, conversion, and the great things to come – which will be more plausible if he was never really *that* bad). He insists that he feels genuine sorrow at his father's sickness ('my heart bleeds inwardly'), but explains that he would be thought a hypocrite if he made a display of grief – as well he might. The testing moment is his legendary taking of the crown from the pillow while his father is asleep. This is usually taken as a fairly unequivocal sign of his eagerness to be king. In Holinshed, when the King wakes up and asks the Prince what on earth he thinks he is doing, the Prince – 'with a good audacity' – simply says: I thought you were dead and thus the crown was mine. At which point, the King shruggingly relinquishes it with a remark to the effect that he didn't have much right to it in the first place. Shakespeare makes much more out of the episode. First, the Prince meditates on the ambivalences, the paradoxes of the crown and all it implies – 'O polished perturbation! Golden care!':

>   O majesty!
> When thou dost pinch thy bearer, thou dost sit
> Like a rich armor worn in heat of day,
> That *scald'st with safety*.
>
>   (IV, v, 27–30, my italics)

Then, thinking his father dead, he takes the crown as his 'due', and shows all his father's tenacity of power in his articulated resolve to hold on to it, come what may:

>   And put the world's whole strength
> Into one giant arm, it shall not force
> This lineal honor from me.
>
>   (IV, v, 43–5)

The King, on waking, reads the worst into the Prince's premature and stealthy purloining of the crown (which he himself, you may remember, had 'snatched'), and feels it as a death blow. This, he says:

>   helps to end me. See, sons, what things you are!
> How quickly nature falls into revolt
> When gold becomes her object!
>
>   (IV, v, 64–6)

which leads on to a powerful speech on filial ingratitude. This is followed by some forty lines of uninterrupted kingly rebuke to his son, ending with the bitter prophecy that, under him, England will 'be a wilderness again' (IV, v, 92–137). The Prince protests that he sincerely thought his father dead, and that he was actually 'upbraiding' the crown for 'eating up' his father. Then:

>   Accusing it, I put it on my head,
> To try with it, as with an enemy
> That had before my face murdered my father,
> The quarrel of a true inheritor.
>
>   (IV, v, 165–8)

He insists that he felt not a trace of 'pride' when he put on the crown, nor did he give it a hint of 'welcome'. Whether this is all said 'with a good audacity' or with an unfeigning heart, we can scarcely decide – the Prince has always been the master of his words, as well as the owner of his face. He certainly *seemed* glad enough to put it on. But the remarkable thing is that the King instantly believes him (his previous contritions have not been notably reliable), giving the act an amazing gloss.

> O my son,
> God put it in thy mind to take it hence,
> That thou mightst win the more thy father's love,
> Pleading so wisely in excuse of it!
>
> (IV, v, 177–80)

'God' again; only invoked by the Bolingbrokes, it seems, when a highly dubious act is to be ascribed to a higher authority. Of course, it is entirely understandable that the dying King should desperately want to believe his son, and the reconciliation is made to seem genuine; just as, I make no doubt, we are intended to believe in the Prince's genuine conversion to just rule and good government – the fruits of which conversion, and his taking on the burdens and responsibilities of office, we duly see in Act V. But Shakespeare has shown up so many of the ambiguities involved in the taking and handling of power (purchased or inherited, eagerly snatched or reluctantly accepted), that I hardly suppose he intends us suddenly to start reading his complex Prince in a monocular way. Whatever else he may have done, the Prince has not converted to an undimensional simplicity. He has decided to put on, or accept, the role of good kingship, and being such a cool and clear-eyed operator, he will do it very well. (In *Henry V*, Shakespeare seems to show that he has *become* a good king – but that is another play.) I don't think Shakespeare's Hal has, really, changed at all; and that, indeed, it is precisely Shakespeare's intention (and wonderful achievement) to show how this might be so, through all the apparent 'transformations' of the Prince, from tavern to battlefield to court. He knows them all – all the time. All this will be good for England; but what might be the cost to the Prince in terms of humanity is much more of an open question – and I think Shakespeare shows that too.

The play ends – again, unusually – with an epilogue (probably a mixture of more than one epilogue). It is 'spoken by a dancer' and is full of play with the idea of 'debtors' and 'creditors', 'debts' paid and unpaid, 'promises' kept and broken. This is clearly the playwright's hope that he has paid his debt, kept his word, to his paying audience; that their expectations have been fulfilled rather than 'mocked'. But then we realize that the whole play has been – at varying levels – about this too. One of the more surprising moments comes right at the end, when the banished Falstaff turns to Shallow and says, with uncharacteristic simple directness: 'Master Shallow, I owe you a thousand pound. ... I will be as good as my word' (V, 74, 86). Were that to happen, it would be an expectation mocked indeed. But perhaps his knightly word is no better than John's 'princely word'. We can never know. And Shakespeare has one more little tease for us. The speaker of the Epilogue promises that 'our humble author will continue the story, with Sir John in it, and make you merry with fair Katharine of France. Where, for anything I know, Falstaff shall die of a sweat ...' The expectations raised *here* are, in due course, mocked. Did Shakespeare already know that he would, indeed, continue the story; but that Sir John would *not* be in it, that Falstaff would never get to France, and he would die, not of a sweat, but a broken heart? I wonder.

*

HENRY V

      for Falstaff he is dead,
And we must earn [grieve] therefore.

                                     (II, iii, 5)

Your Majesty came not like yourself...

                                     (IV, viii, 50)

The unimpeded triumph of Henry V seems to have necessitated the death of Falstaff. The usually accepted reason for his exclusion from the play is the continued opposition of the Brooke family who were Oldcastle's (Falstaff's original name and, perhaps, remote source) descendants. A further justification, or explanation, is often offered – to the effect that Shakespeare couldn't have Falstaff up to his usual deflationary fun and games at Agincourt. Not, that is, if Agincourt was to remain the glorious, indeed almost miraculous, British victory enshrined in history-chronicle-legend. And if – *if* – Henry is to be allowed to appear unequivocally as *the* great saintly warrior English king, he must be entirely protected and insulated from the caustic, irresistible whiff of parody and burlesque which Falstaff's mere presence inevitably diffuses. So far, so understandable. But you can also find a stronger attempt to demonstrate the entire appropriateness of the death of Falstaff on the grounds that he has been superseded, that Henry has truly outgrown him and left him definitively behind. Here is the Arden editor, J. H. Walter: 'The play gains in epic strength and dignity from Falstaff's death, even as the *Aeneid* gains from Dido's death, not only because both accounts are written from the heart with a beauty and power that have moved men's hearts in after time, but because Dido and Falstaff are sacrifices to a larger morality they both ignore.' The account of his death given by the Hostess of the London tavern (Mistress Quickly as was), is indeed not only very moving –

for after I saw him fumble with the sheets, and play with flowers, and smile upon his finger's end, I knew there was but one way; for his nose was as sharp as a pen, and 'a babbled of green fields (see II, iii, 9–27)

– it is also quite unforgettable. But as for being 'sacrificed to a higher morality' – that is more questionable. And Henry will not be compared to Aeneas, but to Alexander – Alexander the Great, certainly; but more specifically, and very pointedly, Alexander the killer of his best friend. Falstaff's death is laid squarely at Henry's door. 'The King has killed his heart' – and:

Nym. The king hath run bad humors on the knight; that's the even of it.
Pistol. Nym, thou hast spoke the right;
His heart is fracted and corroborate.

Nym. The King is a good king, but it must be as it may: he passes some humors, and careers.

(II, i, 124–9)

'Run bad humors' is usually glossed as 'vented his ill humour'; and 'humors and careers' as 'wild and freakish behaviour' (as in 'careering') – we should not forget those 'bad humors' and that wildness, no matter how regal a performance Henry contrives. And for all his terminal banishment, Falstaff is evoked once more and to devastating effect, at what I take to be the most critical point in the play – to which I will come in due course. Falstaff does not haunt Henry – Shakespeare's Henry is hardly a hauntable man: but, I maintain, his absence haunts the play.

Henry V – 'this star of England' as the concluding choric epilogue calls him – was fixed in, or perhaps we should more properly say *by*, both chronicle history and popular legend as the ideal king; both pious saint *and* patriotic hero – unlike Richard II, with whom he was often compared (or, more accurately, contrasted). For Holinshed, Shakespeare's main source for this play, Henry was 'a paterne in princehood, a lode-starr in honour, and mirrour of magnificence'; while Sir Walter Raleigh, looking back on English kings, asserted that 'None of them went to worke like a Conquerour: save onely King *Henrie* the fift.' Many works had been written seeking, or offering, to describe the ideal king, or perfect 'Christian Prince', and the prescribed virtues, gifts, and characteristics, seem obvious enough – he should be learned, just, and merciful; he should not seek vengeance and should always show self-control (no 'running bad humors', perhaps then); he should allow himself to be counselled by wise men, and be gracious and familiar with humble people (supposedly Henry's *forte*, though, as we shall see, 'a little touch of Harry in the night' is not quite what people think it is); he should be constantly concerned with affairs of state, and should banish flatterers and parasites (out goes Falstaff); he should command obedience, remember his responsibility for his people (particularly in war), live as a Christian, and make an honourable marriage (Henry gets round to this last, and tolerably brusquely). You can go through the play – some have – and find evidence that, checked against a list of such requisites, Henry scores nearly one hundred per cent – at times, indeed, in a rather heavy-handed and even too obvious way. He seems to have lost his habit of irony, and makes speeches of such bombastic patriotism that another age would surely have found them unashamedly jingoistic. Curiously – or, perhaps, not so curiously – Henry V has found something less than full favour in the eyes of some of the most English, 'patriotic', critics. Tillyard seems positively to dislike him, writing disparagingly of his lugubrious, pedestrian thoughtfulness; his orotund, detached eloquence; his pious platitudes. Writing of the histories, John Masefield found Henry 'the one commonplace man in the eight plays'. Dr Johnson, more tellingly, says – 'I know not why Shakespeare gives the king nearly such a character as he made him formerly ridicule in *Percy*.' What these, and many other critics are saying – among other things – is that, as Tillyard complained, this Henry is 'utterly inconsistent with his old self' and that 'it is not the same man speaking'. As a result, says Tillyard, 'the play constructed round him shows a great falling off in quality'. Is this right? Did Shakespeare somehow unaccountably 'nod' between writing *Henry IV* Part Two and *Julius Caesar* and *Hamlet* (within a year of *Henry V*)? Was the obligatory theme of the *perfect* king too intractable, or ungrateful, a subject for his questioning, heterodox mind? Did it require too tight a reining in of his wonderful, roaming ironies? Was the elimination of Falstaff too high a price to pay? Is the flat poetry, the conventional piety, the strident patriotism Shakespeare's – or is it Henry's? Is *Henry V* really as triumphalist as it sometimes sounds, and is often thought to be? These are real questions – though it is not clear to me that they are susceptible of definitive answers.

Is Henry the same man? Much has to be made, necessarily, of what legend and chronicle alike held to be his almost miraculous conversion – 'But after he was admitted to the rule of the lande, anon and sodainely he became a newe man, and turned all that rage and wildenesse into sobernesse and wise sadnesse, and the vice into constant virtue' (Fabyon –

Chronicle, 1559). The important point – the miraculous touch in the conversion-transformation – is 'anon and sodainely': 'all at once' as Canterbury says.

> Never was such a sudden scholar made;
> Never came reformation in a flood
> With such a heady currance scouring faults
>
> (I, i, 32–4)

Canterbury, Archbishop that he is, sees the conversion in purely religious terms, with talk of 'th' offending Adam', 'celestial spirits', angels, paradise, and so on. And in this opening scene – doubtless to prepare us for a changed Henry – we are given what might be called the official version of Henry's almost miraculous repentance and conversion ('almost' because, for Protestants, true miracles ended with the revelation of Christ); along with a eulogy by Canterbury of the King as the prince of all perfections. The Bishop of Ely turns to nature for an explanation of the sudden change in Henry:

> The strawberry grows underneath the nettle,
> And wholesome berries thrive and ripen best
> Neighbored by fruit of baser quality;
> And so the Prince obscured his contemplation
> Under the veil of wildness, which (no doubt)
> Grew like the summer grass, fastest by night,
> Unseen, yet crescive in his faculty.
>
> (I, i, 60–66)

Hazlitt thought that, incidentally, this was Shakespeare's account of 'the progress of the poet's mind'. It is an interesting, rather Romantic, thought. In any case, the two prelates give a formal description of the conversion as being brought about by the mysterious processes of both religion and nature, strongly implying that, hereafter, the King enjoys the sanction of both. However, I will just note here that the formulation in Holinshed, perhaps quite unintentionally, allows us at least to consider the possibility of regarding the conversion in a slightly different way. Holinshed writes that Henry 'determined to put on him the shape of a new man'. I don't want to make too much of this, but the point about 'metamorphosis' –

an important process, or phenomenon, or possibility, or almost-miracle, for Shakespeare as I have indicated – is that, though the shape may change, change utterly, some essential part of the person carries through and remains the same. Proteus may make himself appear as a lion, a serpent, water, or a tree – but he is always Proteus. Henry must still, in some way, be Hal, even though he seems to have changed his shape *completely*. He was, anyway, from the beginning, particularly good and adept at 'putting on' new shapes.

The rest of Act I shows the two Bishops – 'we of the spiritualty' – providing genealogical and historical justifications for Henry's claims to France, and indeed urging him 'With blood, and sword and fire, to win your right!' Thus we see the Church giving its authorizing legitimation to a ruthless war of conquest. How much of all this is casuistry and policy is perhaps undecidable – but a good deal, certainly. What is even more undecidable is whether Henry has already resolved to attack France (his dying father advised him to make foreign wars), and merely wants an ever-ready Church to provide a justifying gloss; or whether he is genuinely trying to discover whether his cause is just. For all his protestations of reluctance, pause, and scruple, it is hard (I find) to rule out a sense that the former is, in fact, the case. Whatever, the 'spiritualty' soon gives him all the reassurance he wants, or needs.

> Now we are well resolved, and by God's help
> And yours, the noble sinews of our power,
> France being ours, we'll bend it to our awe,
> *Or break it all to pieces*
>
> (I, ii, 222–5, my italics)

And watch out for Henry's 'bad humors', France! It does not require the Dauphin's silly, and ill-advised, 'gift' of tennis balls to provoke Henry to a determination to invade France; any more than he *really* needed the Church to stiffen his resolve in that direction (to give it a veneer of respectability, yes). For all his coolness in his debate with the Bishops, Henry is hot to go. As his long, often furious and bloodthirsty speech to the French Ambassador surely indicates (I, ii, 259–97). Note that, after some twenty-five lines of violent threats, Henry says:

> But all this lies within the will of God,
> To whom I do appeal, and in whose name,
> Tell you the Dauphin, I am coming on
> To venge me as I may, and to put forth
> My rightful hand in a well-hallowed cause.
>
> (I, ii, 289–93)

He invokes God, as he will continue to do (a Bolingbroke habit), though it is notable that, after Act I, the Bishops never reappear. From now on, Henry will be his own priest. But, though he talks of a 'well-hallowed cause', he is thinking of 'glory' and revenge. Henry hasn't changed, perhaps, quite as much as we thought – or the official version claims.

With a by now familiar shift, Act II moves us from the court to the tavern, or a street before a tavern (I will discuss the choric introductions to each Act later). Here is the Falstaff gang – Nym, Bardolph, Pistol, the Hostess – but, of course, without Falstaff. As Hazlitt said – 'Falstaff is dead, and without him, Pistol, Nym, and Bardolph are satellites without a sun.' They squabble, and swear, and generally 'cynicize' (if I may be allowed the word); but they present no anarchic threat, nor do they offer any seriously subversive ironic parallel to the doings at court. Though Pistol's departing words to the Hostess, now his wife, are worth noting:

> Trust none;
> For oaths are straws, men's faiths are wafer-cakes,
> And Hold-fast is the only dog, my duck ...
> Let us to France, like horse-leeches, my boys,
> To suck, to suck, the very blood to suck!
>
> (II, iii, 51–7)

Oaths, and their (unspoken) breakability, will loom large at the end of the play, where there will also be a reminder that 'Hold-fast' is exactly what England did *not* do, once it had conquered France. As for the rather ghoulish relish at the prospect of sucking French blood – it is not at all certain that a comparable anticipation is not somewhere lurking in Henry's mind as well.

It might be noted here that the play shows (and thus invites) very little sympathy for Nym, Bardolph, and Pistol.

They are the voice of the non-heroic, disaffected, impoverished under-class; but whereas such a voice, elsewhere in
Shakespeare, can exercise a strong claim on our sympathies,
these three are so coarse and snappish (soldiers are commonly
dogs, curs, hounds, in this play), so crassly immoral, cowardly,
and self-serving that, rather than attracting us by touching
our reserves of anti-heroic laughter (Bardolph's rather ludicrous 'On, on, on, on, on, to the breach' is but a limping bit of
mockery of Henry's 'Once more unto the breach, dear friends'
which it follows), they seem more calculated to arouse execration and disgust. The Boy (Falstaff's old servant) leaves
them with a sort of nauseated contempt ('Their villainy goes
against my weak stomach, and therefore I must cast it up,' III,
ii, 54–5); and Gower's verdict on Pistol stands uncorrected
and unchallenged: 'Why, 'tis a gull, a fool, a rogue, that now
and then goes to the wars, to grace himself at his return into
London, under the form of a soldier' (III, vi, 69–71). In the
event, Bardolph and Nym are hanged; and Pistol, suffering the
final humiliation of being forced to eat Fluellen's leek, makes
an exit which is at once pathetic, abject, and squalid.

> Doth Fortune play the huswife with me now?
> News have I, that my Doll is dead i' th' spital
>   of malady of France;
> And there my rendezvous is quite cut off.
> Old do I wax, and from my weary limbs
> Honor is cudgeled. Well, bawd I'll turn,
> And something lean to cutpurse of quick hand.
> To England will I steal, and there I'll steal;
> And patches will I get unto these cudgeled scars,
> And swear I got them in the Gallia wars.

> (V, i, 83–92)

So fades away the last remnant of Falstaff's world. It seems a
cruelly degraded conclusion. Henry (and his rhetoric) deserve
to have had a more persuasive, invigorated challenge from
below than this.

The containment, indeed, the liquidation, of any potential
opposition – the stamping out, or removal (at times, self-
eradication), of any possible points of insurrection or resistance – is a notable feature of the play. This is nowhere made

more obvious than with the implausibly abject and ingratiat-
ingly complete submission and repentance of the (easily
discovered) traitors, Cambridge, Grey, and Scroop. Henry
sets them up by staging a kind of theatre of mercy in front of
them (they do not know he knows about their plotting), in
which he ostentatiously pardons some drunken wretch who
has 'railed against our person' (I wonder what he had to say in
his cups). He thus provokes them into reproaching him for
injudicious leniency – 'That's mercy, but too much security:/
Let him be punished' (II, ii, 45–6). When Henry then
instantly produces proof of their treasonable plot, they are, of
course, in no position to appeal to a mercy they have just so
intransigently censured. There is something of the old cool and
cat-like Hal in these manipulated proceedings. A little touch
of Harry can be a dangerous thing. What strains credulity is
the abject gratitude which they express at their discovery and
consequent sentence:

> But God be thankèd for prevention,
> Which I in sufferance heartily will rejoice. [Cambridge]

> Never did faithful subject more rejoice
> At the discovery of most dangerous treason
> Than I do at this hour joy o'er myself,
> Prevented from a damnèd enterprise. [Grey]
>
> (II, ii, 158–64)

Meeting death with dignity is one thing ('Nothing became his
life like the leaving of it') – but this seems excessive. Dollimore
and Sinfield are justified in their sceptical observation – 'It is
of course one of the most authoritative ideological legitima-
tions available to the powerful: to be sincerely validated by
former opponents.' Certainly, Shakespeare makes any potential source of opposition to Henry fall away – or assimilate
itself – with extraordinary ease. The wily Church disappears
at the end of Act I; the fractious part of the ruling class
troops happily to execution in Act II. We have seen how the
last of the disaffected under-class retreats like a whipped cur
before the end of the play. That leaves a few fellow aristocrats,
and the loyal soldiers, including Irish, Welsh, and Scottish

representatives shown to be (quite unhistorically) cheerfully (and at times rather embarrassingly comically – touches of national caricatures here) subservient to the English king. Compared with previous history plays (for instance, *Richard III*), the British cast of *Henry V* is rather small and circumscribed, giving the impression of a few simplified representatives, rather than a seething and varied population. From this point of view, if from no other, one has to say that, by Shakespeare's standards, this is an impoverished play.

There is another interesting feature of the treatment of the conspirators. Their treachery occasions an impassioned speech from Henry which, occasionally, shows some of the disgust and outrage of Hamlet and even later figures. Calling the conspirators 'dogs' and 'English monsters', he turns to Scroop:

> What shall I say to thee, Lord Scroop, thou cruel,
> Ingrateful, savage, and inhuman creature?
> Thou that didst bear the key of all my counsels,
> That knew'st the very bottom of my soul,
> That (almost) mightst have coined me into gold,
> Wouldst thou have practiced on me for thy use?
>
> (II, ii, 94–9)

(cf. 'do you think I am easier to be played on than a pipe? Call me what instrument you will, though you fret me, you cannot play upon me,' *Hamlet*, III, ii, 377–80). Such an 'evil' can scarcely be credited, even when discovered.

> 'Tis so strange
> That, though the truth of it stands off as gross
> As black and white, my eye will scarcely see it.
>
> (II, ii, 102–4)

Henry invokes 'fiends', 'devils', 'hell', and we hear that Hamletic, indeed ubiquitously Shakespearian, nausea at 'seeming' and 'glist'ring semblances of piety':

> Show men dutiful?
> Why, so didst thou. Seem they grave and learned?
> Why so didst thou. Come they of noble family?
> Why, so didst thou. Seem they religious?
> Why so didst thou ...
> Such and so finely bolted didst thou seem;

And thus thy fall hath left a kind of blot
To mark the full-fraught man and best indued
With some suspicion. I will weep for thee;
For this revolt of thine, methinks, is like
Another fall of man.

(II, ii, 127–42)

There is, indeed, no art to find the mind's construction in the face. This can work two ways – the French have been 'too much mistaken' in Henry. As the Constable says to the Dauphin (shortly after Henry's speech) concerning Henry:

And you shall find vanities forespent
Were but the outside of the Roman Brutus,
Covering discretion with a coat of folly;
As gardeners do with ordure hide those roots
That shall first spring and be most delicate.

(II, iv, 36–40)

What looks like folly might conceal discretion, just as 'ordure' might be overlaying healthy roots. And thus Henry – before and after his 'transformation'. But that, too, is reversible. What now shows as a truly regal 'discretion' (Henry V *now*), might conceal folly and ordure. Might, might not; but you cannot be sure.

So, the conspirators were purely, inexplicably 'evil' – another fall of man. That was perhaps the ultimate mystery and horror for Shakespeare – the Iago phenomenon. But the actual, historical conspiracy was more a matter of politics than theology. As Henry IV's son, Henry V is far from secure on the throne – as he himself reveals:

Not today, O Lord,
O, not today, think not upon the fault
My father made in compassing the crown!

(IV, i, 297–9)

he prays on the eve of battle. Cambridge and his allies were involved in a dynastic contestation with the Bolingbrokes – indeed, Cambridge's son was to claim the crown in the reign of Henry VI, and this Yorkist line would eventually take over the throne. By ascribing pure evil to the conspirators (instead of the impure motivations of factional struggle), Henry is, in effect, purifying himself. And in the total absence of any critical, questioning, contesting voices near him, Shakespeare lets him have it his way.

And that, perhaps, is the trouble with the play. That Henry seems to have it all so effortlessly his own way. No shadows fall on him; he is not beset by doubts; he never loses his mental footing, or misses a step, as it were. There is, effectively, only one soliloquy; in general, (that important soliloquy apart), he never breaks off to explore some troubling inner thoughts; never turns away to utter some questioning aside; never loses himself in doubt or inconsequentiality, or breaks out into an unexpected strangeness (nor does anyone else behave in this way). He is always the central character, invariably appearing and behaving as a public figure; and it is as if we only ever see him in one perspective and in single focus, with no glimpses of peripheral alternatives or possible criticisms or hidden privacies. From this point of view, he does seem to be allowed to appear as the unquestioned, unquestioning English patriot hero – a development of Faulconbridge (in *King John*), though without the latter's irony and wit. (Such comic scenes as there are are fragmentary and undeveloped, lacking in any incendiary or detonative power.) His contemptuous speeches to the French, and his galvanizing exhortations to his troops, are too famous to need citing here. Though we should, perhaps, remind ourselves of the strong strain of sheer brutality in many of his words. To the Governor of Harfleur, for instance, he demands capitulation, or –

> The gates of mercy shall be all shut up,
> And the fleshed soldier, rough and hard of heart,
> In liberty of bloody hand shall range
> With conscience wide as hell, mowing like grass
> Your fresh fair virgins and your flow'ring infants.
> What is it then to me if impious war,
> Arrayed in flames like to the prince of fiends,
> Do with his smirched complexion all fell feats
> Enlinked to waste and desolation? . . .
>   in a moment look to see
> The blind and bloody soldier with foul hand

Defile the locks of your shrill-shrieking daughters;
Your fathers taken by the silver beards,
And their most reverend heads dashed to the walls;
Your naked infants spitted upon pikes,
Whiles the mad mothers with their howls confused
Do break the clouds, as did the wives of Jewry
At Herod's bloody-hunting slaughtermen.

(III, iii, 10–18, 33–41)

and many more bloody lines of the same. I don't wish to be a twentieth-century sensitive about such matters (though the lines *do* put me in mind of Picasso's *Guernica*), and no doubt war at that time was conducted in much such terms. But there is a less than saintly relish in Henry's words – he is clearly enjoying being/playing Herod, famed slaughterer of Innocents. In the event, Harfleur surrenders, and Henry instructs his army – 'Use mercy to them all' (III, iii, 54). But according to the chronicles he *did* sack Harfleur: Shakespeare's omission of that piece of bloodshed may, indeed, represent an inclination to protect Henry's image. Though, as we shall see, the sanitization is not complete.

As traditional enemies, the French were legitimate objects of scorn and ridicule, and, with their bragging and their cowardice, they cut sorry enough figures in the play (the King apart – as father of Katherine who will, in due course, be the mother of the future Henry VII, he is allowed his dignity). But one of the most powerful speeches in the play is an impassioned account by Burgundy of the horrifying ruin and desolation the wars have brought to France – 'this best garden of the world'.

Her vine, the merry cheerer of the heart,
Unprunèd dies; her hedges even-pleached,
Like prisoners wildly overgrown with hair,
Put forth disordered twigs; her fallow leas
The darnel, hemlock, and rank fumitory
Doth root upon, while that the coulter rusts
That should deracinate such savagery
. . .
And all our vineyards, fallows, meads, and hedges,
Defective in their natures, grow to wildness,

xcii

Even so our houses, and ourselves, and children,
Have lost, or do not learn for want of time,
The sciences that should become our country;
But grow like savages – as soldiers will,
That nothing do but meditate on blood –
To swearing, and stern looks, diffused attire,
And everything that seems unnatural.

(see the whole speech – V, ii, 23–67)

Such a vision of utter disorder would have brought a chill to any good Elizabethan heart – irrespective of ancient enmities. The horror of war knows no patriotism.

As usual, Shakespeare omitted many things included in the more meandering progress of the chronicles. These include the conflict with the Lollards, and the capture and execution of Sir John Oldcastle (something too much of Oldcastle, perhaps; the Lollard controversy and troubles were also omitted in *The Famous Victories of Henry V*, from which Shakespeare again took many incidents – as usual, completely transforming them). He also leaves out most of the events of 1416–19 (including the murder of Burgundy and the terrible siege of Rouen), presumably so that he can pass almost immediately from Agincourt to Henry's marriage and the acceptance of his claim to France. This sort of contraction and occlusion is understandable enough – in the interests of focusing on select dramatic moments. More strange, to me, is the complete absence of any reference to the particular battle tactics used by Henry at Agincourt. The English were hopelessly outnumbered; yet, through the skilful deployment of archers (the release of their arrows was perhaps the most memorable moment in the Olivier film), and the famous use of stakes, the heavily armoured French were, indeed, utterly confounded. Holinshed gives *lots* of details:

he caused stakes bound with iron sharpe at both ends, of the length of five or six foot to be pitched before the archers, and at each side the footmen like an hedge, to the intent that if the barded horses ran rashlie upon them, they shortlie be gored and destroied.

the archers in the forefront, and the archers on that side which stood in the medow, so wounded the footmen, galled the horsses, and combred the men of armes, that the footmen durst not go forward, the horssemen ran togither upon plumps without order, some overthrew such as were next to them, and the horsses overthrew their masters, and so at the first joining, the Frenchmen were foulie discomforted, and the Englishmen highlie encouraged.

There is a lot more. Whatever else you may think about this, it was terrific soldiering. And of all this, in Shakespeare's play – nothing. A glimpse of some of the French in panic and disarray, and then –

> *Herald.* The day is yours.
> *King.* Praised be God, and not our strength for it!
>
> (IV, vii, 88–9)

and later:

> O God, thy arm was here!
> And not to us, but to thy arm alone,
> Ascribe we all! When, without stratagem,
> But in plain shock and even play of battle,
> Was ever known so great and little loss
> On one part and on th' other? Take it, God,
> For it is none but thine!
>
> (IV, viii, 108–14)

Without stratagem? What about those stakes and arrows? Bullough rationalizes the omission thus: 'The complex spirit in which the battle was fought, is alone important, the mingling of soaring patriotism with comic gaiety and realism, as English courage brings the French to shame, the victim turning victor and overthrowing the braggart foe.' Perhaps that *is* how we are intended to respond – though it strikes me as a rather breathlessly generous over-reading. What is striking is Henry's persistent and repeated 'ascription' of the whole victory to God. He does this over and over again, culminating in the strangely fierce order:

> And *be it death proclaimèd* through our host
> To boast of this, or take that praise from God
> Which is His only.
>
> (IV, viii, 116–18, my italics)

All commendably pious, no doubt. But we may recall that the

steely 'necessitarian' Bolingbrokes have a way of invoking –
intoning – 'God' at strategic moments when it suits them to
stand aside from their own deeds. Remember John, after the
basely won 'victory' at Gaultree, solemnly saying – 'God, and
not we, hath safely fought today'. (And we may also
remember that Falstaff, on his death-bed, 'cried out "God,
God, God" three or four times' – about the same number of
times as his old drinking companion calls it out after Agincourt.) Not that there was anything treacherous about the
victory at Agincourt; but war is always a dirty business (and
we know from his Harfleur speech that Henry is willing to
abandon all chivalric rules of war and let his men do their
damnedest). Perhaps he prefers to cover the 'ordure' of battle
with a carapace of self-exculpating piety. I did nothing (how
modest): God did *all* (how convenient). I allow myself this
somewhat sceptical reading, because there is one piece of
'ordure' which Henry – as aspirant to saintly reputation –
might well prefer to have hidden with a 'coat' of sanctity. And
this, Shakespeare, notably, *does* include.

This is the incident which has come to be known as 'the
killing of the prisoners'. All the chroniclers regard it as an
indisputable historical fact that, at some point in the battle,
Henry suddenly ordered the slaughter of all the French
prisoners (by any standards of war, then and now, a foul
'stratagem'). It is also agreed that, at some point in the battle,
a group of the French attacked the English baggage train, and
killed the helpless 'boys' looking after it. Whether there was a
(causal) relationship between these two events is the very
reverse of a trivial matter. Some chroniclers simply assert that,
when Henry heard that the French were regrouping for
another attack, he ordered the prisoners killed. Holinshed,
however, links the order to Henry's anger at the attack on
what Fluellen calls 'the poys and the luggage', as well as his
anxiety about the possibility of another attack by the French.
Though even Holinshed seems not to like this 'lamentable
slaughter' much. Henry, he writes:

contrarie to his accustomed gentlenes, commanded by sound of
trumpet, that everie man (upon paine of death) should incontinentlie

slaie his prisoner. When this dolorous decree, and pitifull proclamation was pronounced, pitie it was to see how some Frenchmen were suddenlie sticked with daggers, some were brained with pollaxes, some slaine with malls, others had their throats cut, and some their bellies panched, so that in effect, having respect to the great number, few prisoners were saved.

Some more recent English critics have been far more comfortable with the episode, seemingly finding it not at all 'dolorous', 'pitifull', 'lamentable'. Dover Wilson took the lead in commending Henry for doing exactly what had to be done and no nonsense; and here is the Arden editor – 'Gower's remark, "the King most worthily hath caused every soldier to cut his prisoner's throat. O! 'tis a gallant king!"', shows wholehearted approval of Henry's promptness in decision and his resolute determination. The rage of the epic hero leading to the slaughter of the enemy within his power is not without Virgilian precedent.' I have to confess that I read that opinion with entire incredulity.

But how does Shakespeare show it? The battle is not yet over, despite initial English success, and Henry hears an 'alarum':

> But hark, what new alarum is this same?
> The French have reinforced their scattered men.
> Then every soldier kill his prisoners!
> Give the word through.

(IV, vi, 35–8)

Notice that there is no mention of the French killing the boys minding the baggage – this is cool (or coldly furious) military 'necessity'. Now, immediately *after* this, we shift to Fluellen talking to Gower, and Fluellen's first words follow directly on Henry's order:

Kill the poys and the luggage? 'Tis expressly against the law of arms; 'tis as arrant a piece of knavery, mark you now, as can be offert – in your conscience, now, is it not?

(IV, vii, 1–4)

This *does* refer to the French killing of the boys. But, coming immediately after Henry's order to kill the prisoners, the comment ' 'tis expressly against the law of arms' could equally apply to *that* order, because it was also 'against the law of arms' – in our conscience, now, is it not? In the play, it is certainly not an act justified by the French 'knavery'. And, crucially, there is more. Fluellen rambles on in what seems like his comical Welsh-garrulous way, but what he says could not, in fact, be more pointed. He suddenly starts going on about Alexander, and Macedon and Monmouth:

If you mark Alexander's life well, Harry of Monmouth's life is come after it indifferent well, for there is figures in all things. Alexander, God knows, and you know, in his rages, and his furies, and his wraths, and his cholers, and his moods, and his displeasures, and his indignations, and also being a little intoxicated in his prains, did, in his ales and his angers, look you, kill his best friend, Cleitus ... I speak but in the figures and comparisons of it: as Alexander killed his friend Cleitus, being in his ales and his cups, so also Harry Monmouth, being in his right wits and his good judgments, turned away the fat knight with the great-belly doublet – he was full of jests, and gipes, and knaveries, and mocks; I have forgot his name.
Gower. Sir John Falstaff.
Fluellen. That is he: I'll tell you there is good men porn at Monmouth.
(IV, vii, 33–55)

Let's see – Henry killed his prisoners, the sort of thing Alexander would have done; and that reminds me, didn't he, also like Alexander though without the excuse of drink, effectively kill his best friend – what was the man's name? 'SIR JOHN FALSTAFF'. There he is once more – resurrected, by name, to, I think, devastating effect. The unavoidable implication of Fluellen's inspired concatenation is that this is a king who, when it comes to it, is willing to kill his enemies *and* his friends. And having just had an intimation that, beneath his rather stiffly maintained public exterior of piety, chivalry, regality (he is often described as 'puissant', as if he was turning himself into an archaic heraldic figure), Henry can be a man of 'rages, furies, wraths, cholers, moods'; we may register with a renewed sense of loss the impoverishingly depleting absence of Falstaff's 'jests, gipes, knaveries, and mocks'. Immediately following that exchange, Henry duly enters, indulging one of his rages:

> I was not angry since I came to France
> Until this instant. . . .
>   we'll cut the throats of those we have,
> And not a man of them that we shall take
> Shall taste our mercy.
>
> (IV, vii, 57–8, 65–7)

In an earlier, calmer mood, Henry had declared: 'when lenity and cruelty play for a kingdom, the gentler gamester is the soonest winner' (III, vi, 117–18). 'Use lenity, sweet chuck!' (III, iii, 25) says Pistol, in one of the few possibly ironic echoes in the play. But the only 'lenity' actually shown, displayed is the better word, by Henry in the play, is to the bemused drunkard in Act II, and the sorely tricked, good soldier Williams in Act IV. This is cheap lenity indeed; or rather, no lenity at all. The proposition that these episodes are included to demonstrate Henry's 'magnanimity' – as I have seen advanced – is simply laughable. When the going gets serious, Henry is the very reverse of a 'gentle gamester'. 'O, 'tis a gallant king!'? However unintended, Gower's words have a hollow, ironic ring to them.

An important part of the legend of good King Harry was that he had the common touch, a gift of uncondescending familiarity with the people – presumably a residue of his tavern days. In the play, this is supposedly exemplified by Henry's moving among the soldiers on the night before the battle of Agincourt – though here again, Shakespeare rather complicates the matter. The scene is set by the choric intro-duction to Act IV, and this is perhaps a suitable point to say something about the Chorus in this play. Unlike any other play by Shakespeare, every Act is prefaced by a Chorus – or Prologue – plus an Epilogue. This choric framing has usually been seen as an attempt to make an *epic*-drama, with all the spaciousness and amplitude that that implies. But not quite so. A traditional chorus would help us to see the enacted events in a wider context, a longer perspective. But this triumphalist Chorus is more royalist than the King. I find a comment by Michael Goldman more to the point:

Once it is recognized that the Chorus sounds very much like the

King, much of the play's method becomes clear. Like Henry, the Chorus is a man whose job is to rouse his hearers to unusual effort. The straining note is struck from the start, and may well be the primary reason for the Chorus's existence, since none of the theories usually advanced to account for Shakespeare's unparalleled reliance on the device is satisfactory ... nowhere else does he use it to call attention to the inadequacies of his stage, which is of course no more inadequate to this story than to the material of the other histories. Here, however, the notion of inadequacy is insisted upon, as is the effort we must put forth to make up for it ... The playwright and the resources of his stage are deficient, but so are we, and we are asked to perform all kinds of brain-work to convert the work of actors into a convincing spectacle ... As the Chorus says in his second appearance, the project we are engaged in is to 'force a play'.

'Force' suggests the necessity for unnatural effort; here, it can also mean 'stuff' (courtesy Dover Wilson), and, by definition, the thing that requires/invites 'stuffing' is previously empty. 'Work, Work', says the Chorus to his audience; 'On, on', says Henry to his soldiers. These comparable urgings suggest that they have poor, thin, reluctant material to work on and with. Desperately endeavouring to 'swell' the scene, the Chorus thereby implies that, without his efforts, we would be presented with but a famished, laggardly spectacle. And indeed, nearly all the *action* in the play – the movement (sailing, riding, fighting, running); the noises (boats, horses, voices, instruments); all the turbulent energy released in crowds and war – is in the *speech* of the Chorus (Shakespeare knows that words can do anything). What we *see* is more like a series of tableaux, often curiously still – indeed, stilted. The result of all this choric effort and dramatic inadequacy is more than a slight feeling of unreality. Perhaps – but of course, only perhaps – suggesting that the dramatic portrayal of the ideal, hero-saint King, is an almost impossible (unreal) task. Requiring too much 'forcing'.

And so to the choric introduction to Act IV.

> O, now, who will behold
> The royal captain of this ruined band
> Walking from watch to watch, from tent to tent,
> Let him cry, 'Praise and glory on his head!'

For forth he goes and visits all his host,
Bids them good morrow with a modest smile,
And calls them brothers, friends, and countrymen.
. . .
That every wretch, pining and pale before,
Beholding him, plucks comfort from his looks.
A largess universal, like the sun,
His liberal eye doth give to everyone,
Thawing cold fear, that mean and gentle all
Behold, as may unworthiness define,
A little touch of Harry in the night.

(IV, Cho. 28–34, 41–7)

Which is fine, stirring, and heart-warming. The trouble is, that what we then go on to 'behold' is not remotely like this. For a start, Henry walks about the camp at night in disguise. (This has no basis whatsoever in the chronicles – Bullough suggests that Shakespeare took the idea from Tacitus's *Annals*, II, iii.) Thus, he does not appear as a 'sun' king, beaming rays of comfort and confidence on his sadly straitened soldiers. So far from that, he goes sniffing about for evidence of loyalty – or, probably more to the point, *dis*loyalty. He seems to be seeking the reassurance he should be offering. He gets the sort of (to us embarrassing) praise he wants from Pistol (of all people!) But he runs into a bit of trouble with Bates, Court, and Williams. Famously, he insists on the King's common humanity – 'I think the King is but a man, as I am ... His ceremonies laid by, in his nakedness he appears but a man' and so on (IV, i, 103–7). Bates gives the rather unpromising reply that, whatever the King is, he wishes the King was standing up to his neck in the Thames 'and I by him, at all adventures, so we were quit here' (IV, i, 119). The King then urges that we should be content to die in the King's company, 'his cause being just and his quarrel honorable'. To which Williams makes the utterly justified reply, 'That's more than we know' (IV, i, 131) – and perhaps more than *we* know, too – going on to say: 'I am afeard there are few die well that die in battle; for how can they charitably dispose of anything when blood is their argument? Now, if these men do not die well, it will be a black matter for the King that led them to it; who to disobey, were against all proportion of subjection' (IV, i, 143–9). Henry makes an elaborate case for the innocence of the King in this respect – which the men seem to accept. 'I do not desire he should answer for me, and yet I determine to fight lustily for him,' says Bates (IV, i, 193–4). This is loyalty enough, and the King should be satisfied. But he wants more, and pushes too hard – thus:

King. I myself heard the King say he would not be ransomed.
Williams. Ay, he said so, to make us fight cheerfully; but when our throats are cut, he may be ransomed, and we ne'er the wiser.
King. If I live to see it, I will never trust his word after.
Williams. You pay him then! That's a perilous shot out of an elder-gun, that a poor and a private displeasure can do against a monarch! ... You'll never trust his word after! Come, 'tis a foolish saying.
King. Your reproof is something too round; I should be angry with you, if the time were convenient.
Williams. Let it be a quarrel between us, if you live.
King. I embrace it.
Williams. How shall I know thee again?

(IV, i, 195–212)

And so to the exchange of gloves, which the King will use to play a trick on Williams after the battle. Henry is angry again (we have been warned about these mean moods in *Henry IV* Part Two – 'being incensed, he's flint;/As humorous as winter, and as sudden/As flaws congealed in the spring of day', IV, iv, 33–5); he hasn't got what he came for. But he gets, we must feel, nothing less than he deserves. Who would want a little touch of *this* Harry in the night?

Later, the trick is duly played on Williams; Henry reveals that the glove was, in fact his, and asks – 'How canst thou make me satisfaction?'

Williams. All offenses, my lord, come from the heart: never came any from mine that might offend your Majesty.
King. It was ourself thou didst abuse.
Williams. Your Majesty came not like yourself: you appeared to me but as a common man; witness the night, your garments, your lowliness. And what your Highness suffered under that shape, I beseech you take it for your own fault, and not mine; for had you

been as I took you for, I made no offense. Therefore I beseech your
Highness pardon me.

(IV, viii, 46–56)

Williams's position is unassailable, and his dignity unimpaired
(he refuses the offer of a piddling tip from Fluellen) – the King
was quite unfair, if not something worse, to practise on his
soldiers, sufficiently under strain as they were, in this way – and
it certainly *was* his own fault if he taxed some unwelcome truth-
telling out of them. 'Your Majesty came not like yourself' – but
he never did, he never has. Always Mercury, even when he
looks like Perseus. Emily Dickinson's line, 'Ourself behind
ourself concealed', might have been written for Henry. It is
never certain when he *is* most 'like himself'. When he is 'per-
forming' the good king, as he does for much of this play? Perhaps.
Or perhaps it is in those moments of cold fury ('as humorous as
winter') when he breaks friends' hearts and cuts enemies'
throats. With Henry, this Henry, you can just never know.

By convention, characters are most 'like themselves' in
soliloquy; and Henry has only one, in this notably *un*inward-
looking play. Characteristically, it is not entirely clear what it
reveals about him. It occurs on his night walk, when he has left
the soldiers. Seemingly, it is a bitter lament for the burdens of
high office, and the emptiness of 'Ceremony'.

> What infinite heart's-ease
> Must kings neglect that private men enjoy!
> And what have kings that privates have not too,
> Save ceremony, save general ceremony?
> And what art thou, thou idol Ceremony?
> What kind of god art thou, that suffer'st more
> Of mortal griefs than do thy worshippers?
> What are thy rents? What are thy comings-in?
> O Ceremony, show me but thy worth!
> What is thy soul of adoration?
> Art thou aught else but place, degree, and form,
> Creating awe and fear in other men?
> Wherein thou art less happy, being feared,
> Than they in fearing.

(IV, i, 241–54)

And much more – all seeming to underline the vanity and

pointlessness of 'thrice-gorgeous ceremony'. It is as though the man, Henry, wants to distance, or at least distinguish himself from the ceremonial figure that he is having to become. But by personifying Ceremony, he in fact risks identifying himself *with* it. Because otherwise he is saying that he is simply a helpless creature of Ceremony, as though it had autonomous power. But the power is Henry's, and he *uses* all its ceremonial adjuncts and appurtenances. He may see through all these mystifying accessories, but he would never relinquish or discontinue them. The main burden of the speech is that the responsibilities of a king mean that he cannot sleep the sleep of – no, not the sleep of the just, as we say: the sleep of, to use Henry's preferred terms, the 'beggar', 'lackey', 'wretch', 'slave', all snoring contentedly away with 'body filled, and vacant mind'. This, it would appear, is how he really thinks of his subjects, among them those who, next day, will comprise 'we few, we happy few, we band of brothers'. Does this soliloquy 'come from the heart', as honest Williams would say? If so, then truly the man has a heart of winter.

The last Act wraps things up with France, as Henry's marriage to Katherine is settled (I will say nothing of Henry's 'court-ship' of the poor, hapless Katherine – it is a peremptory business, crudely, and sometimes a little coarsely, done. The 'feminine' is effectively absent from this play.) Oaths are duly taken all round, and the last line of the actual play hopes 'may our oaths well kept and prosp'rous be!' (V, ii, 386). But, as Pistol told his wife – 'oaths are straws, men's faiths are wafer-cakes' (II, iii, 52). And as the Epilogue reminds us, the next king lost all that Henry had fought to win, and precipitated a civil war – 'which oft our stage hath shown'. Shakespeare ends just where he began.

By which time, we can appreciate the aptness and force of W. B. Yeats's imaginative description of him:

He meditated as Solomon, not as Bentham meditated, upon blind ambitions, untoward accidents, and capricious passions, and the world was almost as empty in his eyes as it must be in the eyes of God.

*

HISTORIES

Coda

HENRY VIII

> *Second Gentleman.* These are stars indeed.
> *First Gentleman.* And sometimes falling ones.
> *Second Gentleman.* No more of that.
>
> (IV, i, 53–5)

1613: another *history* play – by *Shakespeare*! It seems somehow
unfitting. When Prospero announced that he was breaking his
staff and drowning his book, in *The Tempest*, most people have
felt that this was Shakespeare's very own way of indicating
that he was doing the same. And yet here it is – *Henry VIII*,
included without any reservations in the first Folio of 1623 by
Heminge and Condell (while they excluded works considered
of more dubious Shakespearian status, such as *Pericles* and *The
Two Noble Kinsmen*). However, in 1850 J. Spedding wrote an
article entitled 'Who Wrote Shakepeare's *Henry VIII*?' in
which he maintained, using plausible stylistic evidence, that
parts of the play were almost certainly written by Fletcher.
Debate and argument about this matter have continued ever
since, with some learned scholars maintaining that there are
good reasons for thinking that, in fact, Shakespeare wrote the
lot, while others are equally sure that they can detect when
Fletcher, as it were, takes over. I have nothing to add to this
debate. That there are stylistic variations (and, if you will,
dips into weakness) is undeniable; that there are lines which
only Shakespeare could have written seems to me incontest-
able. That it is hardly a play, or 'drama', at all, is the
proposition I shall try to advance.[1]

1 Among those who believe in a shared authorship, the generally
accepted division of labour is as follows:
Prologue: Fletcher.
Act One: i and ii: Shakespeare; iii and iv: Fletcher.
Act Two: i and ii: Fletcher; iii and iv: Shakespeare.
Act Three: i: Fletcher; ii: lines 1–203 Shakespeare, lines 204–459
Fletcher.
Act Four: i and ii: Fletcher.
Act Five: i: Shakespeare; ii, iii, iv: Fletcher.
Epilogue: Fletcher.

INTRODUCTION

Why did Shakespeare write it (or part of it – but I shall leave this matter aside in this brief introduction, and simply refer to the play as a whole)? It is, by definition, an unanswerable question; and, more than that, surely no man's motives are less recuperable than Shakespeare's. But one reason is speculatively adduced, which I will simply transcribe. In February 1613, Princess Elizabeth, King James's daughter, was married to Prince Frederick, the Elector Palatine, a leader of the Protestant union in Germany. The wedding was the occasion for the most lavish celebrations – banquets, plays, masques, pageants, fireworks, etc. – and it is suggested that this firm Protestant alliance between Britain and a German power occasioned popular rejoicing as well as court festivities. There was still a slight Popish threat of a Spanish invasion and a second armada in 1613, and many old (patriotic) history plays were revived (see R. A. Foakes, Arden edition). The anti-Catholic implications of the marriage of this second *Elizabeth* was an occasion of great rejoicing; and a play celebrating both the downfall of the last great *Catholic* statesman in England (Wolsey), and the birth of the *first* Elizabeth (Protestant from birth), might have seemed both timely and appropriate. This, anyway, is what we have.

And, it might be said, that's *all* we have: downfall – downfall*s*, actually – and a birth. No rebellions, no usurpations, no invasions, no wars; no serious plotting, no really profound contestations, no irresolvable antagonisms – and no humour (just one – one! – ironic remark). It has been called, variously, 'a sort of historical masque or show-play' (Coleridge), a 'chronicle-pageant', a 'festive history'. And yet this was the reign in which England experienced what must have been the massive trauma of being suddenly, forcibly, violently changed from a Catholic to a Protestant country. About which, be it said, Shakespeare keeps very quiet (so that, to this day, people speculate about his possible Catholic sympathies, going through the plays considering whether unbearable Puritans come off worse than untrustable Catholics). Nothing of that trauma/drama gets into this play, though it ends exactly when it was taking place (in 1533, when Elizabeth was born). This is the court in peace time. We have four trials, three deaths, one marriage, one birth; we have politics, forensic casuistry, some off-the-cuff theology; and a lot of quite uncharacteristically detailed (in the stage directions) ceremony, ritual, and pageantry. We have no serious character development, but instead we have the largest cast of any of the histories. We have no real soliloquies from this King Henry; but, as an innovation, a number of nameless gentlemen who stroll in and out saying – did you hear this, everyone is saying that, and so on. There are three real griefs; but it is a resolutely public play, with everything tending to spectacle. Indeed, so 'spectacular' was the performance that, on one occasion, the discharge of 'chambers', at the King's entry to the masque, set fire to the Globe theatre, which burned down.

The play starts with a description of the famous meeting of Henry VIII and Francis I at the Field of the Cloth of Gold (1520) – a vast Renaissance tournament at which the kings vied to show off their magnificence. It ends with an extended depiction of the baptism of Elizabeth (1533), accompanied by a rapturous 'prophecy' by Cranmer of the glories she will bring to England (not so difficult to write, one might think, with the hindsight of 1613):

> This royal infant – heaven still move about her! –
> Though in her cradle, yet now promises
> Upon this land a thousand thousand blessings,
> Which time shall bring to ripeness.
>
> (V, v, 17–20)

'Thou speakest wonders' says the happy father-king, and that is the note the play ends on, a climax very suitable for a dramatic epithalamion in honour of the just-married *Princess* Elizabeth, as Bullough points out. In between we have, primarily the trial, fall, and death of, in turn, Buckingham, Katherine of Aragon, and Cardinal Wolsey; plus the (thwarted) trial and rise of Archbishop Cranmer. Then – the ground clear – Henry's happy marriage to Anne Boleyn and the rapidly ensuing (historically, somewhat *too* rapidly!) birth of Elizabeth. As usual, Shakespeare does some selecting and rearranging and chronological collapsing. Henry did not marry Anne until 1532, but his meeting with her is placed before Buckingham's condemnation in 1521; while his marriage to Anne is placed before Wolsey's fall and death, which in fact took place in 1530. Katherine of Aragon died in 1536, but in the play this is made to occur before Princess Elizabeth is born (1533), as is the plot against Cranmer, which probably took place in 1540. My details are, as usual, from Bullough, who gives his opinion that the reasons for the changes were 'to give some illusion of enchainment or interconnection to the incidents, and to suggest dramatic parallels or contrasts emergent in a survey of the whole reign'. Cutting the action off where he does means that Shakespeare does not oblige himself to (avoids having to) address the darker and more problematical aspects of Henry's reign, and allows him his triumphant, not to say triumphalist, conclusion, packed with happy auguries under a cloudless sky.

But whatever we make of this conclusion (and truncation), the predominant mood is one of sadness, as indeed the Prologue anticipates:

> I come no more to make you laugh. Things now
> That bear a weighty and a serious brow,
> Sad, high, and working, full of state and woe,
> Such noble scenes as draw the eye to flow,
> We now present. Those that can pity, here
> May, if they think it well, let fall a tear:
> The subject will deserve it ...
> Be sad, as we would make ye. Think ye see
> The very persons of our noble story
> As they were living. Think you see them great,
> And followed with the general throng and sweat
> Of thousand friends. Then, in a moment, see
> How soon this mightiness meets misery;
> And if you can be merry then, I'll say
> A man may weep upon his wedding day.

> (1–7, 25–32)

Sad – not tragic. Sad, rather in the way Hardy describes sadness. 'It is the ongoing – i.e. the becoming – of the world that produces its sadness. If the world stood still at a felicitous moment, there would be no sadness in it.' 'Becoming' also involves 'Be-going' (if I may be allowed the word), just as 'ongoing' must end in 'off-going', and it is the going off of greatness which produces the sadness of this play. 'My soul grows sad with troubles' (III, i, 1), says Queen Katherine, foreseeing her displacement and demise. 'And when you would say something that is sad,/Speak how I fell' (II, i, 135–6) – these are, effectively, Buckingham's last words. The word 'fall' tolls through the play. 'The Cardinal/Will have his will, and she must fall' (II, i, 167).

> I shall fall
> Like a bright exhalation in the evening,
> And no man see me more.
>
> (III, ii, 225–7)

Wolsey rightly predicts. 'Press not a falling man too far' (III, ii, 333), says the compassionate Lord Chamberlain, echoed later by Cromwell – ''tis a cruelty/To load a falling man' (V, iii, 76–7). 'These are stars indeed,' says the Second Gentleman, watching the Coronation procession of Henry and Anne. 'And sometimes falling ones,' rejoins the First Gentleman. He may intend a slight joke about the royal ladies' virtue; but, more generally, the play is, indeed, full of falling stars. 'No more of that,' adds the well-mannered Second Gentleman; and indeed, the play now puts the 'falls' behind, and concentrates on 'ongoing' and 'becoming' – marriage and birth. But the play as a whole has, unmistakably and inexpugnably, a dying fall. (The falls, incidentally, are more fully elaborated, and the 'stars' made more noble in their falling, than they are in Shakespeare's sources. Frank Kermode once described the play as 'an anthology of falls', and thought that it represented a return to the medieval conception of history as found in *The Mirror for Magistrates*.)

One of the falls is fully deserved; one is singularly unjust; and one is curiously indeterminate – but they have one feature in common. The one who falls is, initially, in some way 'chafed' – angry, rebellious, resistant: but they all come to accept their doom with dignity, 'patience', and forgiveness. And they approach their deaths in a state of 'calm of mind, all passion spent'. Reconciliation, both to one's lot, and with former enemies, accusers, opponents, is the order of the day. It is this that has led some critics to see the play as fully consonant with, even a continuation of, Shakespeare's more famous 'last plays'. I will come back to this view with which, while I understand it, I ultimately strongly disagree. But let us consider the fallen in their falling, for these are undoubtedly the most powerful moments, or scenes, in the play.

The play effectively starts with Buckingham in a temper about Wolsey's devious manipulations and ruthless self-advancement. Norfolk warns him against Wolsey's malice, potency, and 'high hatred':

> And let your reason with your choler question
> What 'tis you go about ...
>   Anger is like
> A full hot horse who, being allowed his way,
> Self-mettle tires him ...
> Heat not a furnace for your foe so hot
> That it do singe yourself. We may outrun
> By violent swiftness that which we run at,
> And lose by overrunning. Know you not
> The fire that mounts the liquor till't run o'er
> In seeming to augment it wastes it?
>
>   (I, i, 130–34, 140–45)

This sort of compression of thought and vigour of image is characteristic of parts, but only parts, of the play (and, of course, claimed for Shakespeare by those who want to give the somewhat more soft-focused, languid, even sentimental parts to Fletcher). This power often shows in Buckingham's angry speech; as, for instance, when he is blaming Wolsey for arranging the ruinously pompous expensive Field of the Cloth of Gold show –

> That swallowed so much treasure, and like a glass
> Did break i' th' wrenching.
>
>   (I, i, 166–7)

'Wrenching' is a dialect word for 'rinsing', and more strongly suggests a powerful, even violent, physical act. In this, it is characteristic of many of the images in the play which, as Caroline Spurgeon noted, evoke 'bodily action of almost every kind: walking, stepping, marching, running and leaping;

crawling, hobbling, falling, carrying, climbing and perspiring;
swimming, diving, flinging and peeping; crushing, shaking,
trembling, sleeping, stirring, and – especially and repeatedly –
the picture of the body or back bent and weighed down under
a heavy burden'. At one point, after a distressed Cranmer has
left the King, Henry comments:

> He has strangled
> His language in his tears.
>
> (V, i, 156–7)

That *is* a line, I venture to say, that only Shakespeare could
have written.

Buckingham is soon caught in Wolsey's 'net', and betrayed
by his 'false' surveyor. Henry, about whom more later,
unquestioningly believes the surveyor's slanderous evidence
(that he heard Buckingham say he wanted to kill the King),
and we have another of those kingly speeches of horror at the
unforeseeable treachery of a trusted subject:

> This man so complete,
> Who was enrolled 'mongst wonders ...
> Hath into monstrous habits put the graces
> That once were his, and is become as black
> As if besmeared in hell.
>
> (I, ii, 118–24)

Except that it is very far from clear whether Buckingham *is*
guilty of anything approaching treason, while it is clear
enough that the surveyor has been put up to his lethal
defamations by Wolsey. What is interesting, to me, is that
Buckingham doesn't seem to know whether he is guilty or not
(I find this entirely plausible – *did* I say that? Perhaps I did.
But did I *mean* it? Was I expressing an intention or releasing an
anger? I could kill him – how many unmurderous people have
not said such a thing. And can a man ever know the full extent
of what he harbours in his heart? Even Holinshed is not clear
as to Buckingham's guilt – or innocence.) His last speeches are
those of a resigned and quiescent man, rather than a guilty one
– indeed, even while accepting the verdict against him, he
refers to his 'guiltless blood':

> I have this day received a traitor's judgment,
> And by that name must die. Yet, heaven bear witness,
> And if I have a conscience, let it sink me
> Even as the ax falls, if I be not faithful!
> The law I bear no malice for my death:
> 'T has done, upon the premises, but justice.
> But those that sought it I could wish more Christians.
> Be what they will, I heartily forgive 'em.
>
> (II, i, 58–66)

This strikes me as mild. But, in this play, finally mildness is all. The description of Buckingham, and his bearing, at the bar when he receives the dread sentence, in a way encapsulates the whole play:

> When he was brought again to th' bar, to hear
> His knell rung out, his judgment, he was stirred
> With such an agony he sweat extremely
> And something spoke in choler, ill and hasty.
> But he fell to himself again, and sweetly
> In all the rest showed a most noble patience.
>
> (II, i, 31–6)

From sweat to sweetness; from choler to patience – and seemingly without effort or inner struggle, rather as if it was a miraculous conversion: this is the very stamp of the play. And so this 'noble ruined man' goes to 'the long divorce of steel', speaking of 'sweet sacrifice', 'angels', 'soul', 'heaven' – his nobility intact, indeed enhanced.

Justice, we feel, has not been done. But another 'divorce' is looming – here is the Second Gentleman:

> If the Duke [i.e. Buckingham] be guiltless
> 'Tis full of woe. Yet I can give you inkling
> Of an ensuing evil, if it fall,
> Greater than this.
>
> (II, i, 139–42)

This 'evil' (strong word) is the rumour that the King is going to 'divorce', or rather set aside, Katherine, his wife for twenty years. We have already seen Henry helplessly attracted to Anne 'Bullen' at the masque, so that, despite the legal and theological debates which follow (concerning the 'separation' he clearly both wants and intends to have), we can have no doubts concerning Henry's real reason for wishing to have this separation somehow legitimized. Katherine's speeches, both at her 'trial', and thereafter, are the most moving of the play. She appeals to the King with a simple dignity:

> Alas, sir,
> In what have I offended you? What cause
> Hath my behavior given to your displeasure
> That thus you should proceed to put me off
> And take your good grace from me?
>
> (II, iv, 18–22)

But, remembering that she is a queen, she refrains from weeping, and 'my drops of tears/I'll turn to sparks of fire' (II, iv, 72–3). It is time for some very justifiable 'choler', and we duly get the 'sparks' – or rather, Wolsey does: 'your heart/Is crammed with arrogancy, spleen, and pride' (II, iv, 109–10) and more of the spirited same. She sweeps out of the Hall, saying 'They vex me past my patience' (II, iv, 130). She feels 'the last fit of my greatness' (III, i, 78). To Wolsey she says 'Ye turn me into nothing' (III, i, 114), and, while he rebukes her for her anger and stubbornness, she is tenacious of the rightness and justice of her position:

> I dare not make myself so guilty
> To give up willingly that noble title
> Your master wed me to. Nothing but death
> Shall e'er divorce my dignities.
>
> (III, i, 139–42)

As she fairly complains – 'And am I thus rewarded? 'Tis not well, lords' (III, i, 133). Not – it is *not* well. 'Evil' was, I think, the Gentleman's word.

But, after 'choler' – 'Patience, be near me still' (IV, ii, 76). This is addressed to her maid called Patience, but the larger implication is entirely apt. Although she does permit herself a rather tart remark when Griffith brings her 'commendations' and 'comfort' from the King when she is effectively on her death-bed – ''Tis like a pardon after execution' (IV, ii, 121) – she dies in a spirit of reconciliation. She has a 'Vision' of 'Spirits of peace', in which white-robed figures hold a garland over her head – '*at which, as it were by inspiration, she makes in her sleep signs of rejoicing, and holdeth up her hands to heaven*'. Her last message to the King is:

> Remember me
> In all humility unto his Highness.
> Say his long trouble now is passing
> Out of this world. Tell him in death I blessed him,
> For so I will. Mine eyes grow dim. Farewell,
> My lord.

(IV, ii, 161–5)

It is, one feels, somewhat better than Henry deserves. But that is, here, not the point. She has had her vision, her 'good dreams' (another touch of miracle), and departs in peace – 'unqueened', yet more royal than ever.

But it is the third fall – the absolutely just one – which is in many ways the greatest, for Wolsey came from almost out of nowhere to reach dizzying heights of power, influence – and a sumptuous way of life. Wolsey is the most marked and distinctive character in the play; evil (or ruthless ambition combined with insatiable pride), as ever, having a more complex and dimensioned physiognomy than simple goodness, or even not-so-simple fortitude and forbearance. He is not 'propped by ancestry' (he was a butcher's son), but, in one of Buckingham's images, he is a spider who has made his own spectacular career 'out of his self-drawing web' (I, i, 63). This suggests a 'self-fashioning' of a distinctly venomous kind. We catch glimpses of the range of his influence and power – hosting a banquet for the King, commandeering a lord's horses which he covets ('He will have all, I think'); and we are given clear indications of his dominance and manipulation of the King:

> He dives into the King's soul, and there scatters
> Dangers, doubts, wringing of the conscience,
> Fears and despairs ...

(II, ii, 26–8)

and – 'he hath a witchcraft/Over the King in's tongue' (III, ii, 18–19). The lords both hate and fear him, not least they seem like helpless putty in his scheming hands:

We had need pray,
And heartily, for our deliverance,
Or this imperious man will work us all
From princes into pages. All men's honors
Lie like one lump before him, to be fashioned
Into what pitch he pleases.

(II, ii, 44-9)

As Buckingham complains, Wolsey's ascent and mastery effectively proclaim 'there's difference in no persons' (I, i, 139). He threatens their rank, status, and distinction – seems, indeed, willing and able to subvert hierarchy itself to serve his purposes, and, more dangerously, to further his influence and alliance with Rome. To this end, he tries to delay the Papal dispensation for divorce which Henry initially seeks – because Wolsey wants Henry to marry, not Anne ('a spleeny Lutheran'), but his own choice – the Duchess of Alençon. And this is where he overreaches himself, and everything goes wrong.

All his tricks founder, and he brings his physic
After his patient's death: the King already
Hath married the fair lady.

(III, ii, 40-42)

Henry has already lost patience with the cardinals ('I abhor/ This dilatory sloth and tricks of Rome' (II, iv, 236-7) and called back his 'well-beloved servant, Cranmer' who has duly obliged in providing sound theological justification for the 'divorce' (this is the only oblique reference to the great break from Rome, and the Reformation). But, for Wolsey, it is not just a matter of a foiled plan. His letters to Rome 'miscarried,/ And came to th' eye o' th' King' (III, ii, 30-31); even worse, by a slip so disastrous that it begs to be called 'Freudian', Wolsey includes in some state papers he sends to the King a 'schedule' of all the 'treasure' he has raked and heaped together for himself. 'What piles of wealth hath he accumulated/To his own portion! ... it outspeaks/Possession of a subject' (III, ii, 107-8, 127-8) exclaims the by now angry King. He confronts Wolsey, and gives him the two incriminating papers, adding, grimly enough:

> Read o'er this;
> And after, this; and then to breakfast with
> What appetite you have.
>
> (II, ii, 201–3)

Wolsey knows that the game is up. With something of his old imperious pride, he tries to outface the nobles beginning to gloat over his impending disgrace and ruin. But, left alone, he confronts the truth, in the one powerful soliloquy of the play:

> Farewell! A long farewell to all my greatness!
> This is the state of man: today he puts forth
> The tender leaves of hopes; tomorrow blossoms,
> And bears his blushing honors thick upon him.
> The third day comes a frost, a killing frost,
> And, when he thinks, good easy man, full surely
> His greatness is aripening, nips his root,
> And then he falls, as I do.
>
> (III, ii, 351–8)

This occurs at about the middle of the play, and it may be taken as a central statement of its theme. But, almost immediately, the miraculous transformation or conversion begins:

> Vain pomp and glory of this world, I hate ye.
> I feel my heart new opened. O, how wretched
> Is that poor man that hangs on princes' favors!
> There is betwixt that smile we would aspire to,
> That sweet aspect of princes, and their ruin,
> More pangs and fears than wars or women have.
> And when he falls, he falls like Lucifer,
> Never to hope again.
>
> (III, ii, 365–72)

He tells his 'amazed' servant, Cromwell, that though he is 'fall'n indeed', he was 'never so truly happy', and goes on:

> I know myself now, and I feel within me
> A peace above all earthly dignities,
> A still and quiet conscience. The King hath cured me,
> I humbly thank his Grace; and from these shoulders,
> These ruined pillars, out of pity, taken
> A load would sink a navy – too much honor.

O, 'tis a burden, Cromwell, 'tis a burden
Too heavy for a man that hopes for heaven!

(III, ii, 378–85)

From his radically changed perspective, he gives Cromwell
advice which runs exactly counter to his own life:

Mark but my fall and that that ruined me.
Cromwell, I charge thee, fling away ambition.

(III, ii, 439–40)

Cromwell's last advice is 'Good sir, have patience'; to which
Wolsey replies, as do the other falling stars – 'So I have.' He
dies in 'peace', having 'found the blessedness of being little'
(IV, ii, 66). It is in keeping with the generally benign,
charitable, and forgiving atmosphere of the play that, when
Griffith brings the news of Wolsey's death to the dying
Katherine, while Katherine understandably recalls his 'evil
manners':

He would say untruths and be ever double
Both in his words and meaning. He was never,
But where he meant to ruin, pitiful.

(IV, ii, 38–40)

Griffith asks permission to 'speak his good', and proceeds to do
so. So the last we hear of Wolsey is an account of his abilities
and virtues: it is a moment of imaginative generosity to this
detested Catholic not to be found in the Protestant chronicles.

But what of King Henry himself – the Henry of the play? It
is hardly a very probing study, and, indeed, he speaks fewer
than 450 lines. There is certainly nothing here of the profli-
gate, the gourmand, the sensualist, the wife-killer of popular
image. Bullough finds him 'generous and trusting until he
realizes he has been deceived or that villainy is intended', and
says that 'From being *Defensor Fidei* he becomes the Defender,
not perhaps of Protestantism, but of the rights of the private
conscience; and the enemy of divisions in Church and State.'
The play, he says, 'sets forth a King who is no Prospero
controlling all men and events in justice . . . who can be misled
by self-seekers but who nevertheless does good in the main . . .
growing (unhistorically) in wisdom and benevolence'. R. A.

Foakes, the Arden editor, is even more positive. Of the three falls he asserts – 'in no case is there any recrimination, or blame attached to Henry; the law operates in its normal course ...' I find this an astonishing proposition. The play itself makes it clear that it is at least gullible of Henry to believe the deeply suspect surveyor rather than the every-where respected Buckingham; that he wants to find legalistic reasons for getting rid of old-wife Katherine because he has fallen for Anne; and that he is responsible for allowing Wolsey's unconscionable sway over himself and the land. (Foakes allows that the one ironic exchange in the play does rather glance at Henry's dubious motives in wanting to 'divorce' Katherine:

> *Chamberlain.* It seems the marriage with his brother's wife
> Has crept too near his conscience.
> *Suffolk [Aside].* No, his conscience
> Has crept too near another lady.

(II, ii, 16–18)

– yet he still finds Henry 'blameless'! We will come to Henry's 'creeping' conscience.) But Foakes then makes a larger claim (and he is not alone in this): considering Henry's 'growth in spiritual stature' he contends 'when he administers the law himself, justice as of heaven operates, and in this assumption of control Henry may be compared to Prospero, for he seems to stand above fate, and in all accidents of fortune which befall other characters is praised and blessed ... Like Prospero, he has a kind of vagueness, not a lack of solidity, but a lack of definition, as a representative of benevolent power acting upon others.' This is part of that attempt, which I mentioned, to recruit *Henry VIII* as another of Shakespeare's genuine 'last plays' – *The Tempest* continued in another key, as it were. As against all this rather hagiographic reading of Henry in the play, we may put this burst of uncompromising asperity from Hazlitt: 'The character of Henry VIII is drawn with great truth and spirit. It is like a very disagreeable portrait, sketched by the hand of a master. His gross appearance, his blustering demeanour, his vulgarity, his arrogance, his sensuality, his cruelty, his hypocrisy, his want of common decency and common humanity, are marked in strong lines.' You would hardly think that Foakes and Hazlitt had been to the same play, as it were! As it happens, Hazlitt's account is demonstrably more spirited than accurate; but, at that, hardly as misguided, I think, as the attempt to promote Henry to the status of a Prospero. Power, he has; but no magic.

The play does, admittedly, protect him to some extent; not only by stopping where it does, but in one or two little matters – for instance, by making Anne innocent, demure, totally unambitious, pitiful of Katherine, and clearly chaste; as opposed to the 'scapegrace' (Bullough) she apparently was, already Henry's mistress before the wedding, by which time she was pregnant. And in the matter of taxation. Queen Katherine warns him that the people are being taxed beyond endurance, by the orders of Wolsey, to the point that 'Tongues spit their duties out, and cold hearts freeze/Allegiance in them' (I, ii, 61–2). Henry (in the play) is shocked, and is prompted to one of those strong and vigorous Shakespearian images:

> Why, we take
> From every tree lop, bark, and part o' th' timber,
> And though we leave it with a root, *thus hacked*,
> *The air will drink the sap.*

(I, ii, 95–8, my italics)

He, benevolently, orders the tax to be rescinded, and, magnanimously, all those who refused to pay pardoned. But it was by historical Henry's order that the tax was levied in the first place! It is a small act of sanitization, but perhaps indicative of larger protective intentions.

But he clearly washes his hands of Buckingham:

> If he may
> Find mercy in the law, 'tis his; if none,
> Let him not seek't of us. By day and night!
> He's traitor to th' height.

(I, ii, 211–14)

His evidence for this is of the poorest, and this determined abjuration of 'mercy' does him no kingly credit. We also see him clearly making up to Anne – 'O beauty,/Till now I never

knew thee' (I, iv, 75–6), before we hear his accounts of his
protracted struggles with his conscience (over having married
his brother's widow – but, by any account, twenty years is a
strangely long time to wait for a call of conscience!) Thus,
when we hear him lament about Katherine:

> O, my lord,
> Would it not grieve an able man to leave
> So sweet a bedfellow? But, conscience, conscience!
> O, 'tis a tender place, and I must leave her.
>
> (II, ii, 140–43)

we are bound to be sceptical and hear the words as hollow.
Particularly as in the very next scene, when the so modest and
demure Anne protests to her 'Old Lady' companion that 'I
would not be a queen', the Old Lady (worldly, experienced)
simply retorts 'so would you,/For all this spice of your hypocrisy', and goes on to refer to '(Saving your mincing) the
capacity/Of your soft cheveril conscience' (II, iii, 25–6, 31–2).
There is more than a 'spice of hypocrisy' in more than one part
of this play, and Henry is capable of his own kind of 'mincing'.
'Cheveril' is kidskin, for high-quality gloves and such like, and
the 'cheveril' of *Henry*'s conscience is, as the play shows, of the
softest and most stretchable. By the end, he is indeed in
control, all oppositions and problems in one way or another
dispersed; with Cranmer and Sir Thomas More safely
installed, Cromwell about to begin his reliable work – and
baby Elizabeth to crown it all. Still, the Court of King Henry
VIII is a long way from Prospero's Isle.

The play ends with the dazzling Elizabethan sunrise. But
that sun had set ten years before this play was put on. So what
was it? An exercise in patriotic nostalgia? Larger claims have
been made for it. '*Henry VIII* is a resplendent Finale, ritualisti-
cally expanding through conflict into grace and happy augury
... there is suffering in the play, but the movement on the
whole is towards the triumph of goodness, not through physical battle, as in *Richard II* and *Henry V*, but by dignified
acceptance, by the strength of its own nature' (Bullough).
Foakes sees the play as 'a whole of visionary power, culminating in a mood of joy and reconciliation, and a prospect of

lasting peace and well-being'. Wilson Knight (another Henry as Prospero man) makes the largest possible claims for the play. 'The play is rich with both a grand royalism and a thrilling but solemn Christianity; orthodox religious colouring being present and powerful throughout far in excess of any previous play.' He admires its 'blending of national and religious prophecy', saying 'it is as though time and eternity were seen converging as the play unfurls'. His final verdict is: 'If in *The Tempest* Shakespeare gives us a comprehensive and inclusive statement of his furthest spiritual adventures, in *Henry VIII* he has gone yet further, directly relating those adventures to the religion of his day and the nation of his birth.' I think all these men are describing, not without some material justification, the play they would like it to be. But, despite the themes of reconciliation, resignation, and even miraculous conversion which are undoubtedly there, this is *not*, finally, assimilable to Shakespeare's other 'last plays' (one small piece of overlooked evidence, which *would* work for such critics, is the curiously frequent use of 'strange' in the play – 'strange' is a very 'last play' word). For we must bear in mind the truth claims of the play. The Prologue claims that the audience 'may here find truth too'; and Sir Henry Wotton, who described the burning of the Globe theatre during one performance, tells us that the play was called *All is True* (possibly an alternative title). But, an audience of 1613, invited to watch the play as 'real' history and 'truth', would know very well that that truth included the following historical facts:

that Henry was bitterly disappointed that Elizabeth was not a male heir, and that, when Anne miscarried a deformed son, he was convinced God had damned his second marriage, so he destroyed Anne in a palace coup in 1536;

that Henry went on to have a series of other wives, some also violently removed;

that Henry had Sir Thomas More beheaded in 1535, and Thomas Cromwell beheaded in 1540;

that Archbishop Thomas Cranmer was burnt at the stake by Henry's daughter, Mary, in 1556.

You might keep all such matters out of the *play*, but there is no way you could keep them out of a 1613 audience's mind. It is hard to imagine that Shakespeare was unaware of the sheer irony of what was being depicted on stage. And, certainly, he does not give us a *drama* of the reign of Henry VIII, as he had done, one way or another, for his previous kingly subjects. There is simply no real drama *in* the play. So what is it? Festivity, celebration, nostalgia – a dream of history as it might-have-been, as it ought-to-be? Or is there a deep sadness and irony running inerasably through it all? I, myself, tend to register the sadness and irony; but there will always be individual variation (predisposition?), and presumably a Hazlitt and a Foakes would never agree. And why Shakespeare wrote it – to the extent that he did write it – is simply beyond the reach of informed conjecture.

King's College, Cambridge, 1994   Tony Tanner

TONY TANNER was Professor of English and American Literature in Cambridge University, and Fellow of King's College. His publications include *The Reign of Wonder*, *City of Words*, *Adultery and the Novel* and *Venice Desired*, as well as studies of Jane Austen, Henry James, Saul Bellow and Thomas Pynchon. He died in 1998.

SELECT BIBLIOGRAPHY

BIOGRAPHY
The standard biography is now Samuel Schoenbaum, *William Shakespeare: A Documentary Life*, Oxford University Press, Oxford, 1975. A shortened version of this excellent volume was published in 1977. For those interested in Shakespearian mythology, Schoenbaum has also produced *Shakespeare's Lives*, Clarendon Press, Oxford, 1970, a witty dissection of the myriad theories concerning the playwright's identity and the authorship of the plays. Rather in the same vein is Anthony Burgess, *Shakespeare*, Penguin, London, 1972, a lively introduction to the presumed facts of the poet's life, enhanced by novelistic licence.

BIBLIOGRAPHY
Among the vast quantity of Shakespeare criticism it is probably only useful to list texts which are both outstanding and easily available. This I do below. For further information the serious student may consult the bibliographies of works listed. There are also three major journals which record the flow of critical work: the *Shakespeare Quarterly*; and the *Shakespeare Survey* and *Shakespeare Studies* which are published annually.

CRITICISM
The two indispensable Shakespearian critics are Johnson and Coleridge. Their dispersed comments are collected in *Samuel Johnson on Shakespeare*, ed., H. R. Woodhuysen, Penguin, London, 1989, and S. T. Coleridge, *Shakespearian Criticism*, two vols., Everyman's Library, London, 1960.

THE HISTORY PLAYS: GENERAL

BROCKBANK, J. P., *On Shakespeare*, 1989.
BURDEN, DENNIS H., 'Shakespeare's History Plays: 1952–1983', *Shakespeare's Studies* (1985).
CAMPBELL, LILY B., *Shakespeare's Histories: Mirrors of Elizabethan Policy*, 1947.
DANBY, J. F., *Shakespeare's Doctrine of Nature*, 1961.
DOLLIMORE, JONATHAN, *Political Shakespeare*, 1985.
HAMILTON, A. C., *The Early Shakespeare*, 1967.
HOLDERNESS, GRAHAM, *Shakespeare Recycled*, 1992.
KANTOROWITZ, E. H., *The King's Two Bodies*, 1957.

HISTORIES

KELLY, H. A., *Divine Providence in the England of Shakespeare's Histories*, 1970.

KERNAN, ALVIN B., '*The Henriad*: Shakespeare's major history plays', in *Modern Shakespeare Criticism*, ed. Alvin Kernan, 1970.

KNIGHT, G. WILSON, *The Olive and the Sword*, 1944.

KNIGHTS, L. C., *Some Shakespearean Themes*, 1959.

ORNSTEIN, ROBERT, *A Kingdom for a Stage: the achievement of Shakespeare's history plays*, 1972.

PALMER, JOHN, *Political Characters of Shakespeare*, 1945.

PATER, WALTER, 'Shakespeare's English Kings' in *Appreciations*, 1889.

PIERCE, ROBERT B., *Shakespeare's History Plays: The Family and the State*, 1971.

PRIOR, MOODY E., *The Drama of Power*, 1973.

REESE, MAX MEREDITH, *The Cease of Majesty: A Study of Shakespeare's Plays*, 1961.

RIBNER, IRVING, *The English History Play in the Age of Shakespeare*, 1957.

ROSSITER, A. P., *Angel with Horns*, 1961.

SACCIO, PETER, *Shakespeare's English Kings: History, chronicle and drama*, 1977.

TENNENHOUSE, LEONARD, *Power on Display*, 1986.

TILLYARD, E. M. W., *The Elizabethan World Picture*, 1943.

TILLYARD, E. M. W., *Shakespeare's History Plays*, 1944.

WHIGHAM, FRANK, *Ambition and Privilege*, 1984.

On particular plays the following commentaries are all helpful:

RICHARD II

ALTICK, RICHARD D., Symphonic Imagery in *Richard II*', PMLA LXII, 1947.

DEAN, L. F., '*Richard II*: the State and the Image of the Theatre', PMLA LXVII, 1952.

GURR, ANDREW, (ed.), *Richard II*, 1984.

HUMPHREYS, ARTHUR R., *Shakespeare: King Richard II*, 1967.

MCMILLIN, SCOTT, 'Shakespeare's *Richard II*: Eyes of Sorrow, Eyes of Desire', Shakespeare Quarterly 35, 1984.

NEWLIN, JEANNE T., (ed.), *Richard II: Critical Essays*, 1985.

POTTER, LOIS, 'The Antic Disposition of Richard II', Shakespeare Survey 27, 1974.

REES, MAX M., *The Cease of Majesty*, 1961.

RIBNER, IRVING, 'The Political Problem in Shakespeare's Lancastrian Tetralogy', Studies in Philology, 1952.

Schoenbaum, S., '*Richard II* and the Realities of Power', Shakespeare Survey 28, 1975.

SELECT BIBLIOGRAPHY

TRAVERSI, DEREK, *Shakespeare from 'Richard II' to 'Henry V'*, 1957.

HENRY IV, PART ONE

DICKINSON, HUGH, 'The Reformation of Prince Hal', Shakespeare Quarterly 12, 1961.

DORAN, MADELEINE, 'Imagery in *Richard II* and in *Henry IV*', Modern Language Review 7, 1942.

EVANS, GARETH LLOYD, 'The Comical-tragical-historical Method – *Henry IV*', *Stratford-upon-Avon Studies 3*, 1961.

GOLDMAN, MICHAEL, *Shakespeare and the Energies of Drama*, 1972.

HAWKINS, SHERMAN H., '*Henry IV*: The Structural Problem Revisited', Shakespeare Quarterly 33, 1982.

JENKINS, HAROLD, *The Structural Problem in Shakespeare's Henry the Fourth*, 1956.

KAHN, COPPELIA, *Man's Estate: Masculine Identity in Shakespeare*, 1981.

KELLY, HENRY ANSGAR, *Divine Providence in the England of Shakespeare's Histories*, 1970.

KERNAN, ALVIN, '*The Henriad*: Shakespeare's Major History Plays', Yale Review 59, 1969.

MCLAVERTY, J., 'No Abuse: The Prince and Falstaff in the Tavern Scenes of *Henry IV*', Shakespeare Survey 34, 1982.

PALMER, D. J., 'Casting Off the Old Man: History and St Paul in *Henry IV*', Critical Quarterly 12, 1970.

SELTZER, DANIEL, 'Prince Hal and Tragic Style', Shakespeare Survey 30, 1977.

SPRAGUE, ARTHUR COLBY, 'Gadshill Revisited', Shakespeare Quarterly 4, 1953.

UNGER, LEONARD, *The Man in the Name*, 1956.

WILSON, JOHN DOVER, *The Fortunes of Falstaff*, 1943.

WINNY, JAMES, *The Player King: A Theme of Shakespeare's Histories*, 1968.

HENRY IV, PART TWO

BARBER, C. L., 'Rule and Misrule in Henry IV', in *Shakespeare's Festive Comedy*, 1959.

BERRY, EDWARD I., 'The Rejection Scene in *2 Henry IV*', Studies in English Literature 17, 1971.

BRADLEY, A. C., 'The Rejection of Falstaff', in *Oxford Lectures on Poetry*, 1909.

CALDERWOOD, JAMES L., *Metadrama in Shakespeare's Henriad: Richard II to Henry V*, 1979.

HISTORIES

DAVID, R. W., 'Shakespeare's Historical Plays – Epic or Drama?', Shakespeare Survey 6, 1953.

KNIGHTS, L. C., 'Time's Subjects: The Sonnets and *King Henry IV, Part II*', in *Some Shakespearean Themes*, 1959.

LAWLOR, JOHN, *Tragic Sense in Shakespeare*, 1960.

LEECH, CLIFFORD, 'The Unity of *2 Henry IV*', Shakespeare Survey 6, 1953.

PRIOR, MOODY, 'Comic Theory and the Rejection of Falstaff', Shakespeare Studies 9, 1979.

SPENCER, B. T., '*2 Henry IV* and the Theme of Time', University of Toronto Quarterly, July 1944.

SPIVACK, BERNARD, 'Falstaff and the Psychomachia', Shakespeare Quarterly 8, 1957.

HENRY V

BARTON, ANNE, 'The King Disguised: Shakespeare's *Henry V* and the Comical History' in *The Triple Bond* (ed. Joseph Price), 1975.

COURSEN, H. R., *The Leasing Out of England: Shakespeare's Second Henriad*', 1982.

DANSON, LAWRENCE, '*Henry V*: King, Chorus, and Critics', Shakespeare Quarterly 34, 1983.

GRANVILLE-BARKER, HARLEY, 'From *Henry V* to *Hamlet*', in *Studies in Shakespeare*, 1964.

HOLDERNESS, GRAHAM, *Shakespeare's History*, 1985.

JORGENSEN, PAUL A., *Shakespeare's Military World*, 1956.

MATTHEWS, HONOR, *Character and Symbol in Shakespeare's Plays*, 1962.

PALMER, JOHN, *Political Characters* of Shakespeare, 1945.

HENRY VIII

ALEXANDER, PETER, 'Conjectural History, or Shakespeare's *Henry VIII*', Essays and Studies XVI, 1930.

FELPERIN, HOWARD, 'Shakespeare's *Henry VIII*: History as Myth', Studies in English Literature: 1500–1900, 6, 1966.

KERMODE, FRANK, 'What is Shakespeare's *Henry VIII* About?', Durham University Journal 9, 1947–8.

KNIGHT, G. WILSON, *The Crown of Life*, 1947.

LEECH, CLIFFORD, 'The Structure of the Last Plays', Shakespeare Survey 11, 1958.

LEGGATT, ALEXANDER, '*Henry VIII* and the Ideal England', Shakespeare Survey 38, 1985.

SELECT BIBLIOGRAPHY

MINCOFF, MARCO, '*Henry VIII* and Fletcher', Shakespeare Quarterly 12, 1961.

NOLING, KIM H., 'Grubbing up the Stock: Dramatizing Queens in *Henry VIII*', Shakespeare Quarterly 39, 1988.

SAHEL, PIERRE, 'The Strangeness of a Dramatic Style: Rumour in *Henry VIII*', Shakespeare Survey, 1985.

CHRONOLOGY

DATE	AUTHOR'S LIFE	LITERARY CONTEXT
1564	Born in Stratford, Warwickshire, the eldest surviving son of John Shakespeare, glover and occasional dealer in wool, and Mary Arden, daughter of a prosperous farmer.	Birth of Christopher Marlowe.
1565	John Shakespeare elected Alderman of Stratford.	Clinthio: *Hecatommithi*. Edwards: *Damon and Pythias*.
1566	Birth of Shakespeare's brother Gilbert.	Gascoigne: *Supposes*.
1567		Udall: *Roister Doister*. Golding: *The Stories of Venus and Adonis and of Hermaphroditus and Salamcis*.
1568	His father is elected bailiff.	Gascoigne: *Jocasta*. Wilmot: *Tancred and Gismunda*. Second Edition of Vasari's *Lives of the Artists*.
1569	Probably starts attending the petty school attached to the King's New School in Stratford. Birth of his sister Joan.	
1570	His father involved in money-lending.	
1571	John Shakespeare is elected Chief Alderman and deputy to the new bailiff.	
1572		Whitgift's *Answer* to the 'Admonition' receives Cartwright's *Reply*, beginning the first literary debate between Anglicans and Puritans.
1573		Tasso: *Aminta*.
1574	Probably enters the Upper School (where studies include rhetoric, logic, the Latin poets, and a little Greek). Birth of his brother Richard.	

Death of Michelangelo. Birth of Galileo.

Rebellion against Spain in the Netherlands. Birth of the actor Edward Alleyn.
Birth of the actor Richard Burbage.

Mary Stuart flees to England from Scotland.

Northern Rebellion.

Excommunication of Elizabeth. *Baif's* Academy founded in Paris to promote poetry, music and dance.
Ridolfi Plot. Puritan 'Admonition' to Parliament.

Dutch rebels conquer Holland and Zeeland. Massacre of St Bartholomew's Day in Paris.

Accession of Henry III and new outbreak of civil war in France. First Catholic missionaries arrive in England from Douai. Earl of Leicester's Men obtain licence to perform within the City of London.

DATE	AUTHOR'S LIFE	LITERARY CONTEXT
1575		*Gammer Gurton's Needle* is printed.
1576		Castiglione's *The Book of the Courtier* banned by the Spanish Inquisition. George Gascoigne: *The Steel Glass*.
1577		John Northbrooke's attack in *Treatise wherein Dicing, Dancing, Vain Plays etc are reproved*.
1578	Shakespeare family fortunes are in decline, and John is having to sell off property to pay off his increasing debts.	Sidney writes *The Lady of May* and begins the 'Old' *Arcadia*. George Whetstone: *Promos and Cassandra*. John Lyly: *Euphues, the Anatomy of Wit*. Pierre de Ronsard, leader of the Pléiade, publishes his *Sonnets pour Hélène*. He is said to have exercised a considerable influence on the English sonnet-writers of the sixteenth century.
1579		Spenser: *The Shepherd's Calendar*. North: translation of Plutarch. Gossen: *The School of Abuse, and Pleasant Invective against Poets, Pipers, Players etc*.
1580	Birth of Shakespeare's brother Edmund.	Sidney: *Apologie for Poetrie*. Lodge: *Defense of Plays*.
1581		John Newton's translation of Seneca's *Ten Tragedies*. Barnaby Rich: *Apolonius and Silla*.
1582	Shakespeare marries Anne Hathaway, a local farmer's daughter, 7 or 8 years his senior, who is already pregnant with their first child.	Tasso: *Gerusalemme Liberata*. Watson: *Hekatompathia* (First sonnet sequence published in England). Whetstone: *Heptameron of Civil Discourses*. Sidney begins *Astrophel and Stella* and the 'New' *Arcadia*. Lope de Vega writing for the Corrals in Madrid.

HISTORICAL EVENTS

Kenilworth Revels.

Restricted by the City of London's order that no plays be performed within the City boundaries, James Burbage of The Earl of Leicester's Men builds The Theatre only just outside the boundaries in Shoreditch. The Blackfriars Theatre is built. End of civil war in France. Observatory of Uraniborg built for the Danish astronomer, Tycho Brahe. Death of Titian.
Drake's circumnavigation of the world. The Curtain Theatre built. Birth of Rubens.

First visit to England of the duc d'Alençon as a suitor to Elizabeth, provoking much opposition to a French match. The Corral de la Cruz built in Madrid.

Spanish conquest of Portugal. Jesuit mission arrives in England from Rome led by Edmund Campion and Parsons.
Stricter enforcement of treason laws and increased penalties on recusants. Campion captured and executed. Northern provinces of the Netherlands renounce their allegiance to Phillip II, and invite the duc d'Alençon to be their sovereign.
Sir Walter Ralegh established in the Queen's favour. The Corral del Principe built in Madrid.

DATE	AUTHOR'S LIFE	LITERARY CONTEXT
1583	Birth of their daughter Susanna.	
1583–4	The players' companies of the Earls of Essex, Oxford and Leicester perform in Stratford.	Giordarno Bruno visits England.
1584		Bruno publishes *La cena de le Ceneri* and *Spaccio della bestia trionfante*. Reginald Scott: *The Discovery of Witchcraft*.
1585	Birth of Shakespeare's twins Hamnet and Judith. The following years until 1592 are the 'Lost Years' for which no documentary records of his life survive, only legends such as the one of deer-stealing and flight from prosecution, and conjectures such as ones that he became a schoolmaster, travelled in Europe, or went to London to be an actor as early as the mid 1580s.	Death of Pierre de Ronsard. Bruno: *De gli eroici furori*, dedicated to Sidney.
1586		Timothy Bright: *A Treatise of Melancholy*.
1586–7	Five players' companies visit Stratford, including the Queen's, Essex's, Leicester's and Stafford's.	
1587		Holinshed: *Chronicles of England, Scotland and Ireland*. Marlowe: First part of *Tamburlaine the Great* acted. New edition of *The Mirror for Magistrates*.
1588		Marlowe: Second part of *Tamburlaine*. Thomas Kyd: *The Spanish Tragedy*. Lope de Vega, serving with the Armada, writes some of *The Beauty of Angelica*.

CHRONOLOGY

HISTORIES

DATE	AUTHOR'S LIFE	LITERARY CONTEXT
1589	The earliest likely date at which Shakespeare began composition of his first plays (1 *Henry VI*, *The Taming of the Shrew*) when he would have been working as an actor at The Theatre, with Burbage's company.	Marlowe: *The Jew of Malta*. Thomas Nashe: *The Anatomy of Absurdity*. Richard Hakluyt: *Principal Navigations, Voyages and Discoveries of the English nation*.
1590	2 *Henry VI*, 3 *Henry VI*.	Spenser: first 3 books of *The Faerie Queen*. Publication of Sidney's 'New' *Arcadia*. Nashe: *An Almond for a Parrot*, one of the Marprelate Tracts. Greene: *Menaphon*. Guarina: *The Faithful Shepherd*.
1590–91	*King John* written.	
1590–92	Performances of *Henry VI*, parts 2 and 3, *Titus* and *The Shrew* by the Earl of Pembroke's Men.	
1591	*Richard III* and *The Comedy of Errors* written.	Spenser's *Complaints* which includes his translation of fifteen of Joachim du Bellay's sonnets – du Bellay was a member of the Pléiade and responsible for its manifesto. Sir John Harington's translation of *Orlando Furioso*. Publication of Sidney's *Astrophel and Stella*. Samuel Daniel: *Delia*.
1592	First recorded reference to Shakespeare as an actor and playwright in Greene's attack in *The Groatsworth of Wit* describing him as 'an upstart crow'.	Marlowe's *Edward II* and *Doctor Faustus* performed. *Arden of Feversham* printed. Nashe: *Strange News*.
1592–4	*Titus Andronicus* written.	
1593	Publication of *Venus and Adonis*, dedicated to the Earl of Southampton. The *Sonnets* probably begun.	Marlowe: *Massacre of Paris*. *The Phoenix Nest*, miscellany of poems including ones by Ralegh, Lodge and Breton. Barnabe Barnes: *Parthenophil and Parthenope*. George Peele: *The Honour of the Garter*. Lodge: *Phillis*. Nashe: *Christ's Tears over Jerusalem*.

CHRONOLOGY

HISTORIES

HISTORICAL EVENTS

Henry of Navarre accepted as King in Paris. Rebellion in Ireland. The London theatres re-open. The Swan Theatre is built. Ralegh accused of blasphemy.

France declares war on Spain. Failure of the Indies voyage and death of Hawkins. Ralegh's expedition to Guiana.

England joins France in the war against Spain. Death of Drake. Raid on Cadiz led by Essex. In long-standing power struggle with Essex, Robert Cecil is appointed Secretary of State.

Islands Voyage led by Essex and Ralegh. The government suppresses the *Isle of Dogs* at the Swan and closes the theatres. Despite the continued hostility of the City of London, they soon re-open. James Burbage builds the second Blackfriars Theatre. Death of James Burbage.

Peace between France and Spain. Death of Philip II. Tyrone defeats the English at Armagh. Essex appointed Lord Deputy of Ireland.

DATE	AUTHOR'S LIFE	LITERARY CONTEXT
1598 *cont.*		New edition of Lodge's *Rosalynde*. Lope de Vega: *La Arcadia*. James VI of Scotland: *The True Law of Free Monarchies*.
1598–9	*As You Like It*.	
1598–1600	*Much Ado About Nothing*.	
1599	*Henry V*, *Julius Caesar*. Shakespeare one of the shareholders in the Globe Theatre. He moves lodgings to Bankside. Publication of *The Passionate Pilgrim*, a miscellany of 20 poems, at least 5 by Shakespeare.	Jonson: *Every Man out of his Humour*. Dekker: *The Shoemaker's Holiday*. Sir John Hayward: *The First Part of the Life and Reign of King Henry IV*. Greene's translation of *Orlando Furioso*.
1600		'England's Helicon'.
1600–1	*Hamlet* (performed with Burbage as the Prince and Shakespeare as the Ghost).	
1601	*The Phoenix and the Turtle*. The Lord Chamberlain's Men paid by one of Essex's followers to perform *Richard II* on the day before the rebellion. Death of John Shakespeare.	
1601–2	*Troilus and Cressida*.	
1602	Shakespeare buys more property in Stratford.	
1602–4	*Alls Well That Ends Well*.	
1603	Shakespeare's company now under the patronage of King James. Shakespeare is one of the principal tragedians in Jonson's *Sejanus*.	Montaigne's *Essays* translated into English. Thomas Heywood: *A Woman Killed with Kindness*.
1604	Shakespeare known to be lodging in Silver Street with a Huguenot family called Mountjoy. *Othello*; first performance of *Measure for Measure*.	Chapman: *Bussy d'Ambois*. Marston: *The Malcontent*.
1604–5	Ten of his plays performed at court by the King's Men.	

CHRONOLOGY

The Burbage brothers, Richard and Cuthbert, pull down The Theatre and, with its timbers, build the Globe on Bankside. Essex's campaign fails in Ireland, and after returning without permission to court he is arrested. The government suppresses satirical writings, and burns pamphlets by Nashe and Harvey.

Essex released but still in disgrace. The Fortune Theatre built by Alleyn and Henslowe. Bruno executed for heresy by the Inquisition in Rome.

Essex's Rebellion. Essex and Southampton arrested, and the former executed. Spanish invasion of Ireland. Monopolies debates in Parliament.

Spanish troops defeated in Ireland.

Death of Elizabeth, and accession of James I. Ralegh imprisoned in the Tower. Plague in London. Sir Thomas Bodley re-founds the library of Oxford University.

Peace with Spain. Hampton Court Conference.

DATE	AUTHOR'S LIFE	LITERARY CONTEXT
1605	First performance of *King Lear* at the Globe, with Burbage as the King, and Robert Armin as the Fool. Shakespeare makes further investments in Stratford, buying a half interest in a lease of tithes.	Cervantes: *Don Quixote* (part one). Bacon: *The Proficience and Advancement of Learning*. Jonson and Inigo Jones: *The Masque of Blackness*. Jonson and co-authors imprisoned for libellous references to the court in *Eastward Ho*.
1605–6		Jonson: *Volpone*.
1606	First performance of *Macbeth*.	John Ford's masque *Honour Triumphant*.
1607	*Antony and Cleopatra*. Susanna marries John Hall, a physician. Death of Shakespeare's brother Edmund, an actor.	Tourneur's *The Revenger's Tragedy* printed. Barnes: *The Devil's Charter*.
1607–8	*Timon of Athens*, *Coriolanus*, *Pericles*.	
1608	Shakespeare one of the shareholders in the Blackfriars Theatre. Death of his mother.	Lope de Vega: *Peribanez*. Beaumont and Fletcher: *Philaster*. Jonson and Jones: *The Masque of Beauty*. Donne writes *La Corona*. Twelve books of Homer's *Iliad* (Chapman's translation).
1609	Publication, probably unauthorized, of the quarto edition of the *Sonnets* and *A Lover's Complaint*.	Jonson and Jones: *The Masque of Queens*. Donne's 'The Expiration' printed; 'Liturgie' and 'On the Annunciation' written. Bacon: *De Sapientia Veterum*. Lope de Vega: *New Art of Writing Plays for the Theatre*.
1609–10	*Cymbeline*.	
1610		Donne: *Pseudo-Martyr* printed and *The First Anniversarie* written. Jonson: *The Alchemist*. Beaumont and Fletcher: *The Maid's Tragedy*.
1610–11	*The Winter's Tale*.	
1611	*The Tempest* performed in the Banqueting House, Whitehall. Simon Forman records seeing performances of *Macbeth*, *The Winter's Tale* and *Cymbeline*.	Beaumont and Fletcher: *A King and No King*, *The Knight of the Burning Pestle*. Tourneur: *The Atheist's Tragedy*.

CHRONOLOGY

DATE	AUTHOR'S LIFE	LITERARY CONTEXT
1611 *cont.*		Jonson and Jones: *Masque of Oberon*. Authorized Version of the Bible. Sir John Davies: *The Scourge of Folly*. Donne writes the *The Second Anniversarie* and a 'A Valediction: forbidding mourning'.
1612	Shakespeare appears as a witness in a Court of Requests case involving a dispute over a dowry owed by his former landlord, Mountjoy, to his son-in-law, Belott. Death of his brother Gilbert.	Webster: *The White Devil* printed. Tourneur: *The Nobleman*. Lope de Vega: *Fuente Ovejuna*.
1613	At a performance of his last play, *Henry VIII*, the Globe Theatre catches fire and is destroyed. As part of the court celebrations for the marriage of Princess Elizabeth, The King's Men perform 14 plays, including *Much Ado*, *Othello*, *The Winter's Tale* and *The Tempest*. Death of his brother Richard.	Sir Thomas Overbury: *The Wife*. Donne: 'Good Friday' and 'Epithalamion' on Princess Elizabeth's marriage. Cervantes: *Novelas ejemplares* – a collection of short stories.
1614	In Stratford, Shakespeare protects his property interests during a controversy over a threat to enclose the common fields.	Jonson: *Bartholomew Fair*. Webster: *The Duchess of Malfi*. Ralegh: *The History of the World*.
1615	The Warwick Assizes issue an order to prevent enclosures, which ends the dispute in Stratford.	Cervantes publishes 8 plays and *Don Quixote* (part two).
1616	Marriage of his daughter Judith to Thomas Quincy, a vintner, who a month later is tried for fornication with another woman whom he had made pregnant. Death of Shakespeare (23 April).	Jonson: *The Devil is an Ass*. Jonson publishes his *Works*.
1623	The players Heminge and Condell publish the plays of the First Folio.	

CHRONOLOGY

Death of Henry, Prince of Wales.

Marriage of Princess Elizabeth to Frederick, Elector Palatine. Bacon appointed Attorney-General.

The second Globe and the Hope Theatre built.

Inquiry into the murder of Sir Thomas Overbury in the Tower implicates the wife of the King's favourite, Somerset.

Ralegh released from the Tower to lead an expedition to Guiana; on his return he is executed.

WILLIAM SHAKESPEARE

THE TRAGEDY OF KING RICHARD THE SECOND

Edited by Kenneth Muir

KING RICHARD THE SECOND
EDMUND, Duke of York
JOHN OF GAUNT, Duke of Lancaster } his uncles
HENRY BOLINGBROKE, Gaunt's son
THE DUKE OF AUMERLE, York's son
THOMAS MOWBRAY, Duke of Norfolk
THE EARL OF SALISBURY
THE EARL OF BERKELEY
SIR JOHN BUSHY
SIR WILLIAM BAGOT } Richard's favorites
SIR HENRY GREEN
THE EARL OF NORTHUMBERLAND
HARRY PERCY, his son
LORD ROSS
LORD WILLOUGHBY
THE BISHOP OF CARLISLE
SIR STEPHEN SCROOP
LORD FITZWATER
THE DUKE OF SURREY
THE ABBOT OF WESTMINSTER
SIR PIERCE OF EXTON
LORD MARSHAL
WELSH CAPTAIN
QUEEN ISABEL, Richard's second wife
DUCHESS OF GLOUCESTER, Gaunt's sister-in-law
DUCHESS OF YORK
LADIES, attending on the Queen; GARDENERS; A KEEPER; A
GROOM; LORDS, HERALDS, OFFICERS, SOLDIERS, ATTENDANTS,
SERVANTS.

Scene: England and Wales]

THE TRAGEDY OF
KING RICHARD
THE SECOND

[ACT I

Scene I. *Windsor Castle.*]

*Enter King Richard, John of Gaunt, with other Nobles
and Attendants.*

RICHARD Old John of Gaunt, time-honored Lancaster,
Hast thou according to thy oath and band
Brought hither Henry Hereford, thy bold son,
Here to make good the boist'rous late appeal,   5
Which then our leisure would not let us hear,
Against the Duke of Norfolk, Thomas Mowbray?

GAUNT I have, my liege.

RICHARD Tell me, moreover, hast thou sounded
him,
If he appeal the Duke on ancient malice,
Or worthily, as a good subject should,   10
On some known ground of treachery in him?

GAUNT As near as I could sift him on that
argument,
On some apparent danger seen in him
Aimed at your Highness, no inveterate malice.

Text references are printed in **bold** type; the annotation follows in roman type.
I.i.2 **band** bond   3 **Hereford** (pronounced "Herford")   4 **appeal** accusation of
treason   5 **our** (the royal plural)   9 **appeal** accuse   10 **worthily** according to
desert   12 **sift** examine thoroughly   12 **argument** subject   13 **apparent**
obvious

3

15 RICHARD Then call them to our presence: face to face,
        And frowning brow to brow, ourselves will hear
        The accuser and the accusèd freely speak.
        High-stomached are they both, and full of ire,
        In rage, deaf as the sea, hasty as fire.

Enter Bolingbroke and Mowbray.

20 BOLINGBROKE Many years of happy days befall
        My gracious sovereign, my most loving liege!

MOWBRAY Each day still better other's happiness,
        Until the heavens envying earth's good hap,
        Add an immortal title to your crown!

25 RICHARD We thank you both; yet one but flatters us,
        As well appeareth by the cause you come,
        Namely to appeal each other of high treason.
        Cousin of Hereford, what dost thou object
        Against the Duke of Norfolk, Thomas Mowbray?

BOLINGBROKE First—heaven be the record to my
30   speech!—
        In the devotion of a subject's love,
        Tend'ring the precious safety of my prince,
        And free from other misbegotten hate,
        Come I appellant to this princely presence.
35   Now, Thomas Mowbray, do I turn to thee,
        And mark my greeting well: for what I speak,
        My body shall make good upon this earth,
        Or my divine soul answer it in heaven.
        Thou art a traitor and a miscreant,
40   Too good to be so, and too bad to live;
        Since the more fair and crystal is the sky,
        The uglier seem the clouds that in it fly.
        Once more, the more to aggravate the note,
        With a foul traitor's name stuff I thy throat,
45   And wish—so please my sovereign—ere I move,

18 **High-stomached** high-spirited 20 **Bolingbroke** (pronounced and spelled
"Bullingbrooke" in Shakespeare's time) 32 **Tend'ring** cherishing 34 **appellant** accuser 36 **greeting** address 39 **miscreant** unbeliever, villain 43 **note**
reproach

4

What my tongue speaks my right-drawn sword
    may prove.

MOWBRAY Let not my cold words here accuse my
    zeal:
'Tis not the trial of a woman's war,
The bitter clamor of two eager tongues,
Can arbitrate this cause betwixt us twain;   50
The blood is hot that must be cooled for this.
Yet can I not of such tame patience boast,
As to be hushed, and naught at all to say.
First, the fair reverence of your Highness
    curbs me
From giving reins and spurs to my free speech,   55
Which else would post until it had returned
These terms of treason doubled down his throat.
Setting aside his high blood's royalty,
And let him be no kinsman to my liege,
I do defy him, and I spit at him,   60
Call him a slanderous coward and a villain;
Which to maintain, I would allow him odds,
And meet him were I tied to run afoot
Even to the frozen ridges of the Alps,
Or any other ground inhabitable,   65
Where ever Englishman durst set his foot.
Meantime, let this defend my loyalty:
By all my hopes most falsely doth he lie.

BOLINGBROKE Pale trembling coward, there I throw
    my gage,
Disclaiming here the kindred of the King,   70
And lay aside my high blood's royalty,
Which fear, not reverence, makes thee to except.
If guilty dread have left thee so much strength
As to take up mine honor's pawn, then stoop.

---

46 **right-drawn** drawn to defend the right 47 **accuse my zeal** make me seem
unzealous 49 **eager** sharp 54 **fair reverence** of respect due to 56 **post**
speed 59 **let him be** suppose him to be 63 **tied** obliged 65 **inhabitable**
uninhabitable 67 **this** (his sword) 68 **hopes** i.e., of heaven 70 **Disclaiming**
... **King** (referring to Mowbray's words, lines 58–59) 72 **except** use as excuse
74 **pawn** pledge (his glove or hood, which he throws down)

75 By that, and all the rites of knighthood else,
    Will I make good against thee, arm to arm,
    What I have spoke, or thou canst worse devise.

    MOWBRAY I take it up; and by that sword I swear,
    Which gently laid my knighthood on my shoulder,
80 I'll answer thee in any fair degree
    Or chivalrous design of knightly trial;
    And when I mount, alive may I not light,
    If I be traitor or unjustly fight.

    RICHARD What doth our cousin lay to Mowbray's
        charge?
85 It must be great that can inherit us
    So much as of a thought of ill in him.

    BOLINGBROKE Look what I speak, my life shall prove
        it true:
    That Mowbray hath received eight thousand nobles
    In name of lendings for your Highness' soldiers,
90 The which he hath detained for lewd employments,
    Like a false traitor and injurious villain.
    Besides, I say, and will in battle prove,
    Or here, or elsewhere to the furthest verge
    That ever was surveyed by English eye,
95 That all the treasons for these eighteen years
    Complotted and contrivèd in this land
    Fetch from false Mowbray, their first head and
        spring.
    Further, I say and further will maintain
    Upon his bad life to make all this good,
100 That he did plot the Duke of Gloucester's death,
    Suggest his soon-believing adversaries,
    And, consequently, like a traitor coward,
    Sluiced out his innocent soul through streams of
        blood;
    Which blood, like sacrificing Abel's, cries

80 **degree** manner   82 **light** dismount   85 **inherit us** make us have   88 **nobles** gold coins   89 **lendings** money on trust   90 **lewd** base   93 **Or** either   97 **Fetch** derive   100 **Gloucester** Thomas of Woodstock, who had been murdered at Richard's orders   101 **Suggest** incite   102 **consequently** afterward

6

Even from the tongueless caverns of the earth   105
To me for justice and rough chastisement:
And, by the glorious worth of my descent,
This arm shall do it, or this life be spent.

RICHARD How high a pitch his resolution soars!
Thomas of Norfolk, what say'st thou to this?   110

MOWBRAY O! let my sovereign turn away his face,
And bid his ears a little while be deaf,
Till I have told this slander of his blood
How God and good men hate so foul a liar.

RICHARD Mowbray, impartial are our eyes and ears.   115
Were he my brother, nay, my kingdom's heir,
As he is but my father's brother's son,
Now by my scepter's awe I make a vow,
Such neighbor nearness to our sacred blood
Should nothing privilege him, nor partialize   120
The unstooping firmness of my upright soul.
He is our subject, Mowbray, so art thou:
Free speech and fearless I to thee allow.

MOWBRAY Then, Bolingbroke, as low as to thy heart,
Through the false passage of thy throat, thou
    liest.   125
Three parts of that receipt I had for Calais
Disbursed I duly to his Highness' soldiers;
The other part reserved I by consent,
For that my sovereign liege was in my debt
Upon remainder of a dear account,   130
Since last I went to France to fetch his Queen.
Now swallow down that lie. For Gloucester's death,
I slew him not; but, to my own disgrace,
Neglected my sworn duty in that case.
For you, my noble Lord of Lancaster,   135
The honorable father to my foe,
Once did I lay an ambush for your life,

108 or before 109 pitch peak of a falcon's flight (the King is uneasy that his own guilt will come to light) 120 partialize make partial 126 that receipt I had what I received 130 dear account private or expensive debt 134 duty (either to kill Gloucester, or to reveal the murder)

A trespass that doth vex my grievèd soul;
But, ere I last received the sacrament,
140 I did confess it, and exactly begged
Your grace's pardon, and I hope I had it.
This is my fault: as for the rest appealed,
It issues from the rancor of a villain,
A recreant and most degenerate traitor;
145 Which in myself I boldly will defend,
And interchangeably hurl down my gage
Upon this overweening traitor's foot,
To prove myself a loyal gentleman
Even in the best blood chambered in his bosom.
150 In haste whereof, most heartily I pray
Your Highness to assign our trial day.

RICHARD Wrath-kindled gentlemen, be ruled by me.
Let's purge this choler without letting blood:
This we prescribe, though no physician;
155 Deep malice makes too deep incision;
Forget, forgive, conclude, and be agreed;
Our doctors say this is no month to bleed.
Good uncle, let this end where it begun:
We'll calm the Duke of Norfolk, you your son.

160 GAUNT To be a make-peace shall become my age:
Throw down, my son, the Duke of Norfolk's gage.

RICHARD And Norfolk, throw down his.

GAUNT   When, Harry, when?
Obedience bids I should not bid again.

RICHARD Norfolk, throw down; we bid—there is no
boot.

MOWBRAY Myself I throw, dread sovereign, at thy
165   foot.
My life thou shalt command, but not my shame:
The one my duty owes; but my fair name

---

144 **recreant** renegade   146 **interchangeably** in exchange   153 **choler** anger
153 **letting blood** (pun on bleeding medicinally and bloodshed)   162 **When**
(exclamation of impatience)   164 **boot** remedy

Despite of death that lives upon my grave,
To dark dishonor's use thou shalt not have.
I am disgraced, impeached, and baffled here,   170
Pierced to the soul with slander's venomed spear,
The which no balm can cure but his heart-blood
Which breathed this poison.

RICHARD   Rage must be withstood.
Give me his gage; lions make leopards tame.

MOWBRAY Yea, but not change his spots. Take but
    my shame,   175
And I resign my gage. My dear dear lord,
The purest treasure mortal times afford
Is spotless reputation—that away,
Men are but gilded loam, or painted clay.
A jewel in a ten-times-barred-up chest   180
Is a bold spirit in a loyal breast;
Mine honor is my life, both grow in one;
Take honor from me, and my life is done;
Then, dear my liege, mine honor let me try;
In that I live, and for that will I die.   185

RICHARD Cousin, throw up your gage; do you begin.

BOLINGBROKE O, God defend my soul from such deep
    sin!
Shall I seem crestfallen in my father's sight?
Or with pale beggar-fear impeach my height
Before this out-dared dastard? Ere my tongue   190
Shall wound my honor with such feeble wrong,
Or sound so base a parle, my teeth shall tear
The slavish motive of recanting fear,
And spit it bleeding in his high disgrace,

---

170 **impeached** accused 170 **baffled** treated with infamy 174 **lions make
leopards tame** (alluding to the rampant lion in the King's royal arms and the
standing beast in Mowbray's) 175 **spots** (alluding to the proverb and punning
on spots, meaning stains) 186 **throw up** (perhaps to the upper stage on which
Richard sits) 189 **beggar-fear** fear appropriate to a beggar 189 **height** rank
191 **feeble wrong** a wrong so grave that the man who submits to it exhibits
himself as feeble 192 **parle** parley, truce 193 **motive** moving organ, i.e.,
tongue

195   Where shame doth harbor, even in Mowbray's face.
                                        [*Exit Gaunt.*]

     RICHARD We were not born to sue, but to command:
             Which since we cannot do to make you friends,
             Be ready, as your lives shall answer it,
             At Coventry upon Saint Lambert's day.
200   There shall your swords and lances arbitrate
             The swelling difference of your settled hate:
             Since we cannot atone you, we shall see
             Justice design the victor's chivalry.
             Lord Marshal, command our officers-at-arms
205   Be ready to direct these home alarms.
                                Exit [*Richard with others*].

[Scene II. *London. Gaunt's house.*]

*Enter John of Gaunt with the Duchess
of Gloucester.*

     GAUNT Alas, the part I had in Woodstock's blood
            Doth more solicit me than your exclaims
            To stir against the butchers of his life;
            But since correction lieth in those hands
5   Which made the fault that we cannot correct,
            Put we our quarrel to the will of heaven,
            Who, when they see the hours ripe on earth,
            Will rain hot vengeance on offenders' heads.

     DUCHESS Finds brotherhood in thee no sharper spur?
10   Hath love in thy old blood no living fire?

---

195 s.d. **Exit Gaunt** (Gaunt begins Scene ii, and therefore according to stage
convention must leave the stage before the end of Scene i)   199 **Saint Lambert's
day** (Sept. 17)   202 **atone** reconcile   203 **design the victor's chivalry** indicate
whose prowess will win the victory (i.e., the victor will be vindicated)
I.ii.1 **Woodstock** Gloucester, Gaunt's brother   2 **exclaims** outcries   4 **those
hands** i.e., the King's   7 **they** God and his angels   7 **hours** (two syllables)

Edward's seven sons, whereof thyself art one,
Were as seven vials of his sacred blood,
Or seven fair branches springing from one root.
Some of those seven are dried by nature's course,
Some of those branches by the destinies cut: 15
But Thomas, my dear lord, my life, my Gloucester,
One vial full of Edward's sacred blood,
One flourishing branch of his most royal root,
Is cracked, and all the precious liquor spilt,
Is hacked down, and his summer leaves all faded   20
By Envy's hand and Murder's bloody ax.
Ah! Gaunt, his blood was thine; that bed,
   that womb,
That metal, that self mold that fashioned thee,
Made him a man: and though thou livest and
   breathest,
Yet art thou slain in him; thou dost consent   25
In some large measure to thy father's death,
In that thou seest thy wretched brother die,
Who was the model of thy father's life.
Call it not patience, Gaunt, it is despair:
In suff'ring thus thy brother to be slaught'red,   30
Thou showest the naked pathway to thy life,
Teaching stern Murder how to butcher thee.
That which in mean men we entitle patience
Is pale cold cowardice in noble breasts.
What shall I say? To safeguard thine own life,   35
The best way is to venge my Gloucester's death.

GAUNT God's is the quarrel; for God's substitute,
His deputy anointed in His sight,
Hath caused his death, the which if wrongfully,
Let heaven revenge, for I may never lift   40
An angry arm against His minister.

DUCHESS Where, then, alas, may I complain myself?

---

23 **metal** stuff 23 **self** same 28 **model** copy 30 **suff'ring** allowing
31 **naked pathway** open road (for his murderers) 38 **deputy** (the idea that the
King, however unworthy, is God's deputy is stressed throughout the play)
42 **Where ... myself** to whom shall I complain

GAUNT To God, the widow's champion and defense.

DUCHESS Why, then, I will. Farewell, old Gaunt,
45   Thou goest to Coventry, there to behold
Our cousin Hereford and fell Mowbray fight.
O! sit my husband's wrongs on Hereford's spear,
That it may enter butcher Mowbray's breast;
Or if misfortune miss the first career,
50   Be Mowbray's sins so heavy in his bosom,
That they may break his foaming courser's back,
And throw the rider headlong in the lists,
A caitiff recreant to my cousin Hereford.
Farewell, old Gaunt; thy sometimes brother's wife
55   With her companion, Grief, must end her life.

GAUNT Sister, farewell, I must to Coventry:
As much good stay with thee, as go with me.

DUCHESS Yet one word more: grief boundeth where it
            falls,
Not with the empty hollowness, but weight.
60   I take my leave before I have begun,
For sorrow ends not when it seemeth done.
Commend me to thy brother, Edmund York.
Lo! this is all: nay, yet depart not so;
Though this be all, do not so quickly go.
65   I shall remember more. Bid him ... Ah! what?
With all good speed at Plashy visit me.
Alack! and what shall good old York there see
But empty lodgings and unfurnished walls,
Unpeopled offices, untrodden stones,
70   And what hear there for welcome but my groans?
Therefore commend me, let him not come there,
To seek out sorrow that dwells everywhere.
Desolate, desolate will I hence and die!
The last leave of thee takes my weeping eye.

Exeunt.

46 **cousin** kinsman   46 **fell** ruthless   49 **misfortune** disaster (to Mowbray)
49 **career** encounter   53 **caitiff recreant** captive coward   54 **sometimes** sometime, former   58–59 **grief ... weight** i.e., my grief returns because it is heavy,
not like a ball   62 **York** Duke of York   66 **Plashy** (in Essex)   69 **offices**
kitchens, servants' quarters, etc.

[Scene III. *The lists at Coventry.*]

Enter Lord Marshal and the Duke Aumerle.

MARSHAL My Lord Aumerle, is Harry Hereford armed?

AUMERLE Yea, at all points, and longs to enter in.

MARSHAL The Duke of Norfolk, sprightfully and bold,
Stays but the summons of the appellant's trumpet.

AUMERLE Why, then, the champions are prepared, and
stay   5
For nothing but his Majesty's approach.

*The trumpets sound, and the King enters with his
nobles, [including Gaunt, Bushy, Bagot, Green].
When they are set, enter [Mowbray,] the Duke
of Norfolk, in arms, defendant, [and a Herald].*

RICHARD Marshal, demand of yonder champion
The cause of his arrival here in arms;
Ask him his name; and orderly proceed
To swear him in the justice of his cause.   10

MARSHAL In God's name and the King's, say who thou
art
And why thou comest thus knightly clad in arms,
Against what man thou com'st, and what thy
quarrel.
Speak truly on thy knighthood and thy oath,
As so defend thee heaven and thy valor.   15

MOWBRAY My name is Thomas Mowbray, Duke of
Norfolk,

I.iii.3 **sprightfully** full of spirit

13

Who hither come engagèd by my oath—
Which God defend a knight should violate!
Both to defend my loyalty and truth
20 To God, my king, and my succeeding issue,
Against the Duke of Hereford that appeals me;
And by the grace of God, and this mine arm,
To prove him in defending of myself
A traitor to my God, my king, and me;
25 And as I truly fight, defend me, heaven!

The trumpets sound. Enter [Bolingbroke,] Duke
of Hereford, appellant, in armor.

RICHARD Marshal, demand of yonder knight in arms,
Both who he is, and why he cometh hither
Thus plated in habiliments of war,
And formally, according to our law,
30 Depose him in the justice of his cause.

MARSHAL What is thy name? And wherefore com'st
   thou hither
Before King Richard in his royal lists?
Against whom comest thou? And what's thy
   quarrel?
Speak like a true knight, so defend thee heaven.

35 BOLINGBROKE Harry of Hereford, Lancaster and Derby
Am I, who ready here do stand in arms
To prove by God's grace, and my body's valor
In lists, on Thomas Mowbray, Duke of Norfolk,
That he is a traitor, foul and dangerous,
40 To God of heaven, King Richard and to me:
And as I truly fight, defend me, heaven!

MARSHAL On pain of death, no person be so bold
Or daring-hardy as to touch the lists,
Except the Marshal and such officers
45 Appointed to direct these fair designs.

---

18 **defend** forbid 21 **appeals** accuses 25 **truly** with truth on my side
28 **plated** in plate armor 30 **Depose** examine on oath 43 **daring-hardy**
reckless

BOLINGBROKE Lord Marshal, let me kiss my Sovereign's
    hand,
    And bow my knee before his Majesty;
    For Mowbray and myself are like two men
    That vow a long and weary pilgrimage:
    Then let us take a ceremonious leave   50
    And loving farewell of our several friends.

MARSHAL The appellant in all duty greets your
    Highness,
    And craves to kiss your hand and take his leave.

RICHARD We will descend and fold him in our arms.
    Cousin of Hereford, as thy cause is right,   55
    So be thy fortune in this royal fight:
    Farewell, my blood, which if today thou shed,
    Lament we may, but not revenge thee dead.

BOLINGBROKE O, let no noble eye profane a tear
    For me, if I be gored with Mowbray's spear: 60
    As confident as is the falcon's flight
    Against a bird, do I with Mowbray fight.
    My loving lord, I take my leave of you;
    Of you, my noble cousin, Lord Aumerle,
    Not sick, although I have to do with death,   65
    But lusty, young, and cheerly drawing breath.
    Lo! as at English feasts, so I regreet
    The daintiest last, to make the end most sweet.
    O thou, the earthly author of my blood,
    Whose youthful spirit in me regenerate   70
    Doth with a twofold vigor lift me up
    To reach at victory above my head,
    Add proof unto mine armor with thy prayers,
    And with thy blessings steel my lance's point,
    That it may enter Mowbray's waxen coat   75
    And furbish new the name of John a Gaunt
    Even in the lusty havior of his son.

GAUNT God in thy good cause make thee prosperous;

66 **cheerly** cheerfully 67 **regreet** greet again 70 **regenerate** reborn
73 **proof** invulnerability 75 **waxen** i.e., soft 76 **a** o', of 77 **havior** behavior

Be swift like lightning in the execution,
80 And let thy blows doubly redoubled
Fall like amazing thunder on the casque
Of thy adverse pernicious enemy:
Rouse up thy youthful blood, be valiant and live.

BOLINGBROKE Mine innocency and St. George to
thrive!

85 MOWBRAY However God or fortune cast my lot,
There lives or dies, true to King Richard's throne,
A loyal, just and upright gentleman.
Never did captive with a freer heart
Cast off his chains of bondage, and embrace
90 His golden, uncontrolled enfranchisement
More than my dancing soul doth celebrate
This feast of battle with mine adversary.
Most mighty liege, and my companion peers,
Take from my mouth the wish of happy years;
95 As gentle and as jocund as to jest
Go I to fight: truth hath a quiet breast.

RICHARD Farewell, my lord; securely I espy
Virtue with valor couchèd in thine eye.
Order the trial, Marshal, and begin.

100 MARSHAL Harry of Hereford, Lancaster and Derby,
Receive thy lance, and God defend the right.

BOLINGBROKE Strong as a tower in hope, I cry Amen.

MARSHAL Go bear this lance to Thomas, Duke of
Norfolk.

FIRST HERALD Harry of Hereford, Lancaster and Derby,
105 Stands here for God, his Sovereign and himself,
On pain to be found false and recreant,
To prove the Duke of Norfolk, Thomas Mowbray,
A traitor to his God, his king, and him,

81 **amazing** stupefying 82 **adverse** placed opposite 90 **enfranchisement**
liberation 95 **jest** sport 97 **securely** confidently 98 **couchèd** lying hidden
102 **Strong as a tower in hope** (cf. Psalms 61:3) 106 **On pain** to be at the risk
of being

And dares him to set forward to the fight.

SECOND HERALD Here standeth Thomas Mowbray,
    Duke of Norfolk,   110
On pain to be found false and recreant,
Both to defend himself, and to approve
Henry of Hereford, Lancaster and Derby,
To God, his sovereign, and to him disloyal,
Courageously and with a free desire   115
Attending but the signal to begin.

MARSHAL Sound trumpets; and set forward
    combatants!
        [*A charge sounded.*]
Stay, the King hath thrown his warder down.

RICHARD Let them lay by their helmets and their spears
And both return back to their chairs again.   120
Withdraw with us, and let the trumpets sound,
While we return these dukes what we decree.
        [*A long flourish.*]
Draw near,
And list what with our council we have done.
For that our kingdom's earth should not be soiled   125
With that dear blood which it hath fosterèd;
And for our eyes do hate the dire aspect
Of civil wounds plowed up with neighbor's sword,
And for we think the eagle-wingèd pride
Of sky-aspiring and ambitious thoughts   130
With rival-hating envy set on you
To wake our peace, which in our country's cradle
Draws the sweet infant breath of gentle sleep,
Which so roused up with boist'rous untuned
    drums,
With harsh resounding trumpets' dreadful bray,   135
And grating shock of wrathful iron arms,
Might from our quiet confines fright fair Peace,
And make us wade even in our kindred's blood;

112 **approve** prove 118 **warder** truncheon (a signal to stop the combat)
120 **chairs** (on which the combatants sat before mounting) 122 s.d. **flourish**
trumpet call 124 **list** hear

Therefore we banish you our territories:
140 You, cousin Hereford, upon pain of life,
Till twice five summers have enriched our fields,
Shall not regreet our fair dominions,
But tread the stranger paths of banishment.

BOLINGBROKE Your will be done: this must my
          comfort be,
145 That sun that warms you here shall shine on me,
And those his golden beams to you here lent
Shall point on me, and gild my banishment.

RICHARD Norfolk, for thee remains a heavier doom
Which I with some unwillingness pronounce:
150 The sly slow hours shall not determinate
The dateless limit of thy dear exile;
The hopeless word of "Never to return"
Breathe I against thee, upon pain of life.

MOWBRAY A heavy sentence, my most sovereign
          liege,
155 And all unlooked for from your Highness' mouth:
A dearer merit, not so deep a maim
As to be cast forth in the common air
Have I deservèd at your Highness' hands!
The language I have learnt these forty years,
160 My native English, now I must forgo,
And now my tongue's use is to me no more
Than an unstringèd viol or a harp,
Or like a cunning instrument cased up,
Or being open, put into his hands
165 That knows no touch to tune the harmony.
Within my mouth you have enjailed my tongue,
Doubly portcullised with my teeth and lips,
And dull unfeeling barren ignorance

---

142 **regreet** greet again   143 **stranger** foreign   150 **determinate** put a limit
to   151 **dateless** endless   151 **dear** severe   152 **word** utterance   154 **sentence**
(punning on "word")   156 **dearer merit** better reward   163 **cunning** ingenious
and requiring skill in the playing   167 **portcullised** (a portcullis was a grating
which could be let down in the gateway of a castle to block it)

Is made my jailer to attend on me.
I am too old to fawn upon a nurse,   170
Too far in years to be a pupil now;
What is thy sentence then but speechless death,
Which robs my tongue from breathing native
    breath?

RICHARD It boots thee not to be compassionate:
After our sentence, plaining comes too late.   175

MOWBRAY Then thus I turn me from my country's
    light,
To dwell in solemn shades of endless night.

[*Turns to go.*]

RICHARD Return again, and take an oath with thee.
Lay on our royal sword your banished hands;
Swear by the duty that you owe to God—   180
Our part therein we banish with yourselves—
To keep the oath that we administer:
You never shall—so help you truth and God!—
Embrace each other's love in banishment,
Nor never look upon each other's face,   185
Nor never write, regreet, nor reconcile
This louring tempest of your home-bred hate,
Nor never by advisèd purpose meet
To plot, contrive, or complot any ill
'Gainst us, our state, our subjects, or our land.   190

BOLINGBROKE I swear.

MOWBRAY   And I, to keep all this.

BOLINGBROKE Norfolk, so far as to mine enemy—
By this time, had the King permitted us,
One of our souls had wandered in the air,
Banished this frail sepulcher of our flesh,   195
As now our flesh is banished from this land:

174 **boots** avails   174 **compassionate** expressing passionate feeling   181 **Our
... yourselves** i.e., we absolve you from allegiance to us   188 **advisèd** deliberate
189 **complot** plot with others   195 **sepulcher** (here accented on second syllable)

Confess thy treasons ere thou fly the realm;
Since thou hast far to go, bear not along
The clogging burden of a guilty soul.

200 MOWBRAY No, Bolingbroke, if ever I were traitor,
My name be blotted from the book of life,
And I from heaven banished as from hence!
But what thou art, God, thou, and I, do know,
And all too soon, I fear, the King shall rue.
205 Farewell, my liege, now no way can I stray:
Save back to England all the world's my way.

                                        Exit.

RICHARD Uncle, even in the glasses of thine eyes
I see thy grievèd heart: thy sad aspect
Hath from the number of his banished years
Plucked four away. [*To Bolingbroke*] Six frozen
210   winters spent,
Return with welcome home from banishment.

BOLINGBROKE How long a time lies in one little word.
Four lagging winters and four wanton springs
End in a word—such is the breath of kings.

215 GAUNT I thank my liege that in regard of me
He shortens four years of my son's exile,
But little vantage shall I reap thereby:
For ere the six years that he hath to spend
Can change their moons and bring their times
    about,
220 My oil-dried lamp and time-bewasted light
Shall be extinct with age and endless night;
My inch of taper will be burnt and done,
And blindfold Death not let me see my son.

RICHARD Why! uncle, thou hast many years to live.

225 GAUNT But not a minute, King, that thou canst give;

207 **glasses** (eyes were thought to reflect the heart) 208 **aspect** (accent on second syllable) 213 **wanton** luxuriant 217 **vantage** advantage 219 **times** seasons 223 **blindfold Death** (Death is thought of as eyeless, like a skull, and also as Atropos, Milton's "blind fury with the abhorred shears," cutting short human lives)

Shorten my days thou canst with sullen sorrow
And pluck nights from me, but not lend a morrow;
Thou canst help time to furrow me with age,
But stop no wrinkle in his pilgrimage:
Thy word is current with him for my death,   230
But dead, thy kingdom cannot buy my breath.

RICHARD Thy son is banished upon good advice,
Whereto thy tongue a party-verdict gave:
Why at our justice seem'st thou then to lour?

GAUNT Things sweet to taste prove in digestion sour.   235
You urged me as a judge, but I had rather
You would have bid me argue like a father.
O, had it been a stranger, not my child,
To smooth his fault I should have been more mild:
A partial slander sought I to avoid,   240
And in the sentence my own life destroyed.
Alas! I looked when some of you should say
I was too strict to make mine own away;
But you gave leave to my unwilling tongue
Against my will to do myself this wrong.   245

RICHARD Cousin, farewell, and uncle, bid him so;
Six years we banish him, and he shall go.

[*Flourish.*] *Exit* [*King Richard with his train*].

AUMERLE Cousin, farewell; what presence must not
    know,
From where you do remain let paper show.

MARSHAL My lord, no leave take I, for I will ride   250
As far as land will let me by your side.

GAUNT O, to what purpose dost thou hoard thy words,
That thou returnest no greeting to thy friends?

BOLINGBROKE I have too few to take my leave of you,
When the tongue's office should be prodigal   255

230 **current** valid   233 **party-verdict** one person's share of a joint verdict
240 **partial slander** imputation of partiality   248 **what presence must not
know** (perhaps "as I cannot have your news from you in person," or "what you
cannot say in present company." Aumerle is anxious to know Bolingbroke's
intentions)   255 **prodigal** lavish

21

To breathe the abundant dolor of the heart.

GAUNT Thy grief is but thy absence for a time.

BOLINGBROKE Joy absent, grief is present for that time.

GAUNT What is six winters? They are quickly gone.

BOLINGBROKE To men in joy; but grief makes one hour
260   ten.

GAUNT Call it a travel that thou tak'st for pleasure.

BOLINGBROKE My heart will sigh when I miscall it so,
      Which finds it an enforcèd pilgrimage.

GAUNT The sullen passage of thy weary steps
265   Esteem as foil wherein thou art to set
      The precious jewel of thy home return.

BOLINGBROKE Nay, rather, every tedious stride I make
      Will but remember me what a deal of world
      I wander from the jewels that I love.
270   Must I not serve a long apprenticehood
      To foreign passages, and in the end,
      Having my freedom, boast of nothing else
      But that I was a journeyman to grief?

GAUNT All places that the eye of heaven visits
275   Are to a wise man ports and happy havens.
      Teach thy necessity to reason thus:
      There is no virtue like necessity.
      Think not the King did banish thee,
      But thou the King. Woe doth the heavier sit
280   Where it perceives it is but faintly borne.
      Go, say I sent thee forth to purchase honor,
      And not the King exiled thee; or suppose
      Devouring pestilence hangs in our air,

257 **grief** (1) grievance (2) sorrow 265 **foil** setting (metal leaf serving as a background) 268 **remember** remind 271 **passages** experiences 272 **Having my freedom** at the end of his apprenticeship and of his exile 273 **a journeyman to grief** an employee of Grief (instead of his own master) 273 **journeyman** (1) artisan (2) traveler 274 **eye of heaven** sun (as in Ovid) 277 **virtue** efficacy 280 **faintly** faintheartedly

And thou art flying to a fresher clime.
Look what thy soul holds dear, imagine it   285
To lie that way thou goest, not whence thou com'st.
Suppose the singing birds musicians,
The grass whereon thou tread'st the presence
    strewed,
The flowers fair ladies, and thy steps no more
Than a delightful measure or a dance;   290
For gnarling sorrow hath less power to bite
The man that mocks at it and sets it light.

BOLINGBROKE O, who can hold a fire in his hand
By thinking on the frosty Caucasus?
Or cloy the hungry edge of appetite   295
By bare imagination of a feast?
Or wallow naked in December snow
By thinking on fantastic summer's heat?
O, no! the apprehension of the good
Gives but the greater feeling to the worse.   300
Fell Sorrow's tooth doth never rankle more
Than when he bites, but lanceth not the sore.

GAUNT Come, come, my son, I'll bring thee on thy way.
Had I thy youth and cause, I would not stay.

BOLINGBROKE Then England's ground, farewell; sweet
    soil, adieu;   305
My mother and my nurse that bears me yet!
Where'er I wander, boast of this I can:
Though banished, yet a true-born Englishman.
                                                  Exeunt.

---

285 **Look what** whatever 288 **presence strewed** royal presence chamber
strewn with rushes 291 **gnarling** snarling (with perhaps a suggestion of the
twisting effects of sorrow) 298 **fantastic** imaginary 301 **Fell** fierce
301 **rankle** fester 302 **lanceth** cuts with a surgeon's knife 304 **I would not
stay** i.e., away from England 306 **bears** (1) gives birth to (2) supports me (for a
discussion of these speeches see K. Muir, *Review of English Studies*, X, 1959,
283-86.)

[Scene IV. *The Court*.]

Enter the King, with Bagot, [Green], etc.
at one door, and the Lord Aumerle at another.

RICHARD We did observe. Cousin Aumerle,
How far brought you high Hereford on his way?

AUMERLE I brought high Hereford, if you call him so,
But to the next high way, and there I left him.

RICHARD And say, what store of parting tears were
5   shed?

AUMERLE Faith, none for me, except the northeast
wind,
Which then blew bitterly against our faces,
Awaked the sleeping rheum, and so by chance
Did grace our hollow parting with a tear.

RICHARD What said our cousin when you parted with
10   him?

AUMERLE "Farewell."
And for my heart disdainèd that my tongue
Should so profane the word, that taught me craft
To counterfeit oppression of such grief
15   That words seemed buried in my sorrow's grave.
Marry, would the word "Farewell" have length'ned
hours
And added years to his short banishment,
He should have had a volume of farewells;
But since it would not, he had none of me.

20   RICHARD He is our cousin, cousin, but 'tis doubt,
When time shall call him home from banishment,

I.iv.1 **We did observe** (continuing a conversation) 6 **for me** for my part
20 **cousin** (Richard, Aumerle, and Bolingbroke were cousins)

Whether our kinsman come to see his friends.
Ourself and Bushy, Bagot here and Green,
Observed his courtship to the common people,
How he did seem to dive into their hearts 25
With humble and familiar courtesy,
What reverence he did throw away on slaves,
Wooing poor craftsmen with the craft of smiles
And patient underbearing of his fortune,
As 'twere to banish their affects with him. 30
Off goes his bonnet to an oyster-wench;
A brace of draymen bid God speed him well,
And had the tribute of his supple knee,
With "Thanks, my countrymen, my loving
    friends";
As were our England in reversion his, 35
And he our subjects' next degree in hope.

GREEN Well, he is gone, and with him go these
    thoughts.
Now for the rebels which stand out in Ireland;
Expedient manage must be made, my liege,
Ere further leisure yield them further means 40
For their advantage and your Highness' loss.

RICHARD We will ourself in person to this war,
And for our coffers with too great a court
And liberal largess are grown somewhat light,
We are enforced to farm our royal realm, 45
The revenue whereof shall furnish us
For our affairs in hand. If that come short,
Our substitutes at home shall have blank charters;
Whereto, when they shall know what men are rich,
They shall subscribe them for large sums of gold, 50
And send them after to supply our wants,
For we will make for Ireland presently.
                Enter Bushy.
Bushy, what news?

39 **manage** management   45 **farm** lease (Richard leased the crown lands and
customs dues to his favorites for £7000 a month)   48 **blank charters** (documents
given to Richard's agents, with power to insert what sums they pleased for the rich
to pay)

BUSHY Old John of Gaunt is grievous sick, my Lord,
55   Suddenly taken, and hath sent posthaste
        To intreat your Majesty to visit him.

RICHARD Where lies he?

BUSHY At Ely House.

RICHARD Now put it, God, in the physician's mind
60   To help him to his grave immediately!
        The lining of his coffers shall make coats
        To deck our soldiers for these Irish wars.
        Come, gentlemen, let's all go visit him;
        Pray God we may make haste and come too late!

65   ALL Amen!   *Exeunt.*

61 **lining** contents (with pun on **coats**)

[ACT II

Scene I. *London, Ely House.*]

Enter John of Gaunt, sick, with the Duke of York,
[the Earl of Northumberland, Attendants], etc.

GAUNT Will the King come, that I may breathe my last
   In wholesome counsel to his unstaid youth?

YORK Vex not yourself, nor strive not with your
       breath,
   For all in vain comes counsel to his ear.

GAUNT O, but they say the tongues of dying men   5
   Enforce attention like deep harmony:
   Where words are scarce they are seldom spent
       in vain,
   For they breathe truth that breathe their words
       in pain;
   He that no more must say is listened more
   Than they whom youth and ease have taught to
       glose;   10
   More are men's ends marked than their lives before;
   The setting sun, and music at the close,
   As the last taste of sweets is sweetest last,
   Writ in remembrance more than things long past:

II.i.2 **unstaid** unrestrained   10 **glose** utter pleasing words   12 **close** conclusion
of a musical phrase   13 **last** (because it comes last)

15   Though Richard my life's counsel would not hear,
         My death's sad tale may yet undeaf his ear.

   YORK No, it is stopped with other flattering sounds:
         As praises—of whose taste the wise are fond—
         Lascivious meters, to whose venom sound
20   The open ear of youth doth always listen;
         Report of fashions in proud Italy
         Whose manners still our tardy-apish nation
         Limps after in base imitation.
         Where doth the world thrust forth a vanity—
25   So it be new, there's no respect how vile—
         That is not quickly buzzed into his ears?
         Then all too late comes counsel to be heard,
         Where will doth mutiny with wit's regard.
         Direct not him whose way himself will choose:
         'Tis breath thou lack'st, and that breath wilt
30   thou lose.

   GAUNT Methinks I am a prophet new inspired,
         And thus expiring do foretell of him:
         His rash fierce blaze of riot cannot last,
         For violent fires soon burn out themselves.
         Small showers last long, but sudden storms are
35   short;
         He tires betimes that spurs too fast betimes;
         With eager feeding, food doth choke the feeder.
         Light vanity, insatiate cormorant,
         Consuming means, soon preys upon itself.
40   This royal throne of kings, this scept'red isle,
         This earth of majesty, this seat of Mars,
         This other Eden, demi-paradise,
         This fortress built by Nature for herself

16 **My death's sad tale** my solemn dying words   18 **the wise** even the wise (see Textual Note)   19 **venom** venomous   22 **still** always   22 **tardy-apish** imitative, but behind the fashion   23 **imitation** (five syllables. Complaints of the aping of foreign fashions were common in Elizabethan England. For this speech and the next see K. Muir, *Review of English Studies*, X, 1959, pp. 286–89.)   28 **will** desire   28 **wit's regard** what intelligence ought to regard   31–32 **inspired ... expiring** (pun)   33 **riot** profligacy   36 **betimes** (1) soon (2) early   38 **cormorant** glutton (from the bird)

Against infection and the hand of war,
This happy breed of men, this little world,   45
This precious stone set in the silver sea
Which serves it in the office of a wall,
Or as a moat defensive to a house,
Against the envy of less happier lands,
This blessed plot, this earth, this realm, this
    England,   50
This nurse, this teeming womb of royal kings,
Feared by their breed, and famous by their
    birth,
Renownèd for their deeds as far from home,
For Christian service and true chivalry,
As is the sepulcher in stubborn Jewry   55
Of the world's ransom, blessed Mary's son,
This land of such dear souls, this dear dear land—
Dear for her reputation through the world—
Is now leased out—I die pronouncing it—
Like to a tenement or pelting farm.   60
England, bound in with the triumphant sea,
Whose rocky shore beats back the envious siege
Of wat'ry Neptune, is now bound in with shame,
With inky blots, and rotten parchment bonds.
That England that was wont to conquer others   65
Hath made a shameful conquest of itself.
Ah! would the scandal vanish with my life,
How happy then were my ensuing death!

> *Enter King and Queen, etc.* [*Aumerle, Bushy,*
> *Green, Bagot, Ross, and Willoughby.*]

YORK The King is come; deal mildly with his youth,
    For young hot colts being raged do rage the more.   70

QUEEN How fares our noble uncle, Lancaster?

RICHARD What comfort, man? How is't with aged
    Gaunt?

44 **infection** moral infection   45 **happy breed** fortunate race   45 **little world**
i.e., a world by itself   54 **Christian service** i.e., the Crusades   55 **stubborn**
(because they rejected Christ)   60 **tenement** leased land or property   60 **pelting** paltry   40–60 **This … farm** (the verb comes in line 59)   62 **siege** (perhaps
a partial pun on "surge")   70 **raged** enraged

GAUNT O, how that name befits my composition!
  Old Gaunt indeed, and gaunt in being old!
75 Within me Grief hath kept a tedious fast;
  And who abstains from meat that is not gaunt?
  For sleeping England long time have I watched:
  Watching breeds leanness, leanness is all gaunt.
  The pleasure that some fathers feed upon
80 Is my strict fast—I mean my children's looks—
  And therein fasting hast thou made me gaunt;
  Gaunt am I for the grave, gaunt as a grave
  Whose hollow womb inherits naught but bones.

RICHARD Can sick men play so nicely with their
  names?

85 GAUNT No, misery makes sport to mock itself:
  Since thou dost seek to kill my name in me,
  I mock my name, great King, to flatter thee.

RICHARD Should dying men flatter with those that
  live?

GAUNT No, no, men living flatter those that die.

90 RICHARD Thou, now a-dying, sayest thou flatterest me.

GAUNT O no, thou diest, though I the sicker be.

RICHARD I am in health, I breathe, and see thee ill.

GAUNT Now he that made me knows I see thee ill;
  Ill in myself to see, and in thee seeing ill.
95 Thy deathbed is no lesser than thy land,
  Wherein thou liest in reputation sick;
  And thou, too careless patient as thou art,
  Commit'st thy anointed body to the cure
  Of those physicians that first wounded thee.
100 A thousand flatterers sit within thy crown,

---

80 **Is my strict fast** I must go without   73-82 **name ... grave** (Coleridge
defended the psychological truth of these puns)   83 **inherits** (the grave will get
only bones because Gaunt is wasted away)   84 **nicely** subtly and prettily   86 **kill
my name in me** i.e., by banishing my son and heir   94 **Ill ... ill** (1) bad eyesight
(2) evil   97 **careless patient** one who does not take proper steps to cure himself

Whose compass is no bigger than thy head,
And yet incagèd in so small a verge
The waste is no whit lesser than thy land.
O, had thy grandsire with a prophet's eye
Seen how his son's son should destroy his sons,   105
From forth thy reach he would have laid thy
    shame,
Deposing thee before thou wert possessed,
Which art possessed now to depose thyself.
Why, cousin, wert thou regent of the world,
It were a shame to let this land by lease;   110
But for thy world enjoying but this land
Is it not more than shame to shame it so?
Landlord of England art thou now, not king;
Thy state of law is bondslave to the law,
And thou—

RICHARD [*interrupting*] A lunatic, lean-witted fool,   115
Presuming on an ague's privilege,
Darest with thy frozen admonition
Make pale our cheek, chasing the royal blood
With fury from his native residence.
Now, by my seat's right-royal majesty   120
Wert thou not brother to great Edward's son,
This tongue that runs so roundly in thy head
Should run thy head from thy unreverent
    shoulders.

GAUNT O, spare me not, my brother Edward's son,
For that I was his father Edward's son,   125
That blood already like the pelican

---

102 **verge** limit (and possibly area within a radius of twelve miles around the
court)   103 **waste** (1) destruction of landlord's property by tenant (2) useless
expense (3) wide space   104 **grandsire** i.e., Edward III   105 **sons** i.e., Gloucester and Gaunt   107-108 **possessed ... possessed** (1) possessed of the crown
(2) possessed with devils   109 **cousin** kinsman   111 **world** cf. line 45
114 **state of law** legal status   117 **frozen** (1) frigid in style (2) prompted by ague
(3) cold, and so cooling me   119 **residence** i.e., his cheek   120 **seat's** throne's
122 **roundly** bluntly   126 **pelican** (thought to wound its breast to feed its young
with its blood—a symbol both of parental self-sacrifice and filial ingratitude)

Hast thou tapped out and drunkenly caroused:
My brother Gloucester, plain well-meaning soul—
Whom fair befall in heaven 'mongst happy souls!—
130   May be a precedent and witness good
That thou respect'st not spilling Edward's blood.
Join with the present sickness that I have,
And thy unkindness be like crooked age
To crop at once a too-long-withered flower.
135   Live in thy shame, but die not shame with thee;
These words hereafter thy tormentors be.
Convey me to my bed, then to my grave;
Love they to live that love and honor have.

> *Exit* [*Gaunt, borne by Attendants,
> and Northumberland*].

RICHARD   And let them die that age and sullens have,
140   For both hast thou, and both become the grave.

YORK   I do beseech your Majesty, impute his words
To wayward sickliness and age in him:
He loves you, on my life, and holds you dear
As Harry, Duke of Hereford, were he here.

RICHARD   Right, you say true, as Hereford's love, so
145   his,
As theirs, so mine; and all be as it is.

[*Enter Northumberland.*]

NORTHUMBERLAND   My liege, old Gaunt commends him
to your Majesty.

RICHARD   What says he?

NORTHUMBERLAND   Nay, nothing, all is said;
His tongue is now a stringless instrument;
150   Words, life and all, old Lancaster hath spent.

YORK   Be York the next that must be bankrout so!
Though death be poor, it ends a mortal woe.

RICHARD   The ripest fruit first falls, and so doth he;

133 **crooked** bent (and suggesting Time with a scythe; cf. line 134)   139 **sullens**
sulks   146 **and all be as it is** let what will be, be   151 **bankrout** bankrupt

His time is spent, our pilgrimage must be;
So much for that. Now for our Irish wars.   155
We must supplant those rough rug-headed kernes
Which live like venom, where no venom else,
But only they, have privilege to live.
And for these great affairs do ask some charge,
Towards our assistance we do seize to us   160
The plate, coin, revenues, and movables
Whereof our uncle Gaunt did stand possessed.

YORK   How long shall I be patient? Ah, how long
Shall tender duty make me suffer wrong?
Not Gloucester's death, nor Hereford's banishment,   165
Nor Gaunt's rebukes, nor England's private
    wrongs,
Nor the prevention of poor Bolingbroke
About his marriage, nor my own disgrace,
Have ever made me sour my patient cheek,
Or bend one wrinkle on my Sovereign's face.   170
I am the last of noble Edward's sons,
Of whom thy father, Prince of Wales, was first:
In war was never lion raged more fierce,
In peace was never gentle lamb more mild,
Than was that young and princely gentleman.   175
His face thou hast, for even so looked he,
Accomplished with the number of thy hours;
But when he frowned it was against the French,
And not against his friends; his noble hand
Did win what he did spend, and spent not that   180
Which his triumphant father's hand had won;

153-55 The ... that (cf. Bolingbroke's equally callous reception of Mowbray's death, IV.i.103-04. He also changes the subject in the middle of a line) 156 rug-headed kernes shag-haired light-armed Irish foot soldiers 157 venom reptiles (alluding to the tradition that St. Patrick expelled snakes from Ireland) 166 Gaunt's rebukes rebukes suffered by Gaunt 166 private wrongs wrongs suffered by private citizens 167-68 prevention ... marriage (Richard prevented Bolingbroke's marriage in exile to the French King's cousin) 168 my own disgrace (unexplained; possibly we should accept the equally difficult original reading of Q1, "his own disgrace," corrected in all copies save one) 169 sour make sour 170 wrinkle frown 177 Accomplished ... hours when he was your age

His hands were guilty of no kindred blood,
But bloody with the enemies of his kin.
O, Richard, York is too far gone with grief,
185 Or else he never would compare between—

RICHARD Why, uncle, what's the matter?

YORK   O my liege,
Pardon me, if you please; if not, I pleased
Not to be pardoned, am content withal.
Seek you to seize and gripe into your hands
190 The royalties and rights of banished Hereford?
Is not Gaunt dead? and doth not Hereford live?
Was not Gaunt just? and is not Harry true?
Did not the one deserve to have an heir?
Is not his heir a well-deserving son?
195 Take Hereford's rights away, and take from time
His charters and his customary rights,
Let not tomorrow then ensue today;
Be not thyself. For how art thou a king
But by fair sequence and succession?
200 Now afore God—God forbid I say true—
If you do wrongfully seize Hereford's rights,
Call in the letters patents that he hath
By his attorneys-general to sue
His livery, and deny his off'red homage,
205 You pluck a thousand dangers on your head,
You lose a thousand well-disposèd hearts,
And prick my tender patience to those thoughts
Which honor and allegiance cannot think.

RICHARD Think what you will, we seize into our
        hands
210 His plate, his goods, his money, and his lands.

YORK I'll not be by the while. My liege, farewell.
What will ensue hereof there's none can tell:

189 **gripe** clutch 190 **royalties** gifts from the King 195 **Take** if you take
197 **ensue** follow upon 199 **succession** (four syllables) 202–04 **Call … livery**
if you revoke the royal letters-patent that enable his attorneys to obtain for him his
father's lands 204 **deny** refuse 211 **by** near

But by bad courses may be understood
That their events can never fall out good.   *Exit.*

RICHARD Go, Bushy, to the Earl of Wiltshire
    straight;   215
Bid him repair to us to Ely House,
To see this business. Tomorrow next
We will for Ireland—and 'tis time, I trow;
And we create in absence of ourself
Our uncle York Lord Governor of England,   220
For he is just, and always loved us well.
Come on, our queen, tomorrow must we part;
Be merry, for our time of stay is short.

    [*Flourish.*] *Exeunt King and Queen. Manet*
    Northumberland, [with Willoughby, and Ross].

NORTHUMBERLAND Well, lords, the Duke of Lancaster is
    dead.

ROSS And living too, for now his son is duke.   225

WILLOUGHBY Barely in title, not in revenues.

NORTHUMBERLAND Richly in both, if justice had her
    right.

ROSS My heart is great, but it must break with
    silence
Ere't be disburdened with a liberal tongue.

NORTHUMBERLAND Nay, speak thy mind, and let him
    ne'er speak more   230
That speaks thy words again to do thee harm.

WILLOUGHBY Tends that that thou would'st speak to
    the Duke of Hereford?
If it be so, out with it boldly, man;
Quick is mine ear to hear of good towards him.

ROSS No good at all that I can do for him,   235

213 by concerning 214 events outcomes 215 Wiltshire William le Scrope,
treasurer of England 221 For ... well (in spite of York's criticisms of his
conduct, Richard apparently appreciates his honesty) 223 s.d. Manet remains
229 liberal free

Unless you call it good to pity him,
Bereft, and gelded of his patrimony.

NORTHUMBERLAND Now, afore God, 'tis shame such
        wrongs are borne
    In him a royal prince and many moe
240 Of noble blood in this declining land!
    The King is not himself, but basely led
    By flatterers; and what they will inform
    Merely in hate 'gainst any of us all,
    That will the King severely prosecute
245 'Gainst us, our lives, our children, and our heirs.

ROSS The commons hath he pilled with grievous
        taxes
    And quite lost their hearts. The nobles hath
        he fined
    For ancient quarrels and quite lost their hearts.

WILLOUGHBY And daily new exactions are devised,
250 As blanks, benevolences, and I wot not what:
    But what, a God's name, doth become of this?

NORTHUMBERLAND Wars hath not wasted it, for warred
        he hath not,
    But basely yielded upon compromise
    That which his noble ancestors achieved with blows:
255 More hath he spent in peace than they in wars.

ROSS The Earl of Wiltshire hath the realm in farm.

WILLOUGHBY The King's grown bankrout like a broken
        man.

NORTHUMBERLAND Reproach and dissolution hangeth
        over him.

ROSS He hath not money for these Irish wars,
260 His burdenous taxations notwithstanding,
    But by the robbing of the banished Duke.

---

239 **moe** more   246 **pilled** plundered   250 **blanks** cf. I.iv.48   250 **benevo-**
lences forced loans (an anachronism, as they were introduced in 1473)   251 **a** in

NORTHUMBERLAND His noble kinsman—most degener-
    ate king!
  But, lords, we hear this fearful tempest sing,
  Yet seek no shelter to avoid the storm:
  We see the wind sit sore upon our sails,   265
  And yet we strike not, but securely perish.

ROSS We see the very wrack that we must suffer,
  And unavoided is the danger now,
  For suffering so the causes of our wrack.

NORTHUMBERLAND Not so; even through the hollow
    eyes of death   270
  I spy life peering, but I dare not say
  How near the tidings of our comfort is.

WILLOUGHBY Nay, let us share thy thoughts, as thou
    dost ours.

ROSS Be confident to speak, Northumberland;
  We three are but thyself, and speaking so   275
  Thy words are but as thoughts: therefore be bold.

NORTHUMBERLAND Then thus: I have from le Port
    Blanc, a bay
  In Brittaine, received intelligence
  That Harry, Duke of Hereford, Rainold, Lord
    Cobham,
  [The son of Richard, Earl of Arundel,]   280
  That late broke from the Duke of Exeter,
  His brother, Archbishop, late of Canterbury,
  Sir Thomas Erpingham, Sir Thomas Ramston,
  Sir John Norbery, Sir Robert Waterton, and Francis
    Quoint—   285
  All these well furnished by the Duke of Brittaine
  With eight tall ships, three thousand men of war,
  Are making hither with all due expedience,

266 **strike** (a pun on striking sails and striking blows) 267 **wrack** wreck
278 **Brittaine** Brittany 280 **The ... Arundel** (some such line, necessary for the
sense, is lacking, possibly because an Earl of Arundel was executed in October
1595) 281 **broke** escape 286 **men of war** soldiers 287 **expedience** speed

And shortly mean to touch our northern shore.
Perhaps they had ere this, but that they stay
290   The first departing of the King for Ireland.
If then we shall shake off our slavish yoke,
Imp out our drooping country's broken wing,
Redeem from broking pawn the blemished
    crown,
Wipe off the dust that hides our scepter's gilt,
295   And make high majesty look like itself,
Away with me in post to Ravenspurgh;
But if you faint, as fearing to do so,
Stay, and be secret, and myself will go.

ROSS To horse, to horse, urge doubts to them that
    fear.

WILLOUGHBY Hold out my horse, and I will first be
300   there.   *Exeunt.*

[Scene II. *Windsor Castle.*]

Enter the Queen, Bushy, Bagot.

BUSHY Madam, your Majesty is too much sad.
You promised, when you parted with the King,
To lay aside life-harming heaviness,
And entertain a cheerful disposition.

5   QUEEN To please the King I did: to please myself
I cannot do it; yet I know no cause
Why I should welcome such a guest as Grief,
Save bidding farewell to so sweet a guest

292 **Imp out** engraft new feathers   293 **broking pawn** lending money upon
pawns, which was fraudulent (cf. II.i.113)   294 **gilt** (pun on "guilt")   296 **in
post** with speed, with relays of horses   300 **Hold out my horse** if my horse
holds out

As my sweet Richard. Yet again methinks
Some unborn sorrow ripe in Fortune's womb   10
Is coming towards me; and my inward soul
With nothing trembles—at something it grieves
More than with parting from my lord the King.

BUSHY Each substance of a grief hath twenty
          shadows,
Which shows like the grief itself, but is not so;   15
For Sorrow's eye, glazèd with blinding tears,
Divides one thing entire to many objects,
Like perspectives which, rightly gazed upon,
Show nothing but confusion; eyed awry,
Distinguish form. So your sweet Majesty,   20
Looking awry upon your lord's departure,
Find shapes of grief more than himself to wail,
Which looked on as it is, is nought but shadows
Of what it is not; then, thrice-gracious Queen,
More than your lord's departure weep not:
          more's not seen,   25
Or if it be, 'tis with false Sorrow's eye,
Which for things true weeps things imaginary.

QUEEN It may be so; but yet my inward soul
Persuades me it is otherwise. Howe'er it be,
I cannot but be sad—so heavy sad,   30
As, though on thinking on no thought I think,
Makes me with heavy nothing faint and shrink.

BUSHY 'Tis nothing but conceit, my gracious lady.

QUEEN 'Tis nothing less: conceit is still derived
From some forefather grief; mine is not so,   35
For nothing hath begot my something grief,
Or something hath the nothing that I grieve:

II.ii.14 **shadows** i.e., illusory griefs 18 **perspectives** pictures constructed so that they look distorted when viewed directly ("rightly"), and intelligible when viewed from the side ("awry") 22 **Find** (the subject "you" is understood from "Majesty") 22 **wail** bewail 27 **weeps** weeps for 31 **though ... think** though I try to think about nothing 33 **conceit** fancy 34 **'Tis nothing less** it's anything except mere fancy 37 **something ... grieve** the nothing that I grieve hath something in it

'Tis in reversion that I do possess,
But what it is that is not yet known what,
40   I cannot name; 'tis nameless woe I wot.

[*Enter Green.*]

GREEN God save your Majesty! and well met, gentle-
    men.
I hope the King is not yet shipped for Ireland.

QUEEN Why hopest thou so? 'Tis better hope he is,
For his designs crave haste, his haste good
    hope:
45   Then wherefore dost thou hope he is not shipped?

GREEN That he our hope might have retired his
    power
And driven into despair an enemy's hope,
Who strongly hath set footing in this land:
The banished Bolingbroke repeals himself,
50   And with uplifted arms is safe arrived
At Ravenspurgh.

QUEEN   Now God in heaven forbid!

GREEN Ah, madam! 'tis too true; and that is worse,
The Lord Northumberland, his son, young Henry
    Percy,
The lords of Ross, Beaumond, and Willoughby,
55   With all their powerful friends are fled to him.

BUSHY Why have you not proclaimed Northumberland
And all the rest revolted faction, traitors?

GREEN We have: whereupon the Earl of Worcester
Hath broken his staff, resigned his stewardship,
60   And all the household servants fled with him
To Bolingbroke.

---

38 'Tis ... possess I am heir to it, and I shall know what it is when I experience
it 40 wot know 44 crave demand 48 strongly with a strong force
49 repeals recalls 52 that what 53 young Henry Percy (these words are
repeated in the next scene, and either "Henry" or "his son" may be spurious
here) 57 rest remaining 58 Worcester Northumberland's brother, and the
Lord Steward of the King's household

QUEEN So, Green, thou art the midwife to my woe,
   And Bolingbroke, my sorrow's dismal heir;
   Now hath my soul brought forth her prodigy,
   And I, a gasping, new-delivered mother,   65
   Have woe to woe, sorrow to sorrow, joined.

BUSHY Despair not, madam.

QUEEN   Who shall hinder me?
   I will despair and be at enmity
   With cozening Hope: he is a flatterer,
   A parasite, a keeper-back of Death,   70
   Who gently would dissolve the bands of life
   Which false Hope lingers in extremity.

           [*Enter the Duke of York.*]

GREEN Here comes the Duke of York.

QUEEN With signs of war about his aged neck.
   O, full of careful business are his looks!   75
   Uncle, for God's sake, speak comfortable words.

YORK Should I do so, I should belie my thoughts.
   Comfort's in heaven, and we are on the earth,
   Where nothing lives but crosses, cares, and grief.
   Your husband, he is gone to save far off,   80
   Whilst others come to make him lose at home.
   Here am I left to underprop his land,
   Who, weak with age, cannot support myself.
   Now comes the sick hour that his surfeit made;
   Now shall he try his friends that flattered him.   85

            [*Enter Servingman.*]

SERVINGMAN My lord, your son was gone before I
   came.

YORK He was? Why so, go all which way it will.
   The nobles, they are fled, the commons cold,

63 **heir** offspring   64 **prodigy** monster   71 **dissolve the bands** unloose the bonds   72 **lingers** causes to linger   74 **signs of war** (York is wearing throat armor)   75 **careful business** anxious preoccupation   76 **comfortable** comforting (the phrase "comfortable words" is used in the Anglican communion service)   84 **surfeit** overindulgence

And will, I fear, revolt on Hereford's side.
90   Sirrah, get thee to Plashy to my sister Gloucester;
Bid her send me presently a thousand pound.
Hold, take my ring.

SERVINGMAN My lord, I had forgot to tell your
    lordship:
Today as I came by I callèd there—
95   But I shall grieve you to report the rest.

YORK What is't, knave?

SERVINGMAN An hour before I came the Duchess
    died.

YORK God for his mercy, what a tide of woes
Comes rushing on this woeful land at once.
100   I know not what to do. I would to God—
So my untruth had not provoked him to it—
The King had cut off my head with my brother's.
What! are there no posts dispatched for Ireland?
How shall we do for money for these wars?
Come, sister—cousin, I would say—pray pardon
105   me.
Go fellow, get thee home, provide some carts,
And bring away the armor that is there.

                          [*Exit Servingman.*]

Gentlemen, will you go muster men?
If I know how or which way to order these affairs,
110   Thus disorderly thrust into my hands,
Never believe me. Both are my kinsmen.
Th' one is my sovereign, whom both my oath
And duty bids defend; t'other again
Is my kinsman, whom the King hath wronged,
115   Whom conscience and my kindred bids to right.
Well, somewhat we must do. Come, cousin,
I'll dispose of you. Gentlemen, go muster up
    your men,

90 **sister** sister-in-law   97 **died** (in fact she died later; but Shakespeare wishes to give the effect of a succession of woes)   101 **untruth** disloyalty   117 **dispose of** make arrangements for

And meet me presently at Berkeley.
I should to Plashy too,
But time will not permit. All is uneven,   120
And everything is left at six and seven.

Exeunt Duke, Queen. Manent Bushy,
[Bagot], Green.

BUSHY The wind sits fair for news to go for Ire-
   land,
But none returns. For us to levy power
Proportionable to the enemy
Is all unpossible.   125

GREEN Besides, our nearness to the King in love
Is near the hate of those love not the King.

BAGOT And that is the wavering commons, for their
   love
Lies in their purses, and whoso empties them
By so much fills their hearts with deadly hate.   130

BUSHY Wherein the King stands generally
   condemned.

BAGOT If judgment lie in them, then so do we,
Because we ever have been near the King.

GREEN Well, I will for refuge straight to Bristow
   Castle.
The Earl of Wiltshire is already there.   135

BUSHY Thither will I with you, for little office
The hateful commons will perform for us,
Except like curs to tear us all to pieces.
Will you go along with us?

BAGOT No, I will to Ireland to his Majesty.   140
Farewell; if heart's presages be not vain,
We three here part that ne'er shall meet again.

BUSHY That's as York thrives to beat back Bolingbroke.

121 **six and seven** i.e., in confusion   122 **sits** blows   124 **Proportionable**
proportional   132 **lie in** depends on   134 **Bristow** (old form of Bristol)

GREEN Alas, poor Duke, the task he undertakes
145   Is numb'ring sands, and drinking oceans dry:
         Where one on his side fights, thousands will
              fly.
         Farewell at once, for once, for all, and ever.

BUSHY Well, we may meet again.

BAGOT   I fear me, never.
                                    [*Exeunt.*]

[Scene III. *In Gloucestershire.*]

Enter [Bolingbroke, Duke of] Hereford, [and]
Northumberland [with soldiers].

BOLINGBROKE How far is it, my lord, to Berkeley now?

NORTHUMBERLAND Believe me, noble lord,
         I am a stranger here in Gloucestershire.
         These high wild hills and rough uneven ways
5   Draws out our miles and makes them wearisome;
         And yet your fair discourse hath been as sugar,
         Making the hard way sweet and delectable.
         But I bethink me what a weary way
         From Ravenspurgh to Cotshall will be found
10   In Ross and Willoughby, wanting your company,
         Which I protest hath very much beguiled
         The tediousness and process of my travel:
         But theirs is sweet'ned with the hope to have
         The present benefit which I possess;
15   And hope to joy is little less in joy
         Than hope enjoyed. By this the weary lords

II.iii.7 **delectable** (accents on first and third syllables)   9 **Cotshall** Cotswold
12 **tediousness and process** tedious process

44

Shall make their way seem short as mine hath done,
By sight of what I have, your noble company.

BOLINGBROKE Of much less value is my company
Than your good words. But who comes here?   20

Enter Harry Percy.

NORTHUMBERLAND It is my son, young Harry Percy,
Sent from my brother Worcester whencesoever.
Harry, how fares your uncle?

PERCY I had thought, my lord, to have learned his
health of you.

NORTHUMBERLAND Why, is he not with the Queen?   25

PERCY No, my good lord, he hath forsook the court,
Broken his staff of office, and dispersed
The household of the King.

NORTHUMBERLAND   What was his reason?
He was not so resolved when last we spake
together.

PERCY Because your lordship was proclaimèd
traitor;   30
But he, my lord, is gone to Ravenspurgh
To offer service to the Duke of Hereford,
And sent me over by Berkeley to discover
What power the Duke of York had levied there,
Then with directions to repair to Ravenspurgh.   35

NORTHUMBERLAND Have you forgot the Duke of
Hereford, boy?

PERCY No, my good lord, for that is not forgot
Which ne'er I did remember. To my knowledge
I never in my life did look on him.

NORTHUMBERLAND Then learn to know him now—this is
the Duke.   40

PERCY My gracious lord, I tender you my service,
Such as it is, being tender, raw, and young,

22 **whencesoever** from wherever he is

Which elder days shall ripen and confirm
To more approvèd service and desert.

45 BOLINGBROKE I thank thee, gentle Percy, and be sure
I count myself in nothing else so happy
As in a soul rememb'ring my good friends;
And as my fortune ripens with thy love,
It shall be still thy true love's recompense:
My heart this covenant makes, my hand thus
50   seals it.

NORTHUMBERLAND How far is it to Berkeley, and what
stir
Keeps good old York there with his men of war?

PERCY There stands the castle by yon tuft of trees,
Manned with three hundred men, as I have heard,
And in it are the Lords of York, Berkeley, and
55   Seymour,
None else of name and noble estimate.

[Enter Ross and Willoughby.]

NORTHUMBERLAND Here come the Lords of Ross and
Willoughby,
Bloody with spurring, fiery red with haste.

BOLINGBROKE Welcome, my lords, I wot your love
pursues
60   A banished traitor. All my treasury
Is yet but unfelt thanks, which more enriched
Shall be your love and labor's recompense.

ROSS Your presence makes us rich, most noble lord.

WILLOUGHBY And far surmounts our labor to attain it.

BOLINGBROKE Evermore thank's the exchequer of the
65   poor,
Which till my infant fortune comes to years
Stands for my bounty. But who comes here?

[Enter Berkeley.]

61 **unfelt** intangible 62 **love** love's 66 **infant** (and so unable to possess property)

NORTHUMBERLAND It is my Lord of Berkeley, as I
    guess.

BERKELEY My Lord of Hereford, my message is to
    you.

BOLINGBROKE My lord, my answer is—to Lancaster;   70
    And I am come to seek that name in England;
    And I must find that title in your tongue
    Before I make reply to aught you say.

BERKELEY Mistake me not, my lord; 'tis not my
    meaning
    To race one title of your honor out.   75
    To you, my lord, I come—what lord you will—
    From the most gracious regent of this land,
    The Duke of York, to know what pricks you on
    To take advantage of the absent time,
    And fright our native peace with self-borne arms?   80

          [Enter York, attended.]

BOLINGBROKE I shall not need transport my words by
    you:
    Here comes his Grace in person. My noble uncle!

          [Kneels.]

YORK Show me thy humble heart, and not thy knee,
    Whose duty is deceivable and false.

BOLINGBROKE My gracious uncle—   85

YORK Tut, tut! Grace me no grace, nor uncle me no
    uncle;
    I am no traitor's uncle, and that word "grace"
    In an ungracious mouth is but profane.
    Why have those banished and forbidden legs
    Dared once to touch a dust of England's ground?   90

70 **to Lancaster** (Bolingbroke is about to reply, but in the middle of the sentence he changes his mind, to say that he will answer only in the name of Lancaster) 75 **race one title** erase title (with pun on "tittle") 79 **absent time** time of the King's absence 80 **self-borne** borne for one's own cause 84 **deceivable** deceptive

But then, more "why?" Why have they dared to
   march
So many miles upon her peaceful bosom,
Frighting her pale-faced villages with war,
And ostentation of despisèd arms?
95   Com'st thou because the anointed King is hence?
Why, foolish boy, the King is left behind,
And in my loyal bosom lies his power.
Were I but now the lord of such hot youth
As when brave Gaunt, thy father, and myself
100 Rescued the Black Prince, that young Mars of men,
From forth the ranks of many thousand French,
O, then, how quickly should this arm of mine,
Now prisoner to the palsy, chastise thee,
And minister correction to thy fault!

BOLINGBROKE My gracious uncle, let me know my
105   fault:
On what condition stands it, and wherein?

YORK Even in condition of the worst degree
In gross rebellion and detested treason.
Thou art a banished man, and here art come
110 Before the expiration of thy time,
In braving arms against thy sovereign.

BOLINGBROKE As I was banished, I was banished
    Hereford,
But as I come, I come for Lancaster.
And, noble uncle, I beseech your Grace,
115 Look on my wrongs with an indifferent eye.
You are my father, for methinks in you
I see old Gaunt alive. O, then, my father,
Will you permit that I shall stand condemned,
A wandering vagabond, my rights and royalties
120 Plucked from my arms perforce, and given away
To upstart unthrifts? Wherefore was I born?
If that my cousin king be King in England,

---

94 despisèd despicable   115 indifferent impartial   121 unthrifts prodigals

It must be granted I am Duke of Lancaster.
You have a son, Aumerle, my noble cousin:
Had you first died, and he been thus trod down,   125
He should have found his uncle Gaunt a father,
To rouse his wrongs and chase them to the bay.
I am denied to sue my livery here,
And yet my letters patents give me leave.
My father's goods are all distrained and sold,   130
And these, and all, are all amiss employed.
What would you have me do? I am a subject;
And I challenge law, attorneys are denied me;
And therefore personally I lay my claim
To my inheritance of free descent.   135

NORTHUMBERLAND The noble Duke hath been too much
    abused.

ROSS It stands your Grace upon to do him right.

WILLOUGHBY Base men by his endowments are made
    great.

YORK My lords of England, let me tell you this:
I have had feeling of my cousin's wrongs,   140
And labored all I could to do him right;
But in this kind to come in braving arms,
Be his own carver, and cut out his way,
To find out right with wrong—it may not be:
And you that do abet him in this kind   145
Cherish rebellion, and are rebels all.

NORTHUMBERLAND The noble Duke hath sworn his
    coming is
But for his own; and for the right of that
We all have strongly sworn to give him aid:
And let him never see joy that breaks that oath.   150

YORK Well, well, I see the issue of these arms.
I cannot mend it, I must needs confess,
Because my power is weak and all ill left:

127 **bay** quarry's last stand   133 **And if**   137 **It stands your Grace upon** it behooves your Grace   143 **Be his own carver** i.e., be a law to himself   153 **ill left** left inadequate (?) left in disorder (?)

But if I could, by Him that gave me life,
155 I would attach you all, and make you stoop
Unto the sovereign mercy of the King.
But since I cannot, be it known unto you
I do remain as neuter. So fare you well—
Unless you please to enter in the castle,
160 And there repose you for this night.

BOLINGBROKE An offer, uncle, that we will accept.
But we must win your grace to go with us
To Bristow Castle, which they say is held
By Bushy, Bagot, and their complices,
165 The caterpillars of the commonwealth,
Which I have sworn to weed and pluck away.

YORK It may be I will go with you, but yet I'll pause,
For I am loath to break our country's laws.
Nor friends, nor foes, to me welcome you are.
170 Things past redress are now with me past care.
                                    Exeunt.

[Scene IV. *In Wales.*]

Enter Earl of Salisbury, and a Welsh Captain.

CAPTAIN My Lord of Salisbury, we have stayed ten
    more days,
And hardly keep our countrymen together,
And yet we hear no tidings from the King;
Therefore we will disperse ourselves. Farewell.

5 SALISBURY Stay yet another day, thou trusty Welshman;
The King reposeth all his confidence in thee.

---

155 **attach** arrest   158 **neuter** neutral   164 **complices** accomplices   165 **The
... commonwealth** (common Elizabethan expression, ultimately Biblical, for
those who preyed on society) II.iv.s.d. **Captain** (possibly Owen Glendower,
mentioned in III.i.43)   3 **yet** so far

CAPTAIN 'Tis thought the King is dead: we will not
 stay.
 The bay trees in our country are all withered,
 And meteors fright the fixèd stars of heaven,
 The pale-faced moon looks bloody on the earth,   10
 And lean-looked prophets whisper fearful change;
 Rich men look sad, and ruffians dance and leap,
 The one in fear to lose what they enjoy,
 The other to enjoy by rage and war.
 These signs forerun the death or fall of kings.   15
 Farewell; our countrymen are gone and fled,
 As well assured Richard their king is dead. [*Exit.*]

SALISBURY Ah, Richard! With the eyes of heavy mind
 I see thy glory like a shooting star
 Fall to the base earth from the firmament;   20
 Thy sun sets weeping in the lowly west,
 Witnessing storms to come, woe and unrest;
 Thy friends are fled to wait upon thy foes,
 And crossly to thy good all fortune goes.   [*Exit.*]

---

11 **lean-looked** lean-looking 13 **enjoy** possess 14 **to enjoy by rage** in hope of enjoying by violent action 21–22 **sun … unrest** (Richard's badge was a sun obscured by or breaking from clouds) 24 **crossly** adversely

[ACT III

Scene I. *Bristol. Before the Castle.*]

Enter [Bolingbroke] Duke of Hereford, York, Northumberland,
[other Lords, Soldiers,] Bushy and Green prisoners.

BOLINGBROKE Bring forth these men.
    Bushy and Green, I will not vex your souls,
    Since presently your souls must part your bodies,
    With too much urging your pernicious lives,
5   For 'twere no charity; yet, to wash your blood
    From off my hands, here in the view of men,
    I will unfold some causes of your deaths.
    You have misled a prince, a royal king,
    A happy gentleman in blood and lineaments,
10   By you unhappied and disfigured clean;
    You have in manner with your sinful hours
    Made a divorce betwixt his queen and him,
    Broke the possession of a royal bed,
    And stained the beauty of a fair queen's cheeks
    With tears, drawn from her eyes by your foul
15   wrongs.
    Myself a prince, by fortune of my birth,

III.i.3 **presently** immediately   3 **part** part from   9 **happy** fortunate   11–12 **in manner ... divorce** you have made a kind of divorce   11–15 **You ... wrongs** (there is no suggestion elsewhere in the play that Richard was estranged from his queen, though Holinshed does refer to his adultery. If the accusation is one of homosexuality, it may echo Marlowe's *Edward II*; and in *Woodstock* Queen Ann complains of Richard's favorites. But Bolingbroke is making a propaganda speech)

Near to the King in blood, and near in love
Till you did make him misinterpret me,
Have stooped my neck under your injuries,
And sighed my English breath in foreign clouds,   20
Eating the bitter bread of banishment,
Whilst you have fed upon my signories,
Disparked my parks, and felled my forest woods,
From my own windows torn my household coat,
Raced out my impresse, leaving me no sign,   25
Save men's opinions and my living blood,
To show the world I am a gentleman.
This and much more, much more than twice all this,
Condemns you to the death. See them delivered over
To execution and the hand of death.   30

BUSHY More welcome is the stroke of death to me
Than Bolingbroke to England. Lords, farewell.

GREEN My comfort is that heaven will take our souls
And plague injustice with the pains of hell.

BOLINGBROKE My Lord Northumberland, see them
dispatched.   35

[*Exeunt Northumberland with Bushy and Green.*]

Uncle, you say the Queen is at your house;
For God's sake, fairly let her be intreated.
Tell her I send to her my kind commends;
Take special care my greetings be delivered.

YORK A gentleman of mine I have dispatched   40
With letters of your love to her at large.

BOLINGBROKE Thanks, gentle uncle. Come, Lords, away
To fight with Glendower and his complices;
A while to work, and after holiday.   *Exeunt.*

22 **signories** estates   23 **Disparked** thrown open   24 **From ... coat** broke the
coat of arms in stained glass   25 **Raced out my impresse** erased my impresa
(emblem)   16–27 **Myself ... gentleman** (Bolingbroke's real complaint. He does
not mention the forced loans and the farming of the land)   35 **dispatched**
executed   37 **intreated** treated   38 **commends** commendations, greetings
41 **at large** in full   43 **Glendower** (cf. note in II.iv.s.d. Perhaps Bolingbroke
does not know that the Welsh army has disbanded)

[Scene II. *The coast of Wales, near
Barkloughly Castle.*]

*Enter the King, Aumerle, [the Bishop of]
Carlisle, etc. [Drums, flourish, and colors.]*

RICHARD Barkloughly Castle call they this at hand?

AUMERLE Yea, my lord. How brooks your Grace the
air
After your late tossing on the breaking seas?

RICHARD Needs must I like it well. I weep for joy
5   To stand upon my kingdom once again.
Dear earth, I do salute thee with my hand,
Though rebels wound thee with their horses' hoofs.
As a long-parted mother with her child
Plays fondly with her tears and smiles in meeting,
10   So weeping, smiling, greet I thee, my earth,
And do thee favors with my royal hands.
Feed not thy sovereign's foe, my gentle earth,
Nor with thy sweets comfort his ravenous sense;
But let thy spiders, that suck up thy venom,
15   And heavy-gaited toads lie in their way,
Doing annoyance to the treacherous feet
Which with usurping steps do trample thee;
Yield stinging nettles to mine enemies;
And when they from thy bosom pluck a flower,
20   Guard it, I pray thee, with a lurking adder
Whose double tongue may with a mortal touch
Throw death upon thy sovereign's enemies.
Mock not my senseless conjuration, lords:

III.ii.2 **brooks** enjoys 6 **salute** greet with a gesture 21 **mortal** deadly
23 **senseless** addressed to senseless things

This earth shall have a feeling, and these stones
Prove armèd soldiers, ere her native king   25
Shall falter under foul rebellion's arms.

CARLISLE Fear not, my lord; that power that made
    you king
Hath power to keep you king in spite of all.
The means that heavens yield must be embraced
And not neglected. Else heaven would,   30
And we will not: heaven's offer we refuse,
The proffered means of succor and redress.

AUMERLE He means, my lord, that we are too remiss,
Whilst Bolingbroke through our security
Grows strong and great in substance and in power.   35

RICHARD Discomfortable cousin, know'st thou not
That when the searching eye of heaven is hid
Behind the globe and lights the lower world,
Then thieves and robbers range abroad unseen
In murders and in outrage boldly here: 40
But when from under this terrestrial ball
He fires the proud tops of the eastern pines
And darts his light through every guilty hole,
Then murders, treasons, and detested sins,
The cloak of night being plucked from off their
    backs,
Stand bare and naked, trembling at themselves?   45
So when this thief, this traitor, Bolingbroke,
Who all this while hath reveled in the night
Whilst we were wand'ring with the Antipodes,
Shall see us rising in our throne, the east,   50
His treasons will sit blushing in his face,
Not able to endure the sight of day,
But self-affrighted tremble at his sin.
Not all the water in the rough rude sea
Can wash the balm off from an anointed king;   55
The breath of worldly men cannot depose

30-31 **Else ... not** otherwise we go against the will of heaven   36 **Discomfortable** discomforting   38 **globe** earth   38 **lower world** antipodes   55 **balm** (cf. IV.i.206)   56 **worldly** earthly

The deputy elected by the Lord.
For every man that Bolingbroke hath pressed
To lift shrewd steel against our golden crown,
60   God for his Richard hath in heavenly pay
A glorious angel; then, if angels fight,
Weak men must fall, for heaven still guards the
    right.   *Enter Salisbury.*

Welcome, my lord. How far off lies your power?

SALISBURY Nor near, nor farther off, my gracious
    lord,
65   Than this weak arm. Discomfort guides my tongue,
And bids me speak of nothing but despair.
One day too late, I fear me, noble lord,
Hath clouded all thy happy days on earth.
O, call back yesterday, bid time return,
70   And thou shalt have twelve thousand fighting men.
Today, today, unhappy day too late,
O'erthrows thy joys, friends, fortune, and thy state;
For all the Welshmen, hearing thou wert dead,
Are gone to Bolingbroke, dispersed and fled.

AUMERLE Comfort, my liege, why looks your Grace
75   so pale?

RICHARD But now the blood of twenty thousand men
Did triumph in my face, and they are fled;
And till so much blood thither come again,
Have I not reason to look pale and dead?
80   All souls that will be safe fly from my side,
For Time hath set a blot upon my pride.

AUMERLE Comfort, my liege, remember who you are.

RICHARD I had forgot myself: am I not King?
Awake, thou coward majesty! Thou sleepest.
85   Is not the King's name twenty thousand names?
Arm, arm, my name! a puny subject strikes
At thy great glory. Look not to the ground,

58 **pressed** conscripted   59 **shrewd** sharp   59-61 **crown ... angel** (possibly a
pun on these two coins)   63 **power** army

56

Ye favorites of a king, are we not high?
High be our thoughts. I know my uncle York
Hath power enough to serve our turn. But who
    comes here?   90
                    Enter Scroop.

SCROOP More health and happiness betide my liege
Than can my care-tuned tongue deliver him.

RICHARD Mine ear is open, and my heart prepared;
The worst is worldly loss thou canst unfold.
Say, is my kingdom lost? Why, 'twas my care,   95
And what loss is it to be rid of care?
Strives Bolingbroke to be as great as we?
Greater he shall not be; if he serve God,
We'll serve Him too, and be his fellow so.
Revolt our subjects? That we cannot mend: 100
They break their faith to God as well as us.
Cry woe, destruction, ruin, and decay:
The worst is death, and death will have his day.

SCROOP Glad am I that your Highness is so armed
To bear the tidings of calamity.   105
Like an unseasonable stormy day
Which makes the silver rivers drown their shores
As if the world were all dissolved to tears,
So high above his limits swells the rage
Of Bolingbroke, covering your fearful land   110
With hard bright steel and hearts harder than steel.
White beards have armed their thin and hairless
    scalps
Against thy majesty; boys with women's voices
Strive to speak big, and clap their female joints
In stiff unwieldy arms against thy crown;   115
Thy very beadsmen learn to bend their bows
Of double-fatal yew against thy state;
Yea, distaff-women manage rusty bills

89 **High** i.e., high in name and place   92 **care-tuned** tuned to the key of
sorrow   114 **speak big** assume men's voices   114 **female** weak, effeminate
116 **beadsmen** pensioners who pray for their benefactors   117 **double-fatal** (the
berry is poisonous and the wood used for bows)   118 **manage** wield   118 **bills**
wooden shafts with spiked blades

Against thy seat: both young and old rebel,
120 And all goes worse than I have power to tell.

RICHARD Too well, too well thou tell'st a tale so ill.
Where is the Earl of Wiltshire? Where is Bagot?
What is become of Bushy? Where is Green?
That they have let the dangerous enemy
125 Measure our confines with such peaceful steps?
If we prevail, their heads shall pay for it.
I warrant they have made peace with Bolingbroke.

SCROOP Peace have they made with him indeed, my lord.

RICHARD O, villains, vipers, damned without
redemption!
130 Dogs easily won to fawn on any man!
Snakes in my heart-blood warmed that sting my
heart!
Three Judases, each one thrice worse than Judas!
Would they make peace? Terrible hell
Make war upon their spotted souls for this!

135 SCROOP Sweet love, I see, changing his property,
Turns to the sourest and most deadly hate.
Again uncurse their souls: their peace is made
With heads and not with hands; those whom you
curse
Have felt the worst of death's destroying wound,
140 And lie full low, graved in the hollow ground.

AUMERLE Is Bushy, Green, and the Earl of Wiltshire
dead?

SCROOP Ay, all of them at Bristow lost their heads.

AUMERLE Where is the Duke, my father, with his
power?

RICHARD No matter where—of comfort no man
speak.

---

125 **peaceful** i.e., unopposed   127 **they have** (pronounced "they've")
134 **spotted** sinful   135 **property** distinctive quality   143 **power** army

Let's talk of graves, of worms, and epitaphs,   145
Make dust our paper, and with rainy eyes
Write sorrow on the bosom of the earth.
Let's choose executors and talk of wills:
And yet not so, for what can we bequeath
Save our deposèd bodies to the ground?   150
Our lands, our lives, and all are Bolingbroke's,
And nothing can we call our own, but death
And that small model of the barren earth
Which serves as paste and cover to our bones.
For God's sake let us sit upon the ground   155
And tell sad stories of the death of kings:
How some have been deposed, some slain in war,
Some haunted by the ghosts they have deposed,
Some poisoned by their wives, some sleeping killed,
All murdered—for within the hollow crown   160
That rounds the mortal temples of a king
Keeps Death his court, and there the antic sits,
Scoffing his state and grinning at his pomp,
Allowing him a breath, a little scene,
To monarchize, be feared, and kill with looks,   165
Infusing him with self and vain conceit,
As if this flesh which walls about our life
Were brass impregnable; and, humored thus,
Comes at the last, and with a little pin
Bores thorough his castle wall, and farewell king!   170
Cover your heads, and mock not flesh and blood
With solemn reverence; throw away respect,
Tradition, form, and ceremonious duty;
For you have but mistook me all this while:
I live with bread like you, feel want,   175
Taste grief, need friends—subjected thus,
How can you say to me, I am a king?

153 model (variously explained as mold, grave mound, and microcosm)
154 paste and cover (an image taken from pie crust, since this was sometimes
called a coffin) 160 hollow empty circle, vain, transitory 162 antic clown
165 monarchize play the monarch 166 self and vain conceit empty estimate
of self 168 humored (perhaps "Death thus amused" or "the King thus
indulged") 170 thorough through 176 subjected made a subject and subject
to the ordinary needs of man

CARLISLE My lord, wise men ne'er sit and wail their
    woes,
But presently prevent the ways to wail.
180 To fear the foe, since fear oppresseth strength,
Gives in your weakness strength unto your foe;
And so your follies fight against yourself.
Fear and be slain, no worse can come to fight,
And fight and die is death destroying death,
185 Where fearing dying pays death servile breath.

AUMERLE My father hath a power; inquire of him,
And learn to make a body of a limb.

RICHARD Thou chid'st me well. Proud Bolingbroke, I
    come
To change blows with thee for our day of doom.
190 This ague fit of fear is overblown;
An easy task it is to win our own.
Say, Scroop, where lies our uncle with his power?
Speak sweetly, man, although thy looks be sour.

SCROOP Men judge by the complexion of the sky
195 The state and inclination of the day;
So may you by my dull and heavy eye.
My tongue hath but a heavier tale to say.
I play the torturer by small and small
To lengthen out the worst that must be spoken:
200 Your uncle York is joined with Bolingbroke,
And all your northern castles yielded up,
And all your southern gentlemen in arms
Upon his party.

RICHARD   Thou hast said enough.
Beshrew thee, cousin, which didst lead me
    forth
205 Of that sweet way I was in to despair.

---

179 **presently** immediately   183 **to fight** by fighting   185 **pays ... breath**
makes us slaves to death   187 **body of a limb** make a whole out of a part
189 **change** exchange   190 **overblown** blown over   192 **power** army
198 **small and small** little by little   203 **Upon his party** on his side
204 **Beshrew thee** ill befall you   204 **which** who   205 **way** path, habit

60

What say you now? What comfort have we now?
By heaven, I'll hate him everlastingly
That bids me be of comfort any more.
Go to Flint Castle: there I'll pine away;
A king, woe's slave, shall kingly woe obey.   210
That power I have, discharge, and let them go
To ear the land that hath some hope to grow,
For I have none. Let no man speak again
To alter this, for counsel is but vain.

AUMERLE My liege, one word.

RICHARD   He does me double wrong   215
That wounds me with the flatteries of his tongue.
Discharge my followers, let them hence away,
From Richard's night to Bolingbroke's fair day.
                                                    [*Exeunt.*]

[Scene III. *Wales, before Flint Castle.*]

*Enter [with drum and colors] Bolingbroke, York,
Northumberland, [Attendants and Soldiers].*

BOLINGBROKE So that by this intelligence we learn
The Welshmen are dispersed, and Salisbury
Is gone to meet the King, who lately landed
With some few private friends upon this coast.

NORTHUMBERLAND The news is very fair and good, my
    lord;   5
Richard not far from hence hath hid his head.

YORK It would beseem the Lord Northumberland

---

212 To ... grow to cultivate the fertile ground, i.e., desert to Bolingbroke

To say "King Richard." Alack, the heavy day
When such a sacred king should hide his head.

NORTHUMBERLAND Your Grace mistakes; only to be
10   brief
Left I his title out.

YORK   The time hath been
Would you have been so brief with him, he would
Have been so brief with you to shorten you,
For taking so the head, your whole head's length.

BOLINGBROKE Mistake not, uncle, further than you
15   should.

YORK Take not, good cousin, further than you
    should,
Lest you mis-take: the heavens are over our
    heads.

BOLINGBROKE I know it, uncle, and oppose not myself
Against their will. But who comes here?
              Enter Percy.
20 Welcome, Harry. What, will not this castle yield?

PERCY The castle royally is manned, my lord,
Against thy entrance.

BOLINGBROKE   Royally!
Why, it contains no king?

PERCY   Yes, my good lord,
It doth contain a king: King Richard lies
25 Within the limits of yon lime and stone;
And with him are the Lord Aumerle, Lord
    Salisbury,
Sir Stephen Scroop, besides a clergyman
Of holy reverence—who, I cannot learn.

NORTHUMBERLAND O, belike it is the Bishop of Carlisle.

III.iii.11–12 The ... brief there was a time when if you had been so curt
14 taking so the head (1) chopping off the title (2) acting without restraint
15 Mistake take amiss　17 mis-take transgress, take what is not yours, i.e., the
crown

BOLINGBROKE Noble lord,   30
    Go to the rude ribs of that ancient castle,
    Through brazen trumpet send the breath of parley
    Into his ruined ears, and thus deliver:
    Henry Bolingbroke
    On both his knees doth kiss King Richard's hand,   35
    And sends allegiance and true faith of heart
    To his most royal person; hither come
    Even at his feet to lay my arms and power,
    Provided that my banishment repealed,
    And lands restored again be freely granted;   40
    If not, I'll use the advantage of my power,
    And lay the summer's dust with showers of blood
    Rained from the wounds of slaughtered
       Englishmen—
    The which, how far off from the mind of
       Bolingbroke
    It is such crimson tempest should bedrench   45
    The fresh green lap of fair King Richard's land,
    My stooping duty tenderly shall show.
    Go, signify as much, while here we march
    Upon the grassy carpet of this plain.
    Let's march without the noise of threat'ning drum,   50
    That from this castle's tattered battlements
    Our fair appointments may be well perused.
    Methinks King Richard and myself should meet
    With no less terror than the elements
    Of fire and water, when their thund'ring shock   55
    At meeting tears the cloudy cheeks of heaven.
    Be he the fire, I'll be the yielding water;
    The rage be his, whilst on the earth I rain
    My waters—on the earth, and not on him.
    March on, and mark King Richard how he looks.   60

The trumpets sound [parle without, and answer
within; then a flourish]. Richard appeareth on

31 **ribs** protecting walls 44 **The which** as to which 47 **tenderly** solicitously
51 **tattered** crenelated, dilapidated 52 **appointments** arms and equipment
55 **fire and water** lightning and rain clouds 58 **rain** (pun on "reign")

the walls [with the Bishop of Carlisle, Aumerle,
Scroop, Salisbury].

See, see King Richard doth himself appear,
As doth the blushing discontented sun
From out the fiery portal of the East,
When he perceives the envious clouds are bent
65   To dim his glory, and to stain the track
Of his bright passage to the Occident.

YORK   Yet looks he like a king: behold his eye,
As bright as is the eagle's, lightens forth
Controlling majesty. Alack, alack for woe,
70   That any harm should stain so fair a show.

RICHARD   [*To Northumberland*] We are amazed,
and thus long have we stood
To watch the fearful bending of thy knee,
Because we thought ourself thy lawful king:
And if we be, how dare thy joints forget
75   To pay their awful duty to our presence?
If we be not, show us the hand of God
That hath dismissed us from our stewardship;
For well we know no hand of blood and bone
Can gripe the sacred handle of our scepter,
80   Unless he do profane, steal, or usurp;
And though you think that all, as you have done,
Have torn their souls by turning them from us,
And we are barren and bereft of friends,
Yet know, my master, God omnipotent,
85   Is mustering in his clouds on our behalf
Armies of pestilence, and they shall strike
Your children yet unborn and unbegot
That lift your vassal hands against my head,
And threat the glory of my precious crown.
90   Tell Bolingbroke—for yon methinks he stands—
That every stride he makes upon my land
Is dangerous treason. He is come to open
The purple testament of bleeding war;

68 **lightens forth** flashes   75 **awful** reverential   82 **torn ... turning** (pun)

But ere the crown he looks for live in peace
Ten thousand bloody crowns of mothers' sons　95
Shall ill become the flower of England's face,
Change the complexion of her maid-pale peace
To scarlet indignation, and bedew
Her pastor's grass with faithful English blood.

NORTHUMBERLAND　The King of heaven forbid our lord
　　the King　100
Should so with civil and uncivil arms
Be rushed upon. Thy thrice-noble cousin,
Harry Bolingbroke, doth humbly kiss thy hand,
And by the honorable tomb he swears
That stands upon your royal grandsire's bones,　105
And by the royalties of both your bloods—
Currents that spring from one most gracious
　　head—
And by the buried hand of warlike Gaunt,
And by the worth and honor of himself,
Comprising all that may be sworn or said,　110
His coming hither hath no further scope
Than for his lineal royalties, and to beg
Infranchisement immediate on his knees;
Which on thy royal party granted once,
His glittering arms he will commend to rust,　115
His barbèd steeds to stables, and his heart
To faithful service of your Majesty.
This swears he, as he is a prince and just;
And, as I am a gentleman, I credit him.

RICHARD　Northumberland, say thus the King returns,　120
His noble cousin is right welcome hither,
And all the number of his fair demands
Shall be accomplished without contradiction.
With all the gracious utterance thou hast
Speak to his gentle hearing kind commends.　125

95 **crowns** (punning on the crown of line 94)　99 **pastor's** (the King was the shepherd of his kingdom)　111 **scope** aim　112 **lineal royalties** hereditary rights　113 **Infranchisement** recall from banishment and restitution of his lands　114 **party** side　116 **barbèd** armored　120 **returns** answers　125 **commends** greetings

[*To Aumerle*] We do debase ourselves, cousin,
    do we not,
To look so poorly and to speak so fair?
Shall we call back Northumberland, and send
Defiance to the traitor and so die?

AUMERLE No, good my lord; let's fight with gentle
130   words,
    Till time lend friends, and friends their helpful
    swords.

RICHARD O God! O God! that e'er this tongue of mine,
That laid the sentence of dread banishment
On yon proud man, should take it off again
135   With words of sooth! O, that I were as great
As is my grief, or lesser than my name!
Or that I could forget what I have been!
Or not remember what I must be now!
Swell'st thou, proud heart? I'll give thee scope to
    beat,
140   Since foes have scope to beat both thee and me.

AUMERLE   Northumberland comes back from
    Bolingbroke.

RICHARD What must the King do now? Must he
    submit?
The King shall do it. Must he be deposed?
The King shall be contented. Must he lose
145   The name of king? a God's name, let it go.
I'll give my jewels for a set of beads;
My gorgeous palace for a hermitage;
My gay apparel for an almsman's gown;
My figured goblets for a dish of wood;
150   My scepter for a palmer's walking-staff;
My subjects for a pair of carvèd saints;
And my large kingdom for a little grave,
A little, little grave, an obscure grave;

126 **We** (the speech prefix is repeated in the quarto perhaps because a line of
Northumberland's has dropped out)   127 **poorly** abjectly   135 **sooth** flattery
136 **name** i.e., king   145 **a** in   146 **set of beads** rosary   149 **figured**
ornamented   150 **palmer's** pilgrim's

Or I'll be buried in the King's highway,
Some way of common trade, where subjects' feet   155
May hourly trample on their sovereign's head;
For on my heart they tread now whilst I live,
And buried once, why not upon my head?
Aumerle, thou weep'st, my tender-hearted cousin:
We'll make foul weather with despisèd tears;   160
Our sighs and they shall lodge the summer corn,
And make a dearth in this revolting land:
Or shall we play the wantons with our woes
And make some pretty match with shedding tears,
As thus, to drop them still upon one place,   165
Till they have fretted us a pair of graves
Within the earth; and, therein laid, "there lies
Two kinsmen digged their graves with weeping
    eyes":
Would not this ill do well? Well, well, I see
I talk but idly, and you laugh at me.   170
Most mighty prince, my Lord Northumberland,
What says King Bolingbroke? Will his Majesty
Give Richard leave to live till Richard die?
You make a leg, and Bolingbroke says "Ay."

NORTHUMBERLAND My lord, in the base court he
    doth attend   175
To speak with you; may it please you to come
    down?

RICHARD Down, down I come, like glist'ring
    Phaethon,
Wanting the manage of unruly jades.
In the base court! Base court where kings grow
    base,
To come at traitors' calls, and do them grace: 180
In the base court, come down: down court,
    down king,

155 **trade** coming and going   161 **lodge** beat down   163 **play the wantons** be
unrestrained   165 **still** always   166 **fretted** worn   174 **make a leg** curtsy
175 **base court** basse cour, the lower and outer courtyard   177 **Phaethon** (he
drove the sun chariot of his father, Apollo, and was struck by Zeus's thunderbolt)
178 **manage** art of managing horses

For night owls shriek where mounting larks should
 sing.

BOLINGBROKE What says his Majesty?

NORTHUMBERLAND   Sorrow and grief of heart
Makes him speak fondly like a frantic man;
Yet he is come.

[*Enter King Richard and Attendants, below.*]

185 BOLINGBROKE   Stand all apart,
And show fair duty to his Majesty.

He kneels down.

My gracious Lord.

RICHARD Fair cousin, you debase your princely knee
To make the base earth proud with kissing it.
190 Me rather had my heart might feel your love,
Than my unpleased eye see your courtesy.
Up, cousin, up, your heart is up, I know,
Thus high at least, although your knee be low.

BOLINGBROKE My gracious lord, I come but for mine
 own.

RICHARD Your own is yours, and I am yours, and
195 all.

BOLINGBROKE So far be mine, my most redoubted
 lord,
As my true service shall deserve your love.

RICHARD Well you deserve: they well deserve to have
That know the strong'st and surest way to get.
200 Uncle, give me your hands; nay, dry your eyes;
Tears show their love, but want their remedies.
Cousin, I am too young to be your father,
Though you are old enough to be my heir.
What you will have, I'll give, and willing too,

184 **fondly** foolishly 190 **Me rather** I would sooner 193 **Thus high** (pointing
to his crown) 196 **redoubted** dreaded 201 **want their remedies** i.e., cannot
provide a cure for themselves or for the grief which causes them

For do we must what force will have us do.   205
Set on towards London, cousin, is it so?

BOLINGBROKE Yea, my good Lord.

RICHARD   Then I must not say no.
                                    [*Flourish. Exeunt.*]

[Scene IV. *The Duke of York's garden.*]

*Enter the Queen with [two Ladies,] her
Attendants.*

QUEEN What sport shall we devise here in this garden,
  To drive away the heavy thought of care?

LADY Madame, we'll play at bowls.

QUEEN 'Twill make me think the world is full of rubs,
  And that my fortune runs against the bias.   5

LADY Madame, we'll dance.

QUEEN My legs can keep no measure in delight,
  When my poor heart no measure keeps in grief:
  Therefore no dancing, girl; some other sport.

LADY Madame, we'll tell tales.   10

QUEEN Of sorrow, or of joy?

LADY   Of either, madame.

QUEEN Of neither, girl.
  For if of joy, being altogether wanting,

III.iv.3 **Madame** (spelled thus in the quarto, possibly to suggest that the ladies
came with the Queen from France) 4 **rubs** obstacles by which bowls were
diverted from their proper course 5 **bias** the form of the bowl which imparts an
oblique motion 7-8 **measure ... measure** (1) time to music (2) a stately dance
(3) moderation

It doth remember me the more of sorrow;
15   Or if of grief, being altogether had,
It adds more sorrow to my want of joy:
For what I have I need not to repeat,
And what I want it boots not to complain.

LADY Madame, I'll sing.

QUEEN   'Tis well that thou hast cause;
But thou should'st please me better, would'st thou
20   weep.

LADY I could weep, madame, would it do you good.

QUEEN And I could sing, would weeping do me good,
And never borrow any tear of thee.

    Enter Gardeners, [one the master, the other
                      two his men].

But stay, here come the gardeners.
25   Let's step into the shadow of these trees.
My wretchedness unto a row of pins,
They will talk of state, for every one doth so
Against a change; woe is forerun with woe.

GARDENER [*To one Servant*] Go, bind thou up
    young dangling apricocks,
30   Which like unruly children make their sire
Stoop with oppression of their prodigal weight;
Give some supportance to the bending twigs.
[*To the other*] Go thou, and like an executioner
Cut off the heads of too fast growing sprays
35   That look too lofty in our commonwealth:
All must be even in our government.
You thus employed, I will go root away
The noisome weeds which without profit suck
The soil's fertility from wholesome flowers.

40   MAN Why should we, in the compass of a pale,
Keep law and form and due proportion,

14 **remember** remind   18 **boots** avails   27 **state** the realm   28 **Against a
change** when a change is expected   29 **apricocks** apricots   31 **oppression**
weighing down   31 **prodigal** wasteful   32 **supportance** support   40 **pale**
fenced-in land

Showing, as in a model, our firm estate,
When our sea-wallèd garden, the whole land,
Is full of weeds, her fairest flowers choked up,
Her fruit trees all unpruned, her hedges ruined,   45
Her knots disordered, and her wholesome herbs
Swarming with caterpillars?

GARDENER   Hold thy peace.
He that hath suffered this disordered spring
Hath now himself met with the fall of leaf:
The weeds which his broad spreading leaves did
     shelter,
That seemed in eating him to hold him up,   50
Are plucked up root and all by Bolingbroke—
I mean the Earl of Wiltshire, Bushy, Green.

MAN What, are they dead?

GARDENER   They are; and Bolingbroke
Hath seized the wasteful King. O, what pity is it   55
That he had not so trimmed and dressed his land
As we this garden! We at time of year
Do wound the bark, the skin of our fruit trees,
Lest being overproud in sap and blood
With too much riches it confound itself;   60
Had he done so to great and growing men,
They might have lived to bear, and he to taste
Their fruits of duty. Superfluous branches
We lop away, that bearing boughs may live:
Had he done so, himself had borne the crown,   65
Which waste of idle hours hath quite thrown down.

MAN What, think you the King shall be deposed?

GARDENER Depressed he is already, and deposed
'Tis doubt he will be. Letters came last night
To a dear friend of the good Duke of York's,   70
That tell black tidings.

QUEEN   O, I am pressed to death

42 **as in a model** in miniature   46 **knots** laid-out flower beds   47 **caterpillars**
(cf. II.iii.165)   56 **dressed** tended   68 **depressed** lowered in fortune

Through want of speaking!
                    [*Comes forward.*]
Thou, old Adam's likeness, set to dress this
    garden,
How dares thy harsh rude tongue sound this
    unpleasing news?
75 What Eve, what serpent hath suggested thee
To make a second fall of cursèd man?
Why dost thou say King Richard is deposed?
Dar'st thou, thou little better thing than earth,
Divine his downfall? Say, where, when and how
80 Cam'st thou by this ill tidings? Speak, thou wretch.

GARDENER Pardon me, madam; little joy have I
To breathe this news, yet what I say is true:
King Richard he is in the mighty hold
Of Bolingbroke. Their fortunes both are weighed:
85 In your lord's scale is nothing but himself
And some few vanities that make him light;
But in the balance of great Bolingbroke
Besides himself are all the English peers,
And with that odds he weighs King Richard down.
90 Post you to London, and you will find it so;
I speak no more than everyone doth know.

QUEEN Nimble mischance, that art so light of foot,
Doth not thy embassage belong to me,
And am I last that knows it? O, thou thinkest
95 To serve me last that I may longest keep
Thy sorrow in my breast! Come, ladies, go
To meet at London London's king in woe.
What, was I born to this, that my sad look
Should grace the triumph of great Bolingbroke?
100 Gard'ner, for telling me these news of woe,
Pray God, the plants thou graft'st may never grow.

                          Exit [*with Ladies*].

71-72 O ... speaking (referring to the torture of pressing to death administered
to prisoners who refused to speak)   75 suggested tempted   83 hold custody

GARDENER Poor queen, so that thy state might be no
    worse,
  I would my skill were subject to thy curse.
  Here did she fall a tear; here in this place
  I'll set a bank of rue, sour herb of grace;   105
  Rue even for ruth here shortly shall be seen,
  In the remembrance of a weeping queen.

                      Exeunt.

106 **ruth** pity

[ACT IV

Scene I. *Westminster Hall.*]

*Enter Bolingbroke, with the Lords [Aumerle,
Northumberland, Percy, Fitzwater, Surrey, the Bishop
of Carlisle, the Abbot of Westminster, another Lord,
Herald, and Officers] to Parliament.*

BOLINGBROKE Call forth Bagot.
         Enter Bagot [with Officers].
Now, Bagot, freely speak thy mind,
What thou dost know of noble Gloucester's death,
Who wrought it with the King, and who performed
5   The bloody office of his timeless end.

BAGOT Then set before my face the Lord Aumerle.

BOLINGBROKE Cousin, stand forth, and look upon that
    man.

BAGOT My Lord Aumerle, I know your daring tongue
Scorns to unsay what once it hath delivered.
In that dead time when Gloucester's death was
10   plotted,
I heard you say, "Is not my arm of length,
That reacheth from the restful English court

IV.i.4 **wrought it with** persuaded 5 **timeless** untimely (or everlasting)
10 **dead time** (variously interpreted: past time, deadly time, midnight hour)

74

As far as Callice to mine uncle's head?"
Amongst much other talk that very time
I heard you say that you had rather refuse   15
The offer of an hundred thousand crowns
Than Bolingbroke's return to England;
Adding withal, how blest this land would be
In this your cousin's death.

AUMERLE   Princes and noble Lords,
What answer shall I make to this base man?   20
Shall I so much dishonor my fair stars
On equal terms to give him chastisement?
Either I must, or have mine honor soiled
With the attainder of his slanderous lips.
There is my gage, the manual seal of death,   25
That marks thee out for hell: I say thou liest,
And will maintain what thou hast said is false
In thy heart-blood, though being all too base
To stain the temper of my knightly sword.

BOLINGBROKE Bagot, forbear, thou shalt not take it up.   30

AUMERLE Excepting one, I would he were the best
In all this presence that hath moved me so.

FITZWATER If that thy valor stand on sympathy,
There is my gage, Aumerle, in gage to thine;
By that fair sun which shows me where thou
    stand'st,   35
I heard thee say, and vauntingly thou spak'st it,
That thou wert cause of noble Gloucester's death.
If thou deniest it twenty times, thou liest,
And I will turn thy falsehood to thy heart,
Where it was forgèd, with my rapier's point.   40

AUMERLE Thou dar'st not, coward, live to see that day.

---

13 **Callice** Calais   22 **On equal terms** (Aumerle was Bagot's superior and could therefore refuse to fight with him)   24 **attainder** accusation   25 **manual** by my own hand (punning on a seal fixed to a document and his glove)   29 **temper** i.e., excellence   31-32 **Excepting ... so** I wish I had been angered by the highest in rank present, except Bolingbroke   33 **stand on sympathy** depends on correspondence of rank   34 **in gage** in pledge

FITZWATER Now, by my soul, I would it were this hour!

AUMERLE Fitzwater, thou art damned to hell for this.

PERCY Aumerle, thou liest, his honor is as true
45   In this appeal as thou art all unjust;
      And that thou art so, there I throw my gage,
      To prove it on thee to the extremest point
      Of mortal breathing; seize it if thou dar'st.

AUMERLE And if I do not, may my hands rot off,
50   And never brandish more revengeful steel
      Over the glittering helmet of my foe.

ANOTHER LORD I task the earth to the like, forsworn
          Aumerle,
      And spur thee on with full as many lies
      As may be hollowed in thy treacherous ear
55   From sun to sun: there is my honor's pawn;
      Engage it to the trial if thou darest.

AUMERLE Who sets me else? By heaven, I'll throw
          at all!
      I have a thousand spirits in one breast
      To answer twenty thousand such as you.

60   SURREY My Lord Fitzwater, I do remember well
      The very time Aumerle and you did talk.

FITZWATER 'Tis very true; you were in presence then,
      And you can witness with me this is true.

SURREY As false, by heaven, as heaven itself is true!

FITZWATER Surrey, thou liest.

65   SURREY   Dishonorable boy,
      That lie shall lie so heavy on my sword,
      That it shall render vengeance and revenge,
      Till thou, the lie-giver, and that lie do lie
      In earth as quiet as thy father's skull.

47–48 extremest ... breathing to the death   49 And if if indeed   52 task ...
like lay on the earth the task of bearing another gage   54 hollowed shouted
55 sun to sun sunrise to sunset   56 Engage (pun on "gage" and "engage")
57 Who sets me else who else puts up a stake against me   57 throw (metaphor
from dicing)   62 in presence present (or in attendance at court)

In proof whereof, there is my honor's pawn;   70
Engage it to the trial if thou dar'st.

FITZWATER How fondly dost thou spur a forward
    horse!
If I dare eat, or drink, or breathe, or live,
I dare meet Surrey in a wilderness,
And spit upon him, whilst I say he lies,   75
And lies, and lies. There is my bond of faith,
To tie thee to my strong correction.
As I intend to thrive in this new world,
Aumerle is guilty of my true appeal.
Besides, I heard the banished Norfolk say   80
That thou, Aumerle, did'st send two of thy men
To execute the noble Duke at Callice.

AUMERLE Some honest Christian trust me with a
    gage.
That Norfolk lies, here do I throw down this,
If he may be repealed to try his honor.   85

BOLINGBROKE These differences shall all rest under
    gage
Till Norfolk be repealed; repealed he shall be,
And, though mine enemy, restored again
To all his lands and signories. When he is
    returned,
Against Aumerle we will inforce his trial.   90

CARLISLE That honorable day shall never be seen.
Many a time hath banished Norfolk fought
For Jesu Christ in glorious Christian field,
Streaming the ensign of the Christian cross
Against black pagans, Turks, and Saracens;   95
And, toiled with works of war, retired himself
To Italy, and there at Venice gave
His body to that pleasant country's earth,
And his pure soul unto his captain, Christ,

72 fondly foolishly   72 forward willing   77 correction punishment   78 new
world i.e., of the new reign   83 Some ... gage (he has used both his own
gloves)   86 under gage i.e., prorogued   89 signories estates   94 streaming
flying   96 toiled exhausted with toil

100   Under whose colors he had fought so long.

BOLINGBROKE Why, Bishop, is Norfolk dead?

CARLISLE As surely as I live, my lord.

BOLINGBROKE Sweet peace conduct his sweet soul to
    the bosom
    Of good old Abraham! Lords appellants,
105   Your differences shall all rest under gage,
    Till we assign you to your days of trial.

Enter York.

YORK Great Duke of Lancaster, I come to thee
    From plume-plucked Richard, who with willing
        soul
    Adopts thee heir, and his high scepter yields
110   To the possession of thy royal hand.
    Ascend his throne, descending now from him,
    And long live Henry, fourth of that name!

BOLINGBROKE In God's name, I'll ascend the regal
    throne.

CARLISLE Marry, God forbid!
115   Worst in this royal presence may I speak,
    Yet best beseeming me to speak the truth.
    Would God that any in this noble presence
    Were enough noble to be upright judge
    Of noble Richard. Then true noblesse would
120   Learn him forbearance from so foul a wrong.
    What subject can give sentence on his king?
    And who sits here that is not Richard's subject?
    Thieves are not judged, but they are by to hear,
    Although apparent guilt be seen in them;
125   And shall the figure of God's majesty,
    His captain, steward, deputy elect,
    Anointed, crownèd, planted many years,

104 **Abraham** cf. Luke 16:22   104 **appellants** those who are appealing or
accusing each other   108 **plume-plucked** i.e., humbled   114 **Marry** (a light
oath, from "By the Virgin Mary")   115 **Worst** i.e., least in rank or competence
120 **Learn** teach   124 **apparent** manifest   125 **figure** image   126 **elect** chosen

Be judged by subject and inferior breath,
And he himself not present? O, forfend it, God,
That in a Christian climate souls refined   130
Should show so heinous, black, obscene a deed!
I speak to subjects and a subject speaks,
Stirred up by God thus boldly for his king.
My Lord of Hereford here, whom you call king,
Is a foul traitor to proud Hereford's king;   135
And if you crown him, let me prophesy
The blood of English shall manure the ground,
And future ages groan for this foul act;
Peace shall go sleep with Turks and infidels,
And, in this seat of peace, tumultuous wars   140
Shall kin with kin, and kind with kind, confound;
Disorder, horror, fear, and mutiny
Shall here inhabit, and this land be called
The field of Golgotha and dead men's skulls.
O, if you raise this house against this house,   145
It will the woefullest division prove
That ever fell upon this cursèd earth!
Prevent it, resist it, let it not be so,
Lest child, child's children, cry against you woe.

NORTHUMBERLAND Well have you argued, sir; and for
    your pains   150
Of capital treason we arrest you here.
My Lord of Westminster, be it your charge
To keep him safely till his day of trial.
May it please you, lords, to grant the Commons'
    suit?

BOLINGBROKE Fetch hither Richard, that in common
    view   155
He may surrender; so we shall proceed
Without suspicion.

128 subject of a subject 129 forfend avert 130 refined purified by the
Christian environment 131 obscene offensive 141 with by means of
141 kind race 144 Golgotha cf. Mark 15:22 "a place of dead mens skulles"
(Bishops' Bible) 145 O ... house cf. Mark 3:25 147 cursèd earth earth
cursed by civil war 154 suit (that the charges against the King should be
published)

YORK   I will be his conduct.

Exit.

BOLINGBROKE Lords, you that here are under our
        arrest,
      Procure your sureties for your days of answer.
160   Little are we beholding to your love,
      And little looked for at your helping hands.

Enter Richard and York.

RICHARD Alack, why am I sent for to a king,
      Before I have shook off the regal thoughts
      Wherewith I reigned? I hardly yet have learned
165   To insinuate, flatter, bow, and bend my knee.
      Give Sorrow leave a while to tutor me
      To this submission. Yet I well remember
      The favors of these men: were they not mine?
      Did they not sometime cry "All hail!" to me?
170   So Judas did to Christ: but he in twelve
      Found truth in all but one; I, in twelve thousand,
        none.
      God save the King! Will no man say "Amen"?
      Am I both priest and clerk? Well, then, amen.
      God save the King, although I be not he;
175   And yet amen, if heaven do think him me.
      To do what service am I sent for hither?

YORK To do that office of thine own good will,
      Which tired majesty did make thee offer:
      The resignation of thy state and crown
      To Henry Bolingbroke.

180 RICHARD   Give me the crown.
      Here, cousin, seize the crown. Here, cousin,
      On this side my hand, and on that side yours.
      Now is this golden crown like a deep well
      That owes two buckets, filling one another,

157 **conduct** conductor   165 **insinuate** progress by devious ways   168 **favors**
(1) faces (2) benefits   170 **Judas** cf. Matthew 26:49   170 **twelve** i.e., the
apostles   173 **clerk** (employed to utter responses to the priest's prayers)
177 **office** (York corrects Richard's "service")   184 **owes** owns

The emptier ever dancing in the air,   185
The other down, unseen, and full of water.
That bucket down and full of tears am I,
Drinking my griefs, whilst you mount up on high.

BOLINGBROKE I thought you had been willing to resign.

RICHARD My crown I am, but still my griefs are mine: 190
You may my glories and my state depose,
But not my griefs; still am I King of those.

BOLINGBROKE Part of your cares you give me with
    your crown.

RICHARD Your cares set up, do not pluck my cares
    down.
My care is loss of care, by old care done;   195
Your care is gain of care, by new care won.
The cares I give, I have, though given away;
They 'tend the crown, yet still with me they stay.

BOLINGBROKE Are you contented to resign the crown?

RICHARD Ay, no; no, ay: for I must nothing be.   200
Therefore no, no, for I resign to thee.
Now, mark me how I will undo myself.
I give this heavy weight from off my head,
And this unwieldy scepter from my hand,
The pride of kingly sway from out my heart;   205
With mine own tears I wash away my balm,
With mine own hands I give away my crown,
With mine own tongue deny my sacred state,
With mine own breath release all duteous oaths;
All pomp and majesty I do forswear;   210
My manors, rents, revenues, I forgo;
My acts, decrees, and statutes I deny:
God pardon all oaths that are broke to me.

---

194 **cares** (the word is used in several different senses in lines 194–97—sorrows, responsibilities, diligence or carefulness, anxiety)   195–96 **My . . . won** my sorrow is loss of responsibility by failing to take pains; your anxiety is gain of responsibility won by your new carefulness   198 **'tend** attend on   202 **undo** (1) strip (2) ruin   206 **balm** anointing ointment used at coronation   211 **revenues** (accent on second syllable)

God keep all vows unbroke are made to thee.
215 Make me, that nothing have, with nothing grieved,
And thou with all pleased, that hast all achieved.
Long may'st thou live in Richard's seat to sit,
And soon lie Richard in an earthy pit.
God save King Henry, unkinged Richard says,
220 And send him many years of sunshine days.
What more remains?

NORTHUMBERLAND   No more, but that you read
These accusations, and these grievous crimes,
Committed by your person and your followers,
Against the state and profit of this land:
225 That by confessing them, the souls of men
May deem that you are worthily deposed.

RICHARD Must I do so? and must I ravel out
My weaved-up follies? Gentle Northumberland,
If thy offenses were upon record,
230 Would it not shame thee, in so fair a troop,
To read a lecture of them? If thou would'st,
There should'st thou find one heinous article,
Containing the deposing of a king,
And cracking the strong warrant of an oath,
235 Marked with a blot, damned in the book of heaven.
Nay, all of you that stand and look upon me,
Whilst that my wretchedness doth bait myself,
Though some of you, with Pilate, wash your
          hands,
Showing an outward pity: yet you Pilates
240 Have here delivered me to my sour cross,
And water cannot wash away your sin.

NORTHUMBERLAND My lord, dispatch, read o'er these
articles.

RICHARD Mine eyes are full of tears, I cannot see:
And yet salt water blinds them not so much,

214 **are** that are 226 **worthily** deservedly 227 **ravel out** unweave
229 **record** (accent on second syllable) 230 **troop** assembly 231 **read a
lecture of them** read them aloud 238 **Pilate** cf. Matthew 27:24 240 **sour**
bitter 242 **dispatch** hurry up

82

But they can see a sort of traitors here.   245
Nay, if I turn mine eyes upon myself,
I find myself a traitor with the rest;
For I have given here my soul's consent
T' undeck the pompous body of a king;
Made glory base, and sovereignty a slave,   250
Proud majesty a subject, state a peasant.

NORTHUMBERLAND My lord—

RICHARD No lord of thine, thou haught, insulting
   man,
Nor no man's lord: I have no name, no title,
No, not that name was given me at the font   255
But 'tis usurped. Alack, the heavy day!
That I have worn so many winters out,
And know not now what name to call myself.
O, that I were a mockery king of snow,
Standing before the sun of Bolingbroke,   260
To melt myself away in water drops!
Good king, great king—and yet not greatly good—
And if my word be sterling yet in England,
Let it command a mirror hither straight,
That it may show me what a face I have,   265
Since it is bankrout of his majesty.

BOLINGBROKE Go some of you, and fetch a looking
   glass.   [Exit Attendant.]

NORTHUMBERLAND Read o'er this paper while the glass
   doth come.

RICHARD Fiend, thou torments me, ere I come to hell.

BOLINGBROKE Urge it no more, my Lord Northumber-
   land.   270

NORTHUMBERLAND The Commons will not then be
   satisfied.

RICHARD They shall be satisfied: I'll read enough,

245 **sort** group, pack 249 **pompous** splendid 253 **haught** haughty
255-56 **No ... usurped** (Richard was rumored to be a bastard) 263 **sterling**
current 266 **bankrout** bankrupt

When I do see the very book indeed,
Where all my sins are writ, and that's myself.

Enter one with a glass.

275   Give me the glass, and therein will I read.
No deeper wrinkles yet? Hath Sorrow struck
So many blows upon this face of mine,
And made no deeper wounds? O, flatt'ring glass!
Like to my followers in prosperity,
280   Thou dost beguile me. Was this face the face
That every day under his household roof
Did keep ten thousand men? Was this the face
That, like the sun, did make beholders wink?
Was this the face that faced so many follies,
285   And was at last outfaced by Bolingbroke?
A brittle glory shineth in this face,
As brittle as the glory is the face,

[Throws glass down.]

For there it is, cracked in a hundred shivers.
Mark, silent king, the moral of this sport:
290   How soon my sorrow hath destroyed my face.

BOLINGBROKE The shadow of your sorrow hath
     destroyed
The shadow of your face.

RICHARD   Say that again.
"The shadow of my sorrow"? Ha, let's see.
'Tis very true, my grief lies all within,
295   And these external manners of laments
Are merely shadows to the unseen grief
That swells with silence in the tortured soul.
There lies the substance: and I thank thee, King,
For thy great bounty, that not only giv'st
300   Me cause to wail, but teachest me the way

273-74 **book ... writ** (cf. Psalms 139:16) 283 **sun** (cf. III.ii.50) 284 **faced**
brazened out, countenanced 291 **shadow** outward show 292 **shadow** reflection
294-97 **my ... soul** (Bolingbroke had implied that Richard was putting on an act;
Richard replies that his visible grief is a reflection of a deeper grief he is feeling)

84

How to lament the cause. I'll beg one boon,
And then be gone, and trouble you no more.
Shall I obtain it?

BOLINGBROKE   Name it, fair cousin.

RICHARD Fair cousin? I am greater than a king:
For when I was a king, my flatterers   305
Were then but subjects; being now a subject,
I have a king here to my flatterer.
Being so great, I have no need to beg.

BOLINGBROKE Yet ask.

RICHARD And shall I have?   310

BOLINGBROKE You shall.

RICHARD Then give me leave to go.

BOLINGBROKE Whither?

RICHARD Whither you will, so I were from your
sights.

BOLINGBROKE Go some of you, convey him to the
Tower.   315

RICHARD O, good! "Convey"! Conveyers are you
all,
That rise thus nimbly by a true king's fall.

[*Exeunt Richard, some Lords, and Guards.*]

BOLINGBROKE On Wednesday next we solemnly set
down
Our coronation: Lords, prepare yourselves.

Exeunt. Manent [*the Abbot of*] *Westminster,*
[*the Bishop of*] *Carlisle, Aumerle.*

ABBOT A woeful pageant have we here beheld.   320

---

307 to for   316 Conveyers thieves ("convey" was a euphemism for "steal")
318 set down appoint

CARLISLE The woe's to come; the children yet unborn
Shall feel this day as sharp to them as thorn.

AUMERLE You holy clergymen, is there no plot
To rid the realm of this pernicious blot?

325 ABBOT My lord,
Before I freely speak my mind herein,
You shall not only take the sacrament
To bury mine intents, but also to effect
Whatever I shall happen to devise.
330 I see your brows are full of discontent,
Your hearts of sorrow, and your eyes of tears.
Come home with me to supper: I will lay
A plot shall show us all a merry day.   *Exeunt*.

---

328 **bury mine intents** conceal my plans

[ACT V

Scene I. *London. A Street.*]

Enter the Queen with her Attendants.

QUEEN This way the King will come, this is the way
To Julius Caesar's ill-erected Tower,
To whose flint bosom my condemnèd lord
Is doomed a prisoner by proud Bolingbroke.
Here let us rest, if this rebellious earth   5
Have any resting for her true king's queen.

Enter Richard [and Guard].

But soft, but see, or rather do not see
My fair rose wither; yet look up, behold,
That you in pity may dissolve to dew,
And wash him fresh again with true-love tears.   10
Ah, thou the model where old Troy did stand!
Thou map of honor, thou King Richard's tomb,
And not King Richard, thou most beauteous inn,
Why should hard-favored grief be lodged in thee,
When triumph is become an alehouse guest?   15

RICHARD Join not with grief, fair woman, do not so,
To make my end too sudden; learn, good soul,

V.i.2 **Tower** (the Tower of London was built, according to legend, by Julius Caesar, **ill-erected** because it was used as a prison) 11 **model where old Troy did stand** outline of the walls where Troy once stood, i.e., ruined majesty—suggested by London's old name of Trinovantum, New Troy 15 **alehouse** (Bolingbroke, contrasted with Richard, the beauteous inn)

87

To think our former state a happy dream,
From which awaked, the truth of what we are
20   Shows us but this: I am sworn brother, sweet,
To grim Necessity, and he and I
Will keep a league till death. Hie thee to France,
And cloister thee in some religious house:
Our holy lives must win a new world's crown,
Which our profane hours here have stricken
25   down.

QUEEN What! is my Richard both in shape and mind
Transformed and weakened? Hath Bolingbroke
Deposed thine intellect? Hath he been in thy heart?
The lion dying thrusteth forth his paw
30   And wounds the earth, if nothing else, with rage
To be o'erpow'red, and wilt thou, pupil-like,
Take the correction mildly, kiss the rod,
And fawn on Rage with base humility,
Which art a lion and the king of beasts?

35   RICHARD A king of beasts indeed: if aught but beasts,
I had been still a happy king of men.
Good sometimes queen, prepare thee hence for
France.
Think I am dead, and that even here thou takest
As from my deathbed thy last living leave.
40   In winter's tedious nights sit by the fire
With good old folks, and let them tell thee tales
Of woeful ages long ago betid;
And ere thou bid good night, to quite their griefs
Tell thou the lamentable tale of me,
45   And send the hearers weeping to their beds.
For why, the senseless brands will sympathize
The heavy accent of thy moving tongue,
And in compassion weep the fire out:
And some will mourn in ashes, some coal-black,

23 **religious house** convent   25 **our profane ... down** our careless lives have
endangered our hopes of heaven   37 **sometimes** sometime, former   42 **betid**
happened   43 **quite their griefs** requite, or cap, their tragic stories   46 **For
why** because of this   46 **sympathize** correspond to   49 **some** (of the brands)

For the deposing of a rightful king.   50

Enter Northumberland.

NORTHUMBERLAND My lord, the mind of Bolingbroke is
    changed:
You must to Pomfret, not unto the Tower.
And, madam, there is order ta'en for you:
With all swift speed you must away to France.

RICHARD Northumberland, thou ladder wherewithal   55
    The mounting Bolingbroke ascends my throne,
The time shall not be many hours of age
More than it is, ere foul sin, gathering head,
Shall break into corruption. Thou shalt think,
Though he divide the realm and give thee half,   60
It is too little, helping him to all;
He shall think that thou which knowest the way
To plant unrightful kings, wilt know again,
Being ne'er so little urged another way,
To pluck him headlong from the usurped throne.   65
The love of wicked men converts to fear,
That fear to hate, and hate turns one or both
To worthy danger and deservèd death.

NORTHUMBERLAND My guilt be on my head, and there
    an end.
Take leave and part, for you must part forthwith.   70

RICHARD Doubly divorced! Bad men, you violate
A twofold marriage: 'twixt my crown and me,
And then betwixt me and my married wife.
Let me unkiss the oath 'twixt thee and me—
And yet not so, for with a kiss 'twas made.   75
Part us, Northumberland; I towards the north,
Where shivering cold and sickness pines the clime;

---

52 **Pomfret** Pontefract Castle, in Yorkshire   53 **there is order ta'en** arrangements have been made   58 **gathering head** (metaphor from a boil)   61 **helping him** seeing that you helped him   63 **know** know how   66 **converts** changes   68 **worthy** deserved   69 **there an end** i.e., that's all I have to say   70 **part, for you must part** part from your queen, for you must depart   77 **pines** causes to pine

My wife to France, from whence, set forth in
   pomp,
She came adornèd hither like sweet May,
80   Sent back like Hallowmas, or short'st of day.

QUEEN And must we be divided? Must we part?

RICHARD Ay, hand from hand, my love, and heart
   from heart.

QUEEN Banish us both, and send the King with me.

RICHARD That were some love, but little policy.

85   QUEEN Then whither he goes, thither let me go.

RICHARD So two together weeping make one woe.
Weep thou for me in France, I for thee here;
Better far off than, near, be ne'er the near.
Go count thy way with sighs, I mine with groans.

90   QUEEN So longest way shall have the longest moans.

RICHARD Twice for one step I'll groan, the way being
   short,
And piece the way out with a heavy heart.
Come, come, in wooing sorrow, let's be brief,
Since, wedding it, there is such length in grief.
95   One kiss shall stop our mouths, and dumbly part:
Thus give I mine, and thus take I thy heart.

QUEEN Give me mine own again, 'twere no good part
To take on me to keep and kill thy heart.
So now I have mine own again, be gone,
100   That I may strive to kill it with a groan.

RICHARD We make woe wanton with this fond delay:
Once more adieu, the rest let sorrow say.

Exeunt, [different ways].

---

80 **Hallowmas** Nov. 1   80 **short'st of day** Dec. 22   88 **ne'er the near** never
the nearer (proverbial)   92 **piece the way out** lengthen (with possible pun on
"pace")   94 **Since ... grief** we are wedded to sorrow till death and shall have
plenty of time to grieve   101 **wanton** unrestrained (with secondary sense of
promiscuous)

[Scene II. *The Duke of York's palace.*]

Enter Duke of York and the Duchess.

DUCHESS My lord, you told me you would tell the
          rest,
When weeping made you break the story off,
Of our two cousins' coming into London.

YORK Where did I leave?

DUCHESS   At that sad stop, my lord,
Where rude misgoverned hands from windows'
          tops   5
Threw dust and rubbish on King Richard's head.

YORK Then, as I said, the Duke, great Bolingbroke,
Mounted upon a hot and fiery steed,
Which his aspiring rider seemed to know,
With slow but stately pace kept on his course,   10
Whilst all tongues cried "God save thee,
          Bolingbroke!"
You would have thought the very windows spake:
So many greedy looks of young and old
Through casements darted their desiring eyes
Upon his visage; and that all the walls   15
With painted imagery had said at once,
"Jesu preserve thee! Welcome, Bolingbroke!"
Whilst he, from the one side to the other turning,
Bareheaded, lower than his proud steed's neck,
Bespake them thus: "I thank you, countrymen."   20
And thus still doing, thus he passed along.

V.ii.5 **rude misgoverned** uncivilized and wrongly directed   9 **rider seemed to
know** seemed to know his rider   16 **painted imagery** painted cloths, resembling
tapestry

DUCHESS Alack, poor Richard! Where rode he the
        whilst?

YORK As in a theater the eyes of men,
25   After a well-graced actor leaves the stage,
        Are idly bent on him that enters next,
        Thinking his prattle to be tedious;
        Even so, or with much more contempt, men's eyes
        Did scowl on gentle Richard; no man cried "God
            save him!"
        No joyful tongue gave him his welcome home,
30   But dust was thrown upon his sacred head;
        Which with such gentle sorrow he shook off,
        His face still combating with tears and smiles,
        The badges of his grief and patience,
        That had not God for some strong purpose steeled
        The hearts of men, they must perforce have
35   melted,
        And barbarism itself have pitied him.
        But heaven hath a hand in these events,
        To whose high will we bound our calm contents.
        To Bolingbroke are we sworn subjects now,
40   Whose state and honor I for aye allow.

                    [Enter Aumerle.]

DUCHESS Here comes my son, Aumerle.

YORK   Aumerle that was,
        But that is lost for being Richard's friend;
        And, madam, you must call him Rutland now.
        I am in Parliament pledge for his truth
45   And lasting fealty to the new-made king.

DUCHESS Welcome, my son; who are the violets now
        That strew the green lap of the new-come spring?

AUMERLE Madam, I know not, nor I greatly care not.

24 **well-graced** accomplished 25 **idly** without interest 31 **gentle** noble
33 **badges** signs 35 **perforce** inevitably 38 **bound our calm contents** limit
our wishes to calm content 40 **aye** ever 44 **truth** loyalty 46 **violets** favorites
in the new court

God knows I had as lief be none as one.

YORK Well, bear you well in this new spring of time,   50
Lest you be cropped before you come to prime.
What news from Oxford? Do these jousts and
   triumphs hold?

AUMERLE For aught I know, my lord, they do.

YORK You will be there, I know.

AUMERLE If God prevent me not, I purpose so.   55

YORK What seal is that that hangs without thy
   bosom?
Yea, look'st thou pale? Let me see the writing.

AUMERLE My lord, 'tis nothing.

YORK   No matter, then, who see it.
I will be satisfied: let me see the writing.

AUMERLE I do beseech your Grace to pardon me: 60
It is a matter of small consequence,
Which for some reasons I would not have seen.

YORK Which for some reasons, sir, I mean to see.
I fear, I fear—

DUCHESS   What should you fear?
'Tis nothing but some band that he is ent'red
   into
For gay apparel 'gainst the triumph day.   65

YORK Bound to himself? What doth he with a bond
That he is bound to? Wife, thou art a fool.
Boy, let me see the writing.

AUMERLE I do beseech you, pardon me. I may not
   show it.   70

YORK I will be satisfied. Let me see it, I say!

49 **had as lief** would find it as pleasant   52 **Oxford** (cf. line 99) Aumerle would
give a start   52 **Do ... hold** will these tournaments and triumphal celebrations be
held   56 **seal** (which would be hanging from the document on an attached strip of
parchment)   65 **band** bond   66 **'gainst** in preparation for

He plucks it out of his bosom and reads it.

Treason, foul treason, villain, traitor, slave!

DUCHESS What is the matter, my lord?

YORK Ho, who is within there? Saddle my horse.
75   God for his mercy! What treachery is here!

DUCHESS Why, what is it, my lord?

YORK Give me my boots, I say! Saddle my horse!
Now, by mine honor, by my life, my troth,
I will appeach the villain.

DUCHESS   What is the matter?

80 YORK Peace, foolish woman.

DUCHESS I will not peace. What is the matter,
Aumerle?

AUMERLE Good mother, be content; it is no more
Than my poor life must answer.

DUCHESS   Thy life answer?

YORK Bring me my boots: I will unto the King.

His man enters with his boots.

DUCHESS Strike him, Aumerle. Poor boy, thou art
85   amazed.
Hence, villain, never more come in my sight.

YORK Give me my boots, I say.

DUCHESS Why, York, what wilt thou do?
Wilt thou not hide the trespass of thine own?
90   Have we more sons? Or are we like to have?
Is not my teeming date drunk up with time?
And wilt thou pluck my fair son from mine age?
And rob me of a happy mother's name?
Is he not like thee? Is he not thine own?

95 YORK Thou fond, mad woman,
Wilt thou conceal this dark conspiracy?

75 **God for his mercy** Lord have mercy upon us   79 **appeach** peach, inform
against   85 **amazed** dazed   91 **teeming date** time of childbearing   95 **fond**
foolish

A dozen of them here have ta'en the sacrament
And interchangeably set down their hands
To kill the King at Oxford.

DUCHESS   He shall be none;
We'll keep him here. Then what is that to him?   100

YORK Away, fond woman, were he twenty times my
     son,
I would appeach him.

DUCHESS   Had'st thou groaned for him
As I have done, thou would'st be more pitiful.
But now I know thy mind; thou dost suspect
That I have been disloyal to thy bed,   105
And that he is a bastard, not thy son:
Sweet York, sweet husband, be not of that mind;
He is as like thee as a man may be,
Not like to me, or any of my kin,
And yet I love him.

YORK   Make way, unruly woman.   110

                                        Exit.

DUCHESS After, Aumerle! Mount thee upon his horse;
Spur, post, and get before him to the King,
And beg thy pardon ere he do accuse thee.
I'll not be long behind; though I be old,
I doubt not but to ride as fast as York;   115
And never will I rise up from the ground
Till Bolingbroke have pardoned thee. Away!
Be gone!   [*Exeunt.*]

98 interchangeably reciprocally   112 post hasten

[Scene III. *Windsor Castle.*]

Enter [Bolingbroke, now] the King, with his
Nobles [Percy and others].

BOLINGBROKE Can no man tell me of my unthrifty
    son?
'Tis full three months since I did see him last.
If any plague hang over us, 'tis he.
I would to God, my lords, he might be found:
5   Inquire at London, 'mongst the taverns there,
For there, they say, he daily doth frequent
With unrestrainèd loose companions,
Even such, they say, as stand in narrow lanes,
And beat our watch and rob our passengers;
10   While he, young wanton and effeminate boy,
Takes on the point of honor to support
So dissolute a crew.

PERCY My lord, some two days since I saw the Prince,
And told him of those triumphs held at Oxford.

15 BOLINGBROKE And what said the gallant?

PERCY His answer was, he would unto the stews,
And from the commonest creature pluck a glove,
And wear it as a favor, and with that
He would unhorse the lustiest challenger.

20 BOLINGBROKE As dissolute as desperate; but yet
Through both I see some sparks of better hope,
Which elder years may happily bring forth.

V.iii.1 **unthrifty** prodigal   1 **son** (Prince Hal of *Henry IV*)   3 **plague** (he is thinking of the prophecies of Richard and Carlisle)   9 **watch** watchmen   9 **passengers** wayfarers   10 **effeminate** voluptuous   11 **Takes on the point of honor** undertakes as a point of honor   16 **stews** brothels   21 **both** i.e., dissoluteness and desperateness

But who comes here?

Enter Aumerle, amazed.

AUMERLE   Where is the King?

BOLINGBROKE   What means
Our cousin, that he stares and looks so wildly?

AUMERLE God save your Grace! I do beseech your
    Majesty   25
To have some conference with your Grace
    alone.

BOLINGBROKE Withdraw yourselves, and leave us here
    alone.

                    [Exeunt Percy and Lords.]
What is the matter with our cousin now?

AUMERLE For ever may my knees grow to the earth,

                [Kneels.]

My tongue cleave to my roof within my mouth,   30
Unless a pardon ere I rise or speak.

BOLINGBROKE Intended, or committed, was this fault?
If on the first, how heinous e'er it be,
To win thy after-love I pardon thee.

AUMERLE Then give me leave that I may turn the key,   35
That no man enter till my tale be done.

BOLINGBROKE Have thy desire.

    [Aumerle locks the door.] The Duke of
    York knocks at the door and crieth.

YORK *[Within]* My liege, beware, look to
    thyself:
Thou hast a traitor in thy presence there.

BOLINGBROKE Villain, I'll make thee safe.   40

      [Draws his sword.]

AUMERLE Stay thy revengeful hand; thou hast no cause
    to fear.

26 **conference** conversation   31 **Unless a pardon** unless I have a pardon
33 **on the first** of the former kind   40 **safe** harmless (by killing him)

YORK Open the door, secure, foolhardy King!
　　Shall I for love speak treason to thy face?
　　Open the door, or I will break it open.

[Bolingbroke opens.]

[Enter York.]

45 BOLINGBROKE What is the matter, uncle? Speak.

[He relocks door.]

Recover breath. Tell us, how near is danger,
That we may arm us to encounter it.

YORK Peruse this writing here, and thou shalt know
　　The treason that my haste forbids me show.

AUMERLE Remember, as thou read'st, thy promise
50 　　passed.
　　I do repent me, read not my name there;
　　My heart is not confederate with my hand.

YORK It was, villain, ere thy hand did set it down.
　　I tore it from the traitor's bosom, King:
55 　Fear, and not love, begets his penitence.
　　Forget to pity him, lest thy pity prove
　　A serpent that will sting thee to the heart.

BOLINGBROKE O heinous, strong and bold
　　conspiracy!
　　O loyal father of a treacherous son!
60 Thou sheer immaculate and silver fountain,
　　From whence this stream, through muddy passages,
　　Hath held his current, and defiled himself,
　　Thy overflow of good converts to bad;
　　And thy abundant goodness shall excuse
65 This deadly blot in thy digressing son.

YORK So shall my virtue be his vice's bawd,
　　And he shall spend mine honor with his shame,

42 **secure** overconfident   43 **treason** (by calling him a fool)   49 **haste forbids**
(because he is out of breath)   50 **passed** given   56 **Forget** forget your promise
58 **strong** dangerous   62 **his** its   62 **himself** itself   63 **converts** changes
65 **digressing** transgressing

As thriftless sons their scraping fathers' gold.
Mine honor lives when his dishonor dies,
Or my shamed life in his dishonor lies.   70
Thou kill'st me in his life, giving him breath;
The traitor lives, the true man's put to death.

DUCHESS [*Within*] What ho! My liege, for God's
    sake, let me in!

BOLINGBROKE What shrill-voiced suppliant makes this
    eager cry?

DUCHESS A woman, and thy aunt, great King—'tis I.   75
Speak with me, pity me, open the door;
A beggar begs that never begged before.

BOLINGBROKE Our scene is alt'red from a serious thing,
And now changed to "The Beggar and the King."
My dangerous cousin, let your mother in: 80
I know she is come to pray for your foul sin.

[*Aumerle unlocks door during York's speech.*]

YORK If thou do pardon, whosoever pray,
More sins for this forgiveness prosper may.

[*Enter Duchess.*]

This fest'red joint cut off, the rest rest sound;
This let alone will all the rest confound.   85

DUCHESS O King, believe not this hardhearted man:
Love loving not itself, none other can.

YORK Thou frantic woman, what dost thou make
    here?
Shall thy old dugs once more a traitor rear?

DUCHESS Sweet York, be patient. Hear me, gentle
    liege.   90

[*Kneels.*]

68 scraping parsimonious 79 The Beggar and the King (referring to the title, but not to the contents, of the ballad about King Cophetua and the Beggar Maid) 82 whosoever pray whoever prays 84 rest rest those that remain stay 87 Love ... can i.e., if he does not love his son he cannot love anyone, even you 89 rear raise him to life (with a pun on the usual sense)

BOLINGBROKE Rise up, good aunt.

DUCHESS   Not yet, I thee beseech.
   For ever will I walk upon my knees,
   And never see day that the happy sees,
   Till thou give joy—until thou bid me joy—
95   By pardoning Rutland, my transgressing boy.

AUMERLE Unto my mother's prayers I bend my knee.

               [Kneels.]

YORK Against them both my true joints bended be;

               [Kneels.]

   Ill may'st thou thrive, if thou grant any grace.

DUCHESS Pleads he in earnest? Look upon his face.
100 His eyes do drop no tears, his prayers are in jest;
   His words come from his mouth, ours from our
      breast;
   He prays but faintly, and would be denied;
   We pray with heart and soul, and all beside;
   His weary joints would gladly rise, I know;
105 Our knees still kneel till to the ground they grow;
   His prayers are full of false hypocrisy,
   Ours of true zeal and deep integrity;
   Our prayers do outpray his—then let them have
   That mercy which true prayer ought to have.

BOLINGBROKE Good aunt, stand up.

110 DUCHESS   Nay, do not say "Stand up";
   Say "Pardon" first, and afterwards "Stand up";
   And if I were thy nurse thy tongue to teach,
   "Pardon" should be the first word of thy speech.
   I never longed to hear a word till now.
115 Say "Pardon," King; let pity teach thee how.
   The word is short, but not so short as sweet:
   No word like "pardon" for kings' mouths so meet.

YORK Speak it in French, King; say "Pardonne
   moy."

118 **Pardonne** moy pray excuse me, i.e., "No" (moy rhymes with **destroy**)

DUCHESS Dost thou teach pardon pardon to destroy?
  Ah, my sour husband, my hardhearted lord!   120
  That sets the word itself against the word.
  Speak "Pardon" as 'tis current in our land:
  The chopping French we do not understand.
  Thine eye begins to speak; set thy tongue there,
  Or in thy piteous heart plant thou thine ear,   125
  That hearing how our plaints and prayers do
    pierce,
  Pity may move thee "Pardon" to rehearse.

BOLINGBROKE Good aunt, stand up.

DUCHESS   I do not sue to stand.
  Pardon is all the suit I have in hand.

BOLINGBROKE I pardon him as God shall pardon me.   130

DUCHESS O, happy vantage of a kneeling knee!
  Yet am I sick for fear; speak it again.
  Twice saying "Pardon" doth not pardon twain,
  But makes one pardon strong.

BOLINGBROKE   With all my heart
  I pardon him.

DUCHESS [Standing]   A god on earth thou art.   135

        [York and Aumerle rise.]

BOLINGBROKE But for our trusty brother-in-law, and
  the abbot,
  With all the rest of that consorted crew,
  Destruction straight shall dog them at the heels.
  Good uncle, help to order several powers
  To Oxford, or where'er these traitors are;   140
  They shall not live within this world, I swear,
  But I will have them if I once know where.
  Uncle, farewell, and cousin, too, adieu.

123 **chopping** changing the meaning of words   127 **rehearse** repeat (a perfect rhyme with "pierce" in the 16th century)   129 **suit** (1) suit of cards (2) petition   132 **Yet** still   133 **twain** (1) two people (2) divide   135 **god on earth** (the Homilies taught this; and, as Portia says, "earthly power doth then show likest God's/When mercy seasons justice")   136 **trusty** (ironical)   136 **brother-in-law** (Duke of Exeter, Richard's half-brother, who had married Bolingbroke's sister)

Your mother well hath prayed, and prove you true.

145 DUCHESS Come, my old son, I pray God make thee new.   *Exeunt.*

[Scene IV. *Windsor Castle.*]

Enter Sir Pierce Exton & [a Man].

EXTON Didst thou not mark the King, what words he spake?
"Have I no friend will rid me of this living fear?"
Was it not so?

MAN   These were his very words.

EXTON "Have I no friend?" quoth he: he spake it
5   twice,
And urged it twice together, did he not?

MAN He did.

EXTON And speaking it, he wishtly looked on me,
As who should say, "I would thou wert the man
That would divorce this terror from my heart"—
10   Meaning the King at Pomfret. Come, let's go:
I am the King's friend, and will rid his foe.

                                      [*Exeunt.*]

144 true loyal   145 old unregenerate   V.iv.7 wishtly (probably "wishfully," with an undertone of "wistly," i.e., intently)

[Scene V. *Pomfret Castle*.]

Enter Richard alone.

RICHARD I have been studying how I may compare
This prison where I live unto the world:
And for because the world is populous,
And here is not a creature but myself,
I cannot do it. Yet I'll hammer it out: 5
My brain I'll prove the female to my soul,
My soul the father, and these two beget
A generation of still-breeding thoughts;
And these same thoughts people this little world,
In humors like the people of this world,   10
For no thought is contented. The better sort,
As thoughts of things divine are intermixed
With scruples, and do set the word itself
Against the word; as thus: "Come, little ones";
And then again,   15
"It is as hard to come as for a camel
To thread the postern of a small needle's eye."
Thoughts tending to ambition, they do plot
Unlikely wonders: how these vain weak nails
May tear a passage through the flinty ribs   20
Of this hard world, my ragged prison walls;
And, for they cannot, die in their own pride.
Thoughts tending to content flatter themselves
That they are not the first of fortune's slaves,
Nor shall not be the last, like seely beggars   25
Who sitting in the stocks refuge their shame,

V.v.8 **generation** offspring 8 **still** constantly 10 **humors** psychological
characteristics 13 **scruples** doubts 14 **word** passage of Scripture 14 **Come,
little ones** Matthew 19:14ff. 17 **needle's** (monosyllabic) 16–17 **It ... eye**
Matthew 19:24ff. 21 **ragged** rugged 22 **for** because 22 **pride** prime
25 **seely** (silly) simple-minded 26 **refuge** protect themselves from

That many have, and others must, sit there;
And in this thought they find a kind of ease,
Bearing their own misfortunes on the back
30 Of such as have before endured the like.
Thus play I in one person many people,
And none contented; sometimes am I king,
Then treasons make me wish myself a beggar,
And so I am. Then crushing penury
35 Persuades me I was better when a king.
Then am I kinged again and, by and by,
Think that I am unkinged by Bolingbroke,
And straight am nothing. But whate'er I be,
Nor I, nor any man that but man is,
40 With nothing shall be pleased, till he be eased
With being nothing.

                    The music plays.

                 Music do I hear.
Ha—ha! Keep time! How sour sweet music is
When time is broke, and no proportion kept;
So is it in the music of men's lives:
45 And here have I the daintiness of ear
To check time broke in a disordered string,
But for the concord of my state and time,
Had not an ear to hear my true time broke.
I wasted time, and now doth Time waste me:
For now hath Time made me his numb'ring
50   clock;
My thoughts are minutes, and with sighs they jar
Their watches on unto mine eyes, the outward
        watch
Whereto my finger, like a dial's point,
Is pointing still, in cleansing them from tears.

39-41 **nor any man ... nothing** i.e., man is never content until he is no more   43 **proportion** musical time   46 **check** rebuke   46 **disordered** out of its place, a bar wrong   47 **time** the times   49 **time** measured duration   49 **Time** Father Time   50 **numb'ring** counting hours and minutes   51 **jar** tick (of a clock), making a discord   52 **watches** intervals of time   52 **outward watch** dial (with pun on a man keeping watch)   53 **dial's point** hand of clock   54 **still** continually

Now, sir, the sound that tells what hour it is   55
Are clamorous groans which strike upon my
    heart,
Which is the bell. So sighs, and tears, and groans,
Show minutes, times, and hours; but my time
Runs posting on in Bolingbroke's proud joy,
While I stand fooling here, his Jack-of-the-clock.   60
This music mads me: let it sound no more.
For though it have holp madmen to their wits,
In me it seems it will make wise men mad.
Yet blessing on his heart that gives it me,
For 'tis a sign of love; and love to Richard   65
Is a strange brooch in this all-hating world.

Enter a Groom of the stable.

GROOM Hail, royal Prince!

RICHARD   Thanks, noble peer!
The cheapest of us is ten groats too dear.
What art thou? And how comest thou hither,
Where no man never comes, but that sad dog   70
That brings me food to make misfortune live?

GROOM I was a poor groom of thy stable, King,
When thou wert King, who, traveling towards
    York,
With much ado at length have gotten leave
To look upon my sometimes royal master's face.   75
O, how it erned my heart, when I beheld
In London streets, that coronation day,
When Bolingbroke rode on roan Barbary,
That horse that thou so often hast bestrid,
That horse that I so carefully have dressed.   80

---

60 **Jack-of-the-clock** mannikin to strike the hours   62 **holp** helped   66 **strange brooch** rare jewel   67 **royal ... noble** (a royal was worth ten shillings, a noble six shillings and eight pence; a groat, fourpence. Richard is saying that to call him "royal" now is to price him too high, since he is now the peer, the equal of the groom)   71 **make misfortune live** perpetuate my unfortunate life   75 **sometimes** former   76 **erned** grieved   78 **Barbary** (here the name of the horse, as well as the breed)   80 **dressed** groomed

RICHARD Rode he on Barbary? Tell me, gentle friend,
How went he under him?

GROOM So proudly as if he disdained the ground.

RICHARD So proud that Bolingbroke was on his back!
85   That jade hath eat bread from my royal hand;
This hand hath made him proud with clapping
    him.
Would he not stumble? Would he not fall down,
Since pride must have a fall, and break the neck
Of that proud man that did usurp his back?
90   Forgiveness, horse! Why do I rail on thee,
Since thou created to be awed by man
Wast born to bear? I was not made a horse,
And yet I bear a burden like an ass,
Spurred, galled, and tired by jauncing Boling-
broke.

Enter one, [a Keeper,] to Richard with meat.

95 KEEPER Fellow, give place; here is no longer stay.

RICHARD If thou love me, 'tis time thou wert away.

GROOM What my tongue dares not, that my heart
shall say.   *Exit Groom.*

KEEPER My lord, wilt please you to fall to?

RICHARD Taste of it first, as thou art wont to do.

100 KEEPER My lord, I dare not; Sir Pierce of Exton
Who lately came from the King, commands the
contrary.

RICHARD The devil take Henry of Lancaster, and thee!
Patience is stale, and I am weary of it.

KEEPER Help, help, help!

*The murderers [Exton and Servants]
rush in.*

81 **gentle** (implying groom is of gentle birth) 86 **clapping** patting 94 **galled**
made sore 94 **jauncing** making the horse prance (and perhaps himself prancing
and triumphant) 98 **fall to** start eating 99 **Taste** (he suspects poison)

RICHARD How now! What means Death in this rude
    assault?   105
  Villain, thy own hand yields thy death's instrument.

    [Snatches a weapon and kills one.]

  Go thou, and fill another room in hell!

    [He kills another.] Here Exton strikes
         him down.

  That hand shall burn in never-quenching fire
  That staggers thus my person. Exton, thy fierce
    hand
  Hath with the King's blood stained the King's own
    land.   110
  Mount, mount, my soul; thy seat is up on high,
  Whilst my gross flesh sinks downward here to die.

    [Dies.]

EXTON As full of valor as of royal blood!
  Both have I spilled. O, would the deed were good!
  For now the devil that told me I did well   115
  Says that this deed is chronicled in hell.
  This dead king to the living king I'll bear.
  Take hence the rest, and give them burial here.

                  [Exeunt with the bodies.]

[Scene VI. *Windsor Castle.*]

    [Flourish.] Enter Bolingbroke with the
  Duke of York, [other Lords and Attendants].

BOLINGBROKE Kind uncle York, the latest news we
    hear
  Is that the rebels have consumed with fire

---

105 **What ... assault?** what does death mean by assaulting me so violently?
107 **room** place   109 **staggers** makes to stagger

Our town of Ciceter in Gloucestershire,
But whether they be ta'en or slain we hear not.

Enter Northumberland.

5   Welcome, my lord; what is the news?

NORTHUMBERLAND First, to thy sacred state wish I all
    happiness;
The next news is, I have to London sent
The heads of Salisbury, Spencer, Blunt, and Kent.
The manner of their taking may appear
10   At large discoursèd in this paper here.

BOLINGBROKE We thank thee, gentle Percy, for thy
    pains,
And to thy worth will add right worthy gains.

Enter Lord Fitzwater.

FITZWATER My lord, I have from Oxford sent to
    London
The heads of Brocas and Sir Bennet Seely,
15   Two of the dangerous consorted traitors
That sought at Oxford thy dire overthrow.

BOLINGBROKE Thy pains, Fitzwater, shall not be
    forgot:
Right noble is thy merit well I wot.

Enter Henry Percy [and the Bishop of Carlisle].

PERCY The grand conspirator, Abbot of Westminster,
20   With clog of conscience and sour melancholy,
Hath yielded up his body to the grave;
But here is Carlisle living, to abide
Thy kingly doom, and sentence of his pride.

BOLINGBROKE Carlisle, this is your doom:
Choose out some secret place, some reverend
25   room

V.vi.3 **Ciceter** Cirencester 7 **next** most important 8 **Spencer, Blunt, and
Kent** Lord Spencer, formerly Earl of Gloucester; Sir Thomas Blunt; Earl of Kent
12 **right worthy gains** well-deserved reward 14 **Brocas** Sir Leonard (or
Bernard) Brocas 15 **consorted** associated 25 **reverend room** place of religious
retirement

More than thou hast, and with it joy thy life.
So as thou liv'st in peace, die free from strife;
For though mine enemy thou hast ever been,
High sparks of honor in thee have I seen.

Enter Exton with [Attendants bearing]
the coffin.

EXTON Great King, within this coffin I present   30
Thy buried fear: herein all breathless lies
The mightiest of thy greatest enemies,
Richard of Bordeaux, by me hither brought.

BOLINGBROKE Exton, I thank thee not, for thou hast wrought
A deed of slander with thy fatal hand   35
Upon my head and all this famous land.

EXTON From your own mouth, my lord, did I this deed.

BOLINGBROKE They love not poison that do poison need,
Nor do I thee; though I did wish him dead,
I hate the murderer, love him murderèd.
The guilt of conscience take thou for thy labor,   40
But neither my good word, nor princely favor.
With Cain go wander thorough shades of night,
And never show thy head by day nor light.
                                [Exit Exton.]
Lords, I protest, my soul is full of woe,   45
That blood should sprinkle me to make me grow.
Come, mourn with me for what I do lament,
And put on sullen black incontinent.
I'll make a voyage to the Holy Land,
To wash this blood off from my guilty hand.   50
March sadly after; grace my mournings here,
In weeping after this untimely bier.

                                [Exeunt.]
FINIS

26 **More than thou hast** i.e., more religious and less political   26 **joy** enjoy
27 **So** provided that   31 **buried fear** (cf. living fear, V.iv.2)   33 **Bordeaux**
(Richard's birthplace)   48 **incontinent** forthwith

Textual Note

Richard II was first published in 1597, after 29 August, when it was registered. The First Quarto (Q1) appeared with the following title page: "THE/ Tragedie of King Ri-/ chard the se-/ cond./ *As it hath beene publikely acted/ by the right Honourable the/ Lorde Chamberlaine his Ser-/ uants./* LONDON/ Printed by Valentine Simmes for Androw Wise, and/ are to be sold at his shop in Paules church yard at/ the signe of the Angel./ 1597."

The play is thought to have been printed from a transcript of Shakespeare's manuscript, but it may preserve some of his spelling and punctuation. Some critics (Cairncross, Brooks, Ure) think that the text is memorially contaminated in a few places (i.e., the transcriber introduced mistakes through his memory of other lines of the play and also of *Richard III*). The First Quarto forms the basis of the present edition, except for the abdication scene, which was omitted from the first three quartos and included in the Fourth (1608). The play was included in the First Folio (1623), probably from a corrected text of Q5 (1615). The Folio text (F) enables us to correct Q1 in a number of places, and it provides the best text of the abdication scene; but many of its readings are "sophistications"—unnecessary alterations—for which Shakespeare was not responsible.

The present edition modernizes spelling and punctuation, amplifies abbreviations and regularizes speech prefixes, corrects obvious typographical errors, adjusts the position of stage directions, and in a few cases alters the lineation. Q1 is not divided into acts or scenes; the present edition uses the divisions established by the Globe editors, who used those of F but who added one at V.iv. F indicates the divisions in Latin; they are translated here. Other deviations from Q1 (and for the abdication scene from F) are listed below. The adopted reading is given in bold; if it is not taken from F a note in a bracket explains that it is taken (for example) from Q 5 or (again, for example) from an editor's emendation—indicated by [ed]. Next is given the original reading in roman.

I.i.118 **my scepter's** scepters 139 **But** Ah but 152 **gentlemen** Gentleman 162 **When ... when?** When Harry? when obedience bids 192 **parle** parlee

I.ii.47 **sit** set 58 **it** is

I.iii.26 **demand of** [ed] ask 33 **comest** [Q5] comes 84 **innocency** [ed] innocence 172 **then** but but 180 **you owe** y'owe 221 **night** nightes 238 **had it** [ed] had't

I.iv.1 s.d. **Bagot** [ed] Bushie 20 **cousin, cousin** Coosens Coosin 23 **Bagot ... Green** [Q6] [Q1 omits; F has "heere Bagot and Greene"] 53 **Bushy, what news?** [Q1 omits, but prints the s.d. "Enter Bushie with newes"] 65 **All** [ed; Q and F omit]

II.i.18 **fond** [ed] found [the emendation to "fond" is plausible; but it is possible that "found" was an error caused by the similar endings of adjacent lines— "soundes" and "sound"—or that a line was omitted by mistake] 48 **as a** as 102 **incagèd** inraged 113 **not** [ed] not, not 124 **brother** [Q2] brothers 156 **kernes** kerne 177 **the** a 232 **that** that [ed] that 257 **King's** King 280 **The ... Arundel** [ed; Q and F omit] 283 **Thomas Ramston** [Holinshed] Iohn Ramston 284 **Quoint** Coines

II.ii.16 **eye** eyes 25 **more's** more is 31 **though** thought 53 **Henry** H 88 **cold** [ed] they are cold 112 **Th'one** Tone 137 **The ... will** [ed] Will the hateful commons

II.iii.36 **Hereford** Herefords 98 **the lord** lord

III.ii.32 **succor** [ed] succors 38 **and** [ed] that 40 **boldly** [ed] bouldy 72 **O'erthrows** Ouerthrowes

III.iii.13 **with you** to to 17 **mis-take** [ed] mistake 30 **lord** Lords 59 **waters—on** [ed] water's on 118 **prince and** [ed] princesse

III.iv.11 **joy** [ed] griefe 21 **good.** good? 26 **pins** pines 57 **We at** [ed] at 80 **Cam'st** Canst

IV.i.22 **him** them 54 **As** [ed] As it 55 **sun to sun** [ed] sinne to sinne 76 **my bond** bond 154–319 [for this passage, here printed from F, Q1 has only "Let it be so, and loe on wednesday next,/We solemnly proclaime our Coronation,/Lords be ready all"] 182 **and on** [Q4] on 182 **yours** [Q4] thine 250 **and** [Q4] a 254 **Nor** [Q4] No, nor 275 **the** [Q4] that 284 **was** [Q4] Is 284 **that** [Q4] which 285 **And** [Q4] That 288 **a** [Q4] an 295 **manners** [Q4] manner 322 **I will** [ed] Ile

TEXTUAL NOTE

V.i.25 **stricken** throwne

V.ii.55 **prevent me** [ed] preuent   78 **life, my** [ed] life, by my   116 **And** An

V.iii.10 **While** [ed] Which   20 **but yet** [ed] yet   35 **that I** that   67 **and an**
110 **Bolingbroke** Yorke   134–35 **With ... him** [ed] I pardon him with al my
heart   143 **cousin, too** [Q6] cousin

V.iv.1s.d. **Enter Manet**

V.v.27 **sit** set   79 **bestrid** bestride

V.vi.8 **Salisbury ... Blunt** Oxford, Salisbury, Blunt   12s.d. **Fitzwater** [Q6]
Fitzwaters   43 **thorough** [ed] through [Q] through the [F]

WILLIAM SHAKESPEARE

THE HISTORY OF HENRY IV
PART ONE

Edited by Maynard Mack

KING HENRY THE FOURTH

HENRY, Prince of Wales

PRINCE JOHN OF LANCASTER   }   the King's sons

EARL OF WESTMORELAND

SIR WALTER BLUNT

THOMAS PERCY, Earl of Worcester

HENRY PERCY, Earl of Northumberland

HENRY PERCY ("HOTSPUR"), his son

EDMUND MORTIMER, Earl of March

RICHARD SCROOP, Archbishop of York

ARCHIBALD, Earl of Douglas

OWEN GLENDOWER

SIR RICHARD VERNON

SIR JOHN FALSTAFF

SIR MICHAEL, a friend of the Archbishop of York

POINS

GADSHILL

PETO

BARDOLPH

FRANCIS, a waiter

LADY PERCY, Hotspur's wife and Mortimer's sister

LADY MORTIMER, Glendower's daughter and Mortimer's wife

MISTRESS QUICKLY, hostess of the tavern

SHERIFF, VINTNER, CHAMBERLAIN, TWO CARRIERS, OSTLER, MESSENGERS, TRAVELERS, ATTENDANTS

Scene: England and Wales]

THE HISTORY OF
HENRY IV
[PART ONE]

[ACT I

Scene I. *London. The palace.*]

Enter the King, Lord John of Lancaster, Earl of
Westmoreland, [Sir Walter Blunt,] with others.

KING So shaken as we are, so wan with care,
    Find we a time for frighted peace to pant
    And breathe short-winded accents of new broils
    To be commenced in stronds afar remote.
    No more the thirsty entrance of this soil   5
    Shall daub her lips with her own children's blood,
    No more shall trenching war channel her fields,
    Nor bruise her flow'rets with the armèd hoofs
    Of hostile paces. Those opposèd eyes
    Which, like the meteors of a troubled heaven,   10
    All of one nature, of one substance bred,
    Did lately meet in the intestine shock
    And furious close of civil butchery,
    Shall now in mutual well-beseeming ranks
    March all one way and be no more opposed   15
    Against acquaintance, kindred, and allies.

Text references are printed in **boldface** type; the annotation follows in roman type.
I.i.2 **pant** catch (her) breath 4 **stronds** shores 7 **trenching** (1) cutting (2) encroaching 10 **meteors** atmospheric disturbances 11 **All ... bred** i.e., because believed to originate from vapors 12 **intestine** internal 13 **close** grappling 14 **mutual well-beseeming** interdependent well-ordered

The edge of war, like an ill-sheathèd knife,
No more shall cut his master. Therefore, friends,
As far as to the sepulcher of Christ—
20 Whose soldier now, under whose blessèd cross
We are impressèd and engaged to fight—
Forthwith a power of English shall we levy,
Whose arms were molded in their mother's womb
To chase these pagans in those holy fields
25 Over whose acres walked those blessèd feet
Which fourteen hundred years ago were nailed
For our advantage on the bitter cross.
But this our purpose now is twelvemonth old,
And bootless 'tis to tell you we will go.
30 Therefor we meet not now. Then let me hear
Of you, my gentle cousin Westmoreland,
What yesternight our council did decree
In forwarding this dear expedience.

WESTMORELAND My liege, this haste was hot in
        question
35 And many limits of the charge set down
But yesternight; when all athwart there came
A post from Wales, loaden with heavy news,
Whose worst was that the noble Mortimer,
Leading the men of Herefordshire to fight
40 Against the irregular and wild Glendower,
Was by the rude hands of that Welshman taken,
A thousand of his people butcherèd;
Upon whose dead corpse there was such misuse,
Such beastly shameless transformation
45 By those Welshwomen done, as may not be
Without much shame retold or spoken of.

19 As ... Christ i.e., to Jerusalem 21 impressèd and engaged conscripted and
pledged (i.e., by Henry's vow after the murder of Richard: cf. *Richard II*,
V.vi.45-50) 22 power army 29 bootless useless 30 Therefor ... now that is
not the reason we now meet 31 gentle cousin noble kinsman 33 dear
expedience urgent enterprise 34 hot in question undergoing hot discussion
35 limits of the charge apportionings of tasks and costs 36 athwart crosswise,
i.e., interfering 37 post messenger 40 irregular and wild i.e., as border-raider
and guerrilla 43-46 such ... spoken of (the phrasing in Holinshed, Shakespeare's source, suggests that the dead English were castrated)

KING It seems then that the tidings of this broil
   Brake off our business for the Holy Land.

WESTMORELAND This, matched with other, did, my
     gracious lord;
   For more uneven and unwelcome news   50
   Came from the north, and thus it did import:
   On Holy-rood Day the gallant Hotspur there,
   Young Harry Percy, and brave Archibald,
   That ever-valiant and approvèd Scot,
   At Holmedon met, where they did spend   55
   A sad and bloody hour;
   As by discharge of their artillery
   And shape of likelihood the news was told;
   For he that brought them, in the very heat
   And pride of their contention did take horse,   60
   Uncertain of the issue any way.

KING Here is a dear, a true industrious friend,
   Sir Walter Blunt, new lighted from his horse,
   Stained with the variation of each soil
   Betwixt that Holmedon and this seat of ours,   65
   And he hath brought us smooth and welcome news.
   The Earl of Douglas is discomfited;
   Ten thousand bold Scots, two and twenty knights,
   Balked in their own blood did Sir Walter see
   On Holmedon's plains. Of prisoners, Hotspur took   70
   Mordake, Earl of Fife and eldest son
   To beaten Douglas, and the Earl of Athol,
   Of Murray, Angus, and Menteith.
   And is not this an honorable spoil?
   A gallant prize? Ha, cousin, is it not?   75

WESTMORELAND In faith it is. A conquest for a prince
     to boast of.

---

50 **uneven** cf. "smooth," line 66 52 **Holy-rood Day** September 14
55 **Holmedon** Humbleton in Northumberland 58 **shape of likelihood**
probability 59 **them** i.e., the news 59-60 **heat … contention** peak of battle
61 **issue** outcome 62 **true industrious** loyally zealous 65 **seat** dwelling, i.e.,
the palace 69 **Balked** (1) heaped (2) thwarted

KING Yea, there thou mak'st me sad, and mak'st me sin
In envy that my Lord Northumberland
Should be the father to so blest a son:
80   A son who is the theme of honor's tongue,
Amongst a grove the very straightest plant;
Who is sweet fortune's minion and her pride;
Whilst I, by looking on the praise of him,
See riot and dishonor stain the brow
85   Of my young Harry. O that it could be proved
That some night-tripping fairy had exchanged
In cradle clothes our children where they lay,
And called mine Percy, his Plantagenet!
Then would I have his Harry, and he mine.
90   But let him from my thoughts. What think you, coz,
Of this young Percy's pride? The prisoners
Which he in this adventure hath surprised
To his own use he keeps, and sends me word
I shall have none but Mordake, Earl of Fife.

WESTMORELAND This is his uncle's teaching, this is
95   Worcester,
Malevolent to you in all aspects,
Which makes him prune himself and bristle up
The crest of youth against your dignity.

KING But I have sent for him to answer this;
100   And for this cause awhile we must neglect
Our holy purpose to Jerusalem.
Cousin, on Wednesday next our council we
Will hold at Windsor, so inform the lords:
But come yourself with speed to us again,
105   For more is to be said and to be done
Than out of anger can be utterèd.

WESTMORELAND I will, my liege.   *Exeunt.*

---

82 **minion** darling   86 **fairy** (fairies were thought sometimes to steal a beautiful infant, leaving an ugly "changeling" in its place   88 **Plantagenet** family name of Henry IV   90 **coz** kinsman (short for "cousin")   92 **surprised** taken   96 **Malevolent** ... **aspects** (an astrological expression comparing Worcester to a planet whose influence obstructs Henry's designs)   97 **prune** preen his feathers for action (like a hawk)   106 **utterèd** transacted in public

[Scene II. *London. The Prince's lodging.*]

Enter Prince of Wales and Sir John Falstaff.

FALSTAFF Now, Hal, what time of day is it, lad?

PRINCE Thou art so fat-witted with drinking of old sack, and unbuttoning thee after supper, and sleeping upon benches after noon, that thou hast forgotten to demand that truly which thou wouldest truly know. What a devil hast thou to do with the time of the day? Unless hours were cups of sack, and minutes capons, and clocks the tongues of bawds, and dials the signs of leaping houses, and the blessed sun himself a fair hot wench in flame-colored taffeta, I see no reason why thou shouldst be so superfluous to demand the time of the day.   5   10

FALSTAFF Indeed you come near me now, Hal; for we that take purses go by the moon and the seven stars, and not by Phoebus, he, that wand'ring knight so fair. And I prithee, sweet wag, when thou art a king, as, God save thy Grace—Majesty I should say, for grace thou wilt have none—   15

PRINCE What, none?

I.ii.3 **sack** Spanish white wine 9 **dials** sundials 9 **leaping houses** brothels 12 **so superfluous** to so irrelevant as to 13 **near me** i.e., close to understanding me (as if Hal were shooting at a mark) 14 **go by** (1) walk under (2) tell time by (3) regulate our lives by 14-15 **seven stars** constellation Pleiades 15 **Phoebus** the sun 15-16 **he ... fair** (Falstaff possibly quotes here, or sings, a line of a lost ballad; the sun was readily thought of as an eternal wanderer or "knight-errant") 17 **Grace** (Falstaff puns on "your Grace"—a title which Hal as king will exchange for "your Majesty"—and spiritual grace and, in lines 20-21, on grace before eating)

20   FALSTAFF No, by my troth; not so much as will serve
      to be prologue to an egg and butter.

      PRINCE Well, how then? Come, roundly, roundly.

      FALSTAFF Marry, then, sweet wag, when thou art king,
      let not us that are squires of the night's body be
25   called thieves of the day's beauty. Let us be
      Diana's foresters, gentlemen of the shade, minions
      of the moon; and let men say we be men of good
      government, being governed, as the sea is, by our
      noble and chaste mistress the moon, under whose
30   countenance we steal.

      PRINCE Thou sayest well, and it holds well too; for
      the fortune of us that are the moon's men doth ebb
      and flow like the sea, being governed as the sea is
      by the moon. As, for proof now: a purse of gold
35   most resolutely snatched on Monday night and most
      dissolutely spent on Tuesday morning; got with
      swearing "Lay by," and spent with crying "Bring
      in"; now in as low an ebb as the foot of the ladder,
      and by and by in as high a flow as the ridge of the
40   gallows.

      FALSTAFF By the Lord, thou say'st true, lad—and is
      not my hostess of the tavern a most sweet wench?

---

22 **roundly** i.e., get to the point (but possibly with a glance at Falstaff's girth)
23 **Marry** (a mild oath, from "By the Virgin Mary")   24-25 **squires ... beauty**
(Falstaff's puns on "night/knight"—knights were often attended by body-
squires—and probably on "body/beauty/booty." The "day's beauty" in one of its
senses here is the sun and balances "the night's body," which in one sense is the
moon)   26 **Diana** goddess of the moon and the hunt (by identifying the hunt with
hunting for "booty"—and "beauty"—Falstaff presents himself and his crew as
Diana's companion foresters, her titled "Gentlemen of the Shade," her "minions,"
who "steal"—i.e., [1] move silently [2] take purses under her "countenance"—i.e.,
under [1] her face [2] her protection)   26 **minions** servants and favorites
27-28 **of good government** (1) well-behaved (2) ruled by a good ruler   31 **it
holds well** it's a good comparison   37-38 **Lay by ... Bring in** (the highwayman's commands: the first to his victims, the second to the waiter in the tavern
where he spends his gains)   38 **ladder** (leading up to the gallows)

PRINCE As the honey of Hybla, my old lad of the
castle—and is not a buff jerkin a most sweet robe
of durance?   45

FALSTAFF How now, how now, mad wag? What, in thy
quips and thy quiddities? What a plague have I to
do with a buff jerkin?

PRINCE Why, what a pox have I to do with my
hostess of the tavern?   50

FALSTAFF Well, thou hast called her to a reckoning
many a time and oft.

PRINCE Did I ever call for thee to pay thy part?

FALSTAFF No; I'll give thee thy due, thou hast paid all
there.   55

PRINCE Yea, and elsewhere, so far as my coin would
stretch; and where it would not, I have used my
credit.

FALSTAFF Yea, and so used it that, were it not here apparent that thou art heir apparent—But I prithee,   60
sweet wag, shall there be gallows standing in England
when thou art king? And resolution thus fubbed
as it is with the rusty curb of old father Antic the
law? Do not thou, when thou art king, hang a thief.

PRINCE No; thou shalt.   65

FALSTAFF Shall I? O rare! By the Lord, I'll be a brave
judge.

---

43 **Hybla** Sicilian source of fine honey   43-44 **old lad of the castle** rowdy (with
pun on "Oldcastle," Falstaff's original name, and probably on "The Castle," a
well-known London brothel)   44 **buff jerkin** tan (leather) jacket (a "robe of
durance" because both durable and suggesting imprisonment [durance] because
worn by the sheriff's officers)   46-47 **What ... quiddities** "So you're in a witty
mood, are you?"   49 **pox** (the Prince turns Falstaff's "plague" into a disease more
characteristic of tavern hostesses)   51 **called her to a reckoning** (1) called her to
a showdown (2) asked her for the bill   62 **resolution thus fubbed** courage (i.e.,
in the highwayman) thus cheated of its reward   63 **old father Antic** i.e., "that
old screwball"   66 **brave** (1) excellent (2) handsomely decked out

PRINCE Thou judgest false already. I mean, thou shalt
have the hanging of the thieves and so become a rare
70   hangman.

FALSTAFF Well, Hal, well; and in some sort it jumps
with my humor as well as waiting in the court, I
can tell you.

PRINCE For obtaining of suits?

75   FALSTAFF Yea, for obtaining of suits, whereof the
hangman hath no lean wardrobe. 'Sblood, I am as
melancholy as a gib-cat or a lugged bear.

PRINCE Or an old lion, or a lover's lute.

FALSTAFF Yea, or the drone of a Lincolnshire bagpipe.

80   PRINCE What sayest thou to a hare, or the melancholy
of Moorditch?

FALSTAFF Thou hast the most unsavory similes, and
art indeed the most comparative, rascalliest, sweet
young prince. But, Hal, I prithee trouble me no
85   more with vanity. I would to God thou and I knew
where a commodity of good names were to be
bought. An old lord of the council rated me the
other day in the street about you, sir, but I marked
him not; and yet he talked very wisely, but I re-
90   garded him not; and yet he talked wisely, and in the
street too.

71-72 jumps with my humor agrees with my frame of mind   74 suits petitions
for court favor (but Falstaff takes it in the sense of the victim's garments, which
were forfeit to the executioner)   76 'Sblood by God's (i.e., Christ's) blood
77 gib-cat tomcat   77 lugged i.e., tied to a stake and baited by dogs, as
entertainment   79 drone single note of a bagpipe's bass pipe   80 hare (prover-
bially melancholy)   81 Moorditch foul London drainage ditch   83 comparative full of (insulting) comparisons   85 vanity i.e., worldly considerations
(Falstaff here takes up one of his favorite humorous roles, assuming for the next
several lines the sanctimonious attitudes and vocabulary of Elizabethan
Puritanism)   86 commodity supply   87 rated scolded

PRINCE Thou didst well, for wisdom cries out in the
streets, and no man regards it.

FALSTAFF O, thou hast damnable iteration, and art
indeed able to corrupt a saint. Thou hast done much   95
harm upon me, Hal—God forgive thee for it! Before I knew thee, Hal, I knew nothing; and now
am I, if a man should speak truly, little better than
one of the wicked. I must give over this life, and
I will give it over! By the Lord, and I do not, I   100
am a villain! I'll be damned for never a king's son
in Christendom.

PRINCE Where shall we take a purse tomorrow, Jack?

FALSTAFF Zounds, where thou wilt, lad! I'll make one.
An I do not, call me villain and baffle me.   105

PRINCE I see a good amendment of life in thee—from
praying to purse-taking.

FALSTAFF Why, Hal, 'tis my vocation, Hal. 'Tis no sin
for a man to labor in his vocation.

Enter Poins.

Poins! Now shall we know if Gadshill have set a   110
match. O, if men were to be saved by merit, what
hole in hell were hot enough for him? This is the
most omnipotent villain that ever cried "Stand!" to
a true man.

92-93 **Thou ... it** (Hal quotes Proverbs 1:20-24: "Wisdom crieth without, and
putteth forth her voice in the streets ... saying ... 'I have stretched out my hand,
and no man regarded' ")   94 **damnable iteration** i.e., a sinful way of repenting
and (mis)applying holy texts   99 **the wicked** (Puritan idiom for those who were
not Puritans; cf. "saint" in 95, which glances at the Puritans' way of referring
collectively to themselves)   100 **and** if   104 **Zounds** by God's (i.e., Christ's)
wounds   105 **An** if   105 **baffle** hang upside down (a punishment allotted
perjured knights)   108 **vocation** calling (with reference to the Puritan stress on a
man's being "called" by God to his work)   110-11 **set a match** arranged a
robbery   111 **merit** i.e., good works (in Puritan doctrine wholly insufficient for
salvation)   114 **true** honest

115 PRINCE Good morrow, Ned.

POINS Good morrow, sweet Hal. What says Monsieur Remorse? What says Sir John Sack and Sugar? Jack, how agrees the devil and thee about thy soul, that thou soldest him on Good Friday last for a cup
120 of Madeira and a cold capon's leg?

PRINCE Sir John stands to his word, the devil shall have his bargain; for he was never yet a breaker of proverbs. He will give the devil his due.

POINS Then art thou damned for keeping thy word
125 with the devil.

PRINCE Else he had been damned for cozening the devil.

POINS But, my lads, my lads, tomorrow morning, by four o'clock early, at Gad's Hill! There are pil-
130 grims going to Canterbury with rich offerings, and traders riding to London with fat purses. I have vizards for you all; you have horses for yourselves. Gadshill lies tonight in Rochester. I have bespoke supper tomorrow night in Eastcheap. We may do
135 it as secure as sleep. If you will go, I will stuff your purses full of crowns; if you will not, tarry at home and be hanged!

FALSTAFF Hear ye, Yedward: if I tarry at home and go not, I'll hang you for going.

140 POINS You will, chops?

FALSTAFF Hal, wilt thou make one?

PRINCE Who, I rob? I a thief? Not I, by my faith.

FALSTAFF There's neither honesty, manhood, nor good

---

117 **Sack and Sugar** (sack sweetened with sugar was particularly the drink of the elderly, but there may be a pun, in this context, on sackcloth, symbol of penance) 126 **cozening** cheating 129 **Gad's Hill** (a place notorious for hold-ups on the road from Rochester to London) 130 **offerings** i.e., for the shrine of St. Thomas à Becket 132 **vizards** masks 134 **Eastcheap** London street and district 138 **Yedward** (dialect form of Edward) 140 **chops** "fat-face"

fellowship in thee, nor thou cam'st not of the blood
royal if thou darest not stand for ten shillings.   145

PRINCE Well then, once in my days I'll be a madcap.

FALSTAFF Why, that's well said.

PRINCE Well, come what will, I'll tarry at home.

FALSTAFF By the Lord, I'll be a traitor then, when
thou art king.   150

PRINCE I care not.

POINS Sir John, I prithee, leave the Prince and me
alone. I will lay him down such reasons for this
adventure that he shall go.

FALSTAFF Well, God give thee the spirit of persuasion   155
and him the ears of profiting, that what thou speakest may move and what he hears may be believed,
that the true prince may (for recreation sake) prove
a false thief; for the poor abuses of the time want
countenance. Farewell; you shall find me in East-   160
cheap.

PRINCE Farewell, the latter spring! Farewell, All-
hallow summer!   [*Exit Falstaff.*]

POINS Now, my good sweet honey lord, ride with us
tomorrow. I have a jest to execute that I cannot   165
manage alone. Falstaff, Bardolph, Peto, and Gadshill
shall rob those men that we have already waylaid;
yourself and I will not be there; and when they have
the booty, if you and I do not rob them, cut this
head off from my shoulders.   170

PRINCE How shall we part with them in setting forth?

145 royal (pun on "royal," a ten-shilling coin)   145 stand for (1) pass for (as a
coin) (2) contest for (in a robbery)   155-57 God ... move (mimicry again of the
Puritans, who claimed to act only when the spirit moved in them)   159-60 want
countenance lack protection (royal and aristocratic)   162 the (sometimes used in
the sixteenth century for "thou" and "you")   162-63 All-hallow summer
(Poins compares Falstaff's youthfulness in old age to the belated summer that
occurs around All Hallows day)   167 waylaid set our trap for

POINS Why, we will set forth before or after them and
appoint them a place of meeting, wherein it is at our
pleasure to fail; and then will they adventure upon
175 the exploit themselves, which they shall have no
sooner achieved, but we'll set upon them.

PRINCE Yea, but 'tis like that they will know us by our
horses, by our habits, and by every other appointment, to be ourselves.

180 POINS Tut! Our horses they shall not see—I'll tie them
in the wood; our vizards we will change after we
leave them; and, sirrah, I have cases of buckram
for the nonce, to immask our noted outward garments.

185 PRINCE Yea, but I doubt they will be too hard for us.

POINS Well, for two of them, I know them to be as
true-bred cowards as ever turned back; and for the
third, if he fight longer than he sees reason, I'll
forswear arms. The virtue of this jest will be the
190 incomprehensible lies that this same fat rogue will
tell us when we meet at supper: how thirty, at least,
he fought with; what wards, what blows, what ex-
tremities he endured; and in the reproof of this
lives the jest.

195 PRINCE Well, I'll go with thee. Provide us all things
necessary and meet me tomorrow night in Eastcheap. There I'll sup. Farewell.

POINS Farewell, my lord.   *Exit.*

PRINCE I know you all, and will awhile uphold
200   The unyoked humor of your idleness.

---

178 **habits** dress   178-79 **appointment** piece of equipment   182 **sirrah** (term
of address showing great familiarity)   182-83 **cases ... nonce** outer coverings of
coarse linen for the purpose   185 **doubt** fear   190 **incomprehensible**
unlimited   192 **wards** strategies of defense (in swordsmanship)   193 **reproof**
disproof   196 **tomorrow night** (they will meet for the robbery tomorrow
morning, but Hal is thinking ahead to the jest on Falstaff that night)
200 **unyoked humor** undisciplined inclinations

Yet herein will I imitate the sun,
Who doth permit the base contagious clouds
To smother up his beauty from the world,
That, when he please again to be himself,
Being wanted, he may be more wond'red at   205
By breaking through the foul and ugly mists
Of vapors that did seem to strangle him.
If all the year were playing holidays,
To sport would be as tedious as to work;
But when they seldom come, they wished-for come,   210
And nothing pleaseth but rare accidents.
So when this loose behavior I throw off
And pay the debt I never promisèd,
By how much better than my word I am,
By so much shall I falsify men's hopes;   215
And, like bright metal on a sullen ground,
My reformation, glitt'ring o'er my fault,
Shall show more goodly and attract more eyes
Than that which hath no foil to set it off.
I'll so offend to make offense a skill,   220
Redeeming time when men think least I will.   *Exit*.

---

201 **sun** (royalty's traditional symbol)   202 **contagious** (clouds were thought to breed pestilence)   205 **wanted** lacked, missed   211 **rare accidents** unexpected or uncommon events   215 **hopes** expectations   216 **sullen** dull   219 **foil** contrasting background   221 **Redeeming time** making amends (Hal alludes to Ephesians 5:7ff, which bears in a general way on much that has been said in this scene: "Be not ye therefore partakers with them, for ye were sometimes darkness, but now are ye light in the Lord: walk as children of light.... See then that ye walk circumspectly, not as fools, but as wise. Redeeming the time, because the days are evil").

[Scene III. *Windsor. The council chamber.*]

Enter the King, Northumberland, Worcester,
Hotspur, Sir Walter Blunt, with others.

KING My blood hath been too cold and temperate,
Unapt to stir at these indignities,
And you have found me, for accordingly
You tread upon my patience; but be sure
5   I will from henceforth rather be myself,
Mighty and to be feared, than my condition,
Which hath been smooth as oil, soft as young down,
And therefore lost that title of respect
Which the proud soul ne'er pays but to the proud.

WORCESTER Our house, my sovereign liege, little
10   deserves
The scourge of greatness to be used on it—
And that same greatness too which our own hands
Have holp to make so portly.

NORTHUMBERLAND   My lord—

KING Worcester, get thee gone, for I do see
15   Danger and disobedience in thine eye.
O, sir, your presence is too bold and peremptory,
And majesty might never yet endure
The moody frontier of a servant brow.
You have good leave to leave us: when we need
20   Your use and counsel, we shall send for you.
                                            Exit Worcester.
You were about to speak.

I.iii.3 **found me** found me out   5 **myself** i.e., what I am as king   6 **my
condition** i.e., what I am by nature   13 **holp** helped   13 **portly** stately
18 **frontier** rampart (as if Worcester were an enemy fortress)

NORTHUMBERLAND   Yea, my good lord.
  Those prisoners in your Highness' name demanded
  Which Harry Percy here at Holmedon took,
  Were, as he says, not with such strength denied
  As is deliverèd to your Majesty.   25
  Either envy, therefore, or misprision
  Is guilty of this fault, and not my son.

HOTSPUR My liege, I did deny no prisoners.
  But I remember, when the fight was done,
  When I was dry with rage and extreme toil,   30
  Breathless and faint, leaning upon my sword,
  Came there a certain lord, neat and trimly dressed,
  Fresh as a bridegroom, and his chin new reaped
  Showed like a stubble land at harvest home.
  He was perfumèd like a milliner,   35
  And 'twixt his finger and his thumb he held
  A pouncet box, which ever and anon
  He gave his nose, and took't away again;
  Who therewith angry, when it next came there,
  Took it in snuff; and still he smiled and talked;   40
  And as the soldiers bore dead bodies by,
  He called them untaught knaves, unmannerly,
  To bring a slovenly unhandsome corse
  Betwixt the wind and his nobility.
  With many holiday and lady terms   45
  He questioned me, amongst the rest demanded
  My prisoners in your Majesty's behalf.
  I then, all smarting with my wounds being cold,
  To be so pest'red with a popingay,
  Out of my grief and my impatience   50
  Answered neglectingly, I know not what—
  He should, or he should not; for he made me mad
  To see him shine so brisk, and smell so sweet,

26 envy malice 26 misprision misapprehension 33 reaped i.e., with the
closely clipped beard of a man of fashion 37 pouncet box perfume box
39 Who i.e., his nose 40 Took it in snuff (proverbial, meaning "took offense,"
but here with pun on "snuffing" the perfume) 43 corse corpse 45 holiday
and lady fastidious and effeminate 46 questioned talked to 49 popingay
parrot (here, one who is gaudy in dress and chatters emptily) 50 grief pain

And talk so like a waiting gentlewoman
Of guns and drums and wounds—God save the
55   mark!—
And telling me the sovereignest thing on earth
Was parmacity for an inward bruise,
And that it was great pity, so it was,
This villainous saltpeter should be digged
60   Out of the bowels of the harmless earth,
Which many a good tall fellow had destroyed
So cowardly, and but for these vile guns,
He would himself have been a soldier.
This bald unjointed chat of his, my lord,
65   I answered indirectly, as I said,
And I beseech you, let not his report
Come current for an accusation
Betwixt my love and your high Majesty.

BLUNT The circumstances considerèd, good my lord,
70   Whate'er Lord Harry Percy then had said
To such a person, and in such a place,
At such a time, with all the rest retold,
May reasonably die, and never rise
To do him wrong, or any way impeach
75   What then he said, so he unsay it now.

KING Why, yet he doth deny his prisoners,
But with proviso and exception,
That we at our own charge shall ransom straight
His brother-in-law, the foolish Mortimer;
80   Who, on my soul, hath willfully betrayed
The lives of those that he did lead to fight
Against that great magician, damned Glendower—
Whose daughter, as we hear, that Earl of March
Hath lately married. Shall our coffers, then,
85   Be emptied to redeem a traitor home?

---

55 **God save the mark** (a ritual phrase originally used to invoke a blessing, but here expressing scorn) 56 **sovereignest** best 57 **parmacity** spermaceti (medicinal substance found in sperm whales) 61 **tall** stalwart 65 **indirectly** absently 67 **Come current** (1) be accepted (i.e., as of true coin) (2) intrude 74 **To do him wrong** i.e., to be held against him 75 **so** provided

Shall we buy treason, and indent with fears
When they have lost and forfeited themselves?
No, on the barren mountains let him starve!
For I shall never hold that man my friend
Whose tongue shall ask me for one penny cost   90
To ransom home revolted Mortimer.

HOTSPUR Revolted Mortimer?
He never did fall off, my sovereign liege,
But by the chance of war. To prove that true
Needs no more but one tongue for all those wounds,   95
Those mouthèd wounds, which valiantly he took
When on the gentle Severn's sedgy bank,
In single opposition hand to hand,
He did confound the best part of an hour
In changing hardiment with great Glendower.   100
Three times they breathed, and three times did they
     drink,
Upon agreement, of swift Severn's flood;
Who then affrighted with their bloody looks
Ran fearfully among the trembling reeds
And hid his crisp head in the hollow bank,   105
Bloodstainèd with these valiant combatants.
Never did bare and rotten policy
Color her working with such deadly wounds;
Nor never could the noble Mortimer
Receive so many, and all willingly.   110
Then let not him be slanderèd with revolt.

KING Thou dost belie him, Percy, thou dost belie him!
He never did encounter with Glendower.
I tell thee, he durst as well have met the devil alone
As Owen Glendower for an enemy.   115

86 **indent** bargain 86 **fears** (1) cowards (2) traitors, i.e., those who by "fear"
have yielded to the enemy and so become traitors "to be feared" 96 **mouthèd
wounds** i.e., wounds that speak for him (based on the likeness of a bloody flesh
wound to a mouth) 99 **confound** spend 100 **changing hardiment**
battling 101 **breathed** paused for breath 103 **Who** i.e., the river 105 **crisp**
(used punningly to mean both "curled" [of a man's head] and "rippling" [of a
river]; "head" also refers punningly to a river's force) 107 **policy** cunning
108 **Color** (1) disguise (2) redden (i.e., with blood) 111 **revolt** treason
112 **belie** misrepresent

Art thou not ashamed? But, sirrah, henceforth
Let me not hear you speak of Mortimer.
Send me your prisoners with the speediest means,
Or you shall hear in such a kind from me
120 As will displease you. My Lord Northumberland,
We license your departure with your son.
Send us your prisoners, or you will hear of it.

Exit King, [with Blunt, and train].

HOTSPUR And if the devil come and roar for them,
I will not send them. I will after straight
125 And tell him so, for I will ease my heart,
Albeit I make a hazard of my head.

NORTHUMBERLAND What, drunk with choler? Stay, and
pause awhile.
Here comes your uncle.

Enter Worcester.

HOTSPUR   Speak of Mortimer?
Zounds, I will speak of him, and let my soul
130 Want mercy if I do not join with him!
Yea, on his part I'll empty all these veins,
And shed my dear blood drop by drop in the dust,
But I will lift the downtrod Mortimer
As high in the air as this unthankful king,
135 As this ingrate and cank'red Bolingbroke.

NORTHUMBERLAND Brother, the King hath made your
nephew mad.

WORCESTER Who struck this heat up after I was gone?

HOTSPUR He will forsooth have all my prisoners;
And when I urged the ransom once again
140 Of my wife's brother, then his cheek looked pale,
And on my face he turned an eye of death,
Trembling even at the name of Mortimer.

WORCESTER I cannot blame him. Was not he
proclaimed

116 **sirrah** (term of address to an inferior, here insulting) 123 **And if** if
126 **make a hazard of** risk 127 **choler** anger 135 **cank'red** infected 135 **Bolingbroke** i.e., the king

By Richard that dead is, the next of blood?

NORTHUMBERLAND He was, I heard the proclamation: 145
And then it was when the unhappy king
(Whose wrongs in us God pardon!) did set forth
Upon his Irish expedition;
From whence he intercepted did return
To be deposed, and shortly murderèd.   150

WORCESTER And for whose death we in the world's wide
    mouth
Live scandalized and foully spoken of.

HOTSPUR But soft, I pray you, did King Richard then
Proclaim my brother Edmund Mortimer
Heir to the crown?

NORTHUMBERLAND He did, myself did hear it.   155

HOTSPUR Nay, then I cannot blame his cousin king,
That wished him on the barren mountains starve.
But shall it be that you, that set the crown
Upon the head of this forgetful man,
And for his sake wear the detested blot   160
Of murderous subornation—shall it be
That you a world of curses undergo,
Being the agents or base second means,
The cords, the ladder, or the hangman rather?
O, pardon me that I descend so low   165
To show the line and the predicament
Wherein you range under this subtle king!
Shall it for shame be spoken in these days,
Or fill up chronicles in time to come,
That men of your nobility and power   170
Did gage them both in an unjust behalf
(As both of you, God pardon it, have done)
To put down Richard, that sweet lovely rose,

---

144 **next of blood** i.e., heir to the throne 147 **in us** at our hands
149 **intercepted** interrupted 161 **murderous subornation** confederacy in
murder 166 **line** degree, station (but also "hangman's rope" [cf. line 164] and
"tether" [cf. line 167]) 166 **predicament** category (but also "perilous
position") 171 **gage** pledge

And plant this thorn, this canker Bolingbroke?
175   And shall it in more shame be further spoken
That you are fooled, discarded, and shook off
By him for whom these shames ye underwent?
No, yet time serves wherein you may redeem
Your banished honors and restore yourselves
180   Into the good thoughts of the world again;
Revenge the jeering and disdained contempt
Of this proud king, who studies day and night
To answer all the debt he owes to you
Even with the bloody payment of your deaths.
Therefore I say—

185   WORCESTER   Peace, cousin, say no more;
And now I will unclasp a secret book,
And to your quick-conceiving discontents
I'll read you matter deep and dangerous,
As full of peril and adventurous spirit
190   As to o'erwalk a current roaring loud
On the unsteadfast footing of a spear.

HOTSPUR If he fall in, good night, or sink, or swim!
Send danger from east unto the west,
So honor cross it from the north to south,
195   And let them grapple. O, the blood more stirs
To rouse a lion than to start a hare!

NORTHUMBERLAND Imagination of some great exploit
Drives him beyond the bounds of patience.

HOTSPUR By heaven, methinks it were an easy leap
200   To pluck bright honor from the pale-faced moon,
Or dive into the bottom of the deep,
Where fathom line could never touch the ground,
And pluck up drownèd honor by the locks,
So he that doth redeem her thence might wear
205   Without corrival all her dignities;
But out upon this half-faced fellowship!

174 **canker** dog-rose (an inferior rose, but with suggestions of "cankerworm" and
"ulcer") 187 **quick-conceiving** eagerly responsive 192 **good … swim** i.e.,
the man is doomed whether he sinks at once or is swept away by the current
204 **So** provided 205 **corrival** partner 206 **out … fellowship** down with this
half-and-half sharing (of honors)

WORCESTER He apprehends a world of figures here,
    But not the form of what he should attend.
    Good cousin, give me audience for a while.

HOTSPUR I cry you mercy.   210

WORCESTER Those same noble Scots that are your
    prisoners—

HOTSPUR I'll keep them all.
    By God, he shall not have a Scot of them!
    No, if a Scot would save his soul, he shall not.
    I'll keep them, by this hand!

WORCESTER   You start away   215
    And lend no ear unto my purposes.
    Those prisoners you shall keep.

HOTSPUR   Nay, I will! That's flat!
    He said he would not ransom Mortimer,
    Forbade my tongue to speak of Mortimer,
    But I will find him when he lies asleep,   220
    And in his ear I'll hollo "Mortimer."
    Nay, I'll have a starling shall be taught to speak
    Nothing but "Mortimer," and give it him
    To keep his anger still in motion.

WORCESTER Hear you, cousin, a word.   225

HOTSPUR All studies here I solemnly defy
    Save how to gall and pinch this Bolingbroke;
    And that same sword-and-buckler Prince of Wales,
    But that I think his father loves him not
    And would be glad he met with some mischance,   230
    I would have him poisonèd with a pot of ale.

WORCESTER Farewell, kinsman: I'll talk to you
    When you are better tempered to attend.

---

207 **figures** (1) figures of speech (2) airy fancies (as opposed to substantial "form," line 208)   210 **cry you mercy** beg your pardon   214 **Scot** (pun on "scot," meaning "small payment")   226 **studies** interests   226 **defy** reject   228 **sword-and-buckler** "lowdown" (sword and shield were arms of the lower classes) 231 **ale** (a further glance at Hal's presumed low tastes, gentlemen's drink being wine)

NORTHUMBERLAND Why, what a wasp-stung and
        impatient fool
235   Art thou to break into this woman's mood,
        Tying thine ear to no tongue but thine own!

HOTSPUR Why, look you, I am whipped and scourged
        with rods,
        Nettled, and stung with pismires, when I hear
        Of this vile politician, Bolingbroke.
240   In Richard's time—what do you call the place?
        A plague upon it! It is in Gloucestershire;
        'Twas where the madcap duke his uncle kept,
        His uncle York—where I first bowed my knee
        Unto this king of smiles, this Bolingbroke—
245   'Sblood!—when you and he came back from
        Ravenspurgh—

NORTHUMBERLAND At Berkeley Castle.

HOTSPUR You say true.
        Why, what a candy deal of courtesy
        This fawning greyhound then did proffer me!
250   "Look when his infant fortune came to age,"
        And "gentle Harry Percy," and "kind cousin"—
        O, the devil take such cozeners!—God forgive me!
        Good uncle, tell your tale; I have done.

WORCESTER Nay, if you have not, to it again.
        We will stay your leisure.

255 HOTSPUR   I have done, i' faith.

WORCESTER Then once more to your Scottish prisoners:
        Deliver them up without their ransom straight,
        And make the Douglas' son your only mean
        For powers in Scotland—which, for divers reasons
260   Which I shall send you written, be assured
        Will easily be granted. [To Northumberland] You,
        my lord,

238 pismires ants   242 kept dwelt   245 Ravenspurgh harbor in Yorkshire
(where Hotspur's father had gone to take sides with Bolingbroke—who was
returning from exile on the Continent—against the absent King Richard II)
248 candy deal sugared bit   252 cozeners cheats (with pun on "cousin" of
previous line)

Your son in Scotland being thus employed,
Shall secretly into the bosom creep
Of that same noble prelate well-beloved,
The Archbishop.   265

HOTSPUR Of York, is it not?

WORCESTER True; who bears hard
His brother's death at Bristow, the Lord Scroop.
I speak not this in estimation,
As what I think might be, but what I know   270
Is ruminated, plotted, and set down,
And only stays but to behold the face
Of that occasion that shall bring it on.

HOTSPUR I smell it. Upon my life, it will do well.

NORTHUMBERLAND Before the game is afoot thou still
    let'st slip.   275

HOTSPUR Why, it cannot choose but be a noble plot.
    And then the power of Scotland and of York
    To join with Mortimer, ha?

WORCESTER   And so they shall.

HOTSPUR In faith, it is exceedingly well aimed.

WORCESTER And 'tis no little reason bids us speed 280
    To save our heads by raising of a head;
    For, bear ourselves as even as we can,
    The King will always think him in our debt,
    And think we think ourselves unsatisfied,
    Till he hath found a time to pay us home.   285
    And see already how he doth begin
    To make us strangers to his looks of love.

HOTSPUR He does, he does! We'll be revenged on him.

WORCESTER Cousin, farewell. No further go in this
    Than I by letters shall direct your course.   290

---

267 **bears hard** (because his brother had been executed by Henry) 268 **Bristow**
Bristol 269 **in estimation** as a guess 274 **smell it** i.e., like a hound catching
the scent 275 **let'st slip** let loose (the dogs) 281 **head** army 285 **home** i.e.,
with a "home" thrust

When time is ripe, which will be suddenly,
I'll steal to Glendower and Lord Mortimer,
Where you and Douglas, and our pow'rs at once,
As I will fashion it, shall happily meet,
295   To bear our fortunes in our own strong arms,
Which now we hold at much uncertainty.

NORTHUMBERLAND Farewell, good brother. We shall
   thrive, I trust.

HOTSPUR Uncle, adieu. O, let the hours be short
   Till fields and blows and groans applaud our sport!
                            Exeunt.

[ACT II

Scene I. *Rochester. An inn yard.*]

Enter a Carrier with a lantern in his hand.

FIRST CARRIER Heigh-ho! An it be not four by the day, I'll be hanged. Charles' wain is over the new chimney, and yet our horse not packed. What, ostler!

OSTLER [*Within*] Anon, anon.

FIRST CARRIER I prithee, Tom, beat Cut's saddle, put   5
a few flocks in the point; poor jade is wrung in the withers out of all cess.

Enter another Carrier.

SECOND CARRIER Peas and beans are as dank here as a dog, and that is the next way to give poor jades the bots. This house is turned upside down since Robin   10
Ostler died.

FIRST CARRIER Poor fellow never joyed since the price of oats rose; it was the death of him.

SECOND CARRIER I think this be the most villainous house in all London road for fleas, I am stung like   15
a tench.

II.i.1 **by the day** in the morning 2 **Charles' wain** the Great Bear 5 **beat** i.e., to soften it 6 **a few flocks in the point** a little padding in the pommel 6-7 **wrung in the withers** rubbed raw at the shoulders 7 **out of all cess** to excess 9 **next** nearest 10 **bots** worms 16 **tench** fish with red spots (as if flea-bitten)

FIRST CARRIER Like a tench? By the mass, there is ne'er
a king christen could be better bit than I have been
since the first cock.

20 SECOND CARRIER Why, they will allow us ne'er a jordan, and then we leak in your chimney, and your
chamber-lye breeds fleas like a loach.

FIRST CARRIER What, ostler! Come away and be hanged!
Come away!

25 SECOND CARRIER I have a gammon of bacon and two
razes of ginger, to be delivered as far as Charing
Cross.

FIRST CARRIER God's body! The turkeys in my pannier
are quite starved. What, ostler! A plague on thee,
30 hast thou never an eye in thy head? Canst not hear?
And 'twere not as good deed as drink to break the
pate on thee, I am a very villain. Come, and be
hanged! Hast no faith in thee?

Enter Gadshill.

GADSHILL Good morrow, carriers, what's o'clock?

35 FIRST CARRIER I think it be two o'clock.

GADSHILL I prithee lend me thy lantern to see my
gelding in the stable.

FIRST CARRIER Nay, by God, soft! I know a trick worth
two of that, i' faith.

40 GADSHILL I pray thee lend me thine.

SECOND CARRIER Ay, when? Canst tell? Lend me thy
lantern, quoth he? Marry, I'll see thee hanged first!

17-18 **there ... been** i.e., not even a Christian king (though kings get the best of
everything) could have surpassed my record in flea-bites   19 **the first cock**
midnight   20-21 **jordan** chamberpot   21 **chimney** fireplace   22 **chamber-lye**
urine   22 **loach** fish that breeds often   25 **gammon** haunch   26 **razes** roots
28 **pannier** basket   38 **soft** i.e., "listen to him!"   41 **Ay, when? Canst tell?**
(standard retort to an inopportune request)

GADSHILL Sirrah carrier, what time do you mean to come to London?

SECOND CARRIER Time enough to go to bed with a   45
candle, I warrant thee. Come, neighbor Mugs, we'll
call up the gentlemen, they will along with company,
for they have great charge.   *Exeunt [Carriers].*

GADSHILL What, ho! Chamberlain!

Enter Chamberlain.

CHAMBERLAIN "At hand, quoth pickpurse."   50

GADSHILL That's even as fair as "at hand, quoth the
chamberlain"; for thou variest no more from picking
of purses than giving direction doth from laboring:
thou layest the plot how.

CHAMBERLAIN Good morrow, Master Gadshill. It holds   55
current that I told you yesternight: there's a franklin in the Wild of Kent hath brought three hundred marks with him in gold, I heard him tell it to
one of his company last night at supper—a kind of
auditor, one that hath abundance of charge too,   60
God knows what. They are up already and call for
eggs and butter, they will away presently.

GADSHILL Sirrah, if they meet not with Saint Nicholas'
clerks, I'll give thee this neck.

CHAMBERLAIN No, I'll none of it; I pray thee keep that   65
for the hangman; for I know thou worshippest Saint
Nicholas as truly as a man of falsehood may.

GADSHILL What talkest thou to me of the hangman? If
I hang, I'll make a fat pair of gallows; for if I hang,

45-46 Time ... candle (evasively spoken, the carriers being suspicious of
Gadshill)   48 charge luggage   50 At hand (a popular tag meaning "Ready, sir!"
but relevant here to the Chamberlain's filching way of life, as Gadshill points
out)   56 current true   56-57 franklin rich farmer   57 Wild weald, open
country   57-58 three hundred marks £200 (Elizabethan value)   60 auditor
revenue officer   63-64 Saint Nicholas' clerks highwaymen (St Nicholas was
reckoned the patron of all travelers, including traveling thieves)

70 old Sir John hangs with me, and thou knowest he is
no starveling. Tut! There are other Troyans that
thou dream'st not of, the which for sport sake are
content to do the profession some grace; that would
(if matters should be looked into) for their own
75 credit sake make all whole. I am joined with no foot-
landrakers, no long-staff sixpenny strikers, none
of these mad mustachio purple-hued maltworms;
but with nobility and tranquillity, burgomasters and
great oneyers, such as can hold in, such as will
80 strike sooner than speak, and speak sooner than
drink, and drink sooner than pray—and yet, zounds,
I lie, for they pray continually to their saint, the commonwealth, or rather, not pray to her, but prey on
her, for they ride up and down on her and make her
85 their boots.

CHAMBERLAIN What, the commonwealth their boots?
Will she hold out water in foul way?

GADSHILL She will, she will! Justice hath liquored her.
We steal as in a castle, cocksure. We have the re-
90 ceipt of fernseed, we walk invisible.

CHAMBERLAIN Nay, by my faith, I think you are more
beholding to the night than to fernseed for your
walking invisible.

GADSHILL Give me thy hand. Thou shalt have a share
95 in our purchase, as I am a true man.

CHAMBERLAIN Nay, rather let me have it, as you are a
false thief.

---

71 **Troyans** good fellows   75-76 **foot-landrakers** footloose vagabonds
76 **long-staff sixpenny strikers** men who would pull you from your horse with
long staves even to steal sixpence   77 **mustachio purple-hued maltworms** big-
mustached purple-faced drunkards   78 **tranquillity** (Gadshill's witty coinage, on
the analogy of "nobility": people who don't have to scrounge their living)
79 **oneyers** ones (?)   79 **hold in** keep confidence   80 **speak** i.e., say "hands
up"   85 **boots** (with pun on "boots/booty")   87 **in foul way** on muddy
roads   88 **liquored** (1) greased (as with boots) (2) made her drunk
89-90 **receipt of fernseed** recipe of fernseed (popularly supposed to render one
invisible)   95 **purchase** (euphemism for loot)

GADSHILL Go to; "homo" is a common name to all
men. Bid the ostler bring my gelding out of the
stable. Farewell, you muddy knave.   [*Exeunt*.]   100

[Scene II. *The highway, near Gad's Hill*.]

Enter Prince, Poins, and Peto, etc.

POINS Come, shelter, shelter! I have removed Falstaff's
horse, and he frets like a gummed velvet.

PRINCE Stand close.   [*They step aside*.]

Enter Falstaff.

FALSTAFF Poins! Poins, and be hanged! Poins!

PRINCE [*Comes forward*] Peace, ye fat-kidneyed rascal!   5
What a brawling dost thou keep!

FALSTAFF Where's Poins, Hal?

PRINCE He is walked up to the top of the hill; I'll go
seek him.   [*Steps aside*.]

FALSTAFF I am accursed to rob in that thief's company.   10
The rascal hath removed my horse and tied him I
know not where. If I travel but four foot by the
squire further afoot, I shall break my wind. Well,
I doubt not but to die a fair death for all this, if I
scape hanging for killing that rogue. I have forsworn   15
his company hourly any time this two and twenty
years, and yet I am bewitched with the rogue's company. If the rascal have not given me medicines to
make me love him, I'll be hanged. It could not be
else: I have drunk medicines. Poins! Hal! A plague   20

98-99 homo ... men the Latin for man, *homo* is a term that covers all men, true
(i.e., honest) or false   II.ii.2 frets chafes (with pun on the fretting or fraying of
velvet as the gum used to stiffen it wore away)   13 squire rule

upon you both! Bardolph! Peto! I'll starve ere I'll
rob a foot further. And 'twere not as good a deed
as drink to turn true man and to leave these rogues,
I am the veriest varlet that ever chewed with a tooth.
25   Eight yards of uneven ground is threescore and ten
miles afoot with me, and the stony-hearted villains
know it well enough. A plague upon it when thieves
cannot be true one to another! (*They whistle.*)
Whew! A plague upon you all! Give me my horse,
30   you rogues! Give me my horse and be hanged!

PRINCE [*Comes forward*] Peace, ye fat-guts! Lie down,
lay thine ear close to the ground, and list if thou
canst hear the tread of travelers.

FALSTAFF Have you any levers to lift me up again, being
35   down? 'Sblood, I'll not bear mine own flesh so far
afoot again for all the coin in thy father's exchequer.
What a plague mean ye to colt me thus?

PRINCE Thou liest, thou art not colted, thou art uncolted.

40   FALSTAFF I prithee, good Prince Hal, help me to my
horse, good king's son.

PRINCE Out, ye rogue! Shall I be your ostler?

FALSTAFF Hang thyself in thine own heir-apparent garters! If I be ta'en, I'll peach for this. And I have
45   not ballads made on you all, and sung to filthy tunes,
let a cup of sack be my poison. When a jest is so
forward—and afoot too—I hate it.

Enter Gadshill [and Bardolph].

GADSHILL Stand!

FALSTAFF So I do, against my will.

---

21 **starve** die 37 **colt** trick 38-39 **uncolted** i.e., unhorsed 43-44 **heir-
apparent garters** (Falstaff adapts a proverbial phrase to fit a crown prince)
44 **peach** inform on you

POINS O, 'tis our setter; I know his voice. [*Comes*   50
forward] Bardolph, what news?

BARDOLPH Case ye, case ye! On with your vizards!
There's money of the King's coming down the hill;
'tis going to the King's exchequer.

FALSTAFF You lie, ye rogue! 'Tis going to the King's   55
tavern.

GADSHILL There's enough to make us all—

FALSTAFF To be hanged.

PRINCE Sirs, you four shall front them in the narrow
lane; Ned Poins and I will walk lower: if they scape   60
from your encounter, then they light on us.

PETO How many be there of them?

GADSHILL Some eight or ten.

FALSTAFF Zounds, will they not rob us?

PRINCE What, a coward, Sir John Paunch?   65

FALSTAFF Indeed, I am not John of Gaunt your grandfather, but yet no coward, Hal.

PRINCE Well, we leave that to the proof.

POINS Sirrah Jack, thy horse stands behind the hedge.
When thou need'st him, there thou shalt find him.   70
Farewell and stand fast.

FALSTAFF Now cannot I strike him, if I should be
hanged.

PRINCE [*Aside to Poins*] Ned, where are our disguises?

POINS [*Aside to Prince*] Here, hard by. Stand close.   75
[*Exeunt Prince and Poins.*]

---

50 **setter** one who makes arrangements for a robbery   66 **John of Gaunt** Hal's
grandfather (but in reply to "Sir John Paunch" Falstaff puns on "gaunt/thin"
which Hal evidently is [cf. II.iv.244-48])   68 **proof** test

FALSTAFF Now, my masters, happy man be his dole,
say I. Every man to his business.

Enter the Travelers.

TRAVELER Come, neighbor. The boy shall lead our
horses down the hill; we'll walk afoot awhile and
80　ease our legs.

THIEVES Stand!

TRAVELER Jesus bless us!

FALSTAFF Strike! Down with them! Cut the villains'
throats! Ah, whoreson caterpillars! Bacon-fed
85　knaves! They hate us youth. Down with them!
Fleece them!

TRAVELER O, we are undone, both we and ours forever!

FALSTAFF Hang ye, gorbellied knaves, are ye undone?
No, ye fat chuffs; I would your store were here!
90　On, bacons, on! What, ye knaves, young men must
live. You are grandjurors, are ye? We'll jure ye,
faith!　　*Here they rob them and bind them. Exeunt.*

Enter the Prince and Poins [disguised].

PRINCE The thieves have bound the true men. Now
could thou and I rob the thieves and go merrily to
95　London, it would be argument for a week, laughter
for a month, and a good jest forever.

POINS Stand close! I hear them coming.

[They stand aside.]

Enter the thieves again.

FALSTAFF Come, my masters, let us share, and then to
horse before day. And the Prince and Poins be not
100　two arrant cowards, there's no equity stirring.

76 **happy man be his dole** may happiness be our lot 84 **whoreson caterpillars** miserable parasites 88 **gorbellied** great-bellied 89 **chuffs** misers
89 **store** total wealth 91 **grandjurors** i.e., men of substance (as required for
service on a grand jury) 95 **be argument** make conversation 100 **arrant**
thorough 100 **no equity stirring** i.e., no justice left alive

There's no more valor in that Poins than in a wild
duck.

PRINCE Your money!

POINS Villains!

> *As they are sharing, the Prince
> and Poins set upon them.
> They all run away, and Fal-
> staff, after a blow or two,
> runs away too, leaving the
> booty behind them.*

PRINCE Got with much ease. Now merrily to horse. The   105
thieves are all scattered, and possessed with fear so
strongly that they dare not meet each other: each
takes his fellow for an officer. Away, good Ned. Falstaff sweats to death and lards the lean earth as he
walks along. Were't not for laughing, I should pity   110
him.

POINS How the fat rogue roared!   *Exeunt.*

[Scene III. *Northumberland. Warkworth Castle.*]

Enter Hotspur solus, reading a letter.

HOTSPUR "But, for mine own part, my lord, I could be
well contented to be there, in respect of the love I
bear your house." He could be contented—why is
he not then? In respect of the love he bears our
house! He shows in this he loves his own barn better   5
than he loves our house. Let me see some more. "The
purpose you undertake is dangerous"—why, that's
certain! 'Tis dangerous to take a cold, to sleep, to
drink; but I tell you, my lord fool, out of this nettle,
danger, we pluck this flower, safety. "The purpose   10
you undertake is dangerous, the friends you have

105-11 **Got ... him** (printed as verse by Pope and many later editors, with line
breaks after "horse/fear/other/officer/death/along/him") II.iii.s.d. **solus** alone
(Latin)   3 **house** family

named uncertain, the time itself unsorted, and your
whole plot too light for the counterpoise of so great
an opposition." Say you so, say you so? I say unto
you again, you are a shallow, cowardly hind, and
you lie. What a lack-brain is this! By the Lord, our
plot is a good plot as ever was laid; our friends true
and constant: a good plot, good friends, and full of
expectation; an excellent plot, very good friends.
What a frosty-spirited rogue is this! Why, my Lord
of York commends the plot and the general course
of the action. Zounds, and I were now by this rascal,
I could brain him with his lady's fan. Is there not my
father, my uncle, and myself; Lord Edmund Mortimer, my Lord of York, and Owen Glendower? Is
there not, besides, the Douglas? Have I not all their
letters to meet me in arms by the ninth of the next
month, and are they not some of them set forward
already? What a pagan rascal is this, an infidel! Ha!
you shall see now, in very sincerity of fear and cold
heart will he to the King and lay open all our proceedings. O, I could divide myself and go to buffets
for moving such a dish of skim milk with so honorable an action! Hang him, let him tell the King! We
are prepared. I will set forward tonight.

Enter his Lady.

How now, Kate? I must leave you within these two
hours.

LADY O my good lord, why are you thus alone?
For what offense have I this fortnight been
A banished woman from my Harry's bed?
Tell me, sweet lord, what is't that takes from thee
Thy stomach, pleasure, and thy golden sleep?
Why dost thou bend thine eyes upon the earth,
And start so often when thou sit'st alone?

---

12 **unsorted** unsuitable   15 **hind** menial   20-21 **my Lord of York** the Archbishop of York (cf. I.iii.264 ff)   29 **pagan** faithless   32 **divide ... buffets** split
myself into two, and set the halves fighting   42 **stomach** appetite

Why hast thou lost the fresh blood in thy cheeks   45
And given my treasures and my rights of thee
To thick-eyed musing and cursed melancholy?
In thy faint slumbers I by thee have watched,
And heard thee murmur tales of iron wars,
Speak terms of manage to thy bounding steed,   50
Cry "Courage! To the field!" And thou hast talked
Of sallies and retires, of trenches, tents,
Of palisadoes, frontiers, parapets,
Of basilisks, of cannon, culverin,
Of prisoners' ransom, and of soldiers slain,   55
And all the currents of a heady fight.
Thy spirit within thee hath been so at war,
And thus hath so bestirred thee in thy sleep,
That beads of sweat have stood upon thy brow
Like bubbles in a late-disturbèd stream,   60
And in thy face strange motions have appeared,
Such as we see when men restrain their breath
On some great sudden hest. O, what portents are
     these?
Some heavy business hath my lord in hand,
And I must know it, else he loves me not.   65

HOTSPUR What, ho!

[Enter a Servant.]

                    Is Gilliams with the packet gone?

SERVANT He is, my lord, an hour ago.

HOTSPUR Hath Butler brought those horses from the
     sheriff?

SERVANT One horse, my lord, he brought even now.

HOTSPUR What horse? A roan, a crop-ear, is it not?   70

SERVANT It is, my lord.

47 **cursed** peevish 48 **watched** lain awake 53 **palisadoes** defenses made of
stakes 53 **frontiers** fortifications 54 **basilisks, culverin** (sizes and types of
cannon) 56 **currents** occurrences 56 **heady** violent 63 **hest** (1) command?
(2) resolution?

HOTSPUR That roan shall be my throne. Well, I will
        back him straight. O Esperance! Bid Butler lead
        him forth into the park.

                                                [*Exit Servant.*]

75 LADY But hear you, my lord.

    HOTSPUR What say'st thou, my lady?

    LADY What is it carries you away?

    HOTSPUR Why, my horse, my love—my horse!

    LADY Out, you mad-headed ape! A weasel hath not
80   such a deal of spleen as you are tossed with. In
        faith, I'll know your business, Harry, that I will! I
        fear my brother Mortimer doth stir about his title
        and hath sent for you to line his enterprise; but if
        you go—

85 HOTSPUR So far afoot, I shall be weary, love.

    LADY Come, come, you paraquito, answer me directly
        unto this question that I ask. In faith, I'll break thy
        little finger, Harry, and if thou wilt not tell me all
        things true.

90 HOTSPUR Away, away, you trifler! Love? I love thee not;
        I care not for thee, Kate. This is no world
        To play with mammets and to tilt with lips.
        We must have bloody noses and cracked crowns,
        And pass them current too. Gods me, my horse!
        What say'st thou, Kate? What wouldst thou have
95   with me?

73 **Esperance** hope (part of the Percy motto)   72-74 **That ... park** (Pope and
many later editors print as verse; with line breaks after "throne/Esperance/
park"   77 **away** (1) i.e., from home (2) from your usual self   80 **spleen**
caprice   83 **line** strengthen   79-84 **Out ... go** (printed by Pope and many
later editors as verse, but with a variety of lineations)   86 **paraquito** parrot
86-89 **Come ... true** (printed by Pope and many later editors as verse, with
line breaks after "me/ask/Harry/true"   92 **mammets** dolls   92 **tilt** duel
93 **crowns** (1) heads (2) coins—which when "cracked" were hard to "pass
current" (possibly there is an allusion to the "crown" of kingship, which, though
not genuine when usurped, may be passed current by force)   94 **Gods me** God
save me

LADY Do you not love me? Do you not indeed?
  Well, do not then; for since you love me not,
  I will not love myself. Do you not love me?
  Nay, tell me if you speak in jest or no.

HOTSPUR Come, wilt thou see me ride?   100
  And when I am a-horseback, I will swear
  I love thee infinitely. But hark you, Kate:
  I must not have you henceforth question me
  Whither I go, nor reason whereabout.
  Whither I must, I must, and—to conclude,   105
  This evening must I leave you, gentle Kate.
  I know you wise—but yet no farther wise
  Than Harry Percy's wife; constant you are—
  But yet a woman; and for secrecy,
  No lady closer—for I well believe   110
  Thou wilt not utter what thou dost not know,
  And so far will I trust thee, gentle Kate—

LADY How? So far?

HOTSPUR Not an inch further. But hark you, Kate:
  Whither I go, thither shall you go too;   115
  Today will I set forth, tomorrow you.
  Will this content you, Kate?

LADY   It must of force. *Exeunt.*

[Scene IV. *Eastcheap. The tavern.*]

Enter Prince and Poins.

PRINCE Ned, prithee come out of that fat room and
  lend me thy hand to laugh a little.

POINS Where hast been, Hal?

117 of force of necessity II.iv.s.d. tavern (the tavern is said to be in Eastcheap,
but it is never explicitly named; references to a boar in *Henry IV* [*Part Two*]
suggest it is the Boar's Head) 1 fat hot

PRINCE With three or four loggerheads amongst three
or fourscore hogsheads. I have sounded the very
bass-string of humility. Sirrah, I am sworn brother
to a leash of drawers and can call them all by their
christen names, as Tom, Dick, and Francis. They
take it already upon their salvation that, though I
be but Prince of Wales, yet I am the king of courtesy,
and tell me flatly I am no proud Jack like Falstaff,
but a Corinthian, a lad of mettle, a good boy (by
the Lord, so they call me!), and when I am King of
England I shall command all the good lads in Eastcheap. They call drinking deep, dyeing scarlet; and
when you breathe in your watering, they cry "hem!"
and bid you play it off. To conclude, I am so good
a proficient in one quarter of an hour that I can drink
with any tinker in his own language during my life.
I tell thee, Ned, thou hast lost much honor that thou
wert not with me in this action. But, sweet Ned—
to sweeten which name of Ned, I give thee this
pennyworth of sugar, clapped even now into my
hand by an under-skinker, one that never spake
other English in his life than "Eight shillings and
sixpence," and "You are welcome," with this shrill
addition, "Anon, anon, sir! Score a pint of bastard in the Half-moon," or so—but, Ned, to drive
away the time till Falstaff come, I prithee do thou
stand in some by-room while I question my puny
drawer to what end he gave me the sugar; and do
thou never leave calling "Francis!" that his tale to
me may be nothing but "Anon!" Step aside, and I'll
show thee a precedent.

---

4 **loggerheads** blockheads   7 **leash** trio   7 **drawers** tapsters   9 **take ... salvation** pledge their salvation   11 **Jack** fellow   12 **Corinthian** gay blade
15 **dyeing scarlet** i.e., from the complexion it gives a man   16 **breathe in your
watering** pause for breath while drinking   17 **play it off** down it   23 **sugar** i.e.,
for sweetening wine (cf. I.ii.117)   24 **under-skinker** under-tapster   27 **Anon**
i.e., (I'm coming) at once   27 **Score** charge   27-28 **bastard** Spanish wine
28 **Half-moon** one of the inn's rooms   34 **precedent** example

POINS Francis!   35

PRINCE Thou art perfect.

POINS Francis!   [*Poins steps aside.*]

Enter [Francis, a] Drawer.

FRANCIS Anon, anon, sir. Look down into the Pomgarnet, Ralph.

PRINCE Come hither, Francis.   40

FRANCIS My lord?

PRINCE How long hast thou to serve, Francis?

FRANCIS Forsooth, five years, and as much as to—

POINS [*Within*] Francis!

FRANCIS Anon, anon, sir.   45

PRINCE Five year! By'r Lady, a long lease for the clink-
ing of pewter. But, Francis, darest thou be so valiant
as to play the coward with thy indenture and show
it a fair pair of heels and run from it?

FRANCIS O Lord, sir, I'll be sworn upon all the books   50
in England I could find in my heart—

POINS [*Within*] Francis!

FRANCIS Anon, sir.

PRINCE How old art thou, Francis?

FRANCIS Let me see: about Michaelmas next I shall   55
be—

POINS [*Within*] Francis!

FRANCIS Anon, sir. Pray stay a little, my lord.

PRINCE Nay, but hark you, Francis. For the sugar thou
gavest me—'twas a pennyworth, was't not?   60

38-39 **Pomgarnet** Pomegranate (another of the inn's rooms)   42 **serve** i.e., as an
apprentice (apprenticeship ran for seven years)   46 **By'r Lady** by Our Lady (mild
oath)   48 **indenture** contract   55 **Michaelmas** September 29

FRANCIS O Lord! I would it had been two!

PRINCE I will give thee for it a thousand pound. Ask
me when thou wilt, and thou shalt have it.

POINS [*Within*] Francis!

65   FRANCIS Anon, anon.

PRINCE Anon, Francis? No, Francis; but tomorrow,
Francis; or, Francis, a Thursday; or indeed, Francis,
when thou wilt. But, Francis—

FRANCIS My lord?

70   PRINCE Wilt thou rob this leathern-jerkin, crystal-
button, not-pated, agate-ring, puke-stocking, caddis-
garter, smooth-tongue, Spanish-pouch?

FRANCIS O Lord, sir, who do you mean?

PRINCE Why then, your brown bastard is your only
75   drink; for look you, Francis, your white canvas doublet will sully. In Barbary, sir, it cannot come to so
much.

FRANCIS What, sir?

POINS [*Within*] Francis!

80   PRINCE Away, you rogue! Dost thou not hear them call?

*Here they both call him. The Drawer stands
amazed, not knowing which way to go.*

Enter Vintner.

VINTNER What, stand'st thou still, and hear'st such a
calling? Look to the guests within. [*Exit Francis.*]

---

66 Anon, Francis? (Hal pretends to take Francis' "anon"—at once—to Poins as
meaning he wants the thousand pounds at once)   70-72 this ... Spanish-pouch
i.e., the innkeeper, whose middle-class appearance Hal details: leather jacket with
crystal buttons, short hair, agate ring, wool stockings, plain worsted (not fancy)
garters, ingratiating (and probably unctuous) speech, money pouch of Spanish
leather   74-77 Why ... much (semi-nonsense; but the implication seems clear
that Francis must stick to his trade)   80 s.d. Vintner the innkeeper

My lord, old Sir John, with half a dozen more, are
at the door. Shall I let them in?

PRINCE Let them alone awhile, and then open the door.   85
[*Exit Vintner*.] Poins!

POINS [*Within*] Anon, anon, sir.

Enter Poins.

PRINCE Sirrah, Falstaff and the rest of the thieves are at
the door. Shall we be merry?

POINS As merry as crickets, my lad. But hark ye; what   90
cunning match have you made with this jest of the
drawer? Come, what's the issue?

PRINCE I am now of all humors that have showed themselves humors since the old days of goodman Adam
to the pupil age of this present twelve o'clock at   95
midnight.

[*Enter Francis.*]

What's o'clock, Francis?

FRANCIS Anon, anon, sir.   [*Exit.*]

PRINCE That ever this fellow should have fewer words
than a parrot, and yet the son of a woman! His in-   100
dustry is upstairs and downstairs, his eloquence the
parcel of a reckoning. I am not yet of Percy's mind,
the Hotspur of the North: he that kills me some six
or seven dozen of Scots at a breakfast, washes his
hands, and says to his wife, "Fie upon this quiet   105
life! I want work." "O my sweet Harry," says she,
"how many hast thou killed today?" "Give my roan
horse a drench," says he, and answers "Some fourteen," an hour after, "a trifle, a trifle." I prithee call
in Falstaff. I'll play Percy, and that damned brawn   110

92 **issue** outcome, point (of the jest)   93-96 I ... midnight I am ready for every
kind of gaiety that men have invented since the beginning of the world
100-02 **His industry ... reckoning** his whole activity is running up and down
stairs, his whole conversation the totaling of bills   108 **drench** dose of
medicine   110 **brawn** fat boar

shall play Dame Mortimer his wife. "Rivo!" says
the drunkard. Call in Ribs, call in Tallow.

Enter Falstaff, [Gadshill, Bardolph, and Peto;
Francis follows with wine].

POINS Welcome, Jack. Where hast thou been?

FALSTAFF A plague of all cowards, I say, and a ven-
115   geance too! Marry and amen! Give me a cup of sack,
boy. Ere I lead this life long, I'll sew netherstocks,
and mend them and foot them too. A plague of all
cowards! Give me a cup of sack, rogue. Is there no
virtue extant?   *He drinketh.*

120 PRINCE Didst thou never see Titan kiss a dish of butter
(pitiful-hearted Titan!) that melted at the sweet tale
of the sun's? If thou didst, then behold that compound.

FALSTAFF You rogue, here's lime in this sack too! There
125   is nothing but roguery to be found in villainous man.
Yet a coward is worse than a cup of sack with lime
in it—a villainous coward! Go thy ways, old Jack,
die when thou wilt; if manhood, good manhood, be
not forgot upon the face of the earth, then am I a
130   shotten herring. There lives not three good men un-
hanged in England; and one of them is fat, and grows
old. God help the while! A bad world, I say. I would
I were a weaver; I could sing psalms or anything. A
plague of all cowards, I say still!

135 PRINCE How now, woolsack? What mutter you?

FALSTAFF A king's son! If I do not beat thee out of thy

---

111 **Rivo** (drinking cry of uncertain meaning) 114 **of** on 116 **netherstocks**
stockings 120 **Titan** the sun (of which Hal is possibly reminded by Falstaff's
broad face, and his melting effect on the sack) 124 **lime** (added to make poor
wine seem dry and clear) 130 **shotten herring** herring that has cast its roe (and
is therefore long and lean) 132-33 **God ... psalms** (Falstaff reassumes his role
of comic Puritan: English weavers were often psalm-singing Protestants who had
fled from the Roman Catholic continent)

kingdom with a dagger of lath and drive all thy
subjects afore thee like a flock of wild geese, I'll never
wear hair on my face more. You Prince of Wales?

PRINCE Why, you whoreson round man, what's the 140
matter?

FALSTAFF Are not you a coward? Answer me to that—
and Poins there?

POINS Zounds, ye fat paunch, and ye call me coward,
by the Lord, I'll stab thee.   145

FALSTAFF I call thee coward? I'll see thee damned ere I
call thee coward, but I would give a thousand pound
I could run as fast as thou canst. You are straight
enough in the shoulders; you care not who sees your
back. Call you that backing of your friends? A plague 150
upon such backing, give me them that will face me.
Give me a cup of sack. I am a rogue if I drunk today.

PRINCE O villain, thy lips are scarce wiped since thou
drunk'st last.

FALSTAFF All is one for that. (*He drinketh*.) A plague 155
of all cowards, still say I.

PRINCE What's the matter?

FALSTAFF What's the matter? There be four of us here
have ta'en a thousand pound this day morning.

PRINCE Where is it, Jack, where is it?   160

FALSTAFF Where is it? Taken from us it is. A hundred
upon poor four of us!

PRINCE What, a hundred, man?

FALSTAFF I am a rogue if I were not at half-sword with
a dozen of them two hours together. I have scaped 165
by miracle. I am eight times thrust through the

137 **dagger of lath** wooden dagger (by this phrase Falstaff associates himself with
a character called "the Vice" in the old religious plays, who drove the devil offstage
by beating him with a wooden dagger)   164 **at half-sword** infighting at close
quarters

doublet, four through the hose; my buckler cut through and through; my sword hacked like a handsaw—*ecce signum!* I never dealt better since I was a man. All would not do. A plague of all cowards! Let them speak. If they speak more or less than truth, they are villains and the sons of darkness.

PRINCE Speak, sirs. How was it?

GADSHILL We four set upon some dozen—

175 FALSTAFF Sixteen at least, my lord.

GADSHILL And bound them.

PETO No, no, they were not bound.

FALSTAFF You rogue, they were bound, every man of them, or I am a Jew else—an Ebrew Jew.

180 GADSHILL As we were sharing, some six or seven fresh men set upon us—

FALSTAFF And unbound the rest, and then come in the other.

PRINCE What, fought you with them all?

185 FALSTAFF All? I know not what you call all, but if I fought not with fifty of them, I am a bunch of radish! If there were not two or three and fifty upon poor old Jack, then am I no two-legged creature.

PRINCE Pray God you have not murd'red some of them.

190 FALSTAFF Nay, that's past praying for. I have peppered two of them. Two I am sure I have paid, two rogues in buckram suits. I tell thee what, Hal—if I tell thee a lie, spit in my face, call me horse. Thou knowest

166-67 **doublet** Elizabethan upper garment 167 **hose** Elizabethan breeches 169 **ecce signum** behold the evidence (Latin; spoken as he shows his sword) 169 **dealt** i.e., dealt blows 172 **sons of darkness** i.e., damned (but cf. also I.ii.24) 183 **other** others 186-87 **bunch of radish** (again an object long and lean) 187 **three and fifty** (fifty-three was the number of Spanish ships popularly reputed to have opposed Sir Richard Grenville at the battle of the Azores in 1591; Falstaff thus humorously claims for his fight the status of a national epic) 191 **paid** settled with

my old ward: here I lay, and thus I bore my point.
Four rogues in buckram let drive at me.   195

PRINCE What, four? Thou saidst but two even now.

FALSTAFF Four, Hal. I told thee four.

POINS Ay, ay, he said four.

FALSTAFF These four came all afront and mainly thrust
at me. I made me no more ado but took all their   200
seven points in my target, thus.

PRINCE Seven? Why, there were but four even now.

FALSTAFF In buckram?

POINS Ay, four, in buckram suits.

FALSTAFF Seven, by these hilts, or I am a villain else.   205

PRINCE [*Aside to Poins*] Prithee let him alone. We shall
have more anon.

FALSTAFF Dost thou hear me, Hal?

PRINCE Ay, and mark thee too, Jack.

FALSTAFF Do so, for it is worth the list'ning to. These   210
nine in buckram that I told thee of—

PRINCE So, two more already.

FALSTAFF Their points being broken—

POINS Down fell their hose.

FALSTAFF Began to give me ground; but I followed me   215
close, came in, foot and hand, and with a thought
seven of the eleven I paid.

PRINCE O monstrous! Eleven buckram men grown out
of two!

FALSTAFF But, as the devil would have it, three   220

---

194 **ward** fencing posture 199 **mainly** mightily 209 **mark** pay close attention
to 214 **Down fell their hose** (Poins wittily takes "points" in the sense of laces
holding the breeches to the doublet) 216 **with a thought** quick as a thought

misbegotten knaves in Kendal green came at my back and let drive at me; for it was so dark, Hal, that thou couldest not see thy hand.

PRINCE These lies are like their father that begets them
225 —gross as a mountain, open, palpable. Why, thou clay-brained guts, thou knotty-pated fool, thou whoreson obscene greasy tallow-catch—

FALSTAFF What, art thou mad? Art thou mad? Is not the truth the truth?

230 PRINCE Why, how couldst thou know these men in Kendal green when it was so dark thou couldst not see thy hand? Come, tell us your reason. What sayest thou to this?

POINS Come, your reason, Jack, your reason.

235 FALSTAFF What, upon compulsion? Zounds, and I were at the strappado or all the racks in the world, I would not tell you on compulsion. Give you a reason on compulsion? If reasons were as plentiful as blackberries, I would give no man a reason upon
240 compulsion, I.

PRINCE I'll be no longer guilty of this sin; this sanguine coward, this bed-presser, this horseback-breaker, this huge hill of flesh—

FALSTAFF 'Sblood, you starveling, you eel-skin, you
245 dried neat's-tongue, you bull's pizzle, you stockfish— O for breath to utter what is like thee!—you tailor's yard, you sheath, you bowcase, you vile standing tuck!

PRINCE Well, breathe awhile, and then to it again; and

226 knotty-pated blockheaded   227 tallow-catch (1) pan to catch drippings under roasting meat? (2) tallow-keech, i.e., roll of fat for making candles? 236 strappado instrument of torture   238 reasons (pronounced like "raisins," and hence comparable to blackberries)   241 sanguine ruddy (and hence valorous-seeming)   245 neat's tongue ox-tongue   245 pizzle penis 245 stockfish dried codfish   247-48 standing tuck upright rapier

when thou hast tired thyself in base comparisons, 250
hear me speak but this.

POINS Mark, Jack.

PRINCE We two saw you four set on four, and bound
them and were masters of their wealth. Mark now
how a plain tale shall put you down. Then did we 255
two set on you four and, with a word, outfaced you
from your prize, and have it; yea, and can show it
you here in the house. And, Falstaff, you carried your
guts away as nimbly, with as quick dexterity, and
roared for mercy, and still run and roared, as ever 260
I heard bullcalf. What a slave art thou to hack thy
sword as thou hast done, and then say it was in fight!
What trick, what device, what starting hole canst
thou now find out to hide thee from this open and
apparent shame? 265

POINS Come, let's hear, Jack. What trick hast thou
now?

FALSTAFF By the Lord, I knew ye as well as he that made
ye. Why, hear you, my masters. Was it for me to
kill the heir apparent? Should I turn upon the true 270
prince? Why, thou knowest I am as valiant as Her-
cules, but beware instinct. The lion will not touch
the true prince. Instinct is a great matter. I was now
a coward on instinct. I shall think the better of myself, and thee, during my life—I for a valiant lion, 275
and thou for a true prince. But, by the Lord, lads,
I am glad you have the money. Hostess, clap to the
doors. Watch tonight, pray tomorrow. Gallants,
lads, boys, hearts of gold, all the titles of good fellowship come to you! What, shall we be merry? Shall 280
we have a play extempore?

---

256 with a word (1) in brief? (2) with a mere shout to scare you?   263 starting
hole hiding place 272-73 The lion ... prince (a traditional belief about
lions) 278 Watch ... tomorrow cf. Matthew 26:41 "Watch and pray, that ye
enter not into temptation." (Falstaff puns on "watch," which means " carouse" as
well as "keep vigil")

PRINCE Content—and the argument shall be thy running away.

FALSTAFF Ah, no more of that, Hal, and thou lovest me!

Enter Hostess.

285 HOSTESS O Jesu, my lord the Prince!

PRINCE How now, my lady the hostess? What say'st thou to me?

HOSTESS Marry, my lord, there is a nobleman of the court at door would speak with you. He says he
290 comes from your father.

PRINCE Give him as much as will make him a royal man, and send him back again to my mother.

FALSTAFF What manner of man is he?

HOSTESS An old man.

295 FALSTAFF What doth gravity out of his bed at midnight? Shall I give him his answer?

PRINCE Prithee do, Jack.

FALSTAFF Faith, and I'll send him packing.   *Exit.*

PRINCE Now, sirs. By'r Lady, you fought fair; so did
300 you, Peto; so did you, Bardolph. You are lions too, you ran away upon instinct, you will not touch the true prince; no—fie!

BARDOLPH Faith, I ran when I saw others run.

PRINCE Faith, tell me now in earnest, how came Fal-
305 staff's sword so hacked?

PETO Why, he hacked it with his dagger, and said he would swear truth out of England but he would make you believe it was done in fight, and persuaded us to do the like.

282 **argument** subject   291-92 **royal man** cf. "noble" in the previous speech, but with a pun on the "royal," a coin worth ten shillings, which was of greater value than the "noble," worth six shillings eight pence   295 **gravity** i.e., sober age

BARDOLPH Yea, and to tickle our noses with speargrass   310
to make them bleed, and then to beslubber our garments with it and swear it was the blood of true men.
I did that I did not this seven year before—I
blushed to hear his monstrous devices.

PRINCE O villain! Thou stolest a cup of sack eighteen   315
years ago and wert taken with the manner, and ever
since thou hast blushed extempore. Thou hadst fire
and sword on thy side, and yet thou ran'st away.
What instinct hadst thou for it?

BARDOLPH My lord, do you see these meteors? Do you   320
behold these exhalations?

PRINCE I do.

BARDOLPH What think you they portend?

PRINCE Hot livers and cold purses.

BARDOLPH Choler, my lord, if rightly taken.   325

PRINCE No, if rightly taken, halter.

Enter Falstaff.

Here comes lean Jack; here comes bare-bone. How
now, my sweet creature of bombast? How long is't
ago, Jack, since thou sawest thine own knee?

FALSTAFF My own knee? When I was about thy years,   330
Hal, I was not an eagle's talent in the waist; I could
have crept into any alderman's thumb-ring. A plague
of sighing and grief, it blows a man up like a bladder.
There's villainous news abroad. Here was Sir John
Bracy from your father: you must to the court in   335

313 that what   316 taken with the manner caught with the goods   317 fire
i.e., the alcoholic hue of Bardolph's face   320, 321 meteors, exhalations i.e., the
pimples and other features of Bardolph's face, spoken of as if they were meteoro-
logical portents   324 Hot livers and cold purses (the two notable results of
excessive drink)   325 Choler anger (Bardolph implies that he is choleric, and
therefore no coward; Hal proceeds to understand "choler" as "collar," which in
Bardolph's case will be—if "rightly taken"—the hangman's noose)   328 bombast cotton stuffing   331 talent talon

the morning. That same mad fellow of the north, Percy, and he of Wales that gave Amamon the bastinado, and made Lucifer cuckold, and swore the devil his true liegeman upon the cross of a Welsh
340   hook—what a plague call you him?

POINS Owen Glendower.

FALSTAFF Owen, Owen—the same; and his son-in-law Mortimer, and old Northumberland, and that sprightly Scot of Scots, Douglas, that runs a-horse-
345   back up a hill perpendicular—

PRINCE He that rides at high speed and with his pistol kills a sparrow flying.

FALSTAFF You have hit it.

PRINCE So did he never the sparrow.

350 FALSTAFF Well, that rascal hath good metal in him; he will not run.

PRINCE Why, what a rascal art thou then, to praise him so for running!

FALSTAFF A-horseback, ye cuckoo! But afoot he will not
355   budge a foot.

PRINCE Yes, Jack, upon instinct.

FALSTAFF I grant ye, upon instinct. Well, he is there too, and one Mordake, and a thousand bluecaps more. Worcester is stol'n away tonight; thy father's beard
360   is turned white with the news; you may buy land now as cheap as stinking mack'rel.

PRINCE Why then, it is like, if there come a hot June, and this civil buffeting hold, we shall buy maidenheads as they buy hobnails, by the hundreds.

337-40 **he of Wales ... hook** (Falstaff alludes to Glendower's supposed magical powers: he has cudgeled a devil named Amamon, made horns grow on Lucifer, and forced the devil to swear allegiance to him on the cross of a weapon that has no cross) 350 **good metal** (with pun on "mettle," spirit, courage) 358 **bluecaps** Scots 362-64 **if there ... hundreds** (the Prince applies the analogy of selling cheap what won't keep to the reactions of virgins as they see all the men going off to war)

FALSTAFF By the mass, lad, thou sayest true; it is like we 365
  shall have good trading that way. But tell me, Hal,
  art not thou horrible afeard? Thou being heir apparent, could the world pick thee out three such enemies again as that fiend Douglas, that spirit Percy,
  and that devil Glendower? Art thou not horribly 370
  afraid? Doth not thy blood thrill at it?

PRINCE Not a whit, i' faith. I lack some of thy instinct.

FALSTAFF Well, thou wilt be horribly chid tomorrow
  when thou comest to thy father. If thou love me,
  practice an answer.   375

PRINCE Do thou stand for my father and examine me
  upon the particulars of my life.

FALSTAFF Shall I? Content. This chair shall be my state,
  this dagger my scepter, and this cushion my crown.

PRINCE Thy state is taken for a joined-stool, thy golden 380
  scepter for a leaden dagger, and thy precious rich
  crown for a pitiful bald crown.

FALSTAFF Well, and the fire of grace be not quite out of
  thee, now shalt thou be moved. Give me a cup of
  sack to make my eyes look red, that it may be 385
  thought I have wept; for I must speak in passion,
  and I will do it in King Cambyses' vein.

PRINCE Well, here is my leg.

FALSTAFF And here is my speech. Stand aside, nobility.

HOSTESS O Jesu, this is excellent sport, i' faith!   390

FALSTAFF Weep not, sweet queen, for trickling tears are
  vain.

371 **thrill** shiver (with fear)   378 **state** chair of state   380 **taken for** (either
"seen to be merely," or, alternatively, this is a meditative comment, possibly an
aside, in the detached vein of I.ii.199 and II.iv.481, with "thy" referring to the
King)   387 **King Cambyses' vein** i.e., the old ranting style of Preston's *King
Cambyses* (1569)   389 **nobility** (addressed to his motley ragamuffins)
391 **queen** (addressed to the Hostess, who is evidently tearful with laughter;
probably with a standard pun on *quean* = tart, prostitute)

HOSTESS O, the Father, how he holds his countenance!

FALSTAFF For God's sake, lords, convey my tristful
          queen!
          For tears do stop the floodgates of her eyes.

395 HOSTESS O Jesu, he doth it as like one of these harlotry
          players as ever I see!

FALSTAFF Peace, good pintpot. Peace, good tickle-brain.
          Harry, I do not only marvel where thou spendest
          thy time, but also how thou art accompanied. For
400   though the camomile, the more it is trodden on, the
          faster it grows, so youth, the more it is wasted, the
          sooner it wears. That thou art my son I have partly
          thy mother's word, partly my own opinion, but
          chiefly a villainous trick of thine eye and a foolish
405   hanging of thy nether lip that doth warrant me. If
          then thou be son to me, here lies the point: why,
          being son to me, art thou so pointed at? Shall the
          blessed sun of heaven prove a micher and eat black-
          berries? A question not to be asked. Shall the son
410   of England prove a thief and take purses? A question
          to be asked. There is a thing, Harry, which thou
          hast often heard of, and it is known to many in our
          land by the name of pitch. This pitch (as ancient
          writers do report) doth defile; so doth the company
415   thou keepest. For, Harry, now I do not speak to
          thee in drink, but in tears; not in pleasure, but in
          passion; not in words only, but in woes also: and
          yet there is a virtuous man whom I have often noted
          in thy company, but I know not his name.

---

392 **holds his countenance** keeps a straight face   393 **tristful** sad
395 **harlotry** rascally   400 **camomile** aromatic herb (Falstaff proceeds to satirize
the highflown style of the court by using a manner of speech called euphuism—
from John Lyly's fictional narrative, *Euphues* [1578] which introduced it—based
on similes drawn from natural history, intricate balance, antithesis, and repetition
of sounds, words, and ideas)   401 **so** (some editors emend to "yet," but the
imperfect logical correspondence of "though ... so" may be part of Falstaff's
mockery)   404 **trick** mannerism (possibly a twitch)   408-09 **prove ... blackberries** be a truant from duty and go blackberrying   409 **son** (with pun on
"sun," the royal symbol)

PRINCE What manner of man, and it like your Majesty? 420

FALSTAFF A goodly portly man, i' faith, and a corpulent; of a cheerful look, a pleasing eye, and a most
noble carriage; and, as I think, his age some fifty,
or, by'r Lady, inclining to threescore; and now I remember me, his name is Falstaff. If that man should 425
be lewdly given, he deceiveth me; for, Harry, I see
virtue in his looks. If then the tree may be known by
the fruit, as the fruit by the tree, then, peremptorily
I speak it, there is virtue in that Falstaff. Him keep
with, the rest banish. And tell me now, thou naughty 430
varlet, tell me where hast thou been this month?

PRINCE Dost thou speak like a king? Do thou stand for
me, and I'll play my father.

FALSTAFF Depose me? If thou dost it half so gravely, so
majestically, both in word and matter, hang me up 435
by the heels for a rabbit-sucker or a poulter's hare.

PRINCE Well, here I am set.

FALSTAFF And here I stand. Judge, my masters.

PRINCE Now, Harry, whence come you?

FALSTAFF My noble lord, from Eastcheap. 440

PRINCE The complaints I hear of thee are grievous.

FALSTAFF 'Sblood, my lord, they are false! Nay, I'll tickle
ye for a young prince, i' faith.

PRINCE Swearest thou, ungracious boy? Henceforth
ne'er look on me. Thou art violently carried away 445
from grace. There is a devil haunts thee in the likeness of an old fat man; a tun of man is thy companion. Why dost thou converse with that trunk of

421 **portly** stately 421-22 **corpulent** well filled out 426 **lewdly given**
inclined to evil-doing 427-28 **If ... fruit** cf. Matthew 12:33: "The tree is known
by his fruit" 428 **peremptorily** decisively 436 **rabbit-sucker** suckling
rabbit 442-43 **I'll ... prince** I'll act a prince that will amuse you 447 **tun**
hogshead

humors, that bolting-hutch of beastliness, that
450 swoll'n parcel of dropsies, that huge bombard of
sack, that stuffed cloakbag of guts, that roasted
Manningtree ox with the pudding in his belly, that
reverend vice, that gray iniquity, that father
ruffian, that vanity in years? Wherein is he good,
455 but to taste sack and drink it? Wherein neat and
cleanly, but to carve a capon and eat it? Wherein
cunning, but in craft? Wherein crafty, but in
villainy? Wherein villainous, but in all things?
Wherein worthy, but in nothing?

460 FALSTAFF I would your Grace would take me with you.
Whom means your Grace?

PRINCE That villainous abominable misleader of youth,
Falstaff, that old white-bearded Satan.

FALSTAFF My lord, the man I know.

465 PRINCE I know thou dost.

FALSTAFF But to say I know more harm in him than in
myself were to say more than I know. That he is old,
the more the pity, his white hairs do witness it; but
that he is, saving your reverence, a whoremaster,
470 that I utterly deny. If sack and sugar be a fault, God
help the wicked! If to be old and merry be a sin,
then many an old host that I know is damned. If to
be fat be to be hated, then Pharaoh's lean kine are
to be loved. No, my good lord: banish Peto, banish
475 Bardolph, banish Poins; but for sweet Jack Falstaff,
kind Jack Falstaff, true Jack Falstaff, valiant Jack

448-49 **trunk of humors** receptacle of body fluids (with allusion to the diseases
that were thought to be the product of these fluids) 449 **bolting-hutch** sifting-
bin (where impurities collect) 450 **dropsies** internal fluids 450 **bombard**
leather wine vessel 452 **Manningtree** town in Essex (where at annual fairs plays
were acted and, evidently, great oxen were stuffed and barbecued) 453-54 **vice,
iniquity, ruffian, vanity** (names intended to associate Falstaff with characters of
the old morality plays, all of whom were corrupters of virtue. But unlike Falstaff,
who ought to know better, *they* were young) 456-57 **Wherein cunning but in
craft** i.e., wherein skillful but in underhanded skills 460 **take me with you** let
me follow your meaning 473 **kine** cows (cf. Genesis 41:19-21)

Falstaff, and therefore more valiant being, as he is,
old Jack Falstaff, banish not him thy Harry's company, banish not him thy Harry's company, banish
plump Jack, and banish all the world!   480

PRINCE I do, I will.   [*A knocking heard.*
                    Exeunt Hostess, Francis, and Bardolph.]

                Enter Bardolph, running.

BARDOLPH O, my lord, my lord! The sheriff with a most
monstrous watch is at the door.

FALSTAFF Out, ye rogue! Play out the play, I have much
to say in the behalf of that Falstaff.   485

                Enter the Hostess.

HOSTESS O Jesu, my lord, my lord!

PRINCE Heigh, heigh, the devil rides upon a fiddlestick!
What's the matter?

HOSTESS The sheriff and all the watch are at the door.
They are come to search the house. Shall I let   490
them in?

FALSTAFF Dost thou hear, Hal? Never call a true piece
of gold a counterfeit. Thou art essentially made without seeming so.

PRINCE And thou a natural coward without instinct.   495

FALSTAFF I deny your major. If you will deny the sheriff,
so; if not, let him enter. If I become not a cart as
well as another man, a plague on my bringing up!
I hope I shall as soon be strangled with a halter as
another.   500

PRINCE Go hide thee behind the arras. The rest walk
up above. Now, my masters, for a true face and good
conscience.

483 watch group of constables 492-94 Never ... so (a difficult passage, perhaps
meaning that Falstaff, as a true piece of gold despite appearances, should not be
turned over to the sheriff by a royal friend who is also true gold despite
appearances) 496 major i.e., major premise, with pun on "mayor" 497 cart
hangman's cart 501 arras wall-hanging

FALSTAFF Both which I have had; but their date is out,
505   and therefore I'll hide me.   *Exit.*

PRINCE Call in the sheriff.
                    [*Exeunt all but the Prince and Peto.*]

Enter Sheriff and the Carrier.

Now, master sheriff, what is your will with me?

SHERIFF First, pardon me, my lord. A hue and cry
    Hath followed certain men unto this house.

510   PRINCE What men?

SHERIFF One of them is well known, my gracious lord—
    A gross fat man.

CARRIER   As fat as butter.

PRINCE The man, I do assure you, is not here,
    For I myself at this time have employed him.
515   And, sheriff, I will engage my word to thee
    That I will by tomorrow dinner time
    Send him to answer thee, or any man,
    For anything he shall be charged withal;
    And so let me entreat you leave the house.

520   SHERIFF I will, my lord. There are two gentlemen
    Have in this robbery lost three hundred marks.

PRINCE It may be so. If he have robbed these men,
    He shall be answerable; and so farewell.

SHERIFF Good night, my noble lord.

525   PRINCE I think it is good morrow, is it not?

SHERIFF Indeed, my lord, I think it be two o'clock.
                    Exit [*with Carrier*].

PRINCE This oily rascal is known as well as Paul's. Go
    call him forth.

513-14 **The man ... him** (Hal's reply is equivocal: Falstaff is not "here," in the
heir-apparent's presence, but "employed" behind the arras)

PETO Falstaff! Fast asleep behind the arras, and snorting like a horse.   530

PRINCE Hark how hard he fetches breath. Search his pockets.
      He searcheth his pocket and findeth certain papers.
What hast thou found?

PETO Nothing but papers, my lord.

PRINCE Let's see what they be. Read them.   535

[*Peto reads*] "Item, A capon . . . . . . 2s. 2d.
        Item, Sauce . . . .   4d.
        Item, Sack two gallons . . . 5s. 8d.
        Item, Anchovies and sack
           after supper 2s. 6d.   540
        Item, Bread . . . .   ob."

PRINCE O monstrous! But one halfpennyworth of bread to this intolerable deal of sack! What there is else, keep close; we'll read it at more advantage. There let him sleep till day. I'll to the court in the morn- 545
ing. We must all to the wars, and thy place shall be honorable. I'll procure this fat rogue a charge of foot, and I know his death will be a march of twelve score. The money shall be paid back again with advantage. Be with me betimes in the morning, 550
and so good morrow, Peto.

PETO Good morrow, good my lord.   *Exeunt.*

529-30 **snorting** snoring 541 **ob.** obolus, halfpenny 543 **deal** lot 547-48 **charge of foot** company of infantry 548-49 **twelve score** twelve score paces 550 **advantage** interest 550 **betimes** early

[ACT III

Scene I. *Wales. A room.*]

Enter Hotspur, Worcester, Lord Mortimer, Owen Glendower.

MORTIMER These promises are fair, the parties sure,
And our induction full of prosperous hope.

HOTSPUR Lord Mortimer, and cousin Glendower, will
you sit down? And uncle Worcester. A plague upon
5 it! I have forgot the map.

GLENDOWER No, here it is. Sit, cousin Percy, sit, good
cousin Hotspur, for by that name as oft as Lancaster
doth speak of you, his cheek looks pale, and with
a rising sigh he wisheth you in heaven.

10 HOTSPUR And you in hell, as oft as he hears Owen
Glendower spoke of.

GLENDOWER I cannot blame him. At my nativity
The front of heaven was full of fiery shapes
Of burning cressets, and at my birth
15 The frame and huge foundation of the earth
Shakèd like a coward.

III.i.2 **induction** beginning 3-11 **Lord ... spoke of** (many editors revise to read as verse, with line breaks after "down/it/is/Hotspur/you/sigh/hell/of"; or, leaving Hotspur's lines as prose, revise Glendower's speech to read as verse with breaks after "Percy/name/you/sigh/heaven") 14 **cressets** beacons

HOTSPUR Why, so it would have done at the same season
  if your mother's cat had but kittened, though yourself had never been born.

GLENDOWER I say the earth did shake when I was born. 20

HOTSPUR And I say the earth was not of my mind,
  If you suppose as fearing you it shook.

GLENDOWER The heavens were all on fire, the earth did
  tremble.

HOTSPUR O, then the earth shook to see the heavens on
  fire,
  And not in fear of your nativity.   25
  Diseasèd nature oftentimes breaks forth
  In strange eruptions; oft the teeming earth
  Is with a kind of colic pinched and vexed
  By the imprisoning of unruly wind
  Within her womb, which, for enlargement striving,   30
  Shakes the old beldame earth and topples down
  Steeples and mossgrown towers. At your birth
  Our grandam earth, having this distemp'rature,
  In passion shook.

GLENDOWER   Cousin, of many men
  I do not bear these crossings. Give me leave   35
  To tell you once again that at my birth
  The front of heaven was full of fiery shapes,
  The goats ran from the mountains, and the herds
  Were strangely clamorous to the frighted fields.
  These signs have marked me extraordinary,   40
  And all the courses of my life do show
  I am not in the roll of common men.
  Where is he living, clipped in with the sea
  That chides the banks of England, Scotland, Wales,
  Which calls me pupil or hath read to me?   45
  And bring him out that is but woman's son
  Can trace me in the tedious ways of art
  And hold me pace in deep experiments.

31 **beldame** grandmother (cf. "grandam," line 33)   33 **distemp'rature** physical
disorder   34 **passion** pain   43 **clipped in with** embraced by   45 **read to** tutored
47 **trace** follow   47 **art** magic

HOTSPUR I think there's no man speaks better Welsh.
50   I'll to dinner.

MORTIMER Peace, cousin Percy; you will make him
        mad.

GLENDOWER I can call spirits from the vasty deep.

HOTSPUR Why, so can I, or so can any man;
        But will they come when you do call for them?

55   GLENDOWER Why, I can teach you, cousin, to command
        the devil.

HOTSPUR And I can teach thee, coz, to shame the
        devil—
        By telling truth. Tell truth and shame the devil.
        If thou have power to raise him, bring him hither,
60   And I'll be sworn I have power to shame him hence.
        O, while you live, tell truth and shame the devil!

MORTIMER Come, come, no more of this unprofitable
        chat.

GLENDOWER Three times hath Henry Bolingbroke made
        head
        Against my power; thrice from the banks of Wye
65   And sandy-bottomed Severn have I sent him
        Bootless home and weather-beaten back.

HOTSPUR Home without boots, and in foul weather too?
        How scapes he agues, in the devil's name?

GLENDOWER Come, here is the map. Shall we divide our
        right
70   According to our threefold order ta'en?

MORTIMER The Archdeacon hath divided it
        Into three limits very equally.
        England, from Trent and Severn hitherto,
        By south and east is to my part assigned;

49 **speaks better Welsh** (1) brags better (2) talks more unintelligibly
66 **Bootless** profitless (probably trisyllabic) 68 **agues** i.e., catching cold
69 **our right** i.e., the kingdom they hope to win 72 **limits** regions

All westward, Wales beyond the Severn shore,   75
And all the fertile land within that bound,
To Owen Glendower; and, dear coz, to you
The remnant northward lying off from Trent.
And our indentures tripartite are drawn,
Which being sealèd interchangeably   80
(A business that this night may execute),
Tomorrow, cousin Percy, you and I
And my good Lord of Worcester will set forth
To meet your father and the Scottish power,
As is appointed us, at Shrewsbury.   85
My father Glendower is not ready yet,
Nor shall we need his help these fourteen days.
[*To Glendower*] Within that space you may have
    drawn together
Your tenants, friends, and neighboring gentlemen.

GLENDOWER A shorter time shall send me to you, lords;   90
And in my conduct shall your ladies come,
From whom you now must steal and take no leave,
For there will be a world of water shed
Upon the parting of your wives and you.

HOTSPUR Methinks my moiety, north from Burton
    here,
    95
In quantity equals not one of yours.
See how this river comes me cranking in
And cuts me from the best of all my land
A huge half-moon, a monstrous cantle out.
I'll have the current in this place dammed up,   100
And here the smug and silver Trent shall run
In a new channel fair and evenly.
It shall not wind with such a deep indent
To rob me of so rich a bottom here.

GLENDOWER Not wind? It shall, it must! You see it doth.   105

MORTIMER Yea, but mark how he bears his course, and

79 **indentures tripartite** three-way agreements 80 **interchangeably** i.e., by all three parties 95 **moiety** share 97 **cranking** winding 99 **cantle** piece 101 **smug** smooth 104 **bottom** valley

runs me up with like advantage on the other side,
gelding the opposèd continent as much as on the
other side it takes from you.

WORCESTER Yea, but a little charge will trench him
110   here
And on this north side win this cape of land;
And then he runs straight and even.

HOTSPUR I'll have it so, a little charge will do it.

GLENDOWER I'll not have it alt'red.

115 HOTSPUR Will not you?

GLENDOWER No, nor you shall not.

HOTSPUR Who shall say me nay?

GLENDOWER Why, that will I.

HOTSPUR Let me not understand you then; speak it in
120   Welsh.

GLENDOWER I can speak English, lord, as well as you;
For I was trained up in the English court,
Where, being but young, I framèd to the harp
Many an English ditty lovely well,
125 And gave the tongue a helpful ornament—
A virtue that was never seen in you.

HOTSPUR Marry, and I am glad of it with all my heart!
I had rather be a kitten and cry mew
Than one of these same meter ballad-mongers.
130 I had rather hear a brazen canstick turned
Or a dry wheel grate on the axletree,
And that would set my teeth nothing on edge,
Nothing so much as mincing poetry.

107 **advantage** i.e., disadvantage   108 **gelding the opposèd continent** cutting
out of the opposite bank   106–09 **Yea ... you** (revised by most editors to four or
five lines of verse, with little agreement about lineation)   110 **charge** cost
110 **trench** make a new course for   125 **gave ... ornament** (1) ornamented the
words with music? (2) benefited the English language by my poems?   129 **meter
ballad-mongers** singers of doggerel ballads   130 **canstick turned** i.e., candle-
stick in process of being burnished (and therefore raucously scraped)
133 **mincing** affected

'Tis like the forced gait of a shuffling nag.

GLENDOWER Come, you shall have Trent turned.   135

HOTSPUR I do not care. I'll give thrice so much land
  To any well-deserving friend;
  But in the way of bargain, mark ye me,
  I'll cavil on the ninth part of a hair.
  Are the indentures drawn? Shall we be gone?   140

GLENDOWER The moon shines fair; you may away by
  night.
  I'll haste the writer, and withal
  Break with your wives of your departure hence.
  I am afraid my daughter will run mad,
  So much she doteth on her Mortimer.   *Exit.*   145

MORTIMER Fie, cousin Percy, how you cross my father!

HOTSPUR I cannot choose. Sometime he angers me
  With telling me of the moldwarp and the ant,
  Of the dreamer Merlin and his prophecies,
  And of a dragon and a finless fish,   150
  A clip-winged griffin and a moulten raven,
  A couching lion and a ramping cat,
  And such a deal of skimble-skamble stuff
  As puts me from my faith. I tell you what—
  He held me last night at least nine hours   155
  In reckoning up the several devils' names
  That were his lackeys. I cried "hum," and "Well,
  go to!"
  But marked him not a word. O, he is as tedious
  As a tired horse, a railing wife;
  Worse than a smoky house. I had rather live   160
  With cheese and garlic in a windmill far
  Than feed on cates and have him talk to me
  In any summer house in Christendom.

143 **Break with** inform 148 **moldwarp** mole, i.e., Henry 152 **couching, ramping** (Hotspur ridicules heraldic crouching and rearing beasts; evidently Glendower talked of ancient prophecies which held that the kingdom of the mole should be divided by the lion, dragon and wolf, which were the crests of Percy, Glendower, and Mortimer) 153 **skimble-skamble** meaningless 162 **cates** delicacies

MORTIMER In faith, he is a worthy gentleman,
165   Exceedingly well read and profited
    In strange concealments, valiant as a lion,
    And wondrous affable, and as bountiful
    As mines of India. Shall I tell you, cousin?
    He holds your temper in a high respect
170   And curbs himself even of his natural scope
    When you come 'cross his humor. Faith, he does.
    I warrant you that man is not alive
    Might so have tempted him as you have done
    Without the taste of danger and reproof.
175   But do not use it oft, let me entreat you.

WORCESTER In faith, my lord, you are too willful-blame,
    And since your coming hither have done enough
    To put him quite besides his patience.
    You must needs learn, lord, to amend this fault.
    Though sometimes it show greatness, courage,
180   blood—
    And that's the dearest grace it renders you—
    Yet oftentimes it doth present harsh rage,
    Defect of manners, want of government,
    Pride, haughtiness, opinion, and disdain;
185   The least of which haunting a nobleman
    Loseth men's hearts, and leaves behind a stain
    Upon the beauty of all parts besides,
    Beguiling them of commendation.

HOTSPUR Well, I am schooled. Good manners be your
    speed!
190   Here come our wives, and let us take our leave.

Enter Glendower with the Ladies.

MORTIMER This is the deadly spite that angers me—
    My wife can speak no English, I no Welsh.

165-66 profited ... concealments expert in secret arts   170 scope tendencies
171 come 'cross his humor clash with his temperament   176 two willful-
blame blamable for too much willfulness   180 blood spirit   182 present indicate
183 government self-control   184 opinion arrogance   189 be your speed
bring you success   191 spite misfortune

GLENDOWER My daughter weeps; she'll not part with
   you,
   She'll be a soldier too, she'll to the wars.

MORTIMER Good father, tell her that she and my aunt
   Percy   195
   Shall follow in your conduct speedily.
      Glendower speaks to her in Welsh, and she answers him
                                              in the same.

GLENDOWER She is desperate here.
   A peevish self-willed harlotry, one that no persuasion can do good upon.
                                The Lady speaks in Welsh.

MORTIMER I understand thy looks. That pretty Welsh   200
   Which thou pourest down from these swelling
      heavens
   I am too perfect in; and, but for shame,
   In such a parley should I answer thee.
                                The Lady again in Welsh.
   I understand thy kisses, and thou mine,
   And that's a feeling disputation.   205
   But I will never be a truant, love,
   Till I have learnt thy language; for thy tongue
   Makes Welsh as sweet as ditties highly penned,
   Sung by a fair queen in a summer's bow'r,
   With ravishing division, to her lute.   210

GLENDOWER Nay, if you melt, then will she run mad.
                                The Lady speaks again in Welsh.

MORTIMER O, I am ignorance itself in this!

GLENDOWER She bids you on the wanton rushes lay
   you down
   And rest your gentle head upon her lap,
   And she will sing the song that pleaseth you   215

---

198 harlotry ninny, fool   200 That pretty Welsh i.e., her tears   201 heavens
i.e., her eyes   203 parley meeting (of tears)   205 feeling disputation dialogue
by (1) touching (2) the feelings   208 highly penned i.e., lofty   210 division
musical variation   213 wanton luxurious

And on your eyelids crown the god of sleep,
Charming your blood with pleasing heaviness,
Making such difference 'twixt wake and sleep
As is the difference betwixt day and night
220 The hour before the heavenly-harnessed team
Begins his golden progress in the east.

MORTIMER With all my heart I'll sit and hear her sing.
By that time will our book, I think, be drawn.

GLENDOWER Do so, and those musicians that shall play
    to you
225 Hang in the air a thousand leagues from hence,
And straight they shall be here: sit, and attend.

HOTSPUR Come, Kate, thou art perfect in lying down.
Come, quick, quick, that I may lay my head in thy
lap.

230 LADY PERCY Go, ye giddy goose.   *The music plays.*

HOTSPUR Now I perceive the devil understands Welsh,
And 'tis no marvel he is so humorous,
By'r Lady, he is a good musician.

LADY PERCY Then should you be nothing but musical,
235 For you are altogether governed by humors.
Lie still, ye thief, and hear the lady sing in Welsh.

HOTSPUR I had rather hear Lady, my brach, howl in
Irish.

LADY PERCY Wouldst thou have thy head broken?

240 HOTSPUR No.

LADY PERCY Then be still.

HOTSPUR Neither! 'Tis a woman's fault.

LADY PERCY Now God help thee!

HOTSPUR To the Welsh lady's bed.

216 **crown the god of sleep** i.e., give sleep sovereignty   220 **the heavenly-harnessed team** the horses of the sun   223 **book** agreement   232 **humorous** capricious   237 **brach** bitch-hound

LADY PERCY What's that?   245

HOTSPUR Peace! She sings.

Here the Lady sings a Welsh song.
Come, Kate, I'll have your song too.

LADY PERCY Not mine, in good sooth.

HOTSPUR Not yours, in good sooth? Heart, you swear
like a comfit-maker's wife. "Not you, in good   250
sooth!" and "as true as I live!" and "as God shall
mend me!" and "as sure as day!"
And givest such sarcenet surety for thy oaths
As if thou never walk'st further than Finsbury.
Swear me, Kate, like a lady as thou art,   255
A good mouth-filling oath, and leave "in sooth"
And such protest of pepper gingerbread
To velvet guards and Sunday citizens.
Come, sing.

LADY PERCY I will not sing.   260

HOTSPUR 'Tis the next way to turn tailor or be redbreast-teacher. And the indentures be drawn, I'll
away within these two hours; and so come in when
ye will.   *Exit.*

GLENDOWER Come, come, Lord Mortimer. You are as
slow   265
As hot Lord Percy is on fire to go.
By this our book is drawn; we'll but seal,
And then to horse immediately.

MORTIMER   With all my heart.
                                                      Exeunt.

---

248 **sooth** truth 250 **comfit-maker's** confectioner's 253 **sarcenet surety**
flimsy security ("sarcenet"—a thin silk) 254 **Finsbury** favorite resort near
London (frequented by the middle-class groups whom Hotspur satirizes)
257 **pepper gingerbread** i.e., insubstantial, crumbling in the mouth 258 **velvet**
guards i.e., shopkeepers, who favored velvet trimmings for Sunday wear
261 **tailor** (like weavers, tailors were famed for singing at their work) 261-62
redbreast-teacher singing master to songbirds

[Scene II. *London. The palace.*]

Enter the King, Prince of Wales, and others.

KING Lords, give us leave: the Prince of Wales and I
Must have some private conference; but be near at
    hand,
For we shall presently have need of you.

Exeunt Lords.

I know not whether God will have it so
5   For some displeasing service I have done,
That, in his secret doom, out of my blood
He'll breed revengement and a scourge for me;
But thou dost in thy passages of life
Make me believe that thou art only marked
10 For the hot vengeance and the rod of heaven
To punish my mistreadings. Tell me else,
Could such inordinate and low desires,
Such poor, such bare, such lewd, such mean
    attempts,
Such barren pleasures, rude society,
15 As thou art matched withal and grafted to,
Accompany the greatness of thy blood
And hold their level with thy princely heart?

PRINCE So please your Majesty, I would I could
Quit all offenses with as clear excuse
20 As well as I am doubtless I can purge
Myself of many I am charged withal.
Yet such extenuation let me beg

III.ii.6 **doom** judgment 6 **blood** i.e., heirs 8 **passages** courses 9-11 **thou ...
mistreadings** i.e., (1) heaven is punishing me through you (2) heaven will punish
you to punish me 12 **inordinate** i.e., out of order (for one of your rank)
15 **withal** with 19 **Quit** clear myself of 20 **As well** and as well

As, in reproof of many tales devised,
Which oft the ear of greatness needs must hear
By smiling pickthanks and base newsmongers,   25
I may, for some things true wherein my youth
Hath faulty wand'red and irregular,
Find pardon on my true submission.

KING God pardon thee! Yet let me wonder, Harry,
    At thy affections, which do hold a wing   30
    Quite from the flight of all thy ancestors.
    Thy place in council thou hast rudely lost,
    Which by thy younger brother is supplied,
    And art almost an alien to the hearts
    Of all the court and princes of my blood.   35
    The hope and expectation of thy time
    Is ruined, and the soul of every man
    Prophetically do forethink thy fall.
    Had I so lavish of my presence been,
    So common-hackneyed in the eyes of men,   40
    So stale and cheap to vulgar company,
    Opinion, that did help me to the crown,
    Had still kept loyal to possession
    And left me in reputeless banishment,
    A fellow of no mark nor likelihood.   45
    By being seldom seen, I could not stir
    But, like a comet, I was wond'red at;
    That men would tell their children, "This is he!"
    Others would say, "Where? Which is Bolingbroke?"
    And then I stole all courtesy from heaven,   50
    And dressed myself in such humility
    That I did pluck allegiance from men's hearts,
    Loud shouts and salutations from their mouths
    Even in the presence of the crownèd King.

22-28 Yet ... submission yet let me beg such extenuation that when I have
confuted many manufactured charges (which the ear of greatness is bound to hear
from informers and tattletales) I may be pardoned for some true faults of which
my youth has been guilty   30 affections tastes   36 time reign   42 Opinion
public opinion   43 possession i.e., Richard II   50 I ... heaven I took a godlike
graciousness on myself

55 Thus did I keep my person fresh and new,
 My presence, like a robe pontifical,
 Ne'er seen but wond'red at; and so my state,
 Seldom but sumptuous, showed like a feast
 And won by rareness such solemnity.

60 The skipping King, he ambled up and down
 With shallow jesters and rash bavin wits,
 Soon kindled and soon burnt; carded his state;
 Mingled his royalty with cap'ring fools;
 Had his great name profanèd with their scorns

65 And gave his countenance, against his name,
 To laugh at gibing boys and stand the push
 Of every beardless vain comparative;
 Grew a companion to the common streets,
 Enfeoffed himself to popularity;

70 That, being daily swallowed by men's eyes,
 They surfeited with honey and began
 To loathe the taste of sweetness, whereof a little
 More than a little is by much too much.
 So, when he had occasion to be seen,

75 He was but as the cuckoo is in June,
 Heard, not regarded—seen, but with such eyes
 As, sick and blunted with community,
 Afford no extraordinary gaze,
 Such as is bent on sunlike majesty

80 When it shines seldom in admiring eyes;
 But rather drowsed and hung their eyelids down,
 Slept in his face, and rend'red such aspect
 As cloudy men use to their adversaries,
 Being with his presence glutted, gorged, and full.

85 And in that very line, Harry, standest thou;
 For thou hast lost thy princely privilege
 With vile participation. Not an eye
 But is aweary of thy common sight,

61 **bavin** brushwood (which flares and burns out) 62 **carded** debased 65 **his name** i.e., (1) his kingly title (2) his kingly authority 66 **stand the push** put up with the impudence 67 **comparative** deviser of insulting comparisons 69 **Enfeoffed ... popularity** bound himself to low company 77 **with community** by familiarity (with the king) 83 **cloudy** sullen (but also with reference to "clouds" obscuring the royal "sun") 87 **participation** companionship

Save mine, which hath desired to see thee more;
Which now doth that I would not have it do—   90
Make blind itself with foolish tenderness.

PRINCE I shall hereafter, my thrice-gracious lord,
Be more myself.

KING   For all the world,
As thou art to this hour was Richard then
When I from France set foot at Ravenspurgh;   95
And even as I was then is Percy now.
Now, by my scepter, and my soul to boot,
He hath more worthy interest to the state
Than thou the shadow of succession;
For of no right, nor color like to right,   100
He doth fill fields with harness in the realm,
Turns head against the lion's armèd jaws,
And, being no more in debt to years than thou,
Leads ancient lords and reverend bishops on
To bloody battles and to bruising arms.   105
What never-dying honor hath he got
Against renownèd Douglas! whose high deeds,
Whose hot incursions and great name in arms
Holds from all soldiers chief majority
And military title capital   110
Through all the kingdoms that acknowledge Christ.
Thrice hath this Hotspur, Mars in swathling clothes,
This infant warrior, in his enterprises
Discomfited great Douglas; ta'en him once,
Enlargèd him, and made a friend of him,   115
To fill the mouth of deep defiance up
And shake the peace and safety of our throne.
And what say you to this? Percy, Northumberland,
The Archbishop's grace of York, Douglas, Mortimer
Capitulate against us and are up.   120
But wherefore do I tell these news to thee?

91 **tenderness** i.e., tears   98 **worthy interest** claim based on worth (as compared with a "shadow" claim by inheritance)   100 **color** pretense   101 **harness** armor   109 **majority** preeminence   110 **capital** topmost   116 **To fill ... up** to deepen the noise of defiance   120 **Capitulate** (1) make a "head" or armed force? (2) draw up "heads" of an argument?   120 **up** in arms

Why, Harry, do I tell thee of my foes,
Which art my nearest and dearest enemy?
Thou that art like enough, through vassal fear,
125　Base inclination, and the start of spleen,
To fight against me under Percy's pay,
To dog his heels and curtsy at his frowns,
To show how much thou art degenerate.

PRINCE　Do not think so, you shall not find it so.
130　And God forgive them that so much have swayed
Your Majesty's good thoughts away from me.
I will redeem all this on Percy's head
And, in the closing of some glorious day,
Be bold to tell you that I am your son,
135　When I will wear a garment all of blood,
And stain my favors in a bloody mask,
Which, washed away, shall scour my shame with it.
And that shall be the day, whene'er it lights,
That this same child of honor and renown,
140　This gallant Hotspur, this all-praisèd knight,
And your unthought-of Harry chance to meet.
For every honor sitting on his helm,
Would they were multitudes, and on my head
My shames redoubled! For the time will come
145　That I shall make this northern youth exchange
His glorious deeds for my indignities.
Percy is but my factor, good my lord,
To engross up glorious deeds on my behalf;
And I will call him to so strict account
150　That he shall render every glory up,
Yea, even the slightest worship of his time,
Or I will tear the reckoning from his heart.
This in the name of God I promise here;
The which if he be pleased I shall perform,
155　I do beseech your Majesty may salve
The long-grown wounds of my intemperance.
If not, the end of life cancels all bands,

123 **dearest** (1) most loved (2) costliest　136 **favors** features　147 **factor**
agent　148 engross hoard　151 **worship of his time** honor he has gained in his
lifetime　157 **bands** bonds, promises

And I will die a hundred thousand deaths
Ere break the smallest parcel of this vow.

KING A hundred thousand rebels die in this!   160
Thou shalt have charge and sovereign trust herein.

Enter Blunt.

How now, good Blunt? Thy looks are full of speed.

BLUNT So hath the business that I come to speak of.
Lord Mortimer of Scotland hath sent word
That Douglas and the English rebels met   165
The eleventh of this month at Shrewsbury.
A mighty and a fearful head they are,
If promises be kept on every hand,
As ever off'red foul play in a state.

KING The Earl of Westmoreland set forth today;   170
With him my son, Lord John of Lancaster:
For this advertisement is five days old.
On Wednesday next, Harry, you shall set forward;
On Thursday we ourselves will march. Our meeting
Is Bridgenorth; and, Harry, you shall march   175
Through Gloucestershire; by which account,
Our business valuèd, some twelve days hence
Our general forces at Bridgenorth shall meet.
Our hands are full of business. Let's away:
Advantage feeds him fat while men delay.   *Exeunt.*   180

[Scene III. *Eastcheap. The tavern.*]

Enter Falstaff and Bardolph.

FALSTAFF Bardolph, am I not fall'n away vilely since this
last action? Do I not bate? Do I not dwindle? Why,

159 **parcel** item   163 **So hath the business** i.e., the business too has speed
(must be dealt with speedily)   177 **Our business valuèd** having sized up what
we have to do   180 **him** itself   III.iii.2 **bate** lose weight

my skin hangs about me like an old lady's loose
gown! I am withered like an old apple-john. Well,
I'll repent, and that suddenly, while I am in some
liking. I shall be out of heart shortly, and then I
shall have no strength to repent. And I have not forgotten what the inside of a church is made of, I am
a peppercorn, a brewer's horse. The inside of a
church! Company, villainous company, hath been
the spoil of me.

BARDOLPH Sir John, you are so fretful you cannot live
long.

FALSTAFF Why, there is it! Come, sing me a bawdy song,
make me merry. I was as virtuously given as a gentleman need to be, virtuous enough: swore little, diced
not above seven times a week, went to a bawdy house
not above once in a quarter of an hour, paid money
that I borrowed three or four times, lived well, and
in good compass; and now I live out of all order,
out of all compass.

BARDOLPH Why, you are so fat, Sir John, that you must
needs be out of all compass—out of all reasonable
compass, Sir John.

FALSTAFF Do thou amend thy face, and I'll amend my
life. Thou art our admiral, thou bearest the lantern
in the poop—but 'tis in the nose of thee: thou art
the Knight of the Burning Lamp.

BARDOLPH Why, Sir John, my face does you no harm.

FALSTAFF No, I'll be sworn. I make as good use of it as
many a man doth of a death's-head or a memento
mori. I never see thy face but I think upon hellfire

---

4 **old apple-john** apple with shriveled skin   5-6 **am in some liking** (1) am in
the mood (2) still have some flesh left   6 **out of heart** (1) out of the mood (2) out
of shape   9 **peppercorn, brewer's horse** (Falstaff this time picks objects *not* long
and thin, but dry, withered, decrepit)   16-19 **diced ... times** (probably spoken
with significant pauses after "diced not," "once," "borrowed")   20 **compass**
order (but Bardolph takes it in the sense of "size")   26 **admiral** flagship
(recognizable by its lantern)   31 **death's-head** ring with a skull
31-32 **memento mori** reminder of death

and Dives that lived in purple; for there he is in his
robes, burning, burning. If thou wert any way given
to virtue, I would swear by thy face; my oath should   35
be "By this fire, that's God's angel." But thou art
altogether given over, and wert indeed, but for the
light in thy face, the son of utter darkness. When
thou ran'st up Gad's Hill in the night to catch my
horse, if I did not think thou hadst been an ignis   40
fatuus or a ball of wildfire, there's no purchase in
money. O, thou art a perpetual triumph, an everlasting bonfire-light! Thou hast saved me a thousand
marks in links and torches, walking with thee in the
night betwixt tavern and tavern; but the sack that   45
thou hast drunk me would have bought me lights as
good cheap at the dearest chandler's in Europe.
I have maintained that salamander of yours with
fire any time this two and thirty years. God reward
me for it!   50

BARDOLPH 'Sblood, I would my face were in your belly!

FALSTAFF God-a-mercy! So should I be sure to be heart-
burned.

Enter Hostess.

How now, Dame Partlet the hen? Have you enquired yet who picked my pocket?   55

HOSTESS Why, Sir John, what do you think, Sir John?
Do you think I keep thieves in my house? I have
searched, I have enquired, so has my husband, man
by man, boy by boy, servant by servant. The tithe
of a hair was never lost in my house before.   60

33 **Dives** uncharitable rich man who burns in hell (Luke 16:19-31) 36 **angel**
(alluding to the Scriptural accounts of angels manifesting themselves as fire, or
possibly to the seraphs, highest order of angels, who were fire) 40-41 **ignis
fatuus** will-o'-the-wisp 41 **ball of wildfire** firework 42 **triumph** i.e., of the
Roman kind, with torches 44 **links** flares 47 **good cheap** cheaply
47 **chandler's** candle maker's 48 **salamander** lizard supposed to live in fire
51 **I ... belly** (proverbial retort, to which Falstaff's reply gives new life)
54 **Dame Partlet** (traditional name for a hen, and well suited to the clucking
Hostess) 59 **tithe** tenth part

FALSTAFF Ye lie, hostess. Bardolph was shaved and lost many a hair, and I'll be sworn my pocket was picked. Go to, you are a woman, go!

HOSTESS Who, I? No; I defy thee! God's light, I was 65 never called so in mine own house before!

FALSTAFF Go to, I know you well enough.

HOSTESS No, Sir John; you do not know me, Sir John. I know you, Sir John. You owe me money, Sir John, and now you pick a quarrel to beguile me of it. I 70 bought you a dozen of shirts to your back.

FALSTAFF Dowlas, filthy dowlas! I have given them away to bakers' wives; they have made bolters of them.

HOSTESS Now, as I am a true woman, holland of eight 75 shillings an ell. You owe money here besides, Sir John, for your diet and by-drinkings, and money lent you, four and twenty pound.

FALSTAFF He had his part of it; let him pay.

HOSTESS He? Alas, he is poor; he hath nothing.

80 FALSTAFF How? Poor? Look upon his face. What call you rich? Let them coin his nose, let them coin his cheeks. I'll not pay a denier. What, will you make a younker of me? Shall I not take mine ease in mine inn but I shall have my pocket picked? I have lost a 85 seal ring of my grandfather's worth forty mark.

HOSTESS O Jesu, I have heard the Prince tell him, I know not how oft, that that ring was copper!

FALSTAFF How? The Prince is a Jack, a sneak-up.

---

64 **No** (the Hostess suspects that any word or phrase of Falstaff's may contain hidden innuendoes about her moral character; she sometimes retorts with comments containing amusing innuendoes about herself that she is too ignorant to understand) 71 **Dowlas** coarse linen 72 **bolters** sieves 74 **holland** fine linen 75 **ell** one and a quarter yards 76 **by-drinkings** drinks between meals 81 **rich** (referring to its red gold-and-copper hues) 82 **denier** tenth of a penny 83 **younker** Greenhorn 88 **Jack** rascal 88 **sneak-up** sneak

'Sblood, and he were here, I would cudgel him like
a dog if he would say so.   90

*Enter the Prince [and Poins], marching, and Falstaff
meets them, playing upon his truncheon like a fife.*

How now, lad? Is the wind in that door, i' faith?
Must we all march?

BARDOLPH Yea, two and two, Newgate fashion.

HOSTESS My lord, I pray you hear me.

PRINCE What say'st thou, Mistress Quickly? How doth   95
thy husband? I love him well, he is an honest man.

HOSTESS Good my lord, hear me.

FALSTAFF Prithee let her alone and list to me.

PRINCE What say'st thou, Jack?

FALSTAFF The other night I fell asleep here behind the   100
arras and had my pocket picked. This house is turned
bawdy house; they pick pockets.

PRINCE What didst thou lose, Jack?

FALSTAFF Wilt thou believe me, Hal, three or four bonds
of forty pound apiece and a seal ring of my grand-   105
father's.

PRINCE A trifle, some eightpenny matter.

HOSTESS So I told him, my lord, and I said I heard your
Grace say so; and, my lord, he speaks most vilely of
you, like a foulmouthed man as he is, and said he   110
would cudgel you.

PRINCE What! He did not?

HOSTESS There's neither faith, truth, nor womanhood
in me else.

90s.d. **truncheon** cudgel   91 **Is ... door** i.e., is that how things are going
93 **two and two** i.e., bound in pairs like prisoners on the way to (Newgate) prison

115 FALSTAFF There's no more faith in thee than in a stewed prune, nor no more truth in thee than in a drawn fox; and for womanhood, Maid Marian may be the deputy's wife of the ward to thee. Go, you thing, go!

HOSTESS Say, what thing, what thing?

120 FALSTAFF What thing? Why, a thing to thank God on.

HOSTESS I am no thing to thank God on, I would thou shouldst know it! I am an honest man's wife, and, setting thy knighthood aside, thou art a knave to call me so.

125 FALSTAFF Setting thy womanhood aside, thou art a beast to say otherwise.

HOSTESS Say, what beast, thou knave, thou?

FALSTAFF What beast? Why, an otter.

PRINCE An otter, Sir John? Why an otter?

130 FALSTAFF Why, she's neither fish nor flesh; a man knows not where to have her.

HOSTESS Thou art an unjust man in saying so. Thou or any man knows where to have me, thou knave, thou!

135 PRINCE Thou say'st true, hostess, and he slanders thee most grossly.

HOSTESS So he doth you, my lord, and said this other day you ought him a thousand pound.

PRINCE Sirrah, do I owe you a thousand pound?

140 FALSTAFF A thousand pound, Hal? A million! Thy love is worth a million, thou owest me thy love.

115-16 **stewed prune** (evidently chosen by Falstaff because stewed prunes were associated with bawdy houses) 116 **drawn** drawn from his lair and trying every trick to get back to it 117-18 **Maid Marian ... thee** a disreputable female in country May games is chaste as the wife of the ward's most respectable citizen in comparison with you 138 **ought** owed

HOSTESS Nay, my lord, he called you Jack and said he
would cudgel you.

FALSTAFF Did I, Bardolph?

BARDOLPH Indeed, Sir John, you said so.   145

FALSTAFF Yea, if he said my ring was copper.

PRINCE I say 'tis copper. Darest thou be as good as thy
word now?

FALSTAFF Why, Hal, thou knowest, as thou art but man,
I dare; but as thou art Prince, I fear thee as I fear   150
the roaring of the lion's whelp.

PRINCE And why not as the lion?

FALSTAFF The King himself is to be feared as the lion.
Dost thou think I'll fear thee as I fear thy father?
Nay, and I do, I pray God my girdle break.   155

PRINCE O, if it should, how would thy guts fall about
thy knees! But, sirrah, there's no room for faith,
truth, nor honesty in this bosom of thine. It is all
filled up with guts and midriff. Charge an honest
woman with picking thy pocket? Why, thou whore-   160
son, impudent, embossed rascal, if there were
anything in thy pocket but tavern reckonings, mem-
orandums of bawdy houses, and one poor pennyworth of sugar candy to make thee long-winded—
if thy pocket were enriched with any other injuries   165
but these, I am a villain. And yet you will stand to
it; you will not pocket up wrong. Art thou not
ashamed?

FALSTAFF Dost thou hear, Hal? Thou knowest in the
state of innocency Adam fell, and what should poor   170
Jack Falstaff do in the days of villainy? Thou seest
I have more flesh than another man, and therefore
more frailty. You confess then, you picked my
pocket?

161 embossed (1) swollen (2) foaming at the mouth (of a deer)   161 rascal (1)
rogue (2) lean young deer   165 injuries i.e., things whose loss you call injuries

175 PRINCE It appears so by the story.

FALSTAFF Hostess, I forgive thee, go make ready breakfast, love thy husband, look to thy servants, cherish
thy guests. Thou shalt find me tractable to any honest reason. Thou seest I am pacified still. Nay, prithee
180 be gone.   *Exit Hostess*.
Now, Hal, to the news at court. For the robbery, lad
—how is that answered?

PRINCE O my sweet beef, I must still be good angel to
thee. The money is paid back again.

185 FALSTAFF O, I do not like that paying back! 'Tis a double
labor.

PRINCE I am good friends with my father, and may do
anything.

FALSTAFF Rob me the exchequer the first thing thou
190 doest, and do it with unwashed hands too.

BARDOLPH Do, my lord.

PRINCE I have procured thee, Jack, a charge of foot.

FALSTAFF I would it had been of horse. Where shall I
find one that can steal well? O for a fine thief of the
195 age of two and twenty or thereabouts! I am heinously
unprovided. Well, God be thanked for these rebels,
they offend none but the virtuous: I laud them, I
praise them.

PRINCE Bardolph!

200 BARDOLPH My lord?

PRINCE Go bear this letter to Lord John of Lancaster,
To my brother John; this to my Lord of Westmore-
land.   [*Exit Bardolph*.]
Go, Peto, to horse, to horse; for thou and I
Have thirty miles to ride yet ere dinner time.
                                        [*Exit Peto*.]

---

190 **with unwashed hands** with no delay   194 **thief** i.e., to steal a horse

Jack, meet me tomorrow in the Temple Hall   205
At two o'clock in the afternoon.
There shalt thou know thy charge, and there receive
Money and order for their furniture.
The land is burning, Percy stands on high,
And either we or they must lower lie.   [*Exit.*]   210

FALSTAFF Rare words! Brave world! Hostess, my break-
    fast, come.
  O, I could wish this tavern were my drum!   [*Exit.*]

208 **furniture** equipment   212 **drum** recruiting center

[ACT IV

Scene I. *The rebel camp, near Shrewsbury.*]

[*Enter Hotspur, Worcester, and Douglas.*]

HOTSPUR Well said, my noble Scot. If speaking truth
In this fine age were not thought flattery,
Such attribution should the Douglas have
As not a soldier of this season's stamp
5   Should go so general current through the world.
By God, I cannot flatter, I do defy
The tongues of soothers! But a braver place
In my heart's love hath no man than yourself.
Nay, task me to my word; approve me, lord.

10 DOUGLAS Thou art the king of honor.
No man so potent breathes upon the ground
But I will beard him.

Enter one with letters.

HOTSPUR   Do so, and 'tis well.—
What letters hast thou there?—I can but thank you.

MESSENGER These letters come from your father.

IV.i.3 **attribution** recognition   5 **go so general current** be as widely accepted
(the image is of a coin of recent mintage: "this season's stamp") 6 **defy**
despise 7 **soothers** flatterers 9 **task me** try me, test me 12 **beard** oppose

HOTSPUR Letters from him? Why comes he not himself?   15

MESSENGER He cannot come, my lord, he is grievous
    sick.

HOTSPUR Zounds! How has he the leisure to be sick
    In such a justling time? Who leads his power?
    Under whose government come they along?

MESSENGER His letters bears his mind, not I, my lord.   20

WORCESTER I prithee tell me, doth he keep his bed?

MESSENGER He did, my lord, four days ere I set forth,
    And at the time of my departure thence
    He was much feared by his physicians.

WORCESTER I would the state of time had first been
        whole   25
    Ere he by sickness had been visited.
    His health was never better worth than now.

HOTSPUR Sick now? Droop now? This sickness doth
        infect
    The very lifeblood of our enterprise.
    'Tis catching hither, even to our camp.   30
    He writes me here that inward sickness—
    And that his friends by deputation
    Could not so soon be drawn; nor did he think it meet
    To lay so dangerous and dear a trust
    On any soul removed but on his own.   35
    Yet doth he give us bold advertisement,
    That with our small conjunction we should on,
    To see how fortune is disposed to us;
    For, as he writes, there is no quailing now,
    Because the King is certainly possessed   40
    Of all our purposes. What say you to it?

WORCESTER Your father's sickness is a maim to us.

18 justling jostling, unquiet   19 government command   20 bears (a singular
verb with plural subject is not uncommon in Elizabethan English)   24 feared
feared for   32 deputation a deputy   37 conjunction combination of forces
40 possessed informed

HOTSPUR A perilous gash, a very limb lopped off.
         And yet, in faith, it is not! His present want
45   Seems more than we shall find it. Were it good
         To set the exact wealth of all our states
         All at one cast? To set so rich a main
         On the nice hazard of one doubtful hour?
         It were not good; for therein should we read
50   The very bottom and the soul of hope,
         The very list, the very utmost bound
         Of all our fortunes.

DOUGLAS   Faith, and so we should.
         Where now remains a sweet reversion,
         We may boldly spend upon the hope of what is to
            come in.
55   A comfort of retirement lives in this.

HOTSPUR A rendezvous, a home to fly unto,
         If that the devil and mischance look big
         Upon the maidenhead of our affairs.

WORCESTER But yet I would your father had been here.
60   The quality and hair of our attempt
         Brooks no division. It will be thought
         By some that know not why he is away,
         That wisdom, loyalty, and mere dislike
         Of our proceedings kept the Earl from hence.
65   And think how such an apprehension
         May turn the tide of fearful faction
         And breed a kind of question in our cause.
         For well you know we of the off'ring side
         Must keep aloof from strict arbitrament,
70   And stop all sight-holes, every loop from whence
         The eye of reason may pry in upon us.
         This absence of your father's draws a curtain

---

46 **set** risk   47 **main** (1) stake (in gambling) (2) army   48 **nice** precarious
50 **soul** (1) essence (2) sole (cf. "bottom")   51 **list** limit   53 **reversion**
inheritance still to be received   55 **A comfort of retirement** a security to fall
back on   57 **big** menacingly   60 **hair** nature   61 **Brooks** allows of   66 **fearful**
timid   68 **we of the off'ring side** we who take the offensive   69 **arbitrament**
evaluation   70 **loop** loophole   72 **draws** draws aside

That shows the ignorant a kind of fear
Before not dreamt of.

HOTSPUR   You strain too far.
I rather of his absence make this use: 75
It lends a luster and more great opinion,
A larger dare to our great enterprise,
Than if the Earl were here; for men must think,
If we, without his help, can make a head
To push against a kingdom, with his help   80
We shall o'erturn it topsy-turvy down.
Yet all goes well; yet all our joints are whole.

DOUGLAS As heart can think. There is not such a word
Spoke of in Scotland as this term of fear.

Enter Sir Richard Vernon.

HOTSPUR My cousin Vernon, welcome, by my soul.   85

VERNON Pray God my news be worth a welcome, lord.
The Earl of Westmoreland, seven thousand strong,
Is marching hitherwards; with him Prince John.

HOTSPUR No harm. What more?

VERNON   And further, I have learned
The King himself in person is set forth,   90
Or hitherwards intended speedily,
With strong and mighty preparation.

HOTSPUR He shall be welcome too. Where is his son,
The nimble-footed madcap Prince of Wales,
And his comrades, that daffed the world aside   95
And bid it pass?

VERNON   All furnished, all in arms;
All plumed like estridges that with the wind
Bated like eagles having lately bathed;
Glittering in golden coats like images;
As full of spirit as the month of May   100
And gorgeous as the sun at midsummer;

76 opinion prestige   79 a head (1) an army (2) headway   95 daffed thrust
97 estridges ostriches (ostrich plumes are the emblem of the Prince of Wales)
98 Bated shook their wings

Wanton as youthful goats, wild as young bulls.
I saw young Harry with his beaver on,
His cushes on his thighs, gallantly armed,

105   Rise from the ground like feathered Mercury,
And vaulted with such ease into his seat
As if an angel dropped down from the clouds
To turn and wind a fiery Pegasus
And witch the world with noble horsemanship.

HOTSPUR No more, no more! Worse than the sun in
110   March,
This praise doth nourish agues. Let them come.
They come like sacrifices in their trim,
And to the fire-eyed maid of smoky war
All hot and bleeding will we offer them.

115   The mailèd Mars shall on his altars sit
Up to the ears in blood. I am on fire
To hear this rich reprisal is so nigh,
And yet not ours. Come, let me taste my horse,
Who is to bear me like a thunderbolt

120   Against the bosom of the Prince of Wales.
Harry to Harry shall, hot horse to horse,
Meet, and ne'er part till one drop down a corse.
O that Glendower were come!

VERNON   There is more news.
I learned in Worcester, as I rode along,
125   He cannot draw his power this fourteen days.

DOUGLAS That's the worst tidings that I hear of yet.

WORCESTER Ay, by my faith, that bears a frosty sound.

HOTSPUR What may the King's whole battle reach
unto?

VERNON To thirty thousand.

HOTSPUR   Forty let it be.
130   My father and Glendower being both away,

102 **Wanton** exuberant 103 **beaver** helmet 104 **cushes** thigh armor
108 **wind** wheel about 111 **agues** chills and fever (the spring sun was believed to
set them going) 113 **maid** Bellona, goddess of war 117 **reprisal** prize
128 **battle** army

The powers of us may serve so great a day.
Come, let us take a muster speedily.
Doomsday is near. Die all, die merrily.

DOUGLAS Talk not of dying. I am out of fear
Of death or death's hand for this one half year.   135

Exeunt.

[Scene II. *A road near Coventry.*]

Enter Falstaff [and] Bardolph.

FALSTAFF Bardolph, get thee before to Coventry; fill me
a bottle of sack. Our soldiers shall march through.
We'll to Sutton Co'fil' tonight.

BARDOLPH Will you give me money, captain?

FALSTAFF Lay out, lay out.   5

BARDOLPH This bottle makes an angel.

FALSTAFF And if it do, take it for thy labor; and if it
make twenty, take them all; I'll answer the coinage.
Bid my lieutenant Peto meet me at town's end.

BARDOLPH I will, captain. Farewell.   *Exit.*   10

FALSTAFF If I be not ashamed of my soldiers, I am a
soused gurnet. I have misused the King's press
damnably. I have got, in exchange of a hundred and
fifty soldiers, three hundred and odd pounds. I press
me none but good householders, yeomen's sons;   15

IV.ii.5 **Lay out** i.e., pay out of your own pocket   6 **angel** coin worth, at various
times, six shillings eight pence to ten shillings (Bardolph means that Falstaff now
owes him an angel, but Falstaff jokingly takes "make" in the literal sense—as if the
bottle were minting angels; he tells Bardolph to take them all and he will guarantee
they are not counterfeit)   12 **soused gurnet** pickled fish   12 **press** power of
conscription   15 **good householders, yeomen's sons** i.e., men of some means
who could pay to be let off

inquire me out contracted bachelors, such as had been
asked twice on the banes—such a commodity of
warm slaves as had as lief hear the devil as a drum,
such as fear the report of a caliver worse than a
20   struck fowl or a hurt wild duck. I pressed me none
but such toasts-and-butter, with hearts in their bellies no bigger than pins' heads, and they have bought
out their services; and now my whole charge consists
of ancients, corporals, lieutenants, gentlemen of
25   companies—slaves as ragged as Lazarus in the
painted cloth, where the glutton's dogs licked his
sores; and such as indeed were never soldiers, but
discarded unjust serving-men, younger sons to
younger brothers, revolted tapsters, and ostlers
30   trade-fall'n; the cankers of a calm world and a long
peace; ten times more dishonorable ragged than an
old fazed ancient; and such have I to fill up the
rooms of them as have bought out their services that
you would think that I had a hundred and fifty tat-
35   tered prodigals lately come from swine-keeping, from
eating draff and husks. A mad fellow met me on the
way, and told me I had unloaded all the gibbets and
pressed the dead bodies. No eye hath seen such scare-
crows. I'll not march through Coventry with them,
40   that's flat. Nay, and the villains march wide betwixt
the legs, as if they had gyves on, for indeed I had
the most of them out of prison. There's not a shirt
and a half in all my company, and the half-shirt is
two napkins tacked together and thrown over the
45   shoulders like a herald's coat without sleeves; and
the shirt, to say the truth, stol'n from my host at
Saint Albans, or the red-nose innkeeper of Daventry.

17 **asked twice on the banes** i.e., on the verge of marriage (banns [banes] were
announcements of intent to marry, published usually three times at weekly
intervals) 18 **warm** comfortable 19 **caliver** musket 24 **ancients** ensigns
24-25 **gentlemen of companies** lesser officers 25 **Lazarus** the beggar in the
Dives parable (Luke 16:19-31) 26 **painted cloth** painted wall-hanging
28 **unjust** dishonest 29 **revolted** runaway 30 **trade-fall'n** unemployed
30 **cankers** parasites 32 **fazed ancient** tattered flag 36 **draff** pig-swill (the
prodigal son, in Luke 15:15-16, was so hungry he longed for draff) 41 **gyves**
fetters

But that's all one; they'll find linen enough on every
hedge.

Enter the Prince [and the] Lord of Westmoreland.

PRINCE How now, blown Jack? How now, quilt?   50

FALSTAFF What, Hal? How now, mad wag? What a devil
dost thou in Warwickshire? My good Lord of Westmoreland, I cry you mercy. I thought your honor
had already been at Shrewsbury.

WESTMORELAND Faith, Sir John, 'tis more than time that   55
I were there, and you too, but my powers are there
already. The King, I can tell you, looks for us all, we
must away all night.

FALSTAFF Tut, never fear me: I am as vigilant as a cat
to steal cream.   60

PRINCE I think, to steal cream indeed, for thy theft hath
already made thee butter. But tell me, Jack, whose
fellows are these that come after?

FALSTAFF Mine, Hal, mine.

PRINCE I did never see such pitiful rascals.   65

FALSTAFF Tut, tut, good enough to toss; food for powder, food for powder, they'll fill a pit as well as better.
Tush, man, mortal men, mortal men.

WESTMORELAND Ay, but, Sir John, methinks they are
exceeding poor and bare, too beggarly.   70

FALSTAFF Faith, for their poverty, I know not where
they had that, and for their bareness, I am sure they
never learned that of me.

PRINCE No, I'll be sworn, unless you call three fingers
in the ribs bare. But, sirrah, make haste. Percy is   75
already in the field.   *Exit.*

49 **hedge** i.e., where linen was put out to dry   50 **blown** (1) swelled (2) short of
wind   50 **Jack** (1) Falstaff's name (2) soldier's quilted jacket   66 **toss** i.e., on the
end of a pike   74 **three fingers** i.e., of fat

FALSTAFF What, is the King encamped?

WESTMORELAND He is, Sir John. I fear we shall stay too
　　　long.

80　FALSTAFF Well, to the latter end of a fray and the begin-
　　　ning of a feast fits a dull fighter and a keen guest.
　　　　　　　　　　　　　　　　　　　　　　　　Exeunt.

[Scene III. *The rebel camp, near Shrewsbury.*]

Enter Hotspur, Worcester, Douglas, Vernon.

HOTSPUR We'll fight him tonight.

WORCESTER　　　　　　　　　　　　It may not be.

DOUGLAS You give him then advantage.

VERNON　　　　　　　　　　　　　　　　Not a whit.

HOTSPUR Why say you so? Looks he not for supply?

VERNON So do we.

HOTSPUR　　　　　　　His is certain, ours is doubtful.

5　WORCESTER Good cousin, be advised; stir not tonight.

VERNON Do not, my lord.

DOUGLAS　　　　　　　　　　You do not counsel well.
　　　You speak it out of fear and cold heart.

VERNON Do me no slander, Douglas. By my life—
　　　And I dare well maintain it with my life—
10　If well-respected honor bid me on,
　　　I hold as little counsel with weak fear

---

81 s.d. **Exeunt** (the quarto's "Exeunt," implying that Westmoreland goes off with
Falstaff, may be wrong. Falstaff's last speech sounds as if Westmoreland had
departed, and Falstaff winks at the audience) IV.iii.3 **supply** reinforcement
10 **well-respected** well-considered

As you, my lord, or any Scot that this day lives.
Let it be seen tomorrow in the battle
Which of us fears.

DOUGLAS   Yea, or tonight.

VERNON   Content.

HOTSPUR Tonight, say I.   15

VERNON Come, come, it may not be.
  I wonder much, being men of such great leading as
      you are,
  That you foresee not what impediments
  Drag back our expedition. Certain horse
  Of my cousin Vernon's are not yet come up.   20
  Your uncle Worcester's horse came but today;
  And now their pride and mettle is asleep,
  Their courage with hard labor tame and dull,
  That not a horse is half the half of himself.

HOTSPUR So are the horses of the enemy   25
  In general journey-bated and brought low.
  The better part of ours are full of rest.

WORCESTER The number of the King exceedeth ours.
  For God's sake, cousin, stay till all come in.

                              The trumpet sounds a parley.

                    Enter Sir Walter Blunt.

BLUNT I come with gracious offers from the King,   30
  If you vouchsafe me hearing and respect.

HOTSPUR Welcome, Sir Walter Blunt, and would to God
  You were of our determination.
  Some of us love you well; and even those some
  Envy your great deservings and good name,
  Because you are not of our quality,   35
  But stand against us like an enemy.

---

17 **leading** generalship   19 **expedition** i.e., hastening into battle   26 **journey-bated** travel-weakened   33 **determination** party   36 **quality** company

BLUNT　And God defend but still I should stand so,
　　　So long as out of limit and true rule
40　　You stand against anointed majesty.
　　　But to my charge. The King hath sent to know
　　　The nature of your griefs, and whereupon
　　　You conjure from the breast of civil peace
　　　Such bold hostility, teaching his duteous land
45　　Audacious cruelty. If that the King
　　　Have any way your good deserts forgot,
　　　Which he confesseth to be manifold,
　　　He bids you name your griefs, and with all speed
　　　You shall have your desires with interest,
50　　And pardon absolute for yourself and these
　　　Herein misled by your suggestion.

HOTSPUR　The King is kind, and well we know the King
　　　Knows at what time to promise, when to pay.
　　　My father and my uncle and myself
55　　Did give him that same royalty he wears;
　　　And when he was not six and twenty strong,
　　　Sick in the world's regard, wretched and low,
　　　A poor unminded outlaw sneaking home,
　　　My father gave him welcome to the shore;
60　　And when he heard him swear and vow to God
　　　He came but to be Duke of Lancaster,
　　　To sue his livery and beg his peace,
　　　With tears of innocency and terms of zeal,
　　　My father, in kind heart and pity moved,
65　　Swore him assistance, and performed it too.
　　　Now when the lords and barons of the realm
　　　Perceived Northumberland did lean to him,
　　　The more and less came in with cap and knee;
　　　Met him in boroughs, cities, villages,
70　　Attended him on bridges, stood in lanes,

38 **defend** forbid　39 **limit** i.e., a subject's proper limits　41 **charge** message　51 **suggestion** instigation　62 **sue ... peace** sue for the delivery of his lands (which Richard II had arrogated to the crown) and make his peace with the king　68 **with cap and knee** i.e., with cap off and bended knee (in token of allegiance)　70 **lanes** facing rows

Laid gifts before him, proffered him their oaths,
Gave him their heirs as pages, followed him
Even at the heels in golden multitudes.
He presently, as greatness knows itself,
Steps me a little higher than his vow   75
Made to my father, while his blood was poor,
Upon the naked shore at Ravenspurgh;
And now, forsooth, takes on him to reform
Some certain edicts and some strait decrees
That lie too heavy on the commonwealth;   80
Cries out upon abuses, seems to weep
Over his country's wrongs; and by this face,
This seeming brow of justice, did he win
The hearts of all that he did angle for;
Proceeded further—cut me off the heads   85
Of all the favorites that the absent king
In deputation left behind him here
When he was personal in the Irish war.

BLUNT Tut! I came not to hear this.

HOTSPUR   Then to the point.
In short time after, he deposed the King;   90
Soon after that deprived him of his life;
And in the neck of that tasked the whole state;
To make that worse, suff'red his kinsman March
(Who is, if every owner were well placed,
Indeed his king) to be engaged in Wales,   95
There without ransom to lie forfeited;
Disgraced me in my happy victories,
Sought to entrap me by intelligence;
Rated mine uncle from the council board;
In rage dismissed my father from the court;   100
Broke oath on oath, committed wrong on wrong,
And in conclusion drove us to seek out
This head of safety, and withal to pry

---

74 **as greatness knows itself** as greatness begins to feel its strength   79 **strait**
strict   87 **In deputation** as deputies   88 **personal** personally engaged   92 **in
the neck of that** i.e., next   92 **tasked** taxed   98 **intelligence** spies   99 **Rated**
scolded (cf. I.iii.14-20)   103 **head** army

Into his title, the which we find
105　　Too indirect for long continuance.

BLUNT　Shall I return this answer to the King?

HOTSPUR　Not so, Sir Walter. We'll withdraw awhile.
　　Go to the King; and let there be impawned
　　Some surety for a safe return again,
110　　And in the morning early shall mine uncle
　　Bring him our purposes; and so farewell.

BLUNT　I would you would accept of grace and love.

HOTSPUR　And may be so we shall.

BLUNT　　　　　　　　　Pray God you do. [*Exeunt.*]

[Scene IV. *York. The Archbishop's palace.*]

Enter [the] Archbishop of York [and] Sir Michael.

ARCHBISHOP　Hie, good Sir Michael; bear this sealèd
　　brief
　　With wingèd haste to the Lord Marshal;
　　This to my cousin Scroop; and all the rest
　　To whom they are directed. If you knew
5　　How much they do import, you would make haste.

SIR MICHAEL　My good lord, I guess their tenor.

ARCHBISHOP　Like enough you do.
　　Tomorrow, good Sir Michael, is a day
　　Wherein the fortune of ten thousand men
10　　Must bide the touch; for, sir, at Shrewsbury,
　　As I am truly given to understand,
　　The King with mighty and quick-raisèd power
　　Meets with Lord Harry; and I fear, Sir Michael,

---

105 **indirect** (1) not in the direct line (from Richard) (2) morally oblique　IV.iv.1
brief message　10 **bide the touch** stand the test (as metal is tested by the
touchstone to know if it is gold)

What with the sickness of Northumberland,
Whose power was in the first proportion,   15
And what with Owen Glendower's absence thence,
Who with them was a rated sinew too
And comes not in, overruled by prophecies—
I fear the power of Percy is too weak
To wage an instant trial with the King.   20

SIR MICHAEL Why, my good lord, you need not fear;
There is Douglas and Lord Mortimer.

ARCHBISHOP No, Mortimer is not there.

SIR MICHAEL But there is Mordake, Vernon, Lord Harry
Percy,
And there is my Lord of Worcester, and a head   25
Of gallant warriors, noble gentlemen.

ARCHBISHOP And so there is; but yet the King hath
drawn
The special head of all the land together—
The Prince of Wales, Lord John of Lancaster,
The noble Westmoreland and warlike Blunt,   30
And many moe corrivals and dear men
Of estimation and command in arms.

SIR MICHAEL Doubt not, my lord, they shall be well
opposed.

ARCHBISHOP I hope no less, yet needful 'tis to fear;
And, to prevent the worst, Sir Michael, speed.   35
For if Lord Percy thrive not, ere the King
Dismiss his power, he means to visit us,
For he hath heard of our confederacy,
And 'tis but wisdom to make strong against him.
Therefore make haste. I must go write again   40
To other friends; and so farewell, Sir Michael.

                              Exeunt.

---

15 **proportion** magnitude   17 **rated sinew** highly valued strength   28 **head**
army   31 **moe corrivals** more associates   31 **dear** important

[ACT V

Scene I. *The King's camp, near Shrewsbury.*]

Enter the King, Prince of Wales, Lord John of Lancaster,
Earl of Westmoreland, Sir Walter Blunt, Falstaff.

KING How bloodily the sun begins to peer
Above yon bulky hill! The day looks pale
At his distemp'rature.

PRINCE   The southern wind
Doth play the trumpet to his purposes
5   And by his hollow whistling in the leaves
Foretells a tempest and a blust'ring day.

KING Then with the losers let it sympathize,
For nothing can seem foul to those that win.

The trumpet sounds. Enter Worcester [and Vernon].

How now, my Lord of Worcester? 'Tis not well
10 That you and I should meet upon such terms

V.i.s.d. **Earl of Westmoreland** (in V.ii.28 we learn that Westmoreland has been
held as the "surety" of IV.iii.109, but at this point Shakespeare apparently had not
decided who was the hostage)   **3 his distemp'rature** the sun's apparent
ailment   **4 play the trumpet** (1) act the announcer (2) blow as if playing a
trumpet   **4 his** the sun's

As now we meet. You have deceived our trust
And made us doff our easy robes of peace
To crush our old limbs in ungentle steel.
This is not well, my lord; this is not well.
What say you to it? Will you again unknit   15
This churlish knot of all-abhorrèd war,
And move in that obedient orb again
Where you did give a fair and natural light,
And be no more an exhaled meteor,
A prodigy of fear, and a portent   20
Of broachèd mischief to the unborn times?

WORCESTER Hear me, my liege.
For mine own part, I could be well content
To entertain the lag-end of my life
With quiet hours, for I protest   25
I have not sought the day of this dislike.

KING You have not sought it! How comes it then?

FALSTAFF Rebellion lay in his way, and he found it.

PRINCE Peace, chewet, peace!

WORCESTER It pleased your Majesty to turn your looks   30
Of favor from myself and all our house;
And yet I must remember you, my lord,
We were the first and dearest of your friends.
For you my staff of office did I break
In Richard's time, and posted day and night   35
To meet you on the way and kiss your hand
When yet you were in place and in account
Nothing so strong and fortunate as I.
It was myself, my brother, and his son
That brought you home and boldly did outdare   40
The dangers of the time. You swore to us,
And you did swear that oath at Doncaster,
That you did nothing purpose 'gainst the state,

---

17 **obedient orb** orbit of obedience 19 **exhaled meteor** wandering body (not
subject to orbit, and thought an omen or "prodigy") 21 **broachèd** opened
29 **chewet** (1) jackdaw, i.e., chatterer (2) meat pie. 32 **remember** remind

Nor claim no further than your new-fall'n right,
45 The seat of Gaunt, dukedom of Lancaster.
To this we swore our aid. But in short space
It rained down fortune show'ring on your head,
And such a flood of greatness fell on you—
What with our help, what with the absent King,
50 What with the injuries of a wanton time,
The seeming sufferances that you had borne,
And the contrarious winds that held the King
So long in his unlucky Irish wars
That all in England did repute him dead—
55 And from this swarm of fair advantages
You took occasion to be quickly wooed
To gripe the general sway into your hand;
Forgot your oath to us at Doncaster;
And, being fed by us, you used us so
60 As that ungentle gull, the cuckoo's bird,
Useth the sparrow—did oppress our nest,
Grew by our feeding to so great a bulk
That even our love durst not come near your sight
For fear of swallowing; but with nimble wing
65 We were enforced for safety sake to fly
Out of your sight and raise this present head;
Whereby we stand opposèd by such means
As you yourself have forged against yourself
By unkind usage, dangerous countenance,
70 And violation of all faith and troth
Sworn to us in your younger enterprise.

KING These things, indeed, you have articulate,
Proclaimed at market crosses, read in churches,
To face the garment of rebellion
75 With some fine color that may please the eye
Of fickle changelings and poor discontents,

---

44 **new-fall'n** i.e., by the death of his father, John of Gaunt   57 **gripe** grab
60 **gull,** bird nestling (the cuckoo lays its eggs in other birds' nests, and the young
cuckoos when hatched speedily destroy the other nestlings)   69 **dangerous**
menacing   72 **articulate** spelled out   74 **face** trim   75 **color** (1) hue
(2) rhetorical coloring (hence, pretext)

Which gape and rub the elbow at the news
Of hurlyburly innovation.
And never yet did insurrection want
Such water colors to impaint his cause,   80
Nor moody beggars, starving for a time
Of pell-mell havoc and confusion.

PRINCE In both your armies there is many a soul
Shall pay full dearly for this encounter,
If once they join in trial. Tell your nephew   85
The Prince of Wales doth join with all the world
In praise of Henry Percy. By my hopes,
This present enterprise set off his head,
I do not think a braver gentleman,
More active-valiant or more valiant-young,   90
More daring or more bold, is now alive
To grace this latter age with noble deeds.
For my part, I may speak it to my shame,
I have a truant been to chivalry;
And so I hear he doth account me too.   95
Yet this before my father's majesty—
I am content that he shall take the odds
Of his great name and estimation,
And will, to save the blood on either side,
Try fortune with him in a single fight.   100

KING And, Prince of Wales, so dare we venture thee;
Albeit, considerations infinite
Do make against it. No, good Worcester, no!
We love our people well; even those we love
That are misled upon your cousin's part;   105
And, will they take the offer of our grace,
Both he, and they, and you, yea, every man
Shall be my friend again, and I'll be his.
So tell your cousin, and bring me word
What he will do. But if he will not yield,   110
Rebuke and dread correction wait on us,

77 **rub the elbow** i.e., hug themselves with delight 78 **innovation** revolution 88 **set off his head** removed from his record 96 **this before** let me say this in the presence of 102 **Albeit** on the other hand 106 **grace** pardon 111 **wait on us** are in our service

And they shall do their office. So be gone.
We will not now be troubled with reply.
We offer fair; take it advisedly.

Exit Worcester [with Vernon].

115 PRINCE It will not be accepted, on my life.
The Douglas and the Hotspur both together
Are confident against the world in arms.

KING Hence, therefore, every leader to his charge;
For, on their answer, will we set on them,
120 And God befriend us as our cause is just!

Exeunt. Manent Prince [and] Falstaff.

FALSTAFF Hal, if thou see me down in the battle and
bestride me, so! 'Tis a point of friendship.

PRINCE Nothing but a colossus can do thee that friendship. Say thy prayers, and farewell.

125 FALSTAFF I would 'twere bedtime, Hal, and all well.

PRINCE Why, thou owest God a death.   [*Exit.*]

FALSTAFF 'Tis not due yet: I would be loath to pay him
before his day. What need I be so forward with him
that calls not on me? Well, 'tis no matter; honor
130 pricks me on. Yea, but how if honor prick me off
when I come on? How then? Can honor set to a leg?
No. Or an arm? No. Or take away the grief of a
wound? No. Honor hath no skill in surgery then?
No. What is honor? A word. What is in that word
135 honor? What is that honor? Air—a trim reckoning! Who hath it? He that died a Wednesday. Doth
he feel it? No. Doth he hear it? No. 'Tis insensible
then? Yea, to the dead. But will it not live with the
living? No. Why? Detraction will not suffer it.
140 Therefore I'll none of it. Honor is a mere scutcheon—and so ends my catechism.   *Exit.*

112 **office** duty 120 s.d. **Manent** remain (Latin) 122 **so** i.e., I shan't
object 126 **death** (pronounced like "debt," in which sense Falstaff takes it)
130 **pricks** spurs 130 **prick** check (as a casualty) 135 **trim** fine (spoken
ironically) 139 **Detraction** slander 140-41 **scutcheon** painted shield with
coat of arms identifying a dead nobleman

[Scene II. *The rebel camp, near Shrewsbury.*]

Enter Worcester [and] Sir Richard Vernon.

WORCESTER O no, my nephew must not know, Sir
  Richard,
  The liberal and kind offer of the King.

VERNON 'Twere best he did.

WORCESTER   Then are we all undone.
  It is not possible, it cannot be,
  The King should keep his word in loving us.   5
  He will suspect us still and find a time
  To punish this offense in other faults.
  Supposition all our lives shall be stuck full of eyes;
  For treason is but trusted like the fox,
  Who, never so tame, so cherished and locked up,   10
  Will have a wild trick of his ancestors.
  Look how we can, or sad or merrily,
  Interpretation will misquote our looks,
  And we shall feed like oxen at a stall,
  The better cherished still the nearer death.   15
  My nephew's trespass may be well forgot;
  It hath the excuse of youth and heat of blood,
  And an adopted name of privilege—
  A hare-brained Hotspur, governed by a spleen.
  All his offenses live upon my head   20
  And on his father's. We did train him on;
  And, his corruption being ta'en from us,
  We, as the spring of all, shall pay for all.
  Therefore, good cousin, let not Harry know,
  In any case, the offer of the King.   25

V.ii.8 **Supposition ... eyes** suspicion will always be spying on us 11 **trick**
(1) trait (2) wile 12 **or sad or** either sad or 18 **an ... privilege** a nickname
which carries a privilege (to be impulsive) with it 21 **train** (1) draw (2) aim
22 **ta'en** taken (like an infection)

Enter Hotspur [and Douglas].

VERNON Deliver what you will, I'll say 'tis so.
    Here comes your cousin.

HOTSPUR   My uncle is returned.
    Deliver up my Lord of Westmoreland.
    Uncle, what news?

30 WORCESTER The King will bid you battle presently.

DOUGLAS Defy him by the Lord of Westmoreland.

HOTSPUR Lord Douglas, go you and tell him so.

DOUGLAS Marry, and shall, and very willingly.   *Exit.*

WORCESTER There is no seeming mercy in the King.

35 HOTSPUR Did you beg any? God forbid!

WORCESTER I told him gently of our grievances,
    Of his oath-breaking, which he mended thus,
    By now forswearing that he is forsworn.
    He calls us rebels, traitors, and will scourge
40   With haughty arms this hateful name in us.

Enter Douglas.

DOUGLAS Arm, gentlemen, to arms, for I have thrown
    A brave defiance in King Henry's teeth,
    And Westmoreland, that was engaged, did bear it;
    Which cannot choose but bring him quickly on.

WORCESTER The Prince of Wales stepped forth before
    the King
45   And, nephew, challenged you to single fight.

HOTSPUR O, would the quarrel lay upon our heads,
    And that no man might draw short breath today
    But I and Harry Monmouth! Tell me, tell me,
50   How showed his tasking? Seemed it in contempt?

---

26 **Deliver** report   28 **Westmoreland** (who has been hostage for the safe return of Worcester and Vernon)   43 **engaged** held as hostage   50 **tasking** challenging

VERNON No, by my soul. I never in my life
  Did hear a challenge urged more modestly,
  Unless a brother should a brother dare
  To gentle exercise and proof of arms.
  He gave you all the duties of a man;   55
  Trimmed up your praises with a princely tongue;
  Spoke your deservings like a chronicle;
  Making you ever better than his praise
  By still dispraising praise valued with you;
  And, which became him like a prince indeed,   60
  He made a blushing cital of himself,
  And chid his truant youth with such a grace
  As if he mast'red there a double spirit
  Of teaching and of learning instantly.
  There did he pause; but let me tell the world,   65
  If he outlive the envy of this day,
  England did never owe so sweet a hope,
  So much misconstrued in his wantonness.

HOTSPUR Cousin, I think thou art enamorèd
  On his follies. Never did I hear
  Of any prince so wild a liberty.   70
  But be he as he will, yet once ere night
  I will embrace him with a soldier's arm,
  That he shall shrink under my courtesy.
  Arm, arm with speed! And, fellows, soldiers, friends,   75
  Better consider what you have to do
  Than I, that have not well the gift of tongue,
  Can lift your blood up with persuasion.

Enter a Messenger.

MESSENGER My lord, here are letters for you.

HOTSPUR I cannot read them now—   80
  O gentlemen, the time of life is short!

---

55 **duties of a man** duties that one man can owe another 57 **like a chronicle**
i.e., with the itemized detail characteristic of a chronicle history 59 **dispraising**
... you i.e., because it must fall so far short of your deservings 61 **cital of**
reference to 64 **instantly** simultaneously 67 **owe** own 68 **in** with respect
to 71 **liberty** reckless freedom 74 **That** so that

To spend that shortness basely were too long
If life did ride upon a dial's point,
Still ending at the arrival of an hour.
85 And if we live, we live to tread on kings;
If die, brave death, when princes die with us!
Now for our consciences, the arms are fair,
When the intent of bearing them is just.

Enter another [Messenger].

MESSENGER My lord, prepare. The King comes on
apace.

90 HOTSPUR I thank him that he cuts me from my tale,
For I profess not talking: only this—
Let each man do his best; and here draw I
A sword whose temper I intend to stain
With the best blood that I can meet withal
95 In the adventure of this perilous day.
Now, Esperance! Percy! and set on.
Sound all the lofty instruments of war,
And by that music let us all embrace;
For, heaven to earth, some of us never shall
100 A second time do such a courtesy.
Here they embrace. The trumpets sound. [Exeunt.]

[Scene III. *Shrewsbury. The battlefield.*]

*The King enters with his power. Alarum to the battle.
[Exeunt.] Then enter Douglas, and Sir Walter Blunt
[disguised as the King].*

BLUNT What is thy name, that in battle thus thou
crossest me?
What honor dost thou seek upon my head?

82-84 To ... hour if life were measured by a clock's hand, closing after a single
hour, it would still be too long if basely spent   99 heaven to earth the odds are
as great as heaven to earth

DOUGLAS Know then my name is Douglas,
   And I do haunt thee in the battle thus
   Because some tell me that thou art a king.   5

BLUNT They tell thee true.

DOUGLAS The Lord of Stafford dear today hath bought
   Thy likeness, for instead of thee, King Harry,
   This sword hath ended him: so shall it thee,
   Unless thou yield thee as my prisoner.   10

BLUNT I was not born a yielder, thou proud Scot;
   And thou shalt find a king that will revenge
   Lord Stafford's death.

*They fight. Douglas kills Blunt. Then enter
Hotspur.*

HOTSPUR O Douglas, hadst thou fought at Holmedon
   thus,
   I never had triumphed upon a Scot.   15

DOUGLAS All's done, all's won: here breathless lies the
   King.

HOTSPUR Where?

DOUGLAS Here.

HOTSPUR This, Douglas? No. I know this face full well.
   A gallant knight he was, his name was Blunt;   20
   Semblably furnished like the King himself.

DOUGLAS A fool go with thy soul, whither it goes!
   A borrowed title hast thou bought too dear:
   Why didst thou tell me that thou wert a king?

HOTSPUR The King hath many marching in his coats.   25

DOUGLAS Now, by my sword, I will kill all his coats;
   I'll murder all his wardrobe, piece by piece,
   Until I meet the King.

V.iii.21 **Semblably** similarly   22 **fool** i.e., the title "fool"

HOTSPUR   Up and away!
Our soldiers stand full fairly for the day.   [*Exeunt.*]

Alarum. Enter Falstaff solus.

30   FALSTAFF Though I could scape shot-free at London,
I fear the shot here. Here's no scoring but upon the
pate. Soft! Who are you? Sir Walter Blunt. There's
honor for you! Here's no vanity! I am as hot as
molten lead, and as heavy too. God keep lead out of
35   me. I need no more weight than mine own bowels.
I have led my rag-of-muffins where they are peppered. There's not three of my hundred and fifty
left alive, and they are for the town's end, to beg
during life. But who comes here?

Enter the Prince.

PRINCE What, stands thou idle here? Lend me thy
40   sword.
Many a nobleman lies stark and stiff
Under the hoofs of vaunting enemies, whose deaths
are yet unrevenged. I prithee lend me thy sword.

FALSTAFF O Hal, I prithee give me leave to breathe
45   awhile. Turk Gregory never did such deeds in arms
as I have done this day. I have paid Percy, I have
made him sure.

PRINCE He is indeed, and living to kill thee.
I prithee lend me thy sword.

50   FALSTAFF Nay, before God, Hal, if Percy be alive, thou
gets not my sword; but take my pistol if thou wilt.

PRINCE Give it me. What, is it in the case?

30 **shot-free** without paying the bill   31 **scoring** (1) billing (2) striking
33 **Here's no vanity** (spoken ironically: i.e., here *is* "vanity"—futility, foolishness.
But vanity also implies lightness, which is then set against the "heaviness" of life:
cf. "lead," "heavy," "weight")   36-37 **I ... peppered** (a common practice of
officers, who drew the dead soldiers' pay)   45 **Turk Gregory** (in Shakespeare's
time, "Turk" was a byword for any ruthless man; "Gregory" may refer to the
irascible Pope Gregory VII, or to Elizabeth's enemy, Pope Gregory XIII. Pope
and Turk were regarded as the two great enemies of Protestant Christendom)
46 **paid** killed

FALSTAFF Ay, Hal. 'Tis hot, 'tis hot. There's that will
sack a city.

> *The Prince draws it out and finds*
> *it to be a bottle of sack.*

PRINCE What, is it a time to jest and dally now?   55
> *He throws the bottle at him. Exit.*

FALSTAFF Well, if Percy be alive, I'll pierce him. If he
do come in my way, so; if he do not, if I come in his
willingly, let him make a carbonado of me. I like
not such grinning honor as Sir Walter hath. Give
me life; which if I can save, so; if not, honor comes   60
unlooked for, and there's an end.   [*Exit.*]

[Scene IV. *Shrewsbury. The battlefield.*]

Alarum. Excursions. Enter the King, the Prince,
Lord John of Lancaster, Earl of Westmoreland.

KING I prithee, Harry, withdraw thyself, thou bleedest
too much.
Lord John of Lancaster, go you with him.

JOHN Not I, my lord, unless I did bleed too.

PRINCE I beseech your Majesty make up,
Lest your retirement do amaze your friends.   5

KING I will do so. My Lord of Westmoreland, lead
him to his tent.

WESTMORELAND Come, my lord, I'll lead you to your
tent.

PRINCE Lead me, my lord? I do not need your help;
And God forbid a shallow scratch should drive   10

---

53 **hot** i.e., he has fired it so often he has had to put it away to cool   56 **pierce**
(pronounced "perse")   58 **carbonado** meat slashed open for broiling
V.iv.s.d. **Excursions** sorties   4 **make up** move forward   5 **amaze** dismay

The Prince of Wales from such a field as this,
Where stained nobility lies trodden on,
And rebels' arms triumph in massacres!

JOHN We breathe too long. Come, cousin
　　　Westmoreland,
15　　Our duty this way lies. For God's sake, come.
　　　　　　　[*Exeunt Lancaster and Westmoreland.*]

PRINCE By God, thou hast deceived me, Lancaster!
　　　I did not think thee lord of such a spirit.
　　　Before, I loved thee as a brother, John,
　　　But now I do respect thee as my soul.

20　KING I saw him hold Lord Percy at the point
　　　With lustier maintenance than I did look for
　　　Of such an ungrown warrior.

PRINCE O, this boy lends mettle to us all!　　*Exit.*

　　　　　　　[*Enter Douglas.*]

DOUGLAS Another king? They grow like Hydra's
　　　heads.
25　　I am the Douglas, fatal to all those
　　　That wear those colors on them. What art thou
　　　That counterfeit'st the person of a king?

KING The King himself, who, Douglas, grieves at heart
　　　So many of his shadows thou hast met,
30　　And not the very King. I have two boys
　　　Seek Percy and thyself about the field;
　　　But, seeing thou fall'st on me so luckily,
　　　I will assay thee, and defend thyself.

DOUGLAS I fear thou art another counterfeit;
35　　And yet, in faith, thou bearest thee like a king.
　　　But mine I am sure thou art, whoe'er thou be,
　　　And thus I win thee.

　　　　*They fight, the King being in danger. Enter Prince
　　　　　　　　of Wales.*

14 **breathe** pause　24 **Hydra** a many-headed monster which grew two heads for each one destroyed

222

PRINCE Hold up thy head, vile Scot, or thou art like
    Never to hold it up again. The spirits
    Of valiant Shirley, Stafford, Blunt are in my arms.   40
    It is the Prince of Wales that threatens thee,
    Who never promiseth but he means to pay.

                          They fight: Douglas flieth.
    Cheerly, my lord. How fares your Grace?
    Sir Nicholas Gawsey hath for succor sent,
    And so hath Clifton. I'll to Clifton straight.   45

KING Stay and breathe awhile.
    Thou hast redeemed thy lost opinion,
    And showed thou mak'st some tender of my life,
    In this fair rescue thou hast brought to me.

PRINCE O God, they did me too much injury   50
    That ever said I heark'ned for your death.
    If it were so, I might have let alone
    The insulting hand of Douglas over you,
    Which would have been as speedy in your end
    As all the poisonous potions in the world,   55
    And saved the treacherous labor of your son.

KING Make up to Clifton; I'll to Sir Nicholas Gawsey.
                                 Exit.

Enter Hotspur.

HOTSPUR If I mistake not, thou art Harry Monmouth.

PRINCE Thou speak'st as if I would deny my name.

HOTSPUR My name is Harry Percy.   60

PRINCE Why, then I see a very valiant rebel of the name.
    I am the Prince of Wales, and think not, Percy,
    To share with me in glory any more.
    Two stars keep not their motion in one sphere,
    Nor can one England brook a double reign   65
    Of Harry Percy and the Prince of Wales.

40 **Shirley, Stafford, Blunt** (those whom Douglas has killed wearing the King's coats) 47 **opinion** reputation 48 **tender** value 64 **sphere** orbit 65 **brook** put up with

HOTSPUR Nor shall it, Harry, for the hour is come
　　　　To end the one of us; and would to God
　　　　Thy name in arms were now as great as mine!

70 PRINCE I'll make it greater ere I part from thee,
　　　　And all the budding honors on thy crest
　　　　I'll crop to make a garland for my head.

HOTSPUR I can no longer brook thy vanities. *They fight*.

Enter Falstaff.

FALSTAFF Well said, Hal! To it, Hal! Nay, you shall find
75 no boy's play here, I can tell you.

*Enter Douglas. He fighteth with Falstaff, [who] falls
down as if he were dead. [Exit Douglas.] The Prince
killeth Percy.*

HOTSPUR O Harry, thou hast robbed me of my youth!
　　　　I better brook the loss of brittle life
　　　　Than those proud titles thou hast won of me.
　　　　They wound my thoughts worse than thy sword my
　　　　　flesh.
80　　　But thoughts, the slaves of life, and life, time's fool,
　　　　And time, that takes survey of all the world,
　　　　Must have a stop. O, I could prophesy,
　　　　But that the earthy and cold hand of death
　　　　Lies on my tongue. No, Percy, thou art dust,
85　　　And food for—　　　　　　　　　　　　[*Dies*.]

PRINCE For worms, brave Percy. Fare thee well, great
　　　　　heart.
　　　　Ill-weaved ambition, how much art thou shrunk!
　　　　When that this body did contain a spirit,
　　　　A kingdom for it was too small a bound;
90　　　But now two paces of the vilest earth
　　　　Is room enough. This earth that bears thee dead
　　　　Bears not alive so stout a gentleman.
　　　　If thou wert sensible of courtesy,
　　　　I should not make so dear a show of zeal.

---

80 **slaves ... fool** i.e., because thoughts are dependent on life and because life is
subservient to time　92 **stout** valiant　94 **dear** heartfelt

But let my favors hide thy mangled face;   95
And, even in thy behalf, I'll thank myself
For doing these fair rites of tenderness.
Adieu, and take thy praise with thee to heaven.
Thy ignominy sleep with thee in the grave,
But not rememb'red in thy epitaph.   100
>   *He spieth Falstaff on the ground.*
What, old acquaintance? Could not all this flesh
Keep in a little life? Poor Jack, farewell!
I could have better spared a better man.
O, I should have a heavy miss of thee
If I were much in love with vanity.   105
Death hath not struck so fat a deer today,
Though many dearer, in this bloody fray.
Emboweled will I see thee by-and-by;
Till then in blood by noble Percy lie.   *Exit.*

>   *Falstaff riseth up.*

FALSTAFF Emboweled? If thou embowel me today, I'll   110
give you leave to powder me and eat me too tomorrow. 'Sblood, 'twas time to counterfeit, or that
hot termagant Scot had paid me scot and lot too.
Counterfeit? I lie; I am no counterfeit. To die is to
be a counterfeit, for he is but the counterfeit of a   115
man who hath not the life of a man; but to counterfeit dying when a man thereby liveth, is to be no
counterfeit, but the true and perfect image of life
indeed. The better part of valor is discretion, in the
which better part I have saved my life. Zounds, I am   120
afraid of this gunpowder Percy, though he be dead.
How if he should counterfeit too, and rise? By my
faith, I am afraid he would prove the better counterfeit. Therefore I'll make him sure; yea, and I'll swear

95 **favors** (probably Hal's ostrich plumes, his emblem as Prince of Wales)
104 **heavy miss** "heavy" loss (in two senses)   105 **vanity** frivolity (and lightness)
106 **deer** (with pun on "dear")   107 **dearer** nobler, more valuable   108
Emboweled disemboweled (for embalming)   111 **powder** salt   113 **termagant**
bloodthirsty   113 **paid me scot and lot** killed me (literally, paid me in full;
"scot" and "lot" were parish taxes)   119 **The ... discretion** (Falstaff willfully
misinterprets the maxim that valor is the better for being accompanied by
discretion)

125   I killed him. Why may not he rise as well as I? Noth-
       ing confutes me but eyes, and nobody sees me.
       Therefore, sirrah [*stabs him*], with a new wound in
       your thigh, come you along with me.

       *He takes up Hotspur on his back. Enter Prince
       [and] John of Lancaster.*

PRINCE Come, brother John; full bravely hast thou
       fleshed
       Thy maiden sword.

130 JOHN   But, soft! whom have we here?
       Did you not tell me this fat man was dead?

PRINCE I did; I saw him dead,
       Breathless and bleeding on the ground. Art thou alive,
       Or is it fantasy that plays upon our eyesight?
135   I prithee speak. We will not trust our eyes
       Without our ears. Thou art not what thou seem'st.

FALSTAFF No, that's certain, I am not a double man;
       but if I be not Jack Falstaff, then am I a Jack. There
       is Percy. If your father will do me any honor, so; if
140   not, let him kill the next Percy himself. I look to be
       either earl or duke, I can assure you.

PRINCE Why, Percy I killed myself, and saw thee dead!

FALSTAFF Didst thou? Lord, Lord, how this world is
       given to lying. I grant you I was down, and out of
145   breath, and so was he; but we rose both at an instant
       and fought a long hour by Shrewsbury clock. If I
       may be believed, so; if not, let them that should re-
       ward valor bear the sin upon their own heads. I'll
       take it upon my death, I gave him this wound in the
150   thigh. If the man were alive and would deny it,
       zounds! I would make him eat a piece of my sword.

JOHN This is the strangest tale that ever I heard.

PRINCE This is the strangest fellow, brother John.
       Come, bring your luggage nobly on your back.

137 **double man** (1) wraith (2) twofold man   138 **Jack** rascal

For my part, if a lie may do thee grace,   155
I'll gild it with the happiest terms I have.

A retreat is sounded.

The trumpet sounds retreat; the day is ours.
Come, brother, let us to the highest of the field,
To see what friends are living, who are dead.

Exeunt [Prince Henry and Prince John].

FALSTAFF I'll follow, as they say, for reward. He that   160
rewards me, God reward him. If I do grow great,
I'll grow less; for I'll purge, and leave sack, and
live cleanly, as a nobleman should do.

Exit [bearing off the body].

[Scene V. *Shrewsbury. The battlefield.*]

*The trumpets sound. Enter the King, Prince of Wales,
Lord John of Lancaster, Earl of Westmoreland, with
Worcester and Vernon prisoners.*

KING Thus ever did rebellion find rebuke.
Ill-spirited Worcester, did not we send grace,
Pardon, and terms of love to all of you?
And wouldst thou turn our offers contrary?
Misuse the tenor of thy kinsman's trust?   5
Three knights upon our party slain today,
A noble earl, and many a creature else
Had been alive this hour,
If like a Christian thou hadst truly borne
Betwixt our armies true intelligence.   10

WORCESTER What I have done my safety urged me to;
And I embrace this fortune patiently,
Since not to be avoided it falls on me.

KING Bear Worcester to the death, and Vernon too;
Other offenders we will pause upon.   15

160 **follow** i.e., as hounds do when the quarry is killed, to receive their
reward 162 **purge** repent V.v.10 **intelligence** information

227

[Exeunt Worcester and Vernon, guarded.]
How goes the field?

PRINCE The noble Scot, Lord Douglas, when he saw
The fortune of the day quite turned from him,
The noble Percy slain, and all his men
20 Upon the foot of fear, fled with the rest;
And falling from a hill, he was so bruised
That the pursuers took him. At my tent
The Douglas is, and I beseech your Grace
I may dispose of him.

KING   With all my heart.

25 PRINCE Then, brother John of Lancaster, to you
This honorable bounty shall belong.
Go to the Douglas and deliver him
Up to his pleasure, ransomless and free.
His valors shown upon our crests today
30 Have taught us how to cherish such high deeds,
Even in the bosom of our adversaries.

JOHN I thank your Grace for this high courtesy,
Which I shall give away immediately.

KING Then this remains, that we divide our power.
35 You, son John, and my cousin Westmoreland,
Towards York shall bend you with your dearest
speed
To meet Northumberland and the prelate Scroop,
Who, as we hear, are busily in arms.
Myself and you, son Harry, will towards Wales
40 To fight with Glendower and the Earl of March.
Rebellion in this land shall lose his sway,
Meeting the check of such another day;
And since this business so fair is done,
Let us not leave till all our own be won.   *Exeunt.*

FINIS

43 **business** (trisyllabic)

Textual Note

The text for the present edition as a whole is the first quarto of 1598. This is generally believed to have been set from an earlier edition of the same year (Q0), of which today only four leaves are known—containing the text of the play from I.iii.199 to II.ii.112. Q0, so far as we have it, shows characteristics which relate it closely to an authorial manuscript, probably a corrected working manuscript rather than a fair copy. Q1 may therefore be regarded as still reasonably faithful to what Shakespeare wrote. The later quartos (Q2, 1599; Q3, 1604; Q4, 1608; Q5, 1613), each set from the one preceding, and the Folio (1623), set from Q5, have increasingly less authority.

Apart from spelling and punctuation, which are modernized in this edition, and regularization of speech prefixes, I have followed Q1, and, where it exists, Q0. With one exception (IV.i.12-13), I preserve the lineation of these editions, printing therefore as prose a number of passages so printed in Q1 but now almost invariably divided into lines of verse. It is possible, even probable, that some of these passages were intended to be verse; but the wide differences exhibited by editors in lineating them persuade me to reserve this entertainment for readers who wish to engage in it. I have usually indicated in the footnotes one or more of the traditional patterns of lineation for each passage.

The table below records departures from Q0-Q1. The first reading (bold) is that which I have adopted in the text; the second is that of Q1. Almost all of the emendations were made in the quartos or in the First Folio, indicating that in Shakespeare's own day the passages in question were suspect; but because these early texts have no authority, they are not cited as sources.

Division into acts and scenes is here that of the Folio, save that I follow Capell and most other editors (including those of the Globe edition) in dividing the Folio's V.ii into V.ii and V.iii and renumbering the subsequent scenes. In the quartos

TEXTUAL NOTE

there is no indication of acts or scenes.

I.i.62 **a dear** deere   69 **blood did** bloud. Did   76 **In faith it is** [the quartos and folios give to the King]

I.ii.82 **similes** smiles   166 **Bardolph, Peto** Haruey, Rossill [these are names that Shakespeare evidently meant originally to assign to Falstaff's associates: see below, II.iv.173-76, 180-81]

I.iii.199-206 [Q0-Q4 do not assign to Hotspur, but give as part of Northumberland's speech]

II.ii.16 **two and twenty** xxii

II.iii.4 **respect** the respect   70 **A roan** Roane

II.iv.24 **precedent** present   37 [assigned to Prince]   173-76 [assigned to Gadshill, Ross (=Russell: see above, I.ii.166), Falstaff, Ross]   180-81 [assigned to Ross] 244 **eel-skin** elsskin   341 **Owen** O   393 **tristful** trustfull

III.i.99 **cantle** scantle   132 **on an**

III.ii.115 **Enlargèd** Enlargd

III.iii.36 **that's** that   59 **tithe** tight   90s.d. **them** him   178 **guests** ghesse 206 **o'** of

IV.i.20 **I, my lord** I my mind   54 **is** tis   107 **dropped** drop   125 **cannot** can 126 **yet** it

IV.iii.21 **horse** horses   28 **ours** our   82 **country's** Countrey

V.i.138 **will it** wil

V.ii.3 **undone** vnder one   25s.d. **Hotspur** Percy

V.iii.22 **A** Ah

V.iv.67 **Nor** Now   75s.d. **who he**   157 **ours** our

WILLIAM
SHAKESPEARE

THE SECOND
PART OF
KING HENRY IV

Edited by Norman N. Holland

The Actors' Names

RUMOR, the Presenter

KING HENRY THE FOURTH

PRINCE HENRY, afterwards crowned King Henry the Fifth

PRINCE JOHN OF LANCASTER
HUMPHREY OF GLOUCESTER } sons to Henry IV and
THOMAS OF CLARENCE   brethren to Henry V

[EARL OF] NORTHUMBERLAND
[RICHARD SCROOP] the Arch-
   bishop of York
[LORD] MOWBRAY
[LORD] HASTINGS } opposites against
LORD BARDOLPH   King Henry IV
TRAVERS
MORTON
[SIR JOHN] COLEVILLE

[EARL OF] WARWICK
[EARL OF]
   WESTMORELAND
[EARL OF] SURREY } of the
[SIR JOHN BLUNT]   King's
GOWER   party
HARCOURT
LORD CHIEF JUSTICE

POINS
[SIR JOHN]
   FALSTAFF
BARDOLPH } irregular
PISTOL   humorists
PETO
[FALSTAFF'S]
   PAGE

[ROBERT] SHALLOW } both coun-
SILENCE   try justices

DAVY, servant to Shallow

FANG and SNARE, two sergeants

[RALPH] MOLDY
[SIMON] SHADOW
[THOMAS] WART } country
[FRANCIS] FEEBLE   soldiers
[PETER] BULLCALF

Drawers
Beadles
Grooms

Northumberland's Wife

Percy's Widow

[LADY PERCY]
HOSTESS QUICKLY
DOLL TEARSHEET
[A Dancer as] Epilogue

[PORTER, MESSENGER, SOLDIERS, LORDS, ATTENDANTS
Scene: England]

THE SECOND PART OF [KING] HENRY IV

[INDUCTION]

Enter Rumor, painted full of tongues.

[RUMOR] Open your ears, for which of you will stop
    The vent of hearing when loud Rumor speaks?
    I, from the orient to the drooping west,
    Making the wind my post-horse, still unfold
    The acts commencèd on this ball of earth.   5
    Upon my tongues continual slanders ride,
    The which in every language I pronounce,
    Stuffing the ears of men with false reports.
    I speak of peace while covert enmity
    Under the smile of safety wounds the world.   10
    And who but Rumor, who but only I,
    Make fearful musters and prepared defense
    Whiles the big year, swoln with some other grief,
    Is thought with child by the stern tyrant, war,
    And no such matter? Rumor is a pipe   15
    Blown by surmises, jealousies, conjectures,
    And of so easy and so plain a stop
    That the blunt monster with uncounted heads,
    The still-discordant wav'ring multitude,
    Can play upon it. But what need I thus   20
    My well-known body to anatomize
    Among my household? Why is Rumor here?

Text references are printed in **bold** type; the annotation follows in roman type.

Ind.15 **pipe** wind instrument   18 **blunt** dull   22 **my household** i.e., the audience

I run before King Harry's victory,
Who in a bloody field by Shrewsbury
25 Hath beaten down young Hotspur and his troops,
Quenching the flame of bold rebellion
Even with the rebels' blood. But what mean I
To speak so true at first? My office is
To noise abroad that Harry Monmouth fell
30 Under the wrath of noble Hotspur's sword,
And that the King before the Douglas' rage
Stooped his anointed head as low as death.
This have I rumored through the peasant towns
Between that royal field of Shrewsbury
35 And this worm-eaten hole of ragged stone,
Where Hotspur's father, old Northumberland,
Lies crafty-sick. The posts come tiring on,
And not a man of them brings other news
Than they have learned of me. From Rumor's
        tongues
They bring smooth comforts false, worse than true
40   wrongs.   *Exit Rumor.*

25 **Hotspur** Harry Percy, the Earl of Northumberland's son, a rebel against King Henry IV, killed by the Prince of Wales   29 **Harry Monmouth** the Prince of Wales, Prince Hal   35 **ragged** rough-edged   37 **crafty-sick** feigning sickness   37 **tiring** exhausting themselves

[ACT I

Scene I. *Northumberland's castle.*]

Enter the Lord Bardolph at one door.

LORD BARDOLPH Who keeps the gate here, ho? Where
  is the Earl?

PORTER [*Within*] What shall I say you are?

LORD BARDOLPH   Tell thou the Earl
  That the Lord Bardolph doth attend him here.

PORTER His lordship is walked forth into the orchard.
  Please it your honor, knock but at the gate,   5
  And he himself will answer.

Enter the Earl [of] Northumberland.

LORD BARDOLPH   Here comes the Earl.

NORTHUMBERLAND What news, Lord Bardolph? Every
  minute now
  Should be the father of some stratagem.
  The times are wild. Contention, like a horse
  Full of high feeding, madly hath broke loose   10
  And bears down all before him.

LORD BARDOLPH   Noble Earl,
  I bring you certain news from Shrewsbury.

NORTHUMBERLAND Good, and God will!

LORD BARDOLPH   As good as heart can wish.
  The King is almost wounded to the death;
15 And, in the fortune of my lord your son,
  Prince Harry slain outright; and both the Blunts
  Killed by the hand of Douglas; young Prince John
  And Westmoreland and Stafford fled the field;
  And Harry Monmouth's brawn, the hulk Sir John,
20 Is prisoner to your son. O, such a day,
  So fought, so followed, and so fairly won,
  Came not till now to dignify the times
  Since Caesar's fortunes!

NORTHUMBERLAND   How is this derived?
  Saw you the field? Came you from Shrewsbury?

LORD BARDOLPH I spake with one, my lord, that came
25   from thence,

                    Enter Travers.

  A gentleman well bred and of good name,
  That freely rend'red me these news for true.

NORTHUMBERLAND Here comes my servant Travers,
      who I sent
  On Tuesday last to listen after news.

LORD BARDOLPH My lord, I overrode him on the
30   way,
  And he is furnished with no certainties
  More than he haply may retail from me.

NORTHUMBERLAND Now, Travers, what good tidings
      comes with you?

TRAVERS My lord, Sir John Umfrevile turned me back
35   With joyful tidings, and, being better horsed,
  Outrode me. After him came spurring hard

I.i.13 and if   19 brawn fattened boar   28 Travers (to "traverse" is to deny)
30 overrode outrode   32 haply perhaps

A gentleman, almost forspent with speed,
That stopped by me to breathe his bloodied horse.
He asked the way to Chester, and of him
I did demand what news from Shrewsbury.   40
He told me that rebellion had bad luck,
And that young Harry Percy's spur was cold.
With that, he gave his able horse the head,
And bending forward struck his armèd heels
Against the panting sides of his poor jade   45
Up to the rowel-head, and starting so
He seemed in running to devour the way,
Staying no longer question.

NORTHUMBERLAND   Ha? Again.
Said he young Harry Percy's spur was cold?
Of Hotspur Coldspur? That rebellion   50
Had met ill luck?

LORD BARDOLPH   My lord, I'll tell you what.
If my young lord your son have not the day,
Upon mine honor, for a silken point
I'll give my barony. Never talk of it.

NORTHUMBERLAND Why should that gentleman that
      rode by Travers
Give then such instances of loss?   55

LORD BARDOLPH   Who, he?
He was some hilding fellow that had stol'n
The horse he rode on, and, upon my life,
Spoke at a venture. Look, here comes more news.

Enter Morton.

NORTHUMBERLAND Yea, this man's brow, like to a title-
      leaf,   60
Foretells the nature of a tragic volume.
So looks the strond whereon the imperious flood
Hath left a witnessed usurpation.
Say, Morton, didst thou come from Shrewsbury?

37 **forspent** totally used up   45 **jade** nag   53 **point** lace (used to tie breeches
up)   57 **hilding** base   62 **strond** shore   63 **witnessed** evidence of

65   MORTON I ran from Shrewsbury, my noble lord,
             Where hateful death put on his ugliest mask
             To fright our party.

     NORTHUMBERLAND   How doth my son and brother?
             Thou tremblest, and the whiteness in thy cheek
             Is apter than thy tongue to tell thy errand.
70   Even such a man, so faint, so spiritless,
             So dull, so dead in look, so woebegone,
             Drew Priam's curtain in the dead of night,
             And would have told him half his Troy was burnt.
             But Priam found the fire ere he his tongue
75   And I my Percy's death ere thou report'st it.
             This thou wouldst say, "Your son did thus and
                 thus;
             Your brother thus. So fought the noble Douglas,"
             Stopping my greedy ear with their bold deeds.
             But in the end, to stop my ear indeed,
80   Thou hast a sigh to blow away this praise,
             Ending with "Brother, son, and all are dead."

     MORTON Douglas is living, and your brother—yet;
             But, for my lord your son—

     NORTHUMBERLAND   Why, he is dead!
             See what a ready tongue suspicion hath!
85   He that but fears the thing he would not know
             Hath by instinct knowledge from others' eyes
             That what he feared is chanced. Yet speak, Morton.
             Tell thou an earl his divination lies,
             And I will take it as a sweet disgrace
90   And make thee rich for doing me such wrong.

     MORTON You are too great to be by me gainsaid.
             Your spirit is too true, your fears too certain.

     NORTHUMBERLAND Yet, for all this, say not that Percy's
                 dead.
             I see a strange confession in thine eye.
95   Thou shak'st thy head and hold'st it fear, or sin,
             To speak a truth. If he be slain, say so.
             The tongue offends not that reports his death;

And he doth sin that doth belie the dead,
Not he which says the dead is not alive.
Yet the first bringer of unwelcome news   100
Hath but a losing office, and his tongue
Sounds ever after as a sullen bell,
Rememb'red tolling a departing friend.

LORD BARDOLPH I cannot think, my lord, your son is
    dead.

MORTON I am sorry I should force you to believe   105
    That which I would to God I had not seen.
But these mine eyes saw him in bloody state,
Rend'ring faint quittance, wearied and out-
    breathed,
To Harry Monmouth, whose swift wrath beat down
The never-daunted Percy to the earth,   110
From whence with life he never more sprung up.
In few, his death, whose spirit lent a fire
Even to the dullest peasant in his camp,
Being bruited once, took fire and heat away
From the best-tempered courage in his troops.   115
For from his mettle was his party steeled,
Which once in him abated, all the rest
Turned on themselves, like dull and heavy lead.
And as the thing that's heavy in itself,
Upon enforcement flies with greatest speed,   120
So did our men, heavy in Hotspur's loss,
Lend to this weight such lightness with their fear
That arrows fled not swifter toward their aim
Than did our soldiers, aiming at their safety,
Fly from the field. Then was that noble Worcester   125
So soon ta'en prisoner. And that furious Scot,
The bloody Douglas, whose well-laboring sword
Had three times slain th' appearance of the King,
'Gan vail his stomach and did grace the shame
Of those that turned their backs, and in his flight,   130

---

108 **quittance** repaying (of blows)   112 **few** i.e., few words   114 **bruited** noised
about   128 **th' appearance of the King** noblemen disguised as the King
129 **'Gan vail his stomach** began to abate his courage   129 **grace** favor

Stumbling in fear, was took. The sum of all
Is that the King hath won, and hath sent out
A speedy power to encounter you, my lord,
Under the conduct of young Lancaster
135 And Westmoreland. This is the news at full.

NORTHUMBERLAND For this I shall have time enough to
mourn.
In poison there is physic; and these news,
Having been well, that would have made me sick,
Being sick, have in some measure made me well.
140 And, as the wretch whose fever-weak'ned joints,
Like strengthless hinges, buckle under life,
Impatient of his fit, breaks like a fire
Out of his keeper's arms, even so my limbs,
Weak'ned with grief, being now enraged with
grief,
Are thrice themselves. Hence, therefore, thou nice
145 crutch!
A scaly gauntlet now with joints of steel
Must glove this hand. And hence, thou sickly
quoif!
Thou art a guard too wanton for the head
Which princes, fleshed with conquest, aim to hit.
150 Now bind my brows with iron, and approach
The ragged'st hour that time and spite dare bring
To frown upon th' enraged Northumberland!
Let heaven kiss earth! Now let not Nature's hand
Keep the wild flood confined! Let order die!
155 And let this world no longer be a stage
To feed contention in a ling'ring act!
But let one spirit of the firstborn Cain
Reign in all bosoms, that, each heart being set
On bloody courses, the rude scene may end,
160 And darkness be the burier of the dead!

---

137 physic medicine 138 Having been well, that that, had they been well
144 grief ... grief sickness ... sorrow 145 nice delicate 147 quoif
nightcap 148 wanton light 149 fleshed with having savored 151 ragged'st
roughest 156 act (1) deed (2) section of a play

LORD BARDOLPH This strainèd passion doth you wrong,
   my lord.

MORTON Sweet Earl, divorce not wisdom from your
   honor.
  The lives of all your loving complices
  Lean on your health, the which, if you give o'er
  To stormy passion, must perforce decay.   165
  You cast th' event of war, my noble lord,
  And summed the account of chance, before you
    said,
  "Let us make head." It was your presurmise
  That, in the dole of blows, your son might drop.
  You knew he walked o'er perils, on an edge,   170
  More likely to fall in than to get o'er.
  You were advised his flesh was capable
  Of wounds and scars and that his forward spirit
  Would lift him where most trade of danger ranged.
  Yet did you say, "Go forth." And none of this,   175
  Though strongly apprehended, could restrain
  The stiff-borne action. What hath then befall'n,
  Or what hath this bold enterprise brought forth,
  More than that being which was like to be?

LORD BARDOLPH We all that are engagèd to this loss   180
  Knew that we ventured on such dangerous seas
  That if we wrought out life 'twas ten to one.
  And yet we ventured, for the gain proposed
  Choked the respect of likely peril feared.
  And since we are o'erset, venture again.   185
  Come, we will all put forth, body and goods.

MORTON 'Tis more than time. And, my most noble
   lord,
  I hear for certain, and dare speak the truth:
  The gentle Archbishop of York is up

---

166 **cast th' event** estimated the outcome 168 **make head** raise an army
169 **dole** dealing out 177 **stiff-borne** determinedly carried on 180 **engagèd**
bound by contract 184 **respect** consideration 185 **o'erset** (1) upset, capsized
(2) outwagered 186 **put forth** wager

190 With well-appointed pow'rs. He is a man
 Who with a double surety binds his followers.
 My lord your son had only but the corpse,
 But shadows and the shows of men, to fight.
 For that same word "rebellion" did divide
195 The action of their bodies from their souls,
 And they did fight with queasiness, constrained,
 As men drink potions, that their weapons only
 Seemed on our side. But for their spirits and souls,
 This word "rebellion," it had froze them up
200 As fish are in a pond. But now the Bishop
 Turns insurrection to religion.
 Supposed sincere and holy in his thoughts,
 He's followed both with body and with mind,
 And doth enlarge his rising with the blood
 Of fair King Richard, scraped from Pomfret
205 stones;
 Derives from heaven his quarrel and his cause;
 Tells them he doth bestride a bleeding land,
 Gasping for life under great Bolingbroke;
 And more and less do flock to follow him.

NORTHUMBERLAND I knew of this before; but, to speak
210 truth,
 This present grief had wiped it from my mind.
 Go in with me, and counsel every man
 The aptest way for safety and revenge.
 Get posts and letters, and make friends with
  speed.
215 Never so few, and never yet more need. *Exeunt*.

---

190 **well-appointed pow'rs** well-equipped armies 191 **double** i.e., of body and soul 205 **Pomfret** Pomfret castle (where Richard II was murdered) 208 **Bolingbroke** King Henry IV 209 **more and less** high and low 214 **Get** beget 214 **make** collect

[Scene II. *London*.]

Enter Sir John [Falstaff] alone, with his Page
bearing his sword and buckler.

FALSTAFF Sirrah, you giant, what says the doctor to
    my water?

PAGE He said, sir, the water itself was a good healthy
    water; but, for the party that owed it, he might
    have moe diseases than he knew for.   5

FALSTAFF Men of all sorts take a pride to gird at me.
    The brain of this foolish compounded clay, man
    is not able to invent anything that intends to
    laughter more than I invent or is invented on me.
    I am not only witty in myself, but the cause that   10
    wit is in other men. I do here walk before thee like
    a sow that hath overwhelmed all her litter but one.
    If the Prince put thee into my service for any other
    reason than to set me off, why then I have no judg-
    ment. Thou whoreson mandrake, thou art fitter   15
    to be worn in my cap than to wait at my heels. I
    was never manned with an agate till now, but
    I will inset you neither in gold nor silver, but in
    vile apparel, and send you back again to your
    master, for a jewel—the juvenal, the Prince your   20
    master, whose chin is not yet fledge. I will sooner
    have a beard grow in the palm of my hand than
    he shall get one off his cheek, and yet he will not

I.ii.1 **giant** (the page was played by an unusually small boy, who probably
mimicked Falstaff)   2 **water** urine   4 **owed** owned   5 **moe** more   6 **gird** mock
7 **compounded clay, man** man, compounded of clay   15 **mandrake** man-
shaped root   17 **manned with an agate** attended by a servingman small as a
figure carved in a jewel   20 **juvenal** juvenile (echoing jewel)   21 **fledge**
feathered

stick to say his face is a face-royal. God may fin-
25 ish it when he will, 'tis not a hair amiss yet. He may
keep it still at a face-royal, for a barber shall
never earn sixpence out of it; and yet he'll be crow-
ing as if he had writ man ever since his father was
a bachelor. He may keep his own grace, but he's
30 almost out of mine, I can assure him. What said
Master Dummelton about the satin for my short
cloak and my slops?

PAGE He said, sir, you should procure him better
assurance than Bardolph. He would not take his
35 band and yours; he liked not the security.

FALSTAFF Let him be damned, like the glutton! Pray
God his tongue be hotter! A whoreson Achitophel!
A rascal, yea-forsooth knave! To bear a gentleman in hand, and then stand upon security! The
40 whoreson smooth-pates do now wear nothing but
high shoes, and bunches of keys at their girdles;
and if a man is through with them in honest taking
up, then they must stand upon security. I had as
lief they would put ratsbane in my mouth as offer
45 to stop it with "security." I looked 'a should have
sent me two-and-twenty yards of satin, as I am a
true knight, and he sends me "security." Well, he
may sleep in security, for he hath the horn of
abundance, and the lightness of his wife shines

24, 26 face-royal the King's face on a ten-shilling coin (the royal), which
presumably would not need the attention of a barber 28 writ styled himself
29 grace (1) title, "your Grace," (2) favor 32 slops wide breeches 34 assurance security (Bardolph is not Lord Bardolph, but one of Falstaff's cronies)
35 band bond 36 glutton Dives (who in Luke 16:24 asked for water to cool his
tongue) 37 Achitophel the counselor who betrayed Absalom (II Samuel
15-17) 38 yea-forsooth knave (one who swears sissy oaths like "yea,
forsooth") 40 smooth-pates tradesmen (who wore their hair short, not like a
nobleman's) 41 high shoes (sign of pride) 41 keys (sign of
possessions) 42-43 if a man ... security after a man completes a bargain on
credit with them, they suddenly demand security 45 'a he 48 horn
(1) cornucopia (2) cuckold's horn 49 lightness unchastity

through it. And yet cannot he see, though he have   50
his own lanthorn to light him. Where's Bardolph?

PAGE He's gone into Smithfield to buy your worship
a horse.

FALSTAFF I bought him in Paul's, and he'll buy me a
horse in Smithfield. And I could get me but a wife   55
in the stews, I were manned, horsed, and wived.

Enter Lord Chief Justice [and Servant].

PAGE Sir, here comes the nobleman that committed
the Prince for striking him about Bardolph.

FALSTAFF Wait close—I will not see him.

CHIEF JUSTICE What's he that goes there?   60

SERVANT Falstaff, and't please your lordship.

CHIEF JUSTICE He that was in question for the
robb'ry?

SERVANT He, my lord. But he hath since done good
service at Shrewsbury, and, as I hear, is now going   65
with some charge to the Lord John of Lancaster.

CHIEF JUSTICE What, to York? Call him back again.

SERVANT Sir John Falstaff!

FALSTAFF Boy, tell him I am deaf.

PAGE You must speak louder; my master is deaf.   70

CHIEF JUSTICE I am sure he is—to the hearing of anything good. Go, pluck him by the elbow. I must
speak with him.

SERVANT Sir John!

51 **lanthorn** lantern (in which a light shines through horn panels)   52 **Smith-field** the horse market   54 **Paul's** (unemployed men loitered in St. Paul's cathedral seeking service)   56 **stews** brothels   56 **manned, horsed, and wived** (a proverb: "Who goes to Westminster for a wife, to Paul's for a man, or to Smithfield for a horse, may meet with a whore, a knave, and a jade")   57 **committed** i.e., to prison (notice that the audience needed only this brief allusion to the story about Hal striking the Lord Chief Justice)   62 **in question** suspected   66 **charge** commission for soldiers

75   FALSTAFF What! A young knave, and begging! Is there
     not wars? Is there not employment? Doth not the
     King lack subjects? Do not the rebels need soldiers?
     Though it be a shame to be on any side but one, it
     is worse shame to beg than to be on the worst side,
80   were it worse than the name of rebellion can tell
     how to make it.

     SERVANT You mistake me, sir.

     FALSTAFF Why, sir, did I say you were an honest man?
     Setting my knighthood and my soldiership aside,
85   I had lied in my throat if I had said so.

     SERVANT I pray you, sir, then set your knighthood and
     your soldiership aside and give me leave to tell you
     you lie in your throat if you say I am any other
     than an honest man.

90   FALSTAFF I give thee leave to tell me so! I lay aside
     that which grows to me! If thou get'st any leave of
     me, hang me. If thou tak'st leave, thou wert better
     be hanged. You hunt counter. Hence! Avaunt!

     SERVANT Sir, my lord would speak with you.

95   CHIEF JUSTICE Sir John Falstaff, a word with you.

     FALSTAFF My good lord! God give your lordship good
     time of day. I am glad to see your lordship abroad.
     I heard say your lordship was sick. I hope your
     lordship goes abroad by advice. Your lordship,
100 though not clean past your youth, hath yet some
     smack of an age in you, some relish of the salt-
     ness of time in you; and I most humbly beseech
     your lordship to have a reverent care of your
     health.

105 CHIEF JUSTICE Sir John, I sent for you before your
     expedition to Shrewsbury.

     FALSTAFF And't please your lordship, I hear his Majesty

84 **Setting ... aside** i.e., because knights and soldiers ought not to lie
93 **counter** in the wrong direction   99 **advice** i.e., a physician's advice   101 **age**
(pun on "ague"; cf.IV.i.34)

is returned with some discomfort from Wales.

CHIEF JUSTICE I talk not of his Majesty. You would
not come when I sent for you.   110

FALSTAFF And I hear, moreover, his Highness is fall'n
into this same whoreson apoplexy.

CHIEF JUSTICE Well, God mend him! I pray you, let
me speak with you.

FALSTAFF This apoplexy, as I take it, is a kind of   115
lethargy, and't please your lordship, a kind of
sleeping in the blood, a whoreson tingling.

CHIEF JUSTICE What, tell you me of it? Be it as it is.

FALSTAFF It hath it original from much grief, from
study and perturbation of the brain. I have read the   120
cause of his effects in Galen. It is a kind of deaf-
ness.

CHIEF JUSTICE I think you are fall'n into the disease,
for you hear not what I say to you.

FALSTAFF Very well, my lord, very well. Rather, and't   125
please you, it is the disease of not listening, the
malady of not marking, that I am troubled withal.

CHIEF JUSTICE To punish you by the heels would
amend the attention of your ears, and I care not
if I do become your physician.   130

FALSTAFF I am as poor as Job, my lord, but not so
patient. Your lordship may minister the potion of
imprisonment to me in respect of poverty; but how
I should be your patient to follow your prescrip-
tions, the wise may make some dram of a scruple,   135
or indeed a scruple itself.

CHIEF JUSTICE I sent for you, when there were matters
against you for your life, to come speak with me.

119 it original its origin 121 Galen Greek physician (A.D. 129–199) whose
writings dominated Renaissance medical practice 128 punish you by the heels
put you in fetters or the stocks 135 dram, scruple apothecaries' small weights

FALSTAFF As I was then advised by my learned counsel
140　　in the laws of this land-service, I did not come.

CHIEF JUSTICE Well, the truth is, Sir John, you live in
great infamy.

FALSTAFF He that buckles himself in my belt cannot
live in less.

145　CHIEF JUSTICE Your means are very slender and your
waste is great.

FALSTAFF I would it were otherwise. I would my means
were greater and my waist slender.

CHIEF JUSTICE You have misled the youthful Prince.

150　FALSTAFF The young Prince hath misled me. I am the
fellow with the great belly, and he my dog.

CHIEF JUSTICE Well, I am loath to gall a new-healed
wound. Your day's service at Shrewsbury hath a
little gilded over your night's exploit on Gad's
155　Hill. You may thank th' unquiet time for your quiet
o'erposting that action.

FALSTAFF My lord?

CHIEF JUSTICE But since all is well, keep it so. Wake
not a sleeping wolf.

160　FALSTAFF To wake a wolf is as bad as smell a fox.

CHIEF JUSTICE What! You are as a candle, the better
part burnt out.

FALSTAFF A wassail candle, my lord, all tallow. If I
did say of wax, my growth would approve the
165　　truth.

---

140 **land-service** (a play on military service—in which Falstaff's sword would be
his "learned counsel"—as against the service of a legal summons)　151 **belly** i.e.,
so large he cannot see where he is going and therefore needs a dog to lead him (?), a
reference to some well-known beggar (?)　154 **exploit** (the robbery in
I *Henry IV*, II.ii. and iv)　155-56 **quiet o'erposting** quietly getting past
160 **smell a fox** be suspicious　163 **wassail candle** large candle designed to last
a whole night, as at a feast　164 **wax** a play on (1) beeswax (2) grow

CHIEF JUSTICE There is not a white hair in your face but should have his effect of gravity.

FALSTAFF His effect of gravy, gravy, gravy.

CHIEF JUSTICE You follow the young Prince up and down like his ill angel.   170

FALSTAFF Not so, my lord. Your ill angel is light, but I hope he that looks upon me will take me without weighing. And yet, in some respects, I grant, I cannot go. I cannot tell. Virtue is of so little regard in these costermongers' times that true valor is   175 turned berod. Pregnancy is made a tapster, and hath his quick wit wasted in giving reckonings. All the other gifts appertinent to man, as the malice of this age shapes them, are not worth a gooseberry. You that are old consider not the capacities of us   180 that are young. You do measure the heat of our livers with the bitterness of your galls. And we that are in the vaward of our youth, I must confess, are wags too.

CHIEF JUSTICE Do you set down your name in the   185 scroll of youth, that are written down old with all the characters of age? Have you not a moist eye, a dry hand, a yellow cheek, a white beard, a decreasing leg, an increasing belly? Is not your voice broken, your wind short, your chin double, your   190 wit single, and every part about you blasted with antiquity, and will you yet call yourself young? Fie, fie, fie, Sir John!

FALSTAFF My lord, I was born about three of the clock in the afternoon, with a white head and something   195

---

168 **gravy** with pun on the sense fatty sweat   171 **ill angel** clipped coin
171 **light** (1) not due weight (2) wanton   174 **go** (1) pass for currency
(2) copulate (?)   175 **costermongers'** hucksters'   176 **berod** bear-herd, one
who leads tame bears   176 **Pregnancy** quickness of wit   177 **reckonings** tavern
bills   183 **vaward** vanguard   191 **single** weak

a round belly. For my voice, I have lost it with
hallowing and singing of anthems. To approve
my youth further, I will not. The truth is, I am
only old in judgment and understanding; and he
200 that will caper with me for a thousand marks, let
him lend me the money, and have at him! For the
box of the ear that the Prince gave you, he gave it
like a rude prince, and you took it like a sensible
lord. I have checked him for it, and the young
205 lion repents, marry, not in ashes and sackcloth, but
in new silk and old sack.

CHIEF JUSTICE Well, God send the Prince a better
companion!

FALSTAFF God send the companion a better prince! I
210 cannot rid my hands of him.

CHIEF JUSTICE Well, the King hath severed you and
Prince Harry. I hear you are going with Lord John
of Lancaster against the Archbishop and the Earl
of Northumberland.

215 FALSTAFF Yea, I thank your pretty sweet wit for it. But
look you pray, all you that kiss my lady Peace at
home, that our armies join not in a hot day, for, by
the Lord, I take but two shirts out with me, and
I mean not to sweat extraordinarily. If it be a hot
220 day, and I brandish anything but a bottle, I would
I might never spit white again. There is not a
dangerous action can peep out his head but I am
thrust upon it. Well, I cannot last ever. But it was
alway yet the trick of our English nation, if they
225 have a good thing, to make it too common. If ye
will needs say I am an old man, you should give
me rest. I would to God my name were not so terrible to the enemy as it is. I were better to be eaten
to death with a rust than to be scoured to nothing
230 with perpetual motion.

197 **hallowing** (1) sanctifying (2) "halloing," shouting to hounds   197 **approve**
prove   200 **caper** compete at dancing   204 **checked** reproved   206 **sack** sherry
216 **look you** make sure you   221 **spit white** (1) suffer a dry mouth from
carousing (2) emit semen (?)

CHIEF JUSTICE Well, be honest, be honest, and God
bless your expedition!

FALSTAFF Will your lordship lend me a thousand pound
to furnish me forth?

CHIEF JUSTICE Not a penny, not a penny. You are too   235
impatient to bear crosses. Fare you well. Commend me to my cousin Westmoreland.
                    [*Exeunt Chief Justice and Servant.*]

FALSTAFF If I do, fillip me with a three-man beetle.
A man can no more separate age and covetousness
than 'a can part young limbs and lechery. But the   240
gout galls the one and the pox pinches the other,
and so both the degrees prevent my curses. Boy!

PAGE Sir?

FALSTAFF What money is in my purse?

PAGE Seven groats and twopence.   245

FALSTAFF I can get no remedy against this consumption of the purse. Borrowing only lingers and lingers it out, but the disease is incurable. Go bear this
letter to my Lord of Lancaster, this to the Prince,
this to the Earl of Westmoreland, and this to old   250
Mistress Ursula, whom I have weekly sworn to
marry since I perceived the first white hair of my
chin. About it. You know where to find me. [*Exit
Page.*] A pox of this gout! Or a gout of this pox!
For the one or the other plays the rogue with my   255
great toe. 'Tis no matter if I do halt—I have the
wars for my color, and my pension shall seem the
more reasonable. A good wit will make use of anything. I will turn diseases to commodity.   [*Exit.*]

---

236 **crosses** (1) afflictions (2) coins marked with a cross   238 **fillip** flip
238 **three-man beetle** a battering-ram carried by three men (what it would take
to "fillip" Falstaff)   242 **degrees** stations in life   242 **prevent** act before
245 **groats** fourpenny coins   256 **halt** limp   257 **color** (1) pretense (2) battle
flag   259 **commodity** something to sell

[Scene III. *The rebels' meeting-place*.]

Enter th' Archbishop, Thomas Mowbray (Earl Marshal),
the Lord Hastings and [Lord] Bardolph.

ARCHBISHOP Thus have you heard our cause and
    known our means;
And, my most noble friends, I pray you all,
Speak plainly your opinions of our hopes.
And first, Lord Marshal, what say you to it?

5 MOWBRAY I well allow the occasion of our arms,
    But gladly would be better satisfied
How in our means we should advance ourselves
To look with forehead bold and big enough
Upon the power and puissance of the King.

10 HASTINGS Our present musters grow upon the file
    To five-and-twenty thousand men of choice;
And our supplies live largely in the hope
Of great Northumberland, whose bosom burns
With an incensèd fire of injuries.

LORD BARDOLPH The question then, Lord Hastings,
15   standeth thus:
Whether our present five-and-twenty thousand
May hold up head without Northumberland?

HASTINGS With him, we may.

LORD BARDOLPH   Yea, marry, there's the point.
But if without him we be thought too feeble,
20 My judgment is, we should not step too far
Till we had his assistance by the hand.

I.iii.5 **allow the occasion** approve the cause   9 **puissance** strength   10 **file**
catalog   12 **supplies** reinforcements   18 **marry** by the Virgin Mary (a mild
oath)

For in a theme so bloody-faced as this,
Conjecture, expectation, and surmise
Of aids incertain should not be admitted.

ARCHBISHOP 'Tis very true, Lord Bardolph, for
    indeed   25
It was young Hotspur's case at Shrewsbury.

LORD BARDOLPH It was, my lord, who lined himself
    with hope,
Eating the air and promise of supply,
Flatt'ring himself in project of a power
Much smaller than the smallest of his thoughts,   30
And so, with great imagination
Proper to madmen, led his powers to death
And, winking, leaped into destruction.

HASTINGS But, by your leave, it never yet did hurt
To lay down likelihoods and forms of hope.   35

LORD BARDOLPH Yes, if this present quality of war.
Indeed the instant action, a cause on foot,
Lives so in hope as in an early spring
We see th' appearing buds, which to prove fruit,
Hope gives not so much warrant as despair   40
That frosts will bite them. When we mean to build,
We first survey the plot, then draw the model.
And when we see the figure of the house,
Then must we rate the cost of the erection,
Which if we find outweighs ability,   45
What do we then but draw anew the model
In fewer offices, or at least desist
To build at all? Much more, in this great work,
Which is almost to pluck a kingdom down
And set another up, should we survey   50
The plot of situation and the model,

27 **lined** reinforced (as in tailoring) 29-30 **in project … smaller than** in planning on the basis of an army that in fact was much smaller than 33 **winking** shutting his eyes 36 **Yes … war.** (a famous obscurity, perhaps saying: Yes, it does do hurt to plan if this planning present [i.e. represent, substitute for] quality [i.e., true substance, strength] of war) 40 **despair** (supply: "gives warrant") 42 **model** plan 43 **figure** design 47 **offices** rooms for service 47 **least** worst

Consent upon a sure foundation,
Question surveyors, know our own estate,
How able such a work to undergo,
55   To weigh against his opposite. Or else
We fortify in paper and in figures,
Using the names of men instead of men,
Like one that draws the model of an house
Beyond his power to build it, who, half through,
60   Gives o'er and leaves his part-created cost
A naked subject to the weeping clouds
And waste for churlish winter's tyranny.

HASTINGS Grant that our hopes, yet likely of fair birth,
Should be stillborn, and that we now possessed
65   The utmost man of expectation,
I think we are so, body strong enough
Even as we are, to equal with the King.

LORD BARDOLPH What, is the King but five-and-twenty
thousand?

HASTINGS To us no more, nay, not so much, Lord
Bardolph.
70   For his divisions, as the times do brawl,
Are in three heads: one power against the French,
And one against Glendower, perforce a third
Must take up us. So is the unfirm king
In three divided, and his coffers sound
75   With hollow poverty and emptiness.

ARCHBISHOP That he should draw his several strengths
together
And come against us in full puissance
Need not to be dreaded.

HASTINGS   If he should do so,
He leaves his back unarmed, the French and
Welsh
80   Baying him at the heels. Never fear that.

---

52 **Consent** agree   55 **his opposite** its opposition   60 **part-created cost** half-realized expenditure   76 **several** separate   77 **puissance** power

LORD BARDOLPH Who is it like should lead his forces
  hither?

HASTINGS The Duke of Lancaster and Westmoreland.
  Against the Welsh, himself and Harry Monmouth.
  But who is substituted against the French,
  I have no certain notice.

ARCHBISHOP   Let us on,   85
  And publish the occasion of our arms.
  The commonwealth is sick of their own choice;
  Their overgreedy love hath surfeited.
  An habitation giddy and unsure
  Hath he that buildeth on the vulgar heart.   90
  O thou fond many, with what loud applause
  Didst thou beat heaven with blessing Bolingbroke,
  Before he was what thou wouldst have him be!
  And being now trimmed in thine own desires,
  Thou, beastly feeder, art so full of him   95
  That thou provok'st thyself to cast him up.
  So, so, thou common dog, didst thou disgorge
  Thy glutton bosom of the royal Richard;
  And now thou wouldst eat thy dead vomit up,
  And howl'st to find it. What trust is in these times?   100
  They that when Richard lived would have him die
  Are now become enamored on his grave.
  Thou that threw'st dust upon his goodly head
  When through proud London he came sighing on
  After th' admired heels of Bolingbroke   105
  Criest now, "O earth, yield us that king again,
  And take thou this!" O thoughts of men accursed!
  "Past and to come seems best, things present
    worst."

MOWBRAY Shall we go draw our numbers and set on?

HASTINGS We are time's subjects, and time bids be
    gone.   *Exeunt.*   110

81 **like** likely   91 **fond many** foolish multitude   92 **beat** assault (with noise or
prayer)   94 **trimmed** dressed   99 **thou** the multitude (compared to a dog, as
described in Proverbs 16:11)   103 **Thou** the multitude   108 **Past ... worst**
(proverbial)   109 **draw our numbers** assemble our troops

[ACT II

Scene I. *London.*]

*Enter Hostess of the Tavern and an Officer or
two [Fang and another, followed by Snare].*

HOSTESS Master Fang, have you ent'red the action?

FANG It is ent'red.

HOSTESS Where's your yeoman? Is't a lusty yeoman?
Will 'a stand to't?

5 FANG Sirrah—where's Snare?

HOSTESS O Lord, ay! Good Master Snare!

SNARE Here, here.

FANG Snare, we must arrest Sir John Falstaff.

HOSTESS Yea, good Master Snare, I have ent'red him
10 and all.

SNARE It may chance cost some of us our lives, for he
will stab.

HOSTESS Alas the day! Take heed of him. He stabbed
me in mine own house, and that most beastly. In
15 good faith, 'a cares not what mischief he does, if
his weapon be out. He will foin like any devil; he
will spare neither man, woman, nor child.

II.i.1 ent'red the action filed the lawsuit (with a ribald second meaning)
3 yeoman assistant (i.e., constable) 4 stand to't not collapse in the face of
danger (with a ribald second meaning) 5 Snare (evidently hanging back)
16 foin thrust (with, again, a second meaning)

FANG If I can close with him, I care not for his thrust.

HOSTESS No, nor I neither. I'll be at your elbow.

FANG And I but fist him once, and 'a come but within   20
my vice—

HOSTESS I am undone by his going. I warrant you, he's
an infinitive thing upon my score. Good Master
Fang, hold him sure. Good Master Snare, let him
not 'scape. 'A comes continuantly to Pie Corner   25
—saving your manhoods—to buy a saddle; and he
is indited to dinner to the Lubber's Head in Lumbert Street, to Master Smooth's the silkman. I
pray you, since my exion is ent'red and my case
so openly known to the world, let him be brought   30
in to his answer. A hundred mark is a long one for
a poor lone woman to bear, and I have borne,
and borne, and borne, and have been fubbed off,
and fubbed off, and fubbed off, from this day to
that day, that it is a shame to be thought on. There   35
is no honesty in such dealing, unless a woman
should be made an ass and a beast, to bear every
knave's wrong. Yonder he comes, and that arrant
malmsey-nose knave, Bardolph, with him. Do your
offices, do your offices. Master Fang and Master   40
Snare, do me, do me, do me your offices.

Enter Sir John and Bardolph, and the Boy.

FALSTAFF How now! Whose mare's dead? What's the
matter?

FANG Sir John, I arrest you at the suit of Mistress
Quickly.
45

21 vice grip 23 infinitive infinite 23 score account at the tavern 25 continuantly a mix-up of "continually" and "incontinently" (Mistress Quickly speaks
in a stream of malapropisms, many with indecent second meanings) 25 Pie
Corner the cooks' quarter (with an indecent pun) 26 saving no offense meant
to 27 indited i.e., invited 27 Lubber's Head Libbard's (i.e., Leopard's)
Head 27–28 Lumbert Lombard 29 exion i.e., action 32 borne endured
(with a second, ribald sense) 33 fubbed off put off 39 malmsey-nose nose
reddened from winebibbing 42 Whose mare's dead? what's all the commotion?

FALSTAFF Away, varlets! Draw, Bardolph! Cut me off the villain's head. Throw the quean in the channel.

50 HOSTESS Throw me in the channel! I'll throw thee in the channel. Wilt thou? Wilt thou? Thou bastardly rogue! Murder, murder! Ah, thou honeysuckle villain! Wilt thou kill God's officers and the King's? Ah, thou honeyseed rogue! Thou art a honeyseed, a man-queller, and a woman-queller.

55 FALSTAFF Keep them off, Bardolph.

FANG A rescue! A rescue!

HOSTESS Good people, bring a rescue or two. Thou wo't, wo't thou? Thou wo't, wo't ta? Do, do, thou rogue! Do, thou hempseed!

60 PAGE Away, you scullion! You rampallian! You fustilarian! I'll tickle your catastrophe.

Enter Lord Chief Justice and his Men.

CHIEF JUSTICE What is the matter? Keep the peace here, ho!

65 HOSTESS Good my lord, be good to me. I beseech you, stand to me.

CHIEF JUSTICE How now, Sir John! What are you brawling here?
Doth this become your place, your time and business?
You should have been well on your way to York.
Stand from him, fellow. Wherefore hang'st thou upon him?

47 **quean** scold   47–48 **channel** gutter   50 **bastardly** mixing "dastardly" and "bastard" (1) illegitimate (2) a sweetened wine   51 **honeysuckle** i.e., homicidal   53 **honeyseed** i.e., homicide   54 **man-queller** i.e., man-killer   56 **rescue** forcible taking of persons out of legal custody   59 **hempseed** a child destined for the gallows (but also homicide, as in line 53—Mistress Quickly is referring to the Page)   60 **scullion** kitchen wench   60 **rampallian** rampant whore   61 **fustilarian** (derived from "fustilugs," a frowsy, fat woman)   61 **catastrophe** ending   65 **stand to me** be firm for me (with a second sense)

HOSTESS O my most worshipful lord, and't please your   70
   Grace, I am a poor widow of Eastcheap, and he is
   arrested at my suit.

CHIEF JUSTICE For what sum?

HOSTESS It is more than for some, my lord, it is for
   all I have. He hath eaten me out of house and   75
   home; he hath put all my substance into that fat
   belly of his. But I will have some of it out again,
   or I will ride thee o' nights like the mare.

FALSTAFF I think I am as like to ride the mare, if I
   have any vantage of ground to get up.   80

CHIEF JUSTICE How comes this, Sir John? What man
   of good temper would endure this tempest of exclamation? Are you not ashamed to enforce a poor
   widow to so rough a course to come by her own?

FALSTAFF What is the gross sum that I owe thee?   85

HOSTESS Marry, if thou wert an honest man, thyself
   and the money too. Thou didst swear to me upon a
   parcel-gilt goblet, sitting in my Dolphin chamber,
   at the round table, by a sea-coal fire, upon Wednesday in Wheeson week, when the Prince broke   90
   thy head for liking his father to a singing-man of
   Windsor, thou didst swear to me then, as I was
   washing thy wound, to marry me and make me my
   lady thy wife. Canst thou deny it? Did not good-
   wife Keech, the butcher's wife, come in then and   95
   call me gossip Quickly? Coming in to borrow a
   mess of vinegar, telling us she had a good dish of
   prawns, whereby thou didst desire to eat some,
   whereby I told thee they were ill for a green
   wound? And didst thou not, when she was gone   100
   downstairs, desire me to be no more so familiarity

78 mare nightmare   79 mare female (but also the "two-legged mare," i.e., the
gallows)   80 vantage of ground advantage of higher ground   88 parcel-gilt
partly gilded   88 Dolphin i.e., the sign marking the room   90 Wheeson
Whitsun   91 liking likening   96 gossip friend (a common form of address)
98 prawns shrimp   99 green new

with such poor people, saying that ere long they
should call me "Madam"? And didst thou not kiss
me and bid me fetch thee thirty shillings? I put thee
105   now to thy book-oath. Deny it, if thou canst.

FALSTAFF My lord, this is a poor mad soul, and she
says up and down the town that her eldest son is
like you. She hath been in good case, and the
truth is, poverty hath distracted her. But for these
110   foolish officers, I beseech you I may have redress
against them.

CHIEF JUSTICE Sir John, Sir John, I am well acquainted
with your manner of wrenching the true cause the
false way. It is not a confident brow, nor the throng
115   of words that come with such more than impudent
sauciness from you, can thrust me from a level
consideration. You have, as it appears to me, practiced upon the easy-yielding spirit of this woman,
and made her serve your uses both in purse and in
120   person.

HOSTESS Yea, in truth, my lord.

CHIEF JUSTICE Pray thee, peace. Pay her the debt you
owe her and unpay the villainy you have done with
her. The one you may do with sterling money, and
125   the other with current repentance.

FALSTAFF My lord, I will not undergo this sneap without reply. You call honorable boldness impudent
sauciness. If a man will make curtsy and say nothing, he is virtuous. No, my lord, my humble duty
130   rememb'red, I will not be your suitor. I say to you,
I do desire deliverance from these officers, being
upon hasty employment in the King's affairs.

CHIEF JUSTICE You speak as having power to do
wrong. But answer in th' effect of your reputation,
135   and satisfy the poor woman.

108 **case** situation, i.e., well-to-do 109 **distracted her** driven her mad
116 **level** straight 117-18 **practiced upon** deceived 125 **current** (1) progres-
sive (2) opposite of counterfeit 126 **sneap** snub 134 **in th' effect of** so as to
fulfill

FALSTAFF Come hither, hostess.

Enter a Messenger [Gower].

CHIEF JUSTICE Now, Master Gower, what news?

GOWER The King, my lord, and Harry Prince of Wales
Are near at hand. The rest the paper tells.
[They draw aside.]

FALSTAFF *[To Hostess]* As I am a gentleman!   140

HOSTESS Faith, you said so before.

FALSTAFF As I am a gentleman, come, no more words
of it.

HOSTESS By this heavenly ground I tread on, I must
be fain to pawn both my plate and the tapestry   145
of my dining chambers.

FALSTAFF Glasses, glasses, is the only drinking. And
for thy walls, a pretty slight drollery, or the story
of the Prodigal, or the German hunting in waterwork, is worth a thousand of these bed-hangers   150
and these fly-bitten tapestries. Let it be ten
pound, if thou canst. Come, and 'twere not for thy
humors, there's not a better wench in England.
Go, wash thy face, and draw the action. Come,
thou must not be in this humor with me. Dost not   155
know me? Come, come, I know thou wast set on to
this.

HOSTESS Pray thee, Sir John, let it be but twenty nobles. I' faith, I am loath to pawn my plate, so God
save me, la!   160

FALSTAFF Let it alone; I'll make other shift. You'll be
a fool still.

145 **fain** obliged   147 **glasses, is the only drinking** i.e., glasses are in fashion
now, not metal tankards   148 **drollery** comic picture   149 **German hunting**
hunting the boar   149–50 **waterwork** imitation tapestry   150 **bed-hangers**
bed-curtains   153 **humors** (1) whims (2) general character   154 **draw**
withdraw   158–59 **nobles** coins worth six shillings eight pence   161–62 **be a
fool still** always lose your chance

HOSTESS Well, you shall have it, though I pawn my
gown. I hope you'll come to supper. You'll pay me
165   all together?

FALSTAFF Will I live? [*To Bardolph*] Go, with her, with
her. Hook on, hook on!

HOSTESS Will you have Doll Tearsheet meet you at
supper?

170   FALSTAFF No more words. Let's have her.
Exit Hostess and Sergeant
[*Fang, Bardolph and others*].

CHIEF JUSTICE [*To Gower*] I have heard better news.

FALSTAFF What's the news, my lord?

CHIEF JUSTICE [*Ignoring Falstaff*] Where lay the King
tonight?

175   GOWER At Basingstoke, my lord.

FALSTAFF I hope, my lord, all's well. What is the news,
my lord?

CHIEF JUSTICE Come all his forces back?

GOWER No. Fifteen hundred foot, five hundred horse,
180   Are marched up to my Lord of Lancaster,
Against Northumberland and the Archbishop.

FALSTAFF Comes the King back from Wales, my noble
lord?

CHIEF JUSTICE [*To his men*] You shall have letters of
me presently.
185   Come, go along with me, good Master Gower.

FALSTAFF My lord!

CHIEF JUSTICE What's the matter?

FALSTAFF Master Gower, shall I entreat you with me to
dinner?

167 **Hook on** stick to her   174 **tonight** last night

GOWER I must wait upon my good lord here, I thank   190
you, good Sir John.

CHIEF JUSTICE Sir John, you loiter here too long, being
you are to take soldiers up in counties as you go.

FALSTAFF Will you sup with me, Master Gower?

CHIEF JUSTICE What foolish master taught you these   195
manners, Sir John?

FALSTAFF Master Gower, if they become me not, he was
a fool that taught them me. This is the right fencing grace, my lord—tap for tap, and so part fair.

CHIEF JUSTICE Now the Lord lighten thee! Thou art   200
a great fool.   [*Exeunt.*]

[Scene II. *The Prince's house.*]

Enter the Prince [Henry], Poins, with others.

PRINCE Before God, I am exceeding weary.

POINS Is't come to that? I had thought weariness durst
not have attached one of so high blood.

PRINCE Faith, it does me, though it discolors the complexion of my greatness to acknowledge it. Doth   5
it not show vilely in me to desire small beer?

POINS Why, a prince should not be so loosely studied
as to remember so weak a composition.

PRINCE Belike, then, my appetite was not princely
got, for, by my troth, I do now remember the   10

193 **take soldiers up** recruit men   198 **right** correct   200 **lighten** (1) enlighten
(2) make [you] weigh less   II.ii.1 **weary** (having just ridden from Wales)
3 **attached** arrested   4–5 **discolors the complexion** causes a blush   7 **loosely
studied** carelessly or wantonly applied   8 **so weak a composition** so unstable
and trivial a compound (as small beer)   10 **got** begotten

poor creature, small beer. But indeed these humble
considerations make me out of love with my greatness. What a disgrace is it to me to remember thy
name! Or to know thy face tomorrow! Or to take
15   note how many pair of silk stockings thou hast, viz.
these, and those that were thy peach-colored ones!
Or to bear the inventory of thy shirts, as: one for
superfluity and another for use! But that the tennis-
court-keeper knows better than I; for it is a low
20   ebb of linen with thee when thou keepest not racket
there, as thou hast not done a great while, because
the rest of thy low countries have made a shift to
eat up thy holland. And God knows whether those
that bawl out the ruins of thy linen shall inherit
25   His kingdom. But the midwives say the children are
not in the fault, whereupon the world increases,
and kindreds are mightily strengthened.

POINS How ill it follows, after you have labored so
hard, you should talk so idly! Tell me, how many
30   good young princes would do so, their fathers being
so sick as yours at this time is?

PRINCE Shall I tell thee one thing, Poins?

POINS Yes, faith, and let it be an excellent good thing.

PRINCE It shall serve among wits of no higher breeding
35   than thine.

POINS Go to. I stand the push of your one thing that
you will tell.

PRINCE Marry, I tell thee, it is not meet that I should
be sad, now my father is sick. Albeit I could tell to
40   thee, as to one it pleases me, for fault of a better,

13-14 **disgrace ... remember thy name** i.e., unlike "graceful" courtiers who
affect to forget the names of their inferiors   19-21 **it is ... racket there** i.e., if
you have as many as two shirts, one to play in, a second to change into, you
frequent the tennis courts   22 **low countries** Netherlands (with an obscene
pun)   22 **shift** (1) contrivance (2) shirt   23 **holland** linen made in Holland
26 **in the fault** share the sin (of their illegitimacy, with a pun on French,
foutre = to copulate)   27 **kindreds** clans   36 **push** thrust   38 **meet** fitting

to call my friend, I could be sad, and sad indeed, too.

POINS Very hardly upon such a subject.

PRINCE By this hand, thou thinkest me as far in the devil's book as thou and Falstaff for obduracy and persistency. Let the end try the man. But I tell thee, my heart bleeds inwardly that my father is so sick. And keeping such vile company as thou art hath in reason taken from me all ostentation of sorrow.   45

                                                                          50

POINS The reason?

PRINCE What wouldst thou think of me if I should weep?

POINS I would think thee a most princely hypocrite.

PRINCE It would be every man's thought, and thou art a blessed fellow to think as every man thinks. Never a man's thought in the world keeps the roadway better than thine. Every man would think me an hypocrite indeed. And what accites your most worshipful thought to think so?   55

                                                                          60

POINS Why, because you have been so lewd and so much engraffed to Falstaff.

PRINCE And to thee.

POINS By this light, I am well spoke on; I can hear it with mine own ears. The worst that they can say of me is that I am a second brother and that I am a proper fellow of my hands, and those two things I confess I cannot help. By the mass, here comes Bardolph.   65

Enter Bardolph and Boy [Page].

43 **Very hardly** with great difficulty   46 **end** outcome   49 **ostentation** show   59 **accites** summons (a judicial term)   62 **engraffed** grafted (like a plant)   66 **a second brother** i.e., one who inherits nothing   67 **proper fellow of my hands** skillful with my hands as a fighter (or as a thief?)

70   PRINCE And the boy that I gave Falstaff. 'A had him
     from me Christian, and look if the fat villain have
     not transformed him ape.

     BARDOLPH God save your Grace.

     PRINCE And yours, most noble Bardolph.

75   POINS Come, you virtuous ass, you bashful fool, must
     you be blushing? Wherefore blush you now? What
     a maidenly man-at-arms are you become! Is't such
     a matter to get a pottle-pot's maidenhead?

     PAGE 'A calls me e'en now, my lord, through a red
80   lattice, and I could discern no part of his face
     from the window. At last I spied his eyes, and me-
     thought he had made two holes in the ale-wife's
     petticoat and so peeped through.

     PRINCE Has not the boy profited?

85   BARDOLPH Away, you whoreson upright rabbit, away!

     PAGE Away, you rascally Althaea's dream, away!

     PRINCE Instruct us, boy. What dream, boy?

     PAGE Marry, my lord, Althaea dreamed she was de-
     livered of a firebrand, and therefore I call him her
90   dream.

     PRINCE A crown's worth of good interpretation. There
     'tis, boy. [*Tips him.*]

     POINS O, that this blossom could be kept from
     cankers! Well, there is sixpence to preserve thee.

95   BARDOLPH And you do not make him hanged among
     you, the gallows shall have wrong.

72 **transformed him ape** dressed him fantastically   76 **blushing** redfaced (from
drinking)   78 **pottle-pot** two-quart tankard   79–80 **red lattice** (such a window
was the sign of an alehouse)   84 **profited** i.e., from his association with
Falstaff   86 **Althaea's dream** (the dream he describes in lines 88–90 was actually
Hecuba's. The Fates told Althaea her son would live only as long as a log on the
fire remained unconsumed. Perhaps the boy has not "profited" as much as the
Prince thought)   94 **cankers** plant-destroying worms   94 **preserve** i.e., because
Elizabethan coins bore crosses

PRINCE And how doth thy master, Bardolph?

BARDOLPH Well, my lord. He heard of your Grace's
coming to town. There's a letter for you.

POINS Delivered with good respect. And how doth the   100
martlemas, your master?

BARDOLPH In bodily health, sir.

POINS Marry, the immortal part needs a physician,
but that moves not him. Though that be sick, it
dies not.   105

PRINCE I do allow this wen to be as familiar with me
as my dog, and he holds his place, for look you
how he writes.

POINS [Reads] "John Falstaff, knight"—every man
must know that, as oft as he has occasion to name   110
himself. Even like those that are kin to the King, for
they never prick their finger but they say, "There's
some of the King's blood split." "How comes that?"
says he that takes upon him not to conceive. The
answer is as ready as a borrowed cap, "I am the   115
King's poor cousin, sir."

PRINCE Nay, they will be kin to us, or they will fetch
it from Japhet. But the letter. [Reads] "Sir John
Falstaff, knight, to the son of the King nearest his
father, Harry Prince of Wales, greeting."   120

POINS Why, this is a certificate.

PRINCE Peace! [Reads] "I will imitate the honorable
Romans in brevity."

POINS He sure means brevity in breath, short-winded.

[PRINCE reads] "I commend me to thee, I commend   125
thee, and I leave thee. Be not too familiar with

101 **martlemas** i.e., a beef fattened for slaughter before winter on Martinmas Day
(November 11) 106 **wen** swelling 115 **borrowed cap** (which the borrower
promptly tips) 117-18 **fetch it from Japhet** i.e., fetch their ancestry from that
one of Noah's sons whose offspring peopled Europe 121 **certificate** patent (in
formal style)

Poins, for he misuses thy favors so much that he
swears thou art to marry his sister Nell. Repent at
idle times as thou mayst, and so farewell.

130   "Thine, by yea and no, which is as much as to
say, as thou usest him, JACK FALSTAFF with
my familiars, JOHN with my brothers and sisters, and SIR JOHN with all Europe."

POINS My lord, I'll steep this letter in sack and make
135   him eat it.

PRINCE That's to make him eat twenty of his words.
But do you use me thus, Ned? Must I marry your
sister?

POINS God send the wench no worse fortune! But I
140   never said so.

PRINCE Well, thus we play the fools with the time, and
the spirits of the wise sit in the clouds and mock
us. Is your master here in London?

BARDOLPH Yea, my lord.

145 PRINCE Where sups he? Doth the old boar feed in the
old frank?

BARDOLPH At the old place, my lord, in Eastcheap.

PRINCE What company?

PAGE Ephesians, my lord, of the old church.

150 PRINCE Sup any women with him?

PAGE None, my lord, but old Mistress Quickly and
Mistress Doll Tearsheet.

PRINCE What pagan may that be?

PAGE A proper gentlewoman, sir, and a kinswoman of
155   my master's.

---

146 **frank** sty (presumably a glance at the famous Boar's Head tavern)
149 **Ephesians ... church** libertines (who had to be corrected by St. Paul—
Ephesians 5:3–8)   153 **pagan** prostitute (love-worshipper)

PRINCE Even such kin as the parish heifers are to the
town bull. Shall we steal upon them, Ned, at supper?

POINS I am your shadow, my lord; I'll follow you.

PRINCE Sirrah, you boy, and Bardolph, no word to   160
your master that I am yet come to town. There's
for your silence. [*Tips them.*]

BARDOLPH I have no tongue, sir.

PAGE And for mine, sir, I will govern it.

PRINCE Fare you well; go. [*Exeunt Bardolph and*   165
Page.] This Doll Tearsheet should be some road.

POINS I warrant you, as common as the way between
Saint Alban's and London.

PRINCE How might we see Falstaff bestow himself tonight in his true colors, and not ourselves be seen?   170

POINS Put on two leathern jerkins and aprons, and
wait upon him at his table as drawers.

PRINCE From a God to a bull? A heavy descension!
It was Jove's case. From a prince to a prentice?
A low transformation! That shall be mine, for in   175
everything the purpose must weigh with the folly.
Follow me, Ned.   *Exeunt.*

---

160 **Sirrah** (form of address to an inferior)   166 **road** prostitute (one to be
ridden, open to all)   171 **jerkins** jackets   172 **drawers** tavern waiters
174 **Jove's case** (he transformed himself into a bull to seduce Europa)
176 **weigh with** match

[Scene III. *Northumberland's castle*.]

Enter Northumberland, his Wife [*Lady Northumberland*], *and the Wife to Harry Percy* [*Lady Percy*].

NORTHUMBERLAND I pray thee, loving wife, and gentle
      daughter,
    Give even way unto my rough affairs.
    Put not you on the visage of the times
    And be like them to Percy troublesome.

LADY NORTHUMBERLAND I have given over; I will speak
5   no more.
    Do what you will, your wisdom be your guide.

NORTHUMBERLAND Alas, sweet wife, my honor is at
      pawn,
    And, but my going, nothing can redeem it.

LADY PERCY O yet, for God's sake, go not to these
      wars!
10   The time was, father, that you broke your word,
    When you were more endeared to it than now,
    When your own Percy, when my heart's dear Harry,
    Threw many a northward look to see his father
    Bring up his powers, but he did long in vain.
15   Who then persuaded you to stay at home?
    There were two honors lost, yours and your son's.
    For yours, the God of heaven brighten it!
    For his, it stuck upon him as the sun
    In the gray vault of heaven, and by his light
20   Did all the chivalry of England move
    To do brave acts. He was indeed the glass

II.iii.1 **daughter** daughter-in-law 2 **Give even way** allow free passage
4 **Percy** i.e., Northumberland, "the Percy" 8 **but** except for 21 **glass** looking
glass

Wherein the noble youth did dress themselves.
He had no legs that practiced not his gait;
And speaking thick, which nature made his blemish,
Became the accents of the valiant,   25
For those that could speak low and tardily
Would turn their own perfection to abuse,
To seem like him. So that in speech, in gait,
In diet, in affections of delight,
In military rules, humors of blood,   30
He was the mark and glass, copy and book,
That fashioned others. And him! O wondrous! Him!
O miracle of men! Him did you leave,
Second to none, unseconded by you,
To look upon the hideous god of war   35
In disadvantage, to abide a field
Where nothing but the sound of Hotspur's name
Did seem defensible. So you left him.
Never, O never, do his ghost the wrong
To hold your honor more precise and nice   40
With others than with him! Let them alone.
The Marshal and the Archbishop are strong.
Had my sweet Harry had but half their numbers,
Today might I, hanging on Hotspur's neck,
Have talked of Monmouth's grave.

NORTHUMBERLAND   Beshrew your heart,   45
Fair daughter, you do draw my spirits from me
With new lamenting ancient oversights.
But I must go and meet with danger there,
Or it will seek me in another place
And find me worse provided.

LADY NORTHUMBERLAND   O, fly to Scotland,   50
Till that the nobles and the armèd commons
Have of their puissance made a little taste.

---

23 **He** i.e., any man   23 **his** i.e., Harry Percy's   24 **thick** fast (crowding the
words)   29 **affections of delight** preferences in pleasure   30 **humors of blood**
disposition   36 **abide a field** endure on a battlefield   40 **nice** punctilious
45 **Monmouth's** Prince Hal's   45 **Beshrew** cursed be   50 **Scotland** i.e., far
from the battle   52 **puissance** strength

LADY PERCY If they get ground and vantage of the
          King,
      Then join you with them, like a rib of steel,
55   To make strength stronger. But, for all our loves,
      First let them try themselves. So did your son;
      He was so suff'red. So came I a widow,
      And never shall have length of life enough
      To rain upon remembrance with mine eyes,
60   That it may grow and sprout as high as heaven,
      For recordation to my noble husband.

NORTHUMBERLAND Come, come, go in with me. 'Tis
          with my mind
      As with the tide swelled up unto his height,
      That makes a still-stand, running neither way.
65   Fain would I go to meet the Archbishop,
      But many thousand reasons hold me back.
      I will resolve for Scotland. There am I,
      Till time and vantage crave my company.

                                         Exeunt.

[Scene IV. *Mistress Quickly's tavern.*]

          Enter a Drawer or two [Francis and another].

FRANCIS What the devil hast thou brought there?
      Apple-johns? Thou knowest Sir John cannot en-
      dure an apple-john.

DRAWER Mass, thou say'st true. The Prince once set
5   a dish of apple-johns before him, and told him
      there were five more Sir Johns, and, putting off his
      hat, said, "I will now take my leave of these six

---

57 **suff'red** allowed (to fight alone) 59 **rain** drop tears 61 **recordation**
memorial 68 **vantage** profitable opportunity II.iv.2 **Apple-johns** (apples
ripened on St. John's Day, midsummer, but eaten two years later when withered—
perhaps they remind Sir John of age or impotency)

dry, round, old, withered knights." It ang'red him
to the heart. But he hath forgot that.

FRANCIS Why, then, cover, and set them down. And   10
see if thou canst find out Sneak's noise. Mistress
Tearsheet would fain hear some music.

Enter Will [a third Drawer].

WILL Dispatch! The room where they supped is too
hot. They'll come in straight.

FRANCIS Sirrah, here will be the Prince and Master   15
Poins anon, and they will put on two of our jerkins
and aprons, and Sir John must not know of it.
Bardolph hath brought word.

DRAWER By the mass, here will be old Utis. It will
be an excellent stratagem.   20

FRANCIS I'll see if I can find out Sneak.   *Exit.*

*Enter Mistress Quickly [the Hostess] and
Doll Tearsheet.*

HOSTESS I' faith, sweetheart, methinks now you are in
an excellent good temperality. Your pulsidge
beats as extraordinarily as heart would desire, and
your color, I warrant you, is as red as any rose, in   25
good truth, la! But, i' faith, you have drunk too
much canaries, and that's a marvelous searching
wine, and it perfumes the blood ere one can say,
"What's this?" How do you now?

DOLL Better than I was. Hem!   30

HOSTESS Why, that's well said. A good heart's worth
gold. Lo, here comes Sir John.

Enter Sir John [Falstaff].

FALSTAFF [*Sings*] "When Arthur first in court"—

10 **cover** spread the tablecloth 11 **noise** band of musicians 19 **old Utis** grand
festival (*utaves* was the eighth day or "octave" of a feast) 23 **temperality** i.e.,
temper or temperance 23 **pulsidge** i.e., pulse 27 **canaries** Canary wine
33 **When Arthur first in court** (first line of a ballad)

Empty the jordan!—"And was a worthy king"—
35   How now, Mistress Doll!

HOSTESS Sick of a calm, yea, good faith.

FALSTAFF So is all her sect. And they be once in a
calm, they are sick.

DOLL A pox damn you, you muddy rascal, is that all
40   the comfort you give me?

FALSTAFF You make fat rascals, Mistress Doll.

DOLL I make them? Gluttony and diseases make, I
make them not.

FALSTAFF If the cook help to make the gluttony, you
45   help to make the diseases, Doll. We catch of you,
Doll, we catch of you. Grant that, my poor virtue,
grant that.

DOLL Yea, joy, our chains and our jewels.

FALSTAFF "Your brooches, pearls, and ouches." For
50   to serve bravely is to come halting off, you know.
To come off the breach with his pike bent bravely,
and to surgery bravely; to venture upon the charged
chambers bravely—

DOLL Hang yourself, you muddy conger, hang your-
55   self!

HOSTESS By my troth, this is the old fashion. You
two never meet but you fall to some discord. You
are both, i' good truth, as rheumatic as two
dry toasts. You cannot one bear with another's

---

34 **jordan** chamber pot 36 **calm** i.e., qualm 37 **sect** prostitutes
(love-worshippers) 39 **muddy** filthy 41 **You make fat rascals** (a rascal was a
lean deer—you say or cause the lean to fat, i.e., become bloated or to sweat as a
cure for the pox) 49 **Your brooches, pearls, and ouches** (another scrap of
ballad; "ouches" are both brooches and scabs) 52-53 **charged chambers** loaded
cannon (used, like other words in this speech, with a bawdy second meaning)
54 **conger** eel 58 **rheumatic** (she means splenetic or choleric, the hot and dry
humor—like toast) 58-59 **dry toasts** (that would scratch one another)

confirmities. What the goodyear! One must bear,   60
and that must be you [*to Doll*]. You are the weaker
vessel, as they say, the emptier vessel.

DOLL Can a weak empty vessel bear such a huge full
hogshead? There's a whole merchant's venture of
Bordeaux stuff in him. You have not seen a hulk   65
better stuffed in the hold. Come, I'll be friends
with thee, Jack. Thou art going to the wars, and
whether I shall ever see thee again or no, there is
nobody cares.

Enter Drawer.

DRAWER Sir, Ancient Pistol's below and would speak   70
with you.

DOLL Hang him, swaggering rascal! Let him not
come hither. It is the foul-mouthed'st rogue in
England.

HOSTESS If he swagger, let him not come here. No, by   75
my faith. I must live among my neighbors. I'll no
swaggerers. I am in good name and fame with the
very best. Shut the door, there comes no swaggerers
here. I have not lived all this while to have swaggering now. Shut the door, I pray you.   80

FALSTAFF Dost thou hear, hostess?

HOSTESS Pray ye, pacify yourself, Sir John. There
comes no swaggerers here.

FALSTAFF Dost thou hear? It is mine Ancient.

HOSTESS Tilly-fally, Sir John, ne'er tell me. And your   85
ancient swagg'rer comes not in my doors. I was
before Master Tisick, the debuty, t' other day,
and, as he said to me, 'twas no longer ago than
Wednesday last, "I' good faith, neighbor Quickly,"

59-60 **confirmities** i.e., infirmities 60 **What the goodyear!** what the
plague! 60 **bear** (1) endure (2) support 64-65 **merchant's venture of Bordeaux stuff** shipload of wine 70 **Ancient** ensign, standard-bearer 72 **swaggering** blustering 87 **Tisick** phthisic, consumption (?)

90 says he—Master Dumbe, our minister, was by then
—"neighbor Quickly," says he, "receive those that
are civil, for," said he, "you are in an ill name."
Now 'a said so, I can tell whereupon. "For," says
he, "you are an honest woman, and well thought
95 on; therefore take heed what guests you receive.
Receive," says he, "no swaggering companions."
There comes none here. You would bless you to
hear what he said. No, I'll no swagg'rers.

FALSTAFF He's no swagg'rer, hostess, a tame cheater,
100 i' faith. You may stroke him as gently as a puppy
greyhound. He'll not swagger with a Barbary hen,
if her feathers turn back in any show of resistance.
Call him up, drawer.   [*Exit Drawer.*]

HOSTESS Cheater, call you him? I will bar no honest
105 man my house, nor no cheater. But I do not love
swaggering, by my troth. I am the worse when one
says "swagger." Feel, masters, how I shake, look
you, I warrant you.

DOLL So you do, hostess.

110 HOSTESS Do I? Yea, in very truth, do I, and 'twere
an aspen leaf. I cannot abide swagg'rers.

Enter Ancient Pistol, [Bardolph], and Bardolph's
Boy [Page].

PISTOL God save you, Sir John!

FALSTAFF Welcome, Ancient Pistol. Here, Pistol, I
charge you with a cup of sack. Do you discharge
115 upon mine hostess.

PISTOL I will discharge upon her, Sir John, with two
bullets.

96 **companions** fellows   99 **cheater** cardsharper's decoy   101 **Barbary hen**
guinea hen (whose feathers are already ruffled; also, a prostitute)   113 **Pistol**
(pronounced almost like "pizzle" [=penis] hence leading to this series of obscene
puns)   114 **charge** (1) toast (2) load (a pistol)   114 **discharge** go off (i.e., sound
a return toast, explode like a pistol—or sexually)   117 **bullets** (an indecency)

FALSTAFF She is pistol-proof, sir; you shall not hardily
   offend her.

HOSTESS Come, I'll drink no proofs nor no bullets.   120
   I'll drink no more than will do me good, for no
   man's pleasure, I.

PISTOL Then to you, Mistress Dorothy; I will charge
   you.

DOLL Charge me! I scorn you, scurvy companion.   125
   What! You poor, base, rascally, cheating, lack-
   linen mate! Away, you moldy rogue, away! I am
   meat for your master.

PISTOL I know you, Mistress Dorothy.

DOLL Away, you cut-purse rascal! You filthy bung,   130
   away! By this wine, I'll thrust my knife in your
   moldy chaps, and you play the saucy cuttle with
   me. Away, you bottle-ale rascal! You basket-hilt
   stale juggler, you! Since when, I pray you, sir?
   God's light, with two points on your shoulder?   135
   Much!

PISTOL God let me not live but I will murder your
   ruff for this.

FALSTAFF No more, Pistol; I would not have you go off
   here. Discharge yourself of our company, Pistol.   140

HOSTESS No, good Captain Pistol, not here, sweet
   Captain.

DOLL Captain! Thou abominable damned cheater, art
   thou not ashamed to be called Captain? And captains were of my mind, they would truncheon you   145
   out for taking their names upon you before you

118 **not hardily** by no means   128 **meat** flesh   130 **bung** pickpocket
132 **chaps** cheeks   132 **cuttle** (1) cutthroat (2) cuttlefish (that spews out a fluid
used for sauce)   133 **bottle-ale** cheap (?)   133-34 **basket-hilt stale juggler**
doer of sword-tricks with an old-fashioned sword with hilt shaped like a basket
135 **points** laces for tying on armor   137-38 **murder your ruff** tear your collar
145 **truncheon** cudgel

have earned them. You a captain! You slave, for
what? For tearing a poor whore's ruff in a bawdy
house? He a captain! Hang him, rogue! He lives
150   upon moldy stewed prunes and dried cakes. A
captain! God's light, these villains will make the
word as odious as the word "occupy," which was
an excellent good word before it was ill sorted.
Therefore captains had need look to't.

155   BARDOLPH Pray thee, go down, good Ancient.

FALSTAFF Hark thee hither, Mistress Doll.

PISTOL Not I! I tell thee what, Corporal Bardolph, I
could tear her! I'll be revenged of her!

PAGE Pray thee, go down.

160   PISTOL I'll see her damned first, to Pluto's damnèd
lake, by this hand, to th' infernal deep, with
Erebus and tortures vile also. Hold hook and
line, say I. Down, down, dogs! Down, faitors!
Have we not Hiren here?

165   HOSTESS Good Captain Pizzle, be quiet. 'Tis very late,
i' faith. I beseek you now, aggravate your choler.

PISTOL These be good humors, indeed! Shall pack-
horses
And hollow pampered jades of Asia,
Which cannot go but thirty mile a day,
170   Compare with Caesars, and with Cannibals,
And Trojan Greeks? Nay, rather damn them with

150 **stewed prunes** (put in the windows of brothels, "stews," as a sign)
152 **occupy** (had acquired the sense of "fornicate")   153 **ill sorted** put in bad
company   154 **captains** (Falstaff is a captain)   161 **lake** (he means the river
Styx)   162 **Erebus** passageway to Hades   162 **and tortures vile also** (Pistol
begins to rave in his characteristic way, spewing out garbled scraps from old
declamatory plays—or, indeed, any line that comes to his mind)   162–63 **Hold
hook and line** (a fisherman's cry)   163 **faitors** fates (?)   164 **Hiren** (Pistol
applies this name [Irene] from a play to his sword, punning on "iron")
166 **aggravate** (she means moderate)   168 **jades** nags   170 **Cannibals** (he
means Hannibals)

King Cerberus, and let the welkin roar.
Shall we fall foul for toys?

HOSTESS By my troth, Captain, these are very bitter
words.   175

BARDOLPH Be gone, good Ancient. This will grow to a
brawl anon.

PISTOL Die men like dogs! Give crowns like pins! Have
we not Hiren here?

HOSTESS O' my word, Captain, there's none such here.   180
What the goodyear! Do you think I would deny
her? For God's sake, be quiet.

PISTOL Then feed, and be fat, my fair Calipolis.
Come, give's some sack.
"*Si fortune me tormente, sperato me contento.*"   185
Fear we broadsides? No, let the fiend give fire.
Give me some sack. And, sweetheart, lie thou there.
                                        [*Lays down his sword.*]
Come we to full points here, and are etceteras
    no things?

FALSTAFF Pistol, I would be quiet.

PISTOL Sweet knight, I kiss thy neaf. What! We have   190
seen the seven stars.

DOLL For God's sake, thrust him downstairs. I cannot
endure such a fustian rascal.

PISTOL Thrust him downstairs! Know we not Galloway nags?
                                                                                      195

172 **Cerberus** three-headed dog that guarded Hades   172 **welkin** sky   173 **toys**
trivia (like Doll)   181-82 **deny her** (the Hostess evidently thinks Pistol is calling
for a special girl)   185 **Si fortune ... contento** (a garbled proverb—"If fortune
torments me, hope contents me")   188 **full points** stops, periods (closed
sentences)   188 **etceteras** (open-ended statements—with an obscene sense)
188 **no things** (with a second meaning: women who are "naught." The line as a
whole means: Aren't we going to do anything more here?)   190 **kiss thy neaf** kiss
thy fist (a chivalric gesture)   191 **seven stars** the Pleiades (we have made a night
of it)   193 **fustian** cheap cloth or talk   194-95 **Galloway nags** small Irish
horses (bad to ride)

FALSTAFF Quoit him down, Bardolph, like a shove-groat shilling. Nay, and 'a do nothing but speak nothing, 'a shall be nothing here.

BARDOLPH Come, get you downstairs.

PISTOL What! Shall we have incision? Shall we im-
200   brue?   [*Snatches up his sword.*]
          Then death rock me asleep, abridge my doleful
                    days!
          Why, then, let grievous, ghastly, gaping wounds
          Untwine the Sisters Three! Come, Atropos, I
                    say!

HOSTESS Here's goodly stuff toward!

205 FALSTAFF Give me my rapier, boy.

DOLL I pray thee, Jack, I pray thee, do not draw.

FALSTAFF Get you downstairs!
                    [*Draws, and threatens Pistol.*]

HOSTESS Here's a goodly tumult! I'll forswear keeping
          house afore I'll be in these tirrits and frights. So,
210   murder, I warrant now. Alas, alas! Put up your
          naked weapons, put up your naked weapons.
               [*Falstaff drives Pistol out, Bardolph following.*]

DOLL I pray thee, Jack, be quiet. The rascal's gone.
          Ah, you whoreson little valiant villain, you!

HOSTESS Are you not hurt i' th' groin? Methought 'a
215   made a shrewd thrust at your belly.

                    [*Enter Bardolph.*]

FALSTAFF Have you turned him out o' doors?

BARDOLPH Yea, sir. The rascal's drunk. You have hurt
          him, sir, i' th' shoulder.

FALSTAFF A rascal! To brave me!

---

196 **Quoit** pitch (with a pun on "quiet") 196–97 **shove-groat shilling** coin
used in a game like shuffleboard ("shove-ha'penny") 200 **imbrue** shed blood
203 **Sisters Three** the Fates who spun the thread of life, cut by the third,
Atropos 209 **tirrits** (a blending of terrors and fits?) 219 **brave** defy

DOLL Ah, you sweet little rogue, you! Alas, poor ape, 220
how thou sweat'st! Come, let me wipe thy face.
Come on, you whoreson chops. Ah, rogue! I'
faith, I love thee. Thou art as valorous as Hector
of Troy, worth five of Agamemnon, and ten times
better than the Nine Worthies. Ah, villain!   225

FALSTAFF A rascally slave! I will toss the rogue in a
blanket.

DOLL Do, and thou dar'st for thy heart. And thou dost,
I'll canvas thee between a pair of sheets.

[Enter Musicians.]

PAGE The music is come, sir.   230

FALSTAFF Let them play. Play, sirs. Sit on my knee,
Doll. A rascal bragging slave! The rogue fled from
me like quicksilver.

DOLL I' faith *[aside]* and thou followedst him like a
church. Thou whoreson little tidy Bartholomew   235
boar-pig, when wilt thou leave fighting o' days and
foining o' nights, and begin to patch up thine old
body for heaven?

Enter Prince and Poins [disguised].

FALSTAFF Peace, good Doll! Do not speak like a
death's-head. Do not bid me remember mine end.   240

DOLL Sirrah, what humor's the Prince of?

FALSTAFF A good shallow young fellow. 'A would have
made a good pantler, 'a would ha' chipped bread
well.

DOLL They say Poins has a good wit.   245

222 chops fat-cheeked man 225 Nine Worthies Hector, Alexander, Julius
Caesar, Joshua, David, Judas Maccabaeus, King Arthur, Charlemagne, Godfrey of
Bouillon 229 canvas toss (as in a canvas) 235-36 Bartholomew boar-pig
young male pig fattened as a special delicacy for the Bartholomew Fair on August
24th at West Smithfield 237 foining thrusting (as a sword) 240 death's-head
figure of a skull used to remind one of mortality 240 end (double sense)
241 Prince (Doll may have spied Hal and Poins) 243 pantler pantryworker
243 chipped chopped

FALSTAFF He a good wit? Hang him, baboon! His wit's as thick as Tewksbury mustard. There's no more conceit in him than is in a mallet.

DOLL Why does the Prince love him so, then?

250 FALSTAFF Because their legs are both of a bigness, and 'a plays at quoits well, and eats conger and fennel, and drinks off candles' ends for flap-dragons, and rides the wild-mare with the boys, and jumps upon joined-stools, and swears with a good grace, and 255 wears his boots very smooth, like unto the Sign of the Leg, and breeds no bate with telling of discreet stories; and such other gambol faculties 'a has, that show a weak mind and an able body, for the which the Prince admits him. For the Prince 260 himself is such another; the weight of a hair will turn scales between their avoirdupois.

PRINCE Would not this nave of a wheel have his ears cut off?

POINS Let's beat him before his whore.

265 PRINCE Look, whe'r the withered elder hath not his poll clawed like a parrot.

POINS Is it not strange that desire should so many years outlive performance?

FALSTAFF Kiss me, Doll.

270 PRINCE Saturn and Venus this year in conjunction! What says th' almanac to that?

---

247 **Tewksbury mustard** (Tewksbury was famed for good mustard) 248 **conceit** conception   248 **mallet** i.e., a blockhead   251 **conger and fennel** eel (the eating of which was thought to make one stupid) dressed or flattered by fennel sauce   252 **flap-dragons** (flaming raisins were floated on spirit and the players tried to snap them up; or drink the liquor; here candle ends are used to fool Poins)   253 **wild-mare** seesaw   254 **joined-stools** carefully carpentered stools   255-56 **Sign of the Leg**, sign over a bootmaker's   256 **bate** debate, quarrel   257 **gambol** playful   262 **nave** (1) fat hub on a cart wheel (2) pun on "knave"   265 **whe'r** whether   265 **elder** (1) old man (2) sapless tree   266 **poll** hair   266 **clawed** i.e., by Doll

POINS And look whether the fiery Trigon, his man,
be not lisping to his master's old tables, his notebook, his counsel-keeper.

FALSTAFF Thou dost give me flattering busses.   275

DOLL By my troth, I kiss thee with a most constant
heart.

FALSTAFF I am old, I am old.

DOLL I love thee better than I love e'er a scurvy young
boy of them all.   280

FALSTAFF What stuff wilt have a kirtle of? I shall receive money o' Thursday. Shalt have a cap tomorrow. A merry song, come. 'A grows late; we'll
to bed. Thou'lt forget me when I am gone.

DOLL By my troth, thou'lt set me a-weeping, and thou   285
say'st so. Prove that ever I dress myself handsome
till thy return. Well, hearken o' th' end.

FALSTAFF Some sack, Francis.

PRINCE ⎫
        ⎬ Anon, anon, sir.
POINS ⎭
                              [Coming forward.]

FALSTAFF Ha! A bastard son of the King's? And art not 290
thou Poins his brother?

PRINCE Why, thou globe of sinful continents, what
a life dost thou lead!

FALSTAFF A better than thou. I am a gentleman, thou
art a drawer.   295

PRINCE Very true, sir, and I come to draw you out
by the ears.

272 **fiery Trigon** the conjunction of the three fiery signs of the Zodiac: Aries, Leo,
and Sagittarius (in Bardolph's face)   273 **tables** tablet or engagement book (i.e.,
bawd, Mistress Quickly)   275 **busses** kisses   281 **kirtle** skirt   287 **hearken o'
th' end** i.e., see how it turns out   292 **continents** (1) vast land surfaces
(2) contents (3) pun on "continence"

HOSTESS O, the Lord preserve thy Grace! By my troth, welcome to London. Now, the Lord bless that sweet 300 face of thine! O Jesu, are you come from Wales?

FALSTAFF Thou whoreson mad compound of majesty, by this light flesh and corrupt blood, thou art welcome.

DOLL How, you fat fool! I scorn you.

305 POINS My lord, he will drive you out of your revenge and turn all to a merriment, if you take not the heat.

PRINCE You whoreson candle-mine you, how vilely did you speak of me now before this honest, virtu- 310 ous, civil gentlewoman!

HOSTESS God's blessing of your good heart! And so she is, by my troth.

FALSTAFF Didst thou hear me?

PRINCE Yea, and you knew me, as you did when you 315 ran away by Gad's Hill. You knew I was at your back, and spoke it on purpose to try my patience.

FALSTAFF No, no, no, not so. I did not think thou wast within hearing.

PRINCE I shall drive you then to confess the willful 320 abuse, and then I know how to handle you.

FALSTAFF No abuse, Hal, o' mine honor, no abuse.

PRINCE Not to dispraise me and call me pantler and bread-chipper and I know not what?

FALSTAFF No abuse, Hal.

325 POINS No abuse?

FALSTAFF No abuse, Ned, i' th' world. Honest Ned, none. I dispraised him before the wicked, that the

301 **compound** mixture 302 **light** unchaste (he is referring to Doll) 308 **candle-mine** reservoir of tallow 314-15 **as ... Gad's Hill** (the robbery of the robbers in *1 Henry IV*, II.ii and iv)

wicked might not fall in love with thee. In which
doing, I have done the part of a careful friend and
a true subject, and thy father is to give me thanks   330
for it. No abuse, Hal. None, Ned, none. No, faith,
boys, none.

PRINCE See now, whether pure fear and entire cowardice doth not make thee wrong this virtuous
gentlewoman to close with us. Is she of the   335
wicked? Is thine hostess here of the wicked? Or is
thy boy of the wicked? Or honest Bardolph, whose
zeal burns in his nose, of the wicked?

POINS Answer, thou dead elm, answer.

FALSTAFF The fiend hath pricked down Bardolph irre-   340
coverable, and his face is Lucifer's privy-kitchen,
where he doth nothing but roast malt-worms. For
the boy, there is a good angel about him, but the
devil blinds him too.

PRINCE For the women?   345

FALSTAFF For one of them, she's in hell already, and
burns poor souls. For th' other, I owe her money,
and whether she be damned for that, I know not.

HOSTESS No, I warrant you.

FALSTAFF No, I think thou art not. I think thou art quit   350
for that. Marry, there is another indictment upon
thee, for suffering flesh to be eaten in thy house,
contrary to the law, for the which I think thou wilt
howl.

HOSTESS All victuallers do so. What's a joint of mut-   355
ton or two in a whole Lent?

PRINCE You, gentlewoman—

DOLL What says your Grace?

335 close make peace 340 pricked down checked off 342 malt-worms
(1) weevils in beer (2) drunkards (3) the white material in Bardolph's pimples
347 burns gives burning diseases to 350-51 quit for that paid off for that
352 flesh (1) meat (2) womanflesh 355-56 mutton (also meant a prostitute)

FALSTAFF His Grace says that which his flesh rebels
360   against.   *Peto knocks at door*.

HOSTESS Who knocks so loud at door? Look to th'
door there, Francis.

[*Enter Peto.*]

PRINCE Peto, how now! What news?

PETO The King your father is at Westminster,
365   And there are twenty weak and wearied posts
Come from the north. And as I came along
I met and overtook a dozen captains,
Bareheaded, sweating, knocking at the taverns,
And asking everyone for Sir John Falstaff.

370   PRINCE By heaven, Poins, I feel me much to blame,
So idly to profane the precious time,
When tempest of commotion, like the south
Borne with black vapor, doth begin to melt
And drop upon our bare unarmèd heads.
375   Give me my sword and cloak. Falstaff, good night.
            Exeunt Prince and Poins, [Peto, and Bardolph].

FALSTAFF Now comes in the sweetest morsel of the
night, and we must hence and leave it unpicked.
[*Sound of knocking.*] More knocking at the door?

[*Enter Bardolph.*]

How now! What's the matter?

380   BARDOLPH You must away to court, sir, presently.
A dozen captains stay at door for you.

FALSTAFF [*To the Page*] Pay the musicians, sirrah. Farewell, hostess. Farewell, Doll. You see, my good
wenches, how men of merit are sought after. The
385   undeserver may sleep when the man of action is

359-60 **His Grace ... against** i.e., his Grace calls her a gentlewoman, but his
animal flesh rises up at the idea   365 **posts** messengers   372 **commotion**
rebellion   372 **south** south wind   373 **Borne with black vapor** laden with
black clouds   380 **presently** at present, at once

called on. Farewell, good wenches. If I be not sent
away post, I will see you again ere I go.

DOLL I cannot speak. If my heart be not ready to
burst—well, sweet Jack, have a care of thyself.

FALSTAFF Farewell, farewell.   *Exit [with Bardolph].*   390

HOSTESS Well, fare thee well. I have known thee these
twenty-nine years, come peascod-time, but an
honester and truer-hearted man—well, fare thee
well.

BARDOLPH [*Within*] Mistress Tearsheet!   395

HOSTESS What's the matter?

BARDOLPH [*Within*] Bid Mistress Tearsheet come to
my master.

HOSTESS O, run, Doll, run, run, good Doll. Come. [*To
Bardolph within*] She comes blubbered. Yea, will   400
you come, Doll?   *Exeunt.*

---

387 **post** posthaste   392 **peascod-time** early summer (but there is evidently a
ribald sense, too)   400 **blubbered** disfigured with weeping

[ACT III

Scene I. *The Palace.*]

Enter the King in his nightgown, alone.

KING [*To a Page, within*] Go, call the Earls of Surrey
      and of Warwick.
      But, ere they come, bid them o'erread these letters
      And well consider of them. Make good speed!
      How many thousand of my poorest subjects
5   Are at this hour asleep! O sleep, O gentle sleep,
      Nature's soft nurse, how have I frighted thee,
      That thou no more wilt weigh my eyelids down
      And steep my senses in forgetfulness?
      Why rather, sleep, liest thou in smoky cribs,
10   Upon uneasy pallets stretching thee
      And hushed with buzzing night-flies to thy
         slumber,
      Than in the perfumed chambers of the great,
      Under the canopies of costly state,
      And lulled with sound of sweetest melody?
15   O thou dull god, why li'st thou with the vile
      In loathsome beds, and leavest the kingly couch
      A watchcase or a common 'larum-bell?

III.i.s.d. **nightgown** dressing gown (the customary indoor garment)   9 **smoky
cribs** chimneyless hovels   10 **uneasy pallets** comfortless straw beds   11 **night-
flies** nocturnal insects   12 **perfumed** (Elizabethans who could afford perfume
tried to keep out fresh air)   13 **canopies of costly state** bed-curtains of those in
a wealthy state   17 **watchcase** (1) sentry box (2) case of a constantly ticking
watch   17 **'larum-bell** alarm-bell (hence, constantly watchful)

Wilt thou upon the high and giddy mast
Seal up the ship-boy's eyes, and rock his brains
In cradle of the rude imperious surge   20
And in the visitation of the winds,
Who take the ruffian billows by the top,
Curling their monstrous heads and hanging them
With deafing clamor in the slippery clouds,
That, with the hurly, death itself awakes?   25
Canst thou, O partial sleep, give thy repose
To the wet sea-son in an hour so rude,
And in the calmest and most stillest night,
With all appliances and means to boot,
Deny it to a king? Then happy low, lie down!   30
Uneasy lies the head that wears a crown.

Enter Warwick, Surrey, and Sir John Blunt.

WARWICK Many good morrows to your Majesty!

KING Is it good morrow, lords?

WARWICK 'Tis one o'clock, and past.

KING Why, then, good morrow to you all, my lords.   35
    Have you read o'er the letter that I sent you?

WARWICK We have, my liege.

KING Then you perceive the body of our kingdom
    How foul it is, what rank diseases grow,
    And with what danger, near the heart of it.   40

WARWICK It is but as a body yet distempered,
    Which to his former strength may be restored
    With good advice and little medicine.
    My Lord Northumberland will soon be cooled.

KING O God, that one might read the book of fate,   45
    And see the revolution of the times
    Make mountains level, and the continent,
    Weary of solid firmness, melt itself

24 **deafing** deafening 25 **hurly** hurly-burly 26 **partial** not impartial
29 **means to boot** measures to further (sleep) 30 **low** lowborn 39 **rank** swelling
41 **yet distempered** as yet but sickened 47 **continent** land surface

289

Into the sea! And other times to see
50   The beachy girdle of the ocean
Too wide for Neptune's hips. How chances, mocks,
And changes fill the cup of alteration
With divers liquors! O, if this were seen,
The happiest youth, viewing his progress through,
55   What perils past, what crosses to ensue,
Would shut the book, and sit him down and die.
'Tis not ten years gone
Since Richard and Northumberland, great friends,
Did feast together, and in two years after
60   Were they at wars. It is but eight years since
This Percy was the man nearest my soul,
Who like a brother toiled in my affairs
And laid his love and life under my foot,
Yea, for my sake, even to the eyes of Richard
65   Gave him defiance. But which of you was by—
[*To Warwick*] You, cousin Nevil, as I may
     remember—
When Richard, with his eye brimful of tears,
Then checked and rated by Northumberland,
Did speak these words, now proved a prophecy:
70   "Northumberland, thou ladder by the which
My cousin Bolingbroke ascends my throne"—
Though then, God knows, I had no such intent,
But that necessity so bowed the state
That I and greatness were compelled to kiss—
75   "The time shall come," thus did he follow it,
"The time will come that foul sin, gathering head,
Shall break into corruption." So went on,
Foretelling this same time's condition
And the division of our amity.

80 WARWICK There is a history in all men's lives,
Figuring the nature of the times deceased,

55 **crosses** punishments   59 **Did feast together** (Shakespeare here alters history
for dramatic purposes; this appears neither in Holinshed nor his own *Richard
II*)   63 **under** my foot in subservience to me   66 **Nevil** (historical error for
Beauchamps)   68 **checked, rated** rebuked   76 **gathering head** (1) coming to a
head (2) collecting an army   70–77 **Northumberland ... corruption** (para-
phrased from *Richard II*, V.i.55ff.)   81 **Figuring** symbolizing

The which observed, a man may prophesy,
With a near aim, of the main chance of things
As yet not come to life, who in their seeds
And weak beginning lie intreasurèd.   85
Such things become the hatch and brood of time,
And by the necessary form of this
King Richard might create a perfect guess
That great Northumberland, then false to him,
Would of that seed grow to a greater falseness,   90
Which should not find a ground to root upon,
Unless on you.

KING   Are these things then necessities?
Then let us meet them like necessities.
And that same word even now cries out on us.
They say the Bishop and Northumberland   95
Are fifty thousand strong.

WARWICK   It cannot be, my lord.
Rumor doth double, like the voice and echo,
The numbers of the feared. Please it your Grace
To go to bed. Upon my soul, my lord,
The powers that you already have sent forth   100
Shall bring this prize in very easily.
To comfort you the more, I have received
A certain instance that Glendower is dead.
Your Majesty hath been this fortnight ill,
And these unseasoned hours perforce must add   105
Unto your sickness.

KING   I will take your counsel.
And were these inward wars once out of hand,
We would, dear lords, unto the Holy Land.
                                        Exeunt.

87 **necessary form of this** inevitable operation of this principle of analogy
103 **instance** proof   105 **unseasoned** unusual   107 **inward** internal   107 **out of hand** finished

[Scene II. *Outside Justice Shallow's house.*]

*Enter Justice Shallow and Justice Silence [with
Moldy, Shadow, Wart, Feeble, Bullcalf].*

SHALLOW Come on, come on, come on. Give me your
hand, sir, give me your hand, sir; an early stirrer, by
the rood! And how doth my good cousin Silence?

SILENCE Good morrow, good cousin Shallow.

5   SHALLOW And how doth my cousin, your bedfellow?
And your fairest daughter and mine, my god-
daughter Ellen?

SILENCE Alas, a black ousel, cousin Shallow!

SHALLOW By yea and no, sir, I dare say my cousin
10   William is become a good scholar. He is at Oxford
still, is he not?

SILENCE Indeed, sir, to my cost.

SHALLOW 'A must, then, to the Inns o' Court shortly.
I was once of Clement's Inn, where I think they
15   will talk of mad Shallow yet.

SILENCE You were called "lusty Shallow" then, cousin.

SHALLOW By the mass, I was called anything. And I
would have done anything indeed too, and roundly
too. There was I, and little John Doit of Stafford-
20   shire, and black George Barnes, and Francis Pickbone, and Will Squele, a Cotswold man; you had

III.ii.3 **rood** cross   8 **ousel** blackbird   9 **By yea and no** (a puritan's oath)
13 **Inns o' Court** law schools (which functioned as universities for the gentry)
14 **Clement's Inn** (one of the Inns of Chancery, admitting students unable to get
into the Inns of Court)   18 **roundly** fully   19–21 **Doit ... Barnes ... Pickbone
... Squele** (the names are suggestive of insignificance, a doit being a half-farthing;
country wealth [barns]; stinginess; squealing cowardice)   21 **Cotswold** (a range of
hills in Gloucestershire)

not four such swinge-bucklers in all the Inns o'
Court again. And I may say to you we knew where
the bona-robas were and had the best of them all
at commandment. Then was Jack Falstaff, now Sir   25
John, a boy, and page to Thomas Mowbray, Duke
of Norfolk.

SILENCE This Sir John, cousin, that comes hither anon
about soldiers?

SHALLOW The same Sir John, the very same. I see him   30
break Scoggin's head at the court-gate, when 'a
was a crack not thus high. And the very same day
did I fight with one Sampson Stockfish, a fruiterer,
behind Gray's Inn. Jesu, Jesu, the mad days that
I have spent! And to see how many of my old   35
acquaintance are dead!

SILENCE We shall all follow, cousin.

SHALLOW Certain, 'tis certain, very sure, very sure.
Death, as the Psalmist saith, is certain to all, all
shall die. How a good yoke of bullocks at Stam-   40
ford Fair?

SILENCE By my troth, I was not there.

SHALLOW Death is certain. Is old Double of your
town living yet?

SILENCE Dead, sir.   45

SHALLOW Jesu, Jesu, dead! 'A drew a good bow, and
dead! 'A shot a fine shoot. John a Gaunt loved
him well and betted much money on his head.
Dead! 'A would have clapped i' th' clout at twelve
score, and carried you a forehand shaft a fourteen
and fourteen and a half, that it would have done a   50

22 **swinge-bucklers** shield-beaters (i.e., blusterers)   24 **bona-robas** high-class
whores (Italian *buonaroba*, good material)   31 **Scoggin's** (the name means a coarse
joker)   32 **crack** perky boy   33 **Stockfish** a dried fish (suggestive of an impotent
man)   34 **Gray's Inn** another Inn of Court   40 **How** how much for
43 **Double** (suggests one doubled over with age)   47 **John a Gaunt** Henry IV's
father   49-51 **clapped ... and a half** hit the bull's-eye at 240 yards, and shot a
heavy arrow (for point-blank shooting) 280 or 290 yards

man's heart good to see. How a score of ewes now?

SILENCE Thereafter as they be. A score of good ewes may be worth ten pounds.

55 SHALLOW And is old Double dead?

SILENCE Here come two of Sir John Falstaff's men, as I think.

Enter Bardolph and one with him.

Good morrow, honest gentlemen.

BARDOLPH I beseech you, which is Justice Shallow?

60 SHALLOW I am Robert Shallow, sir, a poor esquire of this county, and one of the King's justices of the peace. What is your good pleasure with me?

BARDOLPH My captain, sir, commends him to you, my captain, Sir John Falstaff, a tall gentleman, by
65 heaven, and a most gallant leader.

SHALLOW He greets me well, sir. I knew him a good backsword man. How doth the good knight? May I ask how my lady his wife doth?

BARDOLPH Sir, pardon, a soldier is better accommo-
70 dated than with a wife.

SHALLOW It is well said, in faith, sir, and it is well said indeed too. "Better accommodated"! It is good, yea, indeed, is it. Good phrases are surely, and ever were, very commendable. "Accommodated"! It
75 comes of "*accommodo*." Very good, a good phrase.

BARDOLPH Pardon, sir. I have heard the word. "Phrase" call you it? By this good day, I know not the phrase, but I will maintain the word with my sword to be a soldier-like word, and a word of ex-
80 ceeding good command, by heaven. "Accommo-dated," that is, when a man is, as they say,

---

53 **Thereafter as they be** according to their condition   60 **esquire** gentleman (ranking just below a knight)   64 **tall** brave   67 **backsword** stick with a hilt used by apprentices in fencing   69–70 **accommodated** provided (a "perfumed term," according to Ben Jonson)

accommodated; or when a man is, being, whereby 'a may be thought to be accommodated, which is an excellent thing.

Enter Falstaff.

SHALLOW It is very just. Look, here comes good Sir   85
John. Give me your good hand, give me your worship's good hand. By my troth, you like well and
bear your years very well. Welcome, good Sir John.

FALSTAFF I am glad to see you well, good Master
Robert Shallow. Master Surecard, as I think?   90

SHALLOW No, Sir John, it is my cousin Silence, in commission with me.

FALSTAFF Good Master Silence, it well befits you should
be of the peace.

SILENCE Your good worship is welcome.   95

FALSTAFF Fie! This is hot weather, gentlemen. Have
you provided me here half a dozen sufficient men?

SHALLOW Marry, have we, sir. Will you sit?

FALSTAFF Let me see them, I beseech you.

SHALLOW Where's the roll? Where's the roll? Where's   100
the roll? Let me see, let me see, let me see. So, so,
so, so, so, so—so. Yea, marry, sir. Rafe Moldy!
Let them appear as I call, let them do so, let them
do so. Let me see, where is Moldy?

MOLDY Here, and't please you.   105

SHALLOW What think you, Sir John? A good-limbed
fellow, young, strong, and of good friends.

FALSTAFF Is thy name Moldy?

MOLDY Yea, and't please you.

FALSTAFF 'Tis the more time thou wert used.   110

85 **just** exact 87 **like** get on 90 **Surecard** absolute winner (at cards)
91–92 **in commission** commissioned as justice of the peace

SHALLOW Ha, ha, ha! Most excellent, i' faith! Things
that are moldy lack use. Very singular good! In
faith, well said, Sir John, very well said.

FALSTAFF Prick him.

115 MOLDY I was pricked well enough before, and you
could have let me alone. My old dame will be undone now for one to do her husbandry and her
drudgery. You need not to have pricked me. There
are other men fitter to go out than I.

120 FALSTAFF Go to. Peace, Moldy, you shall go. Moldy, it
is time you were spent.

MOLDY Spent?

SHALLOW Peace, fellow, peace. Stand aside. Know you
where you are? For th' other, Sir John, let me see.
125 Simon Shadow!

FALSTAFF Yea, marry, let me have him to sit under.
He's like to be a cold soldier.

SHALLOW Where's Shadow?

SHADOW Here, sir.

130 FALSTAFF Shadow, whose son art thou?

SHADOW My mother's son, sir.

FALSTAFF Thy mother's son! Like enough, and thy
father's shadow. So the son of the female is the
shadow of the male. It is often so, indeed, but
135 much of the father's substance!

SHALLOW Do you like him, Sir John?

FALSTAFF Shadow will serve for summer. Prick him,
for we have a number of shadows fill up the muster-
book.

114 **Prick him** check him off   115 **pricked** (1) chosen (2) worried (and a ribald
third meaning)   116 **dame** old wife (or mother)   125 **Shadow** (1) likeness
(2) shade (3) fictitious name in the muster roll for which an officer collected pay
(Falstaff jokes on all three meanings)   133 **son** (he is punning on "sun")
135 **much** little (sarcastic)

SHALLOW Thomas Wart!   140

FALSTAFF Where's he?

WART Here, sir.

FALSTAFF Is thy name Wart?

WART Yea, sir.

FALSTAFF Thou art a very ragged wart.   145

SHALLOW Shall I prick him, Sir John?

FALSTAFF It were superfluous, for his apparel is built upon his back and the whole frame stands upon pins. Prick him no more.

SHALLOW Ha, ha, ha! You can do it, sir! You can do   150
it! I commend you well. Francis Feeble!

FEEBLE Here, sir.

SHALLOW What trade art thou, Feeble?

FEEBLE A woman's tailor, sir.

SHALLOW Shall I prick him, sir?   155

FALSTAFF You may. But if he had been a man's tailor, he'd a' pricked you. Wilt thou make as many holes in an enemy's battle as thou hast done in a woman's petticoat?

FEEBLE I will do my good will, sir. You can have no   160
more.

FALSTAFF Well said, good woman's tailor! Well said, courageous Feeble! Thou wilt be as valiant as the wrathful dove or most magnanimous mouse. Prick the woman's tailor well, Master Shallow, deep,   165
Master Shallow.

FEEBLE I would Wart might have gone, sir.

145 **ragged** having rough projections (referring to his pinned-together clothes) 147 **superfluous** i.e., to "prick him," pin his clothes together 150 **you can do it** you know how to joke 158 **battle** battle line 164 **magnanimous** big-spirited 165 **well, deep** (quibbles on Shallow's name)

FALSTAFF I would thou wert a man's tailor, that thou
mightst mend him and make him fit to go. I can-
170   not put him to a private soldier that is the leader
of so many thousands. Let that suffice, most forcible
Feeble.

FEEBLE It shall suffice, sir.

FALSTAFF I am bound to thee, reverend Feeble. Who is
175   next?

SHALLOW Peter Bullcalf o' th' green!

FALSTAFF Yea, marry, let's see Bullcalf.

BULLCALF Here, sir.

FALSTAFF 'Fore God, a likely fellow! Come, prick
180   Bullcalf till he roar again.

BULLCALF O Lord, good my lord captain—

FALSTAFF What, dost thou roar before thou art
pricked?

BULLCALF O Lord, sir, I am a diseased man.

185   FALSTAFF What disease hast thou?

BULLCALF A whoreson cold, sir, a cough, sir, which I
caught with ringing in the King's affairs upon his
coronation day, sir.

FALSTAFF Come, thou shalt go to the wars in a gown.
190   We will have away thy cold, and I will take such
order that thy friends shall ring for thee. Is here
all?

SHALLOW Here is two more called than your number.
You must have but four here, sir. And so, I pray
195   you, go in with me to dinner.

---

170 **put him to** set him to the occupation of   171 **thousands** i.e., of lice
179 **prick** (here the word refers to the sticking of a bull with a goad in bullbaiting)
187 **ringing in** ringing the church bells to celebrate   189 **gown** dressing gown
191 **ring for thee** i.e., toll your funeral   194 **four** (he settles for three)

FALSTAFF Come, I will go drink with you, but I cannot tarry dinner. I am glad to see you, by my troth, Master Shallow.

SHALLOW O, Sir John, do you remember since we lay all night in the Windmill in Saint George's Field? 200

FALSTAFF No more of that, Master Shallow.

SHALLOW Ha! 'Twas a merry night. And is Jane Nightwork alive?

FALSTAFF She lives, Master Shallow.

SHALLOW She never could away with me. 205

FALSTAFF Never, never, she would always say she could not abide Master Shallow.

SHALLOW By the mass, I could anger her to th' heart. She was then a bona-roba. Doth she hold her own well? 210

FALSTAFF Old, old, Master Shallow.

SHALLOW Nay, she must be old. She cannot choose but be old. Certain she's old, and had Robin Nightwork by old Nightwork before I came to Clement's Inn. 215

SILENCE That's fifty-five year ago.

SHALLOW Ha, cousin Silence, that thou hadst seen that that this knight and I have seen! Ha, Sir John, said I well?

FALSTAFF We have heard the chimes at midnight, 220 Master Shallow.

SHALLOW That we have, that we have, that we have, in faith, Sir John, we have. Our watchword was "Hem, boys!" Come let's to dinner, come, let's to dinner. Jesus, the days that we have seen! Come, 225 come. *Exeunt [Falstaff and the Justices].*

200 Windmill (evidently a brothel) 205 away with put up with 208 anger inflame 224 Hem (the equivalent of "Bottoms up!")

BULLCALF Good Master Corporate Bardolph, stand my friend, and here's four Harry ten shillings in French crowns for you. In very truth, sir, I had as lief be hanged, sir, as go. And yet for mine own part, sir, I do not care, but rather, because I am unwilling, and, for mine own part, have a desire to stay with my friends. Else, sir, I did not care, for mine own part, so much.

230

BARDOLPH Go to, stand aside.

235

MOLDY And, good Master Corporal Captain, for my dame's sake, stand my friend. She has nobody to do anything about her when I am gone, and she is old and cannot help herself. You shall have forty, sir.

240

BARDOLPH Go to, stand aside.

FEEBLE By my troth, I care not. A man can die but once. We owe God a death. I'll ne'er bear a base mind. And't be my destiny, so. And't be not, so. No man's too good to serve's Prince. And let it go which way it will, he that dies this year is quit for the next.

245

BARDOLPH Well said. Th' art a good fellow.

FEEBLE Faith, I'll bear no base mind.

Enter Falstaff and the Justices.

FALSTAFF Come, sir, which men shall I have?

250

SHALLOW Four of which you please.

BARDOLPH Sir, a word with you. [*Aside*] I have three pound to free Moldy and Bullcalf.

FALSTAFF Go to, well.

227 **Corporate** (blunder for "corporal") 228-29 **four Harry ... crowns** (a country way of counting out £1: the amount of four pieces, formerly of ten shillings' value but currently five, rendered in five four-shilling pieces, "French crowns"; Bullcalf is offering around $200 in today's values) 239 **forty** forty shillings (about $400 today) 243 **death** (pronounced like "debt," hence a pun) 246 **is quit** owes nothing

SHALLOW Come, Sir John, which four will you have? 255

FALSTAFF Do you choose for me.

SHALLOW Marry, then, Moldy, Bullcalf, Feeble, and
Shadow.

FALSTAFF Moldy and Bullcalf. For you, Moldy, stay at
home till you are past service. And for your part, 260
Bullcalf, grow till you come unto it. I will none of
you.

SHALLOW Sir John, Sir John, do not yourself wrong.
They are your likeliest men, and I would have you
served with the best. 265

FALSTAFF Will you tell me, Master Shallow, how to
choose a man? Care I for the limb, the thews, the
stature, bulk, and big assemblance of a man? Give
me the spirit, Master Shallow! Here's Wart. You
see what a ragged appearance it is. 'A shall charge 270
you and discharge you with the motion of a pewterer's hammer, come off and on swifter than he that
gibbets on the brewer's bucket. And this same
half-faced fellow, Shadow. Give me this man. He
presents no mark to the enemy: the foeman may 275
with as great aim level at the edge of a penknife.
And for a retreat, how swiftly will this Feeble the
woman's tailor run off! O, give me the spare men,
and spare me the great ones. Put me a caliver into
Wart's hand, Bardolph. 280

BARDOLPH Hold, Wart, traverse. Thus, thus, thus.

FALSTAFF Come, manage me your caliver. So. Very
well. Go to. Very good, exceeding good. O, give me
always a little, lean, old, chopped, bald shot.

---

260 service i.e., (1) military (2) domestic (3) bull's 267 thews bodily
forces 268 assemblance appearance 271–72 motion of a pewterer's hammer i.e., with a rapid tap-tap 273 gibbets on the brewer's bucket hoists with
the beam ("bucket") of a brewer's crane 279 caliver light musket 281 traverse cross over 284 chopped chapped 284 shot shooter (musketeers had to
run nimbly behind the pikemen or spearmen to reload)

285   Well said, i' faith, Wart. Th' art a good scab.
Hold, there's a tester for thee.

SHALLOW He is not his craft's master, he doth not do
it right. I remember at Mile-End Green, when I
lay at Clement's Inn—I was then Sir Dagonet in
290   Arthur's show—there was a little quiver fellow,
and 'a would manage you his piece thus, and 'a
would about and about, and come you in and come
you in. "Rah, tah, tah," would 'a say, "Bounce,"
would 'a say, and away again would 'a go, and
295   again would 'a come. I shall ne'er see such a fellow.

FALSTAFF These fellows would do well, Master Shallow.
God keep you, Master Silence. I will not use many
words with you. Fare you well, gentlemen both.
I thank you. I must a dozen mile tonight. Bardolph,
300   give the soldiers coats.

SHALLOW Sir John, the Lord bless you! God prosper
your affairs! God send us peace! At your return
visit our house, let our old acquaintance be renewed. Peradventure I will with ye to the court.

305   FALSTAFF 'Fore God, would you would.

SHALLOW Go to, I have spoke at a word. God keep
you.

FALSTAFF Fare you well, gentle gentlemen. [*Exeunt
Justices.*] On, Bardolph, lead the men away.
310   [*Exeunt all but Falstaff.*] As I return, I will fetch
off these justices. I do see the bottom of Justice
Shallow. Lord, Lord, how subject we old men are
to this vice of lying! This same starved justice hath
done nothing but prate to me of the wildness of his
315   youth and the feats he hath done about Turnbull
Street, and every third word a lie, duer paid to

285 **scab** i.e., wart   286 **tester** sixpence   290 **Arthur's show** (an annual archery
show at Mile-End Green in which the contestants took the names of knights of the
Round Table. Sir Dagonet was Arthur's fool)   290 **quiver** nimble   306 **at a
word** on an impulse   310-11 **fetch off** trick   315-16 **Turnbull Street** (a red-
light district)   316 **duer** more duly, regularly

the hearer than the Turk's tribute. I do remember
him at Clement's Inn like a man made after supper
of a cheese-paring. When 'a was naked, he was, for
all the world, like a forked radish, with a head   320
fantastically carved upon it with a knife. 'A was so
forlorn that his dimensions to any thick sight were
invisible. 'A was the very genius of famine, yet
lecherous as a monkey, and the whores called him
mandrake. 'A came ever in the rearward of the   325
fashion, and sung those tunes to the overscutched
huswives that he heard the carmen whistle, and
sware they were his fancies or his goodnights. And
now is this Vice's dagger become a squire, and
talks as familiarly of John a Gaunt as if he had   330
been sworn brother to him, and I'll be sworn 'a
ne'er saw him but once in the Tilt-yard, and then
he burst his head for crowding among the marshal's men. I saw it, and told John a Gaunt he beat
his own name, for you might have thrust him and   335
all his apparel into an eel-skin—the case of a treble
hautboy was a mansion for him, a court. And now
has he land and beeves. Well, I'll be acquainted
with him, if I return, and't shall go hard but I'll
make him a philosopher's two stones to me. If the   340
young dace be a bait for the old pike, I see no
reason in the law of nature but I may snap at him.
Let time shape, and there an end.   [*Exit.*]

---

317 **than the Turk's tribute** i.e., than tribute is paid to the Turk   322 **thick**
imperfect   323 **genius** spirit   325 **mandrake** forked root, shaped like the lower
half of a man   326-27 **overscutched huswives** often-whipped whores   328 **his**
fancies or his goodnights musical improvisations of his own or goodnight
songs   329 **Vice's dagger** thin wooden dagger carried by the Vice, clown in the
old morality plays   333 **he** i.e., John of Gaunt   336-37 **treble hautboy** smallest
oboe   340 **philosopher's two stones** (i.e., twice as profitable as one philosopher's stone which would transmute base metals to gold—and a ribald second
sense)   341 **dace** thin, small fish

[ACT IV

Scene I. *With the rebel army.*]

*Enter the Archbishop [of York], Mowbray, Hastings
[and others], within the Forest of Gaultree.*

ARCHBISHOP What is this forest called?

HASTINGS 'Tis Gaultree Forest, and't shall please your
    Grace.

ARCHBISHOP Here stand, my lords, and send
    discoverers forth
    To know the numbers of our enemies.

HASTINGS We have sent forth already.

5   ARCHBISHOP   'Tis well done.
    My friends and brethren in these great affairs,
    I must acquaint you that I have received
    New-dated letters from Northumberland,
    Their cold intent, tenor, and substance, thus:
10   Here doth he wish his person, with such powers
    As might hold sortance with his quality,
    The which he could not levy. Whereupon
    He is retired, to ripe his growing fortunes,
    To Scotland, and concludes in hearty prayers
15   That your attempts may overlive the hazard
    And fearful meeting of their opposite.

IV.i.3 **discoverers** spies 10 **powers** armies 11 **hold sortance with his
quality** accord with his rank 13 **ripe** ripen 15 **overlive** survive
15–16 **hazard/And fearful meeting** of the fearful risk of meeting

MOWBRAY Thus do the hopes we have in him touch
    ground
And dash themselves to pieces.

Enter Messenger.

HASTINGS   Now, what news?

MESSENGER West of this forest, scarcely off a mile,
    In goodly form comes on the enemy,   20
And, by the ground they hide, I judge their number
Upon or near the rate of thirty thousand.

MOWBRAY The just proportion that we gave them
    out.
Let us sway on and face them in the field.

ARCHBISHOP What well-appointed leader fronts us
    here?   25

Enter Westmoreland.

MOWBRAY I think it is my Lord of Westmoreland.

WESTMORELAND Health and fair greeting from our
    general,
The Prince, Lord John and Duke of Lancaster.

ARCHBISHOP Say on, my Lord of Westmoreland, in
    peace.
What doth concern your coming?

WESTMORELAND   Then, my lord,   30
Unto your Grace do I in chief address
The substance of my speech. If that rebellion
Came like itself, in base and abject routs,
Led on by bloody youth, guarded with rage,
And countenanced by boys and beggary,   35
I say, if damned commotion so appeared,
In his true, native and most proper shape,

17 **touch ground** (like a ship) 23 **just proportion ... out** exact number we
allowed for 24 **sway** move 25 **well-appointed** well-furnished 25 **fronts**
confronts 31 **in chief** chiefly 33 **routs** mobs 34 **guarded with rage** trimmed
with false bluster (and pun on "rag") 35 **countenanced** faced out, added to
35 **beggary** beggars 36 **commotion** rebellion

You, reverend father, and these noble lords
Had not been here, to dress the ugly form
40　Of base and bloody insurrection
With your fair honors. You, Lord Archbishop,
Whose see is by a civil peace maintained,
Whose beard the silver hand of peace hath touched,
Whose learning and good letters peace hath tutored,
45　Whose white investments figure innocence,
The dove and very blessèd spirit of peace,
Wherefore do you so ill translate yourself
Out of the speech of peace that bears such grace,
Into the harsh and boisterous tongue of war,
50　Turning your books to graves, your ink to blood,
Your pens to lances, and your tongue divine
To a loud trumpet and a point of war?

ARCHBISHOP　Wherefore do I this? So the question
　　stands.
Briefly to this end: we are all diseased,
55　And with our surfeiting and wanton hours
Have brought ourselves into a burning fever,
And we must bleed for it. Of which disease
Our late king, Richard, being infected, died.
But, my most noble Lord of Westmoreland,
60　I take not on me here as a physician,
Nor do I as an enemy to peace
Troop in the throngs of military men,
But rather show awhile like fearful war,
To diet rank minds sick of happiness
65　And purge th' obstructions which begin to stop
Our very veins of life. Hear me more plainly.
I have in equal balance justly weighed
What wrongs our arms may do, what wrongs we
　　suffer,

---

42 **see** seat, throne, hence diocese　44 **good letters** humane scholarship
45 **investments figure** vestments symbolize　47 **translate** transform (but note
the extended metaphor of language in lines 48–52)　52 **point of war** bugle call
55 **wanton** self-indulgent　57 **bleed** be bled (as a purgative)　60 **I take ...
physician** I do not presume to act as the doctor (to do the bleeding; I will but
"show"—line 63)　64 **rank** swollen　67 **equal** unbiased

And find our griefs heavier than our offenses.
We see which way the stream of time doth run, 70
And are enforced from our most quiet there
By the rough torrent of occasion,
And have the summary of all our griefs,
When time shall serve, to show in articles;
Which long ere this we offered to the King, 75
And might by no suit gain our audience.
When we are wronged and would unfold our griefs,
We are denied access unto his person
Even by those men that most have done us wrong.
The dangers of the days but newly gone, 80
Whose memory is written on the earth
With yet-appearing blood, and the examples
Of every minute's instance, present now,
Hath put us in these ill-beseeming arms,
Not to break peace or any branch of it, 85
But to establish here a peace indeed,
Concurring both in name and quality.

WESTMORELAND When ever yet was your appeal
   denied?
Wherein have you been gallèd by the King?
What peer hath been suborned to grate on you, 90
That you should seal this lawless bloody book
Of forged rebellion with a seal divine?

ARCHBISHOP My brother general, the commonwealth,
   I make my quarrel in particular.

WESTMORELAND There is no need of any such redress, 95
   Or if there were, it not belongs to you.

MOWBRAY Why not to him in part, and to us all
   That feel the bruises of the days before,
   And suffer the condition of these times

69 **griefs** grievances 74 **articles** formal listing 83 **Of every minute's instance** proof in every minute 87 **quality** substance 89 **gallèd** irritated 90 **suborned to grate on** set on to vex 92 **divine** (see Textual Note) 93 **brother general** (brother in a general sense as opposed to my brother by birth; Henry IV had executed the Archbishop's brother—*1 Henry IV*, I.iii; see Textual Note)

100   To lay a heavy and unequal hand
        Upon our honors?

        WESTMORELAND   O, my good Lord Mowbray,
          Construe the times to their necessities,
          And you shall say indeed, it is the time,
          And not the King, that doth you injuries.
105   Yet for your part, it not appears to me
          Either from the King or in the present time
          That you should have an inch of any ground
          To build a grief on. Were you not restored
          To all the Duke of Norfolk's signories,
110   Your noble and right well-rememb'red father's?

        MOWBRAY What thing, in honor, had my father lost,
          That need to be revived and breathed in me?
          The King that loved him, as the state stood then,
          Was force perforce compelled to banish him.
115   And then that Henry Bolingbroke and he,
          Being mounted and both rousèd in their seats,
          Their neighing coursers daring of the spur,
          Their armèd staves in charge, their beavers down,
          Their eyes of fire sparkling through sights of steel,
120   And the loud trumpet blowing them together,
          Then, then, when there was nothing could have
            stayed
          My father from the breast of Bolingbroke—
          O, when the King did throw his warder down
          His own life hung upon the staff he threw.
125   Then threw he down himself and all their lives
          That by indictment and by dint of sword
          Have since miscarried under Bolingbroke.

        WESTMORELAND You speak, Lord Mowbray, now you
            know not what.

100 **unequal** not impartial 102 **Construe ... necessities** interpret the present
state of things according to the forces that inevitably make them the way they
are 109 **signories** lands 114 **force perforce** willy-nilly (for the trial by battle
described in lines 115-37, see *Richard II*, I.iii) 116 **seats** saddles 117 **daring
of** ready for 118 **armèd staves ... beavers** lances at the ready, their
helmet-visors 123 **warder** ceremonial baton 126 **dint** force 127 **miscarried**
perished

The Earl of Hereford was reputed then
In England the most valiant gentleman.   130
Who knows on whom Fortune would then have
    smiled?
But if your father had been victor there,
He ne'er had borne it out of Coventry.
For all the country in a general voice
Cried hate upon him, and all their prayers and love   135
Were set on Hereford, whom they doted on
And blessed and graced—and did more than the
    King.
But this is mere digression from my purpose.
Here come I from our princely general
To know your griefs, to tell you from his Grace   140
That he will give you audience, and wherein
It shall appear that your demands are just,
You shall enjoy them, everything set off
That might so much as think you enemies.

MOWBRAY But he hath forced us to compel this offer,   145
And it proceeds from policy, not love.

WESTMORELAND Mowbray, you overween to take it so.
This offer comes from mercy, not from fear.
For, lo, within a ken our army lies,
Upon mine honor, all too confident   150
To give admittance to a thought of fear.
Our battle is more full of names than yours,
Our men more perfect in the use of arms,
Our armor all as strong, our cause the best.
Then reason will our hearts should be as good.   155
Say you not then our offer is compelled.

MOWBRAY Well, by my will we shall admit no parley.

WESTMORELAND That argues but the shame of your
    offense.

133 it i.e., the prize 133 Coventry (the scene of this trial by battle) 137 did
more than i.e., did so more than for 143 set off put aside, ignored 146 policy
statecraft 147 overween calculate too much 149 ken look 152 battle battle
line 152 names men with warlike reputations 155 reason will it will be
reasonable that

A rotten case abides no handling.

160 HASTINGS Hath the Prince John a full commission,
In very ample virtue of his father,
To hear and absolutely to determine
Of what conditions we shall stand upon?

WESTMORELAND That is intended in the General's
name.
165 I muse you make so slight a question.

ARCHBISHOP Then take, my Lord of Westmoreland,
this schedule,
For this contains our general grievances.
Each several article herein redressed,
All members of our cause, both here and hence
170 That are insinewed to this action,
Acquitted by a true substantial form
And present execution of our wills
To us and our purposes confined,
We come within our awful banks again
175 And knit our powers to the arm of peace.

WESTMORELAND This will I show the General. Please
you, lords,
In sight of both our battles we may meet,
And either end in peace—which God so frame—
Or to the place of diff'rence call the swords
Which must decide it.

180 ARCHBISHOP   My lord, we will do so.
                                        Exit Westmoreland.

MOWBRAY There is a thing within my bosom tells me
That no conditions of our peace can stand.

159 **rotten** fragile (proverbial statement)   161 **In very ample virtue** with
exactly the ample power   164 **intended in the General's name** implicit in the
King's making his son the general   165 **muse** am puzzled   168 **Each ...
redressed** i.e., if each ... is redressed, etc.   169 **hence** elsewhere   170 **insinewed** bound by strong sinews   171 **substantial form** firm formal agreement
172-73 **wills ... confined** demands restricted (in scope) to us and our
grievances   174 **We** i.e., then we   174 **banks** i.e., they will subside like a stream
that had been in flood   179 **diff'rence** conflict   182 **conditions** provisions in
the contract

HASTINGS Fear you not that. If we can make our peace
　　Upon such large terms and so absolute
　　As our conditions shall consist upon,   185
　　Our peace shall stand as firm as rocky mountains.

MOWBRAY Yea, but our valuation shall be such
　　That every slight and false-derivèd cause,
　　Yea, every idle, nice, and wanton reason
　　Shall to the King taste of this action,   190
　　That, were our royal faiths martyrs in love,
　　We shall be winnowed with so rough a wind
　　That even our corn shall seem as light as chaff
　　And good from bad find no partition.

ARCHBISHOP No, no, my lord. Note this. The King is
　　weary   195
　　Of dainty and such picking grievances.
　　For he hath found to end one doubt by death
　　Revives two greater in the heirs of life,
　　And therefore will he wipe his tables clean
　　And keep no telltale to his memory   200
　　That may repeat and history his loss
　　To new remembrance. For full well he knows
　　He cannot so precisely weed this land
　　As his misdoubts present occasion.
　　His foes are so enrooted with his friends   205
　　That, plucking to unfix an enemy,
　　He doth unfasten so and shake a friend.
　　So that this land, like an offensive wife
　　That hath enraged him on to offer strokes,
　　As he is striking, holds his infant up   210
　　And hangs resolved correction in the arm
　　That was upreared to execution.

HASTINGS Besides, the King hath wasted all his rods

187 **valuation** i.e., in the King's eyes 189 **nice, and wanton** petty and
frivolous 191 **were ... love** i.e., even if we were as faithful in love to his
royal self as martyrs 194 **partition** dividing 196 **dainty, picking** finicky
197-98 **to end ... life** i.e., to rid himself of one doubtful subject by executing him
creates two even more treacherous foes in those who live on after the dead man
199 **tables** notebook 203 **precisely** thoroughly 204 **misdoubts** suspicions
211 **resolved correction** a check on his resolution

On late offenders, that he now doth lack
215   The very instruments of chastisement.
So that this power, like to a fangless lion,
May offer, but not hold.

ARCHBISHOP   'Tis very true.
And therefore be assured, my good Lord Marshal,
If we do now make our atonement well,
220   Our peace will, like a broken limb united,
Grow stronger for the breaking.

MOWBRAY   Be it so.
Here is returned my Lord of Westmoreland.

Enter Westmoreland.

WESTMORELAND The Prince is here at hand. Pleaseth
     your lordship
To meet his Grace just distance 'tween our armies.

Enter Prince John [of Lancaster] and his army.

MOWBRAY Your Grace of York, in God's name then,
225   set forward.

ARCHBISHOP Before, and greet his Grace, my lord; we
     come.

[Scene II. *The same.*]

LANCASTER You are well encount'red here, my cousin
     Mowbray.
Good day to you, gentle Lord Archbishop.
And so to you, Lord Hastings, and to all.
My Lord of York, it better showed with you
5   When that your flock, assembled by the bell,
Encircled you to hear with reverence

217 **offer** threaten   219 **atonement** becoming at one   224 **just distance**
halfway IV.ii.s.d. (notice there should be no scene division, the action being
continuous and the stage not having emptied)

Your exposition on the holy text
Than now to see you here an iron man talking,
Cheering a rout of rebels with your drum,
Turning the word to sword and life to death.   10
That man that sits within a monarch's heart
And ripens in the sunshine of his favor,
Would he abuse the countenance of the King,
Alack, what mischiefs might he set abroach
In shadow of such greatness! With you, Lord
    Bishop,   15
It is even so. Who hath not heard it spoken
How deep you were within the books of God?
To us the speaker in His parliament,
To us th' imagined voice of God himself,
The very opener and intelligencer   20
Between the grace, the sanctities of heaven
And our dull workings. O, who shall believe
But you misuse the reverence of your place,
Employ the countenance and grace of heaven,
As a false favorite doth his prince's name,   25
In deeds dishonorable? You have ta'en up,
Under the counterfeited zeal of God,
The subjects of His substitute, my father,
And both against the peace of heaven and him
Have here upswarmed them.

ARCHBISHOP   Good my Lord of Lancaster,   30
I am not here against your father's peace,
But, as I told my Lord of Westmoreland,
The time misord'red doth, in common sense,
Crowd us and crush us to this monstrous form,
To hold our safety up. I sent your Grace   35
The parcels and particulars of our grief,
The which hath been with scorn shoved from the
    court,

---

8 **iron** (1) armored (2) merciless   14 **abroach** open (like a cask)   20 **opener and intelligencer** interpreter and informant   22 **workings** mental operations   26 **ta'en up** enlisted   27 **zeal** (with a pun on "seal")   28 **substitute** deputy   30 **upswarmed** made (them) swarm up   33 **in common sense** to anybody's senses   34 **monstrous** unnatural   36 **parcels** small parts

Whereon this Hydra son of war is born,
Whose dangerous eyes may well be charmed asleep
40   With grant of our most just and right desires,
And true obedience, of this madness cured,
Stoop tamely to the foot of majesty.

MOWBRAY If not, we ready are to try our fortunes
    To the last man.

HASTINGS   And though we here fall down,
45   We have supplies to second our attempt.
If they miscarry, theirs shall second them,
And so success of mischief shall be born
And heir from heir shall hold this quarrel up
Whiles England shall have generation.

LANCASTER You are too shallow, Hastings, much too
50   shallow,
To sound the bottom of the after-times.

WESTMORELAND Pleaseth your Grace to answer them
        directly
How far forth you do like their articles.

LANCASTER I like them all, and do allow them well,
55   And swear here, by the honor of my blood,
My father's purposes have been mistook,
And some about him have too lavishly
Wrested his meaning and authority.
My lord, these griefs shall be with speed redressed.
60   Upon my soul, they shall. If this may please you,
Discharge your powers unto their several counties,
As we will ours. And here between the armies
Let's drink together friendly and embrace,
That all their eyes may bear those tokens home
65   Of our restorèd love and amity.

ARCHBISHOP I take your princely word for these
        redresses.

38 **Hydra** many-headed monster   45 **supplies to second** reinforcements to back
up 46 **theirs** i.e., their supplies 47 **success** succession 49 **generation** offspring 51 **sound** measure the depth of 57 **lavishly** loosely 58 **Wrested**
twisted

LANCASTER I give it you, and will maintain my word.
And thereupon I drink unto your Grace.
                                        [*He drinks.*]

HASTINGS Go, Captain, and deliver to the army
This news of peace. Let them have pay, and part.   70
I know it will well please them. Hie thee, Captain.
                                        [*Exit Officer.*]

ARCHBISHOP To you, my noble Lord of Westmoreland.
                                        [*He drinks.*]

WESTMORELAND I pledge your Grace, and, if you knew
    what pains
I have bestowed to breed this present peace,
You would drink freely. But my love to ye   75
Shall show itself more openly hereafter.

ARCHBISHOP I do not doubt you.

WESTMORELAND   I am glad of it.
Health to my lord and gentle cousin, Mowbray.

MOWBRAY You wish me health in very happy season,
For I am, on the sudden, something ill.   80

ARCHBISHOP Against ill chances men are ever merry,
But heaviness foreruns the good event.

WESTMORELAND Therefore be merry, coz, since sudden
    sorrow
Serves to say thus, "Some good thing comes
    tomorrow."

ARCHBISHOP Believe me, I am passing light in spirit. 85

MOWBRAY So much the worse, if your own rule be
    true.   *Shout* [*within*].

LANCASTER The word of peace is rend'red. Hark, how
    they shout!

MOWBRAY This had been cheerful after victory.

70 **part** depart 80 **something** somewhat 81 **Against** expecting 85 **passing**
surpassingly

ARCHBISHOP A peace is of the nature of a conquest,
90   For then both parties nobly are subdued,
        And neither party loser.

LANCASTER   Go, my lord,
        And let our army be dischargèd too.
                                [*Exit Westmoreland.*]
        And, good my lord, so please you, let our trains
        March by us, that we may peruse the men
        We should have coped withal.

95   ARCHBISHOP   Go, good Lord Hastings,
        And, ere they be dismissed, let them march by.
                                    [*Exit Hastings.*]

LANCASTER I trust, lords, we shall lie tonight together.

                Enter Westmoreland.

        Now cousin, wherefore stands our army still?

WESTMORELAND The leaders, having charge from you
            to stand,
100   Will not go off until they hear you speak.

LANCASTER They know their duties.

                Enter Hastings.

HASTINGS My lord, our army is dispersed already.
        Like youthful steers unyoked, they take their
            courses
        East, west, north, south, or, like a school broke up,
105   Each hurries toward his home and sporting-place.

WESTMORELAND Good tidings, my Lord Hastings, for
            the which
        I do arrest thee, traitor, of high treason.
        And you, Lord Archbishop, and you, Lord
            Mowbray,
        Of capital treason I attach you both.

93 **our trains** those who follow us   95 **coped withal** been matched with
105 **sporting-place** playground   109 **capital** punishable by death   109 **attach**
arrest

MOWBRAY Is this proceeding just and honorable?   110

WESTMORELAND Is your assembly so?

ARCHBISHOP [*To Prince John*] Will you thus break
     your faith?

LANCASTER   I pawned thee none.
  I promised you redress of these same grievances
  Whereof you did complain, which, by mine honor,
  I will perform with a most Christian care.   115
  But for you, rebels, look to taste the due
  Meet for rebellion and such acts as yours.
  Most shallowly did you these arms commence,
  Fondly brought here and foolishly sent hence.
  Strike up our drums, pursue the scatt'red stray.   120
  God, and not we, hath safely fought today.
  Some guard these traitors to the block of death,
  Treason's true bed and yielder up of breath.
                                             [*Exeunt.*]

[Scene III. *The same.*]

Alarum. Enter Falstaff [*and Coleville, meeting*].
                    Excursions.

FALSTAFF What's your name, sir? Of what condition
     are you, and of what place?

COLEVILLE I am a knight, sir, and my name is Coleville
     of the Dale.

FALSTAFF Well, then, Coleville is your name, a knight   5
     is your degree, and your place the Dale. Coleville
     shall be still your name, a traitor your degree, and

112 **pawned** pledged   119 **Fondly** foolishly   IV.iii.s.d. (again, there should be
no scene division; see Textual Note)   s.d. **Excursions** brief combats   1 **condition** rank   4 **Dale** deep place

the dungeon your place, a place deep enough. So
shall you be still Coleville of the Dale.

10   COLEVILLE Are not you Sir John Falstaff?

FALSTAFF As good a man as he, sir, whoe'er I am. Do
ye yield, sir, or shall I sweat for you? If I do sweat,
they are the drops of thy lovers, and they weep for
thy death. Therefore rouse up fear and trembling,
15   and do observance to my mercy.

COLEVILLE I think you are Sir John Falstaff, and in
that thought yield me.

FALSTAFF I have a whole school of tongues in this
belly of mine, and not a tongue of them all speaks
20   any other word but my name. And I had but a belly
of any indifferency, I were simply the most active
fellow in Europe. My womb, my womb, my womb
undoes me. Here comes our general.

*Enter [Prince] John [of Lancaster], Westmore-
land, [Blunt,] and the rest. Retreat [sounded].*

LANCASTER The heat is past, follow no further now.
25   Call in the powers, good cousin Westmoreland.
                              [Exit Westmoreland.]
Now, Falstaff, where have you been all this while?
When everything is ended, then you come.
These tardy tricks of yours will, on my life,
One time or other break some gallows' back.

30   FALSTAFF I would be sorry, my lord, but it should be
thus. I never knew yet but rebuke and check was
the reward of valor. Do you think me a swallow,
an arrow, or a bullet? Have I, in my poor and old
motion, the expedition of thought? I have speeded
35   hither with the very extremest inch of possibility.
I have found'red nine score and odd posts, and

13 **drops of thy lovers** teardrops of those who love you   18 **school** multitude
(he is saying "my belly proclaims my identity as loudly as a multitude")
21 **indifferency** undistinguished quality   22 **womb** belly   23 **undoes** unmans
24 **heat** hot fighting   36 **found'red** lamed   36 **posts** post-horses (Falstaff is,
after all, heavy)

here, travel-tainted as I am, have, in my pure and
immaculate valor, taken Sir John Coleville of the
Dale, a most furious knight and valorous enemy.
But what of that? He saw me, and yielded, that I   40
may justly say, with the hook-nosed fellow of
Rome, "There, cousin, I came, saw, and over-
came."

LANCASTER It was more of his courtesy than your de-
serving.   45

FALSTAFF I know not. Here he is, and here I yield him.
And I beseech your Grace, let it be booked with
the rest of this day's deeds, or, by the Lord, I will
have it in a particular ballad else, with mine own
picture on the top on't, Coleville kissing my foot. 50
To the which course if I be enforced, if you do not
all show like gilt twopences to me, and I in the
clear sky of fame o'ershine you as much as the full
moon doth the cinders of the element, which show
like pins' heads to her, believe not the word of the 55
noble. Therefore let me have right, and let desert
mount.

LANCASTER Thine's too heavy to mount.

FALSTAFF Let it shine, then.

LANCASTER Thine's too thick to shine.   60

FALSTAFF Let it do something, my good lord, that may
do me good, and call it what you will.

LANCASTER Is thy name Coleville?

COLEVILLE It is, my lord.

LANCASTER A famous rebel art thou, Coleville.   65

FALSTAFF And a famous true subject took him.

COLEVILLE I am, my lord, but as my betters are

---

42 **There, cousin** (a gross familiarity to Prince John; the Folio reads "their
Caesar") 49 **particular ballad else** special broadside ballad otherwise 52 **gilt
twopences** (silver twopenny pieces, if gilded, could pass for gold half crowns)
52 **to** in comparison to 54 **cinders of the element** stars

That led me hither. Had they been ruled by me,
You should have won them dearer than you have.

70 FALSTAFF I know not how they sold themselves. But
thou, like a kind fellow, gavest thyself away gratis,
and I thank thee for thee.

Enter Westmoreland.

LANCASTER Now, have you left pursuit?

WESTMORELAND Retreat is made and execution
stayed.

75 LANCASTER Send Coleville with his confederates
To York, to present execution.
Blunt, lead him hence, and see you guard him sure.
        [Exeunt Blunt and others with Coleville.]
And now dispatch we toward the court, my lords.
I hear the King my father is sore sick.
80 Our news shall go before us to his Majesty,
Which, cousin, you shall bear to comfort him,
And we with sober speed will follow you.

FALSTAFF My lord, I beseech you give me leave to go
Through Gloucestershire. And when you come to
court,
85 Stand my good lord in your good report.

LANCASTER Fare you well, Falstaff. I, in my condition,
Shall better speak of you than you deserve.
        [Exeunt all but Falstaff.]

FALSTAFF I would you had the wit. 'Twere better than
your dukedom. Good faith, this same young sober-
90 blooded boy doth not love me, nor a man cannot
make him laugh. But that's no marvel, he drinks
no wine. There's never none of these demure boys
come to any proof, for thin drink doth so over-

---

74 **Retreat is made** the order for retreat has been given   74 **stayed** halted
76 **present** immediate   78 **dispatch** hurry   85 **Stand** act as   86 **condition**
present state of mind (but Falstaff takes his meaning as "rank")   93 **come to any
proof** stand much testing

cool their blood, and making many fish-meals, that
they fall into a kind of male green-sickness, and   95
then, when they marry, they get wenches. They
are generally fools and cowards, which some of us
should be too, but for inflammation. A good
sherris-sack hath a twofold operation in it. It
ascends me into the brain, dries me there all the   100
foolish and dull and cruddy vapors which environ
it, makes it apprehensive, quick, forgetive, full
of nimble, fiery, and delectable shapes, which, delivered o'er to the voice, the tongue, which is the
birth, becomes excellent wit. The second property   105
of your excellent sherris is the warming of the
blood, which, before cold and settled, left the liver
white and pale, which is the badge of pusillanimity
and cowardice. But the sherris warms it and makes
it course from the inwards to the parts extreme. It   110
illumineth the face, which as a beacon gives warning to all the rest of this little kingdom, man, to
arm, and then the vital commoners and inland
petty spirits muster me all to their captain, the
heart, who, great and puffed up with this retinue,   115
doth any deed of courage, and this valor comes of
sherris. So that skill in the weapon is nothing without sack, for that sets it a-work, and learning a
mere hoard of gold kept by a devil, till sack commences it and sets it in act and use. Hereof comes   120
it that Prince Harry is valiant, for the cold blood
he did naturally inherit of his father, he hath, like
lean, sterile, and bare land, manured, husbanded,
and tilled with excellent endeavor of drinking good
and good store of fertile sherris, that he is become   125

95 **green-sickness** anemia common to young girls   96 **get** beget   98 **inflammation** i.e., of the spirits with liquor   99 **sherris-sack** sherry (wine from the
Jerez district in Spain; "sack" is from the French, *sec*, dry)   101 **cruddy**
curded   102 **apprehensive** quick to take in   102 **forgetive** begetting,
procreative   105 **wit** intelligence   107 **liver** (seat of the passions, including
courage)   113-14 **vital ... spirits** (fluids within the body that give it life and
motion)   119-20 **commences it** gives it a university degree (licensing it to
act)   123 **manured** tilled by hand

very hot and valiant. If I had a thousand sons, the
first humane principle I would teach them should
be to forswear thin potations and to addict themselves to sack.

Enter Bardolph.

130   How now, Bardolph?

BARDOLPH The army is discharged all and gone.

FALSTAFF Let them go. I'll through Gloucestershire,
and there will I visit Master Robert Shallow,
Esquire. I have him already temp'ring between
135   my finger and my thumb, and shortly will I seal
with him. Come away.   [*Exeunt.*]

[Scene IV. *Westminster.*]

*Enter the King, Warwick, Kent, Thomas Duke of Clarence,
Humphrey [Duke] of Gloucester, [and others].*

KING Now, lords, if God doth give successful end
To this debate that bleedeth at our doors,
We will our youth lead on to higher fields
And draw no swords but what are sanctified.
5   Our navy is addressed, our power collected,
Our substitutes in absence well invested,
And everything lies level to our wish.
Only, we want a little personal strength
And pause us, till these rebels, now afoot,
10   Come underneath the yoke of government.

WARWICK Both which we doubt not but your Majesty
Shall soon enjoy.

134 **temp'ring** softening (like sealing wax) 135 **seal** (1) squeeze (2) close the
deal IV.iv.4 **sanctified** i.e., in a Crusade 5 **addressed** at the ready 5 **power**
army 6 **invested** clothed (with authority) 7 **level** according 8 **want** lack

KING   Humphrey, my son of Gloucester,
  Where is the Prince your brother?

GLOUCESTER I think he's gone to hunt, my lord, at
    Windsor.

KING And how accompanied?

GLOUCESTER   I do not know, my lord.   15

KING Is not his brother, Thomas of Clarence, with
    him?

GLOUCESTER No, my good lord, he is in presence here.

CLARENCE What would my lord and father?

KING Nothing but well to thee, Thomas of Clarence.
  How chance thou art not with the Prince thy
      brother?
  He loves thee, and thou dost neglect him, Thomas;   20
  Thou hast a better place in his affection
  Than all thy brothers. Cherish it, my boy,
  And noble offices thou mayst effect
  Of mediation, after I am dead,   25
  Between his greatness and thy other brethren.
  Therefore omit him not, blunt not his love,
  Nor lose the good advantage of his grace
  By seeming cold or careless of his will.
  For he is gracious, if he be observed.   30
  He hath a tear for pity and a hand
  Open as day for meeting charity.
  Yet notwithstanding, being incensed, he's flint,
  As humorous as winter and as sudden
  As flaws congealèd in the spring of day.   35
  His temper, therefore, must be well observed.
  Chide him for faults, and do it reverently,
  When you perceive his blood inclined to mirth,
  But, being moody, give him time and scope,
  Till that his passions, like a whale on ground,   40

17 **presence** i.e., the royal presence 30 **gracious** full of royal grace
30 **observed** respected 34 **humorous** given to whims 35 **flaws congealèd**
snowstorms turned to sleet

Confound themselves with working. Learn this, Thomas,
And thou shalt prove a shelter to thy friends,
A hoop of gold to bind thy brothers in,
That the united vessel of their blood,
45 Mingled with venom of suggestion—
As, force perforce, the age will pour it in—
Shall never leak, though it do work as strong
As aconitum or rash gunpowder.

CLARENCE I shall observe him with all care and love.

50 KING Why art thou not at Windsor with him, Thomas?

CLARENCE He is not there today. He dines in London.

KING And how accompanied? Canst thou tell that?

CLARENCE With Poins and other his continual followers.

KING Most subject is the fattest soil to weeds,
55 And he, the noble image of my youth,
Is overspread with them. Therefore my grief
Stretches itself beyond the hour of death.
The blood weeps from my heart when I do shape
In forms imaginary th' unguided days
60 And rotten times that you shall look upon
When I am sleeping with my ancestors.
For when his headstrong riot hath no curb,
When rage and hot blood are his counselors,
When means and lavish manners meet together,
65 O, with what wings shall his affections fly
Towards fronting peril and opposed decay!

WARWICK My gracious lord, you look beyond him quite.
The Prince but studies his companions

41 **Confound** defeat 41 **working** acting out 45 **suggestion** insinuations
46 **force perforce** willy-nilly 48 **aconitum** wolfsbane (a poison) 54 **fattest**
richest 63 **rage** passion 64 **lavish manners** loose behavior 65 **affections**
desires 66 **fronting** confronting 67 **look beyond** misjudge, i.e., you look
further into the future than the evidence warrants

Like a strange tongue, wherein, to gain the
    language,
'Tis needful that the most immodest word   70
Be looked upon and learned, which once attained,
Your Highness knows, comes to no further use
But to be known and hated. So, like gross terms,
The Prince will in the perfectness of time
Cast off his followers, and their memory   75
Shall as a pattern or a measure live,
By which his Grace must mete the lives of others,
Turning past evils to advantages.

KING 'Tis seldom when the bee doth leave her comb
In the dead carrion. Who's here? Westmoreland?   80

Enter Westmoreland.

WESTMORELAND Health to my sovereign, and new
    happiness
Added to that that I am to deliver.
Prince John your son doth kiss your Grace's hand.
Mowbray, the Bishop Scroop, Hastings and all
Are brought to the correction of your law.   85
There is not now a rebel's sword unsheathed,
But Peace puts forth her olive everywhere.
The manner how this action hath been borne
Here at more leisure may your Highness read,
With every course in his particular.   90

KING O Westmoreland, thou art a summer bird,
Which ever in the haunch of winter sings
The lifting up of day.

Enter Harcourt.

Look, here's more news.

HARCOURT From enemies, heavens keep your Majesty,
And, when they stand against you, may they fall   95
As those that I am come to tell you of!

77 **mete** measure, judge   79–80 **'Tis seldom … carrion** i.e., the bee who has
created sweetness in rottenness rarely abandons it   90 **course** occurrence
92 **haunch** back portion

The Earl Northumberland and the Lord Bardolph,
With a great power of English and of Scots,
Are by the shrieve of Yorkshire overthrown.
100   The manner and true order of the fight
This packet, please it you, contains at large.

KING And wherefore should these good news make
    me sick?
Will Fortune never come with both hands full,
But write her fair words still in foulest letters?
105   She either gives a stomach and no food—
Such are the poor, in health—or else a feast
And takes away the stomach—such are the rich
That have abundance and enjoy it not.
I should rejoice now at this happy news,
110   And now my sight fails, and my brain is giddy.
O me! Come near me. Now I am much ill.

GLOUCESTER Comfort, your Majesty!

CLARENCE   O my royal father!

WESTMORELAND My sovereign lord, cheer up yourself,
    look up.

WARWICK Be patient, Princes. You do know these fits
115   Are with his Highness very ordinary.
Stand from him, give him air, he'll straight be well.

CLARENCE No, no, he cannot long hold out these pangs.
Th' incessant care and labor of his mind
Hath wrought the mure that should confine it in
120   So thin that life looks through and will break out.

GLOUCESTER The people fear me, for they do observe
Unfathered heirs and loathly births off nature.
The seasons change their manners, as the year
Had found some months asleep and leaped them
    over.

99 **shrieve** sheriff 104 **still** ever 105 **stomach** appetite 116 **straight**
straightway 119 **wrought the mure** worked the wall 121 **fear me** make me
fear 122 **Unfathered** supernaturally begotten 122 **loathly** monstrous 123 **as**
as if

CLARENCE The river hath thrice flowed, no ebb
　　between,   125
　And the old folk, time's doting chronicles,
　Say it did so a little time before
　That our great-grandsire, Edward, sicked and died.

WARWICK Speak lower, Princes, for the King recovers.

GLOUCESTER This apoplexy will certain be his end.   130

KING I pray you, take me up, and bear me hence
　Into some other chamber. Softly, pray.
　　　　　　　　　[*They bear him to another*
　　　　　　　　　　　　part of the stage.]

　　　　　　　[Scene V. *The same.*]

[KING] Let there be no noise made, my gentle friends,
　Unless some dull and favorable hand
　Will whisper music to my weary spirit.

WARWICK Call for the music in the other room.

KING Set me the crown upon my pillow here.   5

CLARENCE His eye is hollow, and he changes much.

WARWICK Less noise, less noise!

　　　　　　　Enter [Prince] Harry.

PRINCE   Who saw the Duke of Clarence?

CLARENCE I am here, brother, full of heaviness.

125 **river** Thames   125 **flowed** flooded   128 **Edward** Edward III IV.v.s.d. (the stage is not emptied, the King being lifted onto a bed and moved to the inner stage or another part of the outer stage, and the Quarto and the Folio indicate no scene division; the conventional nineteenth-century scene division is superfluous) 2 **dull and favorable** drowsy and kindly   6 **changes** i.e., changes color

PRINCE How now! Rain within doors, and none
    abroad!
10   How doth the King?

GLOUCESTER Exceeding ill.

PRINCE   Heard he the good news yet?
    Tell it him.

GLOUCESTER He altered much upon the hearing it.

PRINCE If he be sick with joy, he'll recover without
    physic.

WARWICK Not so much noise, my lords. Sweet Prince,
15   speak low.
    The King your father is disposed to sleep.

CLARENCE Let us withdraw into the other room.

WARWICK Will't please your Grace to go along with
    us?

PRINCE No, I will sit and watch here by the King.
                       [*Exeunt all but Prince Hal.*]
20   Why doth the crown lie there upon his pillow,
    Being so troublesome a bedfellow?
    O polished perturbation! Golden care!
    That keep'st the ports of slumber open wide
    To many a watchful night! Sleep with it now!
25   Yet not so sound and half so deeply sweet
    As he whose brow with homely biggen bound
    Snores out the watch of night. O majesty!
    When thou dost pinch thy bearer, thou dost sit
    Like a rich armor worn in heat of day,
30   That scald'st with safety. By his gates of breath
    There lies a downy feather which stirs not.
    Did he suspire, that light and weightless down
    Perforce must move. My gracious lord, my father!
    This sleep is sound indeed. This is a sleep

9 **Rain** i.e., tears 23 **ports** city gates (as the eyes are to the mind) 26 **biggen**
nightcap 30 **scald'st with safety** scorches while it protects 30 **gates of
breath** i.e., lips 32 **suspire** breathe

That from this golden rigol hath divorced   35
So many English kings. Thy due from me
Is tears and heavy sorrows of the blood,
Which nature, love, and filial tenderness
Shall, O dear father, pay thee plenteously.
My due from thee is this imperial crown,   40
Which, as immediate from thy place and blood,
Derives itself to me. [*Puts on the crown.*] Lo,
   where it sits,
Which God shall guard. And put the world's whole
   strength
Into one giant arm, it shall not force
This lineal honor from me. This from thee   45
Will I to mine leave, as 'tis left to me.   *Exit.*

KING [*Waking*] Warwick! Gloucester! Clarence!

   Enter Warwick, Gloucester, Clarence.

CLARENCE Doth the King call?

WARWICK What would your Majesty? How fares your
   Grace?

KING Why did you leave me here alone, my lords?   50

CLARENCE We left the Prince my brother here, my
   liege,
Who undertook to sit and watch by you.

KING The Prince of Wales! Where is he? Let me see
   him.
He is not here.

WARWICK This door is open. He is gone this way.   55

GLOUCESTER He came not through the chamber where
   we stayed.

KING Where is the crown? Who took it from my
   pillow?

WARWICK When we withdrew, my liege, we left it here.

35 **rigol** circle   41 **as immediate from** i.e., as nothing is between me and
42 **Derives** flows down   45 **lineal** inherited (as against taken)

KING The Prince hath ta'en it hence. Go, seek him
        out.
60   Is he so hasty that he doth suppose
        My sleep my death?
        Find him, my Lord of Warwick, chide him hither.
                                        [*Exit Warwick.*]
        This part of his conjoins with my disease
        And helps to end me. See, sons, what things you
        are!
65   How quickly nature falls into revolt
        When gold becomes her object!
        For this the foolish overcareful fathers
        Have broke their sleep with thoughts,
        Their brains with care, their bones with industry.
70   For this they have engrossèd and piled up
        The cank'red heaps of strange-achievèd gold;
        For this they have been thoughtful to invest
        Their sons with arts and martial exercises.
        When, like the bee, culling from every flower
75   The virtuous sweets, our thighs packed with wax,
        Our mouths with honey, we bring it to the hive,
        And, like the bees, are murdered for our pains.
        This bitter taste yields his engrossments
        To the ending father.

                        Enter Warwick.

80   Now, where is he that will not stay so long
        Till his friend sickness hath determined me?

WARWICK My lord, I found the Prince in the next
          room,
        Washing with kindly tears his gentle cheeks,
        With such a deep demeanor in great sorrow
85   That tyranny, which never quaffed but blood,
        Would, by beholding him, have washed his knife
        With gentle eye-drops. He is coming hither.

63 **part** act   70 **engrossèd** bought up   71 **cank'red** (1) rusting (2) malignant
71 **strange-achievèd** hard-won   72 **thoughtful** careful   73 **arts** i.e., liberal
arts   78 **yields his engrossments** his accumulations yield   81 **determined**
ended   83 **kindly** natural   84 **deep demeanor** intense manner

KING But wherefore did he take away the crown?

Enter [Prince] Harry.

Lo, where he comes. Come hither to me, Harry.
Depart the chamber, leave us here alone.   90

Exeunt [Warwick and the others].

PRINCE I never thought to hear you speak again.

KING Thy wish was father, Harry, to that thought.
I stay too long by thee, I weary thee.
Dost thou so hunger for mine empty chair
That thou wilt needs invest thee with my honors   95
Before thy hour be ripe? O foolish youth!
Thou seek'st the greatness that will overwhelm thee.
Stay but a little, for my cloud of dignity
Is held from falling with so weak a wind
That it will quickly drop. My day is dim.   100
Thou hast stol'n that which after some few hours
Were thine without offense, and at my death
Thou hast sealed up my expectation.
Thy life did manifest thou lov'dst me not,
And thou wilt have me die assured of it.   105
Thou hid'st a thousand daggers in thy thoughts,
Which thou hast whetted on thy stony heart,
To stab at half an hour of my life.
What! Canst thou not forbear me half an hour?
Then get thee gone and dig my grave thyself,   110
And bid the merry bells ring to thine ear
That thou art crownèd, not that I am dead.
Let all the tears that should bedew my hearse
Be drops of balm to sanctify thy head.
Only compound me with forgotten dust.   115
Give that which gave thee life unto the worms.
Pluck down my officers, break my decrees,
For now a time is come to mock at form.
Harry the Fifth is crowned. Up, vanity!
Down, royal state! All you sage counselors, hence!   120

93 **by thee** (1) with thee (2) in thy opinion   99 **wind** i.e., breath   103 **sealed up**
confirmed   114 **balm** coronation oil   115 **Only compound** just mix
118 **form** order

And to the English court assemble now,
From every region, apes of idleness!
Now, neighbor confines, purge you of your scum.
Have you a ruffian that will swear, drink, dance,
125 Revel the night, rob, murder, and commit
The oldest sins the newest kind of ways?
Be happy, he will trouble you no more.
England shall double gild his treble guilt,
England shall give him office, honor, might,
130 For the fifth Harry from curbed license plucks
The muzzle of restraint, and the wild dog
Shall flesh his tooth on every innocent.
O my poor kingdom, sick with civil blows!
When that my care could not withhold thy riots,
135 What wilt thou do when riot is thy care?
O, thou wilt be a wilderness again,
Peopled with wolves, thy old inhabitants.

PRINCE O, pardon me, my liege! But for my tears,
The moist impediments unto my speech,
140 I had forestalled this dear and deep rebuke
Ere you with grief had spoke and I had heard
The course of it so far. There is your crown,
And He that wears the crown immortally
Long guard it yours. If I affect it more
145 Than as your honor and as your renown,
Let me no more from this obedience rise,
Which my most inward true and duteous spirit
Teacheth, this prostrate and exterior bending.
God witness with me, when I here came in,
And found no course of breath within your
150   Majesty,
How cold it struck my heart. If I do feign,
O, let me in my present wildness die
And never live to show th' incredulous world
The noble change that I have purposèd.
155 Coming to look on you, thinking you dead,

123 **neighbor confines** nearby regions   132 **flesh** sink in flesh   140 **dear**
heartfelt   144 **affect** desire   146 **obedience** low curtsy   150 **course** occurrence

And dead almost, my liege, to think you were,
I spake unto this crown as having sense,
And thus upbraided it: "The care on thee depending
Hath fed upon the body of my father.
Therefore, thou best of gold art worst of gold.   160
Other, less fine in carat, is more precious,
Preserving life in medicine potable,
But thou, most fine, most honored, most renowned,
Hast eat thy bearer up." Thus, my most royal liege,
Accusing it, I put it on my head,   165
To try with it, as with an enemy
That had before my face murdered my father,
The quarrel of a true inheritor.
But if it did infect my blood with joy,
Or swell my thoughts to any strain of pride,   170
If any rebel or vain spirit of mine
Did with the least affection of a welcome
Give entertainment to the might of it,
Let God forever keep it from my head
And make me as the poorest vassal is   175
That doth with awe and terror kneel to it.

KING O my son,
God put it in thy mind to take it hence,
That thou mightst win the more thy father's love,
Pleading so wisely in excuse of it!   180
Come hither, Harry, sit thou by my bed,
And hear, I think, the very latest counsel
That ever I shall breathe. God knows, my son,
By what bypaths and indirect crooked ways
I met this crown, and I myself know well   185
How troublesome it sat upon my head.
To thee it shall descend with better quiet,
Better opinion, better confirmation,
For all the soil of the achievement goes
With me into the earth. It seemed in me   190

---

161 **carat** (with pun on "charact," character) 162 **medicine potable** gold in
solution (prescribed as medicine) 170 **strain** musical theme (i.e., feeling)
182 **latest** last 185 **met** i.e., as one meets one's fate 189 **soil** dirt

But as an honor snatched with boisterous hand,
And I had many living to upbraid
My gain of it by their assistances,
Which daily grew to quarrel and to bloodshed

195 Wounding supposèd peace. All these bold fears
Thou seest with peril I have answered,
For all my reign hath been but as a scene
Acting that argument. And now my death
Changes the mood, for what in me was purchased

200 Falls upon thee in a more fairer sort,
So thou the garland wear'st successively.
Yet, though thou stand'st more sure than I could
     do,
Thou art not firm enough, since griefs are green.
And all my friends, which thou must make thy
     friends,

205 Have but their stings and teeth newly ta'en out,
By whose fell working I was first advanced
And by whose power I well might lodge a fear
To be again displaced. Which to avoid,
I cut them off, and had a purpose now

210 To lead out many to the Holy Land,
Lest rest and lying still might make them look
Too near unto my state. Therefore, my Harry,
Be it thy course to busy giddy minds
With foreign quarrels, that action, hence borne
     out,

215 May waste the memory of the former days.
More would I, but my lungs are wasted so
That strength of speech is utterly denied me.
How I came by the crown, O God forgive,
And grant it may with thee in true peace live!

220 PRINCE My gracious liege,
     You won it, wore it, kept it, gave it me.

191 **boisterous** rough   195 **fears** things causing fear   198 **argument** plot (in a play)   199 **mood** (punning on "mode")   199 **purchased** (a legal term: acquired by deed rather than inheritance)   201 **successively** by hereditary succession   203 **green** fresh and growing   206 **fell** fierce   211-12 **look/Too near** (1) examine (2) aspire too closely   214 **hence borne out** carried on elsewhere

Then plain and right must my possession be,
Which I with more than with a common pain
'Gainst all the world will rightfully maintain.

Enter [Prince John of] Lancaster [and Warwick].

KING Look, look, here comes my John of Lancaster.   225

LANCASTER Health, peace, and happiness to my royal
    father!

KING Thou bring'st me happiness and peace, son
    John,
But health, alack, with youthful wings is flown
From this bare, withered trunk. Upon thy sight
My worldly business makes a period.   230
Where is my Lord of Warwick?

PRINCE   My Lord of Warwick!

KING Doth any name particular belong
Unto the lodging where I first did swoon?

WARWICK 'Tis called "Jerusalem," my noble lord.

KING Laud be to God! Even there my life must end.   235
It hath been prophesied to me many years
I should not die but "in Jerusalem,"
Which vainly I supposed the Holy Land.
But bear me to that chamber; there I'll lie.
In that "Jerusalem" shall Harry die.   [*Exeunt.*]   240

223 **pain** effort (and note the formal rhymes) 234 **Jerusalem** (Holinshed states correctly that the "Jerusalem chamber" is in Westminster Abbey, not Westminster Palace; Shakespeare leaves the setting of IV.iv and v ambiguous until this line—see the stage direction at IV.iv.1) 235 **Laud** praise

[ACT V

Scene I. *Justice Shallow's home.*]

Enter Shallow, Falstaff, and Bardolph [and Page].

SHALLOW By cock and pie, sir, you shall not away
tonight. What, Davy, I say!

FALSTAFF You must excuse me, Master Robert Shallow.

SHALLOW I will not excuse you. You shall not be ex-
5   cused. Excuses shall not be admitted. There is no
excuse shall serve. You shall not be excused. Why,
Davy!

[Enter Davy.]

DAVY Here, sir.

SHALLOW Davy, Davy, Davy, Davy, let me see, Davy.
10   Let me see, Davy, let me see. Yea, marry, William
cook, bid him come hither. Sir John, you shall not
be excused.

DAVY Marry, sir, thus, those precepts cannot be
served. And, again, sir, shall we sow the headland
15   with wheat?

SHALLOW With red wheat, Davy. But for William cook
—are there no young pigeons?

V.i.1 **By cock and pie** (a mild oath) 13 **precepts** orders 14 **headland**
unplowed strip between two plowed fields 16 **red wheat** (sown in late August)

DAVY Yes, sir. Here is now the smith's note for shoeing and plow-irons.

SHALLOW Let it be cast and paid. Sir John, you shall 20 not be excused.

DAVY Now, sir, a new link to the bucket must needs be had. And, sir, do you mean to stop any of William's wages, about the sack he lost the other day at Hinckley Fair? 25

SHALLOW 'A shall answer it. Some pigeons, Davy, a couple of short-legged hens, a joint of mutton, and any pretty little tiny kickshaws, tell William cook.

DAVY Doth the man of war stay all night, sir?

SHALLOW Yea, Davy. I will use him well. A friend i' 30 th' court is better than a penny in purse. Use his men well, Davy, for they are arrant knaves and will backbite.

DAVY No worse than they are backbitten, sir, for they have marvelous foul linen. 35

SHALLOW Well conceited, Davy. About thy business, Davy.

DAVY I beseech you, sir, to countenance William Visor of Woncot against Clement Perkes o' th' hill.

SHALLOW There is many complaints, Davy, against that 40 Visor. That Visor is an arrant knave, on my knowledge.

DAVY I grant your worship that he is a knave, sir, but yet, God forbid, sir, but a knave should have some countenance at his friend's request. An honest 45 man, sir, is able to speak for himself, when a knave is not. I have served your worship truly, sir, this

18 note bill   20 cast checked   22 link to the bucket chain link for the yoke
25 Hinckley Fair (held August 26, thirty miles northeast of Stratford)
28 kickshaws fancy things (French, *quelquechoses*)   34 backbitten i.e., with lice
36 conceited conceived   38 countenance show favor to

eight years—and I cannot once or twice in a quarter bear out a knave against an honest man, I have but a very little credit with your worship. The knave is mine honest friend, sir. Therefore, I beseech you, let him be countenanced.

SHALLOW Go to, I say he shall have no wrong. Look about, Davy! [*Exit Davy*.] Where are you, Sir John? Come, come, come, off with your boots. Give me your hand, Master Bardolph.

BARDOLPH I am glad to see your worship.

SHALLOW I thank thee with my heart, kind Master Bardolph. [*To the Page*] And welcome, my tall fellow. Come, Sir John.

FALSTAFF I'll follow you, good Master Robert Shallow. [*Exit Shallow*.] Bardolph, look to our horses. [*Exeunt Bardolph and Page*.] If I were sawed into quantities, I should make four dozen of such bearded hermits' staves as Master Shallow. It is a wonderful thing to see the semblable coherence of his men's spirits and his. They, by observing him, do bear themselves like foolish justices. He, by conversing with them, is turned into a justice-like servingman. Their spirits are so married in conjunction with the participation of society that they flock together in consent, like so many wild geese. If I had a suit to Master Shallow, I would humor his men with the imputation of being near their master. If to his men, I would curry with Master Shallow that no man could better command his servants. It is certain that either wise bearing or ignorant carriage is caught, as men take diseases, one of another. Therefore let men take heed of their company. I will devise matter enough out of

49 **bear out** help out   53–54 **Look about** look sharp!   64 **quantities** lengths 66 **semblable coherence** visible similarity   71 **society** association   72 **in consent** unanimously   75 **curry** i.e., curry favor   77 **bearing** behavior 79–80 **take heed of their company** (ironical, coming from Falstaff)

this Shallow to keep Prince Harry in continual
laughter the wearing out of six fashions, which is
four terms, or two actions, and 'a shall laugh
without intervallums. O, it is much that a lie with
a slight oath and a jest with a sad brow will do with   85
a fellow that never had the ache in his shoulders! O,
you shall see him laugh till his face be like a wet
cloak ill laid up!

SHALLOW [*Within*] Sir John!

FALSTAFF I come, Master Shallow. I come, Master Shal-   90
low.   [*Exit.*]

[Scene II. *London.*]

*Enter the Earl of Warwick and the
Lord Chief Justice [meeting].*

WARWICK How now, my Lord Chief Justice! Whither
away?

CHIEF JUSTICE How doth the King?

WARWICK Exceeding well. His cares are now all ended.

CHIEF JUSTICE I hope, not dead.

WARWICK   He's walked the way of nature,
And to our purposes he lives no more.   5

CHIEF JUSTICE I would his Majesty had called me with
him.
The service that I truly did his life
Hath left me open to all injuries.

WARWICK Indeed I think the young king loves you not.

83 **terms** court sessions (four in the year) 83 **actions** lawsuits 84 **intervallums** intersessions 88 **ill laid up** put away wrinkled V.ii.5 **our** i.e., living
men's as contrasted to God's 7 **truly** faithfully

10   CHIEF JUSTICE I know he doth not, and do arm myself
              To welcome the condition of the time,
              Which cannot look more hideously upon me
              Than I have drawn it in my fantasy.

          *Enter [Prince] John [of Lancaster], Thomas
          [of Clarence], and Humphrey [of Gloucester].*

      WARWICK Here come the heavy issue of dead Harry.
15   O that the living Harry had the temper
          Of he, the worst of these three gentlemen!
          How many nobles then should hold their places
          That must strike sail to spirits of vile sort!

      CHIEF JUSTICE O God, I fear all will be overturned!

      LANCASTER Good morrow, cousin Warwick, good
20   morrow.

      GLOUCESTER ⎫
                  ⎬ Good morrow, cousin.
      CLARENCE   ⎭

      LANCASTER We meet like men that had forgot to speak.

      WARWICK We do remember, but our argument
          Is all too heavy to admit much talk.

      LANCASTER Well, peace be with him that hath made us
25   heavy.

      CHIEF JUSTICE Peace be with us, lest we be heavier.

      GLOUCESTER O, good my lord, you have lost a friend
              indeed,
          And I dare swear you borrow not that face
          Of seeming sorrow—it is sure your own.

      LANCASTER Though no man be assured what grace to
30   find,
          You stand in coldest expectation.
          I am the sorrier. Would 'twere otherwise.

14 **heavy issue** grieving sons   15 **temper** temperament   16 **he** i.e., whoever is
18 **strike** lower (i.e., submit to pirates)   23 **argument** situation

CLARENCE Well, you must now speak Sir John Falstaff
    fair,
  Which swims against your stream of quality.

CHIEF JUSTICE Sweet Princes, what I did, I did in
    honor,   35
  Led by th' impartial conduct of my soul,
  And never shall you see that I will beg
  A ragged and forestalled remission.
  If truth and upright innocency fail me,
  I'll to the King my master that is dead,   40
  And tell him who hath sent me after him.

WARWICK Here comes the Prince.

Enter the Prince [as King Henry the Fifth] and Blunt.

CHIEF JUSTICE Good morrow, and God save your
    Majesty!

KING This new and gorgeous garment, majesty,
  Sits not so easy on me as you think.
  Brothers, you mix your sadness with some fear.   45
  This is the English, not the Turkish court.
  Not Amurath an Amurath succeeds,
  But Harry Harry. Yet be sad, good brothers,
  For, by my faith, it very well becomes you.
  Sorrow so royally in you appears   50
  That I will deeply put the fashion on
  And wear it in my heart. Why then, be sad,
  But entertain no more of it, good brothers,
  Than a joint burden laid upon us all.
  For me, by heaven, I bid you be assured,   55
  I'll be your father and your brother too.
  Let me but bear your love, I'll bear your cares.
  Yet weep that Harry's dead, and so will I,
  But Harry lives, that shall convert those tears   60
  By number into hours of happiness.

34 **swims ... quality** goes against the current of your disposition and rank
38 **ragged and forestalled remission** beggarly and already prevented pardon
48 **Amurath** Amurath IV of Turkey strangled his brothers on his accession in
1574 51 **appears** (they are wearing black, he royal red) 52 **deeply** (1) solemnly
(2) within

BROTHERS We hope no otherwise from your Majesty.

KING You all look strangely on me. [*To the Chief
     Justice*] And you most.
     You are, I think, assured I love you not.

65   CHIEF JUSTICE I am assured, if I be measured rightly,
     Your Majesty hath no just cause to hate me.

KING No?
     How might a prince of my great hopes forget
     So great indignities you laid upon me?
70   What! Rate, rebuke, and roughly send to prison
     Th' immediate heir of England! Was this easy?
     May this be washed in Lethe, and forgotten?

CHIEF JUSTICE I then did use the person of your
     father.
     The image of his power lay then in me.
75   And, in th' administration of his law,
     Whiles I was busy for the commonwealth,
     Your Highness pleasèd to forget my place,
     The majesty and power of law and justice,
     The image of the King whom I presented,
80   And struck me in my very seat of judgment.
     Whereon, as an offender to your father,
     I gave bold way to my authority
     And did commit you. If the deed were ill,
     Be you contented, wearing now the garland,
85   To have a son set your decrees at nought?
     To pluck down justice from your awful bench?
     To trip the course of law and blunt the sword
     That guards the peace and safety of your person?
     Nay, more, to spurn at your most royal image
90   And mock your workings in a second body?
     Question your royal thoughts. Make the case yours.

70 **Rate** berate   71 **easy** unimportant (the legend was well known; see above, note
to I.ii.57–58).   72 **Lethe** the river of forgetfulness in Hades   73 **use the person**
act in the character   83 **commit** send to prison   86 **awful** causing awe   90 **in a
second body** (i.e., one who uses your person, line 73)

Be now the father and propose a son:
Hear your own dignity so much profaned,
See your most dreadful laws so loosely slighted,
Behold yourself so by a son disdained,   95
And then imagine me taking your part
And in your power soft silencing your son.
After this cold considerance, sentence me,
And, as you are a king, speak in your state
What I have done that misbecame my place,   100
My person, or my liege's sovereignty.

KING You are right, Justice, and you weigh this well.
Therefore still bear the balance and the sword.
And I do wish your honors may increase,
Till you do live to see a son of mine   105
Offend you—and obey you—as I did.
So shall I live to speak my father's words:
"Happy am I, that have a man so bold
That dares do justice on my proper son,
And not less happy, having such a son   110
That would deliver up his greatness so
Into the hands of justice." You did commit me.
For which, I do commit into your hand
Th' unstainèd sword that you have used to bear,
With this remembrance, that you use the same   115
With the like bold, just, and impartial spirit
As you have done 'gainst me. There is my hand.
You shall be as a father to my youth.
My voice shall sound as you do prompt mine ear,
And I will stoop and humble my intents   120
To your well-practiced wise directions.
And, Princes all, believe me, I beseech you,
My father is gone wild into his grave,
For in his tomb lie my affections,
And with his spirits sadly I survive,   125
To mock the expectation of the world,

92 **propose** put the case of (legal term)   98 **cold considerance** cool
consideration   99 **state** station   109 **proper** own   115 **remembrance** entry in
the records (legal term)   123 **wild** uncivilized   124 **affections** appetites
125 **spirits** character (based on his humors)

To frustrate prophecies, and to raze out
Rotten opinion, who hath writ me down
After my seeming. The tide of blood in me
130   Hath proudly flowed in vanity till now.
Now doth it turn and ebb back to the sea,
Where it shall mingle with the state of floods
And flow henceforth in formal majesty.
Now call we our high court of parliament.
135   And let us choose such limbs of noble counsel
That the great body of our state may go
In equal rank with the best-governed nation;
That war, or peace, or both at once, may be
As things acquainted and familiar to us,
140   In which you, father, shall have foremost hand.
Our coronation done, we will accite,
As I before rememb'red, all our state.
And, God consigning to my good intents,
No prince nor peer shall have just cause to say,
145   God shorten Harry's happy life one day!

                                Exit [with the rest].

[Scene III. *Justice Shallow's home.*]

*Enter Sir John [Falstaff], Shallow, Silence, Davy,
Bardolph, Page.*

SHALLOW Nay, you shall see my orchard, where, in an
arbor, we will eat a last year's pippin of mine own
graffing, with a dish of caraways, and so forth.
Come, cousin Silence. And then to bed.

---

127 **raze** erase   129 **my seeming** the way I seem outwardly   132 **state of
floods** majesty of the ocean   141 **accite** summon   142 **rememb'red** noted (cf.
line 115)   142 **state** great men of the land   143 **consigning** signing ratification
(legal term; notice Hal's knowledge of different "languages")   V.iii.2 **pippin** type
of apple   3 **graffing** grafting   3 **caraways** caraway seeds

FALSTAFF 'Fore God, you have here a goodly dwelling   5
and a rich.

SHALLOW Barren, barren, barren. Beggars all, beggars
all, Sir John. Marry, good air. Spread, Davy,
spread, Davy. Well said, Davy.

FALSTAFF This Davy serves you for good uses. He is   10
your servingman and your husband.

SHALLOW A good varlet, a good varlet, a very good
varlet, Sir John. By the mass, I have drunk too
much sack at supper. A good varlet. Now sit down,
now sit down. Come, cousin.   15

SILENCE Ah, sirrah, quoth-a, we shall
    [Sings] Do nothing but eat, and make good cheer,
            And praise God for the merry year,
            When flesh is cheap and females dear,
            And lusty lads roam here and there   20
                    So merrily,
            And ever among so merrily.

FALSTAFF There's a merry heart! Good Master Silence,
I'll give you a health for that anon.

SHALLOW Give Master Bardolph some wine, Davy.   25

DAVY Sweet sir, sit, I'll be with you anon. Most sweet
sir, sit. Master page, good master page, sit. [Makes
them sit down, at another table.] Proface! What
you want in meat, we'll have in drink. But you
must bear, the heart's all.   [Exit.]   30

SHALLOW Be merry, Master Bardolph, and, my little
soldier there, be merry.

SILENCE [Sings] Be merry, be merry, my wife has all,
                    For women are shrews, both short
                        and tall.
                    'Tis merry in hall when beards wag
                        all,   35

11 **husband** housemanager 12 **varlet** servant 16 **quoth-a** said he 19 **flesh**
meat (with a ribald second sense) 28 **Proface!** (a dinner welcome) 29 **want**
lack 30 **bear** endure

And welcome merry Shrovetide.
Be merry, be merry.

FALSTAFF I did not think Master Silence had been a
man of this mettle.

40 SILENCE Who, I? I have been merry twice and once
ere now.

Enter Davy.

DAVY [*To Bardolph*] There's a dish of leather-coats
for you.

SHALLOW Davy!

45 DAVY Your worship! [*To Bardolph*] I'll be with you
straight.—A cup of wine, sir?

SILENCE [*Sings*] A cup of wine that's brisk and fine,
And drink unto the leman mine,
And a merry heart lives long-a.

50 FALSTAFF Well said, Master Silence.

SILENCE [*Sings*] And we shall be merry, now comes in
the sweet o' the night.

FALSTAFF Health and long life to you, Master Silence.

SILENCE [*Sings*] Fill the cup, and let it come,
I'll pledge you a mile to th'
55   bottom.

SHALLOW Honest Bardolph, welcome. If thou want'st
anything, and wilt not call, beshrew thy heart. [*To
the Page*] Welcome, my little tiny thief, and welcome indeed too. I'll drink to Master Bardolph,
60 and to all the cabileros about London.

DAVY I hope to see London once ere I die.

BARDOLPH And I might see you there, Davy—

36 **Shrovetide** period of feasting just before Lent 40 **merry** tipsy (?)
42 **leather-coats** russet apples 48 **leman** sweetheart 55 **pledge you a mile**
drink in one draught though it were a mile deep 57 **beshrew** cursed be
60 **cabileros** cavaliers

SHALLOW By the mass, you'll crack a quart together, ha! Will you not, Master Bardolph?

BARDOLPH Yea, sir, in a pottle-pot.   65

SHALLOW By God's liggens, I thank thee. The knave will stick by thee, I can assure thee that. 'A will not out, 'a. 'Tis true bred.

BARDOLPH And I'll stick by him, sir.

One knocks at door.

SHALLOW Why, there spoke a king. Lack nothing. Be   70
merry. Look who's at door there, ho! Who knocks?

[*Exit Davy.*]

FALSTAFF [*To Silence, seeing him drinking*] Why, now you have done me right.

SILENCE [*Kneels, drinks and sings*] Do me right,
　　　　　　　　　　　And dub me
　　　　　　　　　　　　　knight.   75
　　　　　　　　　Samingo.

Is't not so?

FALSTAFF 'Tis so.

SILENCE Is't so? Why then, say an old man can do somewhat.   80

[*Enter Davy.*]

DAVY And't please your worship, there's one Pistol come from the court with news.

FALSTAFF From the court! Let him come in.

Enter Pistol.

How now, Pistol!

PISTOL Sir John, God save you!   85

63 **crack** split, share 65 **pottle-pot** two-quart tankard 66 **By God's liggens** (an oath of unknown meaning, possibly because Shallow is tipsy) 68 **out** pass out 73 **done me right** i.e., pledged to my pledge 75 **knight** (drinking a deep draught while kneeling entitled one to be called "knight") 76 **Samingo** Monsieur Mingo, the hero of the song

FALSTAFF   What wind blew you hither, Pistol?

PISTOL   Not the ill wind which blows no man to good.
Sweet knight, thou art now one of the greatest men
in this realm.

90   SILENCE   By'r lady, I think 'a be, but goodman Puff
of Barson.

PISTOL   Puff!
Puff i' thy teeth, most recreant coward base!
Sir John, I am thy Pistol and thy friend,
95   And helter-skelter have I rode to thee,
And tidings do I bring and lucky joys
And golden times and happy news of price.

FALSTAFF   I pray thee now, deliver them like a man of
this world.

100   PISTOL   A foutra for the world and worldlings base!
I speak of Africa and golden joys.

FALSTAFF   O base Assyrian knight, what is thy news?
Let King Cophetua know the truth thereof.

SILENCE   [*Sings*] "And Robin Hood, Scarlet, and John."

105   PISTOL   Shall dunghill curs confront the Helicons?
And shall good news be baffled?
Then, Pistol, lay thy head in Furies' lap.

SHALLOW   Honest gentleman, I know not your breeding.

110   PISTOL   Why then, lament therefore.

SHALLOW   Give me pardon, sir. If, sir, you come with
news from the court, I take it there's but two ways,
either to utter them, or conceal them. I am, sir,
under the King, in some authority.

90 **but goodman Puff** except for yeoman Puff (whose name suggests a shape and
size as "great" as Falstaff's)   92 **Puff** swaggerer   98-99 **man of this world**
ordinary man   100 **foutra** (French, *foutre* accompanied by an indecent gesture)
101 **Africa** (where the gold comes from)   102 **Assyrian** pun on "ass" (?) (Falstaff
adopts Pistol's style in hopes of communicating with him)   103 **Cophetua**
African king in a famous ballad   105 **Helicons** poets (?)   106 **baffled** treated
shamefully   110 **therefore** for that

PISTOL Under which king, Besonian? Speak, or die.   115

SHALLOW Under King Harry.

PISTOL   Harry the Fourth, or Fifth?

SHALLOW Harry the Fourth.

PISTOL   A foutra for thine office!
Sir John, thy tender lambkin now is king.
Harry the Fifth's the man. I speak the truth.
When Pistol lies, do this, and fig me, like   120
The bragging Spaniard.

FALSTAFF What, is the old king dead?

PISTOL As nail in door. The things I speak are just.

FALSTAFF Away, Bardolph! Saddle my horse. Master
    Robert Shallow, choose what office thou wilt in the   125
    land, 'tis thine. Pistol, I will double-charge thee
    with dignities.

BARDOLPH O joyful day!
    I would not take a knighthood for my fortune.

PISTOL What! I do bring good news.   130

FALSTAFF Carry Master Silence to bed. Master Shallow,
    my Lord Shallow—be what thou wilt, I am for-
    tune's steward! Get on thy boots! We'll ride all
    night! O sweet Pistol! Away, Bardolph! [*Exit
    Bardolph.*] Come, Pistol, utter more to me, and   135
    withal devise something to do thyself good. Boot,
    boot, Master Shallow. I know the young king is
    sick for me. Let us take any man's horses; the
    laws of England are at my commandment. Blessed
    are they that have been my friends, and woe to my   140
    Lord Chief Justice!

115 **Besonian** beggarly recruit   117 **thine office** (the King's death terminated
Shallow's appointment)   120 **do this** (make an insulting gesture, the "fig," by
putting the thumb between the index and third fingers)   126 **double-charge**
twice-load (a pistol)   130 **What! ... news** (a knighthood is evidently not enough
for Pistol or perhaps he is responding to Silence's sudden collapse)   138 **take any
man's horses** i.e., "press" them (for they are on the King's service)

PISTOL Let vultures vile seize on his lungs also!
"Where is the life that late I led?" say they.
Why, here it is. Welcome these pleasant days!
Exit [with the rest].

[Scene IV. *London.*]

*Enter Beadle and three or four Officers [with
Hostess Quickly and Doll Tearsheet].*

HOSTESS No, thou arrant knave, I would to God that
I might die, that I might have thee hanged. Thou
hast drawn my shoulder out of joint.

BEADLE The constables have delivered her over to
5   me, and she shall have whipping-cheer, I warrant
her. There hath been a man or two killed about
her.

DOLL Nut-hook, nut-hook, you lie. Come on, I'll tell
thee what, thou damned tripe-visaged rascal, and
10   the child I go with do miscarry, thou wert better
thou hadst struck thy mother, thou paper-faced
villain.

HOSTESS O the Lord, that Sir John were come! I
would make this a bloody day to somebody. But
15   I pray God the fruit of her womb miscarry!

BEADLE If it do, you shall have a dozen of cushions
again. You have but eleven now. Come, I charge

---

143 **Where ... led** scrap of an old song V.iv.s.d. **Beadle** parish officer (who
punished petty offenders) 2 **hanged** i.e., for murdering me 5 **whipping-cheer**
hospitality of the whip 6 **about** (1) because of, or (2) in the presence of 8 **Nut-
hook** (slang for the "catchpole" carried by beadles) 9 **tripe-visaged**
pock-marked 11 **paper-faced** thin and pale 15 **miscarry** (she goes along with
Doll's threat) 17 **eleven** (Doll having used one to simulate pregnancy)

you both go with me, for the man is dead that you
and Pistol beat amongst you.

DOLL I'll tell you what, you thin man in a censer, I   20
will have you as soundly swinged for this—you
blue-bottle rogue, you filthy famished correctioner,
if you be not swinged, I'll forswear half-kirtles.

BEADLE Come, come, you she-knight-errant, come.

HOSTESS O God, that right should thus overcome   25
might! Well, of sufferance comes ease.

DOLL Come, you rogue, come. Bring me to a justice.

HOSTESS Ay, come, you starved bloodhound.

DOLL Goodman death, goodman bones!

HOSTESS Thou atomy, thou!   30

DOLL Come, you thin thing! Come, you rascal!

BEADLE Very well.   [*Exeunt.*]

[Scene V. *London.*]

Enter Strewers of rushes.

FIRST STREWER More rushes, more rushes!

SECOND STREWER The trumpets have sounded twice.

THIRD STREWER 'Twill be two o'clock ere they come
from the coronation. Dispatch, dispatch.   [*Exeunt.*]

---

20 **thin man in a censer** figure of a man stamped on the lid of a pan for burning
incense (?) 21 **swinged** beaten 22 **blue-bottle** (beadles, like modern police-
men, wore blue coats) 23 **half-kirtles** skirts 25–26 **O God ... might!** (a
typical Quickly blunder) 26 **of sufferance** out of suffering (but "sufferance"
means tolerance) 30 **atomy** atom (does she mean "anatomy," "cadaver"?)
31 **rascal** lean deer V.v.1 **rushes** (the usual floor covering; here, strewn in the
streets)

*Trumpets sound, and the King and his Train pass over
the stage. After them enter Falstaff, Shallow, Pistol,
Bardolph, and the Boy.*

5   FALSTAFF Stand here by me, Master Shallow. I will
     make the King do you grace. I will leer upon him
     as 'a comes by, and do but mark the countenance
     that he will give me.

     PISTOL God bless thy lungs, good knight.

10   FALSTAFF Come here, Pistol, stand behind me. [*To
     Shallow*] O, if I had had time to have made new
     liveries, I would have bestowed the thousand
     pound I borrowed of you. But 'tis no matter; this
     poor show doth better. This doth infer the zeal I
15   had to see him.

     PISTOL It doth so.

     FALSTAFF It shows my earnestness of affection—

     PISTOL It doth so.

     FALSTAFF My devotion—

20   PISTOL It doth, it doth, it doth.

     FALSTAFF As it were, to ride day and night, and not to
     deliberate, not to remember, not to have patience
     to shift me—

     SHALLOW It is best, certain.

25   FALSTAFF But to stand stained with travel, and sweat-
     ing with desire to see him, thinking of nothing else,
     putting all affairs else in oblivion, as if there were
     nothing else to be done but to see him.

     PISTOL 'Tis "*semper idem*," for "*obsque hoc nihil est.*"
30   'Tis all in every part.

6 **do you grace** show you favor   6 **leer** glance slyly (instead of reverently bowing
his head)   12 **liveries** servants' uniforms   14 **infer** imply   23 **shift me** change
my clothes   29 **semper idem** ever the same   29–30 **obsque hoc nihil est**
without this, nothing (both phrases are mottoes, the second garbled)   30 **all in
every part** absolute (another motto)

352

SHALLOW 'Tis so, indeed.

PISTOL My knight, I will inflame thy noble liver,
And make thee rage.
Thy Doll, and Helen of thy noble thoughts,
Is in base durance and contagious prison,   35
Haled thither by most mechanical and dirty hand.
Rouse up revenge from ebon den with fell
    Alecto's snake,
For Doll is in. Pistol speaks nought but truth.

FALSTAFF I will deliver her.

PISTOL There roared the sea, and trumpet clangor
    sounds.   40

    [*Trumpets sound.*] *Enter the King and his Train*
        [*including the Lord Chief Justice*].

FALSTAFF God save thy Grace, King Hal, my royal Hal!

PISTOL The heavens thee guard and keep, most royal
    imp of fame!

FALSTAFF God save thee, my sweet boy!

KING My Lord Chief Justice, speak to that vain man.   45

CHIEF JUSTICE Have you your wits? Know you what
    'tis you speak?

FALSTAFF My king! My Jove! I speak to thee, my heart!

KING I know thee not, old man. Fall to thy prayers.
How ill white hairs becomes a fool and jester!
I have long dreamt of such a kind of man,   50
So surfeit-swelled, so old, and so profane,
But, being awaked, I do despise my dream.
Make less thy body hence, and more thy grace.
Leave gormandizing. Know the grave doth gape
For thee thrice wider than for other men.   55

32 **liver** seat of the passions (love as well as rage)   35 **contagious** pestilential
36 **mechanical** working-class   37 **ebon** black   37 **Alecto** one of the Furies
43 **imp** (1) scion (2) graft (in falconry or gardening—that which adds to)   48 **I
know thee not** (see Matthew 25:10-12)   53 **hence** henceforth

Reply not to me with a fool-born jest.
Presume not that I am the thing I was,
For God doth know, so shall the world perceive,
That I have turned away my former self.
60   So will I those that kept me company.
When thou dost hear I am as I have been,
Approach me, and thou shalt be as thou wast,
The tutor and the feeder of my riots.
Till then, I banish thee, on pain of death,
65   As I have done the rest of my misleaders,
Not to come near our person by ten mile.
For competence of life I will allow you,
That lack of means enforce you not to evils.
And, as we hear you do reform yourselves,
70   We will, according to your strengths and qualities,
Give you advancement. Be it your charge, my lord,
To see performed the tenor of my word.
Set on.   [*Exeunt the King and his Train.*]

FALSTAFF Master Shallow, I owe you a thousand pound.

75   SHALLOW Yea, marry, Sir John, which I beseech you
          to let me have home with me.

FALSTAFF That can hardly be, Master Shallow. Do not
          you grieve at this. I shall be sent for in private to
          him. Look you, he must seem thus to the world.
80   Fear not your advancements; I will be the man yet
          that shall make you great.

SHALLOW I cannot perceive how, unless you give me
          your doublet and stuff me out with straw. I beseech
          you, good Sir John, let me have five hundred of my
85   thousand.

FALSTAFF Sir, I will be as good as my word. This that
          you heard was but a color.

SHALLOW A color that I fear you will die in, Sir John.

---

56 **fool-born** (note the pun) 67 **competence of life** allowance for
necessaries 87 **color** pretense 88 **color** (punning on "choler," and "collar,"
i.e., noose) 88 **die** (punning on "dye")

FALSTAFF Fear no colors. Go with me to dinner. Come,
Lieutenant Pistol. Come, Bardolph. I shall be sent   90
for soon at night.

*Enter [Lord Chief] Justice and Prince John [of
Lancaster, and Officers].*

CHIEF JUSTICE Go, carry Sir John Falstaff to the Fleet.
Take all his company along with him.

FALSTAFF My lord, my lord—

CHIEF JUSTICE I cannot now speak. I will hear you
soon.   95
Take them away.

PISTOL *"Si fortuna me tormenta, spero contenta."*

Exeunt [all but Prince John and the Chief Justice].

LANCASTER I like this fair proceeding of the King's.
He hath intent his wonted followers
Shall all be very well provided for,   100
But all are banished till their conversations
Appear more wise and modest to the world.

CHIEF JUSTICE And so they are.

LANCASTER The King hath called his parliament, my
lord.

CHIEF JUSTICE He hath.   105

LANCASTER I will lay odds that, ere this year expire,
We bear our civil swords and native fire
As far as France. I heard a bird so sing,
Whose music, to my thinking, pleased the King.
Come, will you hence?   [*Exeunt.*]   110

---

89 **colors** enemy flags (a proverb)   90 **Lieutenant** (note the promotion)
91 **soon at night** at early evening   92 **Fleet** prison for distinguished prisoners
temporarily detained for inquiry ("I will hear you soon"—line 95)   97 **Si fortuna**
... **contenta** if fortune torments me, hope contents me   99 **wonted**
customary   107 **civil swords** i.e., swords presently used in civil war

EPILOGUE

[*Spoken by a Dancer*]

First my fear, then my curtsy, last my speech. My
fear is your displeasure; my curtsy my duty; and my
speech to beg your pardons. If you look for a good
speech now, you undo me, for what I have to say
5 is of mine own making, and what indeed I should say
will, I doubt, prove mine own marring. But to the
purpose, and so to the venture. Be it known to you,
as it is very well, I was lately here in the end of a displeasing play, to pray your patience for it and to
10 promise you a better. I meant indeed to pay you with
this, which, if like an ill venture it come unluckily
home, I break, and you, my gentle creditors, lose.
Here I promised you I would be and here I commit
my body to your mercies. Bate me some and I will
15 pay you some and, as most debtors do, promise you
infinitely, and so I kneel down before you, but, indeed, to pray for the Queen.

If my tongue cannot entreat you to acquit me, will
you command me to use my legs? And yet that were
20 but light payment, to dance out of your debt. But a
good conscience will make any possible satisfaction,
and so would I. All the gentlewomen here have forgiven me. If the gentlemen will not, then the gentlemen do not agree with the gentlewomen, which was
25 never seen in such an assembly.

Epilogue (evidently, as in *Midsummer Night's Dream*, a mingling of epilogues: the
first paragraph is for one occasion, the second and third for another, and epilogues
for any occasion could be built up out of separate parts) 1 **fear** stage fright
(pretended) 4 **undo** ruin 6 **doubt** fear .8–9 **displeasing play** (unidentified)
11 **venture** i.e., business venture 12 **break** (1) break my promise (2) go
bankrupt 14 **Bate me some** forgive part of my debt 22–23 **have forgiven me**
(perhaps the Epilogue was spoken by the Page)

One word more, I beseech you. If you be not too much cloyed with fat meat, our humble author will continue the story, with Sir John in it, and make you merry with fair Katharine of France. Where, for anything I know, Falstaff shall die of a sweat, unless 30 already 'a be killed with your hard opinions, for Oldcastle died martyr, and this is not the man. My tongue is weary. When my legs are too, I will bid you good night.

[*End with a dance.*]

FINIS

28 **Sir John in it** (but Falstaff does not appear in *Henry V*)   31–32 **Oldcastle** (Sir John Oldcastle was the name of the Prince's boon companion in the source play, *The Famous Victories of Henry V*, and, evidently, in Shakespeare's first versions of the *Henry IV* plays. *Old.* appears as a speech tag at Quarto 2 *Henry IV* I.ii.125. [See also this edition of *Part One*, I.ii.43-44]. In this Epilogue, Shakespeare is saying his Falstaff is not the historical Oldcastle, executed in 1417 and honored by Protestant chroniclers as a Lollard martyr [though Catholic chroniclers said he was a drunkard and a robber]. The name was probably removed from Shakespeare's plays at the behest of Oldcastle's descendant, Lord Cobham—who was promptly nicknamed by the Essex faction Sir John Falstaff).

Textual Note

Henry IV [*Part Two*] comes to us in two—or really, three—texts: the Folio of 1623 and the Quarto of 1600; the Quarto, however, occurs in two forms, the second (Qb) a modification of the first, evidently to admit a scene (III.i) omitted in Qa. The researches of a number of scholars[1] have now converged to give us a history of these three texts.

Shakespeare wrote the play in late 1597 or early 1598, and from his manuscript (called "foul papers") the Chamberlain's Men had a transcript made to serve as the promptbook for performances. In 1600, possibly to forestall pirating, the company sold the publication rights to *Much Ado About Nothing* and *2 Henry IV*, which were then entered in the Stationers' Register on August 23. The foul papers were sent to the printshop of Valentine Simmes for publication in quarto form. While there, perhaps while the copy was being cast off into page-length units for the compositors, the sheets containing Act III, scene i were misplaced (perhaps mixed into the sheets of *Much Ado*, which were in the same handwriting). At this point, the deputy of the Bishop of London, whose task it was to censor the play, read the manuscript and ordered the deletion of eight short passages that might conceivably compare Elizabeth to Richard II or otherwise tend to rebellion. He did not, however, see and censor the longer and more important references to Richard in Act III, scene i, for the sheets containing that scene had been mislaid. In due course, Simmes and his men finished and issued the first quarto version of *2 Henry IV*, Qa, and turned to work on *Much Ado*. But then someone discovered a scene was missing, and Simmes had to put aside *Much Ado* and, at some cost to himself, correct his error by resetting two leaves as four to accommodate the

---

[1] Notably J. Dover Wilson, Matthias Shaaber, James McManaway, and John H. Smith.

omitted scene. Simmes then issued this second version of the Quarto, Qb.

Shakespeare's acting company, meanwhile, was using a transcript of the foul papers for their prompt copy and altering it to indicate their stage-practices: removing profanity, omitting mute characters, revising stage business, and so on. There is, of course, no way to tell whether Shakespeare agreed to these changes or whether they simply accumulated over the years. Further, at some point, the prompt copy itself may have been recopied—perhaps for a collector of plays, perhaps preparatory to printing the Folio; if so, the copyist was probably someone used to working with play texts, who systematically took out colloquial and vulgar expressions, improved the punctuation, and rewrote the stage directions. The Folio text of the play was then set up either directly from the altered prompt copy or indirectly through a transcript of it.

Thus, Qa (supplemented by III.i from Qb) comes closest to Shakespeare's original words and imagined staging—though often in the form of "bunched" stage directions (simply an initial listing at the beginning of a scene of the characters who will appear in it). The Folio suggests alterations in staging that Shakespeare may (or may not) have participated in, and it supplies eight passages the censor removed, but for the most part the Folio is authoritative only to correct obvious blunders or otherwise help in deciphering the oddly punctuated quarto text. Accordingly, I have modernized spelling and punctuation, regularized the speech-tags and the printing of prose and verse, and supplied the Globe act and scene divisions used in standard reference books, but otherwise I have followed the quartos closely, with a few exceptions.

The eight passages I have supplied from the Folio that do not appear in Qa or Qb are: I.i.166–79, *You cast ... to be?* I.i.189–209, *The gentle ... follow him.* I.iii.21–24, *Till we ... admitted.* I.iii.36–55, *Yes, if ... Or else.* I.iii.85–108, *Let us ... worst.* II.iii.23–45, *He had ... grave.* IV.i.55–79, *And with ... wrong.* IV.i.101–37, *O, my ... the King.* The Folio also includes many small expansions, some of a word or two, others of whole sentences or phrases. I have included the longer ones, but not those so short as likely to be mere compositors' expansions. Finally, the list of characters appearing at the end of the Folio text I have here reproduced at the beginning.

Occasionally I have adopted certain readings that do not appear in the quartos; these readings are listed in the following, with the accepted reading first in bold, the rejected reading second in roman. Since, in almost all these cases, I have used the Folio reading instead of the quartos', unless otherwise indicated, the accepted reading is from the Folio (F), the rejected from quarto Qa.

Induction   36 **Where** When   40s.d. **Rumor** [ed.] Rumours

I.i.96 **say so** [Q omits]   161 **Lord Bardolph** Vmfr[evile]   162 **Morton** Bard. [Mour. at line 163]   164 **Lean on your** Leaue on you 166–79 [Q omits; F, with editorial *brought* from "bring" at line 178]   189–209 [Q omits]

I.ii.40 **smooth** smoothy   51 **Where's Bardolph** [after "through it" in Q] 52 **into** in   100 **hath** haue   101 **an age** [ed.] an ague [Q] age [F]   179 **this age shapes them, are** his age shapes the one   211–12 **and Prince Harry** [Q omits]

I.iii.s.d. [Q includes a mute character, Fauconbridge]   21–24 [Q omits]   26 **case** [ed.] cause [F, Q]   36–55 [Q omits]   71 **Are** And   79 **He ... Welsh** French and Welch he leaues his/back vnarmde, they   85–108 [Q omits]   109 **Mowbray** Bish.

II.i.14 **and that** [Q omits]   21 **vice** view   25 **continuantly** continually   44 **Sir John** [Q omits]   151 **tapestries** tapestrie   175 **Basingstoke** Billingsgate

II.ii.s.d. **Poins, with** [ed.] Poynes, sir Iohn Russel, with   15 **viz.** with   16 **ones** once   72 **thy** the   22 **made a shift to** [Q omits]   79 **e'en now** [ed.] enow [Q] euen now [F]   89 **rabbit** rabble   125–33 [Q and F give to Poins]   132 **familiars** family

II.iii.11 **endeared** endeere   23–44 [Q omits]

II.iv.12s.d. [occurs after line 18, Q; F omits]   13 **Will Dra[wer]** [Q; F omits]   178 **Die men** Men   226 **A** Ah   273 **master's** master   286 **so to**

III.i.26 **thy** them [Qb]   81 **nature of** natures or [Qb]

III.ii.1 **come on.** [Qa] come on sir [Qb] 114 **Falstaff. Prick him. Iohn prickes him.** [as stage direction, Q] 147 **his** [Q omits] 296 **would** [ed.] will [F] wooll [Q] 308 **Exeunt** [ed.] exit 309-43 [Q assigns this speech to Shallow] 323 **invisible** [ed.] inuincible [Q, F] 325 **ever** ouer

IV.i.s.d. **Mowbray, Hastings** Mowbray, Bardolfe, Hastings 12 **could** ["would" in some copies of Q] 30 **Then, my lord** [omitted in some copies of Q] 36 **appeared** [ed.] appeare 45 **figure** ["figures" in some copies of Q] 55-79 [Q omits] After line 92, line omitted: And consecrate commotions bitter edge. [appears in some copies of Q] After line 93, line omitted: To brother borne an houshold cruelty [appears in some copies of Q, but it seems probable that Shakespeare had marked on his ms. that both these lines were to be deleted] 101-37 [Q omits] 114 **force** [ed.] forc'd [F] 178 **And** [ed.] At [Q, F] 183 **not that. If** [ed.] not, that if [F, Q]

IV.ii.1 [notice that there should be no scene division, the action being continuous, and the stage not having emptied. The stage direction at IV.i.224 follows Q] 8 **Than** That 19 **imagined** [ed.] imagine [Q, F] 24 **Employ** Imply 48 **this** his 67-71 [as in F; Q assigns 67-68 to Bishop, 69-71 to Prince] 117 **and such acts as yours** [Q omits] 122 **these traitors** this traitour

IV.iii.1 [as at IV.ii.1, there should be no scene division]

IV.iv.33 **he's** he is 52 **Canst thou tell that?** [Q omits] 77 **others** other 104 **write** wet 104 **letters** termes 120 **and will break out** [Q omits] 132 **Softly, pray** [Q omits]

IV.v.1 [as at IV.ii.1, there should be no scene division] 13 **altered** vttred [Q, some copies] 49 **How fares your Grace?** [Q omits] 60-61 [one line in Q] 74 **culling** toling 75-79 [text follows F] Our thigh, packt with waxe our mouthes with hony,/We bring it to the hiue: and like the bees,/Are murdred for our paines, this bitter taste/Yeelds his engrossements to the ending father [Q] 79 s.d. at line 81 in Q 81 **hath** hands 107 **Which** Whom 160 **worst of** worse then 161 **is** [Q omits] 177 **O my son** [Q omits] 178 **it** [Q omits] 204 **my** [ed.] thy [Q, F] 220 **My gracious liege** [Q omits]

V.i.24 **the other day** [Q omits] 25 **Hinckley** Hunkly 50 **but a very** [Q omits]

V.ii.s.d. **Enter the Earl of Warwick and the Lord Chief Justice.** Enter Warwike, duke Humphrey, L. chiefe Iustice, Thomas Clarence, Prince, Iohn Westmerland 46 **mix** mixt

V.iii.5-6 **a, a** [Q omits] 35 **wag** wags 129 **knighthood** Knight

V.iv.s.d. **Beadle** Sincklo [Q, and so in the Q speech-tags for this scene; Sincklo was a small-part actor in Shakespeare's company]

V.v.25 **Falstaff** [Q omits] 30 **all** [Q omits]

WILLIAM
SHAKESPEARE

THE LIFE
OF HENRY
THE FIFTH

Edited by John Russell Brown

CHORUS
KING HENRY THE FIFTH
DUKES OF GLOUCESTER AND BEDFORD, brothers of the King
DUKE OF EXETER, uncle of the King
DUKE OF YORK, cousin of the King
EARLS OF SALISBURY, WESTMORELAND, WARWICK, AND
  CAMBRIDGE
ARCHBISHOP OF CANTERBURY
BISHOP OF ELY
LORD SCROOP
SIR THOMAS GREY
SIR THOMAS ERPINGHAM
GOWER, FLUELLEN, MACMORRIS, JAMY, officers in the
  English army
JOHN BATES, ALEXANDER COURT, MICHAEL WILLIAMS,
  soldiers in the English army
PISTOL, NYM, BARDOLPH
BOY
AN ENGLISH HERALD
CHARLES THE SIXTH, King of France
LEWIS, the Dauphin
DUKES OF BURGUNDY, ORLEANS, BOURBON, AND BRETAGNE
THE CONSTABLE OF FRANCE
RAMBURES AND GRANDPRÉ, French lords
GOVERNOR OF HARFLEUR
MONTJOY, a French herald
AMBASSADORS TO KING HENRY
ISABEL, Queen of France
KATHERINE, daughter of the French King and Queen
ALICE, an attendant to Katherine
HOSTESS QUICKLY of an Eastcheap tavern, married to Pistol
LORDS, LADIES, OFFICERS, SOLDIERS, CITIZENS, MESSENGERS
  AND ATTENDANTS

Scene: England; France]

THE LIFE OF
HENRY THE
FIFTH

Enter Prologue.

O for a Muse of fire, that would ascend
The brightest heaven of invention:
A kingdom for a stage, princes to act,
And monarchs to behold the swelling scene!
Then should the warlike Harry, like himself,   5
Assume the port of Mars, and at his heels
(Leashed in, like hounds) should famine, sword, and
    fire
Crouch for employment. But pardon, gentles all,
The flat unraisèd spirits that hath dared
On this unworthy scaffold to bring forth   10
So great an object. Can this cockpit hold
The vasty fields of France? Or may we cram
Within this wooden O the very casques
That did affright the air at Agincourt?
O, pardon—since a crooked figure may   15
Attest in little place a million;

Text references are printed in **boldface** type; the annotation follows in roman
type.
I Prologue 1 **fire** (1) most airy (sublime) of the four elements (2) warlike nature
(cf. line 6 below and II Prologue 1) 2 **invention** imaginative creation
4 **swelling** stately 5 **like himself** (1) incomparable (2) worthy of himself
6 **port of Mars** bearing of the god of war 8 **gentles** gentlefolk 9 **flat unraisèd
spirits** i.e., dull, uninspired actors and playwright 10 **scaffold** stage (technical
term) 13 **wooden O** small wooden circle; i.e., the theater of the King's Men (at
the first performance, this was probably the Curtain) 13 **very casques** i.e.,
helmets, even without the men who wore them 15 **crooked figure** i.e., a nought,
that could change 100,000 into 1,000,000

And let us, ciphers to this great accompt,
On your imaginary forces work.
Suppose within the girdle of these walls
20 Are now confined two mighty monarchies,
Whose high, uprearèd and abutting fronts
The perilous narrow ocean parts asunder.
Piece out our imperfections with your thoughts:
Into a thousand parts divide one man
25 And make imaginary puissance.
Think, when we talk of horses, that you see them
Printing their proud hoofs i' th' receiving earth;
For 'tis your thoughts that now must deck our kings,
Carry them here and there, jumping o'er times,
30 Turning th' accomplishment of many years
Into an hourglass; for the which supply,
Admit me Chorus to this history;
Who, Prologue-like, your humble patience pray,
Gently to hear, kindly to judge our play.   *Exit*.

---

17 **ciphers** nothings   17 **accompt** (1) sum total (2) story   18 **imaginary** imaginative   21 **fronts** frontiers   21-22 **high ... asunder** i.e., the cliffs of Dover and Calais, on opposite sides of the English Channel   25 **puissance** armed force (a trisyllable)   27 **proud** spirited   29 **them** i.e., thoughts (?), kings (?)   31 **for the which supply** to help you in which

ACT I

Scene I. [*London. An antechamber in the King's palace.*]

Enter the two Bishops [the Archbishop] of Canterbury and [the Bishop of] Ely.

CANTERBURY My lord, I'll tell you, that self bill is urged
Which in th' eleventh year of the last king's reign
Was like, and had indeed against us passed
But that the scambling and unquiet time
Did push it out of farther question.   5

ELY But how, my lord, shall we resist it now?

CANTERBURY It must be thought on. If it pass against us,
We lose the better half of our possession;
For all the temporal lands which men devout
By testament have given to the Church   10
Would they strip from us; being valued thus—
As much as would maintain, to the King's honor,
Full fifteen earls and fifteen hundred knights,
Six thousand and two hundred good esquires,
And to relief of lazars, and weak age   15
Of indigent faint souls, past corporal toil,

I.i.1 **self** same   2 **eleventh ... reign** i.e., 1410   3 **like** likely (to be passed)
4 **scambling** scuffling, disordered   9 **temporal** secular (as opposed to sacred)
15 **lazars** lepers

A hundred almshouses right well supplied;
And to the coffers of the King beside,
A thousand pounds by th' year. Thus runs the bill.

ELY This would drink deep.

20 CANTERBURY   'Twould drink the cup and all.

ELY But what prevention?

CANTERBURY The King is full of grace and fair regard.

ELY And a true lover of the holy Church.

CANTERBURY The courses of his youth promised it not.
25   The breath no sooner left his father's body
        But that his wildness, mortified in him,
        Seemed to die too; yea, at that very moment
        Consideration like an angel came
        And whipped th' offending Adam out of him,
30   Leaving his body as a paradise
        T' envelop and contain celestial spirits.
        Never was such a sudden scholar made;
        Never came reformation in a flood
        With such a heady currance scouring faults;
35   Nor never Hydra-headed willfulness
        So soon did lose his seat—and all at once—
        As in this king.

ELY   We are blessèd in the change.

CANTERBURY Hear him but reason in divinity,
        And, all-admiring, with an inward wish
40   You would desire the King were made a prelate;
        Hear him debate of commonwealth affairs,
        You would say it hath been all in all his study;
        List his discourse of war, and you shall hear
        A fearful battle rend'red you in music;

---

22 **regard** repute   26 **mortified** dead (a religious usage)   28 **Consideration**
meditation   29 **whipped th' offending Adam** drove original sin   34 **heady**
currance headlong current   35 **Hydra-headed** Hydra was a mythological beast
with nine heads, growing two more for every one cut off   36 **seat** throne
38 **reason** debate   42 **all in all** all things in all respects   43 **List** listen to
44 **rend'red you in music** recounted with harmonious and stirring eloquence

Turn him to any cause of policy,   45
The Gordian knot of it he will unloose,
Familiar as his garter; that when he speaks,
The air, a chartered libertine, is still,
And the mute wonder lurketh in men's ears
To steal his sweet and honeyed sentences;   50
So that the art and practic part of life
Must be the mistress to this theoric;
Which is a wonder how his Grace should glean it,
Since his addiction was to courses vain,
His companies unlettered, rude, and shallow,   55
His hours filled up with riots, banquets, sports;
And never noted in him any study,
Any retirement, any sequestration
From open haunts and popularity.

ELY The strawberry grows underneath the nettle,   60
And wholesome berries thrive and ripen best
Neighbored by fruit of baser quality;
And so the Prince obscured his contemplation
Under the veil of wildness, which (no doubt)
Grew like the summer grass, fastest by night,   65
Unseen, yet crescive in his faculty.

CANTERBURY It must be so, for miracles are ceased;
And therefore we must needs admit the means
How things are perfected.

ELY   But, my good lord,
How now for mitigation of this bill   70

45 **cause of policy** political problem   46 **Gordian knot** (tied by Gordius when
chosen King of Gordium; the oracle declared that whoever loosened it would rule
Asia; Alexander the Great cut through it with his sword)   48 **chartered libertine**
one licensed to go his own way   49 **wonder** wonderer   50 **sentences** sayings
51-52 **art ... theoric** practice and experience must have taught him theory
53 **Grace** Majesty (a formal title)   55 **companies** companions   59 **open haunts
and popularity** public places and familiarity   63 **contemplation** study of
life   66 **crescive in his faculty** growing because that is its nature   67 **miracles
are ceased** (protestants believed miracles ceased to occur after the revelation of
Christ)   68 **means** i.e., natural cause

Urged by the commons? Doth his Majesty
Incline to it, or no?

CANTERBURY   He seems indifferent;
Or rather swaying more upon our part
Than cherishing th' exhibiters against us;
75 For I have made an offer to his Majesty—
Upon our spiritual Convocation,
And in regard of causes now in hand,
Which I have opened to his Grace at large,
As touching France—to give a greater sum
80 Than ever at one time the clergy yet
Did to his predecessors part withal.

ELY How did this offer seem received, my lord?

CANTERBURY With good acceptance of his Majesty;
Save that there was not time enough to hear,
85 As I perceived his Grace would fain have done,
The severals and unhidden passages
Of his true titles to some certain dukedoms,
And generally to the crown and seat of France,
Derived from Edward, his great-grandfather.

90 ELY What was th' impediment that broke this off?

CANTERBURY The French ambassador upon that instant
Craved audience; and the hour I think is come
To give him hearing. Is it four o'clock?

ELY It is.

95 CANTERBURY Then go we in to know his embassy;
Which I could with a ready guess declare
Before the Frenchman speak a word of it.

ELY I'll wait upon you, and I long to hear it.   *Exeunt*.

---

71 **commons** House of Commons in the parliament of England   72 **indifferent**
impartial   74 **exhibiters** presenters of the bill   76 **Convocation** formal meeting
of the clergy   77 **causes** affairs   78 **opened** revealed   86 **severals and unhidden passages** details and clear (obvious) lines of descent

[Scene II. *The presence chamber in the palace.*]

Enter the King, Humphrey [Duke of Gloucester],
Bedford, Clarence, Warwick, Westmoreland, and Exeter,
[with Attendants].

KING Where is my gracious Lord of Canterbury?

EXETER Not here in presence.

KING   Send for him, good uncle.

WESTMORELAND Shall we call in th' ambassador, my
    liege?

KING Not yet, my cousin. We would be resolved,
Before we hear him, of some things of weight   5
That task our thoughts concerning us and France.

            Enter two Bishops [the Archbishop of
            Canterbury and the Bishop of Ely].

CANTERBURY God and his angels guard your sacred
    throne,
And make you long become it!

KING   Sure we thank you.
My learnèd lord, we pray you to proceed,
And justly and religiously unfold   10
Why the Law Salique, that they have in France,
Or should or should not bar us in our claim.
And God forbid, my dear and faithful lord,
That you should fashion, wrest, or bow your reading,
Or nicely charge your understanding soul   15
With opening titles miscreate, whose right
Suits not in native colors with the truth;

I.ii.4 **cousin** kinsmen   4 **be resolved** have doubts removed   6 **task** burden
12 **Or ... or** either ... or   14 **reading** interpretation   15-16 **nicely ... miscre-**
ate by subtle reasoning lay to the charge of your soul—that knows right and
wrong—the fault of advancing illegitimate claims   16 **right** claim   17 **Suits ...**
truth i.e., plainly told would not be taken as true

371

For God doth know how many now in health
Shall drop their blood in approbation
20   Of what your reverence shall incite us to.
Therefore take heed how you impawn our person,
How you awake our sleeping sword of war.
We charge you in the name of God, take heed;
For never two such kingdoms did contend
25   Without much fall of blood, whose guiltless drops
Are every one a woe, a sore complaint
'Gainst him whose wrongs gives edge unto the
        swords
That makes such waste in brief mortality.
Under this conjuration, speak my lord:
30   For we will hear, note, and believe in heart
That what you speak is in your conscience washed
As pure as sin with baptism.

CANTERBURY Then hear me, gracious Sovereign, and
        you peers,
That owe yourselves, your lives, and services
35   To this imperial throne. There is no bar
To make against your Highness' claim to France
But this which they produce from Pharamond:
"In terram Salicam mulieres ne succedant";
"No woman shall succeed in Salique land."
40   Which Salique land the French unjustly gloze
To be the realm of France, and Pharamond
The founder of this law and female bar.
Yet their own authors faithfully affirm
That the land Salique is in Germany,
45   Between the floods of Sala and of Elbe;
Where Charles the Great having subdued the
        Saxons,
There left behind and settled certain French;
Who, holding in disdain the German women
For some dishonest manners of their life,

---

19 **approbation** support   21 **impawn** pledge, hazard   27 **wrongs** wrongdoings
36 **make** i.e., be made   37 **Pharamond** legendary king of Salian Franks
40 **gloze** interpret   49 **dishonest manners** unchaste conduct

Established then this law: to wit, no female   50
Should be inheritrix in Salique land;
Which Salique (as I said) 'twixt Elbe and Sala
Is at this day in Germany, called Meisen.
Then doth it well appear the Salique Law
Was not devisèd for the realm of France;   55
Nor did the French possess the Salique land
Until four hundred one and twenty years
After defunction of King Pharamond,
Idly supposed the founder of this law,
Who died within the year of our redemption   60
Four hundred twenty-six; and Charles the Great
Subdued the Saxons, and did seat the French
Beyond the river Sala, in the year
Eight hundred five. Besides, their writers say,
King Pepin, which deposèd Childeric,   65
Did, as heir general, being descended
Of Blithild, which was daughter to King Clothair,
Make claim and title to the crown of France.
Hugh Capet also—who usurped the crown
Of Charles the Duke of Lorraine, sole heir male   70
Of the true line and stock of Charles the Great—
To find his title with some shows of truth,
Though in pure truth it was corrupt and naught,
Conveyed himself as heir to th' Lady Lingard,
Daughter to Charlemain, who was the son   75
To Lewis the Emperor, and Lewis the son
Of Charles the Great. Also King Lewis the Tenth,
Who was sole heir to the usurper Capet,
Could not keep quiet in his conscience,
Wearing the crown of France, till satisfied   80
That fair Queen Isabel, his grandmother,
Was lineal of the Lady Ermengard,
Daughter to Charles the foresaid Duke of Lorraine;
By the which marriage the line of Charles the Great
Was reunited to the crown of France.   85

58 **defunction** discharge, death   65 **Pepin** King of Franks   66 **general** through
male or female line of descent   72 **find** provide   74 **Conveyed** passed off
75 **Charlemain** (Holinshed's error for Charles the Bold)   77 **Tenth** (Holinshed's
error for Ninth)   82 **lineal** lineally descended

So that, as clear as is the summer's sun,
King Pepin's title and Hugh Capet's claim,
King Lewis his satisfaction, all appear
To hold in right and title of the female:
90   So do the kings of France unto this day.
Howbeit they would hold up this Salique Law
To bar your Highness claiming from the female,
And rather choose to hide them in a net
Than amply to imbar their crooked titles
95   Usurped from you and your progenitors.

KING   May I with right and conscience make this
claim?

CANTERBURY   The sin upon my head, dread Sovereign!
For in the Book of Numbers is it writ:
When the man dies, let the inheritance
100   Descend unto the daughter. Gracious lord,
Stand for your own, unwind your bloody flag,
Look back into your mighty ancestors;
Go, my dread lord, to your great-grandsire's tomb,
From whom you claim; invoke his warlike spirit,
105   And your great-uncle's, Edward the Black Prince,
Who on the French ground played a tragedy,
Making defeat on the full power of France,
Whiles his most mighty father on a hill
Stood smiling, to behold his lion's whelp
110   Forage in blood of French nobility.
O noble English, that could entertain
With half their forces the full pride of France,
And let another half stand laughing by,
All out of work, and cold for action!

115   ELY   Awake remembrance of these valiant dead
And with your puissant arm renew their feats.

---

88 his satisfaction (see line 80)   93-94 to hide ... titles to take refuge in a
tangle of sophistical arguments than make the most of (bar in, secure) their own
false claims (by admitting female succession)   103 great-grandsire's i.e., Edward
III's (whose mother, Isabella, was daughter of Philip IV of France)   106 a
tragedy i.e., battle of Crécy   107 power army   112 half their forces (one third
was held in reserve with the King)   114 for for lack of

You are their heir; you sit upon their throne;
The blood and courage that renownèd them
Runs in your veins: and my thrice-puissant liege
Is in the very May-morn of his youth   120
Ripe for exploits and mighty enterprises.

EXETER Your brother kings and monarchs of the earth
Do all expect that you should rouse yourself,
As did the former lions of your blood.

WESTMORELAND They know your Grace hath cause
    and means and might;
So hath your Highness. Never king of England   125
Had nobles richer and more loyal subjects,
Whose hearts have left their bodies here in England
And lie pavilioned in the fields of France.

CANTERBURY O, let their bodies follow, my dear liege, 130
With blood, and sword and fire, to win your right!
In aid whereof we of the spiritualty
Will raise your Highness such a mighty sum
As never did the clergy at one time
Bring in to any of your ancestors.   135

KING We must not only arm t' invade the French,
But lay down our proportions to defend
Against the Scot, who will make road upon us
With all advantages.

CANTERBURY They of those marches, gracious
    Sovereign,
Shall be a wall sufficient to defend   140
Our inland from the pilfering borderers.

KING We do not mean the coursing snatchers only;
But fear the main intendment of the Scot,
Who hath been still a giddy neighbor to us;   145
For you shall read that my great-grandfather

119 **thrice-puissant** i.e., for the three reasons just stated 125 **hath**
(accented) 137 **lay down our proportions** estimate the size of our forces
138 **road** raid 139 **With all advantages** at every favorable opportunity, with
everything in their favor 140 **marches** border country 142 **inland** heart of the
country 143 **coursing** marauding 144 **main intendment** general purpose
145 **still** always

Never went with his forces into France
But that the Scot on his unfurnished kingdom
Came pouring like the tide into a breach,
150   With ample and brim fullness of his force,
Galling the gleanèd land with hot assays,
Girding with grievous siege castles and towns;
That England, being empty of defense,
Hath shook and trembled at th' ill neighborhood.

CANTERBURY She hath been then more feared than
155   harmed, my liege;
For hear her but exampled by herself:
When all her chivalry hath been in France,
And she a mourning widow of her nobles,
She hath herself not only well defended
160   But taken and impounded as a stray
The King of Scots; whom she did send to France
To fill King Edward's fame with prisoner kings,
And make her chronicle as rich with praise
As is the ooze and bottom of the sea
165   With sunken wrack and sumless treasuries.

ELY But there's a saying very old and true—
        "If that you will France win,
          Then with Scotland first begin."
For once the eagle (England) being in prey,
170   To her unguarded nest the weasel (Scot)
Comes sneaking, and so sucks her princely eggs
(Playing the mouse in absence of the cat)
To tame and havoc more than she can eat.

EXETER It follows then, the cat must stay at home;
175   Yet that is but a crushed necessity,
Since we have locks to safeguard necessaries,
And pretty traps to catch the petty thieves.

---

148 **unfurnished** undefended 151 **gleanèd** i.e., stripped of defenders
154 **neighborhood** neighborliness 155 **feared** alarmed 156 **exampled** furnished with a precedent 160 **stray** animal found wandering out of bounds
161 **King of Scots** i.e., David II 164 **ooze and bottom** oozy bottom
165 **wrack** wreck 169 **in prey** engaged upon preying 173 **tame** broach (as a
weasel breaks into eggs to suck their meat) 175 **crushed** strained, needless

While that the armèd hand doth fight abroad,
Th' advisèd head defends itself at home;
For government, though high, and low, and lower,   180
Put into parts, doth keep in one consent,
Congreeing in a full and natural close,
Like music.

CANTERBURY   Therefore doth heaven divide
The state of man in divers functions,
Setting endeavor in continual motion;   185
To which is fixèd, as an aim or butt,
Obedience; for so work the honeybees,
Creatures that by a rule in nature teach
The act of order to a peopled kingdom.
They have a king, and officers of sorts,   190
Where some like magistrates correct at home,
Others like merchants venture trade abroad,
Others like soldiers armèd in their stings
Make boot upon the summer's velvet buds,
Which pillage they with merry march bring home   195
To the tent-royal of their emperor—
Who, busied in his majesty, surveys
The singing masons building roofs of gold,
The civil citizens kneading up the honey,
The poor mechanic porters crowding in   200
Their heavy burdens at his narrow gate,
The sad-eyed justice, with his surly hum,
Delivering o'er to executors pale
The lazy yawning drone. I this infer,
That many things, having full reference   205
To one consent, may work contrariously;
As many arrows loosèd several ways

179 **advisèd** prudent   181 **parts** (1) members of the body politic (2) melodies of
the various instruments in concerted music   181 **consent** (1) agreement
(2) harmony   182 **Congreeing** agreeing   182 **close** (1) union (2) conclusion of a
piece of music   184 **state** estate, kingdom   185 **Setting … motion** giving a
perpetual stimulus to effort   188 **in nature** instinctive   189 **act** operation
190 **sorts** various kinds   191 **correct** administer justice   194 **Make boot upon**
plunder   200 **mechanic** engaged in manual labor   202 **surly** stern   203 **executors** executioners   204 **infer** adduce   205 **reference** relation   207 **loosèd
several ways** shot from various places

Come to one mark, as many ways meet in one
   town,
As many fresh streams meet in one salt sea,
210   As many lines close in the dial's center,
So may a thousand actions, once afoot,
End in one purpose, and be all well borne
Without defeat. Therefore to France, my liege!
Divide your happy England into four,
215   Whereof take you one quarter into France,
And you withal shall make all Gallia shake.
If we, with thrice such powers left at home,
Cannot defend our own doors from the dog,
Let us be worried, and our nation lose
220   The name of hardiness and policy.

KING Call in the messengers sent from the Dauphin.
                                 [*Exeunt some Attendants.*]
Now are we well resolved, and by God's help
And yours, the noble sinews of our power,
France being ours, we'll bend it to our awe,
225   Or break it all to pieces. Or there we'll sit,
Ruling in large and ample empery
O'er France and all her (almost) kingly dukedoms,
Or lay these bones in an unworthy urn,
Tombless, with no remembrance over them.
230   Either our history shall with full mouth
Speak freely of our acts, or else our grave,
Like Turkish mute, shall have a tongueless mouth,
Not worshipped with a waxen epitaph.

Enter Ambassadors of France [and Attendants].

Now are we well prepared to know the pleasure
235   Of our fair cousin Dauphin; for we hear
Your greeting is from him, not from the King.

---

212 **borne** carried out   220 **policy** statesmanship   222 **resolved** (1) convinced
(2) determined   224 **ours** i.e., by right of inheritance   224 **bend it to our awe**
subdue it to our authority   226 **empery** dominion   228 **urn** grave
229 **remembrance** memorial inscription   232 **Turkish mute** (certain slaves in
the Turkish royal household had their tongues cut out to ensure secrecy)
233 **worshipped** honored   233 **waxen** easily effaced

AMBASSADOR May't please your Majesty to give us
    leave
    Freely to render what we have in charge;
    Or shall we sparingly show you far off
    The Dauphin's meaning, and our embassy?   240

KING We are no tyrant, but a Christian king,
    Unto whose grace our passion is as subject
    As is our wretches fett'red in our prisons;
    Therefore with frank and with uncurbèd plainness,
    Tell us the Dauphin's mind.

AMBASSADOR   Thus then, in few: 245
    Your Highness, lately sending into France,
    Did claim some certain dukedoms, in the right
    Of your great predecessor, King Edward the Third.
    In answer of which claim, the Prince our master
    Says that you savor too much of your youth,   250
    And bids you be advised: There's naught in
    France
    That can be with a nimble galliard won;
    You cannot revel into dukedoms there.
    He therefore sends you, meeter for your spirit,
    This tun of treasure; and in lieu of this,   255
    Desires you let the dukedoms that you claim
    Hear no more of you. This the Dauphin speaks.

KING What treasure, uncle?

EXETER   Tennis balls, my liege.

KING We are glad the Dauphin is so pleasant with
    us—
    His present, and your pains, we thank you for.   260
    When we have matched our rackets to these balls,
    We will in France (by God's grace) play a set

---

239 **sparingly** with reserve, discreetly   242 **grace** gracious disposition   245 **few**
few words   251 **be advised** take care   252 **galliard** lively dance   255 **tun**
cask   259 **pleasant** jocular, merry   262 **France** (1) tennis court (2) the
country   263 **crown** (1) coin (stake money) (2) throne and power

Shall strike his father's crown into the hazard.
Tell him he hath made a match with such a
      wrangler
265 That all the courts of France will be disturbed
With chases. And we understand him well,
How he comes o'er us with our wilder days,
Not measuring what use we made of them.
We never valued this poor seat of England,
270 And therefore, living hence, did give ourself
To barbarous license; as 'tis ever common
That men are merriest when they are from home.
But tell the Dauphin I will keep my state,
Be like a king, and show my sail of greatness,
275 When I do rouse me in my throne of France.
For that I have laid by my majesty,
And plodded like a man for working days;
But I will rise there with so full a glory
That I will dazzle all the eyes of France,
280 Yea, strike the Dauphin blind to look on us.
And tell the pleasant prince this mock of his
Hath turned his balls to gunstones, and his soul
Shall stand sore chargèd for the wasteful vengeance
That shall fly with them; for many a thousand
      widows
Shall this his mock mock out of their dear hus-
285   bands,
Mock mothers from their sons, mock castles down;
And some are yet ungotten and unborn
That shall have cause to curse the Dauphin's
      scorn.

263 **hazard** (1) opening in the walls of an old-fashioned tennis court; the ball entering it became "dead" and a point was scored (2) peril, jeopardy 264 **wrangler** (1) adversary (2) disputant   265 **courts** (1) tennis courts (2) courts of princes   266 **chases** (1) bouncings twice of tennis ball (scoring points) (2) pursuits   267 **comes o'er us with** affects superiority over us by reason of 269 **seat** throne (lines 269–72 are ironical)   270 **hence** i.e., away from the court 273 **state** position of power   274 **show my sail of greatness** demean myself proudly   276–77 **For that ... working days** i.e., to be able to achieve this I have divested myself of greatness and learned what it is to live as a laboring man 278–80 **But I will ... look on us** (cf. *I Henry IV* I.ii. 217–39)   282 **gunstones** stones used for cannonballs   288 **scorn** taunt

But this lies all within the will of God,
To whom I do appeal, and in whose name,   290
Tell you the Dauphin, I am coming on
To venge me as I may, and to put forth
My rightful hand in a well-hallowed cause.
So get you hence in peace. And tell the Dauphin
His jest will savor but of shallow wit,   295
When thousands weep more than did laugh at it.
Convey them with safe conduct. Fare you well.
                    Exeunt Ambassadors [and Attendants].

EXETER This was a merry message.

KING We hope to make the sender blush at it.
    Therefore, my lords, omit no happy hour   300
    That may give furth'rance to our expedition;
    For we have now no thought in us but France,
    Save those to God, that run before our business.
    Therefore let our proportions for these wars
    Be soon collected, and all things thought upon   305
    That may with reasonable swiftness add
    More feathers to our wings; for, God before,
    We'll chide this Dauphin at his father's door.
    Therefore let every man now task his thought
    That this fair action may on foot be brought.   310
                            Exeunt.

---

289 **lies all within** depends wholly upon   300 **omit no happy hour** lose no favorable occasion   301 **expedition** enterprise   303 **run before** i.e., as prayers precede   304 **proportions** forces and supplies   307 **God before** God leading us   310 **on foot** in active operation

[ACT II]

Flourish. Enter Chorus.

Now all the youth of England are on fire,
And silken dalliance in the wardrobe lies;
Now thrive the armorers, and honor's thought
Reigns solely in the breast of every man.
5   They sell the pasture now, to buy the horse;
Following the mirror of all Christian kings
With wingèd heels, as English Mercuries.
For now sits Expectation in the air
And hides a sword, from hilts unto the point,
10   With crowns imperial, crowns and coronets
Promised to Harry and his followers.
The French, advised by good intelligence
Of this most dreadful preparation,
Shake in their fear, and with pale policy
15   Seek to divert the English purposes.
O England, model to thy inward greatness,
Like little body with a mighty heart,
What mightst thou do, that honor would thee do,
Were all thy children kind and natural!

II Prologue s.d. **Flourish** trumpet fanfare   2 **silken dalliance in the wardrobe
lies** i.e., pastimes and luxuries are laid aside like clothes   4 **solely** alone
6 **mirror** model   7 **Mercuries** (in classical mythology Mercury, or Hermes, was
the gods' messenger; he was pictured as wearing winged helmet and sandals)
9 **hilts** hilt (plural for singular, as frequently)   12 **advised by good intelligence**
informed by efficient espionage   14 **pale policy** contrivance inspired by fear
16 **model** form   19 **kind and natural** loving and naturally affectionate

But see, thy fault France hath in thee found
    out—   20
A nest of hollow bosoms—which he fills
With treacherous crowns; and three corrupted
    men—
One, Richard Earl of Cambridge, and the second,
Henry Lord Scroop of Masham, and the third,
Sir Thomas Grey, knight, of Northumberland—   25
Have, for the gilt of France (O guilt indeed!),
Confirmed conspiracy with fearful France,
And by their hands this grace of kings must die,
If hell and treason hold their promises,
Ere he take ship for France, and in Southampton.   30
Linger your patience on, and we'll digest
Th' abuse of distance; force a play:—
The sum is paid; the traitors are agreed;
The King is set from London; and the scene
Is now transported, gentles, to Southampton.   35
There is the playhouse now, there must you sit,
And thence to France shall we convey you safe
And bring you back, charming the narrow seas
To give you gentle pass; for, if we may,
We'll not offend one stomach with our play.   40
But, till the King come forth, and not till then,
Unto Southampton do we shift our scene.   *Exit.*

---

20 **fault** imperfection 20 **France** the King of France 21 **hollow** (1) false
(2) empty 22 **crowns** coins 26 **gilt** i.e., golden crowns 28 **grace**
ornament 31-32 **digest/Th' abuse of distance** dispose of the wrong done to
fact in moving from place to place in the play's action 32 **force** cram full
38 **charming the narrow seas** laying spells on the English Channel 39 **pass**
passage 40 **offend one stomach** (1) displease anyone (2) make anyone seasick

[Scene I. *London. A street.*]

Enter Corporal Nym and Lieutenant Bardolph.

BARDOLPH Well met, Corporal Nym.

NYM Good morrow, Lieutenant Bardolph.

BARDOLPH What, are Ancient Pistol and you friends
　　　　yet?

5 NYM For my part, I care not; I say little; but when
　　　　time shall serve, there shall be smiles—but that
　　　　shall be as it may. I dare not fight; but I will wink
　　　　and hold out mine iron. It is a simple one; but
　　　　what though? It will toast cheese, and it will endure
10　　　cold, as another man's sword will—and there's
　　　　an end.

BARDOLPH I will bestow a breakfast to make you
　　　　friends, and we'll be all three sworn brothers to
　　　　France. Let 't be so, good Corporal Nym.

15 NYM Faith, I will live so long as I may, that's the
　　　　certain of it; and when I cannot live any longer,
　　　　I will do as I may. That is my rest, that is the
　　　　rendezvous of it.

BARDOLPH It is certain, Corporal, that he is married

II.i.2 **Lieutenant** (Bardolph was a Corporal in 2 *Henry IV* and Nym calls him so
again at III.ii.3, below) 3 **Ancient** Ensign, Standard Bearer 6 **serve** be
opportune 7 **wink** (1) shut my eyes (2) give a meaningful look 8 **iron** sword
9-10 **will endure cold** does not mind being naked 10-11 **there's an end** that's
all there is to it 12 **bestow** treat you to 13 **sworn brothers** comrades pledged
to share each other's fortunes (cf. III.ii.45-46) 17 **I will do as I may** (cf. the
proverb, "He that cannot do as he would must do as he may") 17 **rest** what I
stand to win or lose (the stakes in a game of primero, the loss of which brings about
the end of the game) 18 **rendezvous** last resort

to Nell Quickly, and certainly she did you wrong,   20
for you were troth-plight to her.

NYM I cannot tell. Things must be as they may; men
may sleep, and they may have their throats about
them at that time, and some say knives have edges.
It must be as it may; though patience be a tired   25
mare, yet she will plod; there must be conclusions.
Well, I cannot tell.

Enter Pistol and [Hostess] Quickly.

BARDOLPH Here comes Ancient Pistol and his wife.
Good Corporal, be patient here. How now, mine
host Pistol?   30

PISTOL Base tyke, call'st thou me host?
Now by this hand I swear I scorn the term;
Nor shall my Nell keep lodgers!

HOSTESS No, by my troth, not long; for we cannot
lodge and board a dozen or fourteen gentlewomen   35
that live honestly by the prick of their needles, but
it will be thought we keep a bawdy house straight.
[Nym draws his sword.] O well-a-day, Lady, if he
be not hewn now! We shall see willful adultery
and murder committed.   *[Pistol draws.]*   40

BARDOLPH Good Lieutenant—good Corporal—offer
nothing here.

NYM Pish!

PISTOL Pish for thee, Iceland dog; thou prick-eared
cur of Iceland!   45

HOSTESS Good Corporal Nym, show thy valor, and put
up your sword.

21 **troth-plight** betrothed (more binding than a modern engagement)
25-26 **patience be a tired mare, yet she will plod** patience is wearisome, yet it
achieves its purpose in the end   36 **honestly** (1) decently (2) chastely ("prick" of
the same line sustains the bawdy allusion)   44 **Iceland dog** white sharp-eared
dog, so shaggy that neither its face nor body can be seen (a favorite lapdog)
46-47 **show thy valor, and put up your sword** (unintentionally apposite, for
Nym had such little valor that he could not fight)

NYM Will you shog off? I would have you solus.

PISTOL "Solus," egregious dog? O viper vile!
50   The "solus" in thy most marvelous face!
        The "solus" in thy teeth, and in thy throat,
        And in thy hateful lungs, yea, in thy maw, perdy!
        And, which is worse, within thy nasty mouth!
        I do retort the "solus" in thy bowels;
55   For I can take, and Pistol's cock is up,
        And flashing fire will follow.

NYM I am not Barbason; you cannot conjure me;
      I have an humor to knock you indifferently well.
      If you grow foul with me, Pistol, I will scour you
60   with my rapier, as I may, in fair terms. If you
      would walk off, I would prick your guts a little in
      good terms, as I may, and that's the humor of it.

PISTOL O braggard vile, and damnèd furious wight,
        The grave doth gape, and doting death is near;
65   Therefore exhale!

BARDOLPH Hear me, hear me what I say! He that
      strikes the first stroke, I'll run him up to the hilts,
      as I am a soldier.   [Draws.]

PISTOL An oath of mickle might, and fury shall abate.
                [Pistol and Nym sheathe their swords.]
70   Give me thy fist, thy forefoot to me give.
        Thy spirits are most tall.

48 shog off move off (slang) 48 solus alone (Pistol takes it to mean single, i.e., unmarried; or, ignorant of Latin, some great insult) 49 egregious outsized 52 maw stomach 52 perdy by God 55 take (1) cause harm to befall (by his elaborate exorcism or curse) (2) strike (3) take fire 55 cock is up is cocked for firing (punning on his name) 57 Barbason name of a fiend 57 conjure exorcise 58 indifferently fairly 59-60 If you grow ... my rapier (a pistol was said to be "foul" after firing, and was normally cleaned with a ramrod or scouring rod) 60 in fair terms fairly (a fashionable cliché) 61-62 in good terms on a good footing (another fashionable cliché) 62 humor fancy, inclination (yet another cliché) 63 wight person 64 gape (1) open (2) greedily desire 64 doting loving, fond 65 exhale draw forth 67 run him up to the hilts drive the whole sword blade into him 69 mickle great (already, in Shakespeare's day, archaistic) 70 forefoot paw 71 tall courageous

NYM I will cut thy throat one time or other in fair terms, that is the humor of it.

PISTOL Couple a gorge!   75
  That is the word. I thee defy again.
  O hound of Crete, think'st thou my spouse to get?
  No; to the spital go,
  And from the powd'ring tub of infamy
  Fetch forth the lazar kite of Cressid's kind,   80
  Doll Tearsheet, she by name, and her espouse.
  I have, and I will hold, the quondam Quickly
  For the only she; and—pauca, there's enough.
  Go to!

Enter the Boy.

BOY Mine host Pistol, you must come to my master
  —and your hostess. He is very sick and would to   85
  bed. Good Bardolph, put thy face between his
  sheets, and do the office of a warming pan. Faith,
  he's very ill.

BARDOLPH Away, you rogue!

HOSTESS By my troth, he'll yield the crow a pudding   90
  one of these days. The King has killed his heart.
  Good husband, come home presently.   *Exit*.

BARDOLPH Come, shall I make you two friends? We

---

74 **Couple a gorge** cut the throat (a comic version of the French, *couper la gorge*, appropriate to the coming campaign) 75 **defy** challenge 76 **hound of Crete** (another shaggy dog; cf. line 44, note) 77 **spital** hospital 78 **powd'ring tub** pickling vat (frequently applied to the sweating tub used for curing venereal disease) 79 **lazar kite of Cressid's kind** leprous whore (a stock phrase; a kite is a bird of prey) 80 **Doll Tearsheet** (cf. *2 Henry IV*, II.iii.165-68 and V.iv.) 81 **quondam** former 82 **only she** one woman in the world 82 **pauca** few words (Latin, *pauca verba*) 84 **my master** i.e., Falstaff (the boy is the page given to Falstaff by Prince Hal, *2 Henry IV*, I.ii.) 86 **thy face** (Bardolf's was red like fire) 90 **he'll yield the crow a pudding** i.e., the boy will make food (pudding = stuffed intestines) for crows on the gallows (proverbial) 91 **The King has killed his heart** (by rejecting Falstaff; cf. *2 Henry IV*, V.v.51-77) 92 **presently** immediately

must to France together: why the devil should we
95   keep knives to cut one another's throats?

PISTOL Let floods o'erswell, and fiends for food howl
on!

NYM You'll pay me the eight shillings I won of you
at betting?

PISTOL Base is the slave that pays.

100 NYM That now I will have; that's the humor of it.

PISTOL As manhood shall compound. Push home.
                                    [*They*] *draw.*

BARDOLPH By this sword, he that makes the first
thrust, I'll kill him! By this sword, I will.   [*Draws.*]

PISTOL "Sword" is an oath, and oaths must have their
course.   [*Sheathes his sword.*]

105 BARDOLPH Corporal Nym, and thou wilt be friends,
be friends; and thou wilt not, why then be enemies
with me too. Prithee put up.

NYM I shall have my eight shillings I won of you at
betting?

110 PISTOL A noble shalt thou have, and present pay;
And liquor likewise will I give to thee,
And friendship shall combine, and brotherhood.
I'll live by Nym, and Nym shall live by me.
Is not this just? For I shall sutler be
115 Unto the camp, and profits will accrue.
Give me thy hand.   [*Nym sheathes his sword.*]

NYM I shall have my noble?

PISTOL In cash, most justly paid.

96 Let floods ... howl on let riot thrive and the devils be deprived of their
prey 99 Base is the slave that pays (a corruption of the proverb, "The poor
man always pays") 101 manhood shall compound valor decides 101 Push
thrust (of a sword) 105 and if 107 put up sheathe 110 noble coin worth six
shillings and eight pence 110 present immediate 114 sutler seller of provisions to a camp or garrison

NYM Well then, that's the humor of't.

Enter Hostess.

HOSTESS As ever you come of women, come in   120
quickly to Sir John. Ah, poor heart! he is so shaked
of a burning quotidian tertian that it is most lamentable to behold. Sweet men, come to him.

NYM The King hath run bad humors on the knight;
that's the even of it.   125

PISTOL Nym, thou hast spoke the right;
His heart is fracted and corroborate.

NYM The King is a good king, but it must be as it
may: he passes some humors, and careers.

PISTOL Let us condole the knight; for, lambkins, we
will live.   [*Exeunt.*]   130

[Scene II. *Southampton.*]

Enter Exeter, Bedford, and Westmoreland.

BEDFORD Fore God, his Grace is bold to trust these
traitors.

EXETER They shall be apprehended by and by.

WESTMORELAND How smooth and even they do bear
themselves,
As if allegiance in their bosoms sat,
Crowned with faith and constant loyalty!   5

122 **quotidian tertian** two kinds of intermittent fevers, the first recurring daily,
the second every third day (a nonsensical phrase)   124 **run bad humors** vented
his ill humor   125 **even** truth   127 **fracted and corroborate** broken and joined
together (?)   129 **passes some humors, and careers** indulges some whims and
liveliness   II.ii.2 **apprehended by and by** arrested soon   3 **even** unruffled

BEDFORD The King hath note of all that they intend,
By interception which they dream not of.

EXETER Nay, but the man that was his bedfellow,
Whom he hath dulled and cloyed with gracious
favors—
10 That he should, for a foreign purse, so sell
His Sovereign's life to death and treachery!

*Sound trumpets. Enter the King, Scroop, Cam-
bridge, and Grey, [Lords, and Attendants].*

KING Now sits the wind fair, and we will aboard.
My Lord of Cambridge, and my kind Lord of
Masham,
And you, my gentle knight, give me your thoughts:
15 Think you not that the pow'rs we bear with us
Will cut their passage through the force of France,
Doing the execution and the act
For which we have in head assembled them?

SCROOP No doubt, my liege, if each man do his best.

20 KING I doubt not that, since we are well persuaded
We carry not a heart with us from hence
That grows not in a fair consent with ours,
Nor leave not one behind that doth not wish
Success and conquest to attend on us.

CAMBRIDGE Never was monarch better feared and
25   loved
Than is your Majesty. There's not, I think, a
subject
That sits in heart-grief and uneasiness
Under the sweet shade of your government.

GREY True. Those that were your father's enemies
Have steeped their galls in honey, and do serve
30   you

6 note knowledge 8 bedfellow i.e., Scroop 9 dulled and cloyed bored and
overindulged 18 in head as an organized force 22 grows lives 22 consent
agreement 28 shade protection 30 galls bitterness

With hearts create of duty, and of zeal.

KING We therefore have great cause of thankfulness,
And shall forget the office of our hand
Sooner than quittance of desert and merit
According to the weight and worthiness.   35

SCROOP So service shall with steelèd sinews toil,
And labor shall refresh itself with hope,
To do your Grace incessant services.

KING We judge no less. Uncle of Exeter,
Enlarge the man committed yesterday   40
That railed against our person. We consider
It was excess of wine that set him on,
And on his more advice, we pardon him.

SCROOP That's mercy, but too much security:
Let him be punished, Sovereign, lest example   45
Breed (by his sufferance) more of such a kind.

KING O, let us yet be merciful!

CAMBRIDGE So may your Highness, and yet punish
too.

GREY Sir,
You show great mercy if you give him life   50
After the taste of much correction.

KING Alas, your too much love and care of me
Are heavy orisons 'gainst this poor wretch!
If little faults proceeding on distemper
Shall not be winked at, how shall we stretch our
eye   55
When capital crimes, chewed, swallowed, and
digested,
Appear before us? We'll yet enlarge that man,

31 **create** created 33 **office** proper function 34 **quittance** requital
40 **Enlarge** set at liberty 43 **on his more advice** on maturer reflection
44 **security** want of caution 46 **by his sufferance** by not checking him 47 **yet**
now as always 51 **taste** experience 53 **heavy orisons** weighty pleas
54 **proceeding on distemper** i.e., committed when drunk 55 **winked**
connived 55 **stretch** open wide 56 **capital** punishable by death

Though Cambridge, Scroop, and Grey, in their
        dear care
And tender preservation of our person,
Would have him punished. And now to our French
60   causes.
Who are the late commissioners?

CAMBRIDGE I one, my lord.
        Your Highness bade me ask for it today.

SCROOP So did you me, my liege.

65 GREY And I, my royal sovereign.

KING Then, Richard Earl of Cambridge, there is
        yours;
        There yours, Lord Scroop of Masham; and, sir
        knight,
        Grey of Northumberland, this same is yours:
        Read them, and know I know your worthiness.
70   My Lord of Westmoreland, and uncle Exeter,
        We will aboard tonight.—Why, how now, gentle-
        men?
        What see you in those papers that you lose
        So much complexion?—Look ye, how they
        change!
        Their cheeks are paper.—Why, what read you
        there
75   That have so cowarded and chased your blood
        Out of appearance?

CAMBRIDGE   I do confess my fault,
        And do submit me to your Highness' mercy.

GREY, SCROOP To which we all appeal.

KING The mercy that was quick in us but late,
80   By your own counsel is suppressed and killed.
        You must not dare (for shame) to talk of mercy,
        For your own reasons turn into your bosoms,

---

58 **dear** (1) deeply felt (2) dire   60 **causes** affairs   61 **late** recently appointed
63 **it** i.e., the written commission   73 **complexion** color   76 **appearance** sight

As dogs upon their masters, worrying you.
See you, my princes and my noble peers,
These English monsters! My Lord of Cambridge
    here—   85
You know how apt our love was to accord
To furnish him with all appertinents
Belonging to his honor; and this man
Hath, for a few light crowns, lightly conspired
And sworn unto the practices of France   90
To kill us here in Hampton; to the which
This knight, no less for bounty bound to us
Than Cambridge is, hath likewise sworn. But O,
What shall I say to thee, Lord Scroop, thou cruel,
Ingrateful, savage, and inhuman creature?   95
Thou that didst bear the key of all my counsels,
That knew'st the very bottom of my soul,
That (almost) mightst have coined me into gold,
Wouldst thou have practiced on me for thy use?
May it be possible that foreign hire   100
Could out of thee extract one spark of evil
That might annoy my finger? 'Tis so strange
That, though the truth of it stands off as gross
As black and white, my eye will scarcely see it.
Treason and murder ever kept together,   105
As two yoke-devils sworn to either's purpose,
Working so grossly in a natural cause
That admiration did not hoop at them;
But thou ('gainst all proportion) didst bring in
Wonder to wait on treason and on murder;   110
And whatsoever cunning fiend it was
That wrought upon thee so preposterously
Hath got the voice in hell for excellence;
And other devils that suggest by treasons

---

86 **accord** agree 89 **light ... lightly** trivial ... readily 90 **practices**
intrigues 99 **practiced** on me for thy use plotted against me for your own
profit 103 **off as gross** out as plain 106 **yoke-devils** fellow-devils 107–08 **so
grossly ... at them** so obviously in a matter natural to them that no one cried out
in wonder 109 **proportion** propriety 112 **preposterously** unnaturally
113 **voice** vote 114 **suggest** tempt

115　Do botch and bungle up damnation
　　　With patches, colors, and with forms being fetched
　　　From glist'ring semblances of piety;
　　　But he that tempered thee bade thee stand up,
　　　Gave thee no instance why thou shouldst do
　　　　　treason,
120　Unless to dub thee with the name of traitor.
　　　If that same demon that hath gulled thee thus
　　　Should with his lion gait walk the whole world,
　　　He might return to vasty Tartar back
　　　And tell the legions, "I can never win
125　A soul so easy as that Englishman's."
　　　O, how hast thou with jealousy infected
　　　The sweetness of affiance! Show men dutiful?
　　　Why, so didst thou. Seem they grave and learned?
　　　Why, so didst thou. Come they of noble family?
130　Why, so didst thou. Seem they religious?
　　　Why, so didst thou. Or are they spare in diet,
　　　Free from gross passion, or of mirth or anger,
　　　Constant in spirit, not swerving with the blood,
　　　Garnished and decked in modest complement,
135　Not working with the eye without the ear,
　　　And but in purgèd judgment trusting neither?
　　　Such and so finely bolted didst thou seem;
　　　And thus thy fall hath left a kind of blot
　　　To mark the full-fraught man and best indued
140　With some suspicion. I will weep for thee;
　　　For this revolt of thine, methinks, is like
　　　Another fall of man. Their faults are open.
　　　Arrest them to the answer of the law;

115-17 **Do botch ... piety** disguise the fact of damnation with folly, false pretexts and behavior borrowed from bright outward manifestations of piety　118 **tempered** worked upon　118 **stand up** make a stand straightforwardly　120 **dub** invest (with a title)　122 **lion gait** (cf. I Peter 5:8: "your adversary, the devil, as a roaring lion, walketh about, seeking whom he may devour")　123 **Tartar** Tartarus, hell　124 **legions** i.e., of devils　126 **jealousy infected** suspicion tainted　127 **affiance** confidence　127 **Show seem**　133 **swerving with the blood** erring after the flesh　134 **modest complement** unostentatious demeanor　135 **Not working with the eye without the ear** i.e., listening as well as seeing　137 **bolted** sifted (as flour)　139 **full-fraught** completely gifted　139 **indued** endowed　142 **open** patent　143 **answer** punishment

And God acquit them of their practices!

EXETER I arrest thee of high treason by the name of   145
Richard Earl of Cambridge.
    I arrest thee of high treason by the name of
Henry Lord Scroop of Masham.
    I arrest thee of high treason by the name of
Thomas Grey, knight, of Northumberland.   150

SCROOP Our purposes God justly hath discovered,
And I repent my fault more than my death—
Which I beseech your Highness to forgive,
Although my body pay the price of it.

CAMBRIDGE For me, the gold of France did not
    seduce,   155
Although I did admit it as a motive
The sooner to effect what I intended.
But God be thankèd for prevention,
Which I in sufferance heartily will rejoice,
Beseeching God, and you, to pardon me.   160

GREY Never did faithful subject more rejoice
At the discovery of most dangerous treason
Than I do at this hour joy o'er myself,
Prevented from a damnèd enterprise.
My fault, but not my body, pardon, Sovereign.   165

KING God quit you in His mercy! Hear your
    sentence.
You have conspired against our royal person,
Joined with an enemy proclaimed, and from his
    coffers
Received the golden earnest of our death;
Wherein you would have sold your king to
    slaughter,   170
His princes and his peers to servitude,
His subjects to oppression and contempt,
And his whole kingdom into desolation.
Touching our person, seek we no revenge,

144 acquit requite   158 prevention (four syllables)   159 sufferance suffering
the penalty   159 rejoice i.e., rejoice at   166 quit absolve   169 golden earnest
advance payment

175 But we our kingdom's safety must so tender,
Whose ruin you have sought, that to her laws
We do deliver you. Get you therefore hence
(Poor miserable wretches) to your death;
The taste whereof God of His mercy give
180 You patience to endure, and true repentance
Of all your dear offenses! Bear them hence.

Exeunt [*Cambridge, Scroop, and Grey, guarded*].

Now, lords, for France; the enterprise whereof
Shall be to you as us, like glorious.
We doubt not of a fair and lucky war,
185 Since God so graciously hath brought to light
This dangerous treason, lurking in our way
To hinder our beginnings. We doubt not now
But every rub is smoothèd on our way.
Then, forth, dear countrymen. Let us deliver
190 Our puissance into the hand of God,
Putting it straight in expedition.
Cheerly to sea; the signs of war advance:
No king of England, if not King of France!

Flourish. [*Exeunt.*]

[Scene III. *London. Before a tavern.*]

Enter Pistol, Nym, Bardolph, Boy, and Hostess.

HOSTESS Prithee, honey-sweet husband, let me bring
thee to Staines.

PISTOL No; for my manly heart doth earn.

---

175 **tender** care for   179 **taste** experience   181 **dear** dire   183 **like** equally
188 **rub** obstacle   190 **puissance** armed force   191 **expedition** motion
192 **the signs of war advance** raise up the banners II.iii.2 **Staines** (on the road
to Southampton)   3 **earn** grieve

Bardolph, be blithe; Nym, rouse thy vaunting
  veins;
Boy, bristle thy courage up; for Falstaff he is dead,   5
And we must earn therefore.

BARDOLPH Would I were with him, wheresome'er he is,
either in heaven or in hell!

HOSTESS Nay sure, he's not in hell! He's in Arthur's
bosom, if ever man went to Arthur's bosom. 'A   10
made a finer end, and went away and it had
been any christom child. 'A parted ev'n just between twelve and one, ev'n at the turning o' th'
tide. For after I saw him fumble with the sheets,
and play with flowers, and smile upon his finger's   15
end, I knew there was but one way; for his nose
was as sharp as a pen, and 'a babbled of green
fields. "How now, Sir John?" quoth I. "What, man?
Be o' good cheer." So 'a cried out "God, God,
God!" three or four times. Now I, to comfort him,   20
bid him 'a should not think of God; I hoped there
was no need to trouble himself with any such
thoughts yet. So 'a bade me lay more clothes on
his feet. I put my hand into the bed, and felt them,
and they were as cold as any stone. Then I felt to   25

---

4 **vaunting veins** rising spirits 9-10 **Arthur's bosom** (a mistake for Abraham's
bosom) 10 **'A** he 11 **finer end** i.e., than going to hell 11 **and** as if
12 **christom child** infant in christening robe (the proper form was "chrisom"),
innocent babe 13-14 **at the turning o' th' tide** (according to popular belief,
persons near the sea died at the turn of the tide) 14-17 **fumble ... nose was as
sharp as a pen** (traditionally accepted signs of the imminence of death) 17 **'a
babbled** (the Folio has "a Table," which seems meaningless to most readers.
Lewis Theobald's conjecture, in 1726, that a compositor misread the copy's "'a
babld" has been widely accepted. One might argue that the compositor misread "'a
talkd," but "babbled" is more appropriate than "talked" to the childishness—
referred to earlier in the speech—of an old man's last moments. Recently the Folio
reading has been defended, though not convincingly. One student, for example,
takes "Table" in the sense of "picture" or "tableau," and paraphrases thus:
Falstaff's nose was sharp as the pointed stakes of a pinfold, in a picture of green
fields. Various interpretations are usefully surveyed in E. G. Fogel, *Shakespeare
Quarterly*, IX [1958], 485-92; but Theobald's conjecture seems better sense and
better Shakespeare)

his knees, and so upward, and upward, and all was
as cold as any stone.

NYM   They say he cried out of sack.

HOSTESS   Ay, that 'a did.

30   BARDOLPH   And of women.

HOSTESS   Nay, that 'a did not.

BOY   Yes, that 'a did, and said they were devils incarnate.

HOSTESS   'A could never abide carnation; 'twas a
35   color he never liked.

BOY   'A said once, the devil would have him about
women.

HOSTESS   'A did in some sort, indeed, handle women;
but then he was rheumatic, and talked of the
40   Whore of Babylon.

BOY   Do you not remember 'a saw a flea stick upon
Bardolph's nose, and 'a said it was a black soul
burning in hell?

BARDOLPH   Well, the fuel is gone that maintained that
45   fire: that's all the riches I got in his service.

NYM   Shall we shog? The King will be gone from
Southampton.

PISTOL   Come, let's away. My love, give me thy lips.
Look to my chattels and my movables.
50   Let senses rule. The word is "Pitch and pay."
Trust none;
For oaths are straws, men's faiths are wafer-cakes,

---

28 **cried out of** complained loudly of   32-33 **incarnate** in human shape
34 **carnation** flesh color   38 **handle** speak of   39 **rheumatic** (perhaps a mistake
for "lunatic"; probably pronounced "rome-atic"; see next note)   39-40 **the
Whore of Babylon** (1) the "scarlet woman" of Revelation 17:4-5 (2) the Church
of Rome   44 **fuel** i.e., liquor provided by Falstaff   46 **shog** move off   50 **Let
senses rule. The word is "Pitch and pay"** keep your wits about you. The motto
is "Cash down"   52 **wafer-cakes** i.e., easily broken

And Hold-fast is the only dog, my duck.
Therefore Caveto be thy counselor.
Go, clear thy crystals. Yokefellows in arms,   55
Let us to France, like horse-leeches, my boys,
To suck, to suck, the very blood to suck!

BOY And that's but unwholesome food, they say.

PISTOL Touch her soft mouth, and march.

BARDOLPH Farewell, hostess.   [_Kisses her._] 60

NYM I cannot kiss, that is the humor of it; but adieu!

PISTOL Let housewifery appear; keep close, I thee
command.

HOSTESS Farewell! Adieu!   _Exeunt._

[Scene IV. _France. The French King's palace._]

_Flourish. Enter the French King, the Dauphin, the Dukes
of Berri and Bretagne, [the Constable, and others]._

KING Thus comes the English with full power upon
us,
And more than carefully it us concerns
To answer royally in our defenses.
Therefore the Dukes of Berri and of Bretagne,
Of Brabant and of Orleans, shall make forth,   5
And you, Prince Dauphin, with all swift dispatch
To line and new repair our towns of war
With men of courage, and with means defendant;

---

53 **Hold-fast is the only dog** (cf. the proverb, "Brag is a good dog, but Hold-fast
is a better") 54 **Caveto** take care 55 **clear thy crystals** wipe your eyes
62 **housewifery** good housekeeping 62 **keep close** stay at home II.iv.7 **line**
fortify

For England his approaches makes as fierce
10 As waters to the sucking of a gulf.
It fits us then to be as provident
As fear may teach us out of late examples
Left by the fatal and neglected English
Upon our fields.

DAUPHIN　　　　My most redoubted father,
15 It is most meet we arm us 'gainst the foe;
For peace itself should not so dull a kingdom
(Though war nor no known quarrel were in
　　question)
But that defenses, musters, preparations
Should be maintained, assembled, and collected,
20 As were a war in expectation.
Therefore I say, 'tis meet we all go forth
To view the sick and feeble parts of France;
And let us do it with no show of fear—
No, with no more than if we heard that England
25 Were busied with a Whitsun morris dance;
For, my good liege, she is so idly kinged,
Her scepter so fantastically borne,
By a vain, giddy, shallow, humorous youth,
That fear attends her not.

CONSTABLE　　　　　　O peace, Prince Dauphin!
30 You are too much mistaken in this king.
Question your Grace the late ambassadors,
With what great state he heard their embassy,
How well supplied with noble counselors,
How modest in exception, and withal
35 How terrible in constant resolution;
And you shall find his vanities forespent

10 **gulf** whirlpool 12 **late examples** i.e., battles of Crécy (1346) and
Poitiers (1356) 13 **fatal and neglected** fatally underestimated 19 **maintained, assembled, and collected** (these verbs refer singly to the nouns of the
previous line, in order) 25 **Whitsun morris dance** folk dance celebrating the
coming of summer 27 **Her scepter so fantastically borne** her royal power so
freakishly exercised 28 **humorous** capricious 29 **attends** accompanies
34 **exception** expressing disapproval 36 **forespent** already used up

Were but the outside of the Roman Brutus,
Covering discretion with a coat of folly;
As gardeners do with ordure hide those roots
That shall first spring and be most delicate.   40

DAUPHIN Well, 'tis not so, my Lord High Constable!
But though we think it so, it is no matter;
In cases of defense, 'tis best to weigh
The enemy more mighty than he seems;
So the proportions of defense are filled,   45
Which of a weak and niggardly projection
Doth, like a miser, spoil his coat with scanting
A little cloth.

KING   Think we King Harry strong;
And, princes, look you strongly arm to meet him.
The kindred of him hath been fleshed upon us;   50
And he is bred out of that bloody strain
That haunted us in our familiar paths;
Witness our too much memorable shame
When Crécy battle fatally was struck,
And all our princes captived, by the hand   55
Of that black name, Edward, Black Prince of
      Wales;
Whiles that his mountain sire—on mountain
      standing,
Up in the air, crowned with the golden sun—
Saw his heroical seed, and smiled to see him
Mangle the work of nature, and deface   60
The patterns that by God and by French fathers
Had twenty years been made. This is a stem
Of that victorious stock; and let us fear
The native mightiness and fate of him.

---

37 **Brutus** (Lucius Junius Brutus feigned stupidity in order to escape repressive action when planning to free Rome from the Tarquin tyranny) 45-46 **So the proportions ... niggardly projection** in this way the defending forces are fully mustered which if on a weak and sparing scheme 47 **scanting** stinting 50 **fleshed** (1) encouraged by a foretaste of success (2) initiated to bloodshed 51 **strain** stock 52 **haunted** pursued 57 **mountain sire** father of more than human proportions 59 **seed** issue, son 61 **patterns** i.e., examples of Frenchmen 64 **fate** what he is destined to achieve

Enter a Messenger.

MESSENGER Ambassadors from Harry, King of
65   England,
       Do crave admittance to your Majesty.

KING We'll give them present audience. Go, and bring
       them.   [*Exeunt Messenger and certain Lords.*]
       You see this chase is hotly followed, friends.

DAUPHIN Turn head, and stop pursuit; for coward
       dogs
       Most spend their mouths when what they seem to
70   threaten
       Runs far before them. Good my Sovereign,
       Take up the English short, and let them know
       Of what a monarchy you are the head.
       Self-love, my liege, is not so vile a sin
       As self-neglecting.

Enter [Lords, with] Exeter [and Train].

75 KING   From our brother of England?

EXETER From him, and thus he greets your Majesty:
       He wills you, in the name of God Almighty,
       That you divest yourself, and lay apart
       The borrowed glories that by gift of heaven,
80   By law of nature and of nations, 'longs
       To him and to his heirs—namely, the crown
       And all wide-stretchèd honors that pertain
       By custom, and the ordinance of times,
       Unto the crown of France. That you may know
85   'Tis no sinister nor no awkward claim,
       Picked from the wormholes of long-vanished days,
       Nor from the dust of old oblivion raked,
       He sends you this most memorable line,   [*giving a
       paper*]

67 **present** immediate   69 **Turn head** stand at bay (like stags)   70 **spend their
mouths** give cry   74 **Self-love** i.e., in praising oneself   83 **ordinance of times**
established usage   85 **no sinister nor no awkward** neither irregular nor
illegitimate   86 **Picked from the wormholes** ingeniously derived from neglected (worm-eaten) books   88 **memorable line** noteworthy pedigree

In every branch truly demonstrative;
Willing you overlook this pedigree;   90
And when you find him evenly derived
From his most famed of famous ancestors,
Edward the Third, he bids you then resign
Your crown and kingdom, indirectly held
From him, the native and true challenger.   95

KING Or else what follows?

EXETER Bloody constraint; for if you hide the crown
Even in your hearts, there will he rake for it.
Therefore in fierce tempest is he coming,
In thunder and in earthquake, like a Jove;   100
That if requiring fail, he will compel;
And bids you, in the bowels of the Lord,
Deliver up the crown, and to take mercy
On the poor souls for whom this hungry war
Opens his vasty jaws; and on your head   105
Turning the widows' tears, the orphans' cries,
The dead men's blood, the pining maidens' groans,
For husbands, fathers, and betrothèd lovers
That shall be swallowed in this controversy.
This is his claim, his threat'ning, and my message;   110
Unless the Dauphin be in presence here,
To whom expressly I bring greeting too.

KING For us, we will consider of this further.
Tomorrow shall you bear our full intent
Back to our brother of England.

DAUPHIN   For the Dauphin,   115
I stand here for him: what to him from England?

EXETER Scorn and defiance, slight regard, contempt,
And anything that may not misbecome
The mighty sender, doth he prize you at.
Thus says my King: and if your father's Highness   120

90 **Willing you overlook** desiring you to peruse   91 **evenly** directly
94 **indirectly** wrongfully   95 **native** rightful   101 **requiring** demand   102 **in
the bowels of the Lord** (a phrase found in Holinshed, and derived from
Philippians 1:8)

Do not, in grant of all demands at large,
Sweeten the bitter mock you sent his Majesty,
He'll call you to so hot an answer of it
That caves and womby vaultages of France
125 Shall chide your trespass, and return your mock
In second accent of his ordinance.

DAUPHIN Say: if my father render fair return,
It is against my will; for I desire
Nothing but odds with England. To that end,
130 As matching to his youth and vanity,
I did present him with the Paris balls.

EXETER He'll make your Paris Louvre shake for it,
Were it the mistress court of mighty Europe;
And be assured, you'll find a difference,
135 As we his subjects have in wonder found,
Between the promise of his greener days
And these he masters now. Now he weighs time
Even to the utmost grain: that you shall read
In your own losses, if he stay in France.

140 KING Tomorrow shall you know our mind at full.

                                                        Flourish.

EXETER Dispatch us with all speed, lest that our king
Come here himself to question our delay;
For he is footed in this land already.

KING You shall be soon dispatched, with fair con-
        ditions.
145 A night is but small breath and little pause
To answer matters of this consequence.   *Exeunt.*

---

124 **womby vaultages** hollow caverns   126 **second accent of his ordinance**
echo of his cannon   131 **Paris balls** tennis balls   133 **mistress** chief
136 **greener** more inexperienced   137 **weighs** values

ACT [III]

Flourish. Enter Chorus.

Thus with imagined wing our swift scene flies,
In motion of no less celerity
Than that of thought. Suppose that you have seen
The well-appointed King at Hampton pier
Embark his royalty; and his brave fleet   5
With silken streamers the young Phoebus fanning.
Play with your fancies, and in them behold
Upon the hempen tackle shipboys climbing;
Hear the shrill whistle which doth order give
To sounds confused; behold the threaden sails,   10
Borne with th' invisible and creeping wind,
Draw the huge bottoms through the furrowed sea,
Breasting the lofty surge. O, do but think
You stand upon the rivage, and behold
A city on th' inconstant billows dancing;   15
For so appears this fleet majestical,
Holding due course to Harfleur. Follow, follow!
Grapple your minds to sternage of this navy,
And leave your England, as dead midnight, still,
Guarded with grandsires, babies, and old women,   20
Either past or not arrived to pith and puissance;
For who is he whose chin is but enriched
With one appearing hair that will not follow
These culled and choice-drawn cavaliers to
    France?

III Prologue 1 **imagined** of imagination 5 **brave** splendid 6 **the young
Phoebus fanning** seen fluttering against the rising sun 9 **whistle** (blown by the
master of a ship) 12 **bottoms** ships 14 **rivage** shore 18 **to sternage of** astern
21 **pith** strength 24 **choice-drawn** chosen with special care

405

25   Work, work your thoughts, and therein see a siege:
Behold the ordinance on their carriages,
With fatal mouths gaping on girded Harfleur.
Suppose th' ambassador from the French comes
                 back;
Tells Harry that the King doth offer him
30   Katherine his daughter, and with her to dowry
Some petty and unprofitable dukedoms.
The offer likes not; and the nimble gunner
With linstock now the devilish cannon touches,
                                Alarum, and chambers go off.
And down goes all before them. Still be kind,
35   And eke out our performance with your mind.   _Exit._

[Scene I. _France. Harfleur._]

Enter the King, Exeter, Bedford, and Gloucester. Alarum.
[Enter Soldiers carrying] scaling ladders at Harfleur.

KING Once more unto the breach, dear friends, once
                 more;
Or close the wall up with our English dead!
In peace there's nothing so becomes a man
As modest stillness and humility;
5   But when the blast of war blows in our ears,
Then imitate the action of the tiger:
Stiffen the sinews, conjure up the blood,
Disguise fair nature with hard-favored rage;
Then lend the eye a terrible aspect:
10   Let it pry through the portage of the head

---

26 **ordinance** ordnance, cannon   27 **girded** besieged   33 **linstock** staff holding
lighted match   33 **touches** touches off, fires   33s.d. **chambers** small pieces of
ordnance (usually for ceremonial purposes)   III.i.4 **stillness** silence, staidness (?)
10 **portage** portholes

Like the brass cannon; let the brow o'erwhelm it
As fearfully as doth a gallèd rock
O'erhang and jutty his confounded base,
Swilled with the wild and wasteful ocean.
Now set the teeth, and stretch the nostril wide,   15
Hold hard the breath, and bend up every spirit
To his full height! On, on, you noble English,
Whose blood is fet from fathers of war-proof;
Fathers that like so many Alexanders
Have in these parts from morn till even fought   20
And sheathed their swords for lack of argument.
Dishonor not your mothers; now attest
That those whom you called fathers did beget you!
Be copy now to men of grosser blood
And teach them how to war! And you, good
    yeomen,   25
Whose limbs were made in England, show us here
The mettle of your pasture. Let us swear
That you are worth your breeding; which I doubt
    not,
For there is none of you so mean and base
That hath not noble luster in your eyes.   30
I see you stand like greyhounds in the slips,
Straining upon the start. The game's afoot!
Follow your spirit; and upon this charge,
Cry, "God for Harry, England and Saint George!"
                    [*Exeunt.*] *Alarum, and chambers go off.*

12 **gallèd** sea-beaten   13 **confounded** demolished   14 **Swilled** greedily
swallowed   16 **bend up** strain   18 **fet** fetched   18 **war-proof** proved in war
19 **Alexanders** i.e., sighing for more worlds to conquer   21 **argument** i.e.,
opponents   22 **Dishonor** i.e., by throwing doubts on your paternity   27 **mettle
of your pasture** fine quality of your rearing   31 **slips** leashes   33 **upon this
charge** as you charge

[Scene II. *Harfleur*.]

Enter Nym, Bardolph, Pistol, and Boy.

BARDOLPH On, on, on, on, on, to the breach, to the breach!

NYM Pray thee, Corporal, stay; the knocks are too hot; and, for mine own part, I have not a case of
5 lives. The humor of it is too hot; that is the very plain-song of it.

PISTOL The plain-song is most just; for humors do abound.
　　Knocks go and come; God's vassals drop and die;
　　　　And sword and shield
10 　　　　　　In bloody field
　　　　　Doth win immortal fame.

BOY Would I were in an alehouse in London! I would give all my fame for a pot of ale, and safety.

PISTOL And I:
15 　　　　If wishes would prevail with me,
　　　　My purpose should not fail with me,
　　　　　But thither would I hie.
BOY 　　　As duly, but not as truly,
　　　　As bird doth sing on bough.

Enter Fluellen.

20 FLUELLEN Up to the breach, you dogs! Avaunt, you cullions!

PISTOL Be merciful, great Duke, to men of mold!

III.ii.4 **case** set　6 **plain-song** simple air without variations, i.e., simple truth
18 **truly** (1) honorably (2) in tune　21 **cullions** base fellows　22 **mold** clay

Abate thy rage, abate thy manly rage,
Abate thy rage, great Duke!
Good bawcock, bate thy rage! Use lenity, sweet
  chuck!   25

NYM These be good humors. Your honor wins bad
  humors.   *Exit [with all but Boy].*

BOY As young as I am, I have observed these three
  swashers. I am boy to them all three; but all they
  three, though they would serve me, could not be   30
  man to me; for indeed three such antics do not
  amount to a man. For Bardolph, he is white-livered and red-faced; by the means whereof 'a faces
  it out, but fights not. For Pistol, he hath a killing
  tongue and a quiet sword; by the means whereof 'a   35
  breaks words, and keeps whole weapons. For
  Nym, he hath heard that men of few words are the
  best men, and therefore he scorns to say his
  prayers, lest 'a should be thought a coward; but his
  few bad words are matched with as few good deeds,   40
  for 'a never broke any man's head but his own, and
  that was against a post when he was drunk. They
  will steal anything, and call it purchase. Bardolph
  stole a lute-case, bore it twelve leagues, and sold it
  for three halfpence. Nym and Bardolph are sworn   45
  brothers in filching; and in Calais they stole a fire-
  shovel. I knew by that piece of service the men
  would carry coals. They would have me as familiar with men's pockets as their gloves or their
  handkerchers; which makes much against my man-   50
  hood, if I should take from another's pocket to put
  into mine; for it is plain pocketing up of wrongs.
  I must leave them, and seek some better service.

25 bawcock ... sweet chuck (ingratiating familiarities)   26 good (ironical)
26-27 Your honor wins bad humors valor is dangerous (so he runs off)
31 antics buffoons   32-33 white-livered cowardly   36 breaks words
(1) breaks promises (2) exchanges words   43 purchase booty (thieves' slang)
48 carry coals (1) do dirty work (2) submit to insult   52 pocketing up of
wrongs (1) receiving stolen goods (2) submitting to insult

Their villainy goes against my weak stomach, and
55   therefore I must cast it up.   *Exit*.

Enter Gower [and Fluellen].

GOWER Captain Fluellen, you must come presently
to the mines; the Duke of Gloucester would speak
with you.

FLUELLEN To the mines? Tell you the Duke, it is not
60   so good to come to the mines; for look you, the
mines is not according to the disciplines of the
war. The concavities of it is not sufficient; for look
you, th' athversary, you may discuss unto the
Duke, look you, is digt himself four yard under the
65   countermines. By Cheshu, I think 'a will plow
up all, if there is not better directions.

GOWER The Duke of Gloucester, to whom the order
of the siege is given, is altogether directed by an
Irishman, a very valiant gentleman, i' faith.

70   FLUELLEN It is Captain Macmorris, is it not?

GOWER I think it be.

FLUELLEN By Cheshu, he is an ass, as in the world! I
will verify as much in his beard. He has no more
directions in the true disciplines of the wars, look
75   you, of the Roman disciplines, than is a puppy-dog.

Enter Macmorris and Captain Jamy.

GOWER Here 'a comes, and the Scots captain, Captain
Jamy, with him.

FLUELLEN Captain Jamy is a marvelous falorous gentleman, that is certain, and of great expedition and

---

54 **goes against my weak stomach** (1) is against my disposition (2) makes me
sick   55 **cast it up** (1) run from their service (2) be sick   56 **presently**
immediately   61-62 **disciplines of the war** military experience   63 **discuss**
declare   64-65 **four yard under the countermines** countermines four yards
under the mines   65 **plow** (the first of Fluellen's dialect substitutions of "p" for
"b")   73 **verify as much in his beard** prove it to his face   79 **expedition**
readiness in disputation (rhetorical term)

knowledge in th' aunchient wars, upon my particu- 80
lar knowledge of his directions. By Cheshu, he will
maintain his argument as well as any military man
in the world in the disciplines of the pristine wars
of the Romans.

JAMY I say gud day, Captain Fluellen. 85

FLUELLEN God-den to your worship, good Captain
James.

GOWER How now, Captain Macmorris? Have you quit
the mines? Have the pioners given o'er?

MACMORRIS By Chrish, law, tish ill done! The work 90
ish give over, the trompet sound the retreat. By my
hand I swear, and my father's soul, the work ish
ill done! It ish give over. I would have blowed up
the town, so Chrish save me, law, in an hour. O,
tish ill done, tish ill done! By my hand, tish ill done! 95

FLUELLEN Captain Macmorris, I beseech you now, will
you voutsafe me, look you, a few disputations with
you, as partly touching or concerning the disciplines of the war, the Roman wars?—in the way of
argument, look you, and friendly communication; 100
partly to satisfy my opinion, and partly for the satisfaction, look you, of my mind—as touching the
direction of the military discipline, that is the point.

JAMY It sall be very gud, gud feith, gud captens bath,
and I sall quit you with gud leve, as I may pick 105
occasion. That sall I, mary.

MACMORRIS It is no time to discourse, so Chrish save
me! The day is hot, and the weather, and the wars,
and the King, and the Dukes; it is no time to discourse; the town is beseeched, and the trumpet call 110
us to the breach, and we talk, and, be Chrish, do
nothing; 'tis shame for us all, so God sa' me, 'tis

80-81 **particular** personal 89 **pioners** pioneers, miners 105 **quit** answer
106 **mary** (Jamy's pronunciation of "marry," a mild oath, from "By the Virgin
Mary") 110 **beseeched** (for "besieged")

shame to stand still, it is shame, by my hand! And
there is throats to be cut, and works to be done,
115   and there ish nothing done, so Chrish sa' me, law!

JAMY By the mess, ere theise eyes of mine take themselves to slomber, I'll do gud service, or I'll lig i'
th' grund for it! Ay or go to death! And I'll pay't
as valorously as I may, that sall I suerly do, that
120   is the breff and the long. Mary, I wad full fain
heard some question 'tween you tway.

FLUELLEN Captain Macmorris, I think, look you, under
your correction, there is not many of your nation—

MACMORRIS Of my nation? What ish my nation? Ish
125   a villain, and a basterd, and a knave, and a rascal.
What ish my nation? Who talks of my nation?

FLUELLEN Look you, if you take the matter otherwise
than is meant, Captain Macmorris, peradventure I
shall think you do not use me with that affability
130   as in discretion you ought to use me, look you, being as good a man as yourself, both in the disciplines of war, and in the derivation of my birth, and
in other particularities.

MACMORRIS I do not know you so good a man as my-
135   self; so Chrish save me, I will cut off your head!

GOWER Gentlemen both, you will mistake each
other.

JAMY Ah, that's a foul fault!   *A parley* [*sounded*].

GOWER The town sounds a parley.

140   FLUELLEN Captain Macmorris, when there is more better opportunity to be required, look you, I will be
so bold as to tell you I know the disciplines of war;
and there is an end.   *Exit* [*with others*].

136 will are determined to   141 to be required serves

[Scene III. *Before the gates of Harfleur*.]

Enter the King [*Henry*] *and all his Train
before the gates.*

KING How yet resolves the Governor of the town?
This is the latest parle we will admit:
Therefore to our best mercy give yourselves,
Or, like to men proud of destruction,
Defy us to our worst; for, as I am a soldier,   5
A name that in my thoughts becomes me best,
If I begin the batt'ry once again,
I will not leave the half-achieved Harfleur
Till in her ashes she lie buried.
The gates of mercy shall be all shut up,   10
And the fleshed soldier, rough and hard of heart,
In liberty of bloody hand shall range
With conscience wide as hell, mowing like grass
Your fresh fair virgins and your flow'ring infants.
What is it then to me if impious war,   15
Arrayed in flames like to the prince of fiends,
Do with his smirched complexion all fell feats
Enlinked to waste and desolation?
What is't to me, when you yourselves are cause,
If your pure maidens fall into the hand   20
Of hot and forcing violation?
What rein can hold licentious wickedness
When down the hill he holds his fierce career?
We may as bootless spend our vain command
Upon th' enragèd soldiers in their spoil   25
As send precepts to the leviathan
To come ashore. Therefore, you men of Harfleur,

III.iii.4 **proud of destruction** glorying in death   11 **fleshed** initiated in slaughter
17 **fell** savage   23 **career** gallop   25 **spoil** plundering   26 **precepts** written
instructions   26 **leviathan** legendary aquatic animal of enormous size (common
in Hebrew poetry)

Take pity of your town and of your people
Whiles yet my soldiers are in my command,
30   Whiles yet the cool and temperate wind of grace
O'erblows the filthy and contagious clouds
Of heady murder, spoil, and villainy.
If not—why, in a moment look to see
The blind and bloody soldier with foul hand
35   Defile the locks of your shrill-shrieking daughters;
Your fathers taken by the silver beards,
And their most reverend heads dashed to the walls;
Your naked infants spitted upon pikes,
Whiles the mad mothers with their howls confused
40   Do break the clouds, as did the wives of Jewry
At Herod's bloody-hunting slaughtermen.
What say you? Will you yield, and this avoid?
Or, guilty in defense, be thus destroyed?

Enter Governor [on the wall].

GOVERNOR Our expectation hath this day an end;
45   The Dauphin, whom of succors we entreated,
Returns us that his powers are yet not ready
To raise so great a siege. Therefore, great King,
We yield our town and lives to thy soft mercy.
Enter our gates, dispose of us and ours,
50   For we no longer are defensible.

KING Open your gates. Come, uncle Exeter,
Go you and enter Harfleur; there remain
And fortify it strongly 'gainst the French.
Use mercy to them all. For us, dear uncle,
55   The winter coming on, and sickness growing
Upon our soldiers, we will retire to Calais.
Tonight in Harfleur will we be your guest;
Tomorrow for the march are we addrest.

Flourish, and enter the town.

---

34 blind reckless   43 guilty in defense to blame for holding out   50 defensible able to make a defense   58 addrest prepared

[Scene IV. *Rouen. A room in the palace.*]

Enter Katherine and [*Alice,*] *an old Gentlewoman.*

KATHERINE Alice, tu as été en Angleterre, et tu parles
bien le langage.

ALICE Un peu, madame.

KATHERINE Je te prie m'enseignez; il faut que j'ap-
prenne à parler. Comment appelez-vous la main en   5
Anglais?

ALICE La main? Elle est appelée de hand.

KATHERINE De hand. Et les doigts?

ALICE Les doigts? Ma foi, j'oublie les doigts; mais je
me souviendrai. Les doigts? Je pense qu'ils sont   10
appelés de fingres; oui, de fingres.

KATHERINE La main, de hand; les doigts, le fingres. Je
pense que je suis le bon écolier; j'ai gagné deux
mots d'Anglais vitement. Comment appelez-vous
les ongles?   15

ALICE Les ongles? Nous les appelons de nails.

III.iv. (translated) KATHERINE Alice, you have been in England and
speak the language well.
ALICE A little, my lady.
KATHERINE I pray you, teach me; I have to learn to speak it. What do
you call *la main* in English?
ALICE *La main?* It is called de hand.
KATHERINE De hand. And *les doigts?*
ALICE *Les doigts?* Oh dear, I forget *les doigts;* but I shall remember.
Les doigts? I think that they are called de fingres; yes, de fingres.
KATHERINE *La main*, de hand; *les doigts, le* fingres. I think that I am
an apt scholar; I have learned two words of English quickly. What
do you call *les ongles?*
ALICE *Les ongles?* We call them de nails.

KATHERINE De nails. Ecoutez; dites-moi si je parle bien: de hand, de fingres, et de nails.

ALICE C'est bien dit, madame; il est fort bon Anglais.

20 KATHERINE Dites-moi l'Anglais pour le bras.

ALICE De arm, madame.

KATHERINE Et le coude.

ALICE D' elbow.

25 KATHERINE D' elbow. Je m'en fais la répétition de tous les mots que vous m'avez appris dès à présent.

ALICE Il est trop difficile, madame, comme je pense.

KATHERINE Excusez-moi, Alice; écoutez: d'hand, de fingre, de nails, d'arma, de bilbow.

ALICE D' elbow, madame.

30 KATHERINE O Seigneur Dieu, je m'en oublie! D' elbow. Comment appelez-vous le col?

ALICE De nick, madame.

KATHERINE De nick. Et le menton?

ALICE De chin.

KATHERINE De nails. Listen; tell me if I speak correctly: de hand, de fingres, and de nails.
ALICE Well said, my lady; it is very good English.
KATHERINE Tell me the English for *le bras*.
ALICE De arm, my lady.
KATHERINE And *le coude*.
ALICE D' elbow.
KATHERINE D' elbow. I shall repeat all the words you have taught me so far.
ALICE It is too hard, my lady, I think.
KATHERINE Pardon me, Alice; listen: d' hand, de fingre, de nails, d' arma, de bilbow.
ALICE D' elbow, my lady.
KATHERINE O dear Lord, I forget. D' elbow. What do you call *le col*?
ALICE De nick, my lady.
KATHERINE De nick. And *le menton*?
ALICE De chin.

KATHERINE De sin. Le col, de nick; le menton, de sin.   35

ALICE Oui. Sauf votre honneur, en vérité, vous pro-
noncez les mots aussi droit que les natifs d'Angleterre.

KATHERINE Je ne doute point d'apprendre, par la grace
de Dieu, et en peu de temps.   40

ALICE N'avez-vous pas déjà oublié ce que je vous ai
enseigné?

KATHERINE Non, je réciterai à vous promptement: d'
hand, de fingre, de mails—

ALICE De nails, madame.   45

KATHERINE De nails, de arm, de ilbow—

ALICE Sauf votre honneur, d' elbow.

KATHERINE Ainsi dis-je; d' elbow, de nick, et de sin.
Comment appelez-vous le pied et la robe?

ALICE Le foot, madame; et le count.   50

KATHERINE Le foot et le count! O Seigneur Dieu! Ils
sont les mots de son mauvais, corruptible, gros, et
impudique, et non pour les dames d'honneur d'user:
je ne voudrais prononcer ces mots devant les

KATHERINE De sin. *Le col,* de nick; *le menton,* de sin.
ALICE Yes. By your leave, indeed you pronounce the words just like a native of England.
KATHERINE I have no doubt that I shall learn, with God's help, and in little time.
ALICE Have you not already forgotten what I have taught you?
KATHERINE No, I shall recite to you now: d' hand, de fingre, de mails—
ALICE De nails, my lady.
KATHERINE De nails, de arm, de ilbow—
ALICE By your leave, d' elbow.
KATHERINE That's what I said; d' elbow, de nick, and de sin. What do you call *le pied* and *la robe?*
ALICE The foot, my lady; and the count. [editor's note: these words are similar in sound to the French equivalents of the English "four-letter" words; "count" is an attempt at "gown"]
KATHERINE The foot and the count! O dear Lord! Those are bad words, wicked, vulgar, and indecent, and respectable ladies don't use them. I wouldn't utter those words before French gentlemen

55   seigneurs de France pour tout le monde. Foh, le
        foot et le count! Néanmoins, je réciterai une autre
        fois ma leçon ensemble: d' hand, de fingre, de
        nails, d' arm, d' elbow, de nick, de sin, de foot,
        le count.

60   ALICE Excellent, madame!

     KATHERINE C'est assez pour une fois: allons-nous à
     diner.   *Exit [with Alice].*

                    [Scene V. *Rouen. A room in the palace.*]

           Enter the King of France, the Dauphin, [Bretagne,]
                   the Constable of France, and others.

     KING 'Tis certain he hath passed the river Somme.

     CONSTABLE And if he be not fought withal, my lord,
     Let us not live in France; let us quit all
     And give our vineyards to a barbarous people.

5   DAUPHIN O Dieu vivant! Shall a few sprays of us,
     The emptying of our father's luxury,
     Our scions, put in wild and savage stock,
     Spirt up so suddenly into the clouds
     And overlook their grafters?

     BRETAGNE Normans, but bastard Normans, Norman
10   bastards!
     Mort Dieu! Ma vie! if they march along

---

for the whole world. Fie, the foot and the count! Still, I shall recite
once more my whole lesson: d' hand, de fingre, de nails, d' arm,
d' elbow, de sin, de foot, the count.
ALICE Excellent, my lady.
KATHERINE That's enough for one session: let's go to dinner.
III.v.5 **sprays of us** offshoots, bastards   6 **emptying** expenditure   7 **scions,
put in wild and savage stock** i.e., Norman French mating with Anglo-Saxon
("scions" are shoots, for grafting)   8 **Spirt** sprout, shoot

Unfought withal, but I will sell my dukedom
To buy a slobb'ry and a dirty farm
In that nook-shotten isle of Albion.

CONSTABLE Dieu de batailles! where have they this
    mettle?   15
Is not their climate foggy, raw, and dull,
On whom, as in despite, the sun looks pale,
Killing their fruit with frowns? Can sodden water,
A drench for sur-reined jades, their barley broth,
Decoct their cold blood to such valiant heat?   20
And shall our quick blood, spirited with wine,
Seem frosty? O, for honor of our land,
Let us not hang like roping icicles
Upon our houses' thatch, whiles a more frosty
    people
Sweat drops of gallant youth in our rich fields—   25
"Poor" we call them in their native lords!

DAUPHIN By faith and honor,
Our madams mock at us and plainly say
Our mettle is bred out, and they will give
Their bodies to the lust of English youth,   30
To new-store France with bastard warriors.

BRETAGNE They bid us to the English dancing schools
And teach lavoltas high, and swift corantos,
Saying our grace is only in our heels,
And that we are most lofty runaways.   35

KING Where is Montjoy, the herald? Speed him
    hence;
Let him greet England with our sharp defiance.

---

13 slobb'ry waterlogged 14 nook-shotten full of odd angles, shapeless
14 Albion (an ancient poetical name for Britain alluding to the white cliffs visible
from France) 18 sodden boiled 19 drench for sur-reined jades, their
barley broth medicinal draught (or mash) given to overridden nags, (which is
much the same as) their beer 20 Decoct warm up 23 roping hanging down
together like rope 26 them i.e., "rich fields" of France 29 bred out exhausted,
degenerate 33 lavoltas dances with high leaps 33 corantos dances with a
running step 34 grace virtue, saving grace (?) 34 our heels (1) dancing
(2) running away 35 lofty stately, pompous

Up, Princes, and with spirit of honor edged
More sharper than your swords, hie to the field.
40 Charles Delabreth, High Constable of France,
You Dukes of Orleans, Bourbon, and of Berri,
Alençon, Brabant, Bar, and Burgundy;
Jacques Chatillon, Rambures, Vaudemont,
Beaumont, Grandpré, Roussi, and Faulconbridge,
45 Foix, Lestrale, Bouciqualt, and Charolois,
High dukes, great princes, barons, lords, and
   knights,
For your great seats now quit you of great shames:
Bar Harry England, that sweeps through our land
With pennons painted in the blood of Harfleur;
50 Rush on his host, as doth the melted snow
Upon the valleys whose low vassal seat
The Alps doth spit and void his rheum upon.
Go down upon him—you have power enough—
And in a captive chariot into Rouen
Bring him our prisoner.

55 CONSTABLE   This becomes the great.
Sorry am I his numbers are so few,
His soldiers sick, and famished in their march;
For I am sure, when he shall see our army,
He'll drop his heart into the sink of fear
60 And, for achievement, offer us his ransom.

KING Therefore, Lord Constable, haste on Montjoy,
And let him say to England that we send
To know what willing ransom he will give.
Prince Dauphin, you shall stay with us in Rouen.

65 DAUPHIN Not so, I do beseech your Majesty.

KING Be patient, for you shall remain with us.
Now forth, Lord Constable, and Princes all,
And quickly bring us word of England's fall.
                                        Exeunt.

47 **seats** estates   52 **his** i.e., the Alps's   59 **sink** pit   60 **achievement** acquisition (i.e., for France)

[Scene VI. *France. The English camp in Picardy.*]

Enter Captains, English and Welsh:
Gower and Fluellen.

GOWER How now, Captain Fluellen, come you from
the bridge?

FLUELLEN I assure you, there is very excellent services
committed at the bridge.

GOWER Is the Duke of Exeter safe?   5

FLUELLEN The Duke of Exeter is as magnanimous as
Agamemnon, and a man that I love and honor with
my soul, and my heart, and my duty, and my live,
and my living, and my uttermost power. He is not
—God be praised and blessed!—any hurt in the   10
world, but keeps the bridge most valiantly, with excellent discipline. There is an aunchient lieutenant
there at the pridge, I think in my very conscience he
is as valiant a man as Mark Antony, and he is a
man of no estimation in the world, but I did see him   15
do as gallant service.

GOWER What do you call him?

FLUELLEN He is called Aunchient Pistol.

GOWER I know him not.

Enter Pistol.

FLUELLEN Here is the man.   20

PISTOL Captain, I thee beseech to do me favors;
The Duke of Exeter doth love thee well.

III.vi.2 **the bridge** (over the Ternoise, captured on October 23, 1415, two days
before the battle of Agincourt) 3 **services** exploits 12 **aunchient lieutenant**
sublieutenant

FLUELLEN Ay, I praise God; and I have merited some
love at his hands.

25 PISTOL Bardolph, a soldier firm and sound of heart,
And of buxom valor, hath by cruel fate,
And giddy Fortune's furious fickle wheel—
That goddess blind,
That stands upon the rolling restless stone—

30 FLUELLEN By your patience, Aunchient Pistol. Fortune
is painted blind, with a muffler afore her eyes, to
signify to you that Fortune is blind; and she is
painted also with a wheel, to signify to you, which
is the moral of it, that she is turning and incon-
35 stant, and mutability, and variation; and her foot,
look you, is fixed upon a spherical stone, which
rolls, and rolls, and rolls. In good truth, the poet
makes a most excellent description of it; Fortune
is an excellent moral.

40 PISTOL Fortune is Bardolph's foe, and frowns on him;
For he hath stol'n a pax, and hangèd must 'a be—
A damnèd death!
Let gallows gape for dog; let man go free,
And let not hemp his windpipe suffocate.
45 But Exeter hath given the doom of death
For pax of little price.
Therefore, go speak—the Duke will hear thy voice;
And let not Bardolph's vital thread be cut
With edge of penny cord, and vile reproach.
50 Speak, Captain, for his life, and I will thee requite.

FLUELLEN Aunchient Pistol, I do partly understand
your meaning.

PISTOL Why then, rejoice therefore!

FLUELLEN Certainly, Aunchient, it is not a thing to
55 rejoice at; for if, look you, he were my brother, I
would desire the Duke to use his good pleasure,

26 **buxom** lively   39 **moral** symbolical figure   41 **pax** tablet depicting the
crucifixion, kissed by priest and then communicants at Mass   45 **doom** sentence

and put him to execution; for discipline ought to be used.

PISTOL Die and be damned! and figo for thy friendship!

FLUELLEN It is well.   60

PISTOL The fig of Spain!   *Exit*.

FLUELLEN Very good.

GOWER Why, this is an arrant counterfeit rascal! I remember him now—a bawd, a cutpurse.

FLUELLEN I'll assure you, 'a utt'red as prave words at   65
the pridge, as you shall see in a summer's day. But it is very well. What he has spoke to me, that is well, I warrant you, when time is serve.

GOWER Why, 'tis a gull, a fool, a rogue, that now and then goes to the wars, to grace himself at his   70
return into London, under the form of a soldier. And such fellows are perfect in the great commanders' names, and they will learn you by rote where services were done: at such and such a sconce, at such a breach, at such a convoy; who came off   75
bravely, who was shot, who disgraced, what terms the enemy stood on; and this they con perfectly in the phrase of war, which they trick up with new-tuned oaths; and what a beard of the general's cut and a horrid suit of the camp will do among   80
foaming bottles and ale-washed wits is wonderful to be thought on. But you must learn to know such slanders of the age, or else you may be marvelously mistook.

---

59 **figo** (Spanish for) fig (see next note)   61 **fig of Spain** contemptuous and obscene gesture made by thrusting the thumb between the fingers or into the mouth   63 **arrant** out-and-out   69 **gull** simpleton   74 **services** exploits   74 **sconce** small fort or earthwork   75 **came off** got clear   76–77 **what terms the enemy stood on** what the position of the enemy depended on   77 **con** learn   78–79 **trick up with new-tuned oaths** adorn with newly phrased oaths   79–80 **of the general's cut** shaped in the same fashion as the general's

85 FLUELLEN I tell you what, Captain Gower: I do perceive he is not the man that he would gladly make
show to the world he is. If I find a hole in his coat,
I will tell him my mind. [*Drum within.*] Hark you,
the King is coming, and I must speak with him
90 from the pridge.

Drum and Colors. Enter the King and his poor
Soldiers [and Gloucester].

God pless your Majesty!

KING How now, Fluellen, cam'st thou from the
bridge?

FLUELLEN Ay, so please your Majesty: the Duke of
95 Exeter has very gallantly maintained the pridge; the
French is gone off, look you, and there is gallant
and most prave passages. Marry, th' athversary
was have possession of the pridge, but he is enforced to retire, and the Duke of Exeter is master
100 of the pridge. I can tell your Majesty, the Duke
is a prave man.

KING What men have you lost, Fluellen?

FLUELLEN The perdition of th' athversary hath been
very great, reasonable great: marry, for my part, I
105 think the Duke hath lost never a man, but one that
is liked to be executed for robbing a church—one
Bardolph, if your Majesty know the man. His face
is all bubukles and whelks, and knobs, and flames
o' fire, and his lips blows at his nose, and it is like
110 a coal of fire, sometimes plue and sometimes red;
but his nose is executed, and his fire's out.

KING We would have all such offenders so cut off;
and we give express charge that in our marches
through the country there be nothing compelled

87 a hole in his coat some fault in him   97 passages i.e., of arms
108 bubukles and whelks abscesses-and-carbuncles (a confusion of two words)
and pimples   111 executed i.e., slit (as he stood in the pillory before being
hanged)   111 his its   112 cut off put to death

from the villages, nothing taken but paid for; none 115
of the French upbraided or abused in disdainful
language; for when lenity and cruelty play for a
kingdom, the gentler gamester is the soonest winner.

Tucket. Enter Montjoy.

MONTJOY You know me by my habit.   120

KING Well then, I know thee. What shall I know of
thee?

MONTJOY My master's mind.

KING Unfold it.

MONTJOY Thus says my King: Say thou to Harry of 125
England, though we seemed dead, we did but sleep.
Advantage is a better soldier than rashness. Tell
him, we could have rebuked him at Harfleur, but
that we thought not good to bruise an injury till it
were full ripe. Now we speak upon our cue, and   130
our voice is imperial: England shall repent his folly,
see his weakness, and admire our sufferance. Bid
him therefore consider of his ransom, which must
proportion the losses we have borne, the subjects
we have lost, the disgrace we have digested; which 135
in weight to re-answer, his pettiness would bow
under. For our losses, his exchequer is too poor;
for th' effusion of our blood, the muster of his
kingdom too faint a number; and for our disgrace,
his own person kneeling at our feet but a weak and 140
worthless satisfaction. To this add defiance; and
tell him for conclusion, he hath betrayed his followers, whose condemnation is pronounced. So far
my King and master; so much my office.

KING What is thy name? I know thy quality.   145

119s.d. **Tucket** a personal trumpet call   120 **habit** i.e., the herald's tabard
127 **Advantage** favorable opportunity   129 **bruise an injury** squeeze out a
festering wound   132 **admire our sufferance** wonder at our patience
136-37 **in weight ... bow under** to compensate in full would be too much for
his small resources

MONTJOY   Montjoy.

KING   Thou dost thy office fairly. Turn thee back,
        And tell thy King, I do not seek him now,
        But could be willing to march on to Calais
150   Without impeachment; for, to say the sooth,
        Though 'tis no wisdom to confess so much
        Unto an enemy of craft and vantage,
        My people are with sickness much enfeebled,
        My numbers lessened; and those few I have
155   Almost no better than so many French,
        Who when they were in health, I tell thee, herald,
        I thought upon one pair of English legs
        Did march three Frenchmen. Yet forgive me, God,
        That I do brag thus! This your air of France
160   Hath blown that vice in me. I must repent.
        Go therefore tell thy master, here I am;
        My ransom is this frail and worthless trunk;
        My army but a weak and sickly guard;
        Yet, God before, tell him we will come on,
165   Though France himself and such another neighbor
        Stand in our way. There's for thy labor, Montjoy.
                                        [Gives a purse.]
        Go bid thy master well advise himself:
        If we may pass, we will; if we be hind'red,
        We shall your tawny ground with your red blood
170   Discolor; and so, Montjoy, fare you well.
        The sum of all our answer is but this:
        We would not seek a battle as we are,
        Nor, as we are, we say we will not shun it.
        So tell your master.

175 MONTJOY   I shall deliver so. Thanks to your Highness.
                                        [Exit.]

GLOUCESTER   I hope they will not come upon us now.

KING   We are in God's hand, brother, not in theirs.
        March to the bridge, it now draws toward night;

146 **Montjoy** (title of chief herald of France, not his name)   150 **impeachment**
hindrance   152 **craft and vantage** cunning and superiority

Beyond the river we'll encamp ourselves,
And on tomorrow bid them march away.   *Exeunt.*   180

[Scene VII. *France. The French camp, near
Agincourt.*]

*Enter the Constable of France, the Lord Rambures,
Orleans, Dauphin, with others.*

CONSTABLE Tut! I have the best armor of the world.
Would it were day!

ORLEANS You have an excellent armor; but let my
horse have his due.

CONSTABLE It is the best horse of Europe.   5

ORLEANS Will it never be morning?

DAUPHIN My Lord of Orleans, and my Lord High
Constable, you talk of horse and armor?

ORLEANS You are as well provided of both as any
prince in the world.   10

DAUPHIN What a long night is this! I will not change
my horse with any that treads but on four pasterns.
Ça, ha! He bounds from the earth, as if his entrails
were hairs; le cheval volant, the Pegasus, chez les
narines de feu! When I bestride him, I soar, I am   15
a hawk; he trots the air; the earth sings when he
touches it. The basest horn of his hoof is more
musical than the pipe of Hermes.

ORLEANS He's of the color of the nutmeg.

III.vii.13-14 **as if his entrails were hairs** i.e., as if he were a tennis ball (or
perhaps "hairs" = hares)   14-15 **le cheval ... de feu** the flying horse, Pegasus,
with fiery nostrils   17-18 **The basest horn ... pipe of Hermes** (the winged
horse, Pegasus, struck Mount Helicon with his hoof and the fountain of the Muses
sprang forth; Hermes, alias Mercury, invented the pipe and charmed to sleep
Argus of the hundred eyes)

20 DAUPHIN And of the heat of the ginger. It is a beast
for Perseus: he is pure air and fire; and the dull
elements of earth and water never appear in him,
but only in patient stillness while his rider mounts
him. He is indeed a horse, and all other jades you
25 may call beasts.

CONSTABLE Indeed, my lord, it is a most absolute and
excellent horse.

DAUPHIN It is the prince of palfreys; his neigh is like
the bidding of a monarch, and his countenance en-
30 forces homage.

ORLEANS No more, cousin.

DAUPHIN Nay, the man hath no wit that cannot, from
the rising of the lark to the lodging of the lamb,
vary deservèd praise on my palfrey; it is a theme
35 as fluent as the sea. Turn the sands into eloquent
tongues, and my horse is argument for them all.
'Tis a subject for a sovereign to reason on, and
for a sovereign's sovereign to ride on; and for the
world, familiar to us and unknown, to lay apart
40 their particular functions, and wonder at him. I
once writ a sonnet in his praise and began thus,
"Wonder of nature!"

ORLEANS I have heard a sonnet begin so to one's
mistress.

45 DAUPHIN Then did they imitate that which I com-
posed to my courser, for my horse is my mistress.

ORLEANS Your mistress bears well.

DAUPHIN Me well, which is the prescript praise and
perfection of a good and particular mistress.

21 **Perseus** (Pegasus sprang from the blood of the gorgon, Medusa, when Perseus
cut off her head)   24 **jades** nags   28 **palfreys** saddle horses (too light for use in
battle)   34 **vary** express in different ways   36 **argument** subject   37 **reason**
discourse   47 **bears well** carries her rider well   48 **prescript** prescribed
49 **particular** private

CONSTABLE Nay, for methought yesterday your mis- 50
tress shrewdly shook your back.

DAUPHIN So perhaps did yours.

CONSTABLE Mine was not bridled.

DAUPHIN O, then belike she was old and gentle, and
you rode like a kern of Ireland, your French hose 55
off, and in your strait strossers.

CONSTABLE You have good judgment in horsemanship.

DAUPHIN Be warned by me then: they that ride so,
and ride not warily, fall into foul bogs. I had rather 60
have my horse to my mistress.

CONSTABLE I had as lief have my mistress a jade.

DAUPHIN I tell thee, Constable, my mistress wears his
own hair.

CONSTABLE I could make as true a boast as that, if I 65
had a sow to my mistress.

DAUPHIN "Le chien est retourné à son propre vomiss-
ement, et la truie lavée au bourbier." Thou mak'st
use of anything.

CONSTABLE Yet do I not use my horse for my mistress, 70
or any such proverb so little kin to the purpose.

RAMBURES My Lord Constable, the armor that I saw
in your tent tonight—are those stars or suns upon
it?

CONSTABLE Stars, my lord. 75

DAUPHIN Some of them will fall tomorrow, I hope.

51 **shrewdly** (1) severely (2) shrewishly (cf. line 53)   53 **bridled** (as (1) a horse
(2) a shrew compelled to wear a bridle)   55 **kern** lightly armed Irish foot
soldier   55 **French hose** loose, wide breeches   56 **strait strossers** tight trousers
(i.e., bare-legged)   57–58 **horsemanship** (with a pun on "whores-manship")
62 **jade** (1) poor horse (2) loose woman   63–64 **wears his own hair** i.e., doesn't
need a (fashionable) wig   67–68 **Le chien ... bourbier** cf. 2 Peter 2:22 "The dog
is turned to his own vomit again, and the sow that was washed to her wallowing in
the mire"

CONSTABLE And yet my sky shall not want.

DAUPHIN That may be, for you bear a many super-
fluously, and 'twere more honor some were away.

80 CONSTABLE Ev'n as your horse bears your praises, who
would trot as well, were some of your brags dis-
mounted.

DAUPHIN Would I were able to load him with his
desert! Will it never be day? I will trot tomorrow a
85 mile, and my way shall be paved with English faces.

CONSTABLE I will not say so, for fear I should be faced
out of my way; but I would it were morning, for
I would fain be about the ears of the English.

RAMBURES Who will go to hazard with me for twenty
90 prisoners?

CONSTABLE You must first go yourself to hazard, ere
you have them.

DAUPHIN 'Tis midnight; I'll go arm myself.   *Exit.*

ORLEANS The Dauphin longs for morning.

95 RAMBURES He longs to eat the English.

CONSTABLE I think he will eat all he kills.

ORLEANS By the white hand of my lady, he's a gallant
prince.

CONSTABLE Swear by her foot, that she may tread out
100 the oath.

ORLEANS He is simply the most active gentleman of
France.

CONSTABLE Doing is activity, and he will still be
doing.

105 ORLEANS He never did harm, that I heard of.

86-87 **faced out of my way** (1) put out of countenance (2) driven off   89 **go to
hazard** take a wager   99 **tread out** (1) obliterate (2) treat with contempt
104 **doing** having sexual intercourse

CONSTABLE Nor will do none tomorrow; he will keep
that good name still.

ORLEANS I know him to be valiant.

CONSTABLE I was told that, by one that knows him
better than you.   110

ORLEANS What's he?

CONSTABLE Marry, he told me so himself, and he said
he cared not who knew it.

ORLEANS He needs not; it is no hidden virtue in him.

CONSTABLE By my faith, sir, but it is! Never anybody   115
saw it but his lackey; 'tis a hooded valor, and when
it appears, it will bate.

ORLEANS Ill will never said well.

CONSTABLE I will cap that proverb with "There is
flattery in friendship."   120

ORLEANS And I will take up that with "Give the devil
his due."

CONSTABLE Well placed! There stands your friend for
the devil. Have at the very eye of that proverb with
"A pox of the devil!"   125

ORLEANS You are the better at proverbs, by how much
"a fool's bolt is soon shot."

CONSTABLE You have shot over.

ORLEANS 'Tis not the first time you were overshot.

Enter a Messenger.

MESSENGER My Lord High Constable, the English lie   130
within fifteen hundred paces of your tents.

CONSTABLE Who hath measured the ground?

---

116 **but his lackey** i.e., he has beaten no one but his footboy 116-17 **hooded
valor ... will bate** valor like a hawk hooded before action, which flutters and
beats its wings when its hood is removed 117 **bate** (1) beat its wings (2) become
dejected 128 **over** beyond the mark 129 **overshot** (1) wide of the mark
(2) beaten in shooting

MESSENGER The Lord Grandpré.

CONSTABLE A valiant and most expert gentleman.
135   Would it were day! Alas, poor Harry of England!
He longs not for the dawning, as we do.

ORLEANS What a wretched and peevish fellow is this
King of England, to mope with his fat-brained followers so far out of his knowledge!

140   CONSTABLE If the English had any apprehension, they
would run away.

ORLEANS That they lack; for if their heads had any
intellectual armor, they could never wear such
heavy headpieces.

145   RAMBURES That island of England breeds very valiant
creatures: their mastiffs are of unmatchable
courage.

ORLEANS Foolish curs, that run winking into the
mouth of a Russian bear, and have their heads
150   crushed like rotten apples! You may as well say,
that's a valiant flea, that dare eat his breakfast on
the lip of a lion.

CONSTABLE Just, just! And the men do sympathize
with the mastiffs in robustious and rough coming
155   on, leaving their wits with their wives: and then
give them great meals of beef, and iron and steel;
they will eat like wolves and fight like devils.

ORLEANS Ay, but these English are shrewdly out of
beef.

160   CONSTABLE Then shall we find tomorrow they have
only stomachs to eat, and none to fight. Now is
it time to arm; come, shall we about it?

ORLEANS It is now two o'clock; but let me see—by ten
We shall have each a hundred Englishmen. *Exeunt.*

137 **peevish** senseless 140 **apprehension** understanding, grasp of mind
148 **winking** with eyes shut 158 **shrewdly** very much 161 **stomachs**
disposition

ACT [IV]

Chorus.

Now entertain conjecture of a time
When creeping murmur and the poring dark
Fills the wide vessel of the universe.
From camp to camp, through the foul womb of night,
The hum of either army stilly sounds;   5
That the fixed sentinels almost receive
The secret whispers of each other's watch.
Fire answers fire, and through their paly flames
Each battle sees the other's umbered face.
Steed threatens steed, in high and boastful neighs   10
Piercing the night's dull ear; and from the tents
The armorers accomplishing the knights,
With busy hammers closing rivets up,
Give dreadful note of preparation.
The country cocks do crow, the clocks do toll;   15
And the third hour of drowsy morning named.
Proud of their numbers, and secure in soul,
The confident and over-lusty French
Do the low-rated English play at dice;
And chide the cripple tardy-gaited night   20
Who like a foul and ugly witch doth limp
So tediously away. The poor condemnèd English,
Like sacrifices, by their watchful fires
Sit patiently, and inly ruminate

IV Prologue 2 **poring** eye-straining 5 **stilly** softly 8 **paly** pale (poetic)
9 **battle** army 9 **umbered** shadowed 12 **accomplishing** equipping 14 **note**
indication 17 **secure** confident 18 **over-lusty** too lively 19 **play** play for
23 **watchful** used for keeping watch

433

25 The morning's danger; and their gesture sad,
    Investing lank-lean cheeks and war-worn coats,
    Presenteth them unto the gazing moon
    So many horrid ghosts. O, now, who will behold
    The royal captain of this ruined band

30 Walking from watch to watch, from tent to tent,
    Let him cry, "Praise and glory on his head!"
    For forth he goes and visits all his host,
    Bids them good morrow with a modest smile,
    And calls them brothers, friends, and countrymen.

35 Upon his royal face there is no note
    How dread an army hath enrounded him;
    Nor doth he dedicate one jot of color
    Unto the weary and all-watchèd night;
    But freshly looks, and overbears attaint

40 With cheerful semblance and sweet majesty;
    That every wretch, pining and pale before,
    Beholding him, plucks comfort from his looks.
    A largess universal, like the sun,
    His liberal eye doth give to everyone,

45 Thawing cold fear, that mean and gentle all
    Behold, as may unworthiness define,
    A little touch of Harry in the night.
    And so our scene must to the battle fly;
    Where (O for pity!) we shall much disgrace,

50 With four or five most vile and ragged foils
    Right ill-disposed in brawl ridiculous,
    The name of Agincourt. Yet sit and see,
    Minding true things by what their mock'ries be.

                                            Exit.

25 **gesture** bearing   26 **Investing** accompanying   37-38 **dedicate one jot of color/Unto** look pale on account of   38 **all-watchèd** entirely spent in watches   39 **overbears attaint** overcomes any sign of exhaustion   46 **as may unworthiness define** as far as our unworthy selves can present it   50 **foils** light fencing weapons   53 **mock'ries** imitations

[Scene I. *France. The English camp at Agincourt.*]

Enter the King, Bedford, and Gloucester.

KING Gloucester, 'tis true that we are in great danger;
The greater therefore should our courage be.
Good morrow, brother Bedford. God Almighty!
There is some soul of goodness in things evil,
Would men observingly distill it out;   5
For our bad neighbor makes us early stirrers,
Which is both healthful, and good husbandry.
Besides, they are our outward consciences,
And preachers to us all, admonishing
That we should dress us fairly for our end.   10
Thus may we gather honey from the weed
And make a moral of the devil himself.

Enter Erpingham.

Good morrow, old Sir Thomas Erpingham:
A good soft pillow for that good white head
Were better than a churlish turf of France.   15

ERPINGHAM Not so, my liege. This lodging likes me
        better,
Since I may say, "Now lie I like a king."

KING 'Tis good for men to love their present pains
Upon example: so the spirit is eased;
And when the mind is quick'ned, out of doubt   20
The organs, though defunct and dead before,
Break up their drowsy grave, and newly move
With casted slough and fresh legerity.

IV.i.7 **husbandry** careful management 8 **outward** i.e., not our own inner
10 **dress us** prepare ourselves 12 **moral** improving lesson 19 **Upon** in
pursuance of 21 **organs** parts of the body 21 **defunct** out of use 22 **newly** (a
snake is torpid before casting its slough) 23 **legerity** nimbleness

Lend me thy cloak, Sir Thomas. Brothers both,
25 Commend me to the princes in our camp;
Do my good morrow to them, and anon
Desire them all to my pavilion.

GLOUCESTER We shall, my liege.

ERPINGHAM Shall I attend your Grace?

KING   No, my good knight.
30 Go with my brothers to my lords of England.
I and my bosom must debate awhile,
And then I would no other company.

ERPINGHAM The Lord in heaven bless thee, noble
Harry!   *Exeunt [all but the King].*

KING God-a-mercy, old heart! thou speak'st cheerfully.

Enter Pistol.

35 PISTOL Qui va là?

KING A friend.

PISTOL Discuss unto me; art thou officer,
Or art thou base, common, and popular?

KING I am a gentleman of a company.

40 PISTOL Trail'st thou the puissant pike?

KING Even so. What are you?

PISTOL As good a gentleman as the Emperor.

KING Then you are a better than the King.

PISTOL The king's a bawcock, and a heart of gold,
45 A lad of life, an imp of fame,
Of parents good, of fist most valiant.
I kiss his dirty shoe, and from heartstring

35 **Qui va là** who goes there 37 **Discuss** declare 38 **popular** vulgar
40 **Trail'st thou the puissant pike?** i.e., are you an infantryman? (a pike was held
below its head, the butt trailing behind on the ground) 44 **bawcock** fine fellow
(familiar term) 45 **imp** child

I love the lovely bully. What is thy name?

KING Harry le Roy.

PISTOL Le Roy? A Cornish name. Art thou of Cornish
crew?   50

KING No, I am a Welshman.

PISTOL Know'st thou Fluellen?

KING Yes.

PISTOL Tell him I'll knock his leek about his pate
Upon Saint Davy's day.   55

KING Do not you wear your dagger in your cap that
day, lest he knock that about yours.

PISTOL Art thou his friend?

KING And his kinsman too.

PISTOL The figo for thee then!   60

KING I thank you. God be with you!

PISTOL My name is Pistol called.   *Exit*.

KING It sorts well with your fierceness.
                                             Manet King [aside].

                        Enter Fluellen and Gower.

GOWER Captain Fluellen!

FLUELLEN So! in the name of Jesu Christ, speak fewer.   65
It is the greatest admiration in the universal world,
when the true and aunchient prerogatifes and laws
of the wars is not kept. If you would take the pains
but to examine the wars of Pompey the Great, you
shall find, I warrant you, that there is no tiddle   70
taddle nor pibble babble in Pompey's camp; I warrant you, you shall find the ceremonies of the wars,

48 **bully** fine fellow (familiar, endearing term) 55 **Saint Davy's day**
March 1 60 **figo** fig (Spanish), contemptuous and obscene gesture 63 **sorts**
suits (the Elizabethan pistol was notably noisy and ineffective) 63s.d. **Manet**
remains (Latin) 65 **fewer** less

and the cares of it, and the forms of it, and the
sobriety of it, and the modesty of it, to be other-
75 wise.

GOWER Why, the enemy is loud; you hear him all
night.

FLUELLEN If the enemy is an ass and a fool and a
prating coxcomb, is it meet, think you, that we
80 should also, look you, be an ass and a fool and a
prating coxcomb, in your own conscience now?

GOWER I will speak lower.

FLUELLEN I pray you, and beseech you that you will.
Exit [with Gower].

KING Though it appear a little out of fashion,
85 There is much care and valor in this Welshman.

*Enter three soldiers: John Bates, Alexander Court,
and Michael Williams.*

COURT Brother John Bates, is not that the morning
which breaks yonder?

BATES I think it be; but we have no great cause to
desire the approach of day.

90 WILLIAMS We see yonder the beginning of the day, but
I think we shall never see the end of it. Who goes
there?

KING A friend.

WILLIAMS Under what captain serve you?

95 KING Under Sir Thomas Erpingham.

WILLIAMS A good old commander, and a most kind
gentleman. I pray you, what thinks he of our
estate?

KING Even as men wracked upon a sand, that look to
100 be washed off the next tide.

74 **modesty** moderation   84 **out of fashion** odd   98 **estate** state, condition

438

BATES He hath not told his thought to the King?

KING No; nor it is not meet he should. For though I
speak it to you, I think the King is but a man, as
I am: the violet smells to him, as it doth to me; the
element shows to him, as it doth to me; all his   105
senses have but human conditions. His ceremonies laid by, in his nakedness he appears but a man;
and though his affections are higher mounted than
ours, yet when they stoop, they stoop with the like
wing: therefore, when he sees reason of fears, as   110
we do, his fears, out of doubt, be of the same relish as ours are. Yet, in reason, no man should possess him with any appearance of fear, lest he, by
showing it, should dishearten his army.

BATES He may show what outward courage he will;   115
but I believe, as cold a night as 'tis, he could wish
himself in Thames up to the neck; and so I would
he were, and I by him, at all adventures, so we
were quit here.

KING By my troth, I will speak my conscience of the   120
King: I think he would not wish himself anywhere
but where he is.

BATES Then I would he were here alone; so should he
be sure to be ransomed, and a many poor men's
lives saved.   125

KING I dare say you love him not so ill to wish him
here alone; howsoever you speak this to feel other
men's minds. Methinks I could not die anywhere so
contented as in the King's company, his cause being just and his quarrel honorable.   130

WILLIAMS That's more than we know.

BATES Ay, or more than we should seek after; for we

105 element shows sky appears   106 conditions characteristics   106-07 ceremonies accompaniments of royalty   109 stoop (used of a hawk swooping down
on its prey)   110 of for   118 at all adventures whatever the consequences
119 quit here done with this job   120 conscience inmost thought

know enough if we know we are the King's subjects: if his cause be wrong, our obedience to the
135   King wipes the crime of it out of us.

WILLIAMS But if the cause be not good, the King himself hath a heavy reckoning to make, when all those
legs and arms and heads, chopped off in a battle,
shall join together at the latter day and cry all,
140   "We died at such a place," some swearing, some
crying for a surgeon, some upon their wives left
poor behind them, some upon the debts they owe,
some upon their children rawly left. I am afeard
there are few die well that die in a battle; for how
145   can they charitably dispose of anything when blood
is their argument? Now, if these men do not die
well, it will be a black matter for the King that led
them to it; who to disobey, were against all proportion of subjection.

150   KING So, if a son that is by his father sent about
merchandise do sinfully miscarry upon the sea, the
imputation of his wickedness, by your rule, should
be imposed upon his father that sent him; or if a
servant, under his master's command transporting
155   a sum of money, be assailed by robbers and die in
many irreconciled iniquities, you may call the business of the master the author of the servant's
damnation. But this is not so. The king is not
bound to answer the particular endings of his sol-
160   diers, the father of his son, nor the master of his
servant; for they purpose not their death when they
purpose their services. Besides, there is no king, be
his cause never so spotless, if it come to the arbitrament of swords, can try it out with all unspotted
165   soldiers: some (peradventure) have on them the
guilt of premeditated and contrived murder; some,

143 rawly (1) unprepared (2) at immature age   144 well i.e., a Christian
death   148-49 proportion of subjection due relation of subject to monarch
151 sinfully miscarry perish in his sins   156 irreconciled not atoned for
159 answer render account for

of beguiling virgins with the broken seals of per-
jury; some, making the wars their bulwark, that
have before gored the gentle bosom of peace with
pillage and robbery. Now, if these men have de-   170
feated the law and outrun native punishment,
though they can outstrip men, they have no wings
to fly from God. War is his beadle, war is his vengeance; so that here men are punished for before-
breach of the King's laws in now the King's quar-   175
rel. Where they feared the death, they have borne
life away; and where they would be safe, they
perish. Then if they die unprovided, no more is
the King guilty of their damnation than he was
before guilty of those impieties for the which they   180
are now visited. Every subject's duty is the King's,
but every subject's soul is his own. Therefore should
every soldier in the wars do as every sick man in
his bed—wash every mote out of his conscience;
and dying so, death is to him advantage; or not dy-   185
ing, the time was blessedly lost wherein such preparation was gained; and in him that escapes, it were
not sin to think that, making God so free an offer,
He let him outlive that day, to see His greatness,
and to teach others how they should prepare.   190

WILLIAMS 'Tis certain, every man that dies ill, the ill
upon his own head; the King is not to answer it.

BATES I do not desire he should answer for me, and
yet I determine to fight lustily for him.

KING I myself heard the King say he would not be   195
ransomed.

WILLIAMS Ay, he said so, to make us fight cheerfully;
but when our throats are cut, he may be ransomed,
and we ne'er the wiser.

167 **seals** sealed covenants 168 **bulwark** defense (against pursuing justice)
171 **native** rightful 173 **beadle** parish officer for punishing petty offenders
174-75 **before-breach** previous breach 178 **unprovided** unprepared
181 **visited** punished 188 **free** complete, wholehearted

200 KING If I live to see it, I will never trust his word after.

WILLIAMS You pay him then! That's a perilous shot out of an elder-gun, that a poor and a private displeasure can do against a monarch! You may
205 as well go about to turn the sun to ice with fanning in his face with a peacock's feather. You'll never trust his word after! Come, 'tis a foolish saying.

KING Your reproof is something too round; I should be angry with you, if time were convenient.

210 WILLIAMS Let it be a quarrel between us, if you live.

KING I embrace it.

WILLIAMS How shall I know thee again?

KING Give me any gage of thine, and I will wear it in my bonnet. Then, if ever thou dar'st acknowl-
215 edge it, I will make it my quarrel.

WILLIAMS Here's my glove. Give me another of thine.

KING There.

WILLIAMS This will I also wear in my cap. If ever thou come to me and say, after tomorrow, "This is
220 my glove," by this hand, I will take thee a box on the ear.

KING If ever I live to see it, I will challenge it.

WILLIAMS Thou dar'st as well be hanged.

KING Well, I will do it, though I take thee in the
225 King's company.

WILLIAMS Keep thy word. Fare thee well.

BATES Be friends, you English fools, be friends! We have French quarrels enow, if you could tell how to reckon.

202 **pay him** pay him out   203 **elder-gun** popgun (child's toy)   203 **private** single and common man's   208 **round** plainspoken   213 **gage** pledge   220 **take** strike

KING Indeed the French may lay twenty French   230
crowns to one they will beat us, for they bear
them on their shoulders; but it is no English treason to cut French crowns, and tomorrow the King
himself will be a clipper.   *Exeunt Soldiers.*

"Upon the King! Let us our lives, our souls,   235
Our debts, our careful wives,
Our children, and our sins, lay on the King!"
We must bear all. O hard condition,
Twin-born with greatness, subject to the breath
Of every fool, whose sense no more can feel   240
But his own wringing! What infinite heart's-ease
Must kings neglect that private men enjoy!
And what have kings that privates have not too,
Save ceremony, save general ceremony?
And what art thou, thou idol Ceremony?   245
What kind of god art thou, that suffer'st more
Of mortal griefs than do thy worshippers?
What are thy rents? What are thy comings-in?
O Ceremony, show me but thy worth!
What is thy soul of adoration?   250
Art thou aught else but place, degree, and form,
Creating awe and fear in other men?
Wherein thou art less happy, being feared,
Than they in fearing.
What drink'st thou oft, instead of homage sweet,   255
But poisoned flattery? O, be sick, great greatness,
And bid thy ceremony give thee cure!
Thinks thou the fiery fever will go out
With titles blown from adulation?
Will it give place to flexure and low bending?   260
Canst thou, when thou command'st the beggar's
    knee,

231 **crowns** (1) coins, worth about six shillings each (2) heads 231-32 **for they bear them on their shoulders** i.e., the French can lay such bets because (1) they so outnumber the English (2) they are still alive 232-33 **treason** (it was a treasonable offense to debase the coinage by "clipping," or paring the edges of coins, to take their gold) 236 **careful** anxious 239 **breath** speech 241 **wringing** stomachache 250 **thy soul of adoration** the real nature of thy worship 251 **form** good order 259 **blown** inflated 260 **flexure** obsequious bowing

Command the health of it? No, thou proud dream,
That play'st so subtlely with a king's repose.
I am a king that find thee; and I know
265 'Tis not the balm, the scepter, and the ball,
The sword, the mace, the crown imperial,
The intertissued robe of gold and pearl,
The farcèd title running fore the king,
The throne he sits on, nor the tide of pomp
270 That beats upon the high shore of this world—
No, not all these, thrice-gorgeous ceremony,
Not all these, laid in bed majestical,
Can sleep so soundly as the wretched slave,
Who, with a body filled, and vacant mind,
275 Gets him to rest, crammed with distressful bread;
Never sees horrid night, the child of hell;
But like a lackey, from the rise to set,
Sweats in the eye of Phoebus, and all night
Sleeps in Elysium; next day after dawn,
280 Doth rise and help Hyperion to his horse;
And follows so the ever-running year
With profitable labor to his grave;
And but for ceremony, such a wretch,
Winding up days with toil and nights with sleep,
285 Had the forehand and vantage of a king.
The slave, a member of the country's peace,
Enjoys it; but in gross brain little wots
What watch the king keeps to maintain the peace,
Whose hours the peasant best advantages.

Enter Erpingham.

ERPINGHAM My lord, your nobles, jealous of your
290   absence,

264 **find** discover the true character of 265 **ball** orb 268 **farcèd** stuffed out with
pompous phrases 270 **high shore** exalted places 275 **distressful** gained by
hard toil 277 **lackey** footman who ran by the coach of his master
278 **Phoebus** sun-god 279 **Elysium** (in mythology, the abode of the blessed
after death) 280 **Hyperion** sun-god (more correctly, his father) 284 **Winding
up** passing 285 **forehand** upper hand 286 **member of** sharer in 287 **gross**
stupid 289 **the peasant best advantages** most benefit the peasant 290 **jealous** anxious

Seek through your camp to find you.

KING   Good old knight,
Collect them all together at my tent.
I'll be before thee.

ERPINGHAM   I shall do't, my lord.   *Exit.*

KING O God of battles, steel my soldiers' hearts,
Possess them not with fear! Take from them now   295
The sense of reck'ning, or th' opposèd numbers
Pluck their hearts from them. Not today, O Lord,
O, not today, think not upon the fault
My father made in compassing the crown!
I Richard's body have interrèd new,   300
And on it have bestowed more contrite tears
Than from it issued forcèd drops of blood.
Five hundred poor I have in yearly pay,
Who twice a day their withered hands hold up
Toward heaven, to pardon blood;   305
And I have built two chantries,
Where the sad and solemn priests sing still
For Richard's soul. More will I do:
Though all that I can do is nothing worth;
Since that my penitence comes after all,   310
Imploring pardon.

                   Enter Gloucester.

GLOUCESTER My liege!

KING My brother Gloucester's voice? Ay.
I know thy errand; I will go with thee.
The day, my friends, and all things stay for me.
                                        Exeunt.

298 the fault i.e., the deposition of Richard II, and the suggestion for his
subsequent murder

[Scene II. *France. The French camp.*]

Enter the Dauphin, Orleans, Rambures,
and Beaumont.

ORLEANS The sun doth gild our armor. Up, my lords!

DAUPHIN Montez à cheval! My horse! Varlet,
lacquais! Ha!

ORLEANS O brave spirit!

DAUPHIN Via! les eaux et la terre—

5   ORLEANS Rien puis? L'air et le feu.

DAUPHIN Ciel, cousin Orleans.

Enter Constable.

Now, my Lord Constable?

CONSTABLE Hark how our steeds for present service
neigh!

DAUPHIN Mount them, and make incision in their
hides,

10   That their hot blood may spin in English eyes
And dout them with superfluous courage, ha!

RAMBURES What, will you have them weep our
horses' blood?
How shall we then behold their natural tears?

Enter Messenger.

MESSENGER The English are embattailed, you French
peers.

IV.ii.2 **Montez à cheval!** To horse!   4 **Via! les eaux et la terre** begone, water
and earth (the Dauphin is still thinking of his horse; Orleans asks if he does not
wish to ride further, to "air and fire." The Dauphin replies, "Heaven")   10 **spin**
gush forth   11 **dout them with superfluous courage** extinguish them with
overflowing blood (the supposed source of courage)

CONSTABLE To horse, you gallant Princes! straight to
    horse!   15
Do but behold yond poor and starvèd band,
And your fair show shall suck away their souls,
Leaving them but the shales and husks of men.
There is not work enough for all our hands,
Scarce blood enough in all their sickly veins   20
To give each naked curtle ax a stain
That our French gallants shall today draw out
And sheathe for lack of sport. Let us but blow on
    them,
The vapor of our valor will o'erturn them.
'Tis positive 'gainst all exceptions, lords,   25
That our superfluous lackeys and our peasants,
Who in unnecessary action swarm
About our squares of battle, were enow
To purge this field of such a hilding foe,
Though we upon this mountain's basis by   30
Took stand for idle speculation:
But that our honors must not. What's to say?
A very little little let us do,
And all is done. Then let the trumpets sound
The tucket sonance and the note to mount;   35
For our approach shall so much dare the field
That England shall couch down in fear and yield.

Enter Grandpré.

GRANDPRÉ Why do you stay so long, my lords of
    France?
Yond island carrions, desperate of their bones,
Ill-favoredly become the morning field.   40
Their ragged curtains poorly are let loose,
And our air shakes them passing scornfully.
Big Mars seems bankrout in their beggared host,

---

17 **fair show** spectacular appearance   18 **shales** shells   21 **curtle ax** cutlass
(broad-cutting   sword)   25 **exceptions** objections   29 **hilding** worthless
31 **speculation** looking on   35 **sonance** sound   36 **dare** dazzle   37 **couch**
crouch   39 **carrions** skeletons   39 **desperate** careless, without hope of saving
41 **curtains** i.e., banners   42 **passing** extremely   43 **bankrout** bankrupt

And faintly through a rusty beaver peeps.
45   The horsemen sit like fixèd candlesticks
With torch-staves in their hand; and their poor
            jades
Lob down their heads, dropping the hides and
            hips,
The gum down roping from their pale-dead eyes,
And in their pale dull mouths the gimmaled bit
50   Lies foul with chawed grass, still and motionless;
And their executors, the knavish crows,
Fly o'er them all, impatient for their hour.
Description cannot suit itself in words
To demonstrate the life of such a battle
55   In life so lifeless as it shows itself.

CONSTABLE They have said their prayers, and they stay
      for death.

DAUPHIN Shall we go send them dinners, and fresh
      suits,
And give their fasting horses provender,
And after fight with them?

60   CONSTABLE I stay but for my guard. On to the field!
I will the banner from a trumpet take
And use it for my haste. Come, come away!
The sun is high, and we outwear the day.   *Exeunt.*

[Scene III. *France. The English camp.*]

Enter Gloucester, Bedford, Exeter, Erpingham
with all his Host, Salisbury, and Westmoreland.

GLOUCESTER Where is the King?

44 **beaver** face guard of a helmet   47 **Lob** droop   48 **roping** hanging like rope
49 **gimmaled** jointed   54 **the life of** to the life   61 **trumpet** trumpeter

BEDFORD The King himself is rode to view their
    battle.

WESTMORELAND Of fighting men they have full three-
    score thousand.

EXETER There's five to one; besides they all are fresh.

SALISBURY God's arm strike with us! 'Tis a fearful
    odds.   5
   God bye you, Princes all; I'll to my charge.
   If we no more meet, till we meet in heaven,
   Then joyfully, my noble Lord of Bedford,
   My dear Lord Gloucester, and my good Lord
    Exeter,
   And my kind kinsman, warriors all, adieu!   10

BEDFORD Farewell, good Salisbury, and good luck go
    with thee!

EXETER Farewell, kind lord. Fight valiantly today;
   And yet I do thee wrong to mind thee of it,
   For thou art framed of the firm truth of valor.
                          [*Exit Salisbury.*]

BEDFORD He is as full of valor as of kindness,   15
   Princely in both.

Enter the King.

WESTMORELAND   O that we now had here
   But one ten thousand of those men in England
   That do no work today!

KING   What's he that wishes so?
   My cousin Westmoreland? No, my fair cousin.
   If we are marked to die, we are enow   20
   To do our country loss; and if to live,
   The fewer men, the greater share of honor.
   God's will! I pray thee wish not one man more.
   By Jove, I am not covetous for gold,
   Nor care I who doth feed upon my cost;   25

IV.iii.2 **battle** battle array   **6 bye** be with

It earns me not if men my garments wear;
Such outward things dwell not in my desires:
But if it be a sin to covet honor,
I am the most offending soul alive.
30 No, faith, my coz, wish not a man from England.
God's peace! I would not lose so great an honor
As one man more methinks would share from me
For the best hope I have. O, do not wish one more!
Rather proclaim it, Westmoreland, through my
host,
35 That he which hath no stomach to this fight,
Let him depart; his passport shall be made,
And crowns for convoy put into his purse;
We would not die in that man's company
That fears his fellowship to die with us.
40 This day is called the Feast of Crispian:
He that outlives this day, and comes safe home,
Will stand a-tiptoe when this day is named,
And rouse him at the name of Crispian.
He that shall see this day, and live old age,
45 Will yearly on the vigil feast his neighbors
And say, "Tomorrow is Saint Crispian."
Then will he strip his sleeve and show his scars,
And say, "These wounds I had on Crispin's day."
Old men forget; yet all shall be forgot,
50 But he'll remember, with advantages,
What feats he did that day. Then shall our names,
Familiar in his mouth as household words—
Harry the King, Bedford and Exeter,
Warwick and Talbot, Salisbury and Gloucester—
55 Be in their flowing cups freshly rememb'red.
This story shall the good man teach his son;
And Crispin Crispian shall ne'er go by,
From this day to the ending of the world,
But we in it shall be rememberèd—

---

26 **earns** grieves 35 **stomach** inclination 39 **fellowship** participation
40 **Crispian** (the brothers, Crispin and Crispian [cf. line 57], fled from Rome
during the persecutions of Diocletian and supported and hid themselves as humble
shoemakers; they were martyred in A.D. 286) 50 **advantages** added luster

We few, we happy few, we band of brothers;   60
For he today that sheds his blood with me
Shall be my brother; be he ne'er so vile,
This day shall gentle his condition.
And gentlemen in England, now abed,
Shall think themselves accursed they were not here;   65
And hold their manhoods cheap whiles any speaks
That fought with us upon Saint Crispin's day.

Enter Salisbury.

SALISBURY My sovereign lord, bestow yourself with
    speed:
The French are bravely in their battles set
And will with all expedience charge on us.   70

KING All things are ready, if our minds be so.

WESTMORELAND Perish the man whose mind is back-
    ward now!

KING Thou dost not wish more help from England,
    coz?

WESTMORELAND God's will, my liege! would you and I
    alone,
Without more help, could fight this royal battle!   75

KING Why, now thou hast unwished five thousand
    men!
Which likes me better than to wish us one.
You know your places: God be with you all!

Tucket. Enter Montjoy.

MONTJOY Once more I come to know of thee, King
    Harry,
If for thy ransom thou wilt now compound,   80
Before thy most assurèd overthrow;
For certainly thou art so near the gulf

60-62 **brothers ... brother** (like the brother martyrs; see note, line 40)   62 **vile**
low of birth   63 **gentle his condition** ennoble his rank   69 **bravely** finely
arrayed   70 **expedience** expedition, speed   80 **compound** make terms

Thou needs must be englutted. Besides, in mercy,
The Constable desires thee thou wilt mind
85   Thy followers of repentance, that their souls
May make a peaceful and a sweet retire
From off these fields, where (wretches!) their poor
      bodies
Must lie and fester.

KING   Who hath sent thee now?

MONTJOY The Constable of France.

90   KING I pray thee bear my former answer back:
Bid them achieve me, and then sell my bones.
Good God, why should they mock poor fellows
      thus?
The man that once did sell the lion's skin
While the beast lived, was killed with hunting him.
95   A many of our bodies shall no doubt
Find native graves; upon the which, I trust,
Shall witness live in brass of this day's work.
And those that leave their valiant bones in France,
Dying like men, though buried in your dunghills,
They shall be famed; for there the sun shall greet
100   them
And draw their honors reeking up to heaven,
Leaving their earthly parts to choke your clime,
The smell whereof shall breed a plague in France.
Mark then abounding valor in our English:
105   That, being dead, like to the bullet's grazing,
Break out into a second course of mischief,
Killing in relapse of mortality.
Let me speak proudly. Tell the Constable,
We are but warriors for the working day:
110   Our gayness and our gilt are all besmirched
With rainy marching in the painful field.
There's not a piece of feather in our host—

83 **englutted**   swallowed 84 **mind** remind 86 **retire** retreat (sarcastic)
91 **achieve** kill 101 **reeking** exhaling, rising 107 **relapse of mortality**
(1) renewed deadliness (2) with a deadly rebound (?) 109 **for the working day**
i.e., (1) who mean business (2) who are not dressed in finery 111 **painful** arduous

Good argument, I hope, we will not fly—
And time hath worn us into slovenry.
But, by the mass, our hearts are in the trim;   115
And my poor soldiers tell me, yet ere night
They'll be in fresher robes, or they will pluck
The gay new coats o'er the French soldiers' heads
And turn them out of service. If they do this
(As, if God please, they shall), my ransom then   120
Will soon be levied. Herald, save thou thy labor.
Come thou no more for ransom, gentle herald;
They shall have none, I swear, but these my joints;
Which if they have as I will leave 'em them,
Shall yield them little, tell the Constable.   125

MONTJOY I shall, King Harry. And so fare thee well:
Thou never shalt hear herald any more.   *Exit.*

KING I fear thou wilt once more come again for a
ransom.

Enter York.

YORK My lord, most humbly on my knee I beg   130
The leading of the vaward.

KING Take it, brave York. Now, soldiers, march
away;
And how thou pleasest, God, dispose the day!
Exeunt.

---

115 **in the trim** (1) in fine fettle (2) fashionably attired   117 **in fresher robes**
i.e., in heavenly robes   119 **them** i.e., the soldiers   128-29 **I fear ... for a
ransom** (ironic)   131 **vaward** vanguard

[Scene IV. *France. The field of battle.*]

*Alarum. Excursions. Enter Pistol, French
Soldier, Boy.*

PISTOL Yield, cur!

FRENCH SOLDIER Je pense que vous êtes le gentilhomme
de bonne qualité.

PISTOL Qualtitie calmie custure me! Art thou a gen-
5   tleman? What is thy name? Discuss.

FRENCH SOLDIER O Seigneur Dieu!

PISTOL O Signieur Dew should be a gentleman.
Perpend my words, O Signieur Dew, and mark:
O Signieur Dew, thou diest on point of fox,
10   Except, O signieur, thou do give to me
Egregious ransom.

FRENCH SOLDIER O, prenez miséricorde, ayez pitié de
moi!

PISTOL Moy shall not serve; I will have forty moys,
15   Or I will fetch thy rim out at thy throat
In drops of crimson blood.

FRENCH SOLDIER Est-il impossible d'echapper la force
de ton bras?

IV.iv.2-3 **Je pense ... qualité** I think you are a gentleman of high rank
4 **Qualtitie calmie custure me** (possibly a corruption of an Irish refain to a
popular song: *"Calen o custure me,"* for "the girl from the [river] Suir")
8 **Perpend** consider 9 **fox** kind of sword 11 **Egregious** huge 12-13 **O,
prenez ... de moi** O, have mercy, take pity on me 14 **Moy** (no coin so called
existed; possibly a reference to the measure, about a bushel) 15 **rim** lining of the
stomach 17-18 **Est-il ... bras** is there no way to escape the strength of your arm
(the final "s" in *bras* was still sounded before a pause in Shakespeare's time)

PISTOL Brass, cur?
  Thou damnèd and luxurious mountain goat,   20
  Offer'st me brass?

FRENCH SOLDIER O, pardonnez-moi!

PISTOL Say'st thou me so? Is that a ton of moys?
  Come hither, boy; ask me this slave in French
  What is his name.   25

BOY Ecoutez: comment êtes-vous appelé?

FRENCH SOLDIER Monsieur le Fer.

BOY He says his name is Master Fer.

PISTOL Master Fer? I'll fer him, and firk him, and
  ferret him! Discuss the same in French unto him.   30

BOY I do not know the French for "fer," and "ferret,"
  and "firk."

PISTOL Bid him prepare, for I will cut his throat.

FRENCH SOLDIER Que dit-il, monsieur?

BOY Il me commande de vous dire que vous faites   35
  vous prêt; car ce soldat ici est disposé tout à cette
  heure de couper votre gorge.

PISTOL Owy, cuppele gorge, permafoy!
  Peasant, unless thou give me crowns, brave crowns;
  Or mangled shalt thou be by this my sword.   40

FRENCH SOLDIER O, je vous supplie, pour l'amour de
  Dieu, me pardonner! Je suis gentilhomme de bonne
  maison. Gardez ma vie, et je vous donnerai deux
  cents écus.

PISTOL What are his words?   45

---

20 **luxurious mountain goat** lustful wild lecher   29 **firk** (a euphemistic pronunciation of the common four-letter obscenity)   30 **ferret** go for, search out
34-37 **Que ... gorge** What does he say, sir? BOY He bids me tell you that you
must prepare yourself, for this soldier intends to cut your throat immediately
41-44 **O, je ... écus** O, I pray you, for the love of God, to pardon me. I am a
gentleman of good house. Preserve my life, and I will give you two hundred écus

BOY He prays you to save his life; he is a gentleman of a good house, and for his ransom he will give you two hundred crowns.

PISTOL Tell him my fury shall abate, and I
50   The crowns will take.

FRENCH SOLDIER Petit monsieur, que dit-il?

BOY Encore qu'il est contre son jurement de pardonner aucun prisonnier; néanmoins, pour les écus que vous l'avez promis, il est content de vous
55   donner la liberté, le franchisement.

FRENCH SOLDIER Sur mes genoux je vous donne mille remercîments; et je m'estime heureux que je suis tombé entre les mains d'un chevalier, je pense, le plus brave, vaillant, et très distingué seigneur
60   d'Angleterre.

PISTOL Expound unto me, boy.

BOY He gives you, upon his knees, a thousand thanks, and he esteems himself happy that he hath fall'n into the hands of one (as he thinks) the most
65   brave, valorous, and thrice-worthy signieur of England.

PISTOL As I suck blood, I will some mercy show!
Follow me.

BOY Suivez-vous le grand capitaine.
                    [*Exeunt Pistol and French Soldier.*]
70   I did never know so full a voice issue from so empty a heart; but the saying is true, "The empty vessel makes the greatest sound." Bardolph and Nym had ten times more valor than this roaring devil i' th' old play that everyone may pare his

52-60 Encore ... d' Angleterre I say again that it is against his oath to spare any prisoner; nevertheless, because of the écus you have promised him, he is willing to give you liberty, freedom. FRENCH SOLDIER On my knees I give you a thousand thanks; and I count myself happy that I have fallen into the hands of a knight, as I think, the bravest, most valiant, and eminent gentleman in England   71 empty cowardly

nails with a wooden dagger; and they are both   75
hanged; and so would this be, if he durst steal anything adventurously. I must stay with the lackeys
with the luggage of our camp—the French might
have a good prey of us, if he knew of it, for there
is none to guard it but boys.   *Exit.*   80

[Scene V. *France. Another part of the field.*]

Enter Constable, Orleans, Bourbon, Dauphin,
and Rambures.

CONSTABLE O diable!

ORLEANS O Seigneur! le jour est perdu, tout est
   perdu!

DAUPHIN Mort Dieu, ma vie! all is confounded, all!
   Reproach and everlasting shame
   Sits mocking in our plumes.   *A short alarum.*   5
   O méchante fortune! Do not run away.

CONSTABLE Why, all our ranks are broke.

DAUPHIN O perdurable shame! Let's stab ourselves.
   Be these the wretches that we played at dice for?

ORLEANS Is this the king we sent to for his ransom?   10

BOURBON Shame, and eternal shame, nothing but
      shame!
   Let us die in honor. Once more back again!
   And he that will not follow Bourbon now,
   Let him go hence, and with his cap in hand
   Like a base pander hold the chamber door   15

74-75 **pare his nails** clip his wings (a proverbial phrase)   75 **wooden dagger**
(weapon of the "Vice" in early Elizabethan plays)   IV.v.2 **O Seigneur ... perdu**
O sir, the day is lost, all is lost   6 **méchante** evil, spiteful   8 **perdurable** lasting

Whilst by a slave, no gentler than my dog,
His fairest daughter is contaminated.

CONSTABLE Disorder, that hath spoiled us, friend us
   now!
Let us on heaps go offer up our lives.

20 ORLEANS We are enow yet living in the field
To smother up the English in our throngs,
If any order might be thought upon.

BOURBON The devil take order now! I'll to the
   throng;
Let life be short, else shame will be too long.
                                   Exit [with others].

[Scene VI. *France. Another part of the field.*]

*Alarum. Enter the King and his Train, [Exeter,
and others,] with Prisoners.*

KING Well have we done, thrice-valiant countrymen,
But all's not done; yet keep the French the field.

EXETER The Duke of York commends him to your
   Majesty.

KING Lives he, good uncle? Thrice within this hour
5 I saw him down; thrice up again and fighting.
From helmet to the spur all blood he was.

EXETER In which array, brave soldier, doth he lie,
Larding the plain; and by his bloody side,
Yoke-fellow to his honor-owing wounds,
10 The noble Earl of Suffolk also lies.
Suffolk first died; and York, all haggled over,
Comes to him, where in gore he lay insteeped,

16 **gentler** (1) more noble (2) less rough   18 **spoiled** ruined   19 **on** in
IV.vi.8 **Larding** enriching   9 **owing** owning   11 **haggled** mangled

And takes him by the beard, kisses the gashes
That bloodily did yawn upon his face.
He cries aloud, "Tarry, my cousin Suffolk!   15
My soul shall thine keep company to heaven.
Tarry, sweet soul, for mine, then fly abreast;
As in this glorious and well-foughten field
We kept together in our chivalry!"
Upon these words I came, and cheered him up;   20
He smiled me in the face, raught me his hand,
And, with a feeble gripe, says, "Dear my lord,
Commend my service to my Sovereign."
So did he turn, and over Suffolk's neck
He threw his wounded arm, and kissed his lips;   25
And so, espoused to death, with blood he sealed
A testament of noble-ending love.
The pretty and sweet manner of it forced
Those waters from me which I would have stopped;
But I had not so much of man in me,   30
And all my mother came into mine eyes
And gave me up to tears.

KING   I blame you not;
For, hearing this, I must perforce compound
With mistful eyes, or they will issue too.   *Alarum.*
But hark, what new alarum is this same?   35
The French have reinforced their scattered men.
Then every soldier kill his prisoners!
Give the word through.   *Exit [with others].*

[Scene VII. *France. Another part of the field.*]

Enter Fluellen and Gower.

FLUELLEN Kill the poys and the luggage? 'Tis expressly
    against the law of arms; 'tis as arrant a piece of

21 **raught** reached   28 **pretty** lovely   31 **mother** inherited womanly feeling
33 **compound** come to terms

knavery, mark you now, as can be offert—in your
conscience, now, is it not?

5   GOWER 'Tis certain there's not a boy left alive, and
the cowardly rascals that ran from the battle ha'
done this slaughter; besides, they have burned and
carried away all that was in the King's tent; wherefore the King most worthily hath caused every sol-
10   dier to cut his prisoner's throat. O, 'tis a gallant
king!

FLUELLEN Ay, he was porn at Monmouth, Captain
Gower. What call you the town's name where Alexander the Pig was born?

15   GOWER Alexander the Great.

FLUELLEN Why, I pray you, is not "pig" great? The
pig, or the great, or the mighty, or the huge, or the
magnanimous, are all one reckonings, save the
phrase is a little variations.

20   GOWER I think Alexander the Great was born in
Macedon; his father was called Philip of Macedon,
as I take it.

FLUELLEN I think it is in Macedon where Alexander
is porn. I tell you, Captain, if you look in the maps
25   of the orld, I warrant you sall find, in the comparisons between Macedon and Monmouth, that
the situations, look you, is both alike. There is a
river in Macedon, and there is also moreover a
river at Monmouth. It is called Wye at Monmouth;
30   but it is out of my prains what is the name of the
other river. But 'tis all one; 'tis alike as my fingers
is to my fingers, and there is salmons in both. If
you mark Alexander's life well, Harry of Monmouth's life is come after it indifferent well, for
35   there is figures in all things. Alexander, God
knows, and you know, in his rages, and his furies,
and his wraths, and his cholers, and his moods,

IV.vii.19 variations (for "varied")   35 figures parallels

and his displeasures, and his indignations, and also
being a little intoxicates in his prains, did, in his
ales and his angers, look you, kill his best friend,   40
Cleitus.

GOWER Our King is not like him in that; he never
killed any of his friends.

FLUELLEN It is not well done, mark you now, to take
the tales out of my mouth, ere it is made and   45
finished. I speak but in the figures and comparisons
of it: as Alexander killed his friend Cleitus, being
in his ales and his cups, so also Harry Monmouth,
being in his right wits and his good judgments,
turned away the fat knight with the great-belly   50
doublet—he was full of jests, and gipes, and knaveries, and mocks; I have forgot his name.

GOWER Sir John Falstaff.

FLUELLEN That is he: I'll tell you there is good men
porn at Monmouth.   55

GOWER Here comes his Majesty.

Alarum. Enter King Harry and Bourbon,
[Warwick, Gloucester, Exeter, and others],
with Prisoners. Flourish.

KING I was not angry since I came to France
Until this instant. Take a trumpet, herald,
Ride thou unto the horsemen on yond hill:
If they will fight with us, bid them come down,   60
Or void the field: they do offend our sight.
If they'll do neither, we will come to them,
And make them skirr away, as swift as stones
Enforcèd from the old Assyrian slings.
Besides, we'll cut the throats of those we have,   65
And not a man of them that we shall take
Shall taste our mercy. Go and tell them so.

Enter Montjoy.

50 **great-belly** (1) styled with stuffed lining (2) large-sized (appropriate to
Falstaff's girth)   58 **trumpet** trumpeter   63 **skirr** scurry

EXETER Here comes the herald of the French, my
    liege.

GLOUCESTER His eyes are humbler than they used to be.

KING How now? What means this, herald? Know'st
70   thou not
    That I have fined these bones of mine for ransom?
    Com'st thou again for ransom?

HERALD   No, great King.
    I come to thee for charitable license,
    That we may wander o'er this bloody field
75   To book our dead, and then to bury them;
    To sort our nobles from our common men.
    For many of our princes (woe the while!)
    Lie drowned and soaked in mercenary blood;
    So do our vulgar drench their peasant limbs
80   In blood of princes, and their wounded steeds
    Fret fetlock-deep in gore, and with wild rage
    Yerk out their armèd heels at their dead masters,
    Killing them twice. O, give us leave, great King,
    To view the field in safety, and dispose
    Of their dead bodies!

85 KING   I tell thee truly, herald,
    I know not if the day be ours or no,
    For yet a many of your horsemen peer
    And gallop o'er the field.

HERALD   The day is yours.

KING Praised be God, and not our strength for it!
90   What is this castle called that stands hard by?

HERALD They call it Agincourt.

KING Then call we this the field of Agincourt,
    Fought on the day of Crispin Crispianus.

FLUELLEN Your grandfather of famous memory, an't

71 **fined** paid as a fine (he staked his bones, and having won he now has every
right to them) 75 **book** record 82 **Yerk** kick 87 **peer** are in sight
94 **grandfather** (in fact Edward III was Henry V's great grandfather)

please your Majesty, and your great-uncle Edward   95
the Plack Prince of Wales, as I have read in the
chronicles, fought a most prave pattle here in
France.

KING They did, Fluellen.

FLUELLEN Your Majesty says very true. If your Maj-   100
esties is rememb'red of it, the Welshmen did good
service in a garden where leeks did grow, wearing
leeks in their Monmouth caps; which your Majesty
know to this hour is an honorable badge of the
service; and I do believe your Majesty takes no   105
scorn to wear the leek upon Saint Tavy's day.

KING I wear it for memorable honor;
For I am Welsh, you know, good countryman.

FLUELLEN All the water in Wye cannot wash your
Majesty's Welsh plood out of your pody, I can tell   110
you that: God pless it, and preserve it, as long
as it pleases his Grace, and his Majesty too!

KING Thanks, good my countryman.

FLUELLEN By Jeshu, I am your Majesty's countryman,
I care not who know it! I will confess it to all the   115
orld; I need not to be ashamed of your Majesty,
praised be God, so long as your Majesty is an honest man.

KING God keep me so!

                    Enter Williams.
            Our heralds go with him;
Bring me just notice of the numbers dead   120
On both our parts.
                    [*Exeunt Heralds, Montjoy, and
                        others, including Gower.*]
            Call yonder fellow hither.

101-05 the Welshmen ... badge of service (the custom is usually said to
commemorate a British victory over the Saxons in A.D. 540)

EXETER Soldier, you must come to the King.

KING Soldier, why wear'st thou that glove in thy cap?

125 WILLIAMS And't please your Majesty, 'tis the gage of one that I should fight withal, if he be alive.

KING An Englishman?

WILLIAMS And't please your Majesty, a rascal that swaggered with me last night; who, if alive, and ever dare to challenge this glove, I have sworn to
130 take him a box o' th' ear; or if I can see my glove in his cap, which he swore, as he was a soldier, he would wear (if alive), I will strike it out soundly.

KING What think you, Captain Fluellen, is it fit this soldier keep his oath?

135 FLUELLEN He is a craven and a villain else, and't please your Majesty, in my conscience.

KING It may be his enemy is a gentleman of great sort, quite from the answer of his degree.

FLUELLEN Though he be as good a gentleman as the
140 devil is, as Lucifer and Belzebub himself, it is necessary, look your Grace, that he keep his vow and his oath. If he be perjured, see you now, his reputation is as arrant a villain and a Jack-sauce as ever his black shoe trod upon God's ground and
145 his earth, in my conscience, law!

KING Then keep thy vow, sirrah, when thou meet'st the fellow.

WILLIAMS So I will, my liege, as I live.

KING Who serv'st thou under?

150 WILLIAMS Under Captain Gower, my liege.

FLUELLEN Gower is a good captain, and is good knowledge and literatured in the wars.

130 **take** strike   138 **sort** rank   138 **from the answer of his degree** above that corresponding to his own rank   143 **Jack-sauce** saucy Jack   146 **sirrah** (term of address to an inferior)

KING Call him hither to me, soldier.

WILLIAMS I will, my liege.   *Exit.*

KING Here, Fluellen, wear thou this favor for me,   155
and stick it in thy cap; when Alençon and myself
were down together, I plucked this glove from his
helm. If any man challenge this, he is a friend to
Alençon and an enemy to our person. If thou encounter any such, apprehend him, and thou dost   160
me love.

FLUELLEN Your Grace doo's me as great honors as
can be desired in the hearts of his subjects. I would
fain see the man, that has but two legs, that shall
find himself aggriefed at this glove; that is all. But   165
I would fain see it once, and please God of his
grace that I might see.

KING Know'st thou Gower?

FLUELLEN He is my dear friend, and please you.

KING Pray thee go seek him, and bring him to my   170
tent.

FLUELLEN I will fetch him.   *Exit.*

KING My Lord of Warwick, and my brother
  Gloucester,
Follow Fluellen closely at the heels.
The glove which I have given him for a favor   175
May haply purchase him a box o' th' ear;
It is the soldier's. I by bargain should
Wear it myself. Follow, good cousin Warwick:
If that the soldier strike him—as I judge
By his blunt bearing, he will keep his word—   180
Some sudden mischief may arise of it;
For I do know Fluellen valiant,
And, touched with choler, hot as gunpowder,
And quickly will return an injury.
Follow, and see there be no harm between them.   185
Go you with me, uncle of Exeter.   *Exeunt.*

160 and if   183 touched fired

[Scene VIII. *France. Another part of the field.*]

Enter Gower and Williams.

WILLIAMS I warrant it is to knight you, Captain.

Enter Fluellen.

FLUELLEN God's will and his pleasure, Captain, I beseech you now, come apace to the King. There is
more good toward you peradventure than is in your
5   knowledge to dream of.

WILLIAMS Sir, know you this glove?

FLUELLEN Know the glove? I know the glove is a glove.

WILLIAMS I know this, and thus I challenge it.

Strikes him.

FLUELLEN 'Sblood, an arrant traitor as any's in the uni-
10   versal world, or in France, or in England!

GOWER How now, sir? You villain!

WILLIAMS Do you think I'll be forsworn?

FLUELLEN Stand away, Captain Gower. I will give treason his payment into plows, I warrant you.

15   WILLIAMS I am no traitor.

FLUELLEN That's a lie in thy throat. I charge you in
his Majesty's name apprehend him: he's a friend of
the Duke Alençon's.

Enter Warwick and Gloucester.

WARWICK How now, how now? What's the matter?

20   FLUELLEN My Lord of Warwick, here is (praised be
God for it!) a most contagious treason come to

466

light, look you, as you shall desire in a summer's
day. Here is his Majesty.

Enter King and Exeter.

KING How now? What's the matter?

FLUELLEN My liege, here is a villain and a traitor that,   25
look your Grace, has struck the glove which your
Majesty is take out of the helmet of Alençon.

WILLIAMS My liege, this was my glove, here is the
fellow of it; and he that I gave it to in change
promised to wear it in his cap. I promised to strike   30
him if he did. I met this man with my glove in his cap,
and I have been as good as my word.

FLUELLEN Your Majesty hear now, saving your Majesty's manhood, what an arrant, rascally, beggarly,
lousy knave it is! I hope your Majesty is pear me   35
testimony and witness, and will avouchment, that
this is the glove of Alençon that your Majesty is give
me, in your conscience, now.

KING Give me thy glove, soldier. Look, here is the
fellow of it.
'Twas I indeed thou promisèd'st to strike;   40
And thou hast given me most bitter terms.

FLUELLEN And please your Majesty, let his neck answer for it, if there is any martial law in the world.

KING How canst thou make me satisfaction?   45

WILLIAMS All offenses, my lord, come from the heart:
never came any from mine that might offend your
Majesty.

KING It was ourself thou didst abuse.

WILLIAMS Your Majesty came not like yourself: you   50
appeared to me but as a common man; witness the
night, your garments, your lowliness. And what
your Highness suffered under that shape, I

IV.viii.36 avouchment i.e., acknowledge

55   beseech you take it for your own fault, and not mine;
      for had you been as I took you for, I made no
      offense. Therefore I beseech your Highness pardon
      me.

      KING Here, uncle Exeter, fill this glove with crowns,
          And give it to this fellow. Keep it, fellow,
60   And wear it for an honor in thy cap,
          Till I do challenge it. Give him the crowns;
          And, Captain, you must needs be friends with him.

      FLUELLEN By this day and this light, the fellow has
          mettle enough in his belly. Hold, there is twelve
65   pence for you; and I pray you to serve God, and
          keep you out of prawls and prabbles, and quarrels
          and dissensions, and, I warrant you, it is the better
          for you.

      WILLIAMS I will none of your money.

70   FLUELLEN It is with a good will, I can tell you; it will
          serve you to mend your shoes. Come, wherefore
          should you be so pashful? Your shoes is not so
          good. 'Tis a good silling, I warrant you, or I will
          change it.

                  Enter [an English] Herald.

75   KING Now, herald, are the dead numb'red?

      HERALD Here is the number of the slaught'red French.

                  [*Gives a paper.*]

      KING What prisoners of good sort are taken, uncle?

      EXETER Charles Duke of Orleans, nephew to the King;
          John Duke of Bourbon and Lord Bouciqualt:
80   Of other lords and barons, knights and squires,
          Full fifteen hundred, besides common men.

      KING This note doth tell me of ten thousand French
          That in the field lie slain. Of princes, in this
              number,

77 sort rank

468

And nobles bearing banners, there lie dead
One hundred twenty-six; added to these,   85
Of knights, esquires, and gallant gentlemen,
Eight thousand and four hundred; of the which,
Five hundred were but yesterday dubbed knights.
So that in these ten thousand they have lost
There are but sixteen hundred mercenaries;   90
The rest are princes, barons, lords, knights, squires,
And gentlemen of blood and quality.
The names of those their nobles that lie dead:
Charles Delabreth, High Constable of France;
Jacques of Chatillon, Admiral of France;   95
The master of the crossbows, Lord Rambures;
Great Master of France, the brave Sir Guichard
    Dauphin;
John Duke of Alençon; Anthony Duke of Brabant,
The brother to the Duke of Burgundy;
And Edward Duke of Bar; of lusty earls,
Grandpré and Roussi, Faulconbridge and Foix,   100
Beaumont and Marle, Vaudemont and Lestrale.
Here was a royal fellowship of death!
Where is the number of our English dead?
                            [*Herald gives another paper.*]
Edward the Duke of York, the Earl of Suffolk,   105
Sir Richard Ketly, Davy Gam, esquire;
None else of name; and of all other men
But five-and twenty. O God, thy arm was here!
And not to us, but to thy arm alone,
Ascribe we all! When, without stratagem,   110
But in plain shock and even play of battle,
Was ever known so great and little loss
On one part and on th' other? Take it, God,
For it is none but thine!
EXETER   'Tis wonderful!
KING Come, go we in procession to the village;   115
    And be it death proclaimèd through our host
    To boast of this, or take that praise from God
    Which is His only.

84 **bearing banners** i.e., with coats of arms

FLUELLEN Is it not lawful, and please your Majesty,
120   to tell how many is killed?

KING Yes, Captain; but with this acknowledgment,
That God fought for us.

FLUELLEN Yes, my conscience, he did us great good.

KING Do we all holy rites:
125   Let there be sung "Non nobis" and "Te Deum,"
The dead with charity enclosed in clay,
And then to Calais; and to England then;
Where ne'er from France arrived more happy men.
                                                    Exeunt.

126 **charity** pious concern

ACT V

Enter Chorus.

Vouchsafe to those that have not read the story
That I may prompt them; and of such as have,
I humbly pray them to admit th' excuse
Of time, of numbers, and due course of things
Which cannot in their huge and proper life   5
Be here presented. Now we bear the King
Toward Calais. Grant him there. There seen,
Heave him away upon your wingèd thoughts
Athwart the sea. Behold the English beach
Pales in the flood, with men, wives, and boys,   10
Whose shouts and claps outvoice the deep-mouthed
      sea,
Which, like a mighty whiffler fore the King,
Seems to prepare his way. So let him land,
And solemnly see him set on to London.
So swift a pace hath thought that even now   15
You may imagine him upon Blackheath;
Where that his lords desire him to have borne
His bruisèd helmet and his bended sword
Before him through the city. He forbids it,
Being free from vainness and self-glorious pride;   20
Giving full trophy, signal, and ostent
Quite from himself, to God. But now behold,
In the quick forge and working house of thought,
How London doth pour out her citizens!

V Prologue   3 **th' excuse** i.e., the reasons why the actors rely on the chorus
rather than full stage enactment   10 **Pales in** encloses   12 **whiffler** officer who
clears the way for a procession   21 **trophy, signal, and ostent** token, sign, and
show (of victory)

25 The mayor and all his brethren in best sort—
Like to the senators of th' antique Rome,
With the plebeians swarming at their heels—
Go forth and fetch their conqu'ring Caesar in;
As, by a lower but by loving likelihood,
30 Were now the general of our gracious Empress
(As in good time he may) from Ireland coming,
Bringing rebellion broachèd on his sword,
How many would the peaceful city quit
To welcome him! Much more, and much more
  cause,
35 Did they this Harry. Now in London place him;
As yet the lamentation of the French
Invites the King of England's stay at home;
The Emperor's coming in behalf of France
To order peace between them; and omit
40 All the occurrences, whatever chanced,
Till Harry's back-return again to France.
There must we bring him; and myself have played
The interim, by rememb'ring you 'tis past.
Then brook abridgment; and your eyes advance,
45 After your thoughts, straight back again to France.

             Exit.

[Scene I. *France. The English camp.*]

Enter Fluellen and Gower.

GOWER Nay, that's right. But why wear you your leek
today? Saint Davy's day is past.

---

25 **sort** array 29 **loving** lovingly anticipated 30 **general** i.e., the Earl of Essex, who left to suppress rebellion in Ireland on March 27, 1599 (by the end of June 1599 Essex's failure became obvious) 32 **broachèd** impaled 37 **Invites** i.e., gives excuse and safety for 38 **The Emperor's coming** (the Holy Roman Emperor came to England, May 1, 1416) 42 **played** filled up, represented
44 **brook** tolerate

FLUELLEN There is occasions and causes why and
wherefore in all things. I will tell you ass my friend,
Captain Gower: the rascally, scauld, beggarly,   5
lousy, pragging knave, Pistol—which you and yourself, and all the world, know to be no petter than
a fellow, look you now, of no merits—he is come
to me, and prings me pread and salt yesterday, look
you, and bid me eat my leek. It was in a place   10
where I could not breed no contention with him;
but I will be so bold as to wear it in my cap till
I see him once again, and then I will tell him a
little piece of my desires.

Enter Pistol.

GOWER Why, here he comes, swelling like a turkey   15
cock.

FLUELLEN 'Tis no matter for his swellings nor his turkey cocks. God pless you, Aunchient Pistol! You
scurvy, lousy knave, God pless you!

PISTOL Ha, art thou bedlam? Dost thou thirst, base
Trojan,   20
To have me fold up Parca's fatal web?
Hence! I am qualmish at the smell of leek.

FLUELLEN I peseech you heartily, scurvy, lousy knave,
at my desires, and my requests, and my petitions,
to eat, look you, this leek. Because, look you, you   25
do not love it, nor your affections, and your appetites and your disgestions doo's not agree with
it, I would desire you to eat it.

PISTOL Not for Cadwallader and all his goats.

FLUELLEN There is one goat for you. (*Strikes him.*)   30
Will you be so good, scauld knave, as eat it?

V.i.5 **scauld** scurvy   20 **bedlam** mad   20 **Trojan** boon companion, dissolute
adventurer (slang)   21 **Parca** i.e., Parcae, the three Fates, said to spin the web of
man's destiny (they cut the thread when the pattern was completed, so ending a
life)   29 **Cadwallader** the last British king   29 **goats** (inhabitants of the Welsh
mountains and, hence, used contemptuously of Welshmen)

PISTOL Base Trojan, thou shalt die!

FLUELLEN You say very true, scauld knave, when
God's will is. I will desire you to live in the mean-
35   time, and eat your victuals. Come, there is sauce
for it. [*Strikes him.*] You called me yesterday
mountain-squire; but I will make you today a
squire of low degree. I pray you fall to; if you
can mock a leek, you can eat a leek.

40   GOWER Enough, Captain, you have astonished him.

FLUELLEN I say I will make him eat some part of my
leek, or I will peat his pate four days.—Bite, I pray
you; it is good for your green wound, and your
ploody coxcomb.

45   PISTOL Must I bite?

FLUELLEN Yes, certainly, and out of doubt, and out of
question too, and ambiguities.

PISTOL By this leek, I will most horribly revenge—I
eat and eat—I swear—

50   FLUELLEN Eat, I pray you. Will you have some more
sauce to your leek? There is not enough leek to
swear by.

PISTOL Quiet thy cudgel, thou dost see I eat.

FLUELLEN Much good do you, scauld knave, heartily.
55   Nay, pray you throw none away, the skin is good
for your broken coxcomb. When you take occasions to see leeks hereafter, I pray you mock at
'em; that is all.

PISTOL Good.

---

37 **mountain-squire** owner of worthless land (term of comtempt)   38 **squire of
low degree** (reference to the title of a medieval metrical romance; also a quibble
on "low," as opposed to "mountain," line 37)   40 **astonished** stunned,
dismayed   43 **green** raw   44 **coxcomb** (1) cap worn by a fool (2) head
(ludicrously)   48-49 **By this leek ... I swear** (Pistol changes his tune as his view
of the situation changes; Fluellen probably cudgels him on "revenge" and "swear"
and is placated while he is actually eating)   54 **do** i.e., may it do you

FLUELLEN Ay, leeks is good. Hold you, there is a groat   60
to heal your pate.

PISTOL Me a groat?

FLUELLEN Yes verily, and in truth you shall take it,
or I have another leek in my pocket which you
shall eat.   65

PISTOL I take thy groat in earnest of revenge.

FLUELLEN If I owe you anything, I will pay you in
cudgels; you shall be a woodmonger, and buy nothing of me but cudgels. God bye you, and keep
you, and heal your pate.   *Exit*.   70

PISTOL All hell shall stir for this!

GOWER Go, go; you are a counterfeit cowardly knave.
Will you mock at an ancient tradition, begun upon
an honorable respect, and worn as a memorable
trophy of predeceased valor, and dare not avouch   75
in your deeds any of your words? I have seen you
gleeking and galling at this gentleman twice or
thrice. You thought, because he could not speak
English in the native garb, he could not therefore
handle an English cudgel. You find it otherwise,   80
and henceforth let a Welsh correction teach you a
good English condition. Fare ye well.   *Exit*.

PISTOL Doth Fortune play the huswife with me now?
News have I, that my Doll is dead i' th' spital
Of malady of France;   85
And there my rendezvous is quite cut off.
Old I do wax, and from my weary limbs
Honor is cudgeled. Well, bawd I'll turn,

---

66 in earnest as a token   69 bye be with   74 respect regard, consideration
77 gleeking and galling gibing and annoying   83 huswife hussy   84 my Doll
i.e., Doll Tearsheet (said to be in the spital—i.e., hospital—in II.i.77-80; a change
or confusion in Shakespeare's mind must have been involved here, for Pistol's wife
was Nell Quickly; or, perhaps, for "Doll" the text should read "Nell"—other
proper names are confused in the Folio)   85 malady of France venereal
disease   86 rendezvous refuge, retreat

And something lean to cutpurse of quick hand.
90 To England will I steal, and there I'll steal;
And patches will I get unto these cudgeled scars,
And swear I got them in the Gallia wars.   *Exit.*

[Scene II. *France. An apartment in the French
King's palace.*]

*Enter, at one door, King Henry, Exeter, Bedford,
[Gloucester,] Warwick, [Westmoreland,] and other
Lords; at another, Queen Isabel, the [French] King, the
Duke of Burgundy, [the Princess Katherine, Alice,] and
other French.*

KING HENRY Peace to this meeting, wherefore we are
met!
Unto our brother France and to our sister
Health and fair time of day; joy and good wishes
To our most fair and princely cousin Katherine;
5   And as a branch and member of this royalty,
By whom this great assembly is contrived,
We do salute you, Duke of Burgundy;
And, princes French, and peers, health to you all!

FRANCE Right joyous are we to behold your face,
10   Most worthy brother England; fairly met;
So are you, princes English, every one.

QUEEN So happy be the issue, brother England,
Of this good day and of this gracious meeting
As we are now glad to behold your eyes—
15   Your eyes which hitherto have borne in them,
Against the French that met them in their bent,

89 **something lean** to have a leaning towards the profession of V.ii.1 **Peace to this meeting, wherefore we are met** peace, for which we are here met, be to this meeting   16 **bent** direction

The fatal balls of murdering basilisks.
The venom of such looks, we fairly hope,
Have lost their quality, and that this day
Shall change all griefs and quarrels into love.   20

KING HENRY To cry amen to that, thus we appear.

QUEEN You English princes all, I do salute you.

BURGUNDY My duty to you both, on equal love,
  Great Kings of France and England! That I have
    labored
  With all my wits, my pains, and strong endeavors   25
  To bring your most imperial Majesties
  Unto this bar and royal interview,
  Your Mightiness on both parts best can witness.
  Since, then, my office hath so far prevailed
  That, face to face and royal eye to eye,   30
  You have congreeted, let it not disgrace me
  If I demand before this royal view,
  What rub, or what impediment there is
  Why that the naked, poor, and mangled Peace,
  Dear nurse of arts, plenties, and joyful births,   35
  Should not, in this best garden of the world,
  Our fertile France, put up her lovely visage.
  Alas, she hath from France too long been chased!
  And all her husbandry doth lie on heaps,
  Corrupting in it own fertility.   40
  Her vine, the merry cheerer of the heart,
  Unprunèd dies; her hedges even-pleached,
  Like prisoners wildly overgrown with hair,
  Put forth disordered twigs; her fallow leas
  The darnel, hemlock, and rank fumitory   45
  Doth root upon, while that the coulter rusts
  That should deracinate such savagery;
  The even mead, that erst brought sweetly forth

17 **basilisks** (1) fabulous reptiles, said to kill with their breath and look (2) large
cannon   23 **on** of   27 **bar** place for judgment   31 **congreeted** exchanged
greetings   33 **rub** obstacle   39 **on heaps** fallen in ruin   40 **it** its   42 **even-
pleached** neatly interwoven and trimmed   44 **fallow leas** unsown arable land
45 **darnel** ryegrass (injurious to growing grain)   46 **coulter** knife that precedes
the ploughshare   47 **deracinate** root up

The freckled cowslip, burnet, and green clover,
50 Wanting the scythe, all uncorrected, rank,
Conceives by idleness, and nothing teems
But hateful docks, rough thistles, kecksies, burrs,
Losing both beauty and utility.
And all our vineyards, fallows, meads, and hedges,
55 Defective in their natures, grow to wildness,
Even so our houses, and ourselves, and children,
Have lost, or do not learn for want of time,
The sciences that should become our country;
But grow like savages—as soldiers will,
60 That nothing do but meditate on blood—
To swearing, and stern looks, diffused attire,
And everything that seems unnatural.
Which to reduce into our former favor
You are assembled; and my speech entreats
65 That I may know the let why gentle Peace
Should not expel these inconveniences,
And bless us with her former qualities.

KING HENRY If, Duke of Burgundy, you would the
        peace,
Whose want gives growth to th' imperfections
70 Which you have cited, you must buy that peace
With full accord to all our just demands;
Whose tenors and particular effects
You have, enscheduled briefly, in your hands.

BURGUNDY The King hath heard them; to the which
        as yet
There is no answer made.

75 KING HENRY   Well then, the peace,
Which you before so urged, lies in his answer.

FRANCE I have but with a cursitory eye

---

51 **Conceives by idleness** (cf. proverb, "Idleness is the mother of vice")
51 **teems** is brought forth   52 **kecksies** umbelliferous plants (e.g., cow parsley)
61 **diffused** disorderly   63 **reduce** restore   63 **favor** appearance   65 **let**
hindrance   68 **would** desire   77 **cursitory** cursory

O'erglanced the articles. Pleaseth your Grace
To appoint some of your Council presently
To sit with us once more, with better heed   80
To resurvey them, we will suddenly
Pass our accept and peremptory answer.

KING HENRY Brother, we shall. Go, uncle Exeter,
And brother Clarence, and you, brother Gloucester,
Warwick, and Huntingdon—go with the King,   85
And take with you free power to ratify,
Augment, or alter, as your wisdoms best
Shall see advantageable for our dignity,
Anything in or out of our demands,
And we'll consign thereto. Will you, fair sister,   90
Go with the princes or stay here with us?

QUEEN Our gracious brother, I will go with them;
Haply a woman's voice may do some good
When articles too nicely urged be stood on.

KING HENRY Yet leave our cousin Katherine here
    with us.   95
She is our capital demand, comprised
Within the fore-rank of our articles.

QUEEN She hath good leave.
                    Exeunt omnes. Manet King [Henry] and
                    Katherine [with the Gentlewoman Alice].

KING HENRY   Fair Katherine, and most fair!
Will you vouchsafe to teach a soldier terms
Such as will enter at a lady's ear,   100
And plead his love suit to her gentle heart?

KATHERINE Your Majesty shall mock at me; I cannot
    speak your England.

KING HENRY O fair Katherine, if you will love me

81-82 suddenly/Pass our accept and peremptory answer in very short time
deliver our accepted and conclusive answer   90 consign agree   94 nicely
minutely, scrupulously   94 stood insisted   98s.d. Manet remains (in Elizabethan stage directions the Latin third person singular commonly occurs with a
plural subject)

105 soundly with your French heart, I will be glad to
hear you confess it brokenly with your English
tongue. Do you like me, Kate?

KATHERINE Pardonnez-moi, I cannot tell wat is "like
me."

110 KING HENRY An angel is like you, Kate, and you are
like an angel.

KATHERINE Que dit-il? Que je suis semblable à les
anges?

ALICE Oui, vraiment, sauf votre Grace, ainsi dit-il.

115 KING HENRY I said so, dear Katherine, and I must not
blush to affirm it.

KATHERINE O bon Dieu! les langues des hommes sont
pleines de tromperies.

KING HENRY What says she, fair one? That the
120 tongues of men are full of deceits?

ALICE Oui, dat de tongues of de mans is be full of
deceits:—dat is de Princesse.

KING HENRY The Princess is the better Englishwoman. I' faith, Kate, my wooing is fit for thy
125 understanding; I am glad thou canst speak no better
English, for if thou couldst, thou wouldst find me
such a plain king that thou wouldst think I had sold
my farm to buy my crown. I know no ways to
mince it in love, but directly to say, "I love you."
130 Then, if you urge me farther than to say, "Do you
in faith?" I wear out my suit. Give me your answer, i' faith, do; and so clap hands, and a bargain. How say you, lady?

KATHERINE Sauf votre honneur, me understand well.

112-14 Que ... dit-il what does he say? That I am like the angels? ALICE Yes,
truly, save your Grace, he says so   122 dat is de Princesse that is what the
Princess says   123-24 is the better Englishwoman (because she sees through
flattery)   129 mince it speak prettily   131 wear out my suit spend all my
courtship   132 clap hands shake hands (in token of a bargain)

KING HENRY Marry, if you would put me to verses, or   135
to dance for your sake, Kate, why, you undid me.
For the one I have neither words nor measure;
and for the other, I have no strength in measure,
yet a reasonable measure in strength. If I could
win a lady at leapfrog, or by vaulting into my sad-   140
dle with my armor on my back, under the correction of bragging be it spoken, I should quickly leap
into a wife. Or if I might buffet for my love, or
bound my horse for her favors, I could lay on like
a butcher, and sit like a jackanapes, never off.   145
But, before God, Kate, I cannot look greenly, nor
gasp out my eloquence, nor I have no cunning in
protestation: only downright oaths, which I never
use till urged, nor never break for urging. If thou
canst love a fellow of this temper, Kate, whose face   150
is not worth sunburning, that never looks in his
glass for love of anything he sees there, let thine
eye be thy cook. I speak to thee plain soldier: if
thou canst love me for this, take me; if not, to say
to thee that I shall die, is true—but for thy love,   155
by the Lord, no; yet I love thee too. And while
thou liv'st, dear Kate, take a fellow of plain and
uncoined constancy, for he perforce must do thee
right, because he hath not the gift to woo in other
places; for these fellows of infinite tongue, that can   160
rhyme themselves into ladies' favors, they do always reason themselves out again. What! A speaker
is but a prater; a rhyme is but a ballad; a good
leg will fall, a straight back will stoop, a black
beard will turn white, a curled pate will grow bald,   165
a fair face will wither, a full eye will wax hollow:
but a good heart, Kate, is the sun and the moon,

137 **measure** meter 138 **strength in measure** ability for dancing 140-43 **win
a lady at leapfrog ... leap into a wife** (to "leap" and "vault" were common in
bawdy senses, and clearly used so by Shakespeare in other plays) 145 **jackanapes** ape 146 **greenly** foolishly, sheepishly 151 **not worth sunburning** so
ugly that the sun cannot make it more so 152-53 **thine eye be thy cook** your
eye present me more attractively than I would be without its help 158 **uncoined**
(1) not yet current (2) unalloyed 163 **ballad** (the most popular and unsophisti-
cated verse form)

or rather, the sun, and not the moon, for it shines
bright and never changes, but keeps his course
170   truly. If thou would have such a one, take me; and
take me, take a soldier; take a soldier, take a king.
And what say'st thou then to my love? Speak, my
fair—and fairly, I pray thee.

KATHERINE Is it possible dat I sould love de ennemie
175   of France?

KING HENRY No, it is not possible you should love
the enemy of France, Kate; but in loving me you
should love the friend of France: for I love France
so well, that I will not part with a village of it—I
180   will have it all mine. And, Kate, when France is
mine and I am yours, then yours is France, and
you are mine.

KATHERINE I cannot tell wat is dat.

KING HENRY No, Kate? I will tell thee in French,
185   which I am sure will hang upon my tongue like a
new-married wife about her husband's neck, hardly
to be shook off. Je quand sur le possession de
France, et quand vous avez le possession de moi
(let me see, what then? Saint Denis be my
190   speed!), donc votre est France, et vous êtes
mienne. It is as easy for me, Kate, to conquer the
kingdom as to speak so much more French; I shall
never move thee in French, unless it be to laugh
at me.

195   KATHERINE Sauf votre honneur, le Français que vous
parlez, il est meilleur que l'Anglais lequel je parle.

KING HENRY No, faith, is't not, Kate. But thy speaking
of my tongue, and I thine, most truly-falsely, must
needs be granted to be much at one. But, Kate,

189 **Saint Denis** patron saint of France   187-91 **Je quand ... mienne** when I
have possession of France, and when you have possession of me ... then France is
yours, and you are mine   195-96 **Sauf ... parle** save your honor, the French that
you speak is better than the English that I speak   198 **truly-falsely** in good faith
but bad French and English   199 **at one** (1) alike (2) in sympathy

dost thou understand thus much English? Canst   200
thou love me?

KATHERINE I cannot tell.

KING HENRY Can any of your neighbors tell, Kate?
I'll ask them. Come, I know thou lovest me; and
at night, when you come into your closet, you'll   205
question this gentlewoman about me; and I know,
Kate, you will to her dispraise those parts in me
that you love with your heart; but, good Kate,
mock me mercifully, the rather, gentle Princess,
because I love thee cruelly. If ever thou beest mine,   210
Kate—as I have a saving faith within me tells me
thou shalt—I get thee with scambling, and thou
must therefore needs prove a good soldier-breeder.
Shall not thou and I, between Saint Denis and Saint
George, compound a boy, half French, half Eng-   215
lish, that shall go to Constantinople, and take the
Turk by the beard? Shall we not? What say'st thou,
my fair flower-de-luce?

KATHERINE I do not know dat.

KING HENRY No; 'tis hereafter to know, but now to   220
promise. Do but now promise, Kate, you will endeavor for your French part of such a boy; and for
my English moiety take the word of a king, and a
bachelor. How answer you, la plus belle Katherine
du monde, mon très cher et devin déesse?   225

KATHERINE Your majestee ave fausse French enough
to deceive de most sage demoiselle dat is en France.

KING HENRY Now, fie upon my false French! By mine
honor in true English, I love thee, Kate; by
which honor I dare not swear thou lovest me, yet   230
my blood begins to flatter me that thou dost,

202 I cannot tell (1) I don't know (2) I cannot speak   205 closet private
chamber   212 scambling scrimmaging   216 Constantinople (taken by the
Turks in 1453, thirty-one years after Henry's death; throughout the sixteenth
century Christian princes aspired to crusade against the Turks)   224-25 la plus
... déesse the fairest Katherine in the world, my dearest and divine goddess

notwithstanding the poor and untempering effect of
my visage. Now beshrew my father's ambition! He
was thinking of civil wars when he got me, therefore
235   was I created with a stubborn outside, with an
aspect of iron, that when I come to woo ladies, I
fright them. But in faith, Kate, the elder I wax the
better I shall appear. My comfort is that old age,
that ill layer-up of beauty, can do no more spoil
240   upon my face. Thou hast me, if thou hast me, at
the worst; and thou shalt wear me, if thou wear
me, better and better; and therefore tell me, most
fair Katherine, will you have me? Put off your
maiden blushes; avouch the thoughts of your heart
245   with the looks of an empress; take me by the hand,
and say, "Harry of England, I am thine!" which
word thou shalt no sooner bless mine ear withal, but
I will tell thee aloud, "England is thine, Ireland is
thine, France is thine, and Henry Plantagenet is
250   thine"; who, though I speak it before his face, if
he be not fellow with the best king, thou shalt find
the best king of good fellows. Come, your answer
in broken music; for thy voice is music, and thy
English broken; therefore, Queen of all, Katherine,
255   break thy mind to me in broken English: Wilt thou
have me?

KATHERINE Dat is as it shall please de Roi mon père.

KING HENRY Nay, it will please him well, Kate; it
shall please him, Kate.

260   KATHERINE Den it sall also content me.

KING HENRY Upon that I kiss your hand, and I call
you my queen.

KATHERINE Laissez, mon seigneur, laissez, laissez! Ma
foi, je ne veux point que vous abaissiez votre
265   grandeur en baisant la main d'une de votre

232 untempering without softening influence   239 ill layer-up ill preserver,
wrinkler   241-42 if thou wear me if you possess me   253 broken arranged for
parts

seigneurie indigne serviteur. Excusez-moi, je vous supplie, mon très puissant seigneur.

KING HENRY Then I will kiss your lips, Kate.

KATHERINE Les dames et demoiselles pour être baisées devant leur noces, il n'est pas la coutume de 270 France.

KING HENRY Madam my interpreter, what says she?

ALICE Dat it is not be de fashon pour le ladies of France—I cannot tell wat is "baiser" en Anglish.

KING HENRY To kiss.   275

ALICE Your Majestee entendre bettre que moi.

KING HENRY It is not a fashion for the maids in France to kiss before they are married, would she say?

ALICE Oui, vraiment.   280

KING HENRY O Kate, nice customs cursy to great kings. Dear Kate, you and I cannot be confined within the weak list of a country's fashion: we are the makers of manners, Kate; and the liberty that follows our places stops the mouth of all find- 285 faults, as I will do yours for upholding the nice fashion of your country in denying me a kiss. Therefore patiently, and yielding. [*Kisses her.*] You have witchcraft in your lips, Kate: there is more eloquence in a sugar touch of them than in the 290 tongues of the French Council; and they should sooner persuade Harry of England than a general petition of monarchs. Here comes your father.

Enter the French Power and the English Lords.

263-67 Laissez ... seigneur stop, my lord, stop, stop! Indeed, I do not wish to lower your greatness by kissing the hand of your unworthy servant. Excuse me, I beg you, my most powerful lord   269-71 Les dames ... France it is not customary in France for ladies and young girls to be kissed before their marriage   281 nice fastidious   281 cursy curtsy, bow   283 list limit, bound 285 follows our places is the consequence of our royal status

BURGUNDY God save your Majesty! My royal cousin,
295   Teach you our princess English?

KING HENRY I would have her learn, my fair cousin,
how perfectly I love her, and that is good English.

BURGUNDY Is she not apt?

KING HENRY Our tongue is rough, coz, and my con-
300   dition is not smooth; so that, having neither the
voice nor the heart of flattery about me, I cannot
so conjure up the spirit of love in her that he will
appear in his true likeness.

BURGUNDY Pardon the frankness of my mirth if I an-
305   swer you for that. If you would conjure in her, you
must make a circle; if conjure up love in her in his
true likeness, he must appear naked and blind. Can
you blame her then, being a maid yet rosed over
with the virgin crimson of modesty, if she deny the
310   appearance of a naked blind boy in her naked
seeing self? It were, my lord, a hard condition for
a maid to consign to.

KING HENRY Yet they do wink and yield, as love is
blind and enforces.

315 BURGUNDY They are then excused, my lord, when
they see not what they do.

KING HENRY Then, good my lord, teach your cousin
to consent winking.

BURGUNDY I will wink on her to consent, my lord,
320   if you will teach her to know my meaning; for
maids well summered, and warm kept, are like flies
at Bartholomew-tide, blind, though they have their
eyes; and then they will endure handling which
before would not abide looking on.

299-300 condition temperament   310 naked unprotected   311 condition
(1) stipulation (2) state of being   312 consign agree   313 wink shut their eyes
319 wink give a significant look   322 Bartholomew-tide (St. Bartholomew's
day is August 24th; by this time flies have become torpid)

KING HENRY This moral ties me over to time and a   325
    hot summer; and so I shall catch the fly, your
    cousin, in the latter end, and she must be blind too.

BURGUNDY As love is, my lord, before it loves.

KING HENRY It is so; and you may, some of you,
    thank love for my blindness, who cannot see many   330
    a fair French city for one fair French maid that
    stands in my way.

FRANCE Yes, my lord, you see them perspectively,
    the cities turned into a maid; for they are all girdled
    with maiden walls that war hath never ent'red.   335

KING HENRY Shall Kate be my wife?

FRANCE So please you.

KING HENRY I am content, so the maiden cities you
    talk of may wait on her; so the maid that stood in
    the way for my wish shall show me the way to my   340
    will.

FRANCE We have consented to all terms of reason.

KING HENRY Is't so, my lords of England?

WESTMORELAND The King hath granted every article:
    His daughter first; and in sequel, all,   345
    According to their firm proposèd natures.

EXETER Only he hath not yet subscribed this: Where
    your Majesty demands that the King of France,
    having any occasion to write for matter of grant,
    shall name your Highness in this form, and with   350
    this addition, in French, "Notre très cher fils Henri,
    Roi d'Angleterre, Héritier de France"; and thus in
    Latin, "Praeclarissimus filius noster Henricus, Rex
    Angliae, et Haeres Franciae."

---

325 **ties me over** restricts me   333 **perspectively** as through an optical glass
giving strange, displaced or broken images   341 **will** (1) desire (2) sexual desire
349 **grant** granting lands or titles

355 FRANCE Nor this I have not, brother, so denied
       But your request shall make me let it pass.

KING HENRY I pray you then, in love and dear
       alliance,
       Let that one article rank with the rest,
       And thereupon give me your daughter.

FRANCE Take her, fair son, and from her blood raise
360   up
       Issue to me, that the contending kingdoms
       Of France and England, whose very shores look
       pale
       With envy of each other's happiness,
       May cease their hatred, and this dear conjunction
365   Plant neighborhood and Christian-like accord
       In their sweet bosoms; that never war advance
       His bleeding sword 'twixt England and fair France.

LORDS Amen!

KING HENRY Now, welcome, Kate; and bear me
       witness all,
370   That here I kiss her as my sovereign Queen.

                                                    Flourish.

QUEEN God, the best maker of all marriages,
       Combine your hearts in one, your realms in one!
       As man and wife, being two, are one in love,
       So be there 'twixt your kingdoms such a spousal
375   That never may ill office, or fell jealousy,
       Which troubles oft the bed of blessed marriage,
       Thrust in between the paction of these kingdoms
       To make divorce of their incorporate league;
       That English may as French, French Englishmen,
380   Receive each other! God speak this Amen!

ALL Amen!

362 **pale** (an allusion to the white cliffs bordering the English Channel)
364 **dear** (1) significant (2) loving (3) dearly bought (?) 365 **neighborhood**
neighborliness 375 **office** performance of a function or duty 377 **paction**
compact 378 **incorporate** united in one body (appropriate to both marriage and
peace settlement)

KING HENRY Prepare we for our marriage; on which
    day,
My Lord of Burgundy, we'll take your oath,
And all the peers', for surety of our leagues.
Then shall I swear to Kate, and you to me,   385
And may our oaths well kept and prosp'rous be!
                                        Sennet. Exeunt.

[EPILOGUE]

Enter Chorus.

Thus far with rough, and all-unable pen,
    Our bending author hath pursued the story,
In little room confining mighty men,
    Mangling by starts the full course of their glory.
Small time: but in that small, most greatly lived   5
    This star of England. Fortune made his sword;
By which, the world's best garden he achieved;
    And of it left his son imperial lord.
Henry the Sixth, in infant bands crowned King
    Of France and England, did this king succeed;   10
Whose state so many had the managing,
    That they lost France, and made his England
        bleed:
Which oft our stage hath shown; and for their sake,
In your fair minds let this acceptance take.

FINIS

386s.d. **Sennet** trumpet call for the departure of a procession Epilogue
2 **bending** (1) bending under the weight of his task (2) "stooping to your
clemency" (*Hamlet*, III.ii.155)   4 **starts** fits and starts   7 **world's best garden**
i.e., France (cf. V.ii.36)   13 **oft our stage hath shown** (a reference to *1, 2,* and *3
Henry VI*)   14 **this acceptance take** this play find favor

Textual Note

The first edition of *Henry the Fifth* was a quarto published in 1600 with a title page reading:

THE
CRONICLE
History of Henry the fift,
With his battell fought at *Agin Court* in
France. Togither with *Auntient
Pistoll*.

*As it hath bene sundry times playd by the Right honorable
the Lord Chamberlaine his seruants.*

This was a shortened version and a "bad" text; probably some actors had pieced together their own text, which was subsequently cut and rearranged a little for the convenience of a touring company.

Two more quarto editions followed in 1602 and 1619 (its title page, however, being dated 1608); both were reprints from the first edition.

The first, and only, authoritative edition appeared in the collected folio of Shakespeare's *Comedies, Histories and Tragedies* that was published in 1623. Spellings, punctuation, variations in nomenclature, the nature of some of the stage directions and of some of the errors all suggest that this was printed either from Shakespeare's autograph working-manuscript (or "foul papers" as bibliographers usually term this, despite its general clarity and uniformity), or else from a good copy of Shakespeare's manuscript. A few directions for noises and a duplicate entry suggest that the manuscript may have been annotated lightly by a bookkeeper (or stage manager).

This Folio text is divided into five unequal acts by the occurrence of entries for the Chorus to speak appropriate prologues, but another division, running the first two acts together and dividing Act IV into two after its sixth scene, is marked with Act-Headings. Both arrangements involve difficulties: that of the printed headings disregards the Chorus' prologues that clearly belong to the original composition of the play; that of the Chorus suggests that the play was partly rewritten at some stage of composition. This rewriting must have involved the early Pistol and Mrs. Quickly episodes: the prologue before Act II announces that the scene

> Is now transported, gentles, to Southampton.
> There is the playhouse now, there must you sit,
> And thence to France ...

but in II.i. the scene is still London, in Eastcheap, and then, after one scene at Southampton, II.iii. is again London for the account of Falstaff's death. These confusions are partly covered up by two concluding lines to II Prologue:

> But, till the King come forth, and not till then,
> Unto Southampton do we shift our scene.

Probably II.i. and II.iii. were both invented and inserted after the composition of the first two acts had been completed, or nearly completed, in a form that is now lost. If so, it seems likely that Shakespeare began the play intending to fulfill his promise in the Epilogue to *Part Two, Henry the Fourth* and take Falstaff to France—and that he then decided to omit Falstaff and so had to effect some cutting, rewriting and patching. Such a decision may have affected later parts of the play as well: some editors believe that Pistol has inherited some of the business originally designed for Falstaff (but not his idiom); others that Henry's talk with Pistol and the soldiers before Agincourt is a late addition. There can, of course, be no certain knowledge of such processes of composition; what is undoubted is that the Folio text is a good, authoritative version of the play as Shakespeare wrote or rewrote it.

TEXTUAL NOTE

Obviously the Folio must be the basis for any modern text. This present edition reproduces it wherever possible, modernizing spelling, and altering punctuation and verse lineations where the editor's sense of literary and dramatic fitness dictated. Abbreviations have been expanded and speech prefixes regularized. Stage directions have been amplified where necessary, such additions being printed within square brackets. Obvious typographical errors have been corrected and eccentric spellings regularized where appropriate without notice, but all significant emendations are noted below. In this list the adopted reading is given in bold and is followed by the rejected Folio reading in roman type or a note of the Folio's omission within square brackets. If the adopted reading occurs in the first quarto edition it is followed by "Q" within square brackets.

I.ii.74 **heir** [Q] th'Heire   131 **blood** Bloods   163 **her** their   197 **majesty** [Q] Maiesties   212 **End** [Q] And

II.i.26 **mare** name   44,45 **Iceland** Island   75 **thee defy** [Q] defie thee   82 **enough** enough to   108-09 NYM **I shall … betting?** [Q; F omits]   119 **that's** that   121 **Ah** A

II.ii.87 **him with** with   107 **a** an   139 **mark the** make thee   148 **Henry** [Q] Thomas   159 **I** in in   176 **have sought** [Q] sought   181s.d. **Exeunt** Exit

II.iii.17 **'a babbled** a Table   26 **so upward** [Q] so vp-peer'd   50 **word** [Q] world

II.iv.107 **pining** [Q] priuy

III. Chorus 4 **Hampton** Douer   6 **fanning** fayning

III.i.7 **conjure** commune   17 **noble** Noblish   24 **men** me   32 **Straining** Straying

III.iii.32 **heady** headly   35 **Defile** Desire

III.iv.1 **été** este   1-2 **parles bien** bien parlas   8-13 **Et les doigts … écolier** [F assigns "Et les doigts" to Alice, lines 9-11 to Katherine, and "La main … écolier (in lines 12-13) to Alice]   10 **souviendrai** souemeray   16 **Nous** [F omits]   41 **pas déjà** y desia   43 **Non** Nome   47 **Sauf** Sans

III.v.11 **Dieu** du   45 **Foix** Loys   46 **knights** Kings

III.vi.31 **her** [Q] his   109 **o' fire** a fire   117 **lenity** [Q] Leuitie

III.vii.12 **pasterns** postures   13 **Ça, ha!** ch' ha: 62 **lief** liue   68 **et la truie** est la leuye

IV. Chorus 27 **Presenteth** Presented

492

IV.i.3 **Good** God   35 **Qui va là?** Che vous la?   95 **Thomas** Iohn
184 **mote** Moth   234s.d. **Exeunt Soldiers** Exit Souldiers [after line 229]
250 **What** What?   250 **adoration** Odoration   296 **or** of   315 **friends** [Q]
friend

IV.ii.2 **Montez à** Monte   2 **Varlet** Verlot   4 **eaux et la terre** ewes &
terre   5 **le feu** feu   6 **Ciel** Cein   25 **'gainst** against   49 **gimmaled**
Iymold

IV.iii.13-14 **Exeter. And yet ... truth of valor** [F gives after lines 11 and
12, spoken by Bedford]   26 **earns** yernes   48 **And say ... Crispin's day.**
[Q; F omits]   105 **grazing** crazing

IV.iv.15 **Or** for   36-37 **à cette heure** asture   37 **couper** couppes
54 **l'avez promis** layt a promets   57 **remercîments** remercious   57-58
suis tombé intombe   59 **distingué** distinie   69 **Suivez** Saaue

IV.v.2 **perdu ... perdu** perdia ... perdie   3 **Mort** Mor   12 **in honor** in
16 **by a** [Q] a base

IV.vi.34 **mistful** mixtfull

IV.vii.17 **great** grear   80 **their** with   113 **countryman** [Q] countrymen
119 **God** [Q] Good

IV.viii.44 **martial** Marshall   115 **we** me

V.i.73 **begun** began   85 **Of** of a   92 **swear** swore

V.ii.12 **England** Ireland   50 **all** withall   72 **tenors** Tenures   77 **cursitory**
curselarie   93 **Haply** Happily   118 **pleines** plein   196 **est meilleur &**
melieus   264 **abaissiez** abbaisse   265 **d'une de votre** d'une nostre
269 **baisées** baisee   270 **coutume** costume   274 **baiser** buisse
335 **never ent'red** entred   377 **paction** Pation

WILLIAM SHAKESPEARE

THE FAMOUS HISTORY OF THE LIFE OF KING HENRY THE EIGHTH

Edited by S. Schoenbaum

KING HENRY THE EIGHTH
CARDINAL WOLSEY
CARDINAL CAMPEIUS
CAPUCIUS, ambassador from the Emperor Charles V
CRANMER, Archbishop of Canterbury
DUKE OF NORFOLK
DUKE OF BUCKINGHAM
DUKE OF SUFFOLK
EARL OF SURREY
LORD CHAMBERLAIN
LORD CHANCELLOR
GARDINER, Bishop of Winchester
BISHOP OF LINCOLN
LORD ABERGAVENNY
LORD SANDS
SIR HENRY GUILDFORD
SIR THOMAS LOVELL
SIR ANTHONY DENNY
SIR NICHOLAS VAUX
SECRETARIES TO WOLSEY
CROMWELL, servant to Wolsey
GRIFFITH, gentleman usher to Queen Katherine
THREE GENTLEMEN
DOCTOR BUTTS, physician to the King
GARTER KING-AT-ARMS
SURVEYOR TO THE DUKE OF BUCKINGHAM
BRANDON, and a SERGEANT-AT-ARMS
DOOR-KEEPER OF THE COUNCIL-CHAMBER
PAGE TO GARDINER. A CRIER
PORTER, and his Man

QUEEN KATHERINE, wife to King Henry, afterward divorced
ANNE BULLEN, her Maid of Honor, afterward Queen
AN OLD LADY, friend to Anne Bullen
PATIENCE, woman to Queen Katherine

Several Lords and Ladies in the Dumb Shows; Women attending upon the Queen; Scribes, Officers, Guards, and other Attendants; Spirits

Scene: London; Westminster; Kimbolton]

THE FAMOUS HISTORY
OF THE LIFE OF
KING HENRY
THE EIGHTH

THE PROLOGUE

I come no more to make you laugh. Things now
That bear a weighty and a serious brow,
Sad, high, and working, full of state and woe,
Such noble scenes as draw the eye to flow,
We now present. Those that can pity, here   5
May, if they think it well, let fall a tear:
The subject will deserve it. Such as give
Their money out of hope they may believe
May here find truth too. Those that come to see
Only a show or two, and so agree   10
The play may pass, if they be still and willing,
I'll undertake may see away their shilling

Text references are printed in **boldface** type; the annotation follows in roman type.
Prologue   1 **no more to make you laugh** (the previous play was presumably a comedy)   3 **Sad, high, and working** serious, elevated, and moving   3 **state** dignity   9 **truth** (possibly alluding to the play's alternative title, *All Is True*)   12 **shilling** (the admission price for an expensive seat near the stage)

Richly in two short hours. Only they
That come to hear a merry bawdy play,
15 A noise of targets, or to see a fellow
In a long motley coat guarded with yellow,
Will be deceived; for, gentle hearers, know,
To rank our chosen truth with such a show
As fool and fight is, beside forfeiting
20 Our own brains and the opinion that we bring
To make that only true we now intend,
Will leave us never an understanding friend.
Therefore, for goodness' sake, and as you are known
The first and happiest hearers of the town,
25 Be sad, as we would make ye. Think ye see
The very persons of our noble story
As they were living. Think you see them great,
And followed with the general throng and sweat
Of thousand friends. Then, in a moment, see
30 How soon this mightiness meets misery;
And if you can be merry then, I'll say
A man may weep upon his wedding day.

13 **two short hours** (a conventional reference to performance duration; not to be taken literally)   15 **targets** shields   16 **In a long ... yellow** i.e., in the parti-colored costume of the professional fool, trimmed ("guarded") in yellow   17 **deceived** disappointed   19-21 **beside forfeiting ... intend** besides abandoning any claims to intelligence and our reputation for aiming to present only the truth   22 **an understanding friend** (perhaps alluding to the groundlings—spectators standing under the stage—who were sometimes ironically praised for their "understanding")   24 **first and happiest hearers of the town** i.e., the best and most favorably disposed audience in London   27 **As** as if

ACT I

Scene I. [*London. An antechamber in the palace.*]

Enter the Duke of Norfolk at one door; at the other
the Duke of Buckingham and the Lord Abergavenny.

BUCKINGHAM Good morrow, and well met. How have
    ye done
Since last we saw in France?

NORFOLK   I thank your Grace,
Healthful, and ever since a fresh admirer
Of what I saw there.

BUCKINGHAM   An untimely ague
Stayed me a prisoner in my chamber when   5
Those suns of glory, those two lights of men,
Met in the vale of Andren.

NORFOLK   'Twixt Guynes and Arde.
I was then present; saw them salute on horseback;
Beheld them when they lighted, how they clung
In their embracement, as they grew together;   10
Which had they, what four throned ones could
    have weighed
Such a compounded one?

I.i.2 **saw** saw one another   3 **fresh** ready, eager   4 **ague** fever   6 **suns of glory**
i.e., Henry VIII and Francis I (with perhaps a quibble on "suns" = sons)
7 **Guynes and Arde** (towns in Picardy lying on either side of the valley of Andren;
Guynes was in English, Arde in France hands)   9 **lighted** alighted   10 **as** as if
11 **weighed** equalled in weight

BUCKINGHAM   All the whole time
I was my chamber's prisoner.

NORFOLK   Then you lost
The view of earthly glory. Men might say,
15 Till this time pomp was single, but now married
To one above itself. Each following day
Became the next day's master, till the last
Made former wonders its. Today the French,
All clinquant, all in gold, like heathen gods,
20 Shone down the English; and tomorrow they
Made Britain India: every man that stood
Showed like a mine. Their dwarfish pages were
As cherubins, all gilt. The madams too,
Not used to toil, did almost sweat to bear
25 The pride upon them, that their very labor
Was to them as a painting. Now this masque
Was cried incomparable, and th' ensuing night
Made it a fool and beggar. The two kings,
Equal in luster, were now best, now worst,
30 As presence did present them: him in eye
Still him in praise; and being present both,
'Twas said they saw but one, and no discerner
Durst wag his tongue in censure. When these suns
(For so they phrase 'em) by their heralds
   challenged
35 The noble spirits to arms, they did perform
Beyond thought's compass, that former fabulous
   story,

Being now seen possible enough, got credit,
That Bevis was believed.

BUCKINGHAM   O, you go far.

NORFOLK As I belong to worship, and affect
In honor honesty, the tract of everything   40
Would by a good discourser lose some life
Which action's self was tongue to. All was royal;
To the disposing of it nought rebelled.
Order gave each thing view; the office did
Distinctly his full function.

BUCKINGHAM   Who did guide—   45
I mean, who set the body and the limbs
Of this great sport together, as you guess?

NORFOLK One, certes, that promises no element
In such a business.

BUCKINGHAM   I pray you, who, my lord?

NORFOLK All this was ord'red by the good discretion   50
Of the right reverend Cardinal of York.

BUCKINGHAM The devil speed him! No man's pie
        is freed
From his ambitious finger. What had he
To do in these fierce vanities? I wonder
That such a keech can with his very bulk   55
Take up the rays o' th' beneficial sun,
And keep it from the earth.

---

38 **Bevis** Bevis of Hampton, the legendary Saxon knight celebrated in medieval romance 39 **worship** the nobility 39-40 **affect/ In honor honesty** love truth as a point of honor 40-42 **the tract ... tongue** to the course of all these events, however well narrated, would in the description lose some of the color and spark of the actuality 43 **rebelled** jarred 44 **Order gave each thing view** everything was arranged so that it could easily be viewed 44 **office** official, or officials as a group 45 **Distinctly** i.e., without confusion 47 **sport** entertainment 48 **certes** certainly 48 **promises no element** would not be expected to share 50 **ord'red** arranged 52 **The devil speed him** the Devil, i.e., rather than God, prosper him 54 **fierce** extravagant 55 **keech** animal fat rolled into a lump (with a sneer at Wolsey's reputed origin as a butcher's son; cf. line 120) 56 **Take up** obstruct 56 **sun** i.e., the King

NORFOLK   Surely, sir,
There's in him stuff that puts him to these ends;
For, being not propped by ancestry, whose grace
60 Chalks successors their way, nor called upon
For high feats done to th' crown, neither allied
To eminent assistants, but spider-like,
Out of his self-drawing web, 'a gives us note,
The force of his own merit makes his way—
65 A gift that heaven gives for him, which buys
A place next to the King.

ABERGAVENNY   I cannot tell
What heaven hath given him: let some graver eye
Pierce into that. But I can see his pride
Peep through each part of him. Whence has he
      that?
70 If not from hell, the devil is a niggard,
Or has given all before, and he begins
A new hell in himself.

BUCKINGHAM   Why the devil,
Upon this French going out, took he upon him
(Without the privity o' th' King) t' appoint
75 Who should attend on him? He makes up the file
Of all the gentry, for the most part such
To whom as great a charge as little honor
He meant to lay upon; and his own letter,
The honorable board of council out,
Must fetch him in he papers.

80 ABERGAVENNY   I do know
Kinsmen of mine, three at the least, that have

---

58 **stuff** qualities, capabilities   59-60 **whose grace ... way** whose special
excellence marks a path for followers   60-61 **called ... crown** chosen in recognition of lofty exploits in behalf of the crown   62 **assistants** (1) public officials
(2) supporters   63 **self-drawing** self-spinning   63 **'a gives us note** he lets us
know   64 **makes his way** wins preferment   65 **gift** i.e., merit   70 **If not
... niggard** (the devil is the source of pride, the sin for which Lucifer fell and hell
was created)   73 **going out** expedition   74 **privity** confidential participation
75 **file** list   77 **charge** expense   79 **out** unconsulted   80 **fetch him in he
papers** fetch in whom he puts on his list

By this so sickened their estates that never
They shall abound as formerly.

BUCKINGHAM   O, many
Have broke their backs with laying manors on 'em
For this great journey. What did this vanity   85
But minister communication of
A most poor issue?

NORFOLK   Grievingly I think,
The peace between the French and us not values
The cost that did conclude it.

BUCKINGHAM   Every man,
After the hideous storm that followed, was   90
A thing inspired, and, not consulting, broke
Into a general prophecy: that this tempest,
Dashing the garment of this peace, aboded
The sudden breach on't.

NORFOLK   Which is budded out;
For France hath flawed the league, and hath
     attached
Our merchants' goods at Bordeaux.   95

ABERGAVENNY   Is it therefore
Th' ambassador is silenced?

NORFOLK   Marry, is't.

ABERGAVENNY A proper title of a peace, and
     purchased
At a superfluous rate!

BUCKINGHAM   Why, all this business
Our reverend Cardinal carried.

83 abound prosper 84 broke ... manors on 'em ruined themselves by
pawning their estates to outfit themselves 85 vanity extravagance
86-87 minister ... issue furnish occasion for unproductive talk (with a possible
quibble, "poor issue" = impoverished heirs) 88 not values is not worth
91 not consulting i.e., one another 92 a general prophecy i.e., all prophesied
the same 93 aboded foretold 95 flawed the league, and hath attached
broken the treaty and confiscated 97 Marry (a mild oath, from the name of the
Virgin Mary) 98 A proper title of a peace an excellent contract of peace
(ironic) 99 superfluous rate excessive cost 100 carried managed

100 NORFOLK   Like it your Grace,
       The state takes notice of the private difference
       Betwixt you and the Cardinal. I advise you
       (And take it from a heart that wishes towards you
       Honor and plenteous safety) that you read
105   The Cardinal's malice and his potency
       Together; to consider further that
       What his high hatred would effect wants not
       A minister in his power. You know his nature,
       That he's revengeful, and I know his sword
110   Hath a sharp edge. It's long and 't may be said
       It reaches far, and where 'twill not extend,
       Thither he darts it. Bosom up my counsel;
       You'll find it wholesome. Lo, where comes that
         rock
       That I advise your shunning.

       Enter Cardinal Wolsey, the purse borne before him,
       certain of the Guard, and two Secretaries with papers.
       The Cardinal in his passage fixeth his eye on
       Buckingham, and Buckingham on him, both full of
       disdain.

115 WOLSEY The Duke of Buckingham's surveyor, ha?
       Where's his examination?

       FIRST SECRETARY   Here, so please you.

       WOLSEY Is he in person ready?

       FIRST SECRETARY   Aye, please your Grace.

       WOLSEY Well, we shall then know more, and
         Buckingham
       Shall lessen this big look.
                              Exeunt Cardinal and his train.

100 **Like** it if it please (a courteous formula for volunteering unasked
information) 101 **difference** disagreement 104 **plenteous** ample 104 **read**
construe 105 **potency** power 107-08 **wants not/A minister** does not lack an
agent 111 **extend** reach 112 **Bosom up** conceal within your bosom
113 **wholesome** sound 114s.d. **purse** bag containing the Great Seal that is the
insignia of the Lord Chancellor's office 115 **surveyor** overseer of an estate;
Charles Knyvet, Buckingham's cousin 116 **examination** deposition 119 **big**
haughty

BUCKINGHAM This butcher's cur is venomed-mouthed,
and I   120
Have not the power to muzzle him. Therefore best
Not wake him in his slumber. A beggar's book
Outworths a noble's blood.

NORFOLK   What, are you chafed?
Ask God for temp'rance; that's th' appliance only
Which your disease requires.

BUCKINGHAM   I read in's looks   125
Matter against me, and his eye reviled
Me as his abject object. At this instant
He bores me with some trick. He's gone to th' King;
I'll follow and outstare him.

NORFOLK   Stay, my lord,
And let your reason with your choler question   130
What 'tis you go about. To climb steep hills
Requires slow pace at first. Anger is like
A full hot horse who, being allowed his way,
Self-mettle tires him. Not a man in England
Can advise me like you; be to yourself   135
As you would to your friend.

BUCKINGHAM   I'll to the King,
And from a mouth of honor quite cry down
This Ipswich fellow's insolence, or proclaim
There's difference in no persons.

NORFOLK   Be advised.
Heat not a furnace for your foe so hot   140
That it do singe yourself. We may outrun
By violent swiftness that which we run at,

---

120 **butcher's cur** (referring to Wolsey's parentage)   122-23 **A beggar's ...
blood** a beggar's book-learning is more esteemed than nobility of descent
123 **chafed** angry   124 **appliance only** only remedy   127 **abject object** object
of contempt   128 **bores** cheats   130 **with your choler question** dispute with
your anger   133 **full hot** high-spirited   134 **Self-mettle** his own natural
vigor   137 **from a mouth of honor** speaking as a nobleman   138 **Ipswich**
(Wolsey's birthplace)   138 **fellow's** (usually applied to inferiors; cf. III.ii.279 and
IV.ii.100)   139 **There's ... persons** distinctions of rank no longer matter
139 **Be advised** take care

And lose by overrunning. Know you not
The fire that mounts the liquor till't run o'er
In seeming to augment it wastes it? Be advised.
I say again there is no English soul
More stronger to direct you than yourself,
If with the sap of reason you would quench,
Or but allay, the fire of passion.

BUCKINGHAM   Sir,
I am thankful to you, and I'll go along
By your prescription; but this top-proud fellow
(Whom from the flow of gall I name not, but
From sincere motions) by intelligence
And proofs as clear as founts in July when
We see each grain of gravel, I do know
To be corrupt and treasonous.

NORFOLK   Say not "treasonous."

BUCKINGHAM To th' King I'll say't, and make my
    vouch as strong
As shore of rock. Attend. This holy fox,
Or wolf, or both (for he is equal rav'nous
As he is subtle, and as prone to mischief
As able to perform't, his mind and place
Infecting one another, yea, reciprocally)
Only to show his pomp as well in France
As here at home, suggests the King our master
To this last costly treaty, th' interview,
That swallowed so much treasure, and like a glass
Did break i' th' wrenching.

143 **overrunning** running beyond   144 **mounts the liquor** causes the liquor to
rise   147 **More stronger** better qualified (double comparatives, and also superlatives, are frequent in Shakespeare)   148 **sap** juice, fluid   151 **top-proud** excessively proud   152-53 **Whom ... motions** of whom I thus speak not out of spite
but from sincere motives   153 **intelligence** intelligence reports   154 **founts in
July** i.e., streams no longer muddied by spring floods (the accent in "July" is on
the first syllable)   157 **vouch** allegation   158 **Attend** listen   161 **mind and
place** inclinations and position   163 **pomp** magnificence   164 **suggests**
prompts (used of the devil)   165 **interview** "ceremonial meeting of princes"
(Foakes)   167 **wrenching** rinsing

NORFOLK   Faith, and so it did.

BUCKINGHAM   Pray give me favor, sir. This cunning Cardinal
The articles o' th' combination drew
As himself pleased; and they were ratified   170
As he cried, "Thus let be," to as much end
As give a crutch to th' dead. But our count-cardinal
Has done this, and 'tis well; for worthy Wolsey,
Who cannot err, he did it. Now this follows
(Which, as I take it, is a kind of puppy   175
To th' old dam, treason) Charles the Emperor,
Under pretense to see the Queen his aunt
(For 'twas indeed his color, but he came
To whisper Wolsey) here makes visitation.
His fears were that the interview betwixt   180
England and France might through their amity
Breed him some prejudice, for from this league
Peeped harms that menaced him. He privily
Deals with our Cardinal; and, as I trow
(Which I do well, for I am sure the Emperor   185
Paid ere he promised, whereby his suit was granted
Ere it was asked) but when the way was made
And paved with gold, the Emperor thus desired,
That he would please to alter the King's course
And break the foresaid peace. Let the King know,   190
As soon he shall by me, that thus the Cardinal
Does buy and sell his honor as he pleases,
And for his own advantage.

NORFOLK   I am sorry
To hear this of him, and could wish he were
Something mistaken in't.

BUCKINGHAM   No, not a syllable: 195

168 **Pray give me favor** please hear me out   169 **articles o' th' combination drew** drew up the terms of the peace treaty   176 **dam** mother   178 **color** pretext   179 **makes visitation** pays a visit   183 **privily** secretly   184 **as I trow** as I believe (the principal clause required after the parenthetical comment does not appear; grammar has yielded to the speaker's emotion, but the sense of the passage is clear)   192 **buy and sell** traffic in   195 **Something mistaken** to some extent misinterpreted

I do pronounce him in that very shape
He shall appear in proof.

*Enter Brandon, a Sergeant-at-Arms before him, and
two or three of the Guard.*

BRANDON Your office, sergeant: execute it.

SERGEANT   Sir,
My lord the Duke of Buckingham, and Earl
200 Of Hereford, Stafford, and Northampton, I
Arrest thee of high treason, in the name
Of our most sovereign King.

BUCKINGHAM   Lo you, my lord,
The net has fall'n upon me! I shall perish
Under device and practice.

BRANDON   I am sorry
205 To see you ta'en from liberty, to look on
The business present. 'Tis his Highness' pleasure
You shall to th' Tower.

BUCKINGHAM   It will help me nothing
To plead mine innocence, for that dye is on me
Which makes my whit'st part black. The will of
    heav'n
210 Be done in this and all things! I obey.
O my Lord Aberga'ny, fare you well!

BRANDON Nay, he must bear you company.
[*To Abergavenny*] The King
Is pleased you shall to th' Tower, till you know
How he determines further.

ABERGAVENNY   As the Duke said,
215 The will of heaven be done, and the King's pleasure
By me obeyed!

BRANDON   Here is a warrant from

196 pronounce declare 197 He shall appear in proof experience will reveal
him 202 Lo you behold 204 device and practice plots and intrigues
205-06 to look ... present (1) and to see what is now happening (2) to be
involved in the present affair 207 Tower the Tower of London (where suspected
traitors were imprisoned)

The King t' attach Lord Montacute, and the bodies
Of the Duke's confessor, John de la Car,
One Gilbert Parke, his councillor—

BUCKINGHAM   So, so;
These are the limbs o' th' plot. No more, I hope.   220

BRANDON A monk o' th' Chartreux.

BUCKINGHAM   O, Nicholas Hopkins?

BRANDON   He.

BUCKINGHAM My surveyor is false; the o'er-great
          Cardinal
Hath showed him gold. My life is spanned already.
I am the shadow of poor Buckingham,
Whose figure even this instant cloud puts on,   225
By dark'ning my clear sun. My lord, farewell.

                                        Exeunt.

Scene II. [*The same. The council-chamber.*]

*Cornets. Enter King Henry, leaning on the Cardinal's
shoulder; the Nobles, [a Secretary of the Cardinal's,]
and Sir Thomas Lovell. The Cardinal places himself
under the King's feet on his right side.*

KING My life itself, and the best heart of it,
Thanks you for this great care. I stood i' th' level
Of a full-charged confederacy, and give thanks
To you that choked it. Let be called before us

217 **attach** arrest 217 **bodies** persons 221 **Chartreux** Charterhouse (i.e., a
Carthusian) 223 **spanned** measured out 225-26 **Whose figure ... sun** whose
form is at this instant clouded by misfortune that dims my glory and alienates me
from my King ("sun" may refer to both Buckingham and Henry) I.ii.s.d. **under
the King's feet** at the feet of the King, who is seated on a raised and canopied
"state," or throne 1 **best heart** very core 2 **i' th' level** in direct range 3 **full-
charged confederacy** fully-loaded conspiracy

5   That gentleman of Buckingham's. In person
       I'll hear him his confessions justify,
       And point by point the treasons of his master
       He shall again relate.

          A noise within, crying "Room for the Queen!"
          [*Katherine, who is*] *ushered by the Duke of Norfolk.*
          Enter the Queen, [*Duke of*] *Norfolk and* [*Duke of*]
          Suffolk. She kneels. King riseth from his state, takes her
          up, kisses and placeth her by him.

QUEEN KATHERINE Nay, we must longer kneel: I am
          a suitor.
10 KING Arise, and take place by us. Half your suit
       Never name to us: you have half our power.
       The other moiety ere you ask is given.
       Repeat your will, and take it.

QUEEN KATHERINE   Thank your Majesty.
       That you would love yourself, and in that love
15   Not unconsiderèd leave your honor nor
       The dignity of your office, is the point
       Of my petition.

KING   Lady mine, proceed.

QUEEN KATHERINE I am solicited, not by a few,
       And those of true condition, that your subjects
20   Are in great grievance. There have been
          commissions
       Sent down among 'em, which hath flawed the heart
       Of all their loyalties; wherein although,
       My good Lord Cardinal, they vent reproaches
       Most bitterly on you as putter-on
25   Of these exactions, yet the King our master—
       Whose honor heaven shield from soil!—even he
          escapes not
       Language unmannerly; yea, such which breaks

5 **That gentleman of Buckingham's** (the surveyor referred to at I.i.222)
6 **justify** confirm   10 **take place** be seated   12 **moiety** half   13 **Repeat your
will** state your wish   18 **solicited** informed by petitioners   19 **true condition**
loyal disposition   21 **flawed** broken   24 **putter-on** instigator

The sides of loyalty, and almost appears
In loud rebellion.

NORFOLK   Not almost appears—
It doth appear. For, upon these taxations,   30
The clothiers all, not able to maintain
The many to them 'longing, have put off
The spinsters, carders, fullers, weavers, who,
Unfit for other life, compelled by hunger
And lack of other means, in desperate manner   35
Daring th' event to th' teeth, are all in uproar,
And danger serves among them.

KING   Taxation?
Wherein? And what taxation? My Lord Cardinal,
You that are blamed for it alike with us,
Know you of this taxation?

WOLSEY   .   Please you, sir,   40
I know but of a single part in aught
Pertains to th' state, and front but in that file
Where others tell steps with me.

QUEEN KATHERINE   No, my lord?
You know no more than others? But you frame
Things that are known alike, which are not whole-
     some   45
To those which would not know them, and yet must
Perforce be their acquaintance. These exactions
(Whereof my sovereign would have note), they are
Most pestilent to th' hearing; and to bear 'em
The back is sacrifice to th' load. They say   50

---

32 to them 'longing employed by them   33 spinsters, carders, fullers "spinsters" = spinners (usually female); carders combed out impurities from the wool;
fullers cleansed the cloth by beating   36 Daring th' event to th' teeth defiantly
daring the worst   37 serves among them is welcomed as a comrade   41 a
single part i.e., my own individual share   42-43 front ... with me only march
in the front rank of those who keep in step with me, i.e., share my
responsibility   44-45 frame ... alike devise measures known to all alike (in the
council)   45-46 wholesome/To (1) beneficial to (2) approved by   47 their
acquaintance acquainted with them   48 note knowledge   49 pestilent
offensive

They are devised by you, or else you suffer
Too hard an exclamation.

KING   Still exaction!
The nature of it? In what kind, let's know,
Is this exaction?

QUEEN KATHERINE I am much too venturous
55   In tempting of your patience, but am boldened
Under your promised pardon. The subject's grief
Comes through commissions, which compels from
        each
The sixth part of his substance, to be levied
Without delay; and the pretense for this
Is named your wars in France. This makes bold
60   mouths.
Tongues spit their duties out, and cold hearts freeze
Allegiance in them. Their curses now
Live where their prayers did, and it's come to pass,
This tractable obedience is a slave
65   To each incensèd will. I would your Highness
Would give it quick consideration, for
There is no primer baseness.

KING   By my life,
This is against our pleasure.

WOLSEY   And for me,
I have no further gone in this than by
70   A single voice, and that not passed me but
By learned approbation of the judges. If I am
Traduced by ignorant tongues, which neither know
My faculties nor person, yet will be
The chronicles of my doing, let me say
75   'Tis but the fate of place, and the rough brake
That virtue must go through. We must not stint
Our necessary actions in the fear

52 exclamation reproach   56 grief grievance   59 pretense pretext   62 Allegiance (four syllables)   64-65 This tractable ... will this willing obedience of
theirs has given way to angry passion   67 primer baseness "mischief more
urgently in need of redress" (Foakes)   70 voice vote   73 faculties qualities
75 place high office   75 brake thicket

To cope malicious censurers, which ever,
As rav'nous fishes, do a vessel follow
That is new-trimmed, but benefit no further   80
Than vainly longing. What we oft do best,
By sick interpreters (once weak ones) is
Not ours or not allowed; what worst, as oft,
Hitting a grosser quality, is cried up   85
For our best act. If we shall stand still,
In fear our motion will be mocked or carped at,
We should take root here where we sit,
Or sit state-statues only.

KING   Things done well,
And with a care, exempt themselves from fear.
Things done without example, in their issue   90
Are to be feared. Have you a precedent
Of this commission? I believe, not any.
We must not rend our subjects from our laws,
And stick them in our will. Sixth part of each?
A trembling contribution! Why, we take   95
From every tree lop, bark, and part o' th' timber,
And though we leave it with a root, thus hacked,
The air will drink the sap. To every county
Where this is questioned send our letters with
Free pardon to each man that has denied   100
The force of this commission. Pray look to't;
I put it to your care.

WOLSEY   [*To the Secretary*] A word with you.
Let there be letters writ to every shire
Of the King's grace and pardon. The grievèd
          commons

78 **cope** encounter 80 **new-trimmed** newly made seaworthy 82 **sick**
unsound 82 **once** in short 83 **Not ours or not allowed** denied us or
condemned 84 **Hitting a grosser quality** appealing to the baser sort
86 **motion** (1) movement (2) proposal 88 **state-statues** only mere replicas of
statesmen 90 **example** precedent 90 **issue** consequences 93 **rend** pluck
94 **stick them in our will** i.e., make them creatures of our arbitrary power
95 **trembling** accompanied by, or causing, trembling 96 **lop** smaller branches
and twigs 97 **thus hacked** when it is thus hacked 99 **questioned** disputed
101 **force** validity

105   Hardly conceive of me: let it be noised
       That through our intercession this revokement
       And pardon comes. I shall anon advise you
       Further in the proceeding.   *Exit Secretary.*

                    Enter Surveyor.

       QUEEN KATHERINE I am sorry that the Duke of
            Buckingham
            Is run in your displeasure.

110   KING   It grieves many.
       The gentleman is learned and a most rare speaker;
       To nature none more bound; his training such
       That he may furnish and instruct great teachers,
       And never seek for aid out of himself. Yet see,
115   When these so noble benefits shall prove
       Not well disposed, the mind growing once corrupt,
       They turn to vicious forms, ten times more ugly
       Than ever they were fair. This man so complete,
       Who was enrolled 'mongst wonders, and when we,
120   Almost with ravished listening, could not find
       His hour of speech a minute—he, my lady,
       Hath into monstrous habits put the graces
       That once were his, and is become as black
       As if besmeared in hell. Sit by us. You shall hear—
125   This was his gentleman in trust—of him
       Things to strike honor sad. Bid him recount
       The fore-recited practices, whereof
       We cannot feel too little, hear too much.

       WOLSEY Stand forth, and with bold spirit relate what
            you,
130   Most like a careful subject, have collected
       Out of the Duke of Buckingham.

105 **Hardly conceive** (1) think harshly (2) scarcely have any conception
106 **our** (note his use of the royal pronoun)   107 **anon** soon   110 **Is run in** has
incurred   111 **rare** accomplished   112 **bound** indebted (for his endowments)
114 **out of** from outside   115 **benefits** natural gifts   116 **disposed** applied
120 **Almost with ravished listening** listening almost spellbound   122 **habits**
garments   125 **in trust** trusted   127 **fore-recited practices** already revealed
plots   129 **what** i.e., what information   130 **collected** gathered (by spying)

KING   Speak freely.

SURVEYOR First, it was usual with him—every day
  It would infect his speech—that if the King
  Should without issue die, he'll carry it so
  To make the scepter his. These very words   135
  I've heard him utter to his son-in-law,
  Lord Aberga'ny, to whom by oath he menaced
  Revenge upon the Cardinal.

WOLSEY   Please your Highness, note
  This dangerous conception in this point.
  Not friended by his wish, to your high person   140
  His will is most malignant, and it stretches
  Beyond you to your friends.

QUEEN KATHERINE   My learned Lord Cardinal,
  Deliver all with charity.

KING   Speak on.
  How grounded he his title to the crown
  Upon our fail? To this point hast thou heard him   145
  At any time speak aught?

SURVEYOR   He was brought to this
  By a vain prophecy of Nicholas Henton.

KING What was that Henton?

SURVEYOR   Sir, a Chartreux friar,
  His confessor, who fed him every minute
  With words of sovereignty.

KING   How know'st thou this?   150

SURVEYOR Not long before your Highness sped to
    France,
  The Duke being at the Rose, within the parish
  Saint Lawrence Poultney, did of me demand

134 carry it manage things   139 conception design   140 Not friended by his
wish not granted his wish (that the King should die childless)   145 fail (1) failure
to beget an heir (2) death   147 Henton (his name was in fact Nicholas Hopkins,
Henton being the name of his priory)   150 sovereignty i.e., relating to his
accession to the throne   151 sped to set out for   152 the Rose a manor house
belonging to Buckingham

What was the speech among the Londoners
155 Concerning the French journey. I replied
Men feared the French would prove perfidious,
To the King's danger. Presently the Duke
Said 'twas the fear indeed and that he doubted
'Twould prove the verity of certain words
160 Spoke by a holy monk "that oft," says he,
"Hath sent to me, wishing me to permit
John de la Car, my chaplain, a choice hour
To hear from him a matter of some moment;
Whom after under the confession's seal
165 He solemnly had sworn that what he spoke
My chaplain to no creature living but
To me should utter, with demure confidence
This pausingly ensued: 'Neither the King nor's heirs
(Tell you the Duke) shall prosper. Bid him strive
170 To win the love o' th' commonalty. The Duke
Shall govern England.' "

QUEEN KATHERINE　　　　If I know you well,
You were the Duke's surveyor, and lost your office
On the complaint o' th' tenants. Take good heed
You charge not in your spleen a noble person,
175 And spoil your nobler soul. I say, take heed;
Yes, heartily beseech you.

KING　　　　　　　　　　　Let him on.
Go forward.

SURVEYOR　　　　On my soul, I'll speak but truth.
I told my lord the Duke, by th' devil's illusions
The monk might be deceived, and that 'twas
　　dangerous
180 To ruminate on this so far, until
It forged him some design, which, being believed,
It was much like to do. He answered, "Tush,

154 **speech** report 157 **Presently** instantly 158 **doubted** suspected
162 **choice** suitable 167 **demure** solemn 170 **commonalty** common people
174 **spleen** malice 175 **spoil** destroy 175 **nobler soul** (moral nobility taking
precedence over the nobility of rank mentioned in the previous line) 181 **forged
him** caused him to fashion 181 **which** i.e., the monk's words

It can do me no damage"; adding further,
That, had the King in his last sickness failed,
The Cardinal's and Sir Thomas Lovell's heads   185
Should have gone off.

KING   Ha! What, so rank? Ah, ha!
There's mischief in this man. Canst thou say
    further?

SURVEYOR I can, my liege.

KING   Proceed.

SURVEYOR   Being at Greenwich,
After your Highness had reproved the Duke
About Sir William Bulmer—

KING   I remember   190
Of such a time: being my sworn servant,
The Duke retained him his. But on. What hence?

SURVEYOR "If" (quoth he), "I for this had been
    committed,
As to the Tower I thought, I would have played
The part my father meant to act upon   195
Th' usurper Richard, who, being at Salisbury,
Made suit to come in's presence; which if granted,
As he made semblance of his duty, would
Have put his knife into him."

KING   A giant traitor!

WOLSEY Now, madam, may his Highness live in
    freedom,
And this man out of prison?   200

QUEEN KATHERINE   God mend all!

KING There's something more would out of thee.
    What say'st?

SURVEYOR After "the Duke his father," with the
    "knife,"

184 failed died   186 rank (1) corrupt (2) full grown (the plot)   191 sworn (two
syllables)   198 semblance pretense

He stretched him, and with one hand on his
    dagger,
205   Another spread on's breast, mounting his eyes,
He did discharge a horrible oath whose tenor
Was, were he evil used, he would outgo
His father by as much as a performance
Does an irresolute purpose.

KING   There's his period,
210   To sheathe his knife in us. He is attached.
Call him to present trial. If he may
Find mercy in the law, 'tis his; if none,
Let him not seek't of us. By day and night!
He's traitor to th' height.

Exeunt.

Scene III. [*An antechamber in the palace.*]

Enter Lord Chamberlain and Lord Sands.

CHAMBERLAIN Is't possible the spells of France should
    juggle
Men into such strange mysteries?

SANDS   New customs,
Though they be never so ridiculous
(Nay, let 'em be unmanly) yet are followed.

5   CHAMBERLAIN As far as I see, all the good our English
Have got by the late voyage is but merely
A fit or two o' th' face; but they are shrewd ones,
For when they hold 'em, you would swear directly

204 **stretched him** i.e., stretched himself to his full height   205 **mounting**
raising   207 **evil used** badly treated   209 **irresolute** unfulfilled   209 **period**
goal   210 **attached** arrested   211 **present** immediate   214 **height** utmost degree
I.iii.1-2 **juggle ... mysteries** trick men into such oddly mysterious behavior
7 **A fit or two o' th' face** a grimace or two   7 **shrewd** nasty   8 **hold 'em** i.e.,
screw up their faces in this way

Their very noses had been counsellors
To Pepin or Clotharius, they keep state so.   10

SANDS They have all new legs, and lame ones; one
        would take it,
That never saw 'em pace before, the spavin
Or springhalt reigned among 'em.

CHAMBERLAIN   Death! My lord,
  Their clothes are after such a pagan cut to't,
  That, sure, th' have worn out Christendom.   15

            Enter Sir Thomas Lovell.

                                        How now?
  What news, Sir Thomas Lovell?

LOVELL   Faith, my lord,
  I hear of none but the new proclamation
  That's clapped upon the court gate.

CHAMBERLAIN   What is't for?

LOVELL The reformation of our traveled gallants
  That fill the court with quarrels, talk, and tailors.   20

CHAMBERLAIN I'm glad 'tis there. Now I would pray
        our monsieurs
  To think an English courtier may be wise,
  And never see the Louvre.

LOVELL   They must either
  (For so run the conditions) leave those remnants
  Of fool and feather that they got in France,   25
  With all their honorable points of ignorance
  Pertaining thereunto, as fights and fireworks,

10 **Pepin or Clotharius** sixth- and seventh-century Kings of the Franks
10 **keep state** affect grandeur   11 **new legs** new fashions in walking or bowing
12 **pace** walk (suggesting horse references that follow)   12-13 **spavin/Or springhalt** diseases affecting horses' legs   14 **to't** as well   15 **worn out Christendom**
used up Christian fashions   18 **clapped** fastened   23 **Louvre** palace of the
French kings in Paris; now the art museum   25 **fool and feather** foolish fashions
(alluding to the feathers worn by some gallants in their hats)   26 **honorable
points of ignorance** ignorant conceptions of honorable conduct   27 **fights and
fireworks** i.e., duelling and whoring (with a possible reference to venereal disease
as the outcome)

Abusing better men than they can be
Out of a foreign wisdom, renouncing clean
30   The faith they have in tennis and tall stockings,
Short blist'red breeches, and those types of travel,
And understand again like honest men,
Or pack to their old playfellows. There, I take it,
They may, *cum privilegio*, "*oui*" away
35   The lag-end of their lewdness, and be laughed at.

SANDS   'Tis time to give 'em physic, their diseases
Are grown so catching.

CHAMBERLAIN   What a loss our ladies
Will have of these trim vanities!

LOVELL   Aye, marry,
There will be woe indeed, lords. The sly whoresons
40   Have got a speeding trick to lay down ladies.
A French song and a fiddle has no fellow.

SANDS   The devil fiddle 'em! I am glad they are going,
For, sure, there's no converting of 'em. Now
An honest country lord, as I am, beaten
45   A long time out of play, may bring his plain-song,
And have an hour of hearing; and, by'r lady,
Held current music too.

CHAMBERLAIN   Well said, Lord Sands.
Your colt's tooth is not cast yet?

SANDS   No, my lord,
Nor shall not while I have a stump.

CHAMBERLAIN   Sir Thomas,
Whither were you agoing?

28 **Abusing** (goes with "points of ignorance," and is not parallel with "renouncing" in the next line which continues the thought indicated by "leave" in line
24) 31 **blist'red** puffed 31 **types** insignia 32 **understand** comprehend
things, in general (with a possible quibble on "stand under" [i.e., clothes])
33 **pack** clear out 34 **cum privilegio** with license 35 **lag-end** latter part
36 **physic** medical treatment 38 **trim vanities** spruce fops 40 **speeding**
effective 41 **fellow** equal 45 **plain-song** simple melody 46 **by'r lady** i.e., by
the Virgin Mary (a mild oath) 47 **Held current music** have it accepted as good
music 48 **colt's tooth** i.e., youthful lustiness 49 **stump** (with a bawdy double
meaning)

LOVELL   To the Cardinal's.   50
  Your lordship is a guest too.

CHAMBERLAIN   O, 'tis true.
  This night he makes a supper, and a great one,
  To many lords and ladies. There will be
  The beauty of this kingdom, I'll assure you.

LOVELL That churchman bears a bounteous mind
    indeed,   55
  A hand as fruitful as the land that feeds us.
  His dews fall everywhere.

CHAMBERLAIN   No doubt he's noble.
  He had a black mouth that said other of him.

SANDS He may, my lord; has wherewithal. In him
  Sparing would show a worse sin than ill doctrine.   60
  Men of his way should be most liberal;
  They are set here for examples.

CHAMBERLAIN   True, they are so,
  But few now give so great ones. My barge stays;
  Your lordship shall along. Come, good Sir Thomas,
  We shall be late else, which I would not be,   65
  For I was spoke to, with Sir Henry Guildford
  This night to be comptrollers.

SANDS   I am your lordship's. *Exeunt.*

---

58 **black** evil 60 **Sparing** frugality 61 **way** i.e., of life 66 **spoke to** asked
67 **comptrollers** household officers in charge of the festivities

Scene IV. [*A Hall in York Place.*]

*Hautboys. A small table under a state for the Cardinal, a
longer table for the guests. Then enter Anne Bullen and
divers other Ladies and Gentlemen as guests, at one door;
at another door, enter Sir Henry Guildford.*

GUILDFORD Ladies, a general welcome from his Grace
Salutes ye all. This night he dedicates
To fair content and you. None here, he hopes,
In all this noble bevy, has brought with her
One care abroad. He would have all as merry
As, first, good company, good wine, good welcome,
Can make good people.

*Enter Lord Chamberlain, Lord Sands, and
[Sir Thomas] Lovell.*

                                        O, my lord, y'are tardy.
The very thought of this fair company
Clapped wings to me.

CHAMBERLAIN You are young, Sir Harry Guildford.

SANDS Sir Thomas Lovell, had the Cardinal
But half my lay thoughts in him, some of these
Should find a running banquet, ere they rested,
I think would better please 'em. By my life,
They are a sweet society of fair ones.

LOVELL O, that your lordship were but now confessor
To one or two of these!

SANDS   I would I were;
They should find easy penance.

I.iv.s.d. **Hautboys** oboes s.d. **state** canopy 4 **bevy** company (of ladies)
12 **running banquet** hasty repast (with a bawdy double meaning) 14 **society**
assembly

LOVELL   Faith, how easy?

SANDS As easy as a down bed would afford it.

CHAMBERLAIN Sweet ladies, will it please you sit? Sir
    Harry,
  Place you that side; I'll take the charge of this.   20
  His Grace is ent'ring. Nay, you must not freeze.
  Two women placed together makes cold weather.
  My Lord Sands, you are one will keep 'em waking:
  Pray, sit between these ladies.

SANDS   By my faith,
  And thank your lordship. By your leave, sweet
    ladies.   25
  If I chance to talk a little wild, forgive me;
  I had it from my father.

ANNE   Was he mad, sir?

SANDS O, very mad, exceeding mad, in love too;
  But he would bite none. Just as I do now,
  He would kiss you twenty with a breath.

                         [*Kisses her.*]

CHAMBERLAIN   Well said, my lord.   30
  So, now y'are fairly seated. Gentlemen,
  The penance lies on you if these fair ladies
  Pass away frowning.

SANDS   For my little cure,
  Let me alone.

    Hautboys. Enter Cardinal Wolsey, and takes
                his state.

WOLSEY Y'are welcome, my fair guests. That noble
    lady   35
  Or gentleman that is not freely merry

20 **Place you** i.e., place the guests   30 **kiss you twenty with a breath** kiss
twenty in one breath   30 **said** done   31 **fairly** properly   33 **Pass away** leave
33 **cure** (1) charge, parish (continuing the ecclesiastical metaphor of lines 15ff.)
(2) remedy   34s.d. **state** chair of state

Is not my friend. This, to confirm my welcome;
And to you all, good health.   [*Drinks.*]

SANDS   Your Grace is noble.
Let me have such a bowl may hold my thanks,
And save me so much talking.

40 WOLSEY   My Lord Sands,
I am beholding to you. Cheer your neighbors.
Ladies, you are not merry. Gentlemen,
Whose fault is this?

SANDS   The red wine first must rise
In their fair cheeks, my lord. Then we shall have 'em
Talk us to silence.

45 ANNE   You are a merry gamester,
My Lord Sands.

SANDS   Yes, if I make my play.
Here's to your ladyship; and pledge it, madam,
For 'tis to such a thing—

ANNE   You cannot show me.

SANDS I told your Grace they would talk anon.
                    Drum and trumpet; chambers discharged.

WOLSEY   What's that?

CHAMBERLAIN Look out there, some of ye.
                                        [*Exit Servant.*]

50 WOLSEY   What warlike voice,
And to what end, is this? Nay, ladies, fear not;
By all the laws of war y'are privileged.

                    [*Re-*]*enter a Servant.*

CHAMBERLAIN How now, what is't?

SERVANT   A noble troop of strangers,

---

41 **beholding** beholden   45 **gamester** playful person   46 **make my play** win
my game   49s.d. **chambers** small cannon used for ceremonial purposes
50 **some** some one (cf. also line 60)   52 **privileged** entitled to immunity

For so they seem. Th' have left their barge, and
   landed,
And hither make, as great ambassadors   55
From foreign princes.

WOLSEY   Good Lord Chamberlain,
Go, give 'em welcome: you can speak the French
   tongue;
And pray receive 'em nobly and conduct 'em
Into our presence, where this heaven of beauty
Shall shine at full upon them. Some attend him.   60
         [*Exit Chamberlain, attended.*] *All rise,*
                      and tables removed.
You have now a broken banquet, but we'll mend
   it.
A good digestion to you all; and once more
I show'r a welcome on ye: welcome all.

Hautboys. Enter King and others, as masquers, habited
like shepherds, ushered by the Lord Chamberlain.
They pass directly before the Cardinal, and gracefully
salute him.

A noble company! What are their pleasures?

CHAMBERLAIN Because they speak no English,
   thus they prayed   65
To tell your Grace: that, having heard by fame
Of this so noble and so fair assembly
This night to meet here, they could do no less
(Out of the great respect they bear to beauty)
But leave their flocks and, under your fair conduct,   70
Crave leave to view these ladies and entreat
An hour of revels with 'em.

WOLSEY   Say, Lord Chamberlain,
They have done my poor house grace; for which I
   pay 'em

55 **make** make their way   61 **broken** interrupted, with a possible pun on "poor remains" (of a feast)   63s.d. **masquers** i.e., disguised and vizarded as for a court masque   63s.d. **habited** dressed   66 **fame** report   70 **under your fair conduct** with your kind permission

A thousand thanks and pray 'em take their
    pleasures. *Choose ladies; King and Anne Bullen.*

75   KING   The fairest hand I ever touched! O beauty,
    Till now I never knew thee!   *Music. Dance.*

WOLSEY   My lord!

CHAMBERLAIN   Your Grace?

WOLSEY   Pray tell 'em thus much from me:
    There should be one amongst 'em, by his person,
    More worthy this place than myself, to whom
80   (If I but knew him) with my love and duty
    I would surrender it.

CHAMBERLAIN   I will, my lord.
                  Whisper[s with the masquers].

WOLSEY   What say they?

CHAMBERLAIN   Such a one, they all confess,
    There is indeed, which they would have your Grace
    Find out, and he will take it.

WOLSEY   Let me see then.
85   By all your good leaves, gentlemen; here I'll make
    My royal choice.

KING   [*Unmasking*] Ye have found him, Cardinal.
    You hold a fair assembly; you do well, lord.
    You are a churchman, or, I'll tell you, Cardinal,
    I should judge now unhappily.

WOLSEY   I am glad
    Your Grace is grown so pleasant.

90   KING   My Lord Chamberlain,
    Prithee come hither. What fair lady's that?

CHAMBERLAIN   An't please your Grace, Sir Thomas
    Bullen's daughter,
    The Viscount Rochford, one of her Highness'
    women.

81 **it** i.e., the place of honor   86 **royal choice** choice of a king   89 **unhappily**
unfavorably   90 **pleasant** merry

KING By heaven, she is a dainty one. Sweetheart,
    I were unmannerly to take you out   95
    And not to kiss you. A health, gentlemen!
    Let it go round.

WOLSEY Sir Thomas Lovell, is the banquet ready
    I' th' privy chamber?

LOVELL   Yes, my lord.

WOLSEY   Your Grace,
    I fear, with dancing is a little heated.   100

KING I fear, too much.

WOLSEY   There's fresher air, my lord,
    In the next chamber.

KING Lead in your ladies, every one. Sweet partner,
    I must not yet forsake you. Let's be merry,
    Good my Lord Cardinal. I have half a dozen healths   105
    To drink to these fair ladies, and a measure
    To lead 'em once again; and then let's dream
    Who's best in favor. Let the music knock it.

                        Exeunt with trumpets.

---

95 **to take you out** i.e., to invite you to dance 96 **to kiss you** (customary following a dance) 106 **measure** stately dance 108 **best in favor** (1) prettiest (2) most favored (by the ladies) 108 **knock it** strike up

ACT II

Scene I. [*Westminster. A street.*]

Enter two Gentlemen at several doors.

FIRST GENTLEMAN Whither away so fast?

SECOND GENTLEMAN   O, God save ye!
Ev'n to the Hall, to hear what shall become
Of the great Duke of Buckingham.

FIRST GENTLEMAN   I'll save you
That labor, sir. All's now done but the ceremony
Of bringing back the prisoner.

5   SECOND GENTLEMAN   Were you there?

FIRST GENTLEMAN Yes, indeed was I.

SECOND GENTLEMAN   Pray speak what has happened.

FIRST GENTLEMAN You may guess quickly what.

SECOND GENTLEMAN   Is he found guilty?

FIRST GENTLEMAN Yes, truly is he, and condemned
upon't.

SECOND GENTLEMAN I am sorry for't.

FIRST GENTLEMAN   So are a number more.

II.i.s.d. **several** different 2 **Hall** Westminster Hall

528

HENRY VIII II.i.

SECOND GENTLEMAN But, pray, how passed it? 10

FIRST GENTLEMAN I'll tell you in a little. The great
    Duke
Came to the bar, where to his accusations
He pleaded still not guilty, and allegèd
Many sharp reasons to defeat the law.
The King's attorney on the contrary 15
Urged on the examinations, proofs, confessions
Of divers witnesses; which the Duke desired
To him brought *viva voce* to his face;
At which appeared against him his surveyor;
Sir Gilbert Parke, his councillor; and John Car, 20
Confessor to him; with that devil monk,
Hopkins, that made this mischief.

SECOND GENTLEMAN   That was he
That fed him with his prophecies?

FIRST GENTLEMAN   The same.
All these accused him strongly, which he fain
Would have flung from him; but indeed he could
    not.
And so his peers upon this evidence 25
Have found him guilty of high treason. Much
He spoke, and learnedly, for life, but all
Was either pitied in him or forgotten.

SECOND GENTLEMAN After all this, how did he bear
    himself?
30

FIRST GENTLEMAN When he was brought again to th'
    bar, to hear
His knell rung out, his judgment, he was stirred
With such an agony he sweat extremely

10 **how passed it** i.e., what happened at the trial   11 **in a little** in brief
13 **allegèd** put forward   14 **defeat** frustrate   15 **King's attorney** John Fitz-
James, afterward Chief Justice of the King's Bench   15 **contrary** contrary side
16 **Urged on** (1) argued on the evidence of (intransitive) (2) pressed the evidence
of (transitive)   16 **examinations, proofs** depositions, statements   20 **Sir** (a
courtesy title for a cleric)   24 **which** i.e., which accusations   24 **fain** gladly
29 **Was ... forgotten** either aroused only unavailing pity or had no effect
32 **judgment** sentence (also in line 58)

And something spoke in choler, ill and hasty.
35 But he fell to himself again, and sweetly
In all the rest showed a most noble patience.

SECOND GENTLEMAN I do not think he fears death.

FIRST GENTLEMAN   Sure, he does not;
He never was so womanish. The cause
He may a little grieve at.

SECOND GENTLEMAN   Certainly
The Cardinal is the end of this.

40 FIRST GENTLEMAN   'Tis likely,
By all conjectures: first, Kildare's attainder,
Then Deputy of Ireland, who removed,
Earl Surrey was sent thither, and in haste too,
Lest he should help his father.

SECOND GENTLEMAN   That trick of state
Was a deep envious one.

45 FIRST GENTLEMAN   At his return
No doubt he will requite it. This is noted,
And generally: whoever the King favors,
The Card'nal instantly will find employment,
And far enough from court too.

SECOND GENTLEMAN   All the commons
50 Hate him perniciously, and, o' my conscience,
Wish him ten fathom deep. This Duke as much
They love and dote on; call him bounteous
    Buckingham,
The mirror of all courtesy—

*Enter Buckingham from his arraignment, tipstaves before
him, the ax with the edge towards him, halberds on
each side, accompanied with Sir Thomas Lovell,*

37 **Sure** surely 40 **the end** at the root 41 **attainder** disgrace 44 **father**
father-in-law (cf. III.ii:260-64) 45 **envious** malicious 47 **generally** by all
50 **perniciously** mortally 53s.d. **tipstaves** bailiffs, so called because they carried
silver-tipped staffs 53s.d. **halberds** halberdiers (officers bearing long-handled
weapons with blade-and-spear points)

Sir Nicholas Vaux, Sir Walter Sands, and common
people, etc.

FIRST GENTLEMAN   Stay there, sir,
And see the noble ruined man you speak of.

SECOND GENTLEMAN Let's stand close, and behold him.

BUCKINGHAM   All good people,   55
You that thus far have come to pity me,
Hear what I say, and then go home and lose me.
I have this day received a traitor's judgment,
And by that name must die. Yet, heaven bear
    witness,
And if I have a conscience, let it sink me   60
Even as the ax falls, if I be not faithful!
The law I bear no malice for my death:
'T has done, upon the premises, but justice.
But those that sought it I could wish more
    Christians.
Be what they will, I heartily forgive 'em.   65
Yet let 'em look they glory not in mischief
Nor build their evils on the graves of great men,
For then my guiltless blood must cry against 'em.
For further life in this world I ne'er hope,
Nor will I sue, although the King have mercies   70
More than I dare make faults. You few that loved
    me
And dare be bold to weep for Buckingham,
His noble friends and fellows, whom to leave
Is only bitter to him, only dying,
Go with me like good angels to my end;   75
And as the long divorce of steel falls on me,
Make of your prayers one sweet sacrifice,
And lift my soul to heaven. Lead on, o' God's name.

53s.d. **Sir Walter Sands** (Sir William Sands in Holinshed)   55 **close** (1) out of
view (2) silent   57 **lose** forget   60 **sink** destroy   63 **premises** (1) circumstances
(2) proceedings   64 **more** i.e., more sincere   65 **Be what they will** whoever
they may be   66 **look** look to it   67 **evils** privies (?)   67 **great men** noblemen
74 **only bitter** the only bitterness   76 **divorce of steel** separation of body and
soul caused by the ax   77 **sacrifice** offering

LOVELL I do beseech your Grace, for charity,
80   If ever any malice in your heart
        Were hid against me, now to forgive me frankly.

BUCKINGHAM Sir Thomas Lovell, I as free forgive you
        As I would be forgiven. I forgive all.
        There cannot be those numberless offenses
        'Gainst me that I cannot take peace with. No black
85   envy
        Shall mark my grave. Commend me to his Grace,
        And if he speak of Buckingham, pray tell him
        You met him half in heaven. My vows and prayers
        Yet are the King's and, till my soul forsake,
90   Shall cry for blessings on him. May he live
        Longer than I have time to tell his years!
        Ever beloved and loving may his rule be,
        And when old time shall lead to his end,
        Goodness and he fill up one monument!

95 LOVELL To th' waterside I must conduct your Grace,
        Then give my charge up to Sir Nicholas Vaux,
        Who undertakes you to your end.

VAUX   Prepare there;
        The Duke is coming. See the barge be ready,
        And fit it with such furniture as suits
        The greatness of his person.

100 BUCKINGHAM   Nay, Sir Nicholas,
        Let it alone; my state now will but mock me.
        When I came hither, I was Lord High Constable
        And Duke of Buckingham; now, poor Edward
            Bohun.
        Yet I am richer than my base accusers
105   That never knew what truth meant. I now seal it,
        And with that blood will make 'em one day groan
            for't.

81 **frankly** freely (for Lovell's reference see I.ii.185-86) 85 **take** make
85 **envy** malice 89 **forsake** i.e., part from my body 91 **tell** count
94 **monument** grave 97 **undertakes** has charge of 99 **furniture**
equipment 103 **Bohun** (his family name was actually Stafford, although in the
female line he was descended from the Bohuns) 105 **seal** ratify

My noble father, Henry of Buckingham,
Who first raised head against usurping Richard,
Flying for succor to his servant Banister,
Being distressed, was by that wretch betrayed,   110
And without trial fell. God's peace be with him!
Henry the Seventh succeeding, truly pitying
My father's loss, like a most royal prince,
Restored me to my honors, and out of ruins
Made my name once more noble. Now his son,   115
Henry the Eighth, life, honor, name, and all
That made me happy, at one stroke has taken
Forever from the world. I had my trial,
And must needs say a noble one; which makes me
A little happier than my wretched father.   120
Yet thus far we are one in fortunes: both
Fell by our servants, by those men we loved most—
A most unnatural and faithless service!
Heaven has an end in all. Yet, you that hear me,
This from a dying man receive as certain: 125
Where you are liberal of your loves and counsels
Be sure you be not loose. For those you make
    friends
And give your hearts to, when they once perceive
The least rub in your fortunes, fall away
Like water from ye, never found again   130
But where they mean to sink ye. All good people,
Pray for me! I must now forsake ye; the last hour
Of my long weary life is come upon me.
Farewell!
And when you would say something that is sad,   135
Speak how I fell. I have done, and God forgive me.
                              Exeunt Duke and Train.

FIRST GENTLEMAN O, this is full of pity! Sir, it calls,
    I fear, too many curses on their heads
    That were the authors.

SECOND GENTLEMAN   If the Duke be guiltless,

108 **raised head** gathered troops   108 **Richard** Richard III   124 **end** purpose
127 **loose** careless   129 **rub** check   131 **sink** destroy   133 **long weary life** (he
was forty-three)   139 **authors** originators

140   'Tis full of woe. Yet I can give you inkling
        Of an ensuing evil, if it fall,
        Greater than this.

        FIRST GENTLEMAN Good angels keep it from us!
        What may it be? You do not doubt my faith, sir?

        SECOND GENTLEMAN This secret is so weighty, 'twill
            require
        A strong faith to conceal it.

145   FIRST GENTLEMAN   Let me have it;
        I do not talk much.

        SECOND GENTLEMAN I am confident;
        You shall, sir. Did you not of late days hear
        A buzzing of a separation
        Between the King and Katherine?

        FIRST GENTLEMAN   Yes, but it held
            not;
150   For when the King once heard it, out of anger
        He sent command to the Lord Mayor straight
        To stop the rumor and allay those tongues
        That durst disperse it.

        SECOND GENTLEMAN   But that slander, sir,
        Is found a truth now, for it grows again
155   Fresher than e'er it was, and held for certain
        The King will venture at it. Either the Cardinal
        Or some about him near have, out of malice
        To the good Queen, possessed him with a scruple
        That will undo her. To confirm this too,
160   Cardinal Campeius is arrived, and lately;
        As all think, for this business.

        FIRST GENTLEMAN   'Tis the Cardinal;
        And merely to revenge him on the Emperor

143 **faith** trustworthiness   146 **confident** i.e., of your discretion   147 **shall** i.e.,
shall have it   148 **buzzing** rumor   149 **held** lasted   152 **allay** silence
158 **possessed him with a scruple** put a doubt in his mind   160 **Cardinal ...
lately** (Lorenzo Campeggio, or Campeius, did not actually arrive from Rome until
1528, seven years after Buckingham's execution)   162 **Emperor** (Charles V, Holy
Roman Emperor and King of Spain; nephew to Katherine. See I.i.176-90 and
II.ii.25)

For not bestowing on him at his asking
The archbishopric of Toledo, this is purposed.

SECOND GENTLEMAN I think you have hit the mark. But
  is't not cruel   165
That she should feel the smart of this? The Cardinal
Will have his will, and she must fall.

FIRST GENTLEMAN   'Tis woeful.
We are too open here to argue this;
Let's think in private more.

                                              Exeunt.

Scene II. [*An antechamber in the palace.*]

Enter Lord Chamberlain, reading this letter.

CHAMBERLAIN "My lord, the horses your lordship sent
  for, with all the care I had, I saw well chosen,
  ridden, and furnished. They were young and handsome, and of the best breed in the north. When they
  were ready to set out for London, a man of my   5
  Lord Cardinal's, by commission and main power,
  took 'em from me, with this reason: his master
  would be served before a subject, if not before the
  King; which stopped our mouths, sir."
I fear he will indeed. Well, let him have them.   10
He will have all, I think.

          Enter to the Lord Chamberlain, the Dukes of
                    Norfolk and Suffolk.

NORFOLK Well met, my Lord Chamberlain.

CHAMBERLAIN Good day to both your Graces.

168 open (1) public (2) indiscreet II.ii.3 **ridden** broken in 3 **furnished**
outfitted 6 **commission and main power** warrant and sheer force

SUFFOLK How is the King employed?

CHAMBERLAIN   I left him private,
Full of sad thoughts and troubles.

15 NORFOLK   What's the cause?

CHAMBERLAIN It seems the marriage with his brother's
wife
Has crept too near his conscience.

SUFFOLK [*Aside*]   No, his conscience
Has crept too near another lady.

NORFOLK   'Tis so.
This is the Cardinal's doing; the king-cardinal,
20 That blind priest, like the eldest son of Fortune,
Turns what he list. The King will know him one
day.

SUFFOLK Pray God he do! He'll never know himself
else.

NORFOLK How holily he works in all his business,
And with what zeal! For, now he has cracked the
league
Between us and the Emperor, the Queen's great
25   nephew,
He dives into the King's soul, and there scatters
Dangers, doubts, wringing of the conscience,
Fears and despairs; and all these for his marriage.
And out of all these to restore the King,
30 He counsels a divorce, a loss of her
That like a jewel has hung twenty years
About his neck, yet never lost her luster;
Of her that loves him with that excellence
That angels love good men with, even of her
35 That, when the greatest stroke of fortune falls,
Will bless the King. And is not this course pious?

14 **private** alone 15 **sad** grave (also in lines 57, 62) 20-21 **That blind ... list**
i.e., he takes after Fortune in his disregard for others and his capriciousness
(Fortune was depicted as blind and turning a wheel; eldest sons had special
privileges) 21 **know** understand (also in next line) 27 **wringing** torture
28 **for** because of

CHAMBERLAIN Heaven keep me from such counsel! 'Tis
    most true
    These news are everywhere; every tongue speaks 'em,
    And every true heart weeps for't. All that dare
    Look into these affairs see this main end,   40
    The French King's sister. Heaven will one day
    open
    The King's eyes, that so long have slept upon
    This bold bad man.

SUFFOLK   And free us from his slavery.

NORFOLK We had need pray,
    And heartily, for our deliverance,   45
    Or this imperious man will work us all
    From princes into pages. All men's honors
    Lie like one lump before him, to be fashioned
    Into what pitch he please.

SUFFOLK   For me, my lords,
    I love him not, nor fear him—there's my creed.   50
    As I am made without him, so I'll stand,
    If the King please. His curses and his blessings
    Touch me alike; th'are breath I not believe in.
    I knew him, and I know him; so I leave him
    To him that made him proud—the Pope.

NORFOLK   Let's in,   55
    And with some other business put the King
    From these sad thoughts that work too much upon
    him.
    My lord, you'll bear us company?

CHAMBERLAIN   Excuse me,
    The King has sent me otherwhere. Besides,
    You'll find a most unfit time to disturb him.   60
    Health to your lordships.

41 **The French King's sister** the Duchess of Alençon (see III.ii.85–86)
42 **slept upon** been blind to   48 **lump** i.e., of clay (cf. Romans 9:21)   49 **pitch**
height (figurative), i.e., rank or degree of dignity   55 **the Pope** (the expected
reference would be to the devil)

NORFOLK   Thanks, my good Lord Chamberlain.

Exit Lord Chamberlain, and the King draws
the curtain and sits reading pensively.

SUFFOLK How sad he looks; sure, he is much afflicted.

KING Who's there, ha?

NORFOLK   Pray God he be not angry.

KING Who's there, I say? How dare you thrust your-
    selves
65 Into my private meditations?
    Who am I, ha?

NORFOLK A gracious king that pardons all offenses
    Malice ne'er meant. Our breach of duty this way
    Is business of estate, in which we come
    To know your royal pleasure.

70 KING   Ye are too bold.
    Go to; I'll make ye know your times of business.
    Is this an hour for temporal affairs, ha?

    Enter Wolsey and Campeius, with a commission.

    Who's there? My good Lord Cardinal? O my
        Wolsey,
    The quiet of my wounded conscience,
    Thou art a cure fit for a king. [*To Campeius*] You're
75   welcome,
    Most learnèd reverend sir, into our kingdom:
    Use us and it. [*To Wolsey*] My good lord, have
        great care
    I be not found a talker.

WOLSEY   Sir, you cannot.
    I would your Grace would give us but an hour
    Of private conference.

61s.d. **King draws the curtain** he is thus revealed seated within a curtained
booth or recess 62 **afflicted** disturbed 68 **this way** in this respect 69 **estate**
state 71 **Go to** (an exclamation of impatience or disapproval) 78 **talker** i.e.,
rather than a doer

KING [*To Norfolk and Suffolk*] We are busy; go.   80

NORFOLK [*Aside to Suffolk*] This priest has no pride in
    him?

SUFFOLK [*Aside to Norfolk*] Not to speak of.
    I would not be so sick though for his place.
    But this cannot continue.

NORFOLK [*Aside to Suffolk*] If it do,
    I'll venture one have-at-him.

SUFFOLK [*Aside to Norfolk*]   I another.
                    Exeunt Norfolk and Suffolk.

WOLSEY Your Grace has given a precedent of wisdom   85
    Above all princes, in committing freely
    Your scruple to the voice of Christendom.
    Who can be angry now? What envy reach you?
    The Spaniard, tied by blood and favor to her,
    Must now confess, if they have any goodness,   90
    The trial just and noble. All the clerks
    (I mean the learnèd ones) in Christian kingdoms
    Have their free voices. Rome, the nurse of
        judgment,
    Invited by your noble self, hath sent
    One general tongue unto us, this good man,   95
    This just and learnèd priest, Card'nal Campeius,
    Whom once more I present unto your Highness.

KING And once more in mine arms I bid him welcome,
    And thank the holy conclave for their loves.
    They have sent me such a man I would have wished
        for.   100

CAMPEIUS Your Grace must needs deserve all
        strangers' loves,

82 **so sick though for his place** so sick with pride even if it meant having his position 84 **have-at-him** thrust (the phrase "have at you," meaning "here goes!" or "watch out!" signaled an attack) 88 **envy** malice 89 **Spaniard** Spaniards (Katherine was daughter to Ferdinand of Spain) 91 **clerks** scholars 93 **Have their free voices** may freely express their opinions 95 **One general tongue** one spokesman for all 99 **holy conclave** College of Cardinals 101 **strangers'** foreigners'

You are so noble. To your Highness' hand
I tender my commission; by whose virtue,
The court of Rome commanding, you, my Lord
105   Cardinal of York, are joined with me their servant
In the unpartial judging of this business.

KING Two equal men. The Queen shall be acquainted
Forthwith for what you come. Where's Gardiner?

WOLSEY I know your Majesty has always loved her
110   So dear in heart not to deny her that
A woman of less place might ask by law:
Scholars allowed freely to argue for her.

KING Aye, and the best she shall have, and my favor
To him that does best—God forbid else. Cardinal,
115   Prithee call Gardiner to me, my new secretary;
I find him a fit fellow.

                                    [*Wolsey beckons.*]

                        Enter Gardiner.

WOLSEY [*Aside to Gardiner*] Give me your hand:
        much joy and favor to you.
You are the King's now.

GARDINER [*Aside to Wolsey*] But to be commanded
Forever by your Grace, whose hand has raised me.

120 KING Come hither, Gardiner.

                        Walks and whispers.

CAMPEIUS My Lord of York, was not one Doctor
        Pace
In this man's place before him?

WOLSEY   Yes, he was.

CAMPEIUS Was he not held a learnèd man?

WOLSEY   Yes, surely.

106 **unpartial** impartial   107 **equal** just, impartial   110 **that** that which

540

CAMPEIUS Believe me, there's an ill opinion spread
     then,
  Even of yourself, Lord Cardinal.

WOLSEY   How? Of me?   125

CAMPEIUS They will not stick to say you envied him
  And, fearing he would rise (he was so virtuous),
  Kept him a foreign man still; which so grieved him
  That he ran mad and died.

WOLSEY   Heaven's peace be with him!
  That's Christian care enough. For living murmurers   130
  There's places of rebuke. He was a fool,
  For he would needs be virtuous. That good fellow,
  If I command him, follows my appointment;
  I will have none so near else. Learn this, brother,
  We live not to be griped by meaner persons.   135

KING Deliver this with modesty to th' Queen.
                              Exit Gardiner.
  The most convenient place that I can think of
  For such receipt of learning is Blackfriars;
  There ye shall meet about this weighty business.
  My Wolsey, see it furnished. O, my lord,   140
  Would it not grieve an able man to leave
  So sweet a bedfellow? But, conscience, conscience!
  O, 'tis a tender place, and I must leave her.
                              Exeunt.

---

126 **stick** scruple 128 **a foreign man still** continually on missions abroad
129 **died** (Pace in fact outlived Wolsey by six years) 130 **murmurers** grumblers
133 **appointment** direction 135 **griped** clutched familiarly 136 **Deliver**
relate 138 **receipt** accommodation 138 **Blackfriars** Dominican monastery
buildings in London 140 **furnished** fitted up 141 **able** vigorous

Scene III. [*An antechamber of the Queen's apartments.*]

Enter Anne Bullen and an old Lady.

ANNE Not for that neither. Here's the pang that
     pinches:
  His Highness having lived so long with her, and she
  So good a lady that no tongue could ever
  Pronounce dishonor of her—by my life,
5 She never knew harmdoing—O, now, after
  So many courses of the sun enthronèd,
  Still growing in a majesty and pomp, the which
  To leave a thousandfold more bitter than
  'Tis sweet at first t' acquire—after this process,
10 To give her the avaunt, it is a pity
  Would move a monster.

OLD LADY   Hearts of most hard temper
  Melt and lament for her.

ANNE   O, God's will! Much better
  She ne'er had known pomp; though't be temporal,
  Yet, if that quarrel, Fortune, do divorce
15 It from the bearer, 'tis a sufferance panging
  As soul and body's severing.

OLD LADY   Alas, poor lady!
  She's a stranger now again.

ANNE   So much the more
  Must pity drop upon her. Verily,
  I swear, 'tis better to be lowly born

II.iii.1 **pinches** torments 4 **Pronounce** utter 6 **courses of the sun** years
9 **this process** what has passed 10 **give her the avaunt** order her to go
13 **temporal** worldly 14 **quarrel** quarreler (abstract for concrete) 15 **sufferance panging** suffering as agonizing 17 **stranger** foreigner

542

And range with humble livers in content   20
Than to be perked up in a glist'ring grief
And wear a golden sorrow.

OLD LADY   Our content
Is our best having.

ANNE   By my troth and maidenhead,
I would not be a queen.

OLD LADY   Beshrew me, I would,
And venture maidenhead for't; and so would you,   25
For all this spice of your hypocrisy.
You that have so fair parts of woman on you,
Have too a woman's heart, which ever yet
Affected eminence, wealth, sovereignty;
Which, to say sooth, are blessings; and which gifts   30
(Saving your mincing) the capacity
Of your soft cheveril conscience would receive,
If you might please to stretch it.

ANNE   Nay, good troth.

OLD LADY Yes, troth, and troth. You would not be
    a queen?

ANNE No, not for all the riches under heaven.   35

OLD LADY 'Tis strange. A threepence bowed would
    hire me,
Old as I am, to queen it. But, I pray you,
What think you of a duchess? Have you limbs
To bear that load of title?

ANNE   No, in truth.

OLD LADY Then you are weakly made. Pluck off a
    little;   40

20 **range with humble livers** rank with humble folk   21 **perked up** decked
out   21 **glist'ring** glittering   23 **having** possession   24 **Beshrew me** may evil
befall me! (a mild imprecation)   26 **spice** dash, sample   27 **parts** qualities (of
mind and person)   29 **Affected** aspired to   30 **say sooth** tell the truth
31 **Saving your mincing** despite your coyness   32 **cheveril** kidskin   33 **troth**
faith   36 **bowed** bent (and therefore worthless); with a possible quibble on
"bawd"   37 **queen** (with a pun on "quean" = bawd)   40 **Pluck off** come down
in rank

I would not be a young count in your way,
For more than blushing comes to. If your back
Cannot vouchsafe this burden, 'tis too weak
Ever to get a boy.

ANNE   How you do talk!
45   I swear again, I would not be a queen
For all the world.

OLD LADY   In faith, for little England
You'd venture an emballing. I myself
Would for Caernarvonshire, although there 'longed
No more to th' crown but that. Lo, who comes
    here?

Enter Lord Chamberlain.

CHAMBERLAIN Good morrow, ladies. What were't worth
50   to know
The secret of your conference?

ANNE   My good lord,
Not your demand; it values not your asking.
Our mistress' sorrows we were pitying.

CHAMBERLAIN It was a gentle business, and becoming
55   The action of good women. There is hope
All will be well.

ANNE   Now, I pray God, amen!

CHAMBERLAIN You bear a gentle mind, and heav'nly
      blessings
Follow such creatures. That you may, fair lady,
Perceive I speak sincerely, and high note's
60   Ta'en of your many virtues, the King's Majesty
Commends his good opinion of you, and

41 **count** (with a bawdy double meaning) 41 **way** (1) path (2) virginal
condition 43 **vouchsafe** deign to accept 46 **little England** (perhaps with a
reference to Pembrokeshire, called "little England beyond Wales"; word follows
[line 63] of Anne's promotion to Marchioness—historically, to Marquess—of
Pembroke) 47 **emballing** investment with the ball as emblem of sovereignty
(with a bawdy pun) 48 **Caernarvonshire** a poor Welsh county 51 **conference**
conversation 52 **values not** is not worth 61 **Commends his good opinion of
you** presents his compliments

Does purpose honor to you no less flowing
Than Marchioness of Pembroke; to which title
A thousand pound a year, annual support,
Out of his grace he adds.

ANNE   I do not know   65
What kind of my obedience I should tender.
More than my all is nothing; nor my prayers
Are not words duly hallowed, nor my wishes
More worth than empty vanities. Yet prayers and
    wishes
Are all I can return. Beseech your lordship,   70
Vouchsafe to speak my thanks and my obedience,
As from a blushing handmaid, to his Highness,
Whose health and royalty I pray for.

CHAMBERLAIN   Lady,
I shall not fail t' approve the fair conceit
The King hath of you. [*Aside*] I have perused her
    well.   75
Beauty and honor in her are so mingled
That they have caught the King; and who knows yet
But from this lady may proceed a gem
To lighten all this isle?—I'll to the King,
And say I spoke with you.

ANNE   My honored lord.   80
                    Exit Lord Chamberlain.

OLD LADY Why, this it is: see, see!
I have been begging sixteen years in court,
Am yet a courtier beggarly, nor could
Come pat betwixt too early and too late
For any suit of pounds; and you (O fate!)   85
A very fresh fish here—fie, fie, fie upon
This compelled fortune!—have your mouth filled up
Before you open it.

---

62 **flowing** abundant 66 **kind** expression 67–68 **nor ... not** (the double
negative lends emphasis) 71 **Vouchsafe** be good enough 74 **approve the fair
conceit** confirm the good opinion 81 **this it is** so it goes 83 **beggarly** (1) poor
(2) begging 85 **suit of pounds** i.e., petition for money 87 **compelled** i.e.,
forced upon her

ANNE   This is strange to me.

OLD LADY How tastes it? Is it bitter? Forty pence, no.
90   There was a lady once ('tis an old story)
        That would not be a queen, that would she not,
        For all the mud in Egypt. Have you heard it?

ANNE Come, you are pleasant.

OLD LADY   With your theme, I could
        O'ermount the lark. The Marchioness of
            Pembroke?
95   A thousand pounds a year for pure respect?
        No other obligation? By my life,
        That promises moe thousands: honor's train
        Is longer than his foreskirt. By this time
        I know your back will bear a duchess. Say,
        Are you not stronger than you were?

100 ANNE   Good lady,
        Make yourself mirth with your particular fancy,
        And leave me out on't. Would I had no being,
        If this salute my blood a jot. It faints me
        To think what follows.
105   The Queen is comfortless, and we forgetful
        In our long absence. Pray, do not deliver
        What here y'have heard to her.

OLD LADY   What do you think me?—
                                    Exeunt.

92 **mud in Egypt** riches of Egypt (the mud being the source of its fertility)
94 **O'ermount** fly higher than 95 **for pure respect** simply out of esteem
97 **moe** more 103 **salute my blood** exhilarates me 103 **faints me** makes me
faint 106 **deliver** report

Scene IV. [*A hall in Blackfriars.*]

Trumpets, sennet, and cornets. Enter two Vergers, with short silver wands; next them, two Scribes, in the habit of doctors; after them, the [Arch]bishop of Canterbury alone; after him, the Bishops of Lincoln, Ely, Rochester, and Saint Asaph. Next them, with some small distance, follows a Gentleman bearing the purse, with the Great Seal, and a cardinal's hat; then two priests, bearing each a silver cross; then a Gentleman Usher bareheaded, accompanied with a Sergeant at Arms bearing a silver mace; then two Gentlemen bearing two great silver pillars; after them, side by side, the two Cardinals; two Noblemen with the sword and mace. The King takes place under the cloth of state; the two Cardinals sit under him as judges. The Queen takes place some distance from the King. The Bishops place themselves on each side the court, in manner of a consistory; below them, the Scribes. The Lords sit next the Bishops. The rest of the Attendants stand in convenient order about the stage.

WOLSEY Whilst our commission from Rome is read,
　　Let silence be commanded.

KING　　　　　　　　　　What's the need?
　　It hath already publicly been read,
　　And on all sides th' authority allowed.
　　You may then spare that time.

WOLSEY　　　　　　　　Be't so. Proceed.　　　　5

SCRIBE Say "Henry King of England, come into the
　　court."

II.iv.s.d. **sennet** trumpet fanfare　**habit of doctors** i.e., capped and gowned as doctors of law　**two great silver pillars** Wolsey's insignia **takes place** takes his seat　**cloth of state** canopy　**consistory** College of Cardinals

CRIER Henry King of England, etc.

KING Here.

10 SCRIBE Say "Katherine Queen of England, come into
the court."

CRIER Katherine Queen of England, etc.

> *The Queen makes no answer, rises out of her chair,*
> *goes about the court, comes to the King,*
> *and kneels at his feet; then speaks.*

QUEEN KATHERINE Sir, I desire you do me right and
justice,
And to bestow your pity on me; for
15 I am a most poor woman and a stranger,
Born out of your dominions; having here
No judge indifferent, nor no more assurance
Of equal friendship and proceeding. Alas, sir,
In what have I offended you? What cause
20 Hath my behavior given to your displeasure
That thus you should proceed to put me off
And take your good grace from me? Heaven
witness,
I have been to you a true and humble wife,
At all times to your will conformable,
25 Ever in fear to kindle your dislike,
Yea, subject to your countenance, glad or sorry
As I saw it inclined. When was the hour
I ever contradicted your desire,
Or made it not mine too? Or which of your friends
30 Have I not strove to love, although I knew
He were mine enemy? What friend of mine
That had to him derived your anger did I
Continue in my liking? Nay, gave notice
He was from thence discharged? Sir, call to mind
35 That I have been your wife in this obedience
Upward of twenty years, and have been blessed

17 **indifferent** unbiased 18 **equal friendship and proceeding** impartial
friendship and proceedings 21 **put me off** discard me 22 **grace** (1) self
(2) favor 32 **derived** incurred 33 **gave** i.e., gave not

With many children by you. If, in the course
And process of this time, you can report,
And prove it too, against mine honor aught,
My bond to wedlock or my love and duty,   40
Against your sacred person, in God's name,
Turn me away, and let the foul'st contempt
Shut door upon me, and so give me up
To the sharp'st kind of justice. Please you, sir,
The King, your father, was reputed for   45
A prince most prudent, of an excellent
And unmatched wit and judgment. Ferdinand,
My father, King of Spain, was reckoned one
The wisest prince that there had reigned by many
A year before. It is not to be questioned   50
That they had gathered a wise council to them
Of every realm, that did debate this business,
Who deemed our marriage lawful. Wherefore I
    humbly
Beseech you, sir, to spare me, till I may
Be by my friends in Spain advised, whose counsel   55
I will implore. If not, i' th' name of God,
Your pleasure be fulfilled!

WOLSEY   You have here, lady,
And of your choice, these reverend fathers, men
Of singular integrity and learning,
Yea, the elect o' th' land, who are assembled   60
To plead your cause. It shall be therefore bootless
That longer you desire the court, as well
For your own quiet, as to rectify
What is unsettled in the King.

CAMPEIUS   His Grace
Hath spoken well and justly. Therefore, madam,   65
It's fit this royal session do proceed,
And that without delay their arguments
Be now produced and heard.

41 **Against** (1) i.e., or aught against (?) (2) toward (?)   47 **wit** intelligence
48-49 **one/The wisest** the very wisest   61 **bootless** profitless   62 **longer you
desire the court** longer you draw out the business of the court (by pleading for a
postponement)   63 **quiet** i.e., of mind

QUEEN KATHERINE   Lord Cardinal,
    To you I speak.

WOLSEY   Your pleasure, madam?

QUEEN KATHERINE   Sir,
70   I am about to weep; but, thinking that
    We are a queen, or long have dreamed so, certain
    The daughter of a king, my drops of tears
    I'll turn to sparks of fire.

WOLSEY   Be patient yet.

QUEEN KATHERINE I will, when you are humble; nay,
    before,
75   Or God will punish me. I do believe
    (Induced by potent circumstances) that
    You are mine enemy, and make my challenge
    You shall not be my judge; for it is you
    Have blown this coal betwixt my lord and me—
80   Which God's dew quench! Therefore I say again,
    I utterly abhor, yea, from my soul
    Refuse you for my judge, whom, yet once more,
    I hold my most malicious foe, and think not
    At all a friend to truth.

WOLSEY   I do profess
85   You speak not like yourself, who ever yet
    Have stood to charity and displayed th' effects
    Of disposition gentle and of wisdom
    O'ertopping woman's pow'r. Madam, you do me
      wrong:
    I have no spleen against you, nor injustice
90   For you or any. How far I have proceeded,
    Or how far further shall, is warranted
    By a commission from the consistory,
    Yea, the whole consistory of Rome. You charge me
    That I have blown this coal. I do deny it.

71 **certain** certainly   76 **Induced by potent circumstances** persuaded by
strong reasons   77 **challenge** objection (legal term)   79 **blown this coal** stirred
up this strife (proverbial)   81 **abhor** protest against (legal term)   86 **stood to**
supported   89 **spleen** malice

The King is present. If it be known to him   95
That I gainsay my deed, how may he wound,
And worthily, my falsehood—yea, as much
As you have done my truth. If he know
That I am free of your report, he knows
I am not of your wrong. Therefore in him   100
It lies to cure me, and the cure is to
Remove these thoughts from you; the which before
His Highness shall speak in, I do beseech
You, gracious madam, to unthink your speaking
And to say so no more.

QUEEN KATHERINE   My lord, my lord,   105
I am a simple woman, much too weak
T' oppose your cunning. Y'are meek and
     humble-mouthed.
You sign your place and calling, in full seeming,
With meekness and humility, but your heart
Is crammed with arrogancy, spleen, and pride.   110
You have by fortune and his Highness' favors
Gone slightly o'er low steps, and now are mounted
Where pow'rs are your retainers, and your words
(Domestics to you) serve your will as't please
Yourself pronounce their office. I must tell you, 115
You tender more your person's honor than
Your high profession spiritual; that again
I do refuse you for my judge, and here,
Before you all, appeal unto the Pope,
To bring my whole cause 'fore his Holiness,   120
And to be judged by him.
            She curtsies to the King, and offers to depart.

CAMPEIUS   The Queen is obstinate,
Stubborn to justice, apt to accuse it, and

96 **gainsay my deed** now deny what I have done   99 **free of your report**
innocent of your charges   100 **I am not of your wrong** i.e., I have been wronged
by you   103 in regarding   108-09 **You sign ... humility** to all outward
appearances you set a stamp of meekness and humility on your high spiritual
office   112 **slightly** easily   113 **pow'rs** those in power   113-15 **your words ...
office** i.e., your words are your servants, and you need only speak in order for your
will to be done   116 **tender** value   122 **Stubborn** unpliant   122 **apt to accuse
it** prone to call it in question

Disdainful to be tried by't. 'Tis not well.
She's going away.

125 KING Call her again.

CRIER Katherine Queen of England, come into the
court.

GENTLEMAN USHER Madam, you are called back.

QUEEN KATHERINE What need you note it? Pray you
keep your way;
When you are called, return. Now the Lord help!
130 They vex me past my patience. Pray you, pass on.
I will not tarry; no, nor ever more
Upon this business my appearance make
In any of their courts.

Exit Queen, and her Attendants.

KING　　　　　　　　　　Go thy ways, Kate.
That man i' th' world who shall report he has
135 A better wife, let him in naught be trusted,
For speaking false in that. Thou art, alone—
If thy rare qualities, sweet gentleness,
Thy meekness saint-like, wife-like government,
Obeying in commanding, and thy parts
140 Sovereign and pious else, could speak thee out—
The queen of earthly queens. She's noble born,
And like her true nobility she has
Carried herself towards me.

WOLSEY　　　　　　　　Most gracious sir,
In humblest manner I require your Highness,
145 That it shall please you to declare in hearing
Of all these ears—for where I am robbed and
bound,
There must I be unloosed, although not there
At once and fully satisfied—whether ever I
Did broach this business to your Highness, or

128 keep your way keep going　136 alone without rival　138 government
self-control　139 Obeying in commanding self-restrained when giving orders
139-40 thy parts ... out your other excellent and pious qualities could describe
you fully　144 require beg

Laid any scruple in your way which might   150
Induce you to the question on't? Or ever
Have to you, but with thanks to God for such
A royal lady, spake one the least word that might
Be to the prejudice of her present state,
Or touch of her good person?

KING   My Lord Cardinal,   155
I do excuse you; yea, upon mine honor,
I free you from't. You are not to be taught
That you have many enemies that know not
Why they are so, but, like to village curs,
Bark when their fellows do. By some of these   160
The Queen is put in anger. Y'are excused.
But will you be more justified? You ever
Have wished the sleeping of this business, never
    desired
It to be stirred, but oft have hind'red, oft,
The passages made toward it. On my honor   165
I speak my good Lord Cardinal to this point,
And thus far clear him. Now, what moved me to't,
I will be bold with time and your attention.
Then mark th' inducement. Thus it came; give heed
    to't:
My conscience first received a tenderness,   170
Scruple, and prick, on certain speeches uttered
By th' Bishop of Bayonne, then French ambassador,
Who had been hither sent on the debating
A marriage 'twixt the Duke of Orleans and
Our daughter Mary. I' th' progress of this business, 175
Ere a determinate resolution, he
(I mean the bishop) did require a respite,
Wherein he might the King his lord advertise
Whether our daughter were legitimate,
Respecting this our marriage with the dowager,   180
Sometimes our brother's wife. This respite shook

153 **one the least** a single   155 **touch** sullying   157 **You are not to be taught**
you do not have to be told   165 **passages** proceedings   166 **speak** bear witness
for   176 **determinate resolution** final decision   178 **advertise** inform (accent
on second syllable)   181 **Sometimes** formerly

The bosom of my conscience, entered me,
Yea, with a spitting power, and made to tremble
The region of my breast; which forced such way
185 That many mazed considerings did throng,
And pressed in with this caution. First, methought
I stood not in the smile of heaven, who had
Commanded nature that my lady's womb,
If it conceived a male child by me, should
190 Do no more offices of life to't than
The grave does to th' dead; for her male issue
Or died where they were made, or shortly after
This world had aired them. Hence I took a thought
This was a judgment on me, that my kingdom,
195 Well worthy the best heir o' th' world, should not
Be gladded in't by me. Then follows that
I weighed the danger which my realms stood in
By this my issue's fail, and that gave to me
Many a groaning throe. Thus hulling in
200 The wild sea of my conscience, I did steer
Toward this remedy whereupon we are
Now present here together. That's to say,
I meant to rectify my conscience, which
I then did feel full sick, and yet not well,
205 By all the reverend fathers of the land
And doctors learned. First I began in private
With you, my Lord of Lincoln. You remember
How under my oppression I did reek,
When I first moved you.

LINCOLN   Very well, my liege.

210 KING I have spoke long. Be pleased yourself to say
How far you satisfied me.

LINCOLN   So please your Highness,
The question did at first so stagger me,

---

183 **spitting** as though impaled on a spit, transfixing   185 **mazed considerings**
perplexed thoughts   192 **Or** either   198 **issue's fail** i.e., failure to have a
son   199 **hulling** drifting with sail furled   203 **rectify** set right (cf. line
63)   204 **yet** now still   208 **oppression** heavy burden   208 **reek** sweat (literally
smoke with heat)   209 **moved** proposed the matter

Bearing a state of mighty moment in't
And consequence of dread, that I committed
The daring'st counsel which I had to doubt,   215
And did entreat your Highness to this course
Which you are running here.

KING   I then moved you,
My Lord of Canterbury, and got your leave
To make this present summons. Unsolicited
I left no reverend person in this court,   220
But by particular consent proceeded
Under your hands and seals. Therefore, go on;
For no dislike i' th' world against the person
Of the good Queen, but the sharp thorny points
Of my allegèd reasons, drives this forward.   225
Prove but our marriage lawful, by my life
And kingly dignity, we are contented
To wear our mortal state to come with her,
Katherine our queen, before the primest creature
That's paragoned o' th' world.

CAMPEIUS   So please your Highness,   230
The Queen being absent, 'tis a needful fitness
That we adjourn this court till further day.
Meanwhile must be an earnest motion
Made to the Queen to call back her appeal
She intends unto his Holiness.

KING [*Aside*]   I may perceive   235
These cardinals trifle with me. I abhor
This dilatory sloth and tricks of Rome.
My learned and well-belovèd servant, Cranmer,
Prithee return; with thy approach, I know,
My comfort comes along.—Break up the court;   240
I say, set on.

Exeunt, in manner as they entered.

213-15 **Bearing ... doubt** concerning so momentous a state of affairs, with consequences so dreadful to contemplate, that I did not trust myself to give the boldest advice (i.e., that the marriage be dissolved)   219 **summons** i.e., of the Queen   222 **Under your hands and seals** with your signed and sealed consent   225 **allegèd** stated   229 **primest** foremost   230 **paragoned** held up as a paragon   232 **further** a more distant   233 **motion** appeal

555

ACT III

Scene I. [*London. The Queen's apartments.*]

Enter Queen and her Women, as at work.

QUEEN KATHERINE   Take thy lute, wench. My soul
  grows sad with troubles;
Sing and disperse 'em, if thou canst. Leave
  working.

                    Song
    Orpheus with his lute made trees,
    And the mountain tops that freeze,
5   Bow themselves when he did sing.
    To his music plants and flowers
    Ever sprung, as sun and showers
      There had made a lasting spring.

    Everything that heard him play,
10   Even the billows of the sea,
      Hung their heads, and then lay by.
    In sweet music is such art,
    Killing care and grief of heart
      Fall asleep, or hearing die.

           Enter a Gentleman.

15 QUEEN KATHERINE   How now?

III.i.2 **Leave** leave off   3 **Orpheus** (in mythology the music of his lyre tamed
wild beasts and entranced even inanimate nature)   11 **lay by** subsided

556

GENTLEMAN And't please your Grace, the two great
      cardinals
   Wait in the presence.

QUEEN KATHERINE   Would they speak with me?

GENTLEMAN They willed me say so, madam.

QUEEN KATHERINE   Pray their Graces
   To come near. [*Exit Gentleman.*] What can be their
      business
   With me, a poor weak woman, fall'n from favor?   20
   I do not like their coming, now I think on't.
   They should be good men, their affairs as
      righteous;
   But all hoods make not monks.

   Enter the two Cardinals, Wolsey and Campeius.

WOLSEY   Peace to your Highness!

QUEEN KATHERINE Your Graces find me here part of a
      housewife.
   I would be all, against the worst may happen.   25
   What are your pleasures with me, reverend lords?

WOLSEY May it please you, noble madam, to withdraw
   Into your private chamber, we shall give you
   The full cause of our coming.

QUEEN KATHERINE   Speak it here;
   There's nothing I have done yet, o' my conscience,   30
   Deserves a corner. Would all other women
   Could speak this with as free a soul as I do!
   My lords, I care not (so much I am happy
   Above a number) if my actions
   Were tried by every tongue, every eye saw 'em,   35
   Envy and base opinion set against 'em,
   I know my life so even. If your business

17 **presence** presence chamber   22 **their affairs as righteous** i.e., their business
should be as righteous as they themselves good   24 **part of** to some extent
(because she is sewing)   25 **I would … happen** I would like to be a complete
one, in preparation for the worst (i.e., in case I am divorced and left nothing
else)   36 **Envy and base opinion** malice and unworthy gossip   37 **even** equable

Seek me out, and that way I am wife in,
Out with it boldly: truth loves open dealing.

40 WOLSEY *Tanta est erga te mentis integritas, regina*
serenissima—

QUEEN KATHERINE O, good my lord, no Latin;
I am not such a truant since my coming,
As not to know the language I have lived in.
A strange tongue makes my cause more strange,
45   suspicious;
Pray speak in English. Here are some will thank
you,
If you speak truth, for their poor mistress' sake.
Believe me, she has had much wrong. Lord
Cardinal,
The willing'st sin I ever yet committed
May be absolved in English.

50 WOLSEY   Noble lady,
I am sorry my integrity should breed
(And service to his Majesty and you)
So deep suspicion, where all faith was meant.
We come not by the way of accusation,
55 To taint that honor every good tongue blesses,
Nor to betray you any way to sorrow—
You have too much, good lady—but to know
How you stand minded in the weighty difference
Between the King and you, and to deliver,
60 Like free and honest men, our just opinions
And comforts to your cause.

CAMPEIUS   Most honored madam,
My Lord of York, out of his noble nature,
Zeal and obedience he still bore your Grace,
Forgetting, like a good man, your late censure
65 Both of his truth and him (which was too far)

38 **Seek ... wife in** concerns me, and my behavior as a wife   40-41 **Tanta ...**
serenissima so unprejudiced are we toward you, most serene Queen
45 **strange, suspicious** foreign, and hence suspicious   49 **willing'st** most
deliberate   53 **all** only   63 **still bore** has always borne   65 **far** extreme

Offers, as I do, in a sign of peace,
His service and his counsel.

QUEEN KATHERINE [*Aside*] To betray me.—
My lords, I thank you both for your good wills.
Ye speak like honest men; pray God ye prove so!
But how to make ye suddenly an answer,   70
In such a point of weight, so near mine honor,
More near my life, I fear, with my weak wit,
And to such men of gravity and learning,
In truth I know not. I was set at work
Among my maids, full little, God knows, looking   75
Either for such men or such business.
For her sake that I have been—for I feel
The last fit of my greatness—good your Graces,
Let me have time and counsel for my cause.
Alas, I am a woman friendless, hopeless!   80

WOLSEY Madam, you wrong the King's love with these
    fears.
Your hopes and friends are infinite.

QUEEN KATHERINE   In England
But little for my profit. Can you think, lords,
That any Englishman dare give me counsel
Or be a known friend, 'gainst his Highness'
    pleasure—   85
Though he be grown so desperate to be honest—
And live a subject? Nay, forsooth, my friends,
They that must weigh out my afflictions,
They that my trust must grow to, live not here.
They are, as all my other comforts, far hence   90
In mine own country, lords.

CAMPEIUS   I would your Grace
Would leave your griefs, and take my counsel.

QUEEN KATHERINE   How, sir?

66 in as   70 **suddenly** on the spur of the moment   71 **near** closely affecting
72 **wit** intelligence   74 **set** seated   77 **For her sake that I have been** for what I
once was   78 **fit** seizure (as in an illness)   86 **so desperate to be honest** i.e., so
reckless as to come out honestly in my support   88 **weigh out** attach full weight
to

CAMPEIUS Put your main cause into the King's
    protection;
    He's loving and most gracious. 'Twill be much
95   Both for your honor better and your cause,
    For if the trial of the law o'ertake ye,
    You'll part away disgraced.

WOLSEY   He tells you rightly.

QUEEN KATHERINE Ye tell me what ye wish for both—
    my ruin.
    Is this your Christian counsel? Out upon ye!
100   Heaven is above all yet; there sits a judge
    That no king can corrupt.

CAMPEIUS   Your rage mistakes us.

QUEEN KATHERINE The more shame for ye. Holy men
    I thought ye,
    Upon my soul, two reverend cardinal virtues;
    But cardinal sins and hollow hearts I fear ye.
    Mend 'em, for shame, my lords. Is this your
105   comfort?
    The cordial that ye bring a wretched lady,
    A woman lost among ye, laughed at, scorned?
    I will not wish ye half my miseries:
    I have more charity. But say I warned ye.
    Take heed, for heaven's sake, take heed, lest at
110   once
    The burden of my sorrows fall upon ye.

WOLSEY Madam, this is a mere distraction.
    You turn the good we offer into envy.

QUEEN KATHERINE Ye turn me into nothing. Woe upon
    ye,
115   And all such false professors! Would you have me

95 **Both ... cause** better for both your honor and your cause   97 **part away**
depart   103 **cardinal virtues** the essential virtues (comprising fortitude, justice,
prudence, and temperance); with a pun on the visitors' station   104 **cardinal sins**
(alluding to the seven deadly sins; with pun on "carnal," the Elizabethan
pronunciation of "cardinal")   110 **at once** all at once   112 **mere distraction**
sheer madness   113 **envy** malice   115 **professors** i.e., of Christianity

(If you have any justice, any pity,
If ye be anything but churchmen's habits)
Put my sick cause into his hands that hates me?
Alas, has banished me his bed already;
His love, too long ago! I am old, my lords,   120
And all the fellowship I hold now with him
Is only my obedience. What can happen
To me above this wretchedness? All your studies
Make me a curse like this!

CAMPEIUS   Your fears are worse.

QUEEN KATHERINE Have I lived thus long (let me
    speak myself,   125
Since virtue finds no friends) a wife, a true one?
A woman, I dare say without vainglory,
Never yet branded with suspicion?
Have I with all my full affections
Still met the King? Loved him next heaven? Obeyed
    him?   130
Been, out of fondness, superstitious to him?
Almost forgot my prayers to content him?
And am I thus rewarded? 'Tis not well, lords.
Bring me a constant woman to her husband,
One that ne'er dreamed a joy beyond his pleasure,   135
And to that woman, when she has done most,
Yet will I add an honor: a great patience.

WOLSEY Madam, you wander from the good we aim at.

QUEEN KATHERINE My lord, I dare not make myself so
    guilty
To give up willingly that noble title   140
Your master wed me to. Nothing but death
Shall e'er divorce my dignities.

WOLSEY   Pray hear me.

117 **habits** garb   120 **old** (she was forty-three)   123-24 **All ... this** i.e., let all
your learned efforts make my life any more wretched than it already is
124 **worse** i.e., than your actual situation   125 **speak** describe   131 **superstitious to him** his idolator   134 **constant woman** woman faithful   135 **pleasure**
(1) enjoyment (2) wishes

QUEEN KATHERINE Would I had never trod this English
            earth,
        Or felt the flatteries that grow upon it!
        Ye have angels' faces, but heaven knows your
145   hearts.
        What will become of me now, wretched lady!
        I am the most unhappy woman living.
        Alas, poor wenches, where are now your fortunes?
        Shipwracked upon a kingdom, where no pity,
150   No friends, no hope; no kindred weep for me;
        Almost no grave allowed me. Like the lily,
        That once was mistress of the field, and flourished,
        I'll hang my head and perish.

WOLSEY   If your Grace
        Could but be brought to know our ends are
            honest,
        You'd feel more comfort. Why should we, good
155   lady,
        Upon what cause, wrong you? Alas, our places,
        The way of our profession is against it.
        We are to cure such sorrows, not to sow 'em.
        For goodness' sake, consider what you do;
160 .   How you may hurt yourself, aye, utterly
        Grow from the King's acquaintance, by this
            carriage.
        The hearts of princes kiss obedience,
        So much they love it; but to stubborn spirits
        They swell, and grow as terrible as storms.
165   I know you have a gentle, noble temper,
        A soul as even as a calm. Pray think us
        Those we profess, peacemakers, friends, and
            servants.

CAMPEIUS Madam, you'll find it so. You wrong your
            virtues
        With these weak women's fears. A noble spirit,

145 **Ye have ... hearts** (alluding to the proverbial "Fair face, foul heart")
154 **ends are honest** intentions are honorable   161 **Grow** be estranged
161 **carriage** conduct

As yours was put into you, ever casts　　　　　170
Such doubts, as false coin, from it. The King loves
　you;
Beware you lose it not. For us, if you please
To trust us in your business, we are ready
To use our utmost studies in your service.

QUEEN KATHERINE　Do what ye will, my lords; and pray
　forgive me.　　　　　175
If I have used myself unmannerly,
You know I am a woman, lacking wit
To make a seemly answer to such persons.
Pray do my service to his Majesty.
He has my heart yet, and shall have my prayers　　180
While I shall have my life. Come, reverend fathers,
Bestow your counsels on me. She now begs
That little thought, when she set footing here,
She should have bought her dignities so dear.

　　　　　　　　　　　　　　　Exeunt.

Scene II. [*Antechamber to the King's apartment.*]

*Enter the Duke of Norfolk, Duke of Suffolk,
Lord Surrey, and Lord Chamberlain.*

NORFOLK　If you will now unite in your complaints
And force them with a constancy, the Cardinal
Cannot stand under them. If you omit
The offer of this time, I cannot promise
But that you shall sustain moe new disgraces,　　　5
With these you bear already.

SURREY　　　　　　　　　I am joyful
To meet the least occasion that may give me

174 **studies** endeavors　176 **used myself** behaved　179 **do my service** offer
my respects　183 **footing** foot　III.ii.2 **force them with a constancy** urge
them with determination　3-4 **omit ... time** neglect this opportunity

Remembrance of my father-in-law, the Duke,
To be revenged on him.

SUFFOLK   Which of the peers
10   Have uncontemned gone by him, or at least
Strangely neglected? When did he regard
The stamp of nobleness in any person
Out of himself?

CHAMBERLAIN   My lords, you speak your
            pleasures.
What he deserves of you and me I know;
15   What we can do to him, though now the time
Gives way to us, I much fear. If you cannot
Bar his access to th' King, never attempt
Anything on him, for he hath a witchcraft
Over the King in's tongue.

NORFOLK   O, fear him not;
20   His spell in that is out. The King hath found
Matter against him that forever mars
The honey of his language. No, he's settled,
Not to come off, in his displeasure.

SURREY   Sir,
I should be glad to hear such news as this
Once every hour.

25   NORFOLK   Believe it, this is true.
In the divorce his contrary proceedings
Are all unfolded; wherein he appears
As I would wish mine enemy.

SURREY   How came
His practices to light?

8 my father-in-law, the Duke (Buckingham; see II.i.43-44)   10 uncontemned
undespised   10 at least i.e., have not at least been   13 Out of besides
13 speak your pleasures are free to say what you care to   16 way scope
16 fear doubt   20 His spell in that is out his influence that way is
finished   22-23 he's settled ... displeasure i.e., he (Wolsey) is fixed, not to
escape, in his (the King's) displeasure (but "he" could possibly refer to the King,
in which case "come off" = desist)   26 contrary proceedings (1) proceedings
contradicting their outward appearance (2) adverse proceedings   29 practices
plots

SUFFOLK   Most strangely.

SURREY   O, how? How?

SUFFOLK The Cardinal's letters to the Pope miscar-
    ried,   30
    And came to th' eye o' th' King; wherein was read
    How that the Cardinal did entreat his Holiness
    To stay the judgment o' th' divorce. For if
    It did take place, "I do" (quoth he), "perceive
    My king is tangled in affection to   35
    A creature of the Queen's, Lady Anne Bullen."

SURREY Has the King this?

SUFFOLK   Believe it.

SURREY   Will this work?

CHAMBERLAIN The King in this perceives him how he
    coasts
    And hedges his own way. But in this point
    All his tricks founder, and he brings his physic   40
    After his patient's death: the King already
    Hath married the fair lady.

SURREY   Would he had!

SUFFOLK May you be happy in your wish, my lord!
    For, I profess, you have it.

SURREY   Now, all my joy
    Trace the conjunction!

SUFFOLK   My amen to't!

NORFOLK   All men's!   45

SUFFOLK There's order given for her coronation.
    Marry, this is yet but young, and may be left
    To some ears unrecounted. But, my lords,
    She is a gallant creature and complete

36 **creature** dependent   38-39 **coasts ... way** moves circuitously and stealthily
(i.e., as by coasts and hedgerows) toward his own goals   44-45 **all ... conjunction** all the joy I can wish follow the marriage   49 **complete** fully endowed

50   In mind and feature. I persuade me, from her
          Will fall some blessing to this land, which shall
          In it be memorized.

SURREY   But will the King
          Digest this letter of the Cardinal's?
          The Lord forbid!

NORFOLK   Marry, amen!

SUFFOLK   No, no.
55   There be moe wasps that buzz about his nose
          Will make this sting the sooner. Cardinal Campeius
          Is stol'n away to Rome; hath ta'en no leave;
          Has left the cause o' th' King unhandled, and
          Is posted as the agent of our Cardinal
60   To second all his plot. I do assure you
          The King cried "Ha!" at this.

CHAMBERLAIN   Now God incense him,
          And let him cry "Ha!" louder!

NORFOLK   But, my lord,
          When returns Cranmer?

SUFFOLK He is returned in his opinions, which
65   Have satisfied the King for his divorce,
          Together with all famous colleges
          Almost in Christendom. Shortly, I believe,
          His second marriage shall be published, and
          Her coronation. Katherine no more
70   Shall be called Queen, but Princess Dowager
          And widow to Prince Arthur.

NORFOLK   This same Cranmer's
          A worthy fellow, and hath ta'en much pain
          In the King's business.

SUFFOLK   He has, and we shall see him
          For it an archbishop.

52 **memorized** made memorable   53 **Digest** stomach   59 **posted** hastened
64 **returned in his opinions** i.e., not in person, but in that the opinions have
been received from him   68 **published** proclaimed

NORFOLK   So I hear.

SUFFOLK   'Tis so.

Enter Wolsey and Cromwell.

The Cardinal!

NORFOLK Observe, observe, he's moody.   75

WOLSEY The packet, Cromwell,
Gave't you the King?

CROMWELL   To his own hand, in's bedchamber.

WOLSEY Looked he o' th' inside of the paper?

CROMWELL   Presently
He did unseal them, and the first he viewed,
He did it with a serious mind; a heed   80
Was in his countenance. You he bade
Attend him here this morning.

WOLSEY   Is he ready
To come abroad?

CROMWELL   I think by this he is.

WOLSEY Leave me awhile.

                            Exit Cromwell.

[*Aside*] It shall be to the Duchess of Alençon,   85
The French King's sister; he shall marry her.
Anne Bullen? No. I'll no Anne Bullens for him;
There's more in't than fair visage. Bullen?
No, we'll no Bullens. Speedily I wish
To hear from Rome. The Marchioness of
    Pembroke!   90

NORFOLK He's discontented.

SUFFOLK   Maybe he hears the King
Does whet his anger to him.

76 **packet** parcel of state papers   78 **paper** wrapper   78 **Presently** immediately
90 **Marchioness of Pembroke** (Anne did not in fact receive the title until 1532,
three years after the events of this scene)   92 **to** against

SURREY   Sharp enough,
    Lord, for thy justice!

WOLSEY [*Aside*] The late queen's gentlewoman, a
        knight's daughter,
95   To be her mistress' mistress? The Queen's queen?
    This candle burns not clear. 'Tis I must snuff it;
    Then out it goes. What though I know her virtuous
    And well deserving? Yet I know her for
    A spleeny Lutheran, and not wholesome to
100   Our cause that she should lie i' th' bosom of
    Our hard-ruled King. Again, there is sprung up
    An heretic, an arch one, Cranmer, one
    Hath crawled into the favor of the King,
    And is his oracle.

NORFOLK   He is vexed at something.

    Enter King, reading of a schedule, [and Lovell].

SURREY I would 'twere something that would fret the
105   string,
    The master-cord on's heart.

SUFFOLK   The King, the King!

KING What piles of wealth hath he accumulated
    To his own portion! And what expense by th' hour
    Seems to flow from him! How, i' th' name of thrift,
110   Does he rake this together? Now, my lords,
    Saw you the Cardinal?

NORFOLK   My lord, we have
    Stood here observing him. Some strange commotion
    Is in his brain. He bites his lip, and starts;
    Stops on a sudden, looks upon the ground,
115   Then lays his finger on his temple; straight

96-97 **This candle ... goes** i.e., I will be called on to clear away the impediments
to this marriage, but instead will use the opportunity to quash it altogether
("snuff" = trim the wick) 99 **spleeny** (1) staunch (2) splenetic 101 **hard-
ruled** difficult to manage 103 **Hath** that hath 105 **fret the string** gnaw
through the tendon 106 **on's** of his 111 **Saw you the Cardinal** (the King,
engrossed in the schedule [see s.d.], has not noticed Wolsey's presence)
112 **commotion** turmoil, mutiny (see line 120)

Springs out into fast gait; then stops again,
Strikes his breast hard, and anon he casts
His eye against the moon. In most strange postures
We have seen him set himself.

KING   It may well be
There is a mutiny in's mind. This morning   120
Papers of state he sent me to peruse,
As I required. And wot you what I found
There, on my conscience, put unwittingly?
Forsooth, an inventory, thus importing:
The several parcels of his plate, his treasure,   125
Rich stuffs, and ornaments of household, which
I find at such proud rate that it outspeaks
Possession of a subject.

NORFOLK   It's heaven's will;
Some spirit put this paper in the packet
To bless your eye withal.

KING   If we did think   130
His contemplation were above the earth,
And fixed on spiritual object, he should still
Dwell in his musings; but I am afraid
His thinkings are below the moon, not worth
His serious considering.

            King takes his seat; whispers Lovell, who
                        goes to the Cardinal.

WOLSEY   Heaven forgive me!   135
Ever God bless your Highness!

KING   Good my lord,
You are full of heavenly stuff, and bear the
    inventory
Of your best graces in your mind; the which

118 **against** toward   122 **wot** know   124 **thus importing** conveying this
information   125 **several parcels** various particulars   125 **plate** gold and silver
household plate   126 **stuffs** cloths   127 **proud rate** high value   127-28 **outspeaks ... subject** describes more than a subject should own   132 **spiritual
object** a spiritual objective   134 **below the moon** worldly   137 **stuff** concerns
(with a possible quibble on the household stuff referred to in line 126)

You were now running o'er. You have scarce time
140   To steal from spiritual leisure a brief span
To keep your earthly audit. Sure, in that
I deem you an ill husband, and am glad
To have you therein my companion.

WOLSEY   Sir,
For holy offices I have a time; a time
145   To think upon the part of business which
I bear i' th' state; and Nature does require
Her times of preservation, which perforce
I, her frail son, amongst my brethren mortal,
Must give my tendance to.

KING   You have said well.

150   WOLSEY And ever may your Highness yoke together,
As I will lend you cause, my doing well
With my well saying!

KING   'Tis well said again,
And 'tis a kind of good deed to say well.
And yet words are no deeds. My father loved you;
155   He said he did, and with his deed did crown
His word upon you. Since I had my office
I have kept you next my heart; have not alone
Employed you where high profits might come home,
But pared my present havings, to bestow
My bounties upon you.

160   WOLSEY [*Aside*]   What should this mean?

SURREY [*Aside*] The Lord increase this business!

KING   Have I not made you
The prime man of the state? I pray you tell me
If what I now pronounce you have found true;
And, if you may confess it, say withal,
165   If you are bound to us or no. What say you?

140 **spiritual leisure** religious occupations 142 **husband** manager
148 **amongst my brethren mortal** i.e., in my human (as distinguished from
divine) capacity 149 **tendance** attention 155 **crown** confirm 159 **havings**
possessions

WOLSEY My sovereign, I confess your royal graces,
    Showered on me daily, have been more than could
    My studied purposes requite, which went
    Beyond all man's endeavors. My endeavors
    Have ever come too short of my desires,   170
    Yet filed with my abilities. Mine own ends
    Have been mine so that evermore they pointed
    To th' good of your most sacred person and
    The profit of the state. For your great graces
    Heaped upon me, poor undeserver, I   175
    Can nothing render but allegiant thanks,
    My prayers to heaven for you, my loyalty,
    Which ever has and ever shall be growing
    Till death, that winter, kill it.

KING   Fairly answered;
    A loyal and obedient subject is   180
    Therein illustrated. The honor of it
    Does pay the act of it, as, i' th' contrary,
    The foulness is the punishment. I presume
    That, as my hand has opened bounty to you,
    My heart dropped love, my pow'r rained honor,
        more   185
    On you than any, so your hand and heart,
    Your brain and every function of your power,
    Should, notwithstanding that your bond of duty,
    As 'twere in love's particular, be more
    To me, your friend, than any.

WOLSEY   I do profess   190
    That for your Highness' good I ever labored
    More than mine own; that am, have, and will
        be—
    Though all the world should crack their duty to you

167-68 **more ... requite** more than I could with diligent endeavors repay
171 **filed** kept pace 172 **so that** only to the extent that 176 **allegiant**
loyal 181-83 **The honor ... punishment** i.e., virtue is its own reward, just as
evil is its own punishment 186 **any** on anyone 188 **notwithstanding that**
over and above 189 **in love's particular** out of personal affection 192 **More**
(as in Buckingham's speech, I.i.184ff., the speaker's emotion overcomes the
restraints of normal syntax in the rest of this speech, but the sense is clear)
192 **have** have been

And throw it from their soul; though perils did
195   Abound as thick as thought could make 'em, and
Appear in forms more horrid—yet my duty,
As doth a rock against the chiding flood,
Should the approach of this wild river break,
And stand unshaken yours.

KING   'Tis nobly spoken.
200   Take notice, lords, he has a loyal breast,
For you have seen him open't.   [*Giving him papers.*]
    Read o'er this;
And after, this; and then to breakfast with
What appetite you have.

        Exit King, frowning upon the Cardinal; the nobles
           throng after him, smiling and whispering.

WOLSEY   What should this mean?
What sudden anger's this? How have I reaped it?
205   He parted frowning from me, as if ruin
Leaped from his eyes. So looks the chafèd lion
Upon the daring huntsman that has galled him,
Then makes him nothing. I must read this paper;
I fear, the story of his anger. 'Tis so;
210   This paper has undone me. 'Tis th' account
Of all that world of wealth I have drawn together
For mine own ends; indeed, to gain the popedom,
And fee my friends in Rome. O negligence,
Fit for a fool to fall by! What cross devil
215   Made me put this main secret in the packet
I sent the King? Is there no way to cure this?
No new device to beat this from his brains?
I know 'twill stir him strongly; yet I know
A way, if it take right, in spite of fortune
220   Will bring me off again. What's this? "To th' Pope"?
The letter, as I live, with all the business
I writ to's Holiness. Nay then, farewell!

---

197 **chiding** tumultuous 198 **break** check 206 **chafèd** angry 207 **galled**
wounded 208 **makes him nothing** annihilates him 214 **cross** thwarting
perverse 215 **main** crucial 219 **take right** succeed 220 **bring me off** rescue
me

I have touched the highest point of all my greatness,
And from that full meridian of my glory
I haste now to my setting. I shall fall   225
Like a bright exhalation in the evening,
And no man see me more.

*Enter to Wolsey the Dukes of Norfolk and Suffolk,
the Earl of Surrey, and the Lord Chamberlain.*

NORFOLK Hear the King's pleasure, Cardinal, who
    commands you
To render up the Great Seal presently
Into our hands, and to confine yourself   230
To Asher House, my Lord of Winchester's,
Till you hear further from his Highness.

WOLSEY   Stay:
Where's your commission, lords? Words cannot carry
Authority so weighty.

SUFFOLK   Who dare cross 'em,
Bearing the King's will from his mouth expressly?   235

WOLSEY Till I find more than will or words to do it—
I mean your malice—know, officious lords,
I dare, and must deny it. Now I feel
Of what coarse metal ye are molded—envy;
How eagerly ye follow my disgraces,   240
As if it fed ye! And how sleek and wanton
Ye appear in everything may bring my ruin!
Follow your envious courses, men of malice;
You have Christian warrant for 'em, and no doubt
In time will find their fit rewards. That seal   245
You ask with such a violence, the King,
Mine and your master, with his own hand gave me;
Bade me enjoy it, with the place and honors,

224 **meridian** (a star's highest point)   226 **exhalation** meteor   229 **Great Seal** (insignia of the Lord Chancellor's office; see I.i.114s.d.n.)   229 **presently** at once   231 **Lord of Winchester's** (as Wolsey was himself still Bishop of Winchester, we are perhaps meant to think of his successor, Stephen Gardiner)   234 **cross** oppose   236 **do it** (1) "render up the Great Seal" (line 229) (2) carry such great authority   241 **wanton** unrestrained   244 **Christian warrant** justification by Christian principles (ironical)

During my life; and, to confirm his goodness,
250   Tied it by letters-patents. Now, who'll take it?

SURREY The King, that gave it.

WOLSEY   It must be himself, then.

SURREY Thou art a proud traitor, priest.

WOLSEY   Proud lord, thou liest.
Within these forty hours Surrey durst better
Have burnt that tongue than said so.

SURREY   Thy ambition,
255   Thou scarlet sin, robbed this bewailing land
Of noble Buckingham, my father-in-law.
The heads of all thy brother cardinals,
With thee and all thy best parts bound together,
Weighed not a hair of his. Plague of your policy!
260   You sent me Deputy for Ireland;
Far from his succor, from the King, from all
That might have mercy on the fault thou gav'st him,
Whilst your great goodness, out of holy pity,
Absolved him with an ax.

WOLSEY   This, and all else
265   This talking lord can lay upon my credit,
I answer, is most false. The Duke by law
Found his deserts. How innocent I was
From any private malice in his end,
His noble jury and foul cause can witness.
270   If I loved many words, lord, I should tell you
You have as little honesty as honor,
That in the way of loyalty and truth
Toward the King, my ever royal master,
Dare mate a sounder man than Surrey can be,
And all that love his follies.

275   SURREY   By my soul,

250 **Tied it by letters-patents** confirmed it by documents of formal conveyance
255 **scarlet sin** (referring to the color of his cassock, and also the traditional idea
of scarlet sins, as in Isaiah 1:18)   258 **parts** qualities   259 **Weighed** equaled in
weight   260 **Ireland** (three syllables)   265 **credit** reputation   272 **That** (the
antecedent is "I," line 270)   274 **mate** match

Your long coat, priest, protects you; thou shouldst
    feel
My sword i' th' lifeblood of thee else. My lords,
Can ye endure to hear this arrogance?
And from this fellow? If we live thus tamely,
To be thus jaded by a piece of scarlet,   280
Farewell nobility. Let his Grace go forward,
And dare us with his cap, like larks.

WOLSEY   All goodness
    Is poison to thy stomach.

SURREY   Yes, that goodness
Of gleaning all the land's wealth into one,
Into your own hands, Card'nal, by extortion;   285
The goodness of your intercepted packets
You writ to th' Pope against the King. Your
    goodness,
Since you provoke me, shall be most notorious.
My Lord of Norfolk, as you are truly noble,
As you respect the common good, the state   290
Of our despised nobility, our issues,
Who, if he live, will scarce be gentlemen,
Produce the grand sum of his sins, the articles
Collected from his life. I'll startle you
Worse than the sacring bell, when the brown
    wench   295
Lay kissing in your arms, Lord Cardinal.

WOLSEY How much, methinks, I could despise this
    man,
But that I am bound in charity against it!

NORFOLK Those articles, my lord, are in the King's
    hand;
But, thus much, they are foul ones.

280 **jaded** intimidated   282 **dare us with his cap, like larks** i.e., dazzle us with
his cardinal's hat, as larks were dazed and caught by means of a mirror and piece of
red cloth   289 **Lord of Norfolk** (Norfolk was actually Surrey's father)   291
issues children   293 **articles** charges in an indictment   295 **sacring bell** the
consecrating bell rung at the elevation of the Host, the most solemn portion of the
Mass   300 **thus much** i.e., so much I can say

300 WOLSEY   So much fairer
And spotless shall mine innocence arise,
When the King knows my truth.

SURREY   This cannot save you.
I thank my memory I yet remember
Some of these articles, and out they shall.
305 Now, if you can blush and cry "guilty," Cardinal,
You'll show a little honesty.

WOLSEY   Speak on, sir;
I dare your worst objection. If I blush,
It is to see a nobleman want manners.

SURREY I had rather want those than my head. Have
    at you!
310 First that, without the King's assent or knowledge,
You wrought to be a legate; by which power
You maimed the jurisdiction of all bishops.

NORFOLK Then that in all you writ to Rome, or else
To foreign princes, "*Ego et Rex meus*"
315 Was still inscribed; in which you brought the King
To be your servant.

SUFFOLK   Then, that without the knowledge
Either of King or Council, when you went
Ambassador to the Emperor, you made bold
To carry into Flanders the Great Seal.

320 SURREY Item, you sent a large commission
To Gregory de Cassado, to conclude,
Without the King's will or the state's allowance,
A league between his Highness and Ferrara.

---

308 **want** lack   309 **Have at you** here goes; cf. II.ii.85 (the six charges that
follow are the most serious of the nine leveled against Wolsey)   311 **legate** i.e., the
papal representative in England   314 **Ego et Rex meus** my King and I (the
normal Latin word order, although Shakespeare followed the chroniclers in taking
it to imply that Wolsey put himself before the King)   318 **Emperor** Charles V;
see I.i.176–90   319 **To carry ... Seal** (the Seal, and thus the Lord Chancellor,
were not supposed to leave the country)

SUFFOLK That out of mere ambition you have caused
　Your holy hat to be stamped on the King's coin.   325

SURREY Then that you have sent innumerable
　　substance
　(By what means got, I leave to your own
　　conscience)
　To furnish Rome and to prepare the ways
　You have for dignities, to the mere undoing
　Of all the kingdom. Many more there are,   330
　Which, since they are of you and odious,
　I will not taint my mouth with.

CHAMBERLAIN   O my lord,
　Press not a falling man too far: 'tis virtue.
　His faults lie open to the laws; let them,
　Not you, correct him. My heart weeps to see him   335
　So little of his great self.

SURREY   I forgive him.

SUFFOLK Lord Cardinal, the King's further pleasure
　　is—
　Because all those things you have done of late,
　By your power legative, within this kingdom,
　Fall into th' compass of a præmunire—   340
　That therefore such a writ be sued against you:
　To forfeit all your goods, lands, tenements,
　Chattels, and whatsoever, and to be
　Out of the King's protection. This is my charge.

NORFOLK And so we'll leave you to your meditations   345
　How to live better. For your stubborn answer
　About the giving back the Great Seal to us,
　The King shall know it, and no doubt shall thank
　　you.
　So fare you well, my little good Lord Cardinal.
　　　　　　　　　　　　Exeunt all but Wolsey.

324 **mere** sheer 325 **Your holy ... coin** (a usurpation of royal
prerogative) 326 **innumerable substance** countless treasure 328 **furnish**
supply 333 **virtue** i.e., to relent 339 **legative** as a papal legate 340 **Fall ...
præmunire** i.e., come within the penalties—forfeiture of goods and outlawry—
prescribed by the Statute of Præmunire, which limited papal authority in
England 341 **sued** moved

350 WOLSEY So farewell to the little good you bear me.
        Farewell! A long farewell to all my greatness!
        This is the state of man: today he puts forth
        The tender leaves of hopes; tomorrow blossoms,
        And bears his blushing honors thick upon him.
355   The third day comes a frost, a killing frost,
        And, when he thinks, good easy man, full surely
        His greatness is aripening, nips his root,
        And then he falls, as I do. I have ventured,
        Like little wanton boys that swim on bladders,
360   This many summers in a sea of glory,
        But far beyond my depth. My high-blown pride
        At length broke under me and now has left me,
        Weary and old with service, to the mercy
        Of a rude stream that must forever hide me.
365   Vain pomp and glory of this world, I hate ye.
        I feel my heart new opened. O, how wretched
        Is that poor man that hangs on princes' favors!
        There is betwixt that smile we would aspire to,
        That sweet aspect of princes, and their ruin,
370   More pangs and fears than wars or women have.
        And when he falls, he falls like Lucifer,
        Never to hope again.

              Enter Cromwell, standing amazed.

                      Why, how now, Cromwell?

CROMWELL I have no power to speak, sir.

WOLSEY   What, amazed
        At my misfortunes? Can thy spirit wonder
375   A great man should decline? Nay, and you weep,
        I am fall'n indeed.

CROMWELL   How does your Grace?

WOLSEY   Why, well;
        Never so truly happy, my good Cromwell.

356 **easy** easygoing   359 **wanton** playful   364 **rude** turbulent   369 **their ruin**
the ruin they cause   371 **he falls like Lucifer** (cf. Isaiah 14:12: "How art thou
fallen from heaven, O Lucifer, son of the morning")   375 **and** if

I know myself now, and I feel within me
A peace above all earthly dignities,
A still and quiet conscience. The King has cured me,   380
I humbly thank his Grace; and from these shoulders,
These ruined pillars, out of pity, taken
A load would sink a navy—too much honor.
O, 'tis a burden, Cromwell, 'tis a burden
Too heavy for a man that hopes for heaven!   385

CROMWELL I am glad your Grace has made that right
    use of it.

WOLSEY I hope I have. I am able now, methinks,
Out of a fortitude of soul I feel,
To endure more miseries and greater far
Than my weak-hearted enemies dare offer.   390
What news abroad?

CROMWELL   The heaviest and the worst
Is your displeasure with the King.

WOLSEY   God bless him!

CROMWELL The next is, that Sir Thomas More is
    chosen
Lord Chancellor in your place.

WOLSEY   That's somewhat sudden.
But he's a learnèd man. May he continue   395
Long in his Highness' favor and do justice
For truth's sake and his conscience, that his bones,
When he has run his course and sleeps in blessings,
May have a tomb of orphans' tears wept on him!
What more?

CROMWELL That Cranmer is returned with welcome,   400
Installed Lord Archbishop of Canterbury.

WOLSEY That's news indeed.

CROMWELL   Last, that the Lady Anne,
Whom the King hath in secrecy long married,

---

378 **know myself** i.e., "recognize my limitations and my sins and am able to
transcend them" (Foakes)   386 **made that right use of** derived that benefit from
392 **displeasure** loss of favor

This day was viewed in open as his queen,
405   Going to chapel; and the voice is now
Only about her coronation.

WOLSEY There was the weight that pulled me down.
    O Cromwell,
The King has gone beyond me. All my glories
In that one woman I have lost forever.
410   No sun shall ever usher forth mine honors,
Or gild again the noble troops that waited
Upon my smiles. Go get thee from me, Cromwell;
I am a poor fall'n man, unworthy now
To be thy lord and master. Seek the King
415   (That sun I pray may never set!)—I have told him
What and how true thou art. He will advance thee;
Some little memory of me will stir him
(I know his noble nature) not to let
Thy hopeful service perish too. Good Cromwell,
420   Neglect him not; make use now, and provide
For thine own future safety.

CROMWELL   O my lord,
Must I then leave you? Must I needs forgo
So good, so noble, and so true a master?
Bear witness, all that have not hearts of iron,
425   With what a sorrow Cromwell leaves his lord.
The King shall have my service, but my prayers
Forever and forever shall be yours.

WOLSEY Cromwell, I did not think to shed a tear
In all my miseries, but thou hast forced me,
430   Out of thy honest truth, to play the woman.
Let's dry our eyes—and thus far hear me,
    Cromwell,
And when I am forgotten, as I shall be,
And sleep in dull cold marble where no mention
Of me more must be heard of, say I taught thee,
435   Say, Wolsey, that once trod the ways of glory,
And sounded all the depths and shoals of honor,

405 **voice** talk   408 **gone beyond** overreached   420 **make use** take advantage
422 **forgo** forsake   430 **truth** faith   433 **dull** (1) inanimate (2) cheerless

Found thee a way, out of his wrack, to rise in:
A sure and safe one, though thy master missed it.
Mark but my fall and that that ruined me.
Cromwell, I charge thee, fling away ambition.   440
By that sin fell the angels. How can man then,
The image of his Maker, hope to win by it?
Love thyself last; cherish those hearts that hate thee;
Corruption wins not more than honesty.
Still in thy right hand carry gentle peace   445
To silence envious tongues. Be just, and fear not.
Let all the ends thou aim'st at be thy country's,
Thy God's, and truth's. Then if thou fall'st, O
    Cromwell,
Thou fall'st a blessed martyr. Serve the King;
And prithee, lead me in.   450
There take an inventory of all I have
To the last penny; 'tis the King's. My robe,
And my integrity to heaven, is all
I dare now call mine own. O Cromwell, Cromwell,
Had I but served my God with half the zeal   455
I served my King, he would not in mine age
Have left me naked to mine enemies.

CROMWELL Good sir, have patience.

WOLSEY   So I have. Farewell
The hopes of court! My hopes in heaven do dwell.
                                              Exeunt.

442 win profit   445 Still always   447-49 Let ... martyr (after becoming Earl
of Essex and Lord Great Chamberlain, Cromwell fell from favor and was beheaded
in 1540)   452 robe i.e., cardinal's habit

ACT IV

Scene I. [*A street in Westminster*.]

Enter two Gentlemen, meeting one another.

FIRST GENTLEMAN Y'are well met once again.

SECOND GENTLEMAN   So are you.

FIRST GENTLEMAN You come to take your stand here,
and behold
The Lady Anne pass from her coronation?

SECOND GENTLEMAN 'Tis all my business. At our last
encounter
5   The Duke of Buckingham came from his trial.

FIRST GENTLEMAN 'Tis very true. But that time offered
sorrow;
This, general joy.

SECOND GENTLEMAN   'Tis well. The citizens,
I am sure, have shown at full their royal minds—
As, let 'em have their rights, they are ever
forward—

IV.i.1 **again** (they met previously in II.i) 8 **royal** i.e., well disposed to the
King 9 **let 'em have their rights, they are ever forward** to give them their
due, they are always eager to do

582

In celebration of this day with shows,   10
Pageants, and sights of honor.

FIRST GENTLEMAN   Never greater,
  Nor, I'll assure you, better taken, sir.

SECOND GENTLEMAN May I be bold to ask what that
    contains,
  That paper in your hand?

FIRST GENTLEMAN   Yes. 'Tis the list
  Of those that claim their offices this day   15
  By custom of the coronation.
  The Duke of Suffolk is the first, and claims
  To be High Steward; next, the Duke of Norfolk,
  He to be Earl Marshal. You may read the rest.

SECOND GENTLEMAN I thank you, sir; had I not known
    those customs,   20
  I should have been beholding to your paper.
  But, I beseech you, what's become of Katherine,
  The Princess Dowager? How goes her business?

FIRST GENTLEMAN That I can tell you too. The
    Archbishop
  Of Canterbury, accompanied with other   25
  Learnèd and reverend fathers of his order,
  Held a late court at Dunstable, six miles off
  From Ampthill, where the Princess lay; to which
  She was often cited by them, but appeared not.
  And, to be short, for not appearance and   30
  The King's late scruple, by the main assent
  Of all these learnèd men she was divorced,
  And the late marriage made of none effect;
  Since which she was removed to Kimbolton,
  Where she remains now sick.

SECOND GENTLEMAN   Alas, good lady!   35
                                    [*Trumpets.*]

12 **taken** received   16 **By custom** i.e., in accordance with hereditary privilege
21 **beholding** beholden   27 **late** recent   29 **cited** summoned   31 **main assent**
general agreement   33 **late marriage made of none effect** former marriage
annulled

The trumpets sound: stand close, the Queen is
   coming.

Hautboys.

THE ORDER OF THE CORONATION.

1. *A lively flourish of trumpets.*
2. *Then two judges.*
3. *Lord Chancellor, with purse and mace before him.*
4. *Choristers, singing.*   *Music.*
5. *Mayor of London, bearing the mace. Then Garter, in his
   coat of arms, and on his head he wore a gilt copper crown.*
6. *Marquess Dorset, bearing a scepter of gold, on his head a
   demicoronal of gold. With him, the Earl of Surrey, bearing
   the rod of silver with the dove, crowned with an earl's
   coronet. Collars of S's.*
7. *Duke of Suffolk, in his robe of estate, his coronet on his
   head, bearing a long white wand, as High Steward. With
   him, the Duke of Norfolk, with the rod of marshalship, a
   coronet on his head. Collars of S's.*
8. *A canopy borne by four of the Cinque-ports; under it, the
   Queen in her robe, in her hair, richly adorned with pearl,
   crowned. On each side her, the Bishops of London and
   Winchester.*
9. *The old Duchess of Norfolk, in a coronal of gold, wrought
   with flowers, bearing the Queen's train.*
10. *Certain Ladies or Countesses, with plain circlets of gold
   without flowers.*
*Exeunt, first passing over the stage in order and state, and
then a great flourish of trumpets. [As the procession passes,
the two Gentlemen comment upon it.]*

36s.d. **flourish** fanfare **Music** musicians **Garter** i.e., Garter King-at-Arms
demicoronal small coronet **Collars of S's** gold chains of office fashioned of S-
shaped links **estate** state **four of the Cinque-ports** i.e., four barons of the
channel ports (the ports, five in all, were Dover, Hastings, Hythe, Romney, and
Sandwich) **in her hair** with her hair hanging loosely (the custom for brides)

SECOND GENTLEMAN A royal train, believe me. These
  I know.
Who's that that bears the scepter?

FIRST GENTLEMAN   Marquess Dorset;
And that the Earl of Surrey, with the rod.

SECOND GENTLEMAN A bold brave gentleman. That
  should be   40
The Duke of Suffolk?

FIRST GENTLEMAN   'Tis the same: High Steward.

SECOND GENTLEMAN And that my Lord of Norfolk?

FIRST GENTLEMAN   Yes.

SECOND GENTLEMAN [*Looking on the Queen*] Heaven
  bless thee!
Thou hast the sweetest face I ever looked on.
Sir, as I have a soul, she is an angel;
Our King has all the Indies in his arms,   45
And more and richer, when he strains that lady.
I cannot blame his conscience.

FIRST GENTLEMAN   They that bear
The cloth of honor over her, are four barons
Of the Cinque-ports.

SECOND GENTLEMAN Those men are happy, and so are
  all are near her.   50
I take it, she that carries up the train
Is that old noble lady, Duchess of Norfolk.

FIRST GENTLEMAN It is, and all the rest are countesses.

SECOND GENTLEMAN Their coronets say so. These are
  stars indeed.

FIRST GENTLEMAN And sometimes falling ones.

SECOND GENTLEMAN   No more of that. 55

37 **train** retinue   45 **all the Indies** i.e., the East and the West (the Indies were
celebrated for their riches)   46 **strains** clasps   55 **falling** (with a *double-entendre;*
"falling" = surrendering chastity)

[The last of the procession exits; trumpets sound.]

Enter a third Gentleman.

FIRST GENTLEMAN God save you, sir! Where have you
been broiling?

THIRD GENTLEMAN Among the crowd i' th' abbey,
where a finger
Could not be wedged in more: I am stifled
With the mere rankness of their joy.

SECOND GENTLEMAN   You saw
The ceremony?

THIRD GENTLEMAN That I did.

60 FIRST GENTLEMAN   How was it?

THIRD GENTLEMAN Well worth the seeing.

SECOND GENTLEMAN   Good sir, speak it to us.

THIRD GENTLEMAN As well as I am able. The rich
stream
Of lords and ladies, having brought the Queen
To a prepared place in the choir, fell off
65   A distance from her, while her Grace sat down
To rest awhile, some half an hour or so,
In a rich chair of state, opposing freely
The beauty of her person to the people.
Believe me, sir, she is the goodliest woman
70   That ever lay by man; which when the people
Had the full view of, such a noise arose
As the shrouds make at sea in a stiff tempest,
As loud and to as many tunes; hats, cloaks—
Doublets, I think—flew up, and had their faces
75   Been loose, this day they had been lost. Such joy
I never saw before. Great-bellied women

---

59 **mere rankness** sheer stink   61 **speak** describe   64 **off** back   67 **opposing**
exposing   72 **shrouds** sail-ropes   74 **Doublets** men's close-fitting garments,
with or without sleeves   76 **Great-bellied** pregnant

That had not half a week to go, like rams
In the old time of war, would shake the press,
And make 'em reel before 'em. No man living
Could say "This is my wife" there, all were woven   80
So strangely in one piece.

SECOND GENTLEMAN   But what followed?

THIRD GENTLEMAN At length her Grace rose, and with
    modest paces
Came to the altar, where she kneeled and saintlike
Cast her fair eyes to heaven and prayed devoutly;
Then rose again and bowed her to the people;   85
When by the Archbishop of Canterbury
She had all the royal makings of a queen,
As holy oil, Edward Confessor's crown,
The rod, and bird of peace, and all such emblems
Laid nobly on her; which performed, the choir,   90
With all the choicest music of the kingdom,
Together sung "Te Deum." So she parted,
And with the same full state paced back again
To York Place, where the feast is held.

FIRST GENTLEMAN   Sir,
You must no more call it York Place; that's past.   95
For, since the Cardinal fell, that title's lost:
'Tis now the King's, and called Whitehall.

THIRD GENTLEMAN   I know it,
But 'tis so lately altered that the old name
Is fresh about me.

SECOND GENTLEMAN What two reverend bishops
Were those that went on each side of the Queen?   100

THIRD GENTLEMAN Stokesly and Gardiner; the one of
    Winchester,
Newly preferred from the King's secretary,
The other, London.

77 **rams** battering rams   78 **press** crowd   87 **makings** of things that go to
make   88 **As** namely   91 **music** musicians   92 **parted** departed   93 **state**
pomp   94 **To York ... held** (it was in fact held in Westminster Hall; the change
permits the reference to Wolsey which follows)   96 **lost** erased   102 **preferred
from** promoted from being

SECOND GENTLEMAN   He of Winchester
Is held no great good lover of the Archbishop's,
The virtuous Cranmer.

105 THIRD GENTLEMAN   All the land knows that;
However, yet there is no great breach. When it
    comes,
Cranmer will find a friend will not shrink from
    him.

SECOND GENTLEMAN Who may that be, I pray you?

THIRD GENTLEMAN   Thomas Cromwell,
A man in much esteem with th' King, and truly
110 A worthy friend. The King has made him Master
O' th' Jewel House,
And one, already, of the Privy Council.

SECOND GENTLEMAN He will deserve more.

THIRD GENTLEMAN   Yes, without all doubt.
Come, gentlemen, ye shall go my way,
Which is to th' court, and there ye shall be my
115   guests;
Something I can command. As I walk thither,
I'll tell ye more.

BOTH   You may command us, sir.

                                                Exeunt.

Scene II. [*Kimbolton.*]

*Enter Katherine, Dowager, sick; led between
Griffith, her Gentleman Usher, and
Patience, her woman.*

GRIFFITH How does your Grace?

KATHERINE   O Griffith, sick to death.
My legs like loaden branches bow to th' earth,

107 **will** who will   116 **Something** to some extent

Willing to leave their burden. Reach a chair.
So—now, methinks, I feel a little ease.
Didst thou not tell me, Griffith, as thou led'st me,   5
That the great child of honor, Cardinal Wolsey,
Was dead?

GRIFFITH   Yes, madam; but I think your Grace,
Out of the pain you suffered, gave no ear to't.

KATHERINE Prithee, good Griffith, tell me how he
        died.
If well, he stepped before me happily   10
For my example.

GRIFFITH   Well, the voice goes, madam.
For after the stout Earl Northumberland
Arrested him at York, and brought him forward,
As a man sorely tainted, to his answer,
He fell sick suddenly, and grew so ill   15
He could not sit his mule.

KATHERINE   Alas, poor man!

GRIFFITH At last, with easy roads, he came to
        Leicester,
Lodged in the abbey; where the reverend abbot,
With all his covent, honorably received him;
To whom he gave these words: "O father abbot,   20
An old man broken with the storms of state
Is come to lay his weary bones among ye;
Give him a little earth for charity."
So went to bed, where eagerly his sickness
Pursued him still; and three nights after this,   25
About the hour of eight, which he himself
Foretold should be his last, full of repentance,
Continual meditations, tears, and sorrows,
He gave his honors to the world again,
His blessèd part to heaven, and slept in peace.   30

IV.ii.7 **dead** (Wolsey died in 1530, Katherine in 1536) 10 **happily** (1) appropri-
ately (2) perhaps 11 **the voice goes** people say 14 **sorely tainted** severely
disgraced 17 **roads** stages 19 **covent** convent (used of religious companies of
either sex) 24 **eagerly** sharply 30 **blessèd part** soul

KATHERINE So may he rest. His faults lie gently on
 him!
 Yet thus far, Griffith, give me leave to speak him,
 And yet with charity. He was a man
 Of an unbounded stomach, ever ranking
35 Himself with princes; one that by suggestion
 Tied all the kingdom. Simony was fair play;
 His own opinion was his law. I' th' presence
 He would say untruths and be ever double
 Both in his words and meaning. He was never,
40 But where he meant to ruin, pitiful.
 His promises were, as he then was, mighty,
 But his performance, as he is now, nothing.
 Of his own body he was ill, and gave
 The clergy ill example.

GRIFFITH   Noble madam,
45 Men's evil manners live in brass; their virtues
 We write in water. May it please your Highness
 To hear me speak his good now?

KATHERINE   Yes, good Griffith;
 I were malicious else.

GRIFFITH   This Cardinal,
 Though from an humble stock, undoubtedly
50 Was fashioned to much honor from his cradle.
 He was a scholar, and a ripe and good one;
 Exceeding wise, fair-spoken, and persuading;
 Lofty and sour to them that loved him not,
 But to those men that sought him, sweet as summer.
55 And though he were unsatisfied in getting,
 Which was a sin, yet in bestowing, madam,
 He was most princely: ever witness for him
 Those twins of learning that he raised in you,

---

32 **speak** describe 34 **stomach** arrogance 35-36 **by suggestion/Tied** by
underhand dealing brought into bondage 36 **Simony** the buying and selling of
ecclesiastical preferment 37 **presence** presence chamber, i.e., before the King
38 **double** deceitful 43 **Of his own body he was ill** i.e., he was depraved in his
sexual conduct 47 **speak his good** describe his good qualities 55 **unsatisfied
in getting** insatiably acquisitive 58 **raised in you** i.e., erected in your cities

Ipswich and Oxford; one of which fell with him,
Unwilling to outlive the good that did it;   60
The other, though unfinished, yet so famous,
So excellent in art, and still so rising,
That Christendom shall ever speak his virtue.
His overthrow heaped happiness upon him,
For then, and not till then, he felt himself,   65
And found the blessedness of being little.
And, to add greater honors to his age
Than man could give him, he died fearing God.

KATHERINE After my death I wish no other herald,
No other speaker of my living actions,   70
To keep mine honor from corruption,
But such an honest chronicler as Griffith.
Whom I most hated living, thou hast made me,
With thy religious truth and modesty,
Now in his ashes honor. Peace be with him!   75
Patience, be near me still, and set me lower:
I have not long to trouble thee. Good Griffith,
Cause the musicians play me that sad note
I named my knell, whilst I sit meditating
On that celestial harmony I go to.   80
                                        Sad and solemn music.

GRIFFITH She is asleep. Good wench, let's sit down
      quiet,
For fear we wake her. Softly, gentle Patience.

                        The Vision.

*Enter, solemnly tripping one after another, six personages,
clad in white robes, wearing on their heads garlands of bays,
and golden vizards on their faces; branches of bays or*

60 **good** goodness 61 **other** i.e., Christ Church, Oxford 62 **art** learning
65 **felt himself** truly knew himself 70 **living actions** actions during my life
73 **Whom** (object of "hated"; also of "honor" in line 75) 74 **religious truth
and modesty** strict truth and moderation 78 **note** tune 80 **celestial harmony** (the heavenly spheres in their revolutions were thought to produce a music
accessible only to the liberated soul) 82s.d. **tripping** with light steps **bays** bay
leaves (symbolic of triumph) **vizards** masks (probably to indicate that they are
spirits)

palm in their hands. They first congee unto her, then dance;
and, at certain changes, the first two hold a spare garland over
her head; at which the other four make reverent curtsies. Then
the two that held the garland deliver the same to the other next
two, who observe the same order in their changes, and holding
the garland over her head; which done, they deliver the same
garland to the last two, who likewise observe the same order; at
which, as it were by inspiration, she makes in her sleep signs of
rejoicing, and holdeth up her hands to heaven. And so in their
dancing vanish, carrying the garland with them. The music
continues.

KATHERINE Spirits of peace, where are ye? Are ye all
    gone,
And leave me here in wretchedness behind ye?

GRIFFITH Madam, we are here.

85 KATHERINE   It is not you I call for.
    Saw ye none enter since I slept?

GRIFFITH   None, madam.

KATHERINE No? Saw you not even now a blessèd troop
Invite me to a banquet, whose bright faces
Cast thousand beams upon me, like the sun?
90 They promised me eternal happiness,
And brought me garlands, Griffith, which I feel
I am not worthy yet to wear. I shall, assuredly.

GRIFFITH I am most joyful, madam, such good dreams
Possess your fancy.

KATHERINE   Bid the music leave;
They are harsh and heavy to me.   *Music ceases.*

95 PATIENCE   Do you note
How much her Grace is altered on the sudden?
How long her face is drawn? How pale she looks,
And of an earthy cold? Mark her eyes.

---

congee bow ceremoniously   **changes** movements in the dance   **94 music leave**
musicians stop

GRIFFITH She is going, wench. Pray, pray.

PATIENCE   Heaven comfort her!

Enter a Messenger.

MESSENGER And't like your Grace—

KATHERINE   You are a saucy fellow! 100
Deserve we no more reverence?

GRIFFITH   You are to blame,
Knowing she will not lose her wonted greatness,
To use so rude behavior. Go to, kneel.

MESSENGER I humbly do entreat your Highness'
    pardon:
My haste made me unmannerly. There is staying 105
A gentleman, sent from the King, to see you.

KATHERINE Admit him entrance, Griffith; but this
    fellow
Let me ne'er see again.   *Exit Messenger.*

Enter Lord Capucius.
                    If my sight fail not,
You should be Lord Ambassador from the Em-
    peror,
My royal nephew, and your name Capucius. 110

CAPUCIUS Madam, the same. Your servant.

KATHERINE   O, my lord,
The times and titles now are altered strangely
With me since first you knew me. But I pray you,
What is your pleasure with me?

CAPUCIUS   Noble lady,
First, mine own service to your Grace; the next, 115
The King's request that I would visit you,
Who grieves much for your weakness, and by me

100 **And't like** if it please 102 **lose** give up 105 **staying** waiting 108s.d. **Exit
... Capucius** (most editors have Griffith exit with the messenger and re-enter
with Capucius, but he need not leave the stage in order to usher in the visitor)

Sends you his princely commendations,
And heartily entreats you take good comfort.

KATHERINE O my good lord, that comfort comes too
120   late;
'Tis like a pardon after execution.
That gentle physic, given in time, had cured me,
But now I am past all comforts here but prayers.
How does his Highness?

CAPUCIUS   Madam, in good health.

125 KATHERINE So may he ever do, and ever flourish,
When I shall dwell with worms, and my poor name
Banished the kingdom! Patience, is that letter
I caused you write yet sent away?

PATIENCE   No, madam.
                    [*Giving it to Katherine.*]

KATHERINE Sir, I most humbly pray you to deliver
This to my lord the King.

130 CAPUCIUS   Most willing, madam.

KATHERINE In which I have commended to his
        goodness
The model of our chaste loves, his young
        daughter—
The dews of heaven fall thick in blessings on her!—
Beseeching him to give her virtuous breeding—
135 She is young, and of a noble modest nature;
I hope she will deserve well—and a little
To love her for her mother's sake that loved him
Heaven knows how dearly. My next poor petition
Is that his noble Grace would have some pity
140 Upon my wretched women that so long
Have followed both my fortunes faithfully;
Of which there is not one, I dare avow

---

118 **commendations** greetings 121 **execution** ("-tion" two syllables)
122 **physic** healing art 123 **here** i.e., in this world 132 **model** image
132 **daughter** Mary, afterward Queen (1553-58) 134 **breeding** upbringing
141 **both my fortunes** i.e., my good fortune and bad

(And now I should not lie), but will deserve,
For virtue and true beauty of the soul,
For honesty and decent carriage,   145
A right good husband, let him be a noble;
And, sure, those men are happy that shall have 'em.
The last is, for my men—they are the poorest,
But poverty could never draw 'em from me—
That they may have their wages duly paid 'em,   150
And something over to remember me by.
If heaven had pleased to have given me longer life
And able means, we had not parted thus.
These are the whole contents; and, good my lord,
By that you love the dearest in this world,   155
As you wish Christian peace to souls departed,
Stand these poor people's friend, and urge the King
To do me this last right.

CAPUCIUS   By heaven, I will,
Or let me lose the fashion of a man!

KATHERINE I thank you, honest lord. Remember me   160
In all humility unto his Highness.
Say his long trouble now is passing
Out of this world. Tell him in death I blessed him,
For so I will. Mine eyes grow dim. Farewell,
My lord. Griffith, farewell. Nay, Patience,   165
You must not leave me yet. I must to bed;
Call in more women. When I am dead, good wench,
Let me be used with honor. Strew me over
With maiden flowers, that all the world may know
I was a chaste wife to my grave. Embalm me,   170
Then lay me forth. Although unqueened, yet like
A queen and daughter to a king, inter me.
I can no more.   *Exeunt, leading Katherine.*

---

143 now i.e., at the point of death   146 let him be i.e., even   153 able
sufficient   159 fashion form, nature   169 maiden flowers i.e., flowers appropriate to one who was chaste   173 can i.e., can do

ACT V

Scene I. [*London. A gallery in the palace.*]

Enter Gardiner, Bishop of Winchester,
a Page with a torch before him,
met by Sir Thomas Lovell.

GARDINER It's one o'clock, boy, is't not?

BOY   It hath struck.

GARDINER These should be hours for necessities,
Not for delights; times to repair our nature
With comforting repose, and not for us
To waste these times. Good hour of night, Sir
5   Thomas!
Whither so late?

LOVELL   Came you from the King, my lord?

GARDINER I did, Sir Thomas, and left him at primero
With the Duke of Suffolk.

LOVELL   I must to him too
Before he go to bed. I'll take my leave.

GARDINER Not yet, Sir Thomas Lovell. What's the
10   matter?
It seems you are in haste; and if there be
No great offense belongs to't, give your friend

V.i.7 **primero** a card game

Some touch of your late business. Affairs that walk
(As they say spirits do) at midnight have
In them a wilder nature than the business   15
That seeks dispatch by day.

LOVELL   My lord, I love you,
And durst commend a secret to your ear
Much weightier than this work. The Queen's in
     labor,
They say, in great extremity, and feared
She'll with the labor end.

GARDINER   The fruit she goes with   20
I pray for heartily, that it may find
Good time, and live; but for the stock, Sir
     Thomas,
I wish it grubbed up now.

LOVELL   Methinks I could
Cry thee amen, and yet my conscience says
She's a good creature and, sweet lady, does   25
Deserve our better wishes.

GARDINER   But, sir, sir,
Hear me, Sir Thomas. Y'are a gentleman
Of mine own way; I know you wise, religious;
And, let me tell you, it will ne'er be well—
'Twill not, Sir Thomas Lovell, take't of me—   30
Till Cranmer, Cromwell (her two hands) and she
Sleep in their graves.

LOVELL   Now, sirs, you speak of two
The most remarked i' th' kingdom. As for
     Cromwell,
Beside that of the Jewel House, is made Master
O' th' Rolls, and the King's secretary; further, sir,   35
Stands in the gap and trade of moe preferments,

13 **touch** inkling   22 **Good time** i.e., a safe delivery   22 **stock** trunk (of a tree),
i.e., the Queen   24 **Cry thee amen** i.e., second you   28 **way** i.e., religious
persuasion (anti-Lutheran)   31 **hands** supporters   33 **remarked** in the public
eye   34-35 **Master/O' th' Rolls** Keeper of the Records   36 **gap and trade**
entrance and beaten path

With which the time will load him. Th' Archbishop
Is the King's hand and tongue, and who dare speak
One syllable against him?

GARDINER   Yes, yes, Sir Thomas,
40   There are that dare, and I myself have ventured
To speak my mind of him. And indeed this day,
Sir, I may tell it you, I think I have
Insensed the lords o' th' council that he is
(For, so I know he is, they know he is)
45   A most arch heretic, a pestilence
That does infect the land; with which they moved
Have broken with the King, who hath so far
Given ear to our complaint, of his great grace
And princely care foreseeing those fell mischiefs
50   Our reasons laid before him, hath commanded
Tomorrow morning to the council board
He be convented. He's a rank weed, Sir Thomas,
And we must root him out. From your affairs
I hinder you too long. Good night, Sir Thomas.
Exit Gardiner and Page.

55   LOVELL Many good nights, my lord; I rest your servant.

Enter King and Suffolk.

KING Charles, I will play no more tonight.
My mind's not on't; you are too hard for me.

SUFFOLK Sir, I did never win of you before.

KING But little, Charles,
60   Nor shall not, when my fancy's on my play.
Now, Lovell, from the Queen what is the news?

LOVELL I could not personally deliver to her
What you commanded me, but by her woman
I sent your message; who returned her thanks

---

37 **time** i.e., the trend of the times   43 **Insensed** (1) informed (2) stirred up
("insensed" = incensed)   44 **For ... they know he is** i.e., for if I know he is,
then I can make them know   46 **moved** angered   47 **broken with** broken the
information to   49 **fell** terrible   50 **reasons** account, explanation   50 **hath** i.e.,
that he has   52 **convented** summoned   64 **who** and who (i.e., the Queen)

In the great'st humbleness, and desired your
    Highness   65
Most heartily to pray for her.

KING   What say'st thou, ha?
To pray for her? What, is she crying out?

LOVELL So said her woman, and that her suff'rance
    made
Almost each pang a death.

KING   Alas, good lady!

SUFFOLK God safely quit her of her burden, and   70
With gentle travail, to the gladding of
Your Highness with an heir!

KING   'Tis midnight, Charles;
Prithee, to bed, and in thy prayers remember
Th' estate of my poor queen. Leave me alone,
For I must think of that which company   75
Would not be friendly to.

SUFFOLK   I wish your Highness
A quiet night, and my good mistress will
Remember in my prayers.

KING   Charles, good night. *Exit Suffolk.*

        Enter Sir Anthony Denny.

Well, sir, what follows?

DENNY Sir, I have brought my lord the Archbishop,   80
As you commanded me.

KING   Ha? Canterbury?

DENNY Aye, my good lord.

KING   'Tis true: where is he, Denny?

DENNY He attends your Highness' pleasure.

---

68 **suff'rance** suffering 70 **quit** release 74 **estate** condition 75-76 **that which ... friendly to** i.e., matters for which company would not be helpful

KING   Bring him to us.
                                        [*Exit Denny.*]

LOVELL [*Aside*] This is about that which the bishop
      spake;
85   I am happily come hither.

                    Enter Cranmer and Denny.

KING Avoid the gallery. (*Lovell seems to stay.*) Ha!
      I have said. Be gone.
      What!   *Exeunt Lovell and Denny.*

CRANMER [*Aside*] I am fearful. Wherefore frowns he
      thus?
      'Tis his aspect of terror. All's not well.

KING How now, my lord? You do desire to know
      Wherefore I sent for you.

90   CRANMER [*Kneeling*]   It is my duty
      T' attend your Highness' pleasure.

KING   Pray you, arise,
      My good and gracious Lord of Canterbury.
      Come, you and I must walk a turn together;
      I have news to tell you. Come, come, give me
        your hand.
95   Ah, my good lord, I grieve at what I speak,
      And am right sorry to repeat what follows.
      I have, and most unwillingly, of late
      Heard many grievous, I do say, my lord,
      Grievous complaints of you; which, being
        considered,
100   Have moved us and our council, that you shall
      This morning come before us; where I know
      You cannot with such freedom purge yourself
      But that, till further trial in those charges
      Which will require your answer, you must take
105   Your patience to you and be well contented

84 bishop Gardiner   85 happily opportunely   86 Avoid leave   86 said spoken
87 fearful afraid   88 aspect expression (accent on second syllable)
100 moved persuaded   102 purge i.e., of guilt

To make your house our Tow'r. You a brother of
   us,
It fits we thus proceed, or else no witness
Would come against you.

CRANMER [*Kneeling*] I humbly thank your Highness,
And am right glad to catch this good occasion
Most throughly to be winnowèd, where my chaff   110
And corn shall fly asunder; for I know
There's none stands under more calumnious
   tongues
Than I myself, poor man.

KING   Stand up, good Canterbury;
Thy truth and thy integrity is rooted
In us, thy friend. Give me thy hand; stand up.   115
Prithee, let's walk. Now, by my holidame,
What manner of man are you? My lord, I looked
You would have given me your petition, that
I should have ta'en some pains to bring together
Yourself and your accusers, and to have heard you,   120
Without indurance further.

CRANMER   Most dread liege,
The good I stand on is my truth and honesty.
If they shall fail, I with mine enemies
Will triumph o'er my person; which I weigh not,
Being of those virtues vacant. I fear nothing   125
What can be said against me.

KING   Know you not
How your state stands i' th' world, with the whole
   world?
Your enemies are many, and not small. Their practices

---

106 **make your house our Tow'r** be housed in the Tower (cf.I.i.207)   106 **You
a brother of us** i.e., you being a member of the council   110 **throughly** thoroughly
111 **corn** wheat   112 **stands under** subject to   116 **by my holidame** by my
holiness (a formula of protestation)   121 **indurance further** (1) imprisonment in
addition (2) further hardship   124-25 **I weigh ... vacant** I do not value if it is
devoid of those virtues (i.e., truth and honesty)   125 **nothing** not at all

Must bear the same proportion, and not ever
130   The justice and the truth o' th' question carries
The due o' th' verdict with it. At what ease
Might corrupt minds procure knaves as corrupt
To swear against you? Such things have been done.
You are potently opposed, and with a malice
135   Of as great size. Ween you of better luck—
I mean, in perjured witness—than your master,
Whose minister you are, whiles here he lived
Upon this naughty earth? Go to, go to;
You take a precipice for no leap of danger,
And woo your own destruction.

140 CRANMER   God and your Majesty
Protect mine innocence, or I fall into
The trap is laid for me!

    KING   Be of good cheer;
They shall no more prevail than we give way to.
Keep comfort to you, and this morning see
145   You do appear before them. If they shall chance,
In charging you with matters, to commit you,
The best persuasions to the contrary
Fail not to use, and with what vehemency
Th' occasion shall instruct you. If entreaties
150   Will render you no remedy, this ring
Deliver them, and your appeal to us
There make before them. Look, the good man
    weeps!
He's honest, on mine honor. God's blest mother,
I swear he is true-hearted, and a soul
155   None better in my kingdom. Get you gone,
And do as I have bid you. (*Exit Cranmer.*) He has
    strangled
His language in his tears.

128-29 **Their practices ... proportion** their plots must correspond in number
and scope   129 **ever** always   131 **due** fit reward   131 **At what ease** how easily
135 **Ween you of** do you reckon on   136 **witness** evidence   136 **master** i.e.,
Christ   138 **naughty** wicked   142 **is** that is   143 **way** scope   146 **commit
you** i.e., to imprisonment in the Tower

Enter Old Lady; [Lovell following].

GENTLEMAN (*Within.*) Come back: what mean you?

OLD LADY I'll not come back; the tidings that I bring
    Will make my boldness manners. Now, good angels
    Fly o'er thy royal head, and shade thy person   160
    Under their blessed wings!

KING   Now by thy looks
    I guess thy message. Is the Queen delivered?
    Say "aye," and of a boy.

OLD LADY   Aye, aye, my liege,
    And of a lovely boy. The God of heaven
    Both now and ever bless her! 'Tis a girl   165
    Promises boys hereafter. Sir, your Queen
    Desires your visitation, and to be
    Acquainted with this stranger. 'Tis as like you
    As cherry is to cherry.

KING   Lovell!

LOVELL   Sir?

KING Give her an hundred marks. I'll to the Queen.   170
                                Exit King.

OLD LADY An hundred marks? By this light, I'll ha'
    more.
    An ordinary groom is for such payment.
    I will have more, or scold it out of him.
    Said I for this, the girl was like to him? I'll
    Have more, or else unsay't; and now, while 'tis hot,   175
    I'll put it to the issue.   *[Exeunt.]*

170 **an hundred marks** (one mark = 13s.4d. [two-thirds of a pound]; a hundred
marks = £66.13s.4d. a substantial sum)   172 **for** entitled to

Scene II. [*Before the entrance to the council-chamber.*]

Enter Cranmer, Archbishop of Canterbury; [pursui-
vants, pages, etc., attending at the door].

CRANMER I hope I am not too late; and yet the
        gentleman
    That was sent to me from the council prayed me
    To make great haste. All fast? What means this?
        Ho!
    Who waits there? Sure, you know me?

Enter Keeper.

KEEPER   Yes, my lord,
5   But yet I cannot help you.

CRANMER Why?

KEEPER Your Grace must wait till you be called for.

Enter Doctor Butts.

CRANMER   So.

BUTTS [*Aside*] This is a piece of malice. I am glad
    I came this way so happily. The King
    Shall understand it presently.   *Exit Butts.*

10   CRANMER [*Aside*]   'Tis Butts,
    The King's physician. As he passed along,
    How earnestly he cast his eyes upon me.
    Pray heaven he sound not my disgrace! For
        certain,
    This is of purpose laid by some that hate me

V.ii.s.d. **pursuivants** junior officers attendant upon the heralds   3 **fast** shut
10 **understand it presently** know about it at once   13 **sound** (1) fathom
(2) make known

(God turn their hearts! I never sought their
    malice)   15
To quench mine honor. They would shame to make
    me
Wait else at door, a fellow-councillor,
'Mong boys, grooms, and lackeys. But their
    pleasures
Must be fulfilled, and I attend with patience.

      Enter the King and Butts at a window above.

BUTTS I'll show your Grace the strangest sight—   20

KING   What's that, Butts?

BUTTS I think your Highness saw this many a day.

KING Body o' me, where is it?

BUTTS   There, my lord:
The high promotion of his Grace of Canterbury,
Who holds his state at door 'mongst pursuivants,
Pages, and footboys.

KING   Ha? 'Tis he, indeed.   25
Is this the honor they do one another?
'Tis well there's one above 'em yet. I had thought
They had parted so much honesty among 'em,
At least good manners, as not thus to suffer
A man of his place and so near our favor   30
To dance attendance on their lordships' pleasures,
And at the door too, like a post with packets.
By holy Mary, Butts, there's knavery.
Let 'em alone, and draw the curtain close;
We shall hear more anon.   35

    [*They retire behind the curtain; Cranmer remains
              waiting outside.*]

---

15 turn convert   19s.d. above (i.e., on the upper stage; note the reference to a
curtain, line 34)   24 holds his state maintains the dignity of his position
28 parted so much honesty shared enough decency   32 post with packets
courier with letters

Scene III. [*The council-chamber.*]

A council-table brought in with chairs and stools, and placed under the state. Enter Lord Chancellor, places himself at the upper end of the table on the left hand; a seat being left void above him, as for Canterbury's seat. Duke of Suffolk, Duke of Norfolk, Surrey, Lord Chamberlain, Gardiner, seat themselves in order on each side. Cromwell at lower end, as secretary. [*Keeper at the door.*]

CHANCELLOR Speak to the business, master secretary.
　　Why are we met in council?

CROMWELL　　　　　　　　　Please your honors,
　　The chief cause concerns his Grace of Canterbury.

GARDINER Has he had knowledge of it?

CROMWELL　　　　　　　　　　　Yes.

NORFOLK　　　　　　　　　　Who waits there?

KEEPER Without, my noble lords?

GARDINER　　　　　　　Yes.

5　KEEPER　　　　　　　　　My Lord Archbishop;
　　And has done half an hour, to know your pleasures.

CHANCELLOR Let him come in.

KEEPER　　　　　　　Your Grace may enter now.

Cranmer [*enters and*] *approaches the council-table.*

CHANCELLOR My good Lord Archbishop, I'm very sorry
　　To sit here at this present and behold
10　That chair stand empty. But we all are men,

V.iii.s.d. **state** canopy　**void** empty　4 **had knowledge** been informed
5 **Without** outside the door　9 **at this present** now

In our own natures frail and capable
Of our flesh; few are angels: out of which frailty
And want of wisdom, you, that best should teach
    us,
Have misdemeaned yourself, and not a little,
Toward the King first, then his laws, in filling   15
The whole realm, by your teaching and your
    chaplains'—
For so we are informed—with new opinions,
Divers and dangerous; which are heresies,
And, not reformed, may prove pernicious.

GARDINER Which reformation must be sudden too,   20
My noble lords; for those that tame wild horses
Pace 'em not in their hands to make 'em gentle,
But stop their mouths with stubborn bits and spur
    'em
Till they obey the manage. If we suffer,
Out of our easiness and childish pity   25
To one man's honor, this contagious sickness,
Farewell all physic. And what follows then?
Commotions, uproars, with a general taint
Of the whole state; as of late days our neighbors,
The upper Germany, can dearly witness,   30
Yet freshly pitied in our memories.

CRANMER My good lords, hitherto, in all the progress
Both of my life and office, I have labored,
And with no little study, that my teaching
And the strong course of my authority   35
Might go one way, and safely; and the end
Was ever to do well. Nor is there living
(I speak it with a single heart, my lords)
A man that more detests, more stirs against,
Both in his private conscience and his place,   40

11-12 **capable/Of** i.e., susceptible to the weaknesses of   19 **pernicious** ruinous
22 **Pace 'em not in their hands** do not lead them by hand through their
paces   23 **stubborn** stiff, inflexible   24 **manage** training   28 **taint**
corruption   30 **upper Germany** (possibly referring to the peasants' uprising in
Saxony in 1521-22 or to other insurrections in 1524 and 1535)   38 **with a single
heart** i.e., without duplicity   39 **stirs** bestirs himself

Defacers of a public peace, than I do.
Pray heaven, the King may never find a heart
With less allegiance in it! Men that make
Envy and crookèd malice nourishment
45   Dare bite the best. I do beseech your lordships
That, in this case of justice, my accusers,
Be what they will, may stand forth face to face,
And freely urge against me.

SUFFOLK   Nay, my lord,
That cannot be. You are a councillor,
50   And, by that virtue, no man dare accuse you.

GARDINER My lord, because we have business of more
        moment,
We will be short with you. 'Tis his Highness'
        pleasure,
And our consent, for better trial of you,
From hence you be committed to the Tower;
55   Where, being but a private man again,
You shall know many dare accuse you boldly,
More than, I fear, you are provided for.

CRANMER Ah, my good Lord of Winchester, I thank
        you;
You are always my good friend. If your will pass,
60   I shall both find your lordship judge and juror,
You are so merciful. I see your end:
'Tis my undoing. Love and meekness, lord,
Become a churchman better than ambition.
Win straying souls with modesty again;
65   Cast none away. That I shall clear myself,
Lay all the weight ye can upon my patience,
I make as little doubt as you do conscience
In doing daily wrongs. I could say more,
But reverence to your calling makes me modest.

43-44 make ... nourishment ("make nourishment" = feed on) 46 of
involving 48 urge press their charges 50 that virtue virtue of that 53 our
consent what we have consented to 53 private man i.e., without public
office 59 pass prevail 60 both find your lordship find your lordship
both 64 modesty moderation 67 I make ... conscience I have as little doubt
as you have scruples

GARDINER My lord, my lord, you are a sectary;   70
   That's the plain truth. Your painted gloss
     discovers,
   To men that understand you, words and weakness.

CROMWELL My Lord of Winchester, y'are a little,
   By your good favor, too sharp. Men so noble,
   However faulty, yet should find respect   75
   For what they have been; 'tis a cruelty
   To load a falling man.

GARDINER   Good master secretary,
   I cry your honor mercy; you may, worst
   Of all this table, say so.

CROMWELL   Why, my lord?

GARDINER Do not I know you for a favorer   80
   Of this new sect? Ye are not sound.

CROMWELL   Not sound?

GARDINER Not sound, I say.

CROMWELL   Would you were half so honest!
   Men's prayers then would seek you, not their fears.

GARDINER I shall remember this bold language.

CROMWELL   Do.
   Remember your bold life too.

CHANCELLOR   This is too much;   85
   Forbear, for shame, my lords.

GARDINER   I have done.

CROMWELL   And I.

CHANCELLOR Then thus for you, my lord: it stands
     agreed,
   I take it, by all voices, that forthwith

70 **sectary** follower of a (heretical) sect   71 **painted gloss discovers** deceitful
appearance (or speech) reveals   72 **words** i.e., rather than content   77 **load**
oppress   78 **cry your honor mercy** beg your honor's pardon   78 **worst** with
least justification   81 **sound** loyal

You be conveyed to th' Tower a prisoner,
90   There to remain till the King's further pleasure
Be known unto us. Are you all agreed, lords?

ALL We are.

CRANMER   Is there no other way of mercy,
But I must needs to th' Tower, my lords?

GARDINER   What other
Would you expect? You are strangely trouble-
    some.
Let some o' th' guard be ready there.

Enter the Guard.

95 CRANMER   For me?
Must I go like a traitor thither?

GARDINER   Receive him,
And see him safe i' th' Tower.

CRANMER   Stay, good my lords,
I have a little yet to say. Look there, my lords.
By virtue of that ring, I take my cause
100   Out of the gripes of cruel men, and give it
To a most noble judge, the King my master.

CHAMBERLAIN This is the King's ring.

SURREY   'Tis no counterfeit.

SUFFOLK 'Tis the right ring, by heaven. I told ye all,
When we first put this dangerous stone arolling,
'Twould fall upon ourselves.

105 NORFOLK   Do you think, my lords,
The King will suffer but the little finger
Of this man to be vexed?

CHAMBERLAIN   'Tis now too certain.
How much more is his life in value with him?
Would I were fairly out on't!

94 **strangely** uncommonly   100 **gripes** clutches   106 **suffer but** allow even
108 **in value with** esteemed by

CROMWELL   My mind gave me,
  In seeking tales and informations   110
  Against this man, whose honesty the devil
  And his disciples only envy at,
  Ye blew the fire that burns ye. Now have at ye!

    Enter King, frowning on them; takes his seat.

GARDINER Dread sovereign, how much are we bound
    to heaven
  In daily thanks, that gave us such a prince,   115
  Not only good and wise, but most religious;
  One that in all obedience makes the church
  The chief aim of his honor, and, to strengthen
  That holy duty, out of dear respect,
  His royal self in judgment comes to hear   120
  The cause betwixt her and this great offender.

KING You were ever good at sudden commenda-
    tions,
  Bishop of Winchester. But know, I come not
  To hear such flattery now, and in my presence
  They are too thin and bare to hide offenses.   125
  To me you cannot reach. You play the spaniel,
  And think with wagging of your tongue to win me;
  But, whatsoe'er thou tak'st me for, I'm sure
  Thou hast a cruel nature and a bloody.
  [*To Cranmer*] Good man, sit down. Now let me see
    the proudest,   130
  He that dares most, but wag his finger at thee.
  By all that's holy, he had better starve
  Than but once think this place becomes thee not.

SURREY May it please your Grace—

KING   No, sir, it does not please me.
  I had thought I had had men of some understanding   135
  And wisdom of my council, but I find none.

109 **gave** told   112 **envy at** hate   119 **dear respect** heartfelt care (for the
church)   122 **sudden commendations** extemporaneous compliments
132 **starve** die

Was it discretion, lords, to let this man,
This good man—few of you deserve that title—
This honest man, wait like a lousy footboy
140 At chamber door? And one as great as you are?
Why, what a shame was this! Did my commission
Bid ye so far forget yourselves? I gave ye
Power as he was a councillor to try him,
Not as a groom. There's some of ye, I see,
145 More out of malice than integrity,
Would try him to the utmost, had ye mean;
Which ye shall never have while I live.

CHANCELLOR   Thus far,
My most dread sovereign, may it like your Grace
To let my tongue excuse all. What was purposed
150 Concerning his imprisonment was rather,
If there be faith in men, meant for his trial
And fair purgation to the world, than malice,
I'm sure, in me.

KING   Well, well, my lords, respect him.
Take him and use him well; he's worthy of it.
155 I will say thus much for him, if a prince
May be beholding to a subject, I
Am, for his love and service, so to him.
Make me no more ado, but all embrace him.
Be friends, for shame, my lords! My Lord of
       Canterbury,
160 I have a suit which you must not deny me:
That is, a fair young maid that yet wants baptism;
You must be godfather, and answer for her.

CRANMER The greatest monarch now alive may glory
In such an honor. How may I deserve it,
165 That am a poor and humble subject to you?

KING Come, come, my lord, you'd spare your spoons.
You shall have two noble partners with you: the old

139 **lousy** lice infested   146 **mean** means   148 **like** please   152 **purgation** vindication   161 **wants** lacks   166-67 **spare your spoons** save the expense of giving spoons (traditional christening gifts)   167 **partners** co-sponsors

Duchess of Norfolk, and Lady Marquess Dorset. Will
these please you?
Once more, my Lord of Winchester, I charge you,   170
Embrace and love this man.

GARDINER   With a true heart
And brother-love I do it.

CRANMER   And let heaven
Witness how dear I hold this confirmation.

KING Good man, those joyful tears show thy true
    heart.
The common voice, I see, is verified   175
Of thee, which says thus: "Do my Lord of
    Canterbury
A shrewd turn, and he's your friend forever."
Come, lords, we trifle time away. I long
To have this young one made a Christian.
As I have made ye one, lords, one remain;   180
So I grow stronger, you more honor gain.   *Exeunt.*

Scene IV. [*The palace yard.*]

Noise and tumult within. Enter Porter and his Man.

PORTER You'll leave your noise anon, ye rascals. Do
    you take the court for Parish Garden? Ye rude
    slaves, leave your gaping.

(*Within.*) Good master porter, I belong to th' larder.

PORTER Belong to th' gallows, and be hanged, ye   5
    rogue! Is this a place to roar in? Fetch me a dozen
    crab-tree staves, and strong ones: these are but

175 **common voice** popular report   177 **shrewd** nasty   V.iv.2 **Parish Garden**
Paris Garden, a boisterous bear-baiting arena on the Bankside   2 **rude** uncivilized
3 **leave your gaping** stop your bawling   4 **belong to th' larder** am employed in
the (palace) pantry

switches to 'em. I'll scratch your heads. You must
be seeing christenings? Do you look for ale and
10   cakes here, you rude rascals?

MAN Pray, sir, be patient. 'Tis as much impossible,
Unless we sweep 'em from the door with cannons,
To scatter 'em, as 'tis to make 'em sleep
On May-Day morning, which will never be.
15   We may as well push against Paul's as stir 'em.

PORTER How got they in, and be hanged?

MAN Alas, I know not. How gets the tide in?
As much as one sound cudgel of four foot
(You see the poor remainder) could distribute,
I made no spare, sir.

20   PORTER   You did nothing, sir.

MAN I am not Samson, nor Sir Guy, nor Colbrand,
To mow 'em down before me; but if I spared any
That had a head to hit, either young or old,
He or she, cuckold or cuckold-maker,
25   Let me ne'er hope to see a chine again;
And that I would not for a cow, God save her!

(*Within.*) Do you hear, master porter?

PORTER I shall be with you presently, good master
puppy. Keep the door close, sirrah.

30   MAN What would you have me do?

PORTER What should you do, but knock 'em down by
th' dozens? Is this Moorfields to muster in? Or

---

8 **switches to 'em** twigs in comparison   9-10 **ale and cakes** (traditional fare at
christenings and other celebrations)   14 **May-Day** (a holiday the celebration of
which began before sunrise)   15 **Paul's** St. Paul's Cathedral   20 **made no** did
not   21 **Samson, nor Sir Guy, nor Colbrand** (all three possessed legendary
strength; Guy of Warwick was celebrated in romance for slaying the Danish Giant
Colbrand)   25 **see a chine** i.e., eat beef   26 **for a cow, God save her** (a current
expression of doubtful import; perhaps meaningless)   28 **I shall be with you** I'll
trounce you (Maxwell)   29 **sirrah** (term of address used to inferiors)
32 **Moorfields** a recreation field on the London outskirts

have we some strange Indian with the great tool
come to court, the women so besiege us? Bless me,
what a fry of fornication is at door! On my Chris-   35
tian conscience, this one christening will beget a
thousand; here will be father, godfather, and all together.

MAN The spoons will be the bigger, sir. There is
a fellow somewhat near the door, he should be a   40
brazier by his face, for, o' my conscience, twenty
of the dog days now reign in's nose. All that stand
about him are under the line; they need no other
penance. That firedrake did I hit three times on
the head, and three times was his nose discharged   45
against me; he stands there, like a mortarpiece, to
blow us. There was a haberdasher's wife of small
wit near him, that railed upon me till her pinked
porringer fell off her head, for kindling such a
combustion in the state. I missed the meteor once,   50
and hit that woman, who cried out "Clubs!" when
I might see from far some forty truncheoners draw
to her succor, which were the hope o' th' Strand,
where she was quartered. They fell on; I made
good my place. At length they came to th' broom-   55
staff to me. I defied 'em still; when suddenly a
file of boys behind 'em, loose shot, delivered such
a show'r of pebbles, that I was fain to draw mine

33 some strange Indian with the great tool (American Indians were exhibited
at court; "tool" = penis) 35 fry of fornication (1) swarm of would-be
fornicators (2) swarming offspring of fornication 39 spoons (cf. V.iii.
166-67) 41 brazier by his face brass worker by his (red) face 42 dog days
(the period from about July 3 to August 15, when Sirius, the Dog Star, rises at
almost the same time as the sun; regarded as the hottest and most unwholesome
season of the year) 43 line equator 44 firedrake (1) fiery dragon
(2) meteor 46 mortarpiece squat cannon with a large bore 47 blow us blow
us up 48-49 pinked porringer round cap with scalloped edge or ornamental
perforations 51 Clubs (the rallying cry of the London apprentices) 52 truncheoners truncheon (or cudgel) bearers 53 were the hope o' th' Strand i.e.,
belonged to the shops in the Strand, in Jacobean times a fashionable street
54-55 They fell on; I made good they attacked; I defended 55-56 to th'
broomstaff i.e., to close quarters 57 file small company 57 loose shot
unaffiliated marksmen 58 fain obliged

honor in and let 'em win the work. The devil was
60   amongst 'em, I think, surely.

PORTER These are the youths that thunder at a playhouse and fight for bitten apples; that no audience
but the tribulation of Tower Hill or the limbs of
Limehouse, their dear brothers, are able to en-
65   dure. I have some of 'em in Limbo Patrum, and
there they are like to dance these three days; besides the running banquet of two beadles that is
to come.

Enter Lord Chamberlain.

CHAMBERLAIN Mercy o' me, what a multitude are here!
70   They grow still too; from all parts they are coming,
As if we kept a fair here. Where are these porters,
These lazy knaves? Y'have made a fine hand, fellows;
There's a trim rabble let in. Are all these
Your faithful friends o' th' suburbs? We shall have
75   Great store of room, no doubt, left for the ladies,
When they pass back from the christening.

PORTER   And't please your honor,
We are but men; and what so many may do,
Not being torn apieces, we have done.
An army cannot rule 'em.

CHAMBERLAIN   As I live,
80   If the King blame me for't, I'll lay ye all
By th' heels, and suddenly; and on your heads
Clap round fines for neglect. Y'are lazy knaves,
And here ye lie baiting of bombards when
Ye should do service. Hark! The trumpets sound;

---

59 **work** fort 63 **tribulation** troublemakers 63 **Tower Hill** an unruly
district 63 **limbs** inhabitants, with a possible reference to the limbs of the
devil 64 **Limehouse** the rough dockyard area 65 **Limbo Patrum** i.e., prison
(literally the underworld abode of the souls of the just who died before Christ's
coming) 67 **running banquet of two beadles** i.e., a public whipping, as a
dessert to the "feast" of their confinement 73 **trim** fine 74 **suburbs** disreputable districts outside City jurisdiction 80-81 **I'll lay ... suddenly** I'll have you
all put straightaway into fetters 82 **round** stiff 83 **baiting of bombards**
drinking from leather jugs

Th'are come already from the christening.   85
Go, break among the press, and find a way out
To let the troop pass fairly, or I'll find
A Marshalsea shall hold ye play these two months.

PORTER Make way there for the Princess.

MAN   You great fellow,
Stand close up, or I'll make your head ache.   90

PORTER You i' th' camlet, get up o' th' rail;
I'll peck you o'er the pales else.   *Exeunt*.

Scene V. [*The palace*.]

*Enter trumpets, sounding; then two Aldermen, Lord
Mayor, Garter, Cranmer, Duke of Norfolk with his
marshal's staff, Duke of Suffolk, two Noblemen bearing
great standing-bowls for the christening gifts; then four
noblemen bearing a canopy, under which the Duchess of
Norfolk, godmother, bearing the child richly habited in a
mantle, etc., train borne by a Lady. Then follows the
Marchioness Dorset, the other godmother, and Ladies. The
troop pass once about the stage, and Garter speaks.*

GARTER Heaven, from thy endless goodness, send
prosperous life, long, and ever happy, to the high
and mighty Princess of England, Elizabeth!

Flourish. Enter King and Guard.

CRANMER [*Kneeling*] And to your royal Grace and the
good Queen.

---

86 **press** throng   88 **Marshalsea** prison in Southwark   91 **camlet** a rich fabric
made of Angora wool and other materials   92 **peck you o'er the pales** pitch you
over the palings   V.v.s.d. **Garter** (see IV.i.36s.d., and note)   **standing-bowls**
i.e., bowls with supporting legs or base

5 My noble partners and myself thus pray:
All comfort, joy, in this most gracious lady
Heaven ever laid up to make parents happy
May hourly fall upon ye!

KING   Thank you, good Lord Archbishop.
What is her name?

CRANMER   Elizabeth.

KING   Stand up, lord.
       [The King kisses the child.]
10 With this kiss take my blessing: God protect thee!
Into whose hand I give thy life.

CRANMER   Amen.

KING My noble gossips, y'have been too prodigal.
I thank ye heartily; so shall this lady,
When she has so much English.

CRANMER   Let me speak, sir,
15 For heaven now bids me; and the words I utter
Let none think flattery, for they'll find 'em truth.
This royal infant—heaven still move about her!—
Though in her cradle, yet now promises
Upon this land a thousand thousand blessings,
20 Which time shall bring to ripeness. She shall be
(But few now living can behold that goodness)
A pattern to all princes living with her
And all that shall succeed. Saba was never
More covetous of wisdom and fair virtue
25 Than this pure soul shall be. All princely graces
That mold up such a mighty piece as this is,
With all the virtues that attend the good,
Shall still be doubled on her. Truth shall nurse her,
Holy and heavenly thoughts still counsel her.
She shall be loved and feared. Her own shall bless
30 her;

5 **partners** co-sponsors   12 **gossips** godparents   12 **prodigal** generous with
gifts   17 **still** always   23 **Saba** the Queen of Sheba   26 **mold up such a
mighty piece** go to form so great a personage   30 **own** i.e., own people

Her foes shake like a field of beaten corn,
And hang their heads with sorrow. Good grows
  with her;
In her days every man shall eat in safety
Under his own vine what he plants, and sing
The merry songs of peace to all his neighbors.   35
God shall be truly known, and those about her
From her shall read the perfect ways of honor,
And by those claim their greatness, not by blood.
Nor shall this peace sleep with her; but as when
The bird of wonder dies, the maiden phoenix,   40
Her ashes new create another heir
As great in admiration as herself,
So shall she leave her blessedness to one
(When heaven shall call her from this cloud of
  darkness)
Who from the sacred ashes of her honor   45
Shall star-like rise, as great in fame as she was,
And so stand fixed. Peace, plenty, love, truth,
  terror,
That were the servants to this chosen infant,
Shall then be his, and like a vine grow to him.
Wherever the bright sun of heaven shall shine,   50
His honor and the greatness of his name
Shall be, and make new nations. He shall flourish,
And like a mountain cedar reach his branches
To all the plains about him. Our children's
  children
Shall see this, and bless heaven.

KING   Thou speakest wonders.   55

CRANMER She shall be, to the happiness of England,
An agèd princess; many days shall see her,
And yet no day without a deed to crown it.

31 **corn** wheat   37 **read** learn   40 **phoenix** the fabled Arabian bird—unique in
all the world—that after a life of 660 years rises anew from the ashes in which it
has consumed itself   42 **admiration** "ability to excite wonder" (Foakes)
43 **one** i.e., James I   47 **fixed** i.e., as a fixed star   50-54 **Wherever ... about
him** (inspired by a prophecy in Genesis 17:4-6 which was often cited in
connection with Princess Elizabeth's marriage in 1613 [Foakes]; the "new nations"
may allude to the colonization of Virginia)

Would I had known no more! But she must die:
60   She must, the saints must have her. Yet a virgin,
A most unspotted lily, shall she pass
To th' ground, and all the world shall mourn her.

KING   O Lord Archbishop,
Thou hast made me now a man; never before
65   This happy child did I get anything.
This oracle of comfort has so pleased me
That when I am in heaven I shall desire
To see what this child does, and praise my Maker.
I thank ye all. To you, my good Lord Mayor,
70   And your good brethren, I am much beholding;
I have received much honor by your presence,
And ye shall find me thankful. Lead the way, lords.
Ye must all see the Queen, and she must thank ye;
She will be sick else. This day, no man think
75   Has business at his house; for all shall stay:
This little one shall make it holiday.   *Exeunt*.

THE EPILOGUE

'Tis ten to one this play can never please
All that are here. Some come to take their ease,
And sleep an act or two; but those, we fear,
W'have frighted with our trumpets; so, 'tis clear,
5   They'll say 'tis naught; others, to hear the city
Abused extremely, and to cry "That's witty!"
Which we have not done neither; that, I fear,
All the expected good w'are like to hear
For this play at this time, is only in
10   The merciful construction of good women,
For such a one we showed 'em. If they smile
And say 'twill do, I know, within a while
All the best men are ours; for 'tis ill hap
If they hold when their ladies bid 'em clap.

FINIS

65 **get** beget   74 **no man think** let no man think   75 **Has** he has   75 **stay** stop   Epilogue   5 **naught** worthless   5-6 **others … witty** (a glance at the vogue for satirical comedies of London life)   7 **that** so that   10 **construction** interpretation   13 **hap** luck

Textual Note

The Famous History of the Life of King Henry the Eighth
did not achieve publication until seven years after Shakespeare's death, when it appeared in the collected First
Folio of his works as the last of the history plays. The
1623 Folio furnishes the only authoritative early edition
of *Henry VIII*. Fortunately it is a very good one: behind
the Folio text apparently lies a careful scribal tran-
scription of the authors'—or author's—own manuscript.
To the playwright(s), rather than the prompter, we
presumably owe the very full stage directions called for
by a spectacular historical drama. With few exceptions,
entrances and exits are fully indicated. Speech prefixes are
throughout correct and unambiguous, except for confusion
of the First and Second Gentleman at IV.i.20-23 and 55,
and of the Lord Chamberlain with the Lord Chancellor at
V.iii.85 and 87. Indeed the text as a whole is very clean
and straightforward, with relatively little corruption or
error of any kind, although the language—often complex
in Shakespeare's mature manner—not surprisingly presents a number of interpretative problems.

The Folio text directly or indirectly provides the basis
for all subsequent editions of *Henry VIII*. Wherever possible the present edition reproduces it, modernizing spelling, and altering punctuation and verse lineations where
the editor's sense of literary and dramatic fitness dictated.
The Latin act and scene divisions of the Folio have been
translated, and a new division (as in the Globe text) is
introduced after V.ii.35. Consequently, in the fifth act the
Folio's *Scena Tertia* and *Scena Quarta* are rendered as
V.iv and V.v. respectively. Abbreviations have been expanded
and speech prefixes regularized. Stage directions have been
amplified where necessary, such additions being printed
within square brackets. Obvious typographical errors have
been corrected and eccentric spellings regularized where
appropriate without notice, but all significant emendations
are noted below. In this list the adopted reading is given in

bold and is followed by the rejected Folio reading in roman
type or a note of the Folio's omission within square brackets.

I.i.42-45 **All ... function** [F assigns to Buckingham]   47 **as you guess** [F assigns
to Norfolk]   63 **web,** 'a Web. O   69-70 **that?** ... **hell, that,** ... **Hell?**   183 **He** [F
omits]   200 **Hereford** Hertford   219 **Parke** Pecke   221 **Nicholas** Michaell
227 **lord** Lords
I.ii.156 **feared** feare   164 **confession's** Commissions   170 **win** [F omits]
180 **To** For this to   190 **Bulmer** Blumer
I.iii.12 **saw** see   13 **Or** A   59 **wherewithall. In him** wherewithall in him;

II.i.20 **Parke** Pecke   86 **mark** make
II.iii.14 **quarrel,** quarrell.   61 **you** you, to you
II.iv.174 **A** And   319 **summons. Unsolicited** Summons vnsolicited.

III.i.21 **coming, now I think on't.** comming; now I thinke on't,
23s.d. **Campeius** Campian   61 **your** our
III.ii.142 **glad** gald   171 **filed** fill'd   292 **Who** Whom   343 **Chattels** Castles

IV.i.20-23 **I thank ... business?** [F assigns to First Gentleman]   34 **Kimbolton**
Kymmalton   55 **And sometimes falling ones.** [F assigns to Second Gentleman]
101 **Stokesly** Stokeley
IV.ii.7 **think** thanke   50 **honor from** Honor. From

V.i.24 **thee** the   37 **time** Lime   139 **precipice** Precepit   176s.d. [**Exeunt.**] Exit
Ladie.
V.ii.8 **piece** Peere
V.iii.85-86 **This ... lords.** [F assigns to Lord Chamberlain]   87-91 **Then ...
agreed, lords?** [F assigns to Lord Chamberlain]   125 **bare** base   133 **this** his
174 **heart** hearts
V.v.37 **ways** way   70 **your** you

THE HOUSES OF LANCASTER AND YORK
(Simplified)

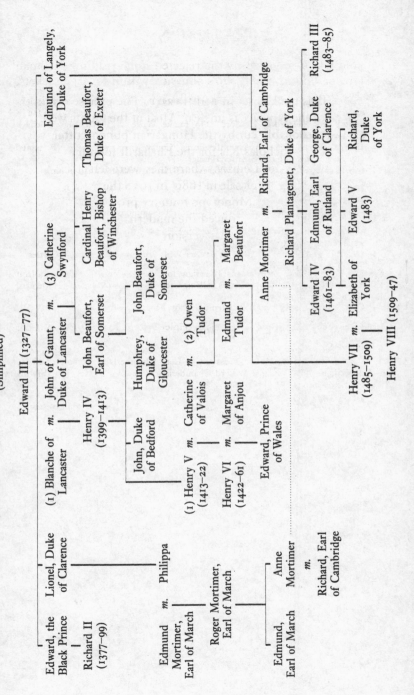

This book is set in EHRHARDT. The precise origin
of the typeface is unclear. Most of the founts were
probably cut by the Hungarian punch-cutter
Nicholas Kis for the Ehrhardt foundry
in Leipzig, where they were left
for sale in 1689. In 1938 the
Monotype foundry pro-
duced the modern
version.